The Victorian Frame of Mind, 1830–1870

The Victorian Frame of Mind

1830-1870

BY WALTER E. HOUGHTON

Published for Wellesley College by

Yale University Press,

New Haven and London

Library of Congress catalog card number 57-6339

ISBN: 978-0-300-00122-8

Printed in the United States of America

*To my father and mother
and my sister Nan*

CONTENTS

Acknowledgments

AS I CALL TO MIND the people who have had a share in the creation of this book, I think first of my colleagues on the Board of Tutors in History and Literature at Harvard College from 1931 to 1940. It was there at our Tuesday lunches in the persistent discussions of intellectual history that this book, though still unthought of, had its deepest roots. In ways too intangible to trace, I owe much to the conversation—sometimes brilliant, often fantastic, always lively—of Paul Doolin, Dana Durand, John Finley, F. O. Matthiessen, Perry Miller, Elliott Perkins, Jack Potter, Dan Sargent, and Ed Whitney. After them, and more immediately helpful, come those who have read and criticized the entire manuscript: the Wellesley College Committee on Publications, especially Katharine Balderston and its chairman, Dean Ella Keats Whiting; Douglas Bush of Harvard; Gordon Haight of Yale; David Horne of the Yale Press; my wife, Esther Rhoads Houghton, who also undertook the immense tasks of proofreading the manuscript and making the index; and my friend and former student (in History and Literature), Robert Stange of Minnesota, who encouraged me to go forward at the critical moment when the idea seemed too large to be attempted, and who later made suggestions ranging from the rewording of a sentence to the recasting of a chapter.

I am also indebted to Marie Edel and Virginia Onderdonk for generously putting their knowledge of English and philosophy at my service; to Margaret Boyce and Elizabeth Olmstead of the Wellesley College Library staff, and Margaret Hackett of the Boston Athenaeum, for research on specific points; and to Elizabeth H. Jones for the energy and patience with which she typed and retyped the manuscript.

Not least am I grateful to those who have given me the free time and the indispensable financial assistance required for writing and publishing a book like this: the trustees of Wellesley College and President Margaret Clapp, for a two-year leave of absence; the Fund for the Advancement of Education for a generous fellowship in 1953–54 (though it must be understood that the Fund is in no way responsible for the statements I have made or the views I have expressed); and the donors of the Sophie C. Hart Fund of Wellesley College for a large contribution to the cost of publication.

Finally, I wish to thank the following publishers for permission to quote from works which are still in copyright: The Clarendon Press for *The Poems of Arthur Hugh Clough*, ed. H. L. Lowry, A. L. P. Norrington, and F. L. Mulhauser; Victor Gollancz for E. E. Kellett's *As I Remember*; Michael Joseph for W. H. Mallock's *The New Republic*; Longmans, Green, and Company for Beatrice Webb's *My Apprenticeship*; Macmillan and Company, St. Martin's Press, and the trustees of the Hardy estate for Thomas Hardy's *Poems*; John Murray for Horatio Brown's *John Addington Symonds. A Biography*; and the Oxford University Press for *The Poems of Gerard Manley Hopkins*, ed. W. H. Gardner, and *The Letters of Matthew Arnold to Arthur Hugh Clough*, ed. H. F. Lowry.

W.E.H.

Wellesley, Massachusetts
September 15, 1956

PREFACE

> To reconstruct a past world, doubtless with a view
> to the highest purposes of truth,—what a work to be
> in any way present at, to assist in, though only as
> a lamp-holder!
>
> *George Eliot*

IT IS OVER forty years since Lytton Strachey decided with a flourish
that we knew too much about the Victorian era to view its culture as
a whole. The truth was rather that in the full tide of reaction it was
impossible to achieve a detached and broad perspective. Since then,
and especially during the past decade, we have had a series of "period
pieces" making the most of the picturesque and the eccentric, as well
as some solid critical and biographical work, and a dozen or so extensive studies of the age. But for all this—to some degree because
of it—the Victorian mind remains for us blurred and obscure. It appears as a bundle of various and often paradoxical ideas and attitudes.
It is fragmentary and incoherent. It is not a mind. I do not mean that
there is only one pattern; still less that the pattern is simple. So complex a thing may be looked at from different points of view, and its
internal economy is intricate. But *some* point of view must be adopted
because otherwise there is no understanding. The very attempt to
describe a mind, whether of a person or a period, is an attempt to
make it intelligible, and intelligibility is a system of relationships. The
general "portraits" of Victorian England are good in their several
ways, but they are limited in range or lacking in integration. We are
still without an extended and rounded synthesis.

This is particularly the case at the fundamental level below that of
formal doctrine and schools of thought. We know a good deal about
Benthamism, Imperialism, Darwinism, and the other isms of the period;
and while a larger book including them, and considering the impact
of institutions like the Church, the Universities, the Inns of Court, or
the Army, might have been written—and called *The Victorian Mind*—
I have chosen a smaller scope (still quite large enough, and one which
in any event will take some account of creeds and organizations). I
have explored those general ideas and attitudes about life which Vic-

torians of the middle and upper classes would have breathed in with the air—the main grounds of hope and uneasiness which they felt, the modes of thought and behavior they followed, often spontaneously, the standards of value they held—in a word, the frame of mind in which they were living and thinking. Studies in this area have emphasized only a few characteristics, notably moral earnestness and optimism, to the obscuring of others, equally important, like enthusiasm and anxiety. Some have never been discussed except briefly here and there in other connections: rigidity, dogmatism, the will to believe. Strange as it may seem, there does not exist a single account as such of Victorian hero worship or Victorian love. And if everyone knows that our great-grand-fathers were hypocritical, what is meant and why they were—if they were—no one can say. Above all, the major attitudes have never been interrelated, nor their simultaneous existence traced to the general character of the age.

The kind of inquiry here undertaken is the more important because to look into the Victorian mind is to see some primary sources of the modern mind. In the area of formal thought, this has now been recognized, and most historical discussions of democracy and socialism, of evolution, of Christianity and agnosticism, deal with Mill and Darwin, Newman and Huxley. But at the deeper level of character and temperament, the old notion of black and white contrast which grew up in the period of reaction continues to prevail. We still imagine that our frame of mind is as different from that of the Victorians as our clothes, and as obviously superior. We need to change the colors to grey and white: to realize that Victorian optimism is still a basic attitude, though the excitement has gone; that our "age of anxiety" suffers from many of the same fears that shook the optimistic surface of Victorian life; that our skepticism is merely a more radical form of the doubt which was even then mining the eternal verities; that the sense of loneliness and isolation we are so aware of was already felt and poignantly expressed by the Victorians; that in their age lie the immediate roots of our commercial spirit, our anti-intellectualism, our appeal to force; and that even the hurry and pressure under which we live is a century old, and Victorian leisure is a myth. I do not mean, of course, that there are not also some striking contrasts, particularly in the area of love and sex. But the very effort to answer the questions we are accustomed to ask, "How *could* the Victorians have been so prudish, or so hypocritical, or so rigid and dogmatic?" leads to some unexpected discoveries which force us to drop the superior tone. We see that there but for the grace of God—or Freud—go we; and that our own candor, sincerity, and measured judgment, so far as we possess these virtues more than the Victorians, have been purchased at the loss of some valuable convictions. In short, to peer through the darkness of a hundred years and turn even a flashlight on the landscape of 1850 is to see our own situation a little more clearly.

As these remarks imply, the attitudes here under scrutiny are those which were conspicuous from about 1830 to 1870; which is to say that taken together and interrelated, they provide a definition of Victorianism. It is quite true that some historians insist on a division at 1850, and others think that no more than a decade can be treated as a unit. In fact, it is now smart to say that of course there was no such thing as Victorianism. But the literature of those years, while indicating shifts and changes of outlook and showing that there are clear distinctions between the frame of mind at the start and at the close of this period, nevertheless so constantly reveals the presence of the same fundamental attitudes in every decade and in every group—among High Churchmen and liberals, agnostics and Tories—that I cannot doubt there was a common culture for which the term Victorianism, though in a wider sense than it usually bears, is appropriate. After 1870, while many of its characteristics persist through the century (as is shown by the quotations occasionally given from writings—or memories—of the seventies and eighties), their dominance and their peculiar coherence were breaking down. Victorianism was dying, and a new frame of mind was emerging, a *late* Victorian frame of mind, which pointed forward to the postwar temper of the 1920's.

For my data I have turned to literature in the full faith that "if we hope to discover the inward thoughts of a generation," as Whitehead once remarked, "it is to literature that we must look." But literature in the broad sense that includes letters and diaries, history, sermons, and social criticism, as well as poetry and fiction. It is there that "the concrete outlook of humanity receives its expression." The wording is precise. If the end proposed, in Newman's words, "is that of delineating, or, as it were, painting what the mind sees and feels," we can do this fully and precisely only through what the mind expresses. That is why I have made extensive use of quotation. Attitudes are elusive. Try to define them and you lose their essence, their special color and tone. They have to be apprehended in their concrete and living formulation.

To rely on literature in this way means to rely on the artist; and by and large the witnesses called in this book are the men of letters—the major Victorian writers and the minor prophets like John Sterling,

W. R. Greg, John Morley, or Baldwin Brown. How far can we trust
their view of the age? And, more important, how far can we assume
that the ideas and attitudes they themselves adopt were widely held
in the upper and middle classes? (The working class as such is not
here under consideration.) These are complex questions which cannot
be explored in a short preface, but one or two relevant factors may
be mentioned.

Certainly the writers are not to be heard uncritically, and we have
always to consider that what they say of society may be true only of
their own literary circles, as is sometimes clearly the case. But to
turn from *Sartor Resartus* and *Past and Present* to a popular handbook
for Victorian Dick Whittingtons called *Self-Help* and discover almost
every one of Carlyle's central ideas reappearing—however stripped
of their "fiery poetic emphasis" in the plain prose of Samuel Smiles—
is simply one instance of many to support the generalization made by
Sir Leslie Stephen in 1876: "How is it that a tacit intellectual cooperation is established between minds placed far apart in the scale of
culture and natural acuteness? How is it that the thought of the intellectual leaders is obscurely reflected by so many darkened mirrors?"
But the process may also work the other way. The writer may 'find'
his ideas already current in the society, waiting only for him to give
them form and authority. Who shall say how much *In Memoriam* gave
artistic embodiment to perceptions already operative, or created new
ones that brought fresh awareness to the generation of the fifties? In
some proportions it must have done both.

Today we tend to think of the intellectuals as a special class, ahead
of their time perhaps and certainly out of touch with professional and
business life; and though exaggerated, the notion has its foundation
in fact. But this divorce between the artist and the public—which can
be seen on the Victorian horizon—did not occur until the last decades
of the century. In the years between 1830 and 1870 the sense of crisis
at the very moment when the traditional authority of the church and
the aristocracy was breaking down, impelled men of letters to focus
on the contemporary scene more consciously, I think, than they had
ever done before; and then, in the light of their analysis, to urge the
adoption of one or another political, religious, or moral philosophy.
Moreover, at a time when middle-class achievements in commerce,
industry, and politics were so extraordinary, the artist-thinkers were
more imbued with bourgeois ideals and more sensitive to bourgeois
needs than was later the case. On the other side, a large public, living
in an age of "doubts, disputes, distractions, fears," looked deliberately

to the literary prophets, and to the famous reviews through which they usually spoke, for guidance or reassurance; and the captains of industry, so long as their formal education was so limited, turned to men of letters for the culture which a rising class is eager to acquire. No doubt certain attitudes—optimism, moral earnestness, and the worship of force, for example—were more common among the men of action, while others like melancholia and enthusiasm were more often found among the intellectuals. But all exist, in varying degrees, in both groups. The intimate connection between literature and life is a significant feature of the Victorian age and one of its chief glories.

Chapter 1

CHARACTER OF THE AGE

In 1858 a Victorian critic, searching for an epithet to describe "the remarkable period in which our own lot is cast," did not call it the age of democracy or industry or science, nor of earnestness or optimism. The one distinguishing fact about the time was "that we are living in *an age of transition.*" [1] This is the basic and almost universal conception of the period.[2] And it is peculiarly Victorian. For although all ages are ages of transition, never before had men thought of their own time as an era of change *from* the past *to* the future. Indeed, in England that idea and the Victorian period began together. When John Stuart Mill in 1831 found transition to be the leading characteristic of the time— "mankind have outgrown old institutions and old doctrines, and have not yet acquired new ones"—he noted that this had been recognized by the more discerning only "a few years ago," and that now "it forces itself upon the most inobservant." [3]

To Mill and the Victorians the past which they had outgrown was not the Romantic period and not even the eighteenth century. It was the Middle Ages. They recognized, of course, that there were differences between themselves and their immediate predecessors, but from their perspective it was the medieval tradition from which they had

1. "The Progress and Spirit of Physical Science," *Edinburgh Review, 108* (1858), 71. The writer (who was kindly identified for me by Professor R. D. Altick) was Sir Henry Holland. The article was reprinted in his *Essays on Scientific and Other Subjects Contributed to the Edinburgh and Quarterly Reviews*, London, 1862.

2. The specific words "transition" or "transitional" are used by Prince Albert, Matthew Arnold, Baldwin Brown, Carlyle, Disraeli, Frederic Harrison, Bulwer Lytton, W. H. Mallock, Harriet Martineau, John Mill, John Morley, William Morris, Herbert Spencer, Hugh Stowell, J. A. Symonds, Tennyson, and no doubt many others.

3. *The Spirit of the Age*, p. 6, and cf. p. 1. Here and throughout the present work the particular edition used for cited and quoted works, if not identified in the note, will be found in the Bibliography.

irrevocably broken—Christian orthodoxy under the rule of the church and civil government under the rule of king and nobility; the social structure of fixed classes, each with its recognized rights and duties; and the economic organization of village agriculture and town guilds. That was "the old European system of dominant ideas and facts" which Arnold saw dissolving in the nineteenth century.[4] But the process had begun much earlier, starting with the Renaissance and the Reformation, gaining momentum, quietly but steadily, through the next two centuries of philosophic rationalism and expanding business, until it finally broke into the open when the French Revolution of 1789 proclaimed the democratic Rights of Man and the atheistical worship of the Goddess of Reason. That was the first overt manifestation, in Mill's opinion, that Europe was in a state of transition.[5] But it was not realized at the time, not in England. There it was not until the rising agitation for a reform bill (finally successful in 1832), the passage of Catholic Emancipation, the attack on the Church by Whig liberals and Benthamite agnostics, together with the outbreak of the 1830 revolutions abroad, that men suddenly realized they were living in an age of radical change.[6] Then they began to say that "old opinions, feelings—ancestral customs and institutions are crumbling away, and both the spiritual and temporal worlds are darkened by the shadow of change."[7]

For "old" and "ancestral" we may read "medieval" or "feudal." When Arnold observed that many people thought it possible to keep a good deal of "the past," his next sentence defined the term: the extremists, indeed, hoped "to retain or restore the whole system of the Middle Ages."[8] "Until quite recently," wrote Baldwin Brown in his important lectures of 1869–70, *The Revolution of the Last Quarter of a Century*, ". . . our modes of thought and speech, our habits of action, our forms

4. "Heine," *Essays in Criticism, First Series*, pp. 186–7.

5. *The Spirit of the Age*, p. 67. Cf. Carlyle, "Signs of the Times," *Essays*, 2, 82.

6. See Mill, "The Claims of Labour," *Dissertations and Discussions*, 2, 188; and George Eliot, *Felix Holt, 1*, chap. 3, pp. 66–7.

7. Edward Bulwer Lytton, *England and the English* (1833), p. 281. This passage may have been written by Mill: see his *Autobiography*, chap. 6, p. 168.

8. "Democracy" (1861), *Mixed Essays*, p. 22. Robert Vaughan began *The Age of Great Cities* (1843) with a section "On the Conflict between Feudalism and Civilization in Modern Society" in which he noticed (pp. 5–6) a reactionary movement that would "diminish everything commercial and civic, so as to place the military and the feudal in its old undisturbed ascendancy" and would "restore the power of the Christian priesthood in much of the form and greatness which distinguished it during the middle age."

of procedure in things social and political, were still feudal." [9] To Carlyle and Ruskin and Thomas Arnold, the period is one of decaying or dying feudalism.[10] This was not an abstract idea. Victorians like Thackeray who had grown up in the 1820's felt they had lived in two distinct worlds:

> It was only yesterday; but what a gulf between now and then! *Then* was the old world. Stage-coaches, more or less swift, riding-horses, pack-horses, highway-men, knights in armour, Norman invaders, Roman legions, Druids, Ancient Britons painted blue, and so forth—all these belong to the old period. I will concede a halt in the midst of it, and allow that gunpowder and printing tended to modernise the world. But your railroad starts the new era, and we of a certain age belong to the new time and the old one. We are of the time of chivalry as well as the Black Prince of Sir Walter Manny. We are of the age of steam.[11]

From a mere glance at the title page of Carlyle's *Past and Present*, any Victorian might have guessed that the book was a comparison of the Middle Ages with the nineteenth century.

By definition an age of transition in which change is revolutionary has a dual aspect: destruction and reconstruction. As the old order of doctrines and institutions is being attacked or modified or discarded, at one point and then another, a new order is being proposed or inaugurated. Both tendencies were apparent by 1830. After his description of the breakup of timeworn landmarks, Bulwer Lytton continued: "The age then is one of *destruction!* . . . Miserable would be our lot were it not also an age of preparation for reconstructing." [12] Twenty years later at the center of the Victorian period, what new construction had emerged? Or rather—for this is the important question for getting at the temper of the age—what did men think distinguished their time

9. *First Principles of Ecclesiastical Truth*, p. 273. The lectures are on pp. 209–364. For their date see p. vii.

10. Thomas Arnold and Carlyle are quoted below, p. 4; for Ruskin, see *The Crown of Wild Olive*, *Works, 18*, Lecture 4, p. 494. Cf. Dowden, quoted below, note 14.

11. "De Juventute" (1860), published in the *Roundabout Papers, Works, 12*, 232. For the tendency to idealize the prerailroad world of the early century, see Kathleen Tillotson, *Novels of the Eighteen-Forties*, pp. 102–9, where Thackeray's essay is quoted.

12. *England and the English*, p. 281; but see note 7. Cf. Carlyle, *Sartor Resartus*, Bk. III, chap. 7, p. 244.

most significantly from the past? What did they think was peculiarly Victorian about "the state of society and of the human mind?"[13]

1. *The State of Society*

By the late nineteenth century it was clear that the feudal and agrarian order of the past had been replaced by a democratic and industrial society.[14] The emergence of democracy meant not only the transference of political power from the aristocracy to the people, mainly by the successive Reform Bills of 1832, 1867, and 1884, but also the arrival of what is often termed a democratic society. The latter, indeed, was so striking that Mill once called the distinguishing feature of modern institutions and of modern life itself the fact "that human beings are no longer born to their place in life . . . but are free to employ their faculties, and such favourable chances as offer, to achieve the lot which may appear to them most desirable."[15] This breakdown of the old conception of status owed something to democratic ideas about the rights of man, but its primary cause was economic. The development of commerce, drawing men off from the land and opening new and independent careers to talent, had been the main instrument in dissolving the feudal nexus of society.[16] In politics, too, the Industrial Revolution underlay the democratic revolution. What Thomas Arnold had in mind when he remarked, on seeing the first train pass through the Rugby countryside, that "feudality is gone for ever,"[17] is made explicit by a passage in *Sartor Resartus*, written on the eve of the Reform Bill of 1832: "Cannot the dullest hear Steam-Engines clanking around him? Has he not seen the Scottish Brassmith's IDEA (and this but a mechanical one) travelling on fire-wings round the Cape, and across two Oceans; and stronger than any other Enchanter's Familiar, on all hands unweariedly fetching and carrying: at home, not only weaving Cloth; but rapidly enough overturning the whole old system of Society; and, for Feudalism and Preservation of the

13. These are Mill's categories in *The Spirit of the Age*, pp. 2, 6.

14. Cf. Dowden, "Victorian Literature" (1887), *Transcripts and Studies* (London, 1896), p. 159: "Society, founded on the old feudal doctrines, has gone to wreck in the storms that have blown over Europe during the last hundred years. A new industrial and democratic period has been inaugurated."

15. *The Subjection of Women*, chap. 1, p. 445. Cf. Brown, *First Principles*, pp. 274–9.

16. Brown, pp. 280–1, and cf. Mill, "Democracy in America," *Dissertations*, 2, 62–71.

17. A. P. Stanley, *Life of Thomas Arnold*, appendix D, p. 723 n., with the journal entry for August 4, 1839.

Game, preparing us, by indirect but sure methods, Industrialism and the Government of the Wisest?" [18]

Whether wisest or not, the bankers and manufacturers who rose to political power through the revolutionary legislation of 1828-1835—the repeal of the Test and Corporation Acts, the Municipal Reform Act, and above all, the Reform Bill—owed their victory to the financial and psychological power they acquired from the Industrial Revolution. Both factors are seen in Disraeli's analysis of the capitalist mind in *Coningsby*. Mr. Millbank is discussing the English peerage: "I have yet to learn they are richer than we are, better informed, wiser, or more distinguished for public or private virtue. Is it not monstrous, then, that a small number of men, several of whom take the titles of Duke and Earl from towns in this very neighbourhood, towns which they never saw, which never heard of them, which they did not form, or build, or establish,—I say, is it not monstrous that individuals so circumstanced should be invested with the highest of conceivable privileges, the privilege of making laws?" [19] Those are the social forces, wealth and outraged pride, which demanded the Reform Bill. And once the middle class attained political as well as financial eminence, their social influence became decisive. The Victorian frame of mind is largely composed of their characteristic modes of thought and feeling.

But far more striking at the time than democracy was the tremendous industrial development that came with the use of new machines for manufacturing and communication.[20] The great inventions date from the later eighteenth century; and in the early decades of the nineteenth the introduction of more canals, macadam roads, railways, and steamboats hastened the growth of large-scale production by making possible a vast expansion of commerce. This development revolutionized the economic life of England. The old system of fixed regulations, which paralleled that in fixed social relations, was abandoned for the new principle of laissez-faire, on which the manufacturer bought his materials in the cheapest market and sold them in the highest, and

18. Bk. II, chap. 4, p. 118. The Scottish Brassmith is James Watt.

19. *Works*, 12, chap. 26, p. 225. Cf. Brougham's speech in the House of Lords advocating the Reform Bill, quoted in A. V. Dicey, *Lectures on the Relation of Law and Public Opinion in England*, pp. 184-5.

20. Cf. T. H. Huxley, "The Progress of Science, 1837-1887," *Method and Results*, p. 42: "The most obvious and the most distinctive feature of the History of Civilisation, during the last fifty years, is the wonderful increase of industrial production by the application of machinery, the improvement of old technical processes and the invention of new ones, accompanied by an even more remarkable development of old and new means of locomotion and intercommunication."

hired his labor wherever he liked, for as long as he pleased, at the lowest wages he could pay. In Southey's *Colloquies on the Progress and Prospects of Society* (1829) and Macaulay's fighting review of it (1830), the world of big business and unlimited competition was debated by the old conservatism and the new liberalism.

To live in this dynamic, free-wheeling society was to feel the enormous pressure of work, far beyond anything known before. When new and more distant sources of supply and demand were constantly being opened up by the railroad and the steamship, the battle for new markets became intense. To neglect them could mean ruin. So could failure to take advantage of the latest invention or adapt one's business methods to the most recent developments. Disraeli's Coningsby is startled to learn from Mr. Head, who is building a new mill at Staleybridge, that Manchester is already gone by. "If you want to see life," he says, "go to Staley-bridge or Bolton. There's high-pressure." Only the Manchester Bank has kept up with the times: "That's a noble institution, full of commercial enterprise; understands the age, sir; high-pressure to the backbone." [21] The masters had to work almost as long hours as their hands—the Messrs. Carson, for example, who did not become acquainted with their agreeable daughters until their mill was burned down: "There were happy family evenings now that the men of business had time for domestic enjoyments." [22] The same pressure was felt in the professions. "The eminent lawyer, the physician in full practice, the minister, and the politician who aspires to be a minister—even the literary workman, or the eager man of science—are one and all condemned to an amount and continued severity of exertion of which our grandfathers knew little." [23] That was due as much to the social system as to business conditions. When class lines broke down and it became possible as never before to rise in the world by one's own strenuous efforts, the struggle for success was complemented by the struggle for rank.[24] Even apart from personal ambitions, the very existence of hundreds of objects, once unknown or within the reach of few, now made widely available and therefore desirable, increased the size of one's expenses and the load of his work.[25] More-

---

21. *Works*, *12*, chap. 24, p. 210. The date is 1844.

22. Mrs. Gaskell, *Mary Barton* (first ed., 1848; London, 1911), chap. 6, p. 67.

23. W. R. Greg, "Life at High Pressure" (1875), *Literary and Social Judgments*, *2*, 272.

24. This is discussed below, Chap. 8.

25. Cf. Mark Pattison, "The Age of Reason," *Fortnightly Review*, 27 (1877), 357: "To live at all is a struggle; to keep within reach of the material advantages which it is the boast of our century to have provided is a competition in which only the strong can succeed—the many fail."

over, the growing wealth of the wealthy advanced the style of living in the middle and upper classes to a point where the Victorian had to struggle for things his father had been able to ignore. George Eliot remarked that £3,000 a year had seemed wealth to provincial families in 1830, "innocent of future gold-fields, and of that gorgeous plutocracy which has so nobly exalted the necessities of genteel life." [26]

Not only the tempo of work but the tempo of living had increased with striking impact, so much so that one observer thought that "the most salient characteristic of life in this latter portion of the 19th century is its SPEED." [27] Until the Victorian period the rate of locomotion and communication had remained almost what it had been for centuries. The horse and the sailing vessel were still the fastest things on earth. But within a few years the speed of travel by land increased from twelve to fifty miles an hour on the new railroads (over 400 per cent) and the new steamships were doing fifteen knots "with wonderful regularity, in spite of wind and tide." [28] But it was less the mechanical speed of the new inventions than the speed of living they produced which impressed the Victorians. Faster locomotion, of goods and letters and people, simply increased the number of things one crowded into a day, and the rush from one to another. Once upon a time "people did not run about the town or the land as we do." They traveled less often, did not hurry to catch trains, wrote one letter a morning instead of ten. Now "we are whirled about, and hooted around, and rung up as if we were all parcels, booking clerks, or office boys." [29] It seems far more modern than Victorian. But if the speed of life has increased in the twentieth century, the sense of speed has declined, for what has become commonplace today was then a startling novelty. Our great-grandfathers may have had more leisure than we do but it seemed less. Even more than ourselves they felt they were living "without leisure and without pause—a life of *haste*—above all a life of excitement, such as haste inevitably involves—a life filled so full . . . that we have no time to reflect where we have been and whither we intend to go . . . still less what is the value, and the purpose, and *the price* of what we have seen, and done, and visited." [30]

26. *Middlemarch, 1,* Bk. I, chap. 1, p. 6; and cf. Greg, p. 278.

27. Greg, p. 263.

28. Ibid., p. 264, quoted from Greg's earlier *Enigmas of Life,* pp. 38–9. Cf. Frederic Harrison, "A Few Words about the Nineteenth Century," *The Choice of Books,* pp. 421–2.

29. Frederic Harrison, *Autobiographic Memoirs, 1,* 12, 18–19. Though he was writing in the 1880's, he was comparing conditions in his later life with those of his youth (he was born in 1831).

30. Greg, p. 268.

This sense of faster and more crowded living had its intellectual as well as its mechanical basis. The spread of education coupled with the enormous expansion of knowledge and the corresponding increase of publication, books and periodicals and newspapers, gave "every man . . . a hundred means of rational occupation and amusement which were closed to his grandfather," [31] and led George Eliot, in a threnody on the death of leisure ("gone where the spinning-wheels are gone, and the pack-horses, and the slow wagons, and the pedlers, who brought bargains to the door on sunny afternoons") to say that "even idleness is eager now,—eager for amusement; prone to excursion-trains, art-museums, periodical literature, and exciting novels; prone even to scientific theorizing, and cursory peeps through microscopes." [32] By the sixties Frances Cobbe was comparing her own generation with that of 1800–30 in words which sound exactly like someone today comparing the generation of 1950 with that of 1850: "That constant sense of being driven—not precisely like 'dumb' cattle, but cattle who must read, write, and talk more in twenty-four hours than twenty-four hours will permit, can never have been known to them." [33]

2. The State of the Human Mind

The radical transition in the human mind was less apparent at first than that in society, but sensitive observers were soon aware that the traditional framework of thought was breaking down. By 1838 Thomas Arnold had noticed a new "atmosphere of unrest and paradox hanging around many of our ablest young men of the present day." He was speaking not merely of religious doubts but "of questions as to great points in moral and intellectual matters; where things which have been settled for centuries seem to be again brought into discussion." [34] This is the atmosphere reflected in the early essays of Macaulay and Car-

31. Kingsley, "Great Cities and Their Influence for Good and Evil" (1857), *Sanitary and Social Essays*, p. 203.

32. *Adam Bede*, 2, chap. 28, p. 339. In editions where the chapters are numbered consecutively this is chap. 52.

33. "The Nineteenth Century," *Fraser's Magazine*, 69 (1864), 482 (for the attribution of this article to Frances Cobbe see the Bibliography, below). Cf. Brown, *First Principles*, pp. 222–3, inviting his hearers in 1869 to compare "the rate at which you are living, . . . the rate of thought, feeling, and energy—in these as compared with those quiet and comfortable times" in the first decades of the century.

34. Stanley, *Life of Arnold*, p. 484, from a letter dated October 5, 1838. The next sentence justifies my insertion of "merely."

lyle, in *Sartor Resartus* and Mill's *Spirit of the Age*, and the novels of Sterling and Maurice. All of them, written between 1825 and 1834, show that the old certitudes are certain no longer and that a reconstruction of thought is now a prime necessity. "The Old has passed away," wrote Carlyle in 1831, "but, alas, the New appears not in its stead; the Time is still in pangs of travail with the New." [35] There was, of course, more destruction to come, for the old was by no means gone (traditional Christianity, indeed, under Wesleyan and presently Tractarian influence was reviving). And there had been earlier efforts to bring forth the new, most notably by Bentham and Coleridge, the respective heirs of the French *philosophes* and the German transcendentalists, "the two great seminal minds of England in their age." [36] But *the New* had not yet appeared by the thirties. All that was then clear to the intellectuals was that their task was precisely what Carlyle found attempted in the two books he had under review in the essay "Characteristics": "Both these Philosophies are of the Dogmatic or Constructive sort: each in its way is . . . an endeavour to bring the Phenomena of man's Universe once more under some theoretic Scheme . . . they strive after a result which shall be positive; their aim is not to question, but to establish." [37]

That is the starting point. What was the situation a generation later? What corresponds in the intellectual world to the establishment of bourgeois industrial society? The answer is—nothing. In 1850 the age is still one "of fusion and transition. . . . Old formula, old opinions, hoary systems are being thrown into the smelting-pan; they are fusing —they must be cast anew: who can tell under what new shapes . . . they will come forth from the moulds?" In the seventies men are still searching—"amid that break-up of traditional and conventional notions respecting our life, its conduct, and its sanctions, which is undeniably befalling our age,—for some clear light and some sure stay." By the eighties "the disintegration of opinion is so rapid that wise men and foolish are equally ignorant where the close of this waning century will find us." [38] Though the Victorians never ceased to look forward to a new period of firm convictions and established beliefs, they

35. "Characteristics," *Essays*, 3, 32.

36. Mill, "Bentham," *Dissertations*, 1, 331.

37. *Essays*, 3, 33.

38. The three quotations are by Hugh Stowell, "The Age We Live In," in *Exeter Hall Lectures*, 6 (London, 1850–51), 45–6; Matthew Arnold, "Bishop Butler and the Zeit-Geist," *Last Essays on Church and Religion*, p. 287; and J. A. Froude, preface to *Short Studies*, 4, v–vi.

had to live in the meantime between two worlds, one dead or dying, one struggling but powerless to be born, in an age of doubt.[39]

The phrase is ambiguous—and at first glance dubious. When one thinks of Macaulay, Spencer, and Huxley, or of Browning, even of Mill and Ruskin, let alone thousands of pious Evangelicals and Anglicans, one is ready to deny it. Indeed, it was still common until very recently to draw a radical contrast between the Victorians and ourselves. One modern critic thought that "a spirit of certitude, wonderful to us who live in an age which has taken the note of interrogation as its emblem, impregnated the great Victorians." Another has claimed that it was only after 1900 that "the old certainties were certainties no longer," and "everything was held to be open to question"; and that "the Victorians seemed to themselves to be living in a house built on unshakable foundations and established in perpetuity . . . the Home, the Constitution, the Empire, the Christian religion—each of these . . . was accepted as a final revelation." [40] From such assumptions we could predict the reversal, under the powerful incitement of nostalgia, of the anti-Victorian movement represented by Lytton Strachey:

> If, after the first World War, we were all debunking the nineteenth century, after the second we are deferring to it, and even yearning nostalgically after it: *tendentesque manus ripae ulterioris amore*. In our own unpleasant century we are mostly displaced persons, and many feel tempted to take flight into the nineteenth as into a promised land . . . In that distant mountain country, all that we now lack seems present in abundance: not only peace, prosperity, plenty and freedom, but faith, purpose and buoyancy.[41]

Though this contrast of the Victorian period with our own has its element of truth, the tendency to invest the past with the virtues one finds lacking in the present has led to a serious misconception. The fact is, while moral values were firm until about 1870, all intellectual

39. See Arnold, "Stanzas from the Grande Chartreuse" (1855), lines 85–8. After Bulwer Lytton in *England and the English* refers (p. 281) to living in an age of transition, he adds in apposition, "an age of disquietude and doubt." Cf. Winwood Reade, *The Martyrdom of Man* (first published in 1872), p. 540: "We are now in the dreary desert that separates two ages of belief." Mill's important statement is quoted below, p. 30.

40. The two critics are D. Willoughby in *The Great Victorians*, ed. H. J. Massingham and Hugh Massingham (Garden City, N.Y., 1932), p. 242, and A. C. Ward, *Twentieth-Century Literature. The Age of Interrogation, 1901–1925* (London, 1930), pp. 2, 4.

41. Basil Willey, *Nineteenth Century Studies*, p. 52.

theories, including those of morality, were insecure. What John Morley said of the fifties and sixties applies to the entire period, though with greater intensity and wider repercussions as the years passed: "It was the age of science, new knowledge, searching criticism, followed by multiplied doubts and shaken beliefs." [42] The very effort to resolve the situation made it worse. New solutions raised new controversies, which raised new questions. "Intellectually," wrote J. A. Froude—with religion in mind, but his remark has broader relevance—"the controversies to which I had listened had unsettled me. Difficulties had been suggested which I need not have heard of, but out of which some road or other had now to be looked for." [43] But which road? The choice was baffling. "None of the ways in which . . . mental regeneration is sought," Mill recognized in 1842, "Bible Societies, Tract Societies, Puseyism, Socialism, Chartism, Benthamism, etc.—will *do*, though doubtless they have all some elements of truth and good in them"; with the result that he was finding it very hard to make up his mind "as to the course which must be taken by the present great transitional movement of opinion and society." [44]

The range of discussion reflected by Mill's list is significant. It was not only in religion that one faced a series of alternatives: is there a God or is there not, and if so, is he a person or an impersonal force? Is there a heaven and a hell? or a heaven but no hell? or neither? If there *is* a true religion, is it Theism or Christianity? And what is Christianity? Roman Catholicism or Protestantism? Is it Church or Chapel? High Church? Broad Church? Low Church? Similar questions, if not so pressing or so widespread, invaded ethical theory and the

42. *Recollections, 1*, 100. The view of the period I am advocating—not that doubt existed, which has long been recognized, but that it was an "age of doubt" rather than of certitude—emerged, here and there, in *Ideas and Beliefs of the Victorians* (1949): see pp. 19, 23–5, 71–7, 423; and in 1953 Gaylord C. LeRoy published a book on Victorian writers called *Perplexed Prophets*. But as recently as June 19, 1953, a critic in the *Times Literary Supplement* (p. 397) wrote of the era: "We may envy the unquestioning firmness of its faith, whether the object of that faith was religion, or science, or humanity."

43. "The Oxford Counter-Reformation," *Short Studies, 4*, 311–12. On p. 252 Froude notices that the Oxford Tracts, designed to check the advance of liberalism and atheism, "provoked doubts, in those whom they failed to persuade, about Christianity itself." Also cf. "The Age We Live In," *Fraser's Magazine, 24* (1841), 5: "The very truths which have come forth have produced doubts . . . and the very lights that have shone in one quarter have only dazzled in others, and this dazzle too often has ended in darkness."

44. From a letter to R. B. Fox printed in Caroline Fox, *Memories of Old Friends,* ed. H. N. Pym (Philadelphia, 1882), pp. 393–4.

conception of man: have we free-will or are we human automatons? and if we have the power of moral choice, what is its basis? a God-given voice of conscience? or rational calculation deciding which of two actions will promote the greatest happiness of the greatest number? Is man a man or simply a higher ape? Even the political-economic order of bourgeois capitalism, if an established fact of the outer environment in 1850, held no unquestioned supremacy in the world of ideas. The sanctity and blessings of private property, laissez-faire, and unlimited competition were challenged, in one aspect or another, by Owen and Mill, Carlyle and Ruskin, the Chartists and the Christian Socialists. The abortive "communism" of 1848 in France further opened Victorian eyes to the possibility that the old political economy was limited and temporary. And the provisional character of middle-class government, suggested by the Chartist agitation of the forties, was confirmed by the Reform Bill of 1867. By 1870 the uncertain future seemed to belong to the unpredictable populace.

It was not, however, the mere existence of competing philosophies which called all in doubt. It was also the prevailing atmosphere. As one prophet after another stepped forward with his program of reconstruction, the hubbub of contending theories, gaining in number as the century advanced, and echoing through lectures, sermons, and periodicals as well as books, created a climate of opinion in which, quite apart from any specific doubts, the habit of doubt was unconsciously bred. One had an uneasy feeling, perhaps only half-conscious, that his beliefs were no longer quite secure. Nor should we forget the complementary effect of the vast increase of knowledge, scientific and historical, that almost inundated the Victorians and left them often baffled by the sheer number and complexity of its implications. The yeasty state of mind which Kingsley ascribed to the young men of 1851 was not only one in which "the various stereotyped systems which they have received by tradition [are] breaking up under them like ice in a thaw"; it was also one in which "a thousand facts and notions, which they know not how to classify, [are] pouring in on them like a flood"; and that fragmentation of knowledge was to increase with increasing specialization.[45] Mill's diary for January 13, 1854, contains what is perhaps the best statement on Victorian doubt:

45. "Epilogue" to *Yeast*, p. 312. Cf. Harrison, "A Few Words about the Nineteenth Century," pp. 437, 442; and Matthew Arnold, *Letters of Arnold to Clough*, p. 130: "Yes—*congestion of the brain* is what we suffer from—I always feel it and say it—and cry for air like my own Empedocles."

> Scarcely any one, in the more educated classes, seems to have any opinions, or to place any real faith in those which he professes to have. . . . It requires in these times much more intellect to marshal so much greater a stock of ideas and observations. This has not yet been done, or has been done only by very few: and hence the multitude of thoughts only breeds increase of uncertainty. Those who should be the guides of the rest, see too many sides to every question. They hear so much said, or find that so much can be said, about everything, that they feel no assurance of the truth of anything.[46]

Without contrary evidence, who would be surprised if the passage were dated 1954?

This evidence—and much more could be given—suggests that continuity rather than contrast is the conclusion to be drawn from comparing the Victorians with ourselves. And yet, if both periods can be called ages of doubt, it is certainly with a difference. Neither the kind of doubt nor the strength of its hold was the same in 1850 as it is today.

In the four decades under inspection, doubt never reached the point of positive or terminal skepticism. It never involved a denial of the mind as a valid instrument of truth. No mid-Victorian ever described his age as Dobrée described the 1930's: "All the previous ages . . . had something they could take for granted. . . . We can be sure of nothing; our civilization is threatened, even the simplest things we live by. . . . In our present confusion our only hope is to be scrupulously honest with ourselves, so honest as to doubt our own minds and the conclusions they arrive at. Most of us have ceased to believe, except provisionally, in truths, and we feel that what is important is not so much truth as the way our minds move towards truths." [47] Though the seeds of that radical doubt were planted by the 1870's, as we shall see in a moment, they did not grow up until the dissolving influences of modern sociology, anthropology, and psychology had done their work, and mined the old confidence with relativism and rationalization.[48]

46. *Letters*, 2, 359.
47. *Modern Prose Style* (Oxford, 1934), p. 220.
48. Cf. W. H. Auden, writing of these modern studies in *Poets of the English Language*, ed. W. H. Auden and N. H. Pearson (5 vols. New York, 1950), 5, xxii–xxiii: "Their exhibition of the mind's capacity for self-deception, of the unconscious effect upon its thinking of social status and sex, their demonstration that the customs and beliefs of other peoples could not be dismissed as merely

The Victorians might be, and often were, uncertain about what theory to accept or what faculty of the mind to rely on; but it never occurred to them to doubt their capacity to arrive at truth. When Mill thought of his age as one of intellectual anarchy, his reaction to such a condition was quite different from ours. He could see it as a momentary and necessary stage in a process of growth: "So long as this intellectual anarchy shall endure, we may be warranted in believing that we are in a fair way to become wiser than our forefathers; but . . . we have not yet advanced beyond the unsettled state, in which the mind is, when it has recently found itself out in a grievous error, and has not yet satisfied itself of the truth." [49] Not yet but soon! "If your opinions, or mine, are right," he told Sterling, "they will in time be unanimously adopted by the instructed classes." [50] It is this faith in the existence of ultimate truths in religion and ethics, in politics, economics, and aesthetics (as well as in the natural sciences), and in the capacity of the human mind to discover them, by some form of reason or of intuition, which unites the partisans of every school. That, one is tempted to say, is the one intellectual certitude in Victorian England. But it is a great one, for on such a foundation the universe can be held together: it can remain rational. That is why Chesterton could claim that the Victorian period was "orderly compared with what came after." (But not, he added, "compared with the centuries that came before.") [51] On that foundation it was still possible, as it no longer is, to find comfort in the thought

> That, though I perish, Truth is so:
> That, howsoe'er I stray and range,
> Whate'er I do, Thou dost not change. [52]

It was still possible to adopt this or that theory of Church or State with full confidence that it might well be true—though not that it *was*.

But less possible after 1870. For about that time a number of things converged to suggest the relativity of knowledge and the subjective character of thought. This radical change, bounding the mid-Victorian temper, is documented in the popular work of Walter Pater.

The historical method, as it was formulated under the influences of

---

savage, irrational, and quaint but must be accepted as rival civilizations complete in themselves, cast doubts on the finality of any truth."

49. *The Spirit of the Age*, pp. 12–13.
50. *Letters*, 1, 6. Cf. *The Spirit of the Age*, p. 33.
51. *The Autobiography of G. K. Chesterton* (New York, 1936), p. 20..
52. Arthur Hugh Clough, "It fortifies my soul to know," *Poems*, p. 75.

Romantic and scientific conceptions of development, meant the study of social phenomena of all kinds, institutions, customs, beliefs, as the natural product of a given time and place; with the result that the type of question one put to the past underwent a crucial change. One no longer asked, What do I think of this? is it good? is it true? For once everything was thought relative, good or true only for a particular society at a particular stage in its cultural evolution, the right questions became: How shall I account for it? Why did men believe that it was good or true? [53]

> In the intellectual as in the organic world the given product, its normal or abnormal characteristics, are determined, as people say, by the "environment." The business of the young scholar therefore, in reading Plato, is not to take his side in a controversy, to adopt or refute Plato's opinions . . . still less, to furnish himself with arguments on behalf of some theory or conviction of his own. His duty is rather to follow intelligently, *but with strict indifference,* the mental process there, as he might witness a game of skill. . . . To put Plato into his natural place, as a result from antecedent and contemporary movements of Greek speculation, of Greek life generally: such is the proper aim of the historic, that is to say, of the really critical study of him. [54]

The phrase I have italicized adds the final touch: nothing could be less Victorian. Though recognized earlier, the awareness that the historical attitude could issue in skepticism did not reach general consciousness, I think, until after 1870 when it came to be debated in the periodicals by men like John Morley, Edward Dowden, and Henry Sidgwick. [55]

At the same time the scientific view that all things, material and human, were in constant flux, changing under the inevitable influences of many and complex factors, could make all truths seem relative only to a particular moment. In the opening paragraphs of the "Coleridge" (1866) and the "Conclusion" to *The Renaissance* (1873), Pater revived the skepticism of Hume and reduced all knowledge to a series of "im-

53. See Morley, *Recollections, 1,* 71–2, and Wilfrid Ward, "The Time-Spirit of the Nineteenth Century," *Edinburgh Review, 194* (1901), 92–131, reprinted in his *Problems and Persons,* London, 1903.
54. Pater, *Plato and Platonism* (New York, 1901), p. 6. The italics are mine.
55. Morley, *On Compromise,* pp. 18–21; Dowden, *Studies in Literature,* pp. 106–9; Sidgwick, "The Historical Method," *Mind, 11* (1886), 213–15.

pressions unstable, flickering, inconsistent," each of which "is the impression of the individual in his isolation, each mind keeping as a solitary prisoner its own dream of a world." [56] On such assumptions the intellectual life was ridiculous. Only the aesthetic life of delicate perceptions and sensitive response had any importance. Not that philosophy or "speculative culture" was ruled out. It still had value for the human spirit—but only "to rouse, to startle it into sharp and eager observation." By suggesting "points of view" it could "help us to gather up what might otherwise pass unregarded by us." [57]

To turn back from Pater to Arnold is to return to the Victorian world. For Arnold threw his whole weight against relativism. Not, it is true, with reference to historical or scientific theories, but to the liberal dogma of individualism and its assertion of private judgment, which in society as a whole was the major force that undermined the belief in absolute truths. By 1864 Arnold was aware of a "baneful notion that there is no such thing as a high, correct standard in intellectual matters; that every one may as well take his own way." [58] To the contemporary boast that every Englishman could believe what he liked, what was true for him, Arnold kept asking whether it was not important that what people were free to believe should be worth believing; whether, in short, the anarchy of individualism should not be checked by the authority of Culture, with its inherent power of discovering truth. For Culture, "bent on seeing things as they are," can dissipate delusions like the worship of freedom for its own sake, and fix "standards of perfection that are real!" [59] What is meant here by things as they are or standards that are real is the very absolutes which Plato affirmed and Pater denied. "To see things as they are" is "to draw towards a knowledge of the universal order which seems to be in-

56. *Appreciations*, pp. 65–7, and *The Renaissance*, pp. 246–9. The quotation is on p. 248. The "Conclusion" was first written in 1868. On Pater's skepticism, see Helen H. Young, *The Writings of Walter Pater. A Reflection of British Philosophical Opinion from 1860 to 1890* (1933), chap. 3, esp. pp. 27–9, and Milton Millhauser, "Walter Pater and the Flux," *Journal of Aesthetics and Art Criticism, 11* (1952–53), 214–23. Cf. Karl Pearson, *The Grammar of Science* (1892), where the same skeptical conclusions were systematically advanced. That book and its impact are discussed in *The Education of Henry Adams*, chap. 31.

57. *Renaissance*, pp. 249, 251.

58. "The Literary Influence of Academies," *Essays in Criticism, First Series*, p. 66.

59. *Culture and Anarchy*, chap. 1, p. 51. Cf. Lionel Trilling, *The New Yorker Magazine* (June 18, 1949), p. 74, where—with Arnold plainly in his mind—he spoke of George Orwell's "commitment to intellect" as "fortified by an old-fashioned faith that the truth can be got at, that we can, if we actually want to, see the object as it really is."

tended and aimed at in the world . . . to learn, in short, the will of God"; and this insight comes from the use of right reason, meaning intuitive judgment, by a man of wide learning and flexible intelligence. Indeed, Arnold cites Plato by name as explicitly denying to the mere man of virtue the Greek instinct for what he (Plato) calls "the true, firm, intelligible law of things." "He reserves it for the lover of pure knowledge, of seeing things as they really are,—the φιλομαθής." [60]

The contrast of Pater with Arnold is pointed by their respective conceptions of the "modern spirit." To Pater, of course, it is the relative spirit, which considers that "truth itself is but a possibility, realisable not as a general conclusion, but rather as the elusive effect of a particular personal experience"; and which "must needs content itself with suspension of judgment, at the end of the intellectual journey, to the very last asking: *Que scais-je?* Who knows?" [61] For Arnold the modern spirit is the awareness that traditional beliefs and institutions are no longer adequate to embody contemporary life; and the representatives of the modern spirit, "the would-be remodellers of the old traditional European order," are "the invokers of reason against custom." For them the end of the intellectual journey is not doubt but reconstruction. [62]

Pater and Arnold face each other across the gulf between two basic conceptions of the human mind that opened up between 1865 and 1875. By 1877, at the house party given by W. H. Mallock where "culture, faith, and philosophy" are discussed in a new "Republic," the Paters have become a society, still small but destined to rise to fame, or notoriety, in the nineties. Mr. Herbert, who speaks for the mid-Victorians (he is Ruskin) berates the younger generation because, in the face of conflicting opinions, they persuade themselves "that neither opinion is of much moment—that the question cannot be decided absolutely—that it should not be decided absolutely." [63] This is as true of morality as of everything else. "There is no recognised rule of life

60. *Culture and Anarchy*, chaps. 1, 4, 5, pp. 46, 134, 147. Arnold was also indebted to Cicero and the Stoic theory of natural law: see p. 54 of the essay cited in note 58. It is true that Arnold sometimes uses "things as they are" to mean as they "objectively exist" or "as they are in fact," in contrast with how they appear to a prejudiced mind.

61. *Plato*, pp. 156–7. As the quotation suggests, Pater found the beginning of the modern, relative spirit in Montaigne.

62. "Heine," *Essays in Criticism, First Series*, pp. 185, 189–90. Though I develop it somewhat differently, this contrast between Pater and Arnold was suggested to me by Graham Hough, *The Last Romantics*, pp. 134–41.

63. W. H. Mallock, *The New Republic, or, Culture, Faith, and Philosophy in an English Country House*, p. 279.

anywhere," comments Mr. Leslie. "Every one who does right at all
only does what is right in his own eyes. All society, it seems, is going
to pieces." To which another guest replies:

> "I," said Mr. Rose, "look upon social dissolution as the true con-
> dition of the most perfect life. For the centre of life is the individ-
> ual, and it is only through dissolution that the individual can re-
> emerge. All the warrings of endless doubts, all the questionings of
> matter and of spirit, which I have myself known, I value only
> because, remembering the weariness of them, I take a profounder
> and more exquisite pleasure in the colour of a crocus, the pulsa-
> tions of a chord of music, or a picture of Sandro Botticelli's." [64]

Mr. Rose, I need hardly say, is Pater—a caricature of Pater. A decade
later Canon Liddon, who like Arnold and Ruskin was a mid-Victorian,
observed that "a morbidly active imagination which cannot acquiesce
in the idea of fixed and unalterable truth" had become a malady of
modern society.[65]

Though the Victorians were certain that truth existed and the mind
could discover it, they found themselves involved in two forms of
doubt: either what is sometimes called negative skepticism, when the
judgment is suspended between alternate conclusions, one of which
is considered true; or the affirmation of a belief which they only half
believed—and half doubted. Both types of insecurity are present in
the important passage from Mill's diary quoted earlier: "Scarcely any
one, in the more educated classes seems to have any opinions [because
he sees "too many sides to every question"] or to place any real faith
in those which he professes to have." [66]

When Alfred North Whitehead spoke of the nineteenth century as
being disturbed by the conflicting claims of incompatible doctrines,

64. Pages 54–5.

65. Quoted by R. H. Hutton, *Aspects of Religious and Scientific Thought*, p. 17.
For a similar account of "the intellectual revolution of our time," which he sees
beginning somewhat later, viz. "about 1890," see H. Stuart Hughes, *An Essay for
Our Times* (New York, 1950), pp. 15–17. For an extended discussion of the Victorian
faith in absolute and universal laws, see below, Chap. 6, sec. 2.

66. Reference in note 46, above. In discussions of the period, both contemporary
and modern, the word "doubt" is sometimes used to mean religious unbelief. In
this book I restrict it to the two definitions just given, which apply to all areas of
thought, but especially religious thought, and use "religious skepticism," "unbelief,"
"agnosticism," or "atheism" for outright disbelief in a divine reality.

he pointed out that Cardinal Newman in his *Apologia pro Vita Sua*
found it a peculiarity of Pusey, the great Anglican ecclesiastic, that
"he was haunted by no intellectual perplexities." "In this respect,"
Whitehead continued, "Pusey recalls Milton, Pope, Wordsworth, as in
contrast with Tennyson, Clough, Matthew Arnold, and Newman himself." [67] A letter of George Eliot's, written in 1839, gives a characteristic
illustration of this new state of mind, and with reference to a topic
which for Newman was especially baffling:

> I think no one feels more difficulty in coming to a decision on
> controverted matters than myself. . . . The other day Montaigne's
> motto came to my mind (it is mentioned by Pascal) as an ap-
> propriate one for me,—"Que sais-je?"—beneath a pair of balances,
> though, by the by, it is an ambiguous one, and may be taken in a
> sense that I desire to reprobate. . . . I use it in a limited sense
> as a representation of my oscillating judgment. On no subject do I
> veer to all points of the compass more frequently than on the
> nature of the visible Church. I am powerfully attracted in a
> certain direction, but when I am about to settle there, counter-
> assertions shake me from my position.[68]

Nothing could better describe the negative skepticism of the time, including, as it does, the rejection of the positive skepticism which Pater
drew from the same passage in Montaigne.[69] It was not, of course,
limited to religion. In the forties Disraeli found society "in the midst
of a convulsion in which the very principles of our political and social
systems are called in question," and created a hero in its image—"confused, perplexed," his mind "a chaos"; but his spirit sustained "by a
profound, however vague, conviction, that there are still great truths,
if we could but work them out." [70] In the same years, worried because
the condition-of-England problem was "shaking many old beliefs, and
leading him whither he knew not," Tom Brown at Oxford plunged
into works on political economy, then consulted an Anglo-Catholic
friend about High Church teaching on social questions, and finally
read *Past and Present*—and so filled his head "full of a set of contra-

67. *Science and the Modern World*, p. 120.

68. J. W. Cross, *George Eliot's Life as Related in Her Letters and Journals, 1,*
41, letter to Miss Lewis, May 20, 1839.

69. For the Victorian view of Montaigne, see John Sterling's essay in the
Westminster Review, 29 (1838), 321–52, reprinted in his *Essays and Tales, 1,*
129–87.

70. *Coningsby*, in *Works, 12*, chap. 23, pp. 196–7.

dictory notions and beliefs." By the time he graduated, reading and discussion had combined to drag him into "perplexities, and doubts, and dreams, and struggles." [71] The Victorian plight was summed up by Clough in a poem which deals with still another area of doubt, the nature of man: *Is* he a human automaton?

> Oh say it, all who think it,
> Look straight, and never blink it!
> If it is so, let it be so,
> And we will all agree so;
> But the plot has counterplot,
> It may be, and yet be not.[72]

It must not be supposed, however, that the normal state of the Victorian mind was one of indecision or suspended judgment. The confidence in reason or intuition and the powerful will to believe made doubt itself unstable. It came and went. Individuals passed through it. Mill confessed in 1833 that "I am often in a state almost of scepticism, and have no theory of Human Life at all, or seem to have conflicting theories, or a theory which does not amount to a belief"; but he added at once, "This is only a *recent* state, and, as I well know, a passing one, and my convictions will be firmer." [73] Passing but recurrent. What he says of his own transition (from his early Benthamism through doubt to his later liberalism) applies in general to all the mid-Victorian intellectuals. For reasons we shall have to consider, Carlyle, Newman, Disraeli, Froude, Eliot, Arnold—none was any more content than Mill to remain "confused and unsettled." [74] All like him succeeded in weaving new ideas and old dogmas into a fresh pattern of thought.

Not until the sixties does a settled state of baffled judgment and a mind empty of beliefs begin to appear. It was then, when the *Origin of Species* and *Essays and Reviews* intensified the difficulties of decision, especially in religion, while at the same time positive skepticism was emerging, that Frances Cobbe was struck by a new disposition "to accept as a finality that condition of hesitation and uncertainty

71. Thomas Hughes, *Tom Brown at Oxford* (which describes the university when Hughes was there from 1842 to 1845), chaps. 35 and 50, pp. 415–19, 572.

72. *Poems*, p. 44, from an untitled poem beginning, "Is it true, ye gods, who treat us."

73. *Letters*, 1, 48–9.

74. *Autobiography*, chap. 5, pp. 132–3. For the "reasons," see below, Chap. 4, sec. 2, on the will to believe.

which in the nature of things should be one of transition." [75] Such a condition, as we might expect, is habitual in the society of Mallock's *New Republic*, where "nobody knows what to believe, and most people believe nothing," [76] but it did not exist a generation earlier. It had only afflicted individuals for shorter or longer intervals. Most of the time the Victorian mind contained beliefs and not doubts—but the beliefs were shaky. [77]

What *is* constantly present, therefore, is the fear or suspicion, or simply the vague uneasy feeling, that one was not sure he believed what he believed. I do not mean that no one had any strong beliefs. The traditional morality was firmly held by almost everyone until the seventies and by a vast majority until after World War I; and there were certainly many people whose religious or political convictions remained unshaken. But the more one studies the period, the more certain he is that most Victorians were aptly described by Mill himself in *The Spirit of the Age*: "The men of the present day rather incline to an opinion than embrace it; few . . . have full confidence in their own convictions"; or, in a variant phrase, people "have no strong or deep-rooted convictions at all." [78] How could it have been otherwise in a period of dissolving creeds and clashing theories? If one's formal

75. *Fraser's Magazine*, 69 (1864), 491. A few years later Henry Sidgwick (*Henry Sidgwick: A Memoir*, p. 158) detected signs that "an age of general indecisiveness" seemed to be commencing; and Symonds (Horatio F. Brown, *John Addington Symonds*, pp. 316–17) referred to "the *habitual* condition of scepticism" in which the soul is denuded of "moral ideas and fixed principles," and went on to say that nowadays a man "is *always* saying like Montaigne: 'Ni comme ceci, ni comme cela, ni même autrement'; or again, 'Peut-être oui, peut-être non, peut-être ni l'un ni l'autre.'" The italics are mine.

76. Page 50. Cf. Harrison, *Autobiographic Memoirs*, 1, 24, in 1882; Beatrice Webb, *My Apprenticeship*, p. 165, in 1884 (and cf. pp. 49–50); Mark Rutherford, *Mark Rutherford's Deliverance*, pp. 28, 75–6, in 1885.

77. This was particularly true of religious beliefs; and in calling the period one of doubt, I do not mean to imply that it was one of religious skepticism. On the contrary, Christian faith was characteristic of the frame of mind. If most Victorians had reservations about one or more theological doctrines, they instinctively looked for the hand of God in the events of life; interpreted success as the reward for virtue, or suffering as the punishment for sin. They thought of death quite literally as a reunion with the loved ones who had gone ahead. The churches were crowded; Bibles (on chains!) were placed in railroad stations; sermons outsold novels. But here, too, as in other areas, belief was shaky.

78. *The Spirit of the Age*, pp. 12, 13. These remarks were made in 1831, but the quotation from his diary given above (p. 13) shows that he would have thought them entirely applicable in 1854.

doubts were sooner or later discarded for one creed or another, the taint of doubt remained. A prayer attributed to the Victorians is a witty distortion of the truth: "O God—if there is a God—save my soul—if I have a soul." Like Spencer in later life (and the example is significant, since no one could seem more certain or dogmatic), one clung to his dogmas, old or new or a mixture of both, "but without confident faith." [79] Or like Tennyson. In the representative poem of the age, the key words are "trust," "hope," "guess":

> Behold, we know not anything;
>   I can but trust that good shall fall
>   At last—far off—at last, to all.

> I trust I have not wasted breath:
>   I think we are not wholly brain,
>   Magnetic mockeries.

> The Power in darkness whom we guess. [80]

In Memoriam is not a poem of belief or of unbelief. It is a poem of doubt, that is, of doubtful beliefs. In our generation, Kingsley noted, "few of us deeply believe anything." [81]

The two outstanding features of their world which most impressed the Victorians are now before us. No one could escape them. No one could take them, as we can take them now, with the indifference or the neutrality adopted toward the customary. Everyone in all classes to some degree felt their impact. We might well expect, therefore, that the major Victorian attitudes would have been mainly determined by the powerful influence (as much from the reaction they provoked as from their positive effect) of these two things, one or both of which are implicit in every reference to "the age of transition"—bourgeois industrial society and widespread doubt about the nature of man, society, and the universe. In the analysis that follows this is the central thread in a pattern planned to include, in due relation to it, other important influences, especially that of the so-called Puritan or Evangelical revival. [82]

79. Beatrice Webb, *My Apprenticeship*, p. 32.
80. *In Memoriam* (1850), secs. 54, 120, 124.
81. *Letters and Memories*, *1*, 113 (unabridged ed., *1*, 141).
82. Elie Halévy's well-known thesis (a typical statement is in the "Conclusion" to his *England in 1815*) that Victorian culture was the child of Evangelicalism

At the threshold stand two emotional attitudes, in the broad sense of pleasure-pain responses, which were bound to occur in a period of conscious and radical change, and which were nourished by many of the same social and intellectual developments. The Victorians reacted to their age with hope and dismay, optimism and anxiety.

and Industrialism has been widely adopted; indeed, this has been the only general key to the period. Valuable as it is, I think it gives too much importance in the total picture to the Puritan revival, however central that was for a few attitudes, mainly moral earnestness (though even there other factors must be reckoned with, as we shall see in Chap. 10); and it ignores the widespread and demonstrable influence of doubt upon the Victorian frame of mind.

Part I

EMOTIONAL ATTITUDES

Chapter 2

OPTIMISM

> Look around you and see what is the characteristic of
> your country and of your generation at this moment.
> What a yearning, what an expectation, amid infinite
> falsehoods and confusions, of some nobler, more chiv-
> alrous, more god-like state! Your very costermonger
> trolls out his belief that 'there's a good time coming,'
> and the hearts of *gamins*, as well as millenarians,
> answer, 'True!' . . . And as for flesh, what new ma-
> terials are springing up among you every month . . .
> railroads, electric telegraphs . . . chemical agriculture,
> a matchless school of inductive science, an equally
> matchless school of naturalist painters,—and all this
> in the very workshop of the world!
>
> *Kingsley, 1851* [1]

1. *Reconstruction and History: the Revival of Hope*

By 1830 it was no longer bliss to be alive; nor was the time dawn. The
Utopian dreams of human perfectibility which had grown up in the
eighteenth century and seemed on the point of fulfillment when the
French Revolution broke out had been undermined by the Reign of
Terror, the dictatorship of Napoleon, the long years of war with the succeeding period of depression and social unrest, and by the speculations of Malthus. "Man has walked by the light of conflagrations, and
amid the sound of falling cities; and now there is darkness, and long
watching till it be morning." [2]

Now, but not for long. For the darkest hour is nearest the dawn;
and though "deep and sad as is our feeling that we stand yet in the
bodeful Night; equally deep, indestructible is our assurance that the
Morning also will not fail. Nay, already, as we look round, streaks of
a dayspring are in the east . . . when the time shall be fulfilled, it will

1. *Yeast*, chap. 17, pp. 293–4.
2. Carlyle, "Characteristics" (1831), *Essays, 3,* 32.

be day." [3] In another pattern of imagery the time is described in terms of illness. The destructive period of the disease is over; the stage is now one of convalescence in which the principle of life is reviving. Or, more exactly, it is laboring to produce fresh health and vigor; for in this period, progress is associated with strenuous effort. Though the time is racked and torn, men are "struggling towards the light." In the midst of promise and threatening, "human society is, as it were, struggling to body itself forth anew, and so many *coloured rays* are springing up in this quarter and in that, which only by their union can produce *pure light*." [4]

This renewal of hope about 1830 had its basis in the idea of progress, which had first clearly emerged in the Renaissance. The Baconian argument from advancing knowledge, each age possessing and profiting from a constantly increasing body of positive truth, was well established by the eighteenth century. To this the rational philosophers, assuming the almost omnipotent effect of external circumstances on the shaping of mind and character, added the particular argument that by the control of environment human life might be vastly improved. Wise laws, democratic government, and universal education would end the twin reign of tyranny and superstition and usher in the millennium. In this fine faith Mill was brought up by his father and Jeremy Bentham. The Utilitarian creed meant:

> In politics, an almost unbounded confidence in the efficacy of two things: representative government, and complete freedom of discussion. So complete was my father's reliance on the influence of reason over the minds of mankind, whenever it is allowed to reach them, that he felt as if all would be gained if the whole population were taught to read, if all sorts of opinions were allowed to be addressed to them by word and in writing, and if by means of the suffrage they could nominate a legislature to give effect to the opinions they adopted. . . .
>
> In psychology, his fundamental doctrine was the formation of all human character by circumstances, through the universal Principle of Association, and the consequent unlimited possibility of

3. Ibid., p. 37. Cf. "The Age We Live In," *Fraser's Magazine*, 24 (1841), 4: "We are . . . still in that twilight where the stars are retreating one by one, but where the day is not yet distinct."

4. The quotations are from John Sterling, "Poems by Alfred Tennyson," *Quarterly Review*, 70 (1842), 390, reprinted in his *Essays and Tales*, 1, 422–62; and Carlyle, "State of German Literature" (1827), *Essays*, 1, 30. Cf. Carlyle, *Essays*, 3, 32, 40, and Mill, *The Spirit of the Age* (written in 1831), p. 13.

improving the moral and intellectual condition of mankind by education.[5]

Even Carlyle in his earlier years, though hostile to Utilitarianism, thought the age was advancing because "knowledge, education are opening the eyes of the humblest; are increasing the number of thinking minds without limit."[6]

In the late eighteenth century another theory of progress was founded on a new conception of history, adopted by both Carlyle and Mill. History was not a "stop-and-go" process in which advance waited upon particular events, but a natural and organic development in which each age was the child of the previous one; and since the contrast between contemporary civilization and its small and inferior beginnings seemed obvious, the development was plainly one of progress. In Mill, drawing on French interpretations, this process was viewed scientifically as a series of causes and effects, governed by some law of historical evolution.[7] In Carlyle, more influenced by the metaphysical speculations of the Germans, it was conceived as a gradual realization of ideals, in the philosophic sense, a progressive unfolding of the capabilities of humanity. The crude beginnings of justice develop in course of time into closer and closer approximation to Justice. Carlyle's assurance that a new and brighter day will follow the present darkness rests explicitly on his faith in "the progress of man towards higher and nobler developments of whatever is highest and noblest in him. . . . Under the mortal body lies a *soul* which is immortal; which anew incarnates itself in fairer revelation."[8] But this distinction between a scientific and an idealist interpretation was made by only a few philosophers. The idea of progress as it actually existed in Victorian minds

5. *Autobiography,* chap. 4, pp. 89, 91.

6. "Signs of the Times" (1829), *Essays, 2,* 80.

7. A succinct statement by Mill is in his "Michelet's History of France," *Dissertations, 2,* 129. In general see Bury, *The Idea of Progress,* chaps. 15 and 16, on Saint-Simon and Comte.

8. "Characteristics," *Essays, 3,* 37, 39. On the speculations of Lessing, Herder, Kant, and Hegel, see Bury, chap. 13, and R. G. Collingwood, *The Idea of History* (Oxford, 1946), pp. 86–122. Kant's theory was described by Southey in *Sir Thomas More: or, Colloquies on the Progress and Prospects of Society, 2,* 408–11. René Wellek, "Carlyle and the Philosophy of History," *Philological Quarterly, 23* (1944), 55–76, suggests some distinctions between Carlyle and the German idealists which may be valid. But the statements I quote bring him into general line with their point of view. Cf. Hill Shine, "Carlyle's Early Writings and Herder's *Ideen:* the Concept of History," *Booker Memorial Studies,* ed. Hill Shine (Chapel Hill, N.C., 1950), pp. 3–33.

was a loose blending of both into a general notion of progressive development. Without asking about whys and wherefores, they would have agreed with Carlyle's summary: "As Phlogiston is displaced by Oxygen, and the Epicycles of Ptolemy by the Ellipses of Kepler; so does Paganism give place to Catholicism, Tyranny to Monarchy, and Feudalism to Representative Government,—where also the process does not stop. Perfection of Practice, like completeness of Opinion, is always approaching, never arrived; Truth, in the words of Schiller, *immer wird, nie ist;* never *is,* always *is a-being.*" [9]

The forward movement, however, was not continuous. Progress occurred through a series of alternating periods. Because Mill's exposition defines the historical character of an age of transition, with its tripartite divisions of destruction, reconstruction, and doubt, and places the present period against the Middle Ages, I quote it at length. He is speaking of the Saint-Simonians, though he was aware that the theory "was the general property of Europe."

> I was greatly struck with the connected view which they for the first time presented to me, of the natural order of human progress; and especially with their division of all history into organic periods and critical periods. During the organic periods (they said) mankind accept with firm conviction some positive creed, claiming jurisdiction over all their actions, and containing more or less of truth and adaptation to the needs of humanity. Under its influence they make all the progress compatible with the creed, and finally outgrow it; when a period follows of criticism and negation, in which mankind lose their old convictions without acquiring any new ones, of a general or authoritative character, except the conviction that the old are false. The period of Greek and Roman polytheism, so long as really believed in by instructed Greeks and Romans, was an organic period, succeeded by the critical or sceptical period of the Greek philosophers. Another organic period came in with Christianity. The corresponding critical period began with the Reformation, has lasted ever since, still lasts, and cannot altogether cease until a new organic period has been inaugurated by the triumph of a yet more advanced creed. [10]

This is also Carlyle's philosophy of history (where the two periods are called those of "belief" and "unbelief" and the metaphor of the phoenix

9. "Characteristics," *Essays,* 3, 38.

10. *Autobiography,* chap. 5, pp. 138–9. The opening sentence refers to 1829–30, when he first read the Saint-Simonians.

for society is introduced): "Find Mankind where thou wilt, thou find-est it in living movement, in progress faster or slower: the Phoenix soars aloft, hovers with outstretched wings, filling Earth with her music; or, as now, she sinks, and with spheral swan-song immolates herself in flame, that she may soar the higher and sing the clearer." [11] It is this confidence in a new and greater age of organic belief, whether religious or secular, which makes the present period of doubt and confusion seem tolerable because temporary. "If our era is the Era of Unbelief, why murmur under it; is there not a better coming, nay come?" [12] Indeed, denial itself can thus be viewed as having a vital if negative function: "The fever of Scepticism must needs burn itself out, and burn out thereby the Impurities that caused it; then again will there be clearness, health." [13]

The note of hopeful expectation was increased by the position as-signed to the modern period in the cyclical pattern of history. By Herder, Novalis, and Goethe, as well as by the Saint-Simonians, the present moment was considered the end of the critical phase and therefore the springtime of renewal or rebirth. It is true that the autumn fulfillment now seemed much further off than it had on the eve of the French Revolution; perhaps it would take two centuries.[14] But meanwhile the organic filaments of the new age were forming, even now as the last of the old age were being destroyed. "Amid the rushing and the waving of the Whirlwind-element come tones of a melodious Deathsong, which end not but in tones of a more melodious Birthsong." [15]

Carlyle and Mill were not reflecting the general outlook in the England of 1830. They were attempting—and successfully—to form it. They were trying to revive the idea of progress which had lost its hold on the generation of the twenties, and by doing so, to check the impotent dismay which the revolutionary changes of the period pro-duced in many minds. In itself, insists Carlyle, there is "nothing ter-rible, nothing supernatural" about change; it is the normal condition of

11. *Sartor Resartus*, Bk. III, chap. 7, p. 248. Carlyle too was influenced here by the Saint-Simonians: see Hill Shine, *Carlyle and the Saint-Simonians: The Concept of Historical Periodicity*, Baltimore, 1941.

12. *Sartor Resartus*, Bk. II, chap. 3, p. 112.

13. "Characteristics," *Essays*, 3, 40; and cf. pp. 32–3. The temporary utility of doubt is also found, as we should expect, in Mill: see *The Spirit of the Age*, pp. 12–13.

14. Carlyle's estimate in *Sartor*, Bk. III, chap. 7, p. 244.

15. Ibid., pp. 244–5.

life, from day to day, age to age.[16] And though often painful, it is a wholly beneficent process. Change is *progress*, and the age is one of *transition to a greater age*—that is the underlying message of "Signs of the Times" (1829), "Characteristics" (1831), and *Sartor Resartus* (1833). In similar fashion, when Mill gave his "Speech on Perfectibility" in 1828, he began by admitting that "if I had much anxiety to save my credit as a wise and practical person I should not venture to stand forth in defence of the progressiveness of the human mind. I know that among all that class of persons who consider themselves to be *par excellence* the wise and the practical, it is esteemed a proof of consummate judgement to despair of doing good."[17] The speech that follows is then an attempt to revive the faith in progress in its Utilitarian form, emphasizing the potential benefits of education and representative institutions. It might be thought that Macaulay's essays of this period, with their massive evidence for the progress of wealth and population, of knowledge and liberty—and their glamorous prophecies of greater things to come—tell a different story and justify the notion that the early thirties "was one of those springtide periods when life seems aglow with new-born energy," a "glad, confident morning."[18] But Macaulay himself testified to just the opposite state of mind. "Though in every age," he wrote in 1830, "everybody knows that up to his own time progressive improvement has been taking place, nobody seems to reckon on any improvement during the next generation. We cannot absolutely prove that those are in error who tell us that society has reached a turning point, that we have seen our best days."[19] But he will try to do so. The year 1830 *was* a turning point of another kind, the point when the decline of faith in progress was reversed and its upward movement began again—partly through the persuasive efforts of Carlyle, Mill, and Macaulay.

A generation later, and like Carlyle's phoenix it has soared higher and sings more clearly than ever before, or since. In Frederic Harrison's "Words on the Nineteenth Century" we hear the full voice of Victorian optimism: "We all feel a-tiptoe with hope and confidence. We *are* on the threshold of a great time, even if our time is not great itself. In science, in religion, in social organisation, we all know what great things are in the air. 'We shall see it, but not *now*'—or rather

16. "Characteristics," *Essays*, 3, 39.

17. *Autobiography*, appendix of unpublished speeches, p. 288.

18. Wingfield-Stratford, *Those Earnest Victorians*, p. 111.

19. "Southey's Colloquies on Society," *Critical, Historical, and Miscellaneous Essays*, 2, 186.

our children and our children's children will see it. . . . It is *not* the
age of money-bags and cant, soot, hubbub, and ugliness. It is the age
of great expectation and unwearied striving after better things." [20]
Because Utopia is now in sight, the striving is now unwearied. This
is the note of ecstatic anticipation which marked the period after 1850.
Though political and economic developments formed a favorable environment, it was largely scientific theory and scientific invention that
together created an atmosphere of supreme optimism about the present
and the future.

2. *Two Utopias of Science: Great Expectations*

Perhaps the most important development in nineteenth-century intellectual history was the extension of scientific assumptions and methods from the physical world to the whole life of man. In itself this was
not a new idea, but never before had the questions Mill raised in his
System of Logic (1843) been widely asked, or answered so confidently
in the affirmative: "Are the actions of human beings, like all other
natural events, subject to invariable laws? Does that constancy of
causation, which is the foundation of every scientific theory of successive phenomena, really obtain among them?" [21] The affirmative answer
of the rationalists reawakened the dream of Bacon in the Victorian
consciousness. "The End of our Foundation," he had said of his scientific academy called Solomon's House, "is the knowledge of Causes,
and secret motions of things; and the enlarging of the bounds of
Human Empire, to the effecting of all things possible." [22] Indeed,
under the influence of Comte, that came to be thought of as the historical end of the nineteenth century. For in Comte's analysis the
intellectual progress of mankind was divided into three stages: in the
first, the theological, phenomena were explained by supernatural agen-
cies; in the second by metaphysical abstractions; in the third and final
by positive, scientific laws. Now at long last the human mind, freed
from the false methods of theology and metaphysics, possesses the key
to truth. That was the theme of George Henry Lewes' *Biographical*

20. "A Few Words about the Nineteenth Century," *The Choice of Books*,
p. 425. The date is 1882 but the same note begins to be struck in the fifties: see
below, in the next section, and above, the epigraph from Kingley's *Yeast* (1851)
prefixed to this chapter.

21. Bk. VI, chap. 1, sec. 2 (New York, 1874), p. 581.

22. The *New Atlantis*, in *The Works of Francis Bacon*, ed. Spedding, Ellis,
and Heath (7 vols. London, 1857–59), 3, 156. The passage has been related to the
Victorians by G. M. Young and Basil Willey.

History of Philosophy (1845–46), which, with Mill's *System of Logic,* introduced Comte to England. Lewes' last section on the nineteenth century, called "Philosophy finally relinquishing its place in favor of positive science," is the happy ending foretold in the Introduction:

> Philosophy has been ever in movement, but the movement has been circular; and this fact is thrown into stronger relief by contrast with the linear progress of Science. Instead of perpetually finding itself, after years of gigantic endeavor, returned to the precise point from which it started, Science finds itself year by year, and almost day by day, advancing step by step, each accumulation of power adding to the momentum of its progress. . . . *Onward, and forever onward, mightier and forever mightier, rolls this wondrous tide of discovery,* and the "thoughts of men are widened by the process of the suns." [23]

After Darwin had made the greatest 'discovery' of the period in 1859, the imagination of young liberals was fired by the vision of a life spent in contributing, no matter how little, to the great revelation of all knowledge.[24] "It reminds one almost of the crusades," wrote one observer, "of the search for the Holy Grail,—this strange determined resolution to go out in pursuit of the Truth. Solitary souls—groups of two or three—have gone forth in all ages; but here was a whole army with its enthusiasts, its raw recruits, its mercenaries, its troop of mere camp-followers." [25]

The goal was by no means merely intellectual. It included the practical elimination of physical suffering through medicine, and even of moral evil through the new science of sociology, founded by Comte

23. *The Biographical History of Philosophy* (2 vols. in 1, New York, 1885), Introduction, p. xi. The italics are mine. The quotation, which also stands on the title page, is from Tennyson's "Locksley Hall." This introduction first appeared in the 1857 ed.

24. Cf. Huxley's reference in "On Species and Races, and Their Origin" (1860), quoted in J. R. A. Davis, *Thomas Henry Huxley* (London and New York, 1907), p. 51, to "those whose life is spent, to use Newton's noble words, in picking up here a pebble and there a pebble on the shores of the great ocean of truth— who watch, day by day, the slow but sure advance of that mighty tide, bearing on its bosom the thousand treasures wherewith man ennobles and beautifies his life."

Single quotation marks (e.g. Darwin's 'discovery,' above) indicate that a word or phrase is used in a broad sense, not strictly true, as it might be used in conversation.

25. Margaret Todd, *Windyhaugh*, written under the pseudonym of Graham Travers, p. 352. Though first published in 1898, the time of the story (see p. 31) is the sixties. On this excited march toward the utopia of truth, other source passages may be found in Amy Cruse, *The Victorians and their Reading*, pp. 96–8, where *Windyhaugh* is mentioned, and in Noel Annan, *Leslie Stephen*, pp. 144–9.

and first discussed in England by Mill. Since the historical process was an organic process, the possible discovery of its dynamic law or laws, through the combined study of history and human nature, held out immense possibilities. For once that was done, men would be able by the knowledge of causes to determine "what artificial means may be used, and to what extent, to accelerate the natural progress in so far as it is beneficial; to compensate for whatever may be its inherent inconveniences or disadvantages." [26] That theory and its promise, stated by Mill in the *Logic*, were widely popularized in the following decades by H. T. Buckle, Herbert Spencer, John Morley, and others, until "the reconstruction of society on a scientific basis" became an assumption of the time.[27] Precisely how this was to be done remained obscure—the laws of social dynamics proving more elusive than was expected—but the belief that it could be done gave the search for truth a practical bearing of the most optimistic kind. "Because evil and wrong-doing and darkness," said Morley, "are acknowledged to be effects of causes, sums of conditions, terms in a series, they are to be brought to their end, or weakened and narrowed, by right action and endeavour." Once the laws of sociology are mastered, predicted W. K. Clifford, we may "rationally organize society for the training of the best citizens. . . . Those who can read the signs of the times read in them that the kingdom of Man is at hand." [28]

To appreciate how ecstatic this faith in science became one must turn to the concluding pages of Winwood Reade's *The Martyrdom of Man* (1872), with their glowing prophecy of human perfectibility in body, mind, and character:

> The God of Light, the Spirit of Knowledge, the Divine Intellect, is gradually spreading over the planet and upward to the skies. . . . Satan will be overcome; Virtue will descend from heaven, surrounded by her angels, and reign over the hearts of men. Earth, which is now a purgatory, will be made a paradise . . .
>
> Hunger and starvation will then be unknown, and the best part

26. Mill, *Logic*, Bk. VI, chap. 10, sec. 8 (New York, 1874), p. 643.

27. The "others" include Kingsley, Huxley, Henry Sidgwick, Frederic Harrison, and W. K. Clifford. Kingsley, *Letters and Memories*, 2, 255 (unabridged ed., 2, 294) wrote to Mill in 1869: "In five-and-twenty years my ruling idea has been that which my friend Huxley has lately set forth as common to him and Comte; that 'the reconstruction of society on a scientific basis is not only possible, but the only political object much worth striving for.'"

28. Morley, "Byron" (1870), *Critical Miscellanies, 1,* 239; Clifford, "Cosmic Emotion" (1877), *Lectures and Essays, 2,* 284–5.

of the human life will no longer be wasted in the tedious process
of cultivating the fields. . . .

Disease will be extirpated; the causes of decay will be removed;
immortality will be invented. And then, the earth being small,
mankind will migrate into space, and will cross the airless Saharas
which separate planet from planet, and sun from sun. The earth
will become a Holy Land which will be visited by pilgrims from
all the quarters of the universe. Finally, men will master the forces
of Nature; they will become themselves architects of systems,
manufacturers of worlds. Man then will be perfect; he will then
be a Creator; he will therefore be what the vulgar worship as
a God.[29]

Two world wars and the imminent threat of another, the science of
atomic explosion, and a realistic look at the rapidity with which we
are consuming our natural resources have ended the optimism, but they
have not, I think, destroyed an underlying faith that the progress of
science must mean the progress of civilization.[30]

The other vision of Utopia had nothing to do with scientific advance.
It was a metaphysical conception of the universe erected on the narrow
foundation of natural evolution. By 1850 the evidence of paleontology
made it possible to read the history of animal life as a great progressive
development from the amoeba up through fishes to reptiles, to birds,
to mammals, culminating—so far—in man. But need it stop there? "Is
our race," asked Robert Chambers in his *Vestiges of the Natural History of Creation* (1844), "but the initial of the grand crowning type?
Are there yet to be species superior to us in organization, purer in feeling, more powerful in device and act, and who shall take a rule over
us!"[31] Six years later Tennyson, who knew both Lyell and Chambers,
fused the new evolution with the Romantic belief in "the progress of
man towards higher and nobler developments,"[32] and hailed Arthur
Hallam as

a closer link
Betwixt us and the crowning race

29. Pages 512–14.
30. A good account of "The Cult of Science," to which I am indebted for the
references to Lewes and Reade, is in Beatrice Webb, *My Apprenticeship*, pp. 112–
23. On p. 123 she calls "the belief in science and the scientific method . . . certainly the most salient, as it was the most original, element of the mid-Victorian
Time-Spirit."
31. Page 276.
32. Carlyle's phrase, quoted above, p. 29.

Of those that, eye to eye, shall look
 On knowledge; under whose command
 Is Earth and Earth's, and in their hand
Is Nature like an open book;

No longer half-akin to brute,
 For all we thought and loved and did,
 And hoped, and suffer'd, is but seed
Of what in them is flower and fruit;

Whereof the man that with me trod
 This planet was a noble type
 Appearing ere the times were ripe,
That friend of mine who lives in God,

That God, which ever lives and loves,
 One God, one law, one element,
 And one far-off divine event,
To which the whole creation moves.[33]

In contrast to the faith in science, where progress depends on the application of scientific methods to all the problems of life, this is a faith in progress as a law of the universe, a world-process which must occur regardless of human efforts.

That is apparent in a chapter of Herbert Spencer's *Social Statics*, called "The Evanescence of Evil." Adopting from Lamarck the doctrine that all animals instinctively strive to adapt themselves to their environment, Spencer argued that men would more and more discard those characteristics suitable to a predatory life, and more and more acquire those appropriate to a social life: "Progress, therefore, is not an accident, but a necessity. . . . As surely as there is . . . any meaning in such terms as habit, custom, practice"; so surely must "evil and immorality disappear; so surely must man become perfect." [34] It only remained for Darwin to assure his readers that as his own particular theory of evolution by natural selection "works solely by and for the

33. Epilogue to *In Memoriam*, lines 127–44. Cf. Mill, "Guizot's Essays and Lectures on History" (1845), *Dissertations*, 2, 221, on the idealist theory of history as that "of a progressive unfolding of the capabilities of humanity—of a tendency of man and society towards some distant result—of a *destination*, as it were, of humanity."

34. *Social Statics*, p. 65. The first edition appeared the year after *In Memoriam*, 1851. For a critique of this general theory of progress as a law of nature, see Collingwood, *The Idea of History*, pp. 144–5, 321–3.

good of each being, all corporeal and mental endowments will tend
to progress towards perfection" to unloose a flood of evolutionary
utopias.[35] Though Huxley was to insist that the natural process promotes only the tiger instincts (the fittest who survive are not ethically
the best but "the strongest, the most self-assertive"), and that moral
progress could be achieved only by the slow effort of man to conquer
his inherited passions,[36] the "myth of evolution" fitted so perfectly
into the general atmosphere of Victorian progress that it was accepted
without critical scrutiny. The young Lord Balfour reported in the
sixties that his barber talked of "the doctrine of evolution, Darwin
and Huxley and the lot of them—hashed up somehow with the good
time coming and the universal brotherhood, and I don't know what
else."[37]

3. Applied Science and Bigger Business: Pride and Complacency

It has been said that while the eighteenth century was satisfied with
what it was, the nineteenth century was satisfied with what it was
becoming. But with the exception of the working class, the Victorians
were very well satisfied indeed with what they *had* become; and their
faith in future progress was based less on the theories we have been
exploring than on the confident expectation of becoming more of what
they were already. Frederic Harrison's essay on the nineteenth century begins with a reference to the cantata played every morning by
the chamberlains before a great satrap in Voltaire's *Zadig:*

> Every third minute there came a refrain to this effect—
>
> > "Que son mérite est extrême!
> > Que de grâces! que de grandeur!
> > Ah! combien Monseigneur
> > Doit être content de lui-même!" . . .
>
> I sometimes think this nineteenth century with its material
> progress and its mechanical inventions, its steam and electricity,
> gas, and patents, is being treated by the press, and its other public

35. *The Origin of Species,* chap. 15, p. 373. See Leo G. Henkin, *Darwinism in
the English Novel, 1860–1910: the Impact of Evolution on Victorian Fiction*
(New York, 1940), chap. 11, "Evolution and the Idea of Progress."

36. "Evolution and Ethics" (1893), *Evolution and Ethics and Other Essays,*
pp. 80–5.

37. Quoted in the introduction to *English Prose of the Victorian Era,* ed.
C. F. Harrold and W. D. Templeman (New York, 1938), p. lvii.

admirers, much as the chamberlains in *Zadig* treated the satrap.
The century is hardly awake of a morning before thousands of
newspapers, speeches, lectures, and essays appear at its bedside,
or its breakfast table, repeating as in chorus—

> "Que son mérite est extrême!
> Que de grâces! que de grandeur!"

Surely no century in all human history was ever so much
praised to its face for its wonderful achievements, its wealth and
its power, its unparalleled ingenuity and its miraculous capacity
for making itself comfortable and generally enjoying life. British
Associations, and all sorts of associations, economic, scientific, and
mechanical, are perpetually executing cantatas in honour of the
age of progress, cantatas which (alas!) last much longer than
three hours. . . . The journals perform the part of orchestra, bang-
ing big drums and blowing trumpets—penny trumpets, twopenny,
threepenny, or sixpenny trumpets—and the speakers before or
after dinner, and the gentlemen who read papers in the sections
perform the part of chorus, singing in unison—

> "Ah! combien Monseigneur
> Doit être content de lui-même!" [38]

This cantata was first performed, and best performed, by the most
popular writer of the age, T. B. Macaulay. As the period opened, his
essays on Southey, Mackintosh, and Bacon, followed in 1846 by the
contrast of Restoration with nineteenth-century England in his *History*,
were so many variations on a single theme: that the English have
become "the greatest and most highly civilised people that ever the
world saw, have spread their dominion over every quarter of the
globe . . . have created a maritime power which would annihilate
in a quarter of an hour the navies of Tyre, Athens, Carthage, Venice,
and Genoa together, have carried the science of healing, the means of
locomotion and correspondence, every mechanical art, every manufacture, every thing that promotes the convenience of life, to a perfection which our ancestors would have thought magical." In short,
"the history of England is emphatically the history of progress." [39]
Most of this achievement Macaulay attributed to science and the influence of Bacon,[40] but it was the material "fruits" of the Baconian

38. "A Few Words about the Nineteenth Century," pp. 417–19.
39. "Sir James Mackintosh" (1835), *Critical Essays, 3,* 279.
40. Quite erroneously: see below, p. 113.

philosophy and not its theoretical implications that concerned him. And when he looked forward to even greater progress in the future, he had no theories in mind, sociological or evolutionary, and no transformation of purgatory into paradise. He simply saw the endless continuation of applied science producing greater and greater industrial civilizations. In 1930 a far larger and wealthier population will be "better fed, clad, and lodged" than in 1830, live longer and healthier lives in bigger cities, travel only by railroad and steam, and have "machines constructed on principles yet undiscovered . . . in every house." [41] Macaulay might have sat for a famous cartoon by Max Beerbohm depicting a portly and bewhiskered bourgeois pointing proudly to a larger replica of himself called "The Future as Beheld by the Nineteenth Century." Beside it Beerbohm placed another of a thin, frightened young man with a black band on his arm, staring at a question mark—"The Future as Beheld by the Twentieth Century." But the faith in material progress through applied science still continues, though without the original zest, or any of the early confidence that it meant moral and intellectual progress as well.

The zest was partly the vulgar enthusiasm for sheer size and quantity—bigger populations, longer lines of railroad, more tons of coal—which Arnold ridiculed in *Culture and Anarchy*.[42] But it was also an excited tribute to the power of man to conquer nature; to the human mind that could discover her secrets and transform her material resources into productive usefulness. "Within the last half century," wrote one Victorian in the year of the Great Exhibition, "there have been performed upon our island, unquestionably, the most prodigious feats of human industry and skill witnessed in any age of time or in any nation of the earth." [43] Equally significant, because his attitude toward science and industrialism was not uncritical, is Carlyle's excited recognition of the "wonderful accessions," which the century was making to the physical power of mankind. "We remove mountains, and make seas our smooth highway; nothing can resist us. We war with rude Nature; and, by our resistless engines, come off always

41. "Southey's Colloquies on Society," *Critical Essays*, 2, 185. Cf. the end of chap. 3, *The History of England from the Accession of James II*, in *Complete Writings of Macaulay*, 12, 108–9. Also see Froude on "the England of the future as pictured in the imagination of the sanguine Liberal statesman," "England and Her Colonies" (1870), *Short Studies*, 2, 193–5, 198–9.

42. Chap. 1, pp. 49–53. For a good example, see "The First Half of the Nineteenth Century," *Fraser's Magazine*, 43 (1851), 1–15, which proudly gives the statistics, in heads and pounds and miles.

43. E. P. Hood, *The Age and Its Architects*, pp. 138; and cf. p. 20.

victorious, and loaded with spoils." [44] The same spirit infected the manufacturers themselves. They seemed to Mrs. Gaskell "to defy the old limits of possibility, in a kind of fine intoxication, caused by the recollection of what had been achieved, and what yet should be. . . . There was much to admire . . . in their anticipated triumphs over all inanimate matter at some future time, which none of them should live to see." [45] That fine intoxication was only possible in the days when big business and applied science were still young, and the material world was all before them.

Both were often associated with moral and intellectual progress. Newman might ridicule the liberal doctrine that "education, railroad travelling, ventilation, drainage, and the arts of life, when fully carried out, serve to make a population moral and happy," but it had its element of truth. [46] To improve the physical conditions of life, especially in the new towns, through the alliance of legislation and science, was to improve not only health but moral habits as well. Good drains, good water, decent light and air could reduce the amount of vice; and by making the working classes more contented with their lot, could make them more law-abiding—and less dangerous. [47] As for Newman's reference to railroad traveling, it was a Victorian commonplace that "every improvement of the means of locomotion benefits mankind morally and intellectually as well as materially," because it "not only facilitates the interchange of the various productions, of nature and art, but tends to remove national and provincial antipathies, and to bind together all the branches of the great human family"—to bind them together, that is, in universal brotherhood and peace. [48]

Nothing Victorian is now so curious and ironic as the confident expectation that industrial progress would mean the end of war. The argument that the advance of international communications would displace the prejudice of ignorance by the friendliness of understanding was supplemented by another: that the control of society was passing out

44. "Signs of the Times" (1829), *Essays, 2*, 60. It is worth noticing that even Coleridge, *On the Constitution of the Church and State* (first ed. 1830; London, 1839), p. 63, reported that he finished reading a history of English and Scotch inventions, "docks, rail-ways, canals, and the like . . . under the strongest impressions of awe, and admiration akin to wonder."

45. *North and South*, chap. 20, pp. 193–4. On this topic cf. G. M. Young, *Victorian England*, pp. 6–8.

46. Note on "Liberalism," *Apologia pro Vita Sua*, p. 501.

47. See particularly Kingsley's *Sanitary and Social Lectures and Essays*. Cf. Young, *Victorian England*, p. 7, where he quotes Newman's remark.

48. Macaulay, *History of England*, in *Complete Writings, 12*, chap. 3, pp. 44–5.

of the hands of the old aristocratic-military class into those of an industrial middle class interested only in peaceful trade and civic affairs.[49] But the most hopeful sign was the displacement of the old mercantile theory of trade by the new political economy. In the past, wrote Buckle, "every commercial treaty was an attempt made by one nation to outwit another; every new tariff was a declaration of hostility; and that which ought to be the most peaceable of all pursuits became one of the causes of those national jealousies and national animosities, by which war is mainly promoted."[50] For this great evil the new theory of free trade between nations, each of which produces what it can manufacture most easily and efficiently, seemed the perfect solution. In the summary by W. E. H. Lecky, the major historian of ideas in the period, political economy had taught men an enlightened interest in the prosperity of nations they traded with (as the shopman had an interest in the wealth of his customers) and in the enormous value of peace, since the markets of the world were now so interconnected that any derangement in one of them brought evil on all. By infallible logic he concluded that every fresh commericial enterprise was "an additional guarantee of peace," and that the most successful industrial nations, and therefore those with the greatest power to wage war, were precisely those which were "the most pacific."[51] Optimism indeed!

Five years after the repeal of the Corn Laws had announced the new era of free trade, the Great Exhibition of 1851 was opened at

49. See H. T. Buckle, *History of Civilization in England, 1,* chap. 4, pp. 192–202; and W. E. H. Lecky, *History of Rationalism, 2,* chap. 6, p. 341.

50. Buckle, pp. 216–17.

51. Lecky, pp. 335–42. He is drawing on Mill (cf. *Principles of Political Economy,* Bk. III, chap. 17, and the start of chap. 25) as well as on Buckle. Cf. Tennyson, "Locksley Hall," lines 11–16, 119–22, 127–30. The most elaborate case for the related progress of industry and peace was made out by Spencer in *The Principles of Sociology:* see the two chapters placed side by side: "The Militant Type of Society" and "The Industrial Type of Society" (3d ed. New York, 1888–90), 2, 568–602, 603–42. It is amusing to notice Buckle's weasel about the recent Crimean War, which on the face of it seemed to weigh against the whole theory, since England was the most industrial nation in the world: the peace was broken, he says (1, 195), not "by a quarrel between two civilized nations, but by the encroachments of the uncivilized Russians on the still more uncivilized Turks." By the seventies, the note of disillusionment was appearing (see J. B. Brown, *First Principles,* pp. 283–4) as the swords, especially German swords, seemed to be resisting transformation into ploughshares. But the faith continued until the first World War: see the opening stanzas of Yeats' "Nineteen Hundred and Nineteen."

London. In its impressive display of industrial achievements, both English and foreign, the Prince Consort found concrete evidence of "a period of most wonderful transition, which tends rapidly to accomplish that great end to which indeed all history points—*the realisation of the unity of mankind*"; and *The Times* in its leading article thought it marked "a great crisis in the history of the world," foreshadowing universal peace.[52] In such a context, the identification of progress with the spirit of God was less—a little less—of a rationalization than it otherwise would have been. As Kingsley entered the Great Exhibition "he was moved to tears; to him it was like going into a sacred place." Four days later he preached a notable sermon in which he said: "If these forefathers of ours could rise from their graves this day they would be inclined to see in our hospitals, in our railroads, in the achievements of our physical science, confirmation of that old superstition of theirs, proofs of the kingdom of God, realizations of the gifts which Christ received for men, vaster than any of which they had dreamed."[53] Earlier in the same year his *Yeast* had contained a letter from the hero, Lancelot Smith, to his Roman Catholic cousin which would be even more incredible than it is but for the environment I have been sketching:

> When your party compare sneeringly Romish Sanctity, and English Civilization, I say, "Take you the Sanctity, and give me the Civilization!" . . . Give me the political economist, the sanitary reformer, the engineer; and take your saints and virgins, relics and miracles. The spinning-jenny and the railroad, Cunard's liners and the electric telegraph, are to me, if not to you, signs that we are,

In fact, it still exists, or at any rate is still affirmed. In an advertisement in *The New York Times* (April 27, 1954), p. 42, Harvey S. Firestone, Jr., chairman of the board of the Firestone Tire and Rubber Corp., had occasion to say about trade with other countries: "Beyond any financial return from international business, there is the more lasting benefit of international friendship brought about by mutually beneficial commerce and person-to-person meetings between our people and those of other nations. The growing interchange of goods and services throughout the free world will do much to increase the opportunities for international economic co-operation, a fundamental step towards lasting peace."

52. Both quoted from Bury, *Idea of Progress*, pp. 330, 331. On the Exhibition there are good essays by E. L. Woodward, "1851 and the Visibility of Progress," in *Ideas and Beliefs of the Victorians*, pp. 53–62, and Asa Briggs, "The Crystal Palace and the Men of 1851," *Victorian People*, chap. 2.

53. *Letters and Memories*, 1, 239, 240 (unabridged ed., 1, 280, 281).

on some points at least, in harmony with the universe; that there is a mighty spirit working among us, who cannot be your anarchic and destroying Devil, and therefore may be the Ordering and Creating God.[54]

But for all the fine talk about brotherhood and the unity of mankind, the Great Exhibition was an obvious expression of British industrial power, and no one went away without the complacent thought of England's superiority to the less gifted and less fortunate nations of the world. Some years earlier, in Macaulay, pride in the power of man to conquer nature had already passed into pride in the power of the *English*man to subdue the earth, both material and human. Macaulay was soon echoed by Carlyle. "This Nation," announces Herr Professor Sauerteig, in the days before Germany and the United States became successful rivals, "now has . . . war-fleets, spinning-jennies, ware-houses and West-India Docks: see what it has built and done, what it can and will yet build and do!" For "to this English People in World-History" has been assigned "the grand Industrial task of conquering some half or more of this Terraqueous Planet for the use of man." [55] Perhaps the best—or worst—example of this optimism of national bravado among even the leaders of Victorian thought is found in a passage from Kingsley's lecture "How to Study Natural History." One could hardly ask for a more beautiful *mélange* of power and nationalism and empire, of Bacon and the import-export trade—and of God:

> Remember that . . . England is . . . the nation which above all others has conquered nature by obeying her; that as it pleased God that the author of that proverb, the father of inductive science, Bacon Lord Verulam, should have been an Englishman, so it has pleased Him that we, Lord Bacon's countrymen, should improve that precious heirloom of science, inventing, producing, exporting, importing, till it seems as if the whole human race, and every land from the equator to the pole must henceforth bear the indelible impress and sign manual of English science. . . .
>
> Do you not see, then, that by following these studies . . . you are training in yourselves that habit of mind which God has approved as the one which He has ordained for Englishmen, and are doing what in you lies toward carrying out, in after life, the glori-

54. Chap. 5, p. 82.
55. "Chartism" (1839), *Essays*, 4, 171, 175. There is an even higher strain of the same kind in *Past and Present*, Bk. III, chap. 6, pp. 168–9.

ous work which God seems to have laid on the English race, to replenish the earth and subdue it? [56]

4. *Liberation from the Burdens of the Past: Relief and Joy*

If the decline of the old order in political institutions and religious doctrine was viewed by some Victorians with dismay, it was greeted by others with whole-hearted satisfaction. There was a happy sense that the burdens and errors of the past were now yielding before the march of civilization.

> The year is dying in the night;
> Ring out, wild bells, and let him die.

One observer was glad to report in 1850 that "old formula, old opinions, hoary systems are being thrown into the smelting-pan"; and Dickens took pleasure in a set of dummy books called "The Wisdom of our Ancestors," with such titles as *The Block, The Stake, Ignorance, Superstition.*[57] The victory over nature was being complemented by the victory over tradition, and both victories, men felt, attested their immeasurable superiority to their forefathers.[58] At last they were casting off the fetters of aristocratic privilege and theological dogma.

56. *Scientific Lectures and Essays*, p. 308. The national conceit was also founded on the superiority of the British Constitution and the English moral character, especially when compared with what existed in France. The first is discussed just below. Kingsley, *Sanitary and Social Lectures and Essays*, p. 238, takes the French to task for their "ruinous self-conceit," and then proceeds to point out that "we . . . have been trained at once in a sounder school of morals, and in a greater respect for facts." Traveling abroad made Thomas Arnold realize (Stanley's *Life*, appendix D, pp. 701, 720, under Aug. 3, 1829, and July 16, 1839) that the English were "one of the chosen people of history." "The safety of the English people," said Lord Shaftesbury (quoted in Christie, *The Transition from Aristocracy*, p. 104), "is the special care of Providence." In one of the stalls along the Seine I once saw a book entitled *Dieu, est-il Anglais?*

57. Tennyson, *In Memoriam*, sec. 106; Hugh Stowell, "The Age We Live In," in *Exeter Hall Lectures*, 6 (1850–1), 46. For Dickens, see *Ideas and Beliefs of the Victorians*, p. 72.

58. Cf. Froude, "On Progress" (1870), *Short Studies*, 2, 352: "Our lights are before us, and all behind is shadow. In every department of life—in its business and in its pleasures . . . in its material developments and in its spiritual convictions—we thank God that we are not like our fathers." Collingwood, *The Idea of History*, pp. 145–6, gives a digest of a third-rate historical work (Robert Mackenzie, *The Nineteenth Century—a History*, London and New York, 1880), "depicting that century as a time of progress from a state of barbarism, ignorance, and bestiality which can hardly be exaggerated, to a reign of science, enlightenment, and democracy."

Shelley's Jupiter, at once political tyrant and evil God of Christianity, was being pushed from the throne and Prometheus released from chains.

Among the Chartists and the liberals of the forties who supported them, the dream of democracy exercised again its old promise of the golden age. Young intellectuals, like Tom Brown at Oxford, "very truly" believed "that that state of the world which this universal democracy was to bring about, and which was coming no man could say how soon, was to be in fact that age of peace and goodwill which men had dreamt of in all times, when the lion should lie down with the kid, and nation should not vex nation any more." [59] Mill's hopes were more restrained; and in any event, outside of the working class few Victorians were democrats. The optimism of political progress rested rather on the advance of social freedom than on social equality. The reform of the civil law under Benthamite influence, the repeal of class legislation like the Test and Corporation Acts in 1828, the extension of the suffrage in 1832 with the realignment of the electoral districts, the admission of Dissenters to seats on the town councils (1835) and to degrees at Oxford and Cambridge (1871), the reform of the civil service (1850–70), and the whole shift in economic policy from interference and regulation to laissez-faire, culminating in the free trade legislation which repealed the Corn Laws in 1846 and the Navigation Acts in 1849, was a record of political emancipation more than sufficient to warrant as much satisfaction as the middle class felt in its material wealth and power. It is significant that Millbank, the new capitalist in *Coningsby*, calls himself a "disciple of progress," not because he exults in the industrial achievements of his class but because in his father's time "the displeasure of a peer of England was like a sentence of death to a man," while now "we may defend ourselves . . . and, perhaps, do something more. I defy any peer to crush me." [60] Millbank, it may be noticed, was not a democrat. "I am no leveller; I look upon an artificial equality as equally pernicious with a factitious aristocracy; both depressing the energies, and checking the enterprise of a nation. I like man to be free, really free: free in his industry as well as his body." And free, Carlyle would have retorted, to starve. The Victorian hymn to liberty, political and economic, was distinctly addressed to middle-class liberty. But whatever their criticisms, or

59. Hughes, *Tom Brown at Oxford*, chap. 42, p. 487. This is autobiography: see his *Memoir of a Brother* (London, 1873), p. 89.
60. Disraeli, *Works, 12*, chap. 26, pp. 228–9. The next quotation is on p. 227.

their awareness of the loss involved, most of the intellectuals were well satisfied to see the end of aristocratic power and privilege. Froude spoke for his group as well as his class when he summed up the social progress of the age: "The people have at last political power. All interests are now represented in Parliament. All are sure of consideration. Class government is at an end. Aristocracies, landowners, established churches, can abuse their privileges no longer. The age of monopolies is gone. England belongs to herself. We are at last free." [61]

Besides being a genuine source of pride, this freedom could be a matter of self-congratulation almost as bumptious as that inspired by English business. John Roebuck's fatuous remarks were immortalized by Arnold: "I look around me and ask what is the state of England? Is not every man able to say what he likes? I ask you whether the world over, or in past history, there is anything like it? Nothing. I pray that our unrivalled happiness may last." [62] There was also our unrivaled superiority, not only to our ancestors, but to our less fortunate neighbors, as poorly off politically as they were economically. The edifying contrast in 1848 between affairs at home and abroad, and again in 1851 when Louis Napoleon brought off his *coup d'état*, were so much tangible proof of the blessings of English liberty. [63] Tennyson burst forth with a series of popular poems on the theme:

> To this great cause of Freedom drink, my friends,
> And the great name of England, round and round. [64]

The founding of new Anglo-Saxon colonies was inspired, it was said— and believed—by the generous and altruistic "desire of spreading throughout the habitable globe all the characteristics of Englishmen— their energy, their civilization, their religion and their freedom." [65] Praise of the British constitution, with its ingenious system of checks "which stops and paralyses any power in interfering with the free

61. "On Progress," pp. 376–7. Cf. *The Spectator* (1851) quoted in John W. Dodds, *The Age of Paradox. A Biography of England, 1841–1851* (New York and Toronto, 1952), p. 487: "At home the half-century has changed the aspect of society: where all was Tory suppression at the beginning, all is thrown open now. We have gained freedom, political, religious, and commercial."

62. *Culture and Anarchy*, chap. 3, p. 121, and see chap. 2, "Doing as One Likes," passim.

63. See Arthur Bryant, *English Saga*, pp. 108–9.

64. In "Hands All Round"; and cf. "The Third of February, 1852," and "Britons, Guard Your Own": in *Poetic Works*, pp. 515, 269, and 792 respectively.

65. Charles Adderley, quoted by Halévy, *History of the English People*, Vol. 4, *Victorian Years*, p. 411.

action of individuals," became the stock-in-trade of political speeches
and dinner-table conversation, of Gladstone and John Bright—and
Mr. Podsnap.⁶⁶ The last had a famous conversation with a visiting
Frenchman:

"And Do You Find, Sir," pursued Mr. Podsnap, with dignity,
"Many Evidences that Strike You, of our British Constitution in
the Streets Of The World's Metropolis, London, Londres, London? . . . We Englishmen are Very Proud of our Constitution,
Sir. It Was Bestowed Upon Us By Providence. No Other Country
is so Favoured as This Country." . . .

"And *other* countries," said the foreign gentleman. "They do
how?"

"They do, Sir," returned Mr. Podsnap, gravely shaking his head;
"they do—I am sorry to be obliged to say it—*as* they do."

"It was a little particular of Providence," said the foreign gentleman, laughing; "for the frontier is not large."

"Undoubtedly," assented Mr. Podsnap; "But So it is. It was the
Charter of the Land. This Island was Blest, Sir, to the Direct Exclusion of such Other Countries as—as there may happen to be."

The disintegration of Christian theology and even religious belief
which was so often agonizing was also an enormous relief. The new
vision of a 'scientific' universe was a nightmare—and it was a glorious
dream, as men discovered that much or all of dogmatic Christianity
was sheer superstition, thank God, and looked forward, with joyful
anticipation in some cases, to a new revelation of man's destiny. To
put the situation another way, if modernism for most Victorians
threatened to destroy the comforts of belief, for a substantial minority
it promised to end the *dis*comforts of belief.⁶⁷

These discomforts, from which the liberals escaped into theism or a
Broad Church or mere agnosticism,⁶⁸ were of two kinds. The first was

66. Arnold, *Culture and Anarchy*, chap. 2, p. 74, who refers to Bright. Halévy,
loc. cit., mentions Gladstone. Mr. Podsnap is in Dickens, *Our Mutual Friend*,
from which the next quotation is taken, *1*, Bk. I, chap. 11, pp. 138–40.

67. Cf. Huxley, "Agnosticism," *Science and Christian Tradition*, p. 242: "People
who talk about the comforts of belief appear to forget its discomforts."

68. I use the term theism to describe the belief in a personal god and a divine
moral law intuitively grasped by the conscience. Where, in addition, Christ is
accepted as the son of God sent to earth to give that moral law special revelation,
we have Christian theism, which is not very different from the Broad Church
Christianity of Thomas Arnold and A. P. Stanley. See the interesting account of

the intellectual burden of accepting the miraculous character of Christian theology: the story of creation in *Genesis*, the incarnation, the virgin birth, the vicarious sacrifice, and all the biblical miracles and supernatural rites and ceremonies of the Church. A liberal effort to free the mind from these "Hebrew old clothes" seemed to many thinkers the major need of the age. Only then could religious truth be re-embodied in a believable form. "It was clearly the part of every noble heart," said Carlyle, thinking of himself and his work, "to expend all its lightnings and energies burning-up without delay, and sweeping into their native Chaos" these "incredible uncredited traditions, solemnly sordid hypocrisies, and beggarly deliriums old and new." [69] That is the first step. Until it is taken, men cannot escape the alternatives which Froude saw being thrust upon his generation, "of believing nothing, or believing everything which superstition, disguised as Church authority, had been pleased to impose; or, as a third course, and a worse one, of acquiescing, for worldly convenience, in the established order of things, which had been made intellectually incredible." [70] From this dilemma thousands of Victorians, like Froude himself, found joyful release in the gospel according to Carlyle: "Amidst the controversies, the arguments, the doubts, the crowding uncertainties of forty years ago, Carlyle's voice was to the young generation of Englishmen like the sound of 'ten thousand trumpets' in their ears." In his writings "dogma and tradition had melted like a mist, and the awful central fact [of God's reality and His moral law] burnt clear once more in the midst of heaven." [71] Within the Church various liberal movements brought a similar response. The Broad Churchmen in the *New Republic* (Jowett and Matthew Arnold) are quick to oppose anyone who thinks the decline of theology an ominous sign of the times. On the contrary, "we have already got rid of a vast amount of superstition and ignorance, and are learning what Christianity really is"—not a body of impossible dogma, but simply a life of piety and virtue.[72] The

Frances Cobbe's religious progress from Evangelical Christianity to agnosticism to theism in her autobiography: *Life of Frances Power Cobbe. By Herself* (2 vols. Boston and New York, 1895), *1*, chap. 4, pp. 70–95.

69. *The Life of John Sterling*, Pt. I, chap. 4, p. 37; and cf. Pt. II, chap. 4, pp. 139–40, as well as "Shooting Niagara: and After?" *Essays, 5*, 29–30, where he uses the epithet he coined of "Hebrew old clothes."

70. Froude, *Carlyle: Life in London, 1*, chap. 11, p. 296.

71. Ibid., pp. 292, 293. Froude was writing in 1884.

72. *New Republic*, pp. 51, 227–8. Mallock has Arnold's *Literature and Dogma* (1873) particularly in mind, with its attempt to separate the *Aberglaube* in the Bible from the true religion, viz. the "morality touched with emotion." The happy

full impact of religious liberalism can be felt from a nostalgic remark of Margaret Todd's in 1898. Because everyone is now "dashed with free-thought, modern science, and German philosophy . . . we have lost the subtle thrill of intense delight with which an awakening mind scented a kindred mind from afar; we have lost the exhilarating sensation of being in the vanguard." But we can never forget "the time 'when we felt the days before us.'" "To us too it was given to see the sun rise." [73]

Though for them the revelation was not religious but scientific, the same note of joy, part relief, part excited hope of discovering a new philosophy of man and the universe, is found among the rationalists. When George Eliot, for example, cast off her Evangelical faith under the influence of biblical criticism, she did so with a "feeling of exultation and strong hope." Her soul, she said, was "liberated from the wretched giant's bed of dogmas on which it has been racked and stretched over since it began to think"; and she was now eager to join "that glorious crusade that is seeking to set Truth's Holy Sepulchre free from a usurped dominion." [74] This is the crusade of the rationalists with their faith in scientific method, but with a significant shift in emphasis. The truth is not so much to be found as to be set free—that is to say, *men* are to be set free from a painful delusion. It is the battle-cry of militant atheism. Carlyle, whose own escape from superstition stopped short at theism, was surprised and horrified to notice the "joyful exultant humour" with which the scientific pamphlets and journals of the sixties were spouting out atheism. [75] How *could* men delight in the blank prospect of a mechanistic universe? In his fear of materialism he forgot the release it could bring from the weary and frustrating effort to reconcile religion and science. In itself there might be nothing to recommend the belief that human beings were simply atoms in a vast complex of forces moving by inexorable natural laws, but under the conditions of the time it could make a powerful negative appeal. Accept it, wrote John Morley, with his own experience in mind (the

---

arrival of this new religion is expressed by Arnold in "Obermann Once More," lines 281–96, 345–8, in the imagery of a brilliant sunrise.

73. *Windyhaugh,* p. 31. The reference is to Thomas Erskine, Macleod Campbell, F. D. Maurice, and F. W. Robertson, a group less 'broad' than Jowett and his school but united in their shift of focus from the fall and the sinful nature of man to divine forgiveness and universal salvation.

74. Cross, *George Eliot's Life, 1,* 80, 91, letters to Mrs. Pears, February 1842, and Sara Hennell, October 19, 1843.

75. Froude, *Carlyle: Life in London,* 2, chap. 31, pp. 372–3; cf. pp. 386, 388.

trying struggle to maintain his Christianity, followed by the happy conversion to agnosticism), and "the active energies are not [any longer] paralysed by the possibilities of enfeebling doubt, nor the reason drawn down and stultified by apprehension lest its methods should discredit a document, or its inferences clash with a dogma, or its light flash unseasonably on a mystery." [76] The mind is freed from the whole pressure, social and personal, to think within a traditional context which has become incredible. [77]

Casting off the old theology, especially in its popular Puritan form, brought another relief: from emotional fears as well as intellectual difficulties. The conception of a jealous God of wrath, punishing most of the human race with eternal torture in hell, and of human nature innately corrupt and powerless to attain salvation except by an act of divine grace; the anxious self-examination in a frantic effort to determine whether one was among the elect or the damned; the realization that the slightest moral failing or the least theological error was a dangerous sin—all this formed a context of living fear from which any escape, even at the cost of all religious faith, might seem at times a blessed event. [78] And once freed of this "fatalist creed," one might experience an upsurge of fresh energy and self-reliance. Take the case of George Holyoake. After years of being agitated by doubt and perturbation as to whether he was of the "elect," he read in Robert Owen that the clue to moral progress lay in the control of the social environment, and at once was "delivered by reason alone," he says, "from the prison-house in which I had dwelt with its many terrors." By this lucky escape he passed into a new "land of self-effort and improvement; and entered into the fruitful kingdom of material endeavour, where help and hope dwelt." [79] The protagonists of Tennyson's "De-

76. "Byron," *Critical Miscellanies, 1,* 237–8. On the happy conversion to agnosticism, see Leslie Stephen, "An Apology for Plainspeaking," *Essays on Freethinking and Plainspeaking,* pp. 374–6. Of his own experience, he says ("Some Early Impressions, II," *Atlantic Monthly, 92* [1903], 532): "I did not feel that the solid ground was giving way beneath my feet, but rather that I was being relieved of a cumbrous burden."

77. On this pressure see below, pp. 128, 397–9, 422–4.

78. When Huxley spoke of the discomforts of belief (note 67 above), he specifically mentioned "the introspective hunting after sins of the mint and cummin type, the fear of theological error, and the overpowering terror of possible damnation, which have accompanied the Churches like their shadow." For examples of the state of mind which this theology could induce, see below, Chap. 3, sec. 4.

79. *Bygones Worth Remembering* (2 vols. New York, 1905), *2,* 238. E. E. Kellett, *Religion and Life in the Early Victorian Age,* p. 75, recalls "a lady who had been

spair" found the same comfort (temporarily) in the scientific picture of the universe:

> See, we were nursed in the drear nightfold
>   of your fatalist creed,
> And we turn'd to the growing dawn, we had
>   hoped for a dawn indeed,
> When the light of a sun that was coming
>   would scatter the ghosts of the past,
> And the cramping creeds that had madden'd
>   the peoples would vanish at last,
> And we broke away from the Christ, our human
>   brother and friend,
> For He spoke, or it seem'd that He spoke,
>   of a hell without help, without end.[80]

The fullest account of such an experience is in Harriet Martineau's *Autobiography*. When she came to believe in "eternal and irreversible laws, working in every department of the universe, without any interference from any random will, human or divine," she ended forever the painful anxiety of feeling that her salvation depended either on her own weak will or on God's arbitrary will. "My labouring brain and beating heart grew quiet, and something more like peace than I had ever yet known settled down upon my anxious mind. . . . A new vigour pervaded my whole life, a new light spread through my mind, and I began to experience a steady growth in self-command, courage, and consequent integrity and disinterestedness." [81] Later, when she expounded the full creed of scientific materialism in the *Letters on the Laws of Man's Nature and Development* (1851), written in collaboration with Henry Atkinson, the tone of the book was even more shocking to Victorian readers than its content. Far from offering any apology, the authors put forward their philosophy as a new gospel (literally), good tidings of great value to mankind. "The strangest thing," wrote Charlotte Brontë, "is, that we are called on to rejoice over this hopeless blank . . . to welcome this unutterable desolation as a state of

---

through months of this torment, and had renounced all religion in consequence," telling him "that no conversion could have brought her more joy than the sudden resolve to have done with the whole thing."

80. Stanza 4.

81. *Autobiography, 1,* Period III, sec. 1, pp. 109–11.

pleasant freedom." [82] Miss Martineau's reply was to insist the more strongly on what she knew she had felt:

> When I experienced the still new joy of feeling myself to be a portion of the universe, resting on the security of its everlasting laws, certain that its Cause was wholly out of the sphere of human attributes . . . how could it matter to me that the adherents of a decaying mythology,—(the Christian following the heathen, as the heathen followed the barbaric-fetish) were fiercely clinging to their Man-God, their scheme of salvation, their reward and punishment, their arrogance, their selfishness, their essential pay-system, as ordered by their mythology? . . . To the emancipated, it is a small matter that those who remain imprisoned are shocked at the daring which goes forth into the sunshine and under the stars, to study and enjoy, without leave asked, or fear of penalty.[88]

To the personal relief was added, we notice, the happy sense of superiority to one's foolish or timid neighbors. But they too, as the creed of science gains sway, will come out into the sunshine. For "the last of the mythologies is about to vanish before the flood of a brighter light"; and in the new day men will no longer have to "work out *their own* salvation with fear and trembling." [84]

82. Elizabeth Gaskell, *Life of Charlotte Brontë*, chap. 23, p. 329.

83. Vol. 2, Period VI, sec. 6, pp. 355–6.

84. Vol. 2, p. 461, at the very end of the book. Two essays by R. H. Hutton on the "triumphant relief" among "all the Positivists" of throwing off the superstitions of the past are in his *Contemporary Thought and Thinkers*, 1, 281–7, 296–302, under the titles "Ardent Agnosticism" and "The Magnanimity of Unbelief." But Hutton is so irritated by the whole attitude he cannot give any credit to the need for release from the intellectual difficulties and the emotional fears that were bound up with religious belief. For him it was simply an act of human pride, a deliberate casting off of all moral obligation to a superior being.

Chapter 3

ANXIETY

> Whoever looks abroad upon the world, comparing
> the Past with the Present, may find that the practical
> condition of man in these days is one of the saddest;
> burdened with miseries which are in a considerable
> degree peculiar.
>
> *Carlyle*
>
> One thing is certain; as a nation, as a people we are
> unhappy.
>
> *E. P. Hood* [1]

To THINK IT STRANGE that the great age of optimism was also an age
of anxiety is to overlook the ambivalent reaction which the main social
and intellectual tendencies of the period provoked. Expanding business, scientific development, the growth of democracy, and the decline
of Christianity were sources of distress as well as of satisfaction. But
since optimism was expressed more often than anxiety (partly because
it was more widely felt, and partly because any pessimistic attitude
toward the human situation was considered weak or unmanly), we are
still unaware of the degree to which the Victorian consciousness—and
especially the subconsciousness—was haunted by fear and worry, by
guilt and frustration and loneliness.

1. *Fear of Revolution*

Bertrand Russell tells us that his grandfather, lying on his deathbed
in 1869, "heard a loud noise in the street and thought it was the revolution breaking out." [2] The incident is symbolic. For all its solid and

1. Carlyle, "Characteristics," *Essays*, 3, 28; Edwin P. Hood, *The Age and Its
Architects*, p. 81.
2. *Ideas and Beliefs of the Victorians*, p. 20.

imposing strength, Victorian society, particularly in the period before 1850, was shot through, from top to bottom, with the dread of some wild outbreak of the masses that would overthrow the established order and confiscate private property. The note of warning sounded in Burke's *Reflections on the French Revolution* (1790), echoes through Southey's *Colloquies on the Progress and Prospects of Society* (1829), and rings in tones of fright through the literature of the forties. Carlyle's *French Revolution* (1837) and even Dickens' *Tale of Two Cities* (1859) are tracts for the times.

The possibility that it might happen here was abundantly supported, a priori, by the spread of radical propaganda, both political and religious, among the working classes. The two most influential books, Tom Paine's *The Rights of Man* and *The Age of Reason*, hardly seem dangerous now, for the former did not go beyond democracy nor the latter beyond deism. But democracy, to consider that first, carried connotations much like those of communism today. "The last time I saw Southey," Carlyle recorded in his *Reminiscences*, ". . . our talk was long and earnest; topic ultimately the usual one, steady approach of democracy, with revolution (probably *explosive*) and a *finis* incomputable to man." [3] That is standard conservatism. But a liberal like Macaulay regarded universal suffrage with "dread and aversion" because it was "incompatible with property, and . . . consequently incompatible with civilization." Grant the petition, he said in his speech on "The People's Charter" (1842), and the first use which a democracy will make of its new political power "will be to plunder every man in the kingdom who has a good coat on his back and a good roof over his head." [4] Rhetorical exaggeration, no doubt, but still, there *was* the Reign of Terror, recently brought to life again in the vivid pages of Carlyle's *History*.

Moreover, specific theories of socialism, derived from Godwin, Owen, and Thomas Spence, were pushing their way into the radical program. [5] Although the Chartists' demands were entirely political, chiefly for the extension of the franchise, their petition suggested the radical use to which the left-wing, at least, would have put its political power. The intention was to end "all monopoly and oppression," including "the existing monopolies . . . of paper-money, of machinery, of land, of

3. Page 355. For Southey, see *Colloquies on Society*, 1, 106–7, 114–15; 2, 201–2, 415–16.

4. *Complete Writings of Lord Macaulay*, 9, 308–9. See in general, pp. 308–17.

5. On socialism in the Chartist movement, see Mark Hovell, *The Chartist Movement* (Manchester, London, and New York, 1925), pp. 28–51.

the public press, of religion, of the means of travelling and transit." [6]
Though unfair to the majority, the epithet "communist" sometimes
hurled at the Chartists [7] was not without foundation. And Chartism
was a potent force in England for ten years.

Another calamity associated with democracy is equally modern.
With France again as chief exhibit, it was argued that if society were
to be saved from plunder, a military despotism would have to inter-
vene. In the United States, therefore, the day was bound to come,
Macaulay predicted, when "either some Caesar or Napoleon will seize
the rein of Government with a strong hand or your republic will be
as fearfully plundered and laid waste by barbarians in the Twentieth
Century as the Roman Empire was in the Fifth." So it would be in
England, too, if universal suffrage were enacted. For democracy must
lead either to communism and the end of "civilization" or to dictatorship and the end of liberty. [8] And to make these possibilities the more
disturbing, the Victorians were quite sure that democracy was inevitable, sooner or later.

But if the implications of radical thought were menacing, then as
now (our very different view of democracy tends to conceal the close
connection here between the 1850's and the 1950's), the growing
bitterness of class feeling, often issuing in physical violence and repressive force, made the threat of revolution tangible and immediate
to an extent unknown in England or the United States today. From
1815 to 1850 the tension between what Disraeli called "the Two Nations" was almost constantly at the breaking point. After the war

6. *Hansard's Parliamentary Debates: Third Series*, 62, col. 1379, under date
of May 2, 1842.

7. See, for example, Kingsley's *Alton Locke*, chaps. 2 and 35, pp. 26, 366.

8. Letter on democracy, written to Commodore H. S. Randall of the New York
Yacht Club, May 23, 1857; *Review of Reviews and World's Work*, 90 (July 1934),
38–9. Cf. *The Times* for Feb. 24, 1849, p. 5, commenting on the events in Europe,
1848–49, as a warning to all time that purely democratic government must lead to
the alternative of "social dissolution or military despotism." Macaulay uses the
same example at the start of his letter. The fear of dictatorship is found in Thomas
Arnold, *Life*, p. 259, letter of April 1831; Frederick Maurice, *Life of F. D. Maurice*,
2, 129; and Hallam Tennyson, *Memoir of Tennyson*, 2, 338. I do not, of course,
mean to imply that democracy did not have its champions, or that everyone thought
it must lead to the extreme left or the extreme right. Mill, Morley, and Matthew
Arnold could be brought forward to answer Macaulay on one count or another. On
the general subject, see B. E. Lippincott, *Victorian Critics of Democracy: Carlyle,
Ruskin, Arnold, Stephen, Maine, Lecky* (London and Minneapolis, 1938), and
an essay by Asa Briggs with special reference to the Reform Bill of 1867, "Robert
Lowe and the Fear of Democracy," in *Victorian People*.

economic depression and a reactionary Tory policy created the social
atmosphere in which a whole generation of Victorians grew up:

> The young men of the labouring classes were "the cads," "the
> snobs," "the blackguards"; looked on with a dislike, contempt,
> and fear, which they were not backward to return. . . . The old
> feudal ties between class and class, employer and employed, had
> been severed. Large masses of working people had gathered in
> the manufacturing districts in savage independence. The agricul-
> tural labourers had been debased by the abuses of the Old Poor-
> law . . . Then arose Luddite mobs, meal mobs, farm riots, riots
> everywhere; Captain Swing and his rickburners, Peterloo "mas-
> sacres," Bristol conflagrations, and all the ugly sights and rumours
> which made young lads, thirty or forty years ago, believe (and
> not so wrongly) that "the masses" were their natural enemies, and
> that they might have to fight, any year, or any day, for the safety
> of their property and the honour of their sisters.[9]

By 1830 Thomas Arnold was citing Arthur Young's *Travels in France
in 1789 and 1790* for its "applicability to our own times and country"
and predicting that reform "long repulsed and scorned," was again
"on the point of changing her visage to that of Revolution." [10] The
prediction was soon borne out. For more than a year the country
seemed in a state of near civil war. In Norfolk, to cite a typical account,
there were "meetings of five or six hundred desperadoes in every village." Every house was "in a state of defence, and all the farmers,
shopkeepers, servants, etc., etc., sworn in special constables."

> Truly the hearts of men are full of fear;
> You cannot reason almost with a man
> That looks not heavily and full of dread.[11]

It was that panic which carried the Reform Bill.

After its passage came a period of calm, but not for long. The new
Poor Law with its workhouse "bastilles," the laissez-faire policy of the
Whigs, and the refusal of both parties to repeal the Corn Laws showed
clearly enough that the Reformed Parliament was a middle-class government, and recreated in more ominous form (because better organ-

9. *Alton Locke,* xci–xcii, from the 1862 preface.
10. Stanley, *Life,* pp. 250–3, in letters of November and December 1830, and
February 1831.
11. The contemporary quotations are taken from O. F. Christie, *The Transition
from Aristocracy,* pp. 44–7.

ized under the Chartists) the unrest and violence of the postwar period.[12] The crisis came in 1848. In February revolutions burst out on the continent. In March there were riots in London, Liverpool, Glasgow, and other large towns. In April the government filled London with troops under the Duke of Wellington, who barricaded the bridges and Downing Street, and garrisoned the Bank. In June the Houses of Parliament were provisioned for a siege. The strong measures were successful and the Chartist movement, already weakened by internal dissension, collapsed.[13] In the fifties, the combination of national prosperity and the new direction of working-class reform, toward co-operatives and trade unions, ended the revolutionary period. But the threat was revived by the Hyde Park riots of 1866,[14] and the anxiety was kept alive by the existence of "masses of dark, impenetrable, subterranean blackguardism" in the slums of every city. "Our civilisation" seemed to Mark Rutherford "nothing but a thin film or crust lying over a volcanic pit," and he often wondered "whether some day the pit would not break up through it and destroy us all." [15]

2. The Danger of Atheism

Another source of alarm came from quite a different quarter. The decline of Christianity and the prospect of atheism had social implications which now seem curious (though they may have more bearing on our contemporary situation than we suppose). It was then assumed, in spite of rationalist denials, that any collapse of faith would destroy the sanctions of morality; and morality gone, society would disintegrate. Mill described the age as one in which the opinion that religious belief was necessary for moral and social purposes was universal, and yet real belief was feeble and precarious—a situation well calculated

12. There is a good description of the forties in Hughes, *Tom Brown at Oxford*, chap. 39, pp. 460–1.

13. Hughes, "Prefatory Memoir," first printed in the 1876 ed., *Alton Locke*, pp. xii–xiii; Froude, *Carlyle: Life in London, 1*, chap. 16, pp. 434–6.

14. See Arnold, *Culture and Anarchy*, pp. xxvi–xxix, 76, 80–2, 105. Cf. the passage by Lionel Trilling, *Arnold*, p. 218, beginning: "Arnold, we must perceive, labors always under the fear of revolution."

15. *Mark Rutherford's Deliverance*, p. 65. Cf. Huxley, "The Struggle for Existence in Human Society," *Evolution and Ethics*, pp. 213–19. Both are late (1885 and 1888), but Kingsley's "Great Cities and Their Influence for Good and Evil" (1857), *Sanitary and Social Essays*, pp. 187–222, and Tom All-Alone's in *Bleak House* (1853) show that the same fear was felt at least a generation earlier. On the general subject of this section, see J. L. and Barbara Hammond, *The Age of the Chartists, 1832–1854; a Study in Discontent*, London and New York, 1930.

to arouse anxiety.[16] When men like Froude were saying that "an established religion . . . is the sanction of moral obligation; it gives authority to the commandments, creates a fear of doing wrong, and a sense of responsibility for doing it," they were naturally concluding that "to raise a doubt about a creed established by general acceptance is a direct injury to the general welfare." [17] But just such doubts were being raised on every side. Even so honest and courageous a thinker as Henry Sidgwick was reluctant to publish his skeptical views about immortality because the loss of such a hope, "from the minds of average human beings as now constituted, would be an evil of which I cannot pretend to measure the extent,"—if not the actual "dissolution of the existing social order," at least the increased danger of such a catastrophe.[18]

What gave edge to these general speculations on the causal relationship of disbelief and disorder was their particular application to the lower classes. For 'everyone' agreed that any discarding of the Christian sanctions of duty, obedience, patience under suffering, and brotherly love was obviously "fraught with grievous danger to property and the State." [19] Nothing could illustrate that assumption more tellingly than the reviews of *The Descent of Man* (1871) in the most important newspapers, where Darwin was severely censured for "revealing his zoological [anti-Christian] conclusions to the general public at a moment when the sky of Paris was red with the incendiary flames of the Commune." [20]

That explains why the decline of faith among members of the working class doubled the fear of revolution. A number of things combined to make atheism more common in this class than in any other single group: the skeptical character of radical thought, explicit in the work of Paine, Shelley, and the early free-thinkers; the neglect of the new town population by the Church of England (a neglect only partly offset by Methodism); the prejudice against the Church raised by the general adherence of the clergy to Tory and aristocratic principles,

16. *Autobiography*, chap. 3, p. 59.

17. "The Oxford Counter-Reformation," *Short Studies*, 4, 237.

18. *Henry Sidgwick: a Memoir*, p. 357.

19. E. Belfort Bax, *Reminiscences*, p. 189. For other illustrations, see below, pp. 241-2.

20. Morley, *Recollections, 1*, 101. Cf. a quotation from a letter of Newman's in 1871 and his comment on it, in Wilfrid Ward, *Life of John Henry, Cardinal Newman* (2 vols. London and New York, 1912), 2, 344: " 'The lowest class, which is most numerous, and is infidel, will rise up from the depths of the modern cities, and will be the new scourges of God.' This great prophecy, as it may be called, is first fulfilled in Paris."

and by their conservative reading of the Bible; above all, the suffering which seemed incompatible with the existence of a just and merciful God.[21] A Chartist advocating democracy might be called a communist, but he was certain with more justification to be called an infidel—which made him twice as dangerous.[22]

3. Worry and Fatigue

On the faces passing down Cheapside, there was little sign of personal or national optimism. In every countenance one read "the authentic signature of care and anxiety." [23] Most of the men were artisans and laborers. Their grueling toil, often for wages barely sufficient to keep alive, their constant fear of unemployment, the slums in which they existed, form a record of suffering unparalleled in the history of the working class. By the later nineteenth century the growth of trade unionism and of legislative action brought some relief, but meanwhile the unions were still too weak and the theory of laissez-faire too strong to make any major alleviation possible. All this is now a commonplace of Victorian history, though to realize even faintly the appalling conditions of lower-class life we have to reread some of the Blue Books, the poetry of Hood, novels like *Mary Barton, Alton Locke, Bleak House*, and *Hard Times*, or a tract like Kingsley's "Cheap Clothes and Nasty." [24]

What is often forgotten is that many of the faces in Cheapside were those of the business and professional class, some even of wealthy and prominent men. For the strain and severity of the struggle for existence was "by no means confined to the lower orders. Throughout the whole community we are all called to labour too early and compelled to labour too severely and too long. We live sadly too fast." [25] Arthur

21. See Kingsley, *Alton Locke*, in chaps. 1, 4, 16, 20, 30, 40, pp. 8–9, 50–1, 187, 213–14, 321–3, 422–3; "The Religious Heresies of the Working Class," *Westminster Review*, 77 (1862), 60–97; Arnold, *Literature and Dogma*, pp. vi–vii; *The Life of Thomas Cooper, Written by Himself* (first published 1872; London, 1886), pp. 173, 260–1.

22. The moral and social functions of religion, and therefore the anxiety caused by religious doubts, are discussed by Gaylord C. LeRoy, *Perplexed Prophets*, pp. 108–13.

23. John Cumming, "The Age We Live In," in *Exeter Hall Lectures*, 3 (1848), p. 364.

24. There is a good collection of documentary evidence in S. Gordon and T. G. B. Cocks, *A People's Conscience* (London, 1952), and some lurid statistics in G. M. Young, *Victorian England*, p. 24.

25. W. R. Greg, "England as It Is," *Edinburgh Review*, 93 (1851), 325. For the pressure of work and the speed of life, see above, pp. 6–8.

Helps wanted a statue to Worry erected in the City, "on which the cunning sculptor should have impressed the marks of haste, anxiety, and agitation."[26] The major worry was "failure." In a period when hectic booms alternated with financial panics and there was no such thing as limited liability, the business magnate and the public investor were haunted by specters of bankruptcy and the debtor's jail.[27] So great was the physical and mental strain that many men, it was said, were forced "to break off (or to break down) in mid-career, shattered, paralysed, reduced to premature inaction or senility."[28] Even the "anxiety to be in time, the hurrying pace—often the running to catch trains"—was causing a daily wear and tear which it was thought contributed to the increase of heart disease between 1851 and 1870.[29] There were also the social worries which were inseparable from the ambition to move up the social ladder. Many a self-made man dreaded the fatal exposure of his humble origins or, like Bulstrode in *Middlemarch*, of some dubious cutting of corners on the way up. Anyone toiling and scheming on the new principle of *l'art de parvenir* had to live, Frances Cobbe pointed out, "in constant fear of every chance disclosure which may throw down his hardly-erected edifice of respectability like a house of cards."[30] Or in constant fear of a loss from financial failure even worse than money—social status. To "have the bailiff in the house" and "to be sold up" were phrases which Tom Tulliver in *The Mill on the Floss* had been used to even as a boy. "They were part of the disgrace and misery of 'failing', of losing all one's money, and being ruined,—sinking into the condition of poor working-people."[31]

4. *The Strain of Puritanism*

While some Victorians experienced a profound sense of relief and new hope from casting off their Puritan theology, many who held to its dogmas—a majority of the society—remained under the psycho-

26. *Friends in Council, New Series*, 1, 24.

27. For a good example see Mrs. Craik, *John Halifax, Gentleman*, chap. 22, pp. 297–9.

28. W. R. Greg, "Life at High Pressure," *Literary and Social Judgments*, 2, 272. Cf. a paragraph in *Meliora*, 6 (1864), 199, under the running title, "The Sad Intensity of Modern Life."

29. Greg, pp. 267–8. In his *Enigmas of Life*, pp. 10–11, he cites statistics on the increase of heart disease from the *British Medical Journal*.

30. "The Nineteenth Century," *Fraser's Magazine*, 69 (1864), 483.

31. *The Mill on the Floss*, 1, Bk. III, chap. 2, p. 282.

logical burden they often imposed.[32] Conscientious souls who tried to achieve a life of absolute purity and self-denial might experience an almost daily sense of failure, distressing in itself and frightening in its implications; or at the least they were dismayed to find quite different ideals glaringly apparent in the world around them.[33] What it could mean to live with a 'Puritan' conscience, hardly less common among Anglo-Catholics than Evangelicals and Dissenters, can be seen in the diary of F. W. Robertson, the famous preacher, where all of his sins and errors are set down, selfishness discovered in every effort and resolve, and lists made out of duties he was struggling in vain to fulfill.[34] Even a convert to agnosticism like George Eliot never rid herself "of a mind morbidly desponding, of a consciousness tending more and more to consist in memories of error and imperfection rather than in a strengthening sense of achievement." [35] One wonders if the tremendous optimism of outward success was not often checked or even nullified by an inward sense of moral failure.

The sufferings of the conscience, however, were as nothing compared with its fears. The favorite Evangelical texts tell their own story: "The Lord our God is a consuming fire, even a jealous God." "Depart from me, ye cursed, into everlasting fire, prepared for the devil and his angels." "Because I have called, and ye refused; I have stretched out my hand, and no man regarded; but ye have set at naught all my counsel, and would none of my reproof: I also will laugh at your calamity; I will mock when your fear cometh; when your fear cometh as desolation, and your destruction cometh as a whirlwind." Is it possible, asked William Wilberforce, from whose *Practical View of Christianity*, often called the Bible of Evangelicism, the quotations have

32. See above, pp. 51–3, which bears directly on what follows.

33. Cf. Lecky, *The Map of Life*, chap. 4, p. 31: "Conscience, indeed, when it is very sensitive and very lofty, is far more an element of suffering than the reverse. It aims at an ideal higher than we can attain. It takes the lowest view of our own achievements. It suffers keenly from the many shortcomings of which it is acutely sensible. Far from indulging in the pleasurable retrospect of a well-spent life, it urges men to constant, painful, and often unsuccessful effort. A nature that is strung to the saintly or the heroic level will find itself placed in a jarring world, will provoke much friction and opposition, and will be pained by many things in which a lower nature would placidly acquiesce." The classic example of the last sentence is Arthur Clough, bred under Thomas Arnold at Rugby, and the classic text his *Dipsychus*, written to show (*Poems*, p. 294) "the conflict between the tender conscience and the world." On Victorian conscience, see below, pp. 231–3.

34. Stopford Brooke, *Life of F. W. Robertson*, p. 62.

35. Cross, *George Eliot's Life*, 2, 347, from a letter to Frederic Harrison, August 15, 1866.

been taken, "that these declarations should not strike terror, or at least excite serious and fearful apprehension in the lightest and most inconsiderate mind?" [36] It *was* possible among the worldly Christians of the 1790's to whom Wilberforce was preaching, but not possible once the movement started by the Wesleys had made its way into middle- and upper-class society. By then the reaction of J. A. Symonds had become a common one. From listening to "dismal sermons," he developed by the age of seven "a morbid sense of sin, and screamed at night about imaginary acts of disobedience." "I was persuaded," he said, "that the devil lived near the doormat, in a dark corner of the passage by my father's bedroom. I thought that he appeared to me there under the shape of a black shadow, scurrying about upon the ground, with the faintest indication of a swiftly whirling tail." In this context the finger he saw in a recurrent nightmare was clearly that of an avenging God:

> I dreamed that we were all seated in our well-lit drawing-room, when the door opened of itself, just enough to admit a little finger. The finger, disconnected from any hand, crept slowly into the room, and moved about through the air, crooking its joints and beckoning. No one saw it but myself. What was the horror that would happen if it should touch me or any other present, I never discovered, for   woke before the catastrophe occurred.[37]

Alton Locke, reflecting Kingsley's own experience, describes the same terrifying world of Victorian childhood: "Believing, in obedience to my mother's assurances, and the solemn prayers of the ministers about me, that I was a child of hell, and a lost and miserable sinner, I used to have accesses of terror, and fancy that I should surely wake next morning in everlasting flames." [38]

Alton would remain a child of Hell unless he were "converted, born again." This tremendous experience when the inrush of divine grace brought eternal forgiveness of sin was at the center of religious life among the Dissenting sects and the Evangelicals. It was proof of election. Without it damnation was a terrible certainty. Anxious parents watched their children for the slightest sign of a "saving knowledge of

36. Chap. 4, sec. 5, p. 225. That and chap.   sec. 2, pp. 41, 43, are the sources of the texts.

37. Horatio Brown, *Life of Symonds*, pp. 7–8.

38. *Alton Locke*, chap. 1, p. 8. Cf. Wingfield-Stratford's chapter "The Lord," *Those Earnest Victorians*, pp. 62–75, where he quotes from Watts' *Hymns* and Margaret Sherwood's *The Fairchild Family*.

God," and often subjected them to probing questions that heightened their own anxiety.[39] After persistent demands that she search her heart and persistent failures to find there any reassurance, Wilhelmina Galbraith, in Mrs. Todd's *Windyhaugh*, is awakened one night by a storm and looks out at the swaying trees: "It terrified her to see them, —now grovelling with head and arms down to earth, and again sweeping themselves up as if in a last despairing appeal to Heaven. . . . The season was late, and a crowd of green and yellow leaves went whirling and eddying past the window-panes. 'The harvest is past; the summer is ended,' they wailed in their fearsome flight,—'and *you are not saved!*' " Suddenly she thinks that the end of the world has come and Christ will appear to judge the quick and the dead. With "terrified eyes," she peers into the blackness: "Suddenly—suddenly—while she stood, such a light as the child had never seen flashed out over sky and sea, and distant hills. It was too much. Poor tortured self-control gave way, and the little bare feet went pattering—flying—into the nurse's room. '*Jane!*' cried a choking voice. '*Jane! Wake up! wake up! Christ is coming, and I am not saved!*' " [40]

Such experiences of terror were confined, no doubt, to childhood, but in many adults, as Newman pointed out, the introspective focus on the spiritual condition of the heart led "to a feverish anxiety about their religious state and prospects," and fears lest they were under "the reprobation of their All-merciful Saviour." [41]

5. *Ennui and Doubt*

In his opening lecture as professor of poetry at Oxford (1856), Arnold spoke of "depression and *ennui*" as "characteristics stamped on how many of the representative works of modern times!" They were symptoms, he said, "of the disease of the most modern societies, the most advanced civilizations!" [42] They were what Pater was to call "that inexhaustible discontent, languor, and home-sickness, that endless regret, the chords of which ring all through our modern literature." [43] It is the mood of Werther and René, Obermann and Lélia, of Childe Harold and all the Byronic heroes, of Carlyle's Teufelsdröckh. It appears in Browning's *Pauline* and many of Tennyson's earlier poems,

39. See E. E. Kellett, *Religion and Life in the Early Victorian Age*, pp. 74–5.
40. Pages 38–40.
41. Sermon entitled "Self-Contemplation," *Parochial and Plain Sermons*, 2, 173.
42. "On the Modern Element in Literature," *Essays by Matthew Arnold* (London, 1914), p. 468.
43. Pater, "Coleridge," *Appreciations*, pp. 105–6.

from the "Confessions" to *In Memoriam* and *Maud*, and is a major theme in both Arnold and Clough. For longer or shorter periods it swept over Sterling, Maurice, Robertson, Kingsley, and Mill. It dominated the early lives of Symonds and Mallock and to some extent was felt by nearly all educated Victorians.

The disease was well analyzed, in its most extreme form, by Arnold's niece, Mrs. Humphry Ward, in a passage in *Robert Elsmere*. Mr. Langham, intended as a portrait of Amiel, whose *Journals* are a major record of the malady, is giving a sketch of his life. It was at college, he says, that he first became aware "of something cold, impotent, and baffling in himself, which was to stand for ever between him and action, between him and human affection; the growth of the critical pessimist sense which laid the axe to the root of enthusiasm after enthusiasm, friendship after friendship—which made other men feel him inhuman, intangible, a skeleton at the feast; and the persistence through it all of a kind of hunger for life and its satisfactions, which the will was more and more powerless to satisfy." [44] The central note is that of weakness and frustration. The will is impotent; action is thwarted; friendship is impossible. Carlyle, indeed, spoke more than once of the fatal misery of "languor and paralysis." [45] In psychological terms this is plainly a neurosis, and in every genuine instance (setting aside literary imitations) personal factors, now for the most part beyond reach of recovery, were undoubtedly at its root. But a mood so widespread was indebted to the general environment—in particular, to the breakdown of traditional thought. It was, in truth, the *mal du siècle*. "We live in an age of visible transition," wrote Bulwer Lytton, "—an age of disquietude and doubt. . . . To me such epochs appear . . . the times of greatest unhappiness to our species." [46] Especially because so much of the doubt was religious. When Ruskin defined the despondency characteristic of the modern mind as "ennui, and jaded intellect, and uncomfortableness of soul and body," he attributed it to "our want of faith." "There never yet was a generation of men (savage or civilized) who . . . so wofully fulfilled the words 'having no hope, and without God in the world,' as the present civilized European race." [47]

44. Chap. 16, p. 249. Cf. the definition by J. A. Symonds quoted below, in note 64.

45. "Sir Walter Scott," *Essays*, 4, 50, 56, 59; *Heroes and Hero-Worship*, Bk. 5, p. 170; and cf. *Life of Sterling*, p. 6.

46. *England and the English*, p. 281.

47. *Modern Painters*, 3 (1856), chap. 16, secs. 9 and 10, in *Works*, 5, 321–2.

Though they could see in retrospect that the ground had been mined by eighteenth-century rationalism and the revolutionary dogmas of 1789—and even earlier, it was thought, by the Reformation appeal to liberty of judgment—the Victorians were utterly unprepared for the radical crisis in thought and society which burst over England in the thirties and forties. The assumptions of the old order had been bred into the young minds of almost all mid-Victorians; and now in the nineteenth century, in the early manhood of individuals like Carlyle and Kingsley, Froude and Arnold, they suddenly began to crumble. Froude spoke for all his contemporaries when late in life he remembered the 1840's: "All round us, the intellectual lightships had broken from their moorings, and it was then a new and trying experience. The present generation which has grown up in an open spiritual ocean, which has got used to it and has learned to swim for itself, will never know what it was to find the lights all drifting, the compasses all awry, and nothing left to steer by except the stars." [48] What he says of the "present generation" of the 1880's, when he was writing, is even truer of our own generation. Those who have never been disinherited because they have never known the absence of doubt can only imagine the distress of the first, sudden catastrophe.

Another metaphor described the state of mind more precisely. Symonds found "the whole fabric of humanity, within and without, rocking and surging in earthquake throes"; Kingsley, wondering where the destructive process was going to stop, felt as though he were standing "on a cliff which is crumbling beneath one, and falling piecemeal into the dark sea." [49] What makes this figure so appropriate is the suggestion of a series of shocks, keeping the mind in a state of frightened anticipation: "Those who dwell in the tower of ancient faiths look about them in constant apprehension, misgiving, and wonder, with the hurried uneasy mien of people living amid earthquakes. The

48. Carlyle: *Life in London, 1*, chap. 11, pp. 290–1. Cf. J. B. Brown, "The Revolution of the Last Quarter of a Century," *First Principles*, p. 279: "It is evident that an old order of things is breaking up into fragments; and men watch it, as they watch all wrecks, fearfully. There is a sense of repose in a settled order, in fixed relations, duties, and appointed work. And now nothing is fixed, nothing is appointed. . . . This state of things, in which the elements of an old order are, as it were, held in solution, before beginning to crystallize afresh, fills the majority of men with distress and apprehension. The old landmarks, the old habits, are a kind of social Bible to them. When these vanish, it is as though a guiding light, a supporting hand, were taken out of the world."

49. Brown, *Life of Symonds*, p. 260, under date of 1867; Kingsley, letter of 1855, referring specifically to biblical criticism, quoted in Thorp, *Kingsley*, p. 125.

air seems full of missiles, and all is doubt, hesitation, and shivering expectancy." [50] The history of thought from 1830 on, religious thought in particular, is a history of successive blows. Each advance in knowledge, every new theory, raises fresh difficulties; the entrenched position to which one retreats today is under threatening attack tomorrow. "The struggle with what Carlyle used to call 'Hebrew old clothes' is over," cries out Henry Sidgwick of the sixties; "Freedom is won"—that is, a simple faith in God and immortality has been freed at last from the theological dogmas in which it was imbedded. "And what," he continues, "does Freedom bring us to? It brings us face to face with atheistic science." [51] Always a fresh assault makes the last defense obsolete and raises again the ghost of doubt which one thought—or hoped—he had laid. To read an article like "On Tendencies towards the Subversion of Faith," written in 1848, and to discover that the author deals only with German rationalism and biblical criticism and is not aware of Lyell or Mill's *Logic* or *The Vestiges of Creation*, let alone such future bombshells as *The Origin of Species* and Huxley's "Physical Basis of Life," is to realize how terribly exposed the Victorians were to a constant succession of shattering developments. [52]

> For what wears out the life of mortal men?
>   'Tis that from change to change their being rolls;
>   'Tis that repeated shocks, again, again,
>   Exhaust the energy of strongest souls
>   And numb the elastic powers.

> But we, brought forth and rear'd in hours
> Of change, alarm, surprise—
> What shelter to grow ripe is ours?
> What leisure to grow wise?

> Like children bathing on the shore,
> Buried a wave beneath,
> The second wave succeeds, before
> We have had time to breathe. [53]

50. Morley, *On Compromise*, p. 25.

51. Sidgwick, letter to Hallam Tennyson, *Memoir of Tennyson*, 1, 302, reprinted in *Henry Sidgwick: a Memoir*, p. 539.

52. *The English Review*, 10 (1848), 399–444.

53. Matthew Arnold, "The Scholar-Gipsy," lines 142–6, and "Stanzas in Memory of the Author of 'Oberman,'" lines 69–76.

What made religious doubt peculiarly painful to the Victorians was the direction toward which it pointed. As the Christian view of the universe receded, another took its place—the scientific picture of a vast mechanism of cause and effect, acting by physical laws that governed even man himself. Rationalists might hail that vision with Utopian optimism, but most Victorians felt the same horrified shock which Charlotte Brontë recorded on her reading of the Atkinson-Martineau *Letters on the Laws of Man's Nature and Development:*

> It is the first exposition of avowed atheism and materialism I have ever read; the first unequivocal declaration of disbelief in the existence of a God or a future life I have ever seen. In judging of such exposition and declaration, one would wish entirely to put aside the sort of instinctive horror they awaken, and to consider them in an impartial spirit and collected mood. This I find it difficult to do. . . . If this be Truth, man or woman who beholds her can but curse the day he or she was born.[54]

For if that be truth, man and nature are reduced to inhuman and godless "circlings of force."

In spite of some notable anticipations, in Hobbes, for example, nature had been thought of as the manifestation of a good and beneficent God. Natural theology, culminating in Paley, had emphasized the order and design of a creative intelligence; the romantic sensibility had found the divine spirit rolling through all things, and had worshiped nature as the nurse and guide of life. But once Lyell's *Principles of Geology* had appeared (1830–33), followed by Chambers' *Vestiges of Creation* (1844) and Darwin's *Origin of Species* (1859), nature became a battleground in which individuals and species fought for their lives and every acre of land was the scene of untold violence and suffering. If *this* nature was the creation of God, then God, as Tennyson put it, "is disease, murder and rapine." [55] Or if not, then

54. Gaskell, *Life of Charlotte Brontë*, chap. 23, p. 329. Cf. Elizabeth Barrett's comment (*The Letters of Robert Browning and Elizabeth Barrett, 2,* 136–7) on how she would feel were she a materialist who believed in no soul and no future life: "My whole nature would cry aloud against that most pitiful result of the struggle here—a wrestling only for the dust, and not for the crown. What a resistless melancholy would fall upon me if I had such thoughts!—and what a dreadful indifference. . . . I should not have strength to love you, I think, if I had such a miserable creed. And for life itself, . . would it be worth holding on such terms,—with our blind Ideals making mocks and mows at us wherever we turned?"

55. Tennyson, *Memoir of Tennyson, 1,* 314.

either there is no God and no immortality, but only Nature, indifferent
to all moral values, impelling all things to a life of instinctive cruelty
ending in death; or else God and Nature are locked in an incredible
and inexplicable strife. These terrible alternatives are all present, directly or by implication, in the famous passage on evolution in *In
Memoriam:*

> Are God and Nature then at strife,
>   That Nature lends such evil dreams?
>   So careful of the type she seems,
> So careless of the single life,
>
> That I, considering everywhere
>   Her secret meaning in her deeds,
>   And finding that of fifty seeds
> She often brings but one to bear,
>
> I falter where I firmly trod,
>   And falling with my weight of cares
>   Upon the great world's altar-stairs
> That slope thro' darkness up to God,
>
> I stretch lame hands of faith, and grope,
>   And gather dust and chaff, and call
>   To what I feel is Lord of all,
> And faintly trust the larger hope.

Can it be true that man

> Who trusted God was love indeed
>   And love Creation's final law—
>   Tho' Nature, red in tooth and claw
> With ravine, shriek'd against his creed—

simply dies the death of all animals?

> O life as futile, then, as frail! . . .
>   What hope of answer, or redress?
> Behind the veil, behind the veil.[56]

56. From secs. 55, 56; and cf. "Maud," Pt. I, lines 123–5, and "Despair," stanza
5. For similar views of nature see John Sterling, *Arthur Coningsby* (1833), 3,
380–1; Kingsley, *Letters and Memories*, 2, 22, 319–20 (unabridged ed., *1*, 486,
for the first passage; the second is apparently not in this ed.); Arnold, "In Harmony with Nature."

Death is not all that man now shares with the other animals. Carlyle fought against Darwin's theory, "though . . . he dreaded that it might turn out true," because if man were no more than a developed animal, conscience and intellect were "but developments of the functions of animals." [57] Far from being the special gift of God, they would be natural mechanisms which all the higher animals had acquired, perhaps by "natural selection," and developed because of their enormous utility in the long struggle for existence. Family and gregarious instincts in certain animals, tribal law in primitive races, would have made for better survival by cooperation and group cohesiveness; and tribal punishment would in time have built a conscience into human nature. From this standpoint the moral sentiments were simply a disguised form of selfishness, and the moral life had no moral purpose.[58]

Furthermore, man found himself reduced not only to the animal but to the material world as well. He was descended recently from the apes, but originally from some bit of primordial slime. Darwin might talk of God breathing life into the first sperm, but Huxley and other scientists would not believe that in the vast evolution of all things from some purely material beginning, like a spiral nebula, there was any moment of supernatural intervention. Why was not life itself a natural result of certain chemical elements uniting under exactly the right, fortuitous conditions? In his lecture "On the Physical Basis of Life" (1868), Huxley argued that the property of "life" or "vitality" was as much a product of the combination of oxygen, hydrogen, nitrogen, and carbon which forms the protoplasm that is common to all living beings as the property of "aquosity" is of the combination of oxygen and hydrogen which forms water. If so, man has no spirit or soul independent of the body, but only a brain in which molecular changes, determined by external stimuli, give automatic rise to all his thoughts and all his actions.[59] For Huxley, as for many physiologists and biologists today, man is simply a human automaton.[60] It was not

57. Froude, Carlyle: Life in London, 2, chap. 26, p. 259.

58. See K. F. Gantz, "The Beginnings of Darwinian Ethics, 1859–1871," University of Texas Publications, Studies in English, 1939 (Austin, 1939), pp. 180–97. For later illustrations, see Mallock, The New Republic, p. 92; St. George Mivart, Nature and Thought (London, 1882), p. 168; A. J. Balfour, The Foundations of Belief (New York and London, 1895), pp. 16–19.

59. Method and Results, pp. 150–4.

60. Cf. J. H. Randall, Jr., The Making of the Modern Mind (Boston, 1926), p. 559: "Turn to the psychologist or biologist, and he answers that man is a com-

yet proved, but it seemed certain, that the advance of science would
extend the realm of matter and law until it was "co-extensive with
knowledge, with feeling, and with action." [61]

> The consciousness of this great truth weighs like a nightmare, I
> believe, upon many of the best minds of these days. They watch
> what they conceive to be the progress of materialism, in such fear
> and powerless anger as a savage feels, when, during an eclipse,
> the great shadow creeps over the face of the sun. The advancing
> tide of matter threatens to drown their souls; the tightening grasp
> of law impedes their freedom; they are alarmed lest man's moral
> nature be debased by the increase of his wisdom.

The combined effect of a dissolving tradition of thought and the new
scientific conception of man and nature was to drive sensitive minds
into the mood of ennui and frustration. So long as one lives within an
accepted structure of belief and value, he follows customary lines
without raising fundamental questions, and human energy flows un-
impeded into activity. By and large that way of life still obtained in
England until the commencement of the Victorian period. Once upon
a time, wrote Carlyle in 1831, "action . . . was easy, was voluntary,
for the divine worth of human things lay acknowledged." Now "doubt
storms-in . . . through every avenue; inquiries of the deepest, pain-
fulest sort must be engaged with; and the invincible energy of young
years waste itself in sceptical, suicidal cavillings; in passionate 'questionings of Destiny,' whereto no answer will be returned." [62] One finds
himself caught in a maze of introspection; the dialogue of the mind
with itself has commenced. By the seventies Mallock could argue that
through the nineteenth century "man has been curiously changing.
Much of his old spontaneity of action has gone from him. He has become a creature looking before and after; and his native hue of resolution has been sicklied over by thought. We admit nothing now without question; we have learnt to take to pieces all motives to actions.
We not only know more than we have done before, but we are per-

plex physico-chemical organism, the lineal descendant of some bit of primordial
slime; all his hopes and aspirations, all his loves and fears, all his self-sacrifice
and knowledge, are the result of the peculiar laws governing the chemical reactions that ultimately go to produce his behavior."

61. Huxley, *Method*, p. 159; for the next quotation, p. 160. A good contemporary
account of materialist developments in the period is in Tyndall's "Belfast Address"
(1874), in *Fragments of Science*, 2, 170–201.

62. "Characteristics," *Essays*, 3, 30; cf. *Sartor*, Bk. II, chap. 7, p. 161.

petually chewing the cud of our knowledge." [63] The "we" applies more exactly to Mallock's contemporaries, but the paralyzing effect of introversion and analysis is clearly seen in Arnold's correspondence with Clough in the forties and fifties, and in their poetry. Empedocles cannot act because he has become "nothing but a devouring flame of thought—but a naked, eternally restless mind." [64]

Action is not only short-circuited by speculation, it is frustrated by indecision. So long as one has a "vague feeling of potential right in all things when there seems to be actual right in nothing," no conviction is strong enough to call out energetic support. [65] Disraeli's Tancred is without faith in anything, "whether it be religion, or government, or manners, sacred or political or social life"; and "if there be no faith," he asks, "how can there be duty?" [66] More commonly, especially in the shrill atmosphere of sectarian controversy, one was not merely faced, he was battered, by conflicting theories and competing parties. "We are crushed," wrote F. D. Maurice in 1833, "by the spirit of this world, by the horrible Babylonian oppression . . . of contradictory opinions, strifes, divisions, heresies, selfishness. We feel this spirit around us, above us, within us. It cramps our energies, kills our life, destroys our sympathy." [67] Ten years later Eustace Lyle in Disraeli's Coningsby was not only "confused, perplexed, harassed" from being solicited by all parties to throw the weight of his influence in one scale or another—he was "paralysed." [68] In the sixties the situation, if anything, was worse. Symonds felt "paralysed," he said, "by the confusion round me, science and religion clashing, no creeds emergent. . . . The nervous fluids of our brains, instead of being concentrated upon single thoughts, are dispersed through a thousand channels. There is little

63. Is Life Worth Living? pp. 25–6.

64. Act II, lines 329–30. In his essay on Clough, Fortnightly Review, 10 (1868), 602, J. A. Symonds defined "the maladie du siècle" as "the nondescript cachexy, in which aspiration mingles with disenchantment, satire and scepticism with a childlike desire for the tranquility of reverence and belief—in which self-analysis has been pushed to the verge of monomania, and all springs of action are clogged and impeded by the cobwebs of speculation." On introspection as a "note" of the thirties and forties, see Kathleen Tillotson, Novels of the Eighteen-Forties, pp. 131–4.

65. Maurice, Life of F. D. Maurice, 1, 339, in 1843.

66. Works, 15, chap. 7, p. 63. The date is 1847.

67. Quoted in Richard C. Trench, Letters and Memorials, ed. by the author of "Charles Lowder" (Mrs. Trench) (2 vols. London, 1888), 1, 138.

68. Works, 12, chap. 23, p. 197.

productive energy, much . . . real blindness and impotent drifting, on all sides." [69]

Prolonged introspection, analysis, and indecision; or the sudden collapse of a philosophy or a religion which had been the motivation of action, with nothing to take its place; or the vision of a mechanistic universe without purpose or meaning—any or all of these possibilities latent in the intellectual situation can mean the destruction of all values whatsoever. How a succession of doubts may finally merge into one overwhelming doubt that anything is worth doing or life worth living is poignantly described in an autobiographical passage of Frederick Robertson's:

> It is an awful moment when the soul begins to find that the props on which it has blindly rested so long are, many of them, rotten, and begins to suspect them all; when it begins to feel the nothingness of many of the traditionary opinions which have been received with implicit confidence, and in that horrible insecurity begins also to doubt whether there be any thing to believe at all. It is an awful hour—let him who has passed through it say how awful—when this life has lost its meaning, and seems shrivelled into a span; when the grave appears to be the end of all, human goodness nothing but a name, and the sky above this universe a dead expanse, black with the void from which God himself has disappeared. [70]

Ennui has become despair. Frustration is absolute and the pain of existence great enough to make suicide a serious consideration.

It is the experience of Carlyle in the "black" years of 1818–26, recreated in the story of Teufelsdröckh. The materialism latent in eighteenth-century rationalism drove him from faith to doubt to unbelief, and left the universe "all void of Life, of Purpose, of Volition, even of Hostility . . . one huge, dead, immeasurable Steam-engine, rolling on, in its dead indifference, to grind me limb from limb." "From Suicide

69. Brown, *Life of Symonds*, p. 260. The frustrating effect of vacillation was well analyzed by Canon H. P. Liddon, *Christmastide in St. Paul's* (First ed. 1889; London, 1893), pp. 14–15: "No man acts with decision upon a motive which one half of his mind accepts, while the other questions or rejects it. As St. James says, a man with two souls or minds is unstable in all his ways. He cannot make up his mind, for he has no one mind to make up. And while he is balancing helplessly between the conflicting views which in their equipoise produce the doubt, the time for decisive action passes, and nothing has been done."

70. Brooke, *Life of Robertson*, p. 86.

a certain aftershine . . . of Christianity withheld me." [71] At almost the same time, a man utterly unlike Carlyle in temperament and breeding suffered the same fate. For Mill, Utilitarianism was not only a philosophy of ethics and politics which he believed; it was the inspiration of his life. From 1821 "when I first read Bentham . . . I had what might truly be called an object in life; to be a reformer of the world." And then in 1826 the very cornerstone of this edifice—the association of his own happiness with social progress—suddenly gave way. "The whole formulation on which my life was constructed fell down. . . . I seemed to have nothing left to live for." He described his suffering in lines from Coleridge's "Dejection":

> A grief without a pang, void, dark and drear,
> A drowsy, stifled, unimpassioned grief,
> Which finds no natural outlet or relief
> In word, or sigh, or tear.

He frequently asked himself if he could go on living in such a condition, and generally answered he could not bear it beyond a year.[72] The basic cause of this breakdown probably lay in Mill's personal relationship with his father.[73] But the sudden loss of a philosophy that gave life meaning and purpose played its important role.

Though the similar breakdowns of Kingsley were attributed to overwork, they too were the result, in part, of a periodic collapse of his religious faith under the pressure of his scientific studies. He felt at times "accessible to no hints from anything but matter." [74] He knew the agonizing impact of Huxley's nightmare:

Science frees us in many ways . . . from the bodily terror which the savage feels. But she replaces that, in the minds of many, by a moral terror which is far more overwhelming. Am I—a man is driven to ask—am I, and all I love, the victims of an organised

71. *Sartor Resartus*, Bk. II, chap. 7, "The Everlasting No." The quotations are on pp. 164–5. Cf. "Characteristics," *Essays*, 3, 30: "Not Godhead, but an iron, ignoble circle of Necessity embraces all things. . . . Heroic Action is paralysed; for what worth now remains unquestionable?" For the biographical background see Froude, *Carlyle: First Forty Years*, 1, chaps. 5–20, and note in particular, *1*, chap. 12, pp. 199–200.

72. *Autobiography*, chap. 5, pp. 112–19.

73. See A. W. Levi, "The 'Mental Crisis' of John Stuart Mill," *Psychoanalytic Review*, 32 (1945), 86–101. In his analysis, M. St. J. Packe, *The Life of John Stuart Mill*, pp. 74–82, does not find Levi's interpretation as persuasive as I do.

74. *Letters and Memories*, 2, 57 (unabridged ed., 2, 19).

tyranny, from which there can be no escape—for there is not even
a tyrant from whom I may perhaps beg mercy? Are we only help-
less particles, at best separate parts of the wheels of a vast machine, which will use us till it has worn us away, and ground us
to powder? Are our bodies—and if so, why not our souls?—the
puppets, yea, the creatures of necessary circumstances, and all
our strivings and sorrows only vain beatings against the wires of
our cage? . . . Tell us not that the world is governed by universal
law; the news is not comfortable, but simply horrible.[75]

The account of his illness in 1859 should be read with a passage like
that in mind.

I can't think; I can't write; I can't run; I can't ride—I have neither
wit, nerve, nor strength for anything; and if I try I get a hot head,
and my arms and legs begin to ache. I was so ten years ago:
worse than now. . . . Oh life—life, life! why do folks cling to
this half existence, and call that life?

> " 'Tis life, not death, for which I pant,
> 'Tis life, whereof my nerves are scant,
> More life and fuller that I want." [76]

The stanza (quoted from memory) is from Tennyson's dialogue "The
Two Voices." It is Faith's answer to the plea for suicide from Skepticism. But in the complementary poem, originally called "Supposed
Confessions of a Second-rate Sensitive Mind Not in Unity with Itself,"
there is no resolution. It ends with a cry of pain:

> O weary life! O weary death!
> O spirit and heart made desolate!
> O damned vacillating state!

No Victorian, I think, suffered from that state of mind more acutely
than J. A. Symonds, for in his case, aided by the bad condition of his
health, it lasted for many years. At what was literally the crisis of his
life in the winter of 1867–68, "all the evil humours which were fer-

75. "The Meteor Shower," preached on November 26, 1866, *The Water of
Life and Other Sermons,* in *Works, 26,* 179–80. Kingsley goes on to try and
remove the horror by arguing that a law must have a lawgiver, who is God; but
this leaves man still imprisoned in a network of law, even though it must be
'good.'

76. *Letters and Memories, 2,* 114–15 (unabridged ed., *2,* 93–4). Cf. *1,* 387–8
(not in unabridged ed.) for a similar attack in 1855.

menting in my petty state of man— . . . physical maladies of nerve-substance and of lung-tissue, decompositions of habitual creeds, sentimental vapours, doubts about the existence of a moral basis to human life, thwarted intellectual activity, ambitions rudely checked by impotence—all these miserable factors of a wretched inner life" drove him into an "utter blackness of despair." "I contemplated suicide. But death is not acceptable—it offers no solution. I loathe myself, and turn in every direction to find strength. What I want is life; the source of life fails me. I try to rest upon my will and patience. Doing so, I faint; for there is no force in me to keep the resolves I form." [77]

Against this background of case histories we can appreciate the full relevance of Arnold's classic statement of Victorian melancholia in "The Scholar-Gipsy." There in the integrity of experience are blended together the paralyzing introversion, the frustration of indecision, and the ultimate despair of finding no aim, no business, no desire that is worth living for:

> For early didst thou leave the world . . .
>   Free from the sick fatigue, the languid doubt,
>   Which much to have tried, in much been baffled, brings.
>   O life unlike to ours!
>   Who fluctuate idly without term or scope,
>   Of whom each strives, nor knows for what he strives,
>   And each half lives a hundred different lives;
>   Who wait like thee, but not, like thee, in hope.
>
> Thou waitest for the spark from heaven! and we,
>   Light half-believers of our casual creeds,
>   Who never deeply felt, nor clearly will'd,
>   Whose insight never has borne fruit in deeds,
>   Whose vague resolves never have been fulfill'd;
>   For whom each year we see
>   Breeds new beginnings, disappointments new;
>   Who hesitate and falter life away,
>   And lose to-morrow the ground won to-day—
>   Ah! do not we, wanderer! await it too?
>
> Yes, we await it!—but it still delays,
>   And then we suffer! . . .

77. Brown, *Life of Symonds*, pp. 254–5. Cf. Mallock, *The New Republic*, pp. 67–72, and Beatrice Webb, *My Apprenticeship*, pp. 85, 88–9, and 341, for the continuation of this mood into the seventies and eighties.

And wish the long unhappy dream would end,
  And waive all claim to bliss, and try to bear;
With close-lipp'd patience for our only friend,
  Sad patience, too near neighbour to despair . . .[78]

6. Isolation, Loneliness, and Nostalgia

The feeling of isolation and loneliness, so characteristic of modern man, first appeared in the nineteenth century. With the breakup of a long-established order and the resulting fragmentation of both society and thought, the old ties were snapped, and men became acutely conscious of separation. They felt isolated by dividing barriers; lonely for a lost companionship, human and divine; nostalgic for an earlier world of country peace and unifying belief.

In one sense democratic-industrial society was not a society at all. Men and classes were no longer integral parts of a Christian-feudal organism where everyone had his recognized place and function and was united to Church and State by established rights and duties. In the new liberal theory all men were free, politically and economically, owing no one any service beyond the fulfillment of legal contracts; and society was simply a collection of individuals, each motivated—naturally and rightly—by self-interest. The result was described by Carlyle's Teufelsdröckh: "Call ye that a Society," cries he again, "where there is no longer any Social Idea extant; not so much as the Idea of a common Home, but only of a common over-crowded Lodging-house? Where each, isolated, regardless of his neighbour, turned against his neighbour, clutches what he can get, and cries 'Mine!' " [79]

In *Past and Present*, a similar passage centers on the cold war between capital and labor:

We call it a Society; and go about professing openly the totalest separation, isolation. Our life is not a mutual helpfulness; but

78. Lines 161, 164–82, 192–5. In a letter to Clough on July 27, 1853 (*Letters of Arnold to Clough*, p. 138), Arnold speaks of himself as "deplorably ennuyé" and applies to himself the lines above on each year breeding "new beginnings, disappointments new." The chief literary sources which influenced Arnold's descriptions of ennui were Senancour's *Obermann*, 1804, George Sand's *Lélia*, 1833 (especially chap. 29, "Dans le Désert"), and her preface to the 1840 edition of *Obermann*. There is a sketch of this background in I. E. Sells, *Matthew Arnold and France. The Poet* (Cambridge, 1935), chaps. 2–4. Also see Trilling, *Arnold*, pp. 82–8. For other reasons why doubt, especially religious doubt, was painful, see below in the next section, pp. 81–9, and above, sec. 2, "The Dangers of Atheism."

79. *Sartor Resartus*, Bk. III, chap. 5, p. 232.

rather, cloaked under due laws-of-war, named "fair competition"
and so forth, it is a mutual hostility. We have profoundly forgotten
everywhere that *Cash-payment* is not the sole relation of human
beings; we think, nothing doubting, that *it* absolves and liquidates
all engagements of man. "My starving workers?" answers the
rich mill-owner: "Did not I hire them fairly in the market? Did
I not pay them, to the last sixpence, the sum covenanted for?
What have I to do with them more?" [80]

This new relationship—without relatedness—was founded as much
on fact as on theory. When machinery was driven by water power,
factories were scattered in small villages. Owners and foremen and
workers all knew each other. They had grown up together; they were
neighbors. But as soon as steam power was introduced, factories were
concentrated in towns near the coal fields, and large-scale production
paved the way to large-scale employment. Now a mill owner might
assemble, as Scott pointed out, "500 workmen one week and dismiss
them next without having any farther connection with them than to
receive a weeks work for a weeks wages nor any further solicitude
about their future fate than if they were so many old shuttles." [81]
Such economic causes are overlooked by Carlyle. What he sees is
the destruction of the binding obligations and loyalties of the feudal
past by the present philosophy of liberalism. It is true that Gurth with
a brass collar around his neck was forced to tend Cedric's pigs, but
he was certain of the supper and lodging which Cedric owed him.
If he was a serf, he had the "satisfaction of feeling himself related
indissolubly . . . to his fellow-mortals in this Earth." He was happier,
therefore, than "many a Lancashire and Buckinghamshire man of
these days, not born thrall of anybody"; born free, to live as he could
—if he could—in "social isolation," which might well mean freedom to
starve.[82] And the employer too, on his side, unlike the feudal baron
watching over his loyal troops with rigor yet with love, lived in "hostile
isolation," surrounded by potential or active enemies, ready to ruin him
with a strike or to burn his house in revenge for being laid off. The
"you" in Carlyle's summary statement is purposely ambiguous: it fits
both the capitalist and the worker; it applies to every individual in the
new economic order: "To be cut off, to be left solitary: to have a world

80. Bk. III, chap. 2, pp. 146–7.
81. Letter to John B. S. Morritt, May 19, 1820, *The Letters of Sir Walter Scott*,
ed. H. J. C. Grierson (12 vols. London, 1932), *6*, 190.
82. *Past and Present*, Bk. III, chap. 13, pp. 211–12.

alien, not your world; all a hostile camp for you; not a home at all, of hearts and faces who are yours, whose you are! It is the frightfulest enchantment; too truly a work of the Evil One. To have neither superior, nor inferior, nor equal, united manlike to you. Without father, without child, without brother. Man knows no sadder destiny." [83]

The modern city was the creation and the symbol of liberal-industrial society. When the ties that had bound men to their country neighbors and their ancestral village were snapped by the exodus to the factory towns and metropolitan London, the sense of community was permanently lost. For the huge, impersonal city is simply a "place" where a mass of unassorted atoms is collected together for greater business efficiency. What human as distinct from commercial intercourse exists is largely casual and amorphous. A miscellaneous crowd of people comes and goes. Social relations, as Beatrice Webb found them in London, had "no roots in neighbourhood, in vocation, in creed, or for that matter in race." [84] Furthermore, because density of population intensifies the struggle for existence, economic isolation is increased. Carlyle on his first visit to London in 1831 said to himself: "Miserable is the scandal-mongery and evil speaking of the country population: more frightful still the total ignorance and mutual heedlessness of these poor souls in populous city pent. 'Each passes on quick, transient, regarding not the other or his woes.' Each must button himself together, and take no thought (not even for evil) of his neighbour." [85]

In this environment the romantic love of nature passed into a new phase. It became the nostalgia for a lost world of peace and companionship, of healthy bodies and quiet minds. The image had its basis in memory, for every Victorian in the city had either grown up in the country or in a town small enough for ready contact with the rural environment. "When I was a child [in the 1830's]," Harrison remembered, "in every city of the kingdom, and even in most parts of London, an easy walk would take a man into quiet fields and pure air. We did not live in a pall of smoke and yellow fog" or in the "prison . . . of brick and pavement" which has made the life of man what it never

83. Ibid., Bk. IV, chap. 4, p. 274. Cf. chap. 15, "Masters and Men," in Mrs. Gaskell's North and South, in particular p. 142.

84. My Apprenticeship, pp. 35–6.

85. Froude, Carlyle: First Forty Years, 2, chap. 9, p. 207. For Victorian reactions to the modern city, see the references above in note 15; Froude, "England and Her Colonies," Short Studies, 2, 201–7; Robert Vaughan, The Age of Great Cities (1843); and Sir Arthur Helps, Social Pressure (London, 1875), pp. 7–58 and passim.

was before.[86] This is the background against which we should read
the nature poetry of the Victorians (and understand the popularity of
Wordsworth), or look at their landscapes. Kingsley's essay of 1848 on
the National Gallery gives the perspective:

> Picture-galleries should be the townsman's paradise of refresh-
> ment. . . . There, in the space of a single room, the townsman
> may take his country walk—a walk beneath mountain peaks,
> blushing sunsets, with broad woodlands spreading out below it; a
> walk through green meadows, under cool mellow shades, and
> overhanging rocks, by rushing brooks, where he watches and
> watches till he seems to *hear* the foam whisper, and to *see* the
> fishes leap; and his hard-worn heart wanders out free, beyond
> the grim city-world of stone and iron, smoky chimneys, and roar-
> ing wheels, into the world of beautiful things.[87]

To Ruskin even architecture, let alone painting, was to counterbalance
"our loss of fellowship with Nature." Its function in the age of cities
"is, as far as may be . . . to tell us about Nature; to possess us with
memories of her quietness; to be solemn and full of tenderness, like
her, and rich in portraitures of her; full of delicate imagery of the
flowers we can no more gather, and of the living creatures now far
away from us in their own solitude." [88]

It is clear that this function is more than mere escape. Whether in
fact or in art, the countryside is to save the 'spiritual' values now being
destroyed in the unspiritual city. It is, in Harrison's words, to rescue
men from the infection of urban life—its utilitarian aims, its greed,
its hard selfishness, its wear and tear on body and soul—by withdrawing them "from time to time into the only 'rest-cure,' the true spiritual
'retreat.'" [89] In Kensington Gardens, which remind him of Rugby and
the Lakes, Arnold meditates:

86. *Autobiographic Memoirs,* 1, 4, 19. Cf. Basil Willey, in *Ideas and Beliefs
of the Victorians,* p. 43: "The nineteenth century, for all its buoyancy and optimism, was homesick for an idealised but not wholly imaginary past, for the days
'When life ran gaily as the sparkling Thames,' and for the 'cool, flowery lap of
earth,' where Nature 'laid us at our birth.'" It is worth noticing that in the passage where Carlyle contrasts Gurth with the modern worker (*Past and Present,*
p. 212), Gurth lives "with the sky above him, with the free air and tinted boscage
and umbrage round him."

87. *Letters and Memories,* 1, 138–9 (unabridged ed., *1,* 168–9).

88. *Stones of Venice,* 1, chap. 30, sec. 6, in *Works,* 9, 411.

89. *Autobiographic Memoirs, 1,* 14. Cf. Kingsley's essay "Great Cities," *Sanitary
and Social Essays,* pp. 217–18 and passim.

In the huge world, which roars hard by,
Be others happy if they can!
But in my helpless cradle I
Was breathed on by the rural Pan. . . .

Calm soul of all things! make it mine
To feel, amid the city's jar,
That there abides a peace of thine,
Man did not make, and cannot mar.

The will to neither strive nor cry,
The power to feel with others give!
Calm, calm me more! nor let me die
Before I have begun to live.[90]

What is true of anxiety in general is equally true of isolation: it has
roots in both environments, the intellectual as well as the social. Men
felt divided by sectarian as well as business conflict; estranged from
family and friends by intellectual differences; alienated by doubts
from parties or circles they might otherwise have joined. An age when
"ancient assumptions [are] rudely questioned, ancient inferences utterly denied" is an age "when each man has a different view from his
neighbor, when an intellectual change has set father and son at vari-
ance, when a man's own household are the special foes of his favorite
and self-adopted creed." [91] Under those conditions isolation often pro-
vokes loneliness. It is quite possible, of course, to stand apart from the
group with pride or hostility or indifference; but one may also feel the
haunting sense of being alone, without anyone to sympathize with his
thinking, or cooperate in the pursuit of a common cause.

To feel alone is always, no doubt, the lot of original thinkers, but
their number is small. In the Victorian period a great many thoughtful
people shared the same fate. For to think at all in that environment of
clashing theories and onrushing knowledge was to arrive at some individual cross-blend of ideas that was, or seemed to be, different from
anybody else's. If one wrote, he was conscious of an audience more
likely to be argumentative than sympathetic—if indeed he had an

90. "Lines Written in Kensington Gardens." Cf. Brown, *Life of Symonds*, pp.
241-2; and see Trilling, *Arnold*, pp. 91-2.
91. Bagehot, "The First Edinburgh Reviewers," *Works, 1*, 12. Ostensibly he is
referring to the early years of the century, but I think he is reading back into the
past a good deal of what he saw around him in 1855 as he was writing.

audience in the heterogeneous mass of readers which now had replaced the relatively small and homogeneous reading public of the past. "The Thinker," Carlyle noted in 1831, "must, in all senses, wander homeless, too often aimless, looking . . . round to an Earth which is deaf." [92] And he welcomed the correspondence with Mill because "a most wholesome feeling of *communion* comes over me in your neighbourhood; the agreeable memento: Thou art *not* alone, then!" [93] Mill himself, when he had cut his family and party ties with Benthamism, spoke of "the comparative loneliness of my probable future lot. . . . By loneliness I mean the absence of that feeling which has accompanied me through the greater part of my life, that which one fellow-traveller, or one fellow-soldier has towards another—the feeling of being engaged in the pursuit of a common object, and of mutually cheering one another on, and helping one another in an arduous undertaking." Years later, even when he had formed a school, the same feeling persisted. In reply to a letter in which F. D. Maurice had spoken of his own "mental loneliness," Mill wrote: "In our age and country every person with any mental power at all, who both thinks for himself and has a conscience, must feel himself, to a very great degree, alone"; and believed that he had even fewer people than Maurice had "in real communion of thoughts, feelings, and purposes" with him. [94]

A particular factor that isolated men whose ideas, like Mill's, were the least bit radical was the powerful pressure of public opinion, demanding a high degree of conformity to what was considered safe and proper. [95] To be a democrat or a socialist or a religious liberal, let alone an agnostic, when any of these terms could suggest a person who might be undermining Church and State, was to feel excluded from society, and more alone than one really was, since prudent reticence concealed the number of one's sympathizers. When Harriet Martineau embraced scientific materialism, Henry Atkinson warned her that "the sense of loneliness will accompany you more or less through much of your social intercourse." [96] Even "honest doubt" in a period so fright-

92. "Characteristics," *Essays*, 3, 29–30.

93. *Letters of Carlyle to Mill, Sterling, and Browning*, p. 37, dated February 22, 1833.

94. *Letters*, 1, 2, dated April 15, 1829; ibid., 2, 29, dated May 11, 1865. Cf. 1, 98, where he remarks to Carlyle in 1834: "Every increase of insight carries with it the uncomfortable feeling of being separated more and more widely from almost all other human beings." Cf. Ruskin, quoted in the introduction to *Fors Clavigera*, in *Works*, 27, xxvi.

95. This pressure is discussed below, pp. 395–6, 397–9.

96. Martineau, *Autobiography*, 2, Period VI, sec. 4, p. 286.

ened of the social consequences of irreligion and so ready to consider
doubt a sin was usually met with moral censure, often from the very
people whose sympathetic understanding one most needed. As if his
personal agonies were not bad enough, Robertson had also to endure
"that fearful loneliness of spirit" when those who should have been his
friends and counselors only frowned upon his misgivings.[97] "You can't
conceive how lonely I am," cries out Ruskin, in grave perplexity about
questions of faith. "All my old religious friends are casting me off; or,
if they speak, their words are as the brass and the cymbal."[98] That
experience was most painful in the family circle, where many young
Victorians had to live in the atmosphere described by the hero of
Froude's Nemesis of Faith:

> Things grow worse and worse at home. Little things I have let
> fall are turned against me. The temperature is getting very cold,
> and our once warm and happy family, where every feeling used to
> flow so sweetly together in one common stream, seems freezing
> up, at least wherever I am, into disunited ice crystals. . . . They
> talk in whispers before me. Religious subjects are pointedly
> avoided. If I say anything myself, I am chilled with frosty mono-
> syllables, and to no one soul around me can I utter out a single
> thought.[99]

When doubts issued in conversions to another Church or to outright
agnosticism, Victorian families were torn asunder. The Wilberforces,
the Newmans, the Arnolds, the Froudes, the Martineaus are simply
the most famous examples.[100] In the case of Catholicism, the break
was particularly violent because anti-Catholic feeling, strong in England since the sixteenth century, had been inflamed by the Oxford

97. Brooke, Life of Robertson, p. 86.
98. Works, 36, 364.
99. Page 27; cf. pp. 116–17.
100. In the preface to Yeast (1851), Kingsley noticed (p. xxii) that "the young
men and women of our day are fast parting from their parents and each other;
the more thoughtful are wandering either towards Rome, towards sheer materialism, or towards an unchristian and unphilosophic spiritualism." Indeed, he wrote
the novel (p. xxiii) partly to teach the older generation "something of the reasons
of that calamitous estrangement between themselves and those who will succeed
them." The pain of religious doubt was often, in fact, the pain of a potential
or actual breaking of the family bond in a period when family life was exalted.
Norman May found doubt a "cruel agony" (Mrs. Yonge, The Daisy Chain, Pt. II,
chap. 16, p. 461) partly because, as his sister explains, his "dear home" had made
faith "our joy, our union." For the households of Carlyle, George Eliot, and
Stevenson, see Basil Willey, Nineteenth Century Studies, p. 217; for Frederic
Harrison's, see his Autobiographic Memoirs, 1, 147.

Movement; and because to enter the Roman Church was literally to exile oneself from English life. The cost can be read in Newman's *Apologia:* he had to part from all his deepest attachments—family, friends, Oxford. "You may think how lonely I am," he wrote soon after his conversion, as he prepared to leave the university forever. " 'Obliviscere populum tuum et domum patris tui' has been in my ears for the last twelve hours. . . . It is like going on the open sea." [101] Gerard Hopkins, whose conversion in 1866 owed much to Newman's influence, felt the same wrench of separation from family and country:

> To seem the stranger lies my lot, my life
> Among strangers. Father and mother dear,
> Brothers and sisters are in Christ not near
> And he my peace my parting, sword and strife;

and his parting also, as he goes on to say, from England.[102]

Finally, the mood of depression and despair, like all intense suffering, could drive the individual into himself, in lonely or in savage isolation. Mill could not turn, in his misery, to anyone, least of all to his father.[103] In the dark mood of doubt engendered by the death of Hallam, Tennyson had to resist the desire to shut himself from his kind and eat his heart alone.[104] The immediate impact of such an experience at its most painful is recorded by Carlyle in *Sartor Resartus:*

> A feeble unit in the middle of a threatening Infinitude, I seemed to have nothing given me but eyes, whereby to discern my own wretchedness. Invisible yet impenetrable walls, as of Enchantment, divided me from all living. . . . It was a strange isolation I then lived in. The men and women around me, even speaking with me, were but Figures. . . . In the midst of their crowded streets and assemblages, I walked solitary; and (except as it was my own heart, not another's that I kept devouring) savage also, as the tiger in his jungle.[105]

101. At end of Pt. VI, p. 327; cf. pp. 319–20, 323. The quotation is from Psalms 45:10.

102. Poem No. 68, *Poems,* ed. W. H. Gardner (New York and London, 1948), p. 109. Cf. Morley on conversions to agnosticism, *On Compromise,* p. 129: "The future faith, like the faith of the past, brings not peace but a sword. It is a tale not of concord, but of households divided against themselves." Clough's poem entitled "Qua Cursum Ventus" may refer to the breakup of his friendship with W. G. Ward when the latter became a Roman Catholic in 1845.

103. *Autobiography,* chap. 5, pp. 114–15; and cf. *Letters, 1,* 48.

104. *In Memoriam,* sec. 108.

105. Bk. II, chap. 7, pp. 163–4; and cf. the previous chap., p. 154. Also see the

Where the loss of faith was accompanied, as it usually was (and as it is in this example from Carlyle), by the image of Nature ruling all things with blind indifference, another kind of isolation swept over the Victorians, with an emotional impact more painful than sadness or bitterness—cosmic isolation and the terror of absolute solitude.

> O, we poor orphans of nothing—alone on
>   that lonely shore—
> Born of the brainless Nature who knew not
>   that which she bore! [106]

A sensitive boy like Charles Kingsley, driven by his studies in natural history into religious doubts, found himself not only cut off from his parents, whom he dared not talk with, but completely detached "from every other being in a cold passionless universe." [107] Even a man who held to some form of pantheism and believed in an impersonal power or a stream of tendency making for righteousness had to say to himself, as J. A. Symonds did, "I have no living God in constant relation to myself, no father, no future host and friend and master in the immortal houses." [108] Or, more exactly, he had lost the living God he had known and loved. What made the sense of cosmic isolation so acute was the sudden destruction of a divine spirit uniting man to the universe. We are the generation, wrote W. K. Clifford, who have had to see "the spring sun shine out of an empty heaven, to light up a soulless earth; we have felt with utter loneliness that the Great Companion is dead." [109]

In Clifford's voice we hear the note of nostalgia which is inseparable from loneliness. The longing for an earlier world of religious hope and the social communion of a common faith fastens on two images, historical and personal. The lost world is 'placed' either in a previous

---

quotation above, p. 65, from *Robert Elsmere;* Act II of "Empedocles on Etna"; and Mallock, *The New Republic,* pp. 70–1, where Laurence closes his account of "the intense restless misery that a man endures when he can find nothing to do which he really feels worth doing" by saying: "And so here I am utterly alone—friendless, and with nothing to help me."

106. Tennyson, "Despair," lines 33–4. The date is late (1881), but earlier examples follow.

107. Thorp, *Kingsley,* pp. 10–11. Cf. Carlyle, "Characteristics," *Essays,* 3, 31: "A noble Friedrich Schlegel [is] stupefied in that fearful loneliness" of a world from which "the Godlike has vanished." The dates are 1835 and 1831.

108. Brown, *Life of Symonds,* p. 237.

109. *Lectures and Essays, 2,* 247. Clifford was born in 1845.

period, in the childhood of the race,[110] or in one's own childhood, where the early home can readily become the symbol of a companionship that was once both divine and human. The child that one remembers is the boy who prayed to a listening Father and who walked in the family circle to the Sunday service, in the happy days before the exile from both. Few Victorians would have laughed at the sentimentality of a passage in *The Nemesis of Faith;* they knew the same feelings too well:

> I would gladly give away all I am, and all I ever may become, all the years, every one of them, which may be given me to live, but for one week of my old child's faith, to go back to calm and peace again, and then to die in hope. Oh, for one look of the blue sky, as it looked then when we called it Heaven! . . . The old family prayers, which taught us to reverence prayer, however little we understood its meaning; the far dearer private prayers at our own bedside; the dear friends for whom we prayed; the still calm Sunday, with its best clothes and tiresome services, which we little thought were going so deep into our heart, when we thought them so long and tedious; yes, it is among these so trifling seeming scenes, these, and a thousand more, that our faith has wound among our heartstrings; and it is the thought of these scenes now which threatens me with madness as I call them up again.[111]

The various strands of intellectual isolation, loneliness, and nostalgia are brought together and expressed with poignant sensitivity in the poetry of Arnold. His own experience in the forties when rationalism undermined his childhood faith and estranged him from his home lies behind the "Stanzas from the Grande Chartreuse," parts of "Empedocles," and "Dover Beach."

> The Sea of Faith
> Was once, too, at the full, and round earth's shore

110. Ruskin, "St. Mark's Rest," *Works, 24,* chap. 5, pp. 258-9, described the attitude of a Victorian who grew up in the environment of scientific and historical studies as one "of true respect for the Christian faith, and sympathy with the passions and imaginations it excited, while yet, in security of modern enlightenment, the observer regards the faith itself only as an exquisite dream of mortal childhood, and the acts of its votaries as a beautifully deceived heroism of vain hope."

111. Froude, *The Nemesis of Faith,* pp. 30-1; and cf. pp. 116-17. Also see Tennyson, "Supposed Confessions of a Second-Rate Sensitive Mind," lines 33-122.

> Lay like the folds of a bright girdle furl'd.
> But now I only hear
> Its melancholy, long, withdrawing roar,
> Retreating, to the breath
> Of the night-wind, down the vast edges drear
> And naked shingles of the world.

The metaphor manages at once to describe the ebb tide and to suggest the emotional response: Arnold, too, is standing, melancholy, on the shore of the world, alone and unprotected from the chill night-wind of an indifferent Nature.[112] The poem ends:

> Ah, love, let us be true
> To one another! for the world, which seems
> To lie before us like a land of dreams,
> So various, so beautiful, so new,
> Hath really neither joy, nor love, nor light,
> Nor certitude, nor peace, nor help for pain;
> And we are here as on a darkling plain
> Swept with confused alarms of struggle and flight,
> Where ignorant armies clash by night.

The clash of the armies reflects (it is not to be interpreted literally as expressing) the clash of contending theories—the disputes, distractions, fears of an iron time which not only make certitude and peace impossible but isolate the individual, and so provoke the cry for the companionship of love.[113] In "The Forsaken Merman" the haunting note of separation gives depth and contemporary relevance to a poem of faëry fantasy in the Romantic manner. The family is divided by opposing beliefs, or, more exactly, opposing values, which suggest (again any specific or literal reading is to be avoided) the Christian-

112. "Dover Beach." Cf. Bertrand Russell, "A Free Man's Worship" (1902), *Selected Papers of Bertrand Russell* (New York, n.d.), pp. 11–12: "We see . . . the dark ocean on whose rolling waves we toss for a brief hour; from the great night without, a chill blast breaks in upon our refuge; all the loneliness of humanity amid hostile forces is concentrated upon the individual soul, which must struggle alone, with what of courage it can command, against the whole weight of a universe that cares nothing for its hopes and fears."

113. This interpretation of the battle is supported by Clough's patent use of the same passage in Thucydides to describe the contemporary situation: see "The Bothie of Tober-na-Vuolich" (1848), Pt. IX, lines 51–4. The parallel was noticed by Paul Turner, " 'Dover Beach' and 'The Bothie of Tober-na-Vuolich,' " *English Studies*, 28 (1947), 173–8.

Protestant life of religious faith and active work on the one side, and on the other the life of pagan and sensuous naturalism.[114] Margaret stops her wheel, stares out across the sand to the sea:

> And anon there breaks a sigh,
> And anon there drops a tear,
> From a sorrow-clouded eye,
> And a heart sorrow-laden,
> A long, long sigh;
> For the cold strange eyes of a little Mermaiden
> And the gleam of her golden hair.

The merman and the children from the depths of the sea are

> Singing: 'Here came a mortal,
> But faithless was she!
> And alone dwell for ever
> The kings of the sea.'. . .

> Singing: 'There dwells a loved one,
> But cruel is she!
> She left lonely for ever
> The kings of the sea.'

Though apparently unconnected with this poem, Arnold's love affair with Marguerite comes readily to mind. This episode, indeed, may have been central in making him the poet of Victorian loneliness. It acted on his imagination, I suggest, like a catalytic agent, drawing out and intensifying by its symbolic implications the sense of general isolation which otherwise would have been less sharp, and less clamorous for expression. It is significant that his principal statement appears in the group of lyrics inspired by that event, entitled "Switzerland," where we can see the personal experience of thwarted love being transmuted into the universal experience of loneliness and nostalgia that first came to modern consciousness in the Victorian period:

> Yes! in the sea of life enisled,
> With echoing straits between us thrown,
> Dotting the shoreless watery wild,
> We mortal millions live *alone*.
> The islands feel the enclasping flow,
> And then their endless bounds they know.

114. The same contrast is seen in "Morality."

But when the moon their hollows lights,
And they are swept by balms of spring,
And in their glens, on starry nights,
The nightingales divinely sing;
And lovely notes, from shore to shore,
Across the sounds and channels pour—

Oh! then a longing like despair
Is to their farthest caverns sent;
For surely once, they feel, we were
Parts of a single continent!
Now round us spreads the watery plain—
Oh might our marges meet again!

Who order'd, that their longing's fire
Should be, as soon as kindled, cool'd?
Who renders vain their deep desire?—
A God, a God their severance ruled!
And bade betwixt their shores to be
The unplumb'd, salt, estranging sea.[115]

115. Poem No. 5. "A God" here means a fate or destiny. Cf. No. 4.

Part II

INTELLECTUAL ATTITUDES

Chapter 4

THE CRITICAL SPIRIT—AND
THE WILL TO BELIEVE

> This is the age of experiment, everything is passed
> through some alembic; there is a strange absence truly
> of all present faith and belief, but the cheerful fact
> is, that almost all men are yearning after a faith.
>
> *E. P. Hood* [1]

IN THE AGE of Victoria, the Voice of Authority was accepted in religion, in politics, in literature, in family life. It was not until the twentieth century that everything was held to be an open question; and the modern spirit was initiated by Samuel Butler and Bernard Shaw with their watchwords, "Question! Examine! Test!"

That is the traditional notion, the floating impression that still persists.[2] It is a curious mixture of error and truth. The error is exposed at once by Baldwin Brown's lectures of 1870. The distinguishing feature of the Victorian revolution, he pointed out, was "the utter overthrow of ancient and venerated authority, the searching and to a large. extent destructive criticism of ideas and institutions, on which, as on an immovable rock, the order of society was believed to rest; the submission of every thing and every method to the free judgment of reason." [3] To the judgment, that is, of a man's own reason. The individual questions, examines, and decides. But if that were the whole truth, it would be difficult to account for such a representative Victorian as Gladstone: "In every field of thought and

1. *The Age and Its Architects*, pp. 66–7.
2. See, for example, A. C. Ward, *Twentieth-Century Literature. The Age of Interrogation, 1901–1925* (London, 1930), pp. 1–6, and later editions, which I am partly paraphrasing. As Ward reveals, this view and the notion that the Victorian period was one of certitude instead of doubt (see above, p. 10) naturally go together.
3. Lectures, "The Revolution of the Last Quarter of a Century" (1869–70), in *First Principles*, p. 224.

life he started from the principle of authority; it fitted in with his
reverential instincts, his temperament, above all, his education." [4]
And that could be said of thousands of his contemporaries, eminent
and obscure. We have to conclude that although the critical spirit
was characteristic of the age, nevertheless what specially distinguished
the Victorian was "his insistent *attitude* of acceptance, his persistent
belief in (but only rare examination of) the credentials of authority,
his innate desire to affirm and conform rather than to reject or to
question." [5] The truth is that to a large extent the will to believe
overrode the desire to question, and private judgment was renounced,
both deliberately and unconsciously, for external authority.

1. *Rise of the Critical Spirit*

What Mill called "the disposition to demand the *why* of everything" was a direct inheritance from the eighteenth-century philosophers, notably from Voltaire and Hume, but its immediate Victorian
source was Bentham. He was "the great questioner of things established . . . the great *subversive*, or, in the language of continental
philosophers, the great *critical*, thinker of his age and country."
"Great," Mill explains, because under his influence "the yoke of
authority has been broken, and innumerable opinions, formerly received on tradition as incontestable, are put upon their defence, and
required to give an account of themselves." [6] Moreover, he was not
merely a negative or destructive philosopher. He made a positive
contribution to Victorian thought, and one more important than the
Utilitarian doctrines he formulated. "It was not his opinions," in the
judgment of Mill, " . . . but his method, that constituted the novelty
and the value of what he did." He introduced into morals and
politics "those habits of thought and modes of investigation, which
are essential to the idea of science." [7] In short, more than anyone
else, Bentham shaped the liberal frame of mind, and made the subjection of all authority to the judgment of reason its central characteristic.

His influence was then broadened and deepened, naturally enough,
by the scientific movement, with its Baconian attack on the principle

---

4. Morley, *Life of Gladstone, 1,* 202; and see his own essay, "On the Influence
of Authority in Matters of Opinion," *The Nineteenth Century, 1* (1877), 2–22.

5. Ward, *Twentieth-Century Literature* (1940 ed., which gives a slight revision
of the original text), p. 3.

6. "Bentham" (1838), *Dissertations, 1,* 332–4.

7. Ibid., pp. 338–9.

of authority and its insistent appeal to experiment and observation. "The improver of natural knowledge," as Huxley kept repeating through his popular essays, "absolutely refuses to acknowledge authority, as such. For him, scepticism is the highest of duties; blind faith the one unpardonable sin." He clinched the point with an epigram: "The man of science has learned to believe in justification, not by faith, but by verification." [8] Furthermore, the general spread of knowledge and discussion, implemented by new periodicals and newspapers, tended to weaken the hold of traditional ideas. As early as 1831 Mill could report that "men may not reason better concerning the great questions in which human nature is interested, but they reason more. Large subjects are discussed more, and longer, and by more minds." But "to discuss," as he goes on to say, "and to question established opinions, are merely two phrases for the same thing." [9]

Rational inquiry of this kind means that the individual reaches his own conclusion.[10] This fact had theoretical support. Since the root of liberalism was "respect for the dignity and worth of the individual," the right, even the obligation, of private judgment was a dogma widely affirmed. The individual should be free to decide for himself, and he *should* decide for himself, what is true, useful, or virtuous; he should bring all things to the bar of his own mind and conscience.[11] That liberal principle was often traced back to the Reformation (especially by the scientists, who in this way could turn the flank on a clerical opposition pleading for religious authority). "We are in the midst of a gigantic movement," wrote Huxley, "greater than that which preceded and produced the Reformation, and really only the continuation of that movement. . . . There is nothing new in the ideas which lie at the bottom of the movement, nor is any reconcilement possible between free thought and traditional authority." [12] That is much too simple, as Huxley came to realize; [13] and in any event, whatever the exact relationship between Protestantism

8. "On the Advisableness of Improving Natural Knowledge" (1866), *Method and Results*, pp. 40–1.

9. *The Spirit of the Age*, pp. 13–14.

10. Cf. "The Age We Live In," *Fraser's Magazine*, 24 (1841), 8: "Knowledge is now sociable. . . . We can all talk about it . . . and each in a different way. . . . The more we think for ourselves, the less inclined we feel to take the thoughts of others."

11. Cf. Morley, *Recollections*, 1, 21.

12. Leonard Huxley, *Life of T. H. Huxley*, 1, 427–8, from a letter of Aug. 8, 1873. Cf. Baldwin Brown, *Our Theology in Relation to the Intellectual Movement of Our Times* (London, 1876), pp. 12–14, where he traces both private judgment

and freedom of thought, there was nothing Protestant about the notion that *everyone* was to rely on his own judgment, that the common man, so to speak, should be free to "select his own credo, construct his own opinions." [14] It was only with the French Revolution that democratic theories of popular sovereignty and the equality of man extended the right of private judgment to the masses. In 1817 Coleridge noted that *all* men were now considered able to judge; and by 1831 Mill was uneasily aware that the new liberalism was "for making every man his own guide and sovereign-master, and letting him think for himself, and do exactly as he judges best for himself, giving other men leave to persuade him if they can by evidence, but forbidding him to give way to authority." [15] That result, indeed, was indigenous to an age of transition. The very breakdown of traditional beliefs and the declining prestige of both the clergy and the aristocracy tended to throw the individual back upon himself, whether he would or no. "As the old doctrines have gone out, and the new ones have not yet come in, every one must judge for himself as he best may." [16]

2. The Will to Believe

The critical movement, like Jupiter in the old myth, produced a son destined for the time being to be stronger than its father. Because it often issued, as we have seen, not in reconstruction but in fresh perplexity, it gave birth to an anxious will to believe. There was "abroad a strange consciousness of doubt, instability, and incoherence; *and, withal,* a secret yearning after certainty and reorganisation in thought and in life." "Even the special merits of this time," Frederic Harrison went on to say, "its candour, tolerance, and spirit of inquiry, exaggerate our consciousness of mental anarchy, and give a strange fascination to anything that promises to end it." [17] The emotional

---

and the critical spirit to the Reformation; Mill, *Autobiography*, chap. 2, p. 36; Spencer, *Education*, pp. 97, 100; Leslie Stephen (see next note).

13. "Prologue" (1892), *Science and Christian Tradition*, pp. 8–14. For a criticism of this theory, see Noel Annan, *Leslie Stephen*, pp. 128–9.

14. Hood, *The Age and Its Architects*, p. 102.

15. Coleridge, *Biographia Literaria*, ed. J. Shawcross (2 vols. Oxford, 1907), *1*, 42; Mill, *Letters, 1*, 15, and cf. *The Spirit of the Age*, p. 30.

16. Mill, *The Spirit of the Age*, p. 33.

17. Frederic Harrison, "The Positivist Problem," *Fortnightly Review, 12* (1869), 471. The italics are mine. Cf. Mill, "Utility of Religion" (written between 1850 and 1858), *Three Essays on Religion*, p. 70: "We are in an age of weak beliefs, and in which such belief as men have is much more determined by their wish to believe than by any mental appreciation of evidence."

attraction of belief is plainly counteracting the desire to question and examine. By the sixties this tendency was common enough to draw fire from the rationalists. John Tyndall saw one very obvious danger besetting the more earnest spirits of the time—"the danger of *haste* in endeavouring to give the feelings repose." They should adopt a more scientific attitude:

> There are periods when the judgment ought to remain in suspense, the data on which a decision might be based being absent. This discipline of suspending the judgment is a common one in science, but not so common as it ought to be elsewhere. . . . We ought to learn to wait. We ought assuredly to pause before closing with the advances of those expounders of the ways of God to men, who offer us intellectual peace at the modest cost of intellectual life.[18]

If Tyndall was ironic in using the word "modest," to many Victorians the cost seemed little enough. For they were not merely seeking repose; they were craving relief from the social fears and personal distress which religious doubt in particular was exciting. In 1836 Carlyle described the age as "at once destitute of faith and terrified at scepticism"—at the prospect of social disintegration or outright revolution if religion were abandoned, or by the appalling vision of a mechanistic universe devoid of spiritual life or moral value.[19] Terror does not think. It demands, compels, a recoil to faith. In a universe from which God has vanished, a noble soul, "stupefied in that fearful loneliness, as of a silenced battle-field," flies back to his church, "as a child might to its slain mother's bosom, and cling there."[20] That is precisely what Kingsley found true of the "mass" of his contemporaries. They were "losing most fearfully and rapidly the living spirit of Christianity, and . . . for that very reason, clinging all the more convulsively . . . to the outward letter of it, whether High Church or Evangelical."[21] Those Victorians whose doubts had carried them beyond the harbor of a church cried out for a *new* faith that would end their distress of mind. After Symonds referred

18. *Fragments of Science*, 2, 98–9.
19. Carlyle, "Sir Walter Scott," *Essays*, 4, 49. For other uses of the word "terror" see Froude and Stowell, below, pp. 100–1; Harriet Martineau, *Autobiography*, 2, Period VI, sec. 7, p. 368.
20. Carlyle, referring in particular to Friedrich Schlegel, "Characteristics," *Essays*, 3, 31–2.
21. *Yeast*, p. xxii.

to the "anxious, yearning, impotent, God-desiring, hungry and thirsty, exiled, footsore, feverish, blind, passionate, unhappy scepticism in the present day," he went on at once to say: "Give a man possessed by this fiend one creed, throw him a mustard seed of faith, and he will move mountains. It does not much matter what a man believes; but for power and happiness he must believe something—he must have his foot 'tenoned and morticed' somewhere, not planted for ever on a shifting sand-heap." [22] The agony is so intense, be it noted, that it hardly matters much *what* a man believes so long as by believing it he can exorcise the agony of skeptical negation—which is to abandon any pretense of making a rational choice among various beliefs. Lucky if he can get hold of one. To meet "the curse of our generation . . . that so few of us deeply believe anything . . . we must pray to God," said Kingsley, "to give us faith." In Himself? in immortality? in Christianity? No, simply "faith in something—something that we can live for, and would die for. Then we shall be ready and able to do good in our generation." [23] That is to say, we shall then escape from the paralysis of doubt and be able to act.

This feeling of near panic was limited to the more sensitive intellectuals. But the general apprehension was common enough to provoke a defense of religious beliefs on the ground not of their truth—not now when their truth was so dubious—but of their utility. It is significant that when Mill described this tendency in *On Liberty*, he began his discussion with the very quotation from Carlyle whose implications we have been exploring: "In the present age—which has been described as 'destitute of faith, but terrified at scepticism' —in which people feel sure, not so much that their opinions are true, as that they should not know what to do without them—the claims of an opinion to be protected from public attack are rested not so much on its truth, as on its importance to society." [24] To refrain from attack is to refrain from critical analysis; and if some individuals did so from fear of public opinion,[25] others were quite willing to accept beliefs as useful which, in point of fact, they

22. Brown, *Life of Symonds*, p. 318.

23. *Letters and Memories*, *1*, 113 (unabridged ed., *1*, 141).

24. *On Liberty*, chap. 2, p. 110. Cf. Morley, "Of the Possible Utility of Error," *On Compromise*, chap. 2.

25. The pressure of public opinion to accept biblical authority, to hold orthodox opinions, and not to question or examine or exert any private judgment, is, of course, a factor opposing the critical spirit; but since this is rather the necessity than the will to believe, I deal with it in the next chapter on Anti-Intellectualism, in sec. 2.

thought doubtful or even false. Froude's comment on the tragic story of Markham Sutherland, whose life was destroyed by skepticism, is that "we little know what we are doing when we cast adrift from system. . . . Even superstition [by which he means biblical Christianity] is a bracing girdle, which the frame that is trained to it can ill afford to lose." [26] And perhaps, therefore, had best not examine. By the end of the century Lecky could see that a new intellectual habit had been growing up among educated men. Those who had once discussed religious questions simply as questions of truth or falsehood, in later years came frequently to "accept their creed as a working hypothesis of life; as a consolation in innumerable calamities; as the one supposition under which life is not a melancholy anti-climax; as the indispensable sanction of moral obligation; as the gratification and reflection of needs, instincts and longings which are planted in the deepest recesses of human nature; as one of the chief pillars on which society rests." [27] From this multiple motivation the will to believe was setting aside the appeal to reason.

3. Recoil to Authority

The desire to cling to the old faith or seize on a new one under emotional stress, or more coolly to accept Christianity for all its superstition in the interests of social order and personal need, has its complementary aspect in the readiness to abandon private judgment for some external authority. "The passionate resolve" of religious people, noticed by Arnold, "to keep hold on what is slipping away from them by giving up more and more the use of reason in religion" carried with it the corollary of "resting more and more on authority" —that of either a Church or a prophet.[28]

The Church, naturally enough, was the Catholic Church, Anglican or Roman. Both were gaining converts in large numbers through the middle decades of the century. By 1853 half the most amiable men whom Ruskin knew at Oxford (1837–42) were Roman Catholics,

26. *The Nemesis of Faith*, pp. 178–9.

27. *Map of Life*, chap. 11, pp. 227–8. Specifically Lecky is referring to a general change in habits of thought as men grew older; but his previous paragraph applies the change to the later nineteenth century.

28. *Literature and Dogma*, chap. 11, p. 307. The particular reference in the passage is to Roman Catholicism. Cf. his *God and the Bible* (First ed. 1875; New York, 1895), preface, p. xxx: "For fear of losing their religious convictions, the pious part of our people would fain shut off from themselves the intellectual current, which they fear might carry them away to shores of desolations." Cf. Morley, *Life of Gladstone, I*, 209, and Gladstone's article cited above, note 4.

"the others altogether unsettled in purpose and principle." [29] Had he said "still unsettled," he would have expressed more clearly what was surely in his mind: that the converts had been originally in the same state of doubt. In a period when religious differences and perplexities were not only painful in themselves but so much evidence of the fallibility or impotence of the unassisted human reason, men were glad enough, in many cases, to exchange their vaunted private judgment for a divine teacher.[30] Moreover, as the Bible, which had been "the religion of Protestants," was losing its old status as a sacred and inspired authority, the claim of the Catholic Church to that supreme rôle became more persuasive, and in the context of fear and despair more compelling. Froude was quite right to see the Catholic revival in Oxford as part of the general movement toward Roman Catholicism in Europe, and to find for both the same basic cause: "Pious Protestants had trusted themselves upon the Bible as their sole foundation. They found their philosophers and professors assuming that the Bible was a human composition—parts of it of doubtful authenticity, other parts bearing marks on them of the mistaken opinions of the age when these books were written; and they were flying terrified back into the Church from which they had escaped at the Reformation, like ostriches hiding their heads in a bush." [31]

In the last phrase we hear the tone of the Protestant apologist. The standard explanation for Catholic conversions to either the High Church or the Roman Church was quite simple, and allowing for its patent exaggeration and prejudice, substantially true. When the rationalist was suddenly startled by finding he was cutting away all the ground from under his feet, he took "a desperate leap," according to Thomas Arnold, "into a blind fanaticism"—that is, into Newmanism. Or, in the complementary statement by Hugh Stowell, "minds which shrink with horror from the gulph-stream of infidelity, blinded by

29. *Works*, 36, 155.

30. See W. E. H. Lecky, *The Religious Tendencies of the Age*, pp. 103–4 (published anonymously; for the attribution to Lecky see the Bibliography, below), and the revealing passage in Beatrice Webb's diary, Nov. 14, 1880, *My Apprenticeship*, pp. 86–7. I wonder if Gladstone's reliance upon authority in general (noticed in the first paragraph of this chapter), and the authority of a High Church in particular, may not have been related to the fact that the history of his inner life, as he said himself (Morley, *Life of Gladstone*, 1, 13), was "extraordinarily dubious, vacillating, and above all complex."

31. "The Oxford Counter-Reformation," *Short Studies*, 4, 312–13.

their very terror, plunge into the opposite gulph-stream, which hurries them along in the direction of Rome." [32]

But Catholicism had so long been an object of fear and distaste in England, and ecclesiastical control so long foreign to English tradition, that this solution appealed only to a minority. Most Victorians who could not cling to a Protestant Church, and were therefore ready in their "confusion and perplexity" to turn anywhere, as Maurice tells us, "for the help which they cannot find among divines," [33] looked to literature for authority and to the writer as prophet. Men of letters became in fact, as they often boasted they were in theory, a modern priesthood, supplying the help and guidance, religious and moral, which the old priesthood could no longer provide. [34] Every writer had his congregation of devoted or would-be devoted disciples who read his work in much the spirit they had once read the Bible. We have noticed the dilemma in which men found themselves in the forties, of "believing nothing, or believing everything which superstition, disguised as Church authority, had been pleased to impose." [35] The resulting impact of *Sartor Resartus* and *Past and Present* —or rather of their author—is recorded by Froude: "Carlyle taught me a creed which I could then accept as really true; which I have held ever since, with increasing confidence, as the interpretation of my existence and the guide of my conduct, so far as I have been able

32. Stanley, *Life of Arnold*, p. 484, in a letter of October 5, 1838; Stowell, "The Age We Live In," in *Exeter Hall Lectures, 6* (1850–51), 55. The necessity of abridging private judgment if the "all-corroding, all-dissolving scepticism of the intellect in religious inquiries" were to be avoided (*Apologia*, p. 335) is the central teaching of Newman, and the thesis of his *Lectures on the Prophetical Office of the Church* (1837)—that is, the duty of the Church to prophesy the truth—which is sometimes called the bible of Anglo-Catholicism. For the essence of his attack on liberalism see the note affixed to the *Apologia*, pp. 491–502, especially propositions 1, 9, and 10 on pp. 499–500. In *The Idea of a University*, Discourse II, p. 37, he remarks: "In a state of society . . . in which free discussion and fallible judgment are prized as the birthright of each individual, I must be excused if I exercise towards this age, as regards its belief in this doctrine, some portion of that scepticism which it exercises itself towards every received but unscrutinized assertion whatever."

33. Frederick Maurice, *Life of F. D. Maurice, 1*, 508.

34. For the theory, see below, pp. 152–4. For the fact, besides the evidence that follows, there is Lecky's remark, *Religious Tendencies of the Age*, p. 316: "It is our lay writers who are moulding the characters and forming the opinions of the age"; they have superseded "the clergy in the direction of the thought of England."

35. Above, p. 49.

to act up to it. *Then and always I looked, and have looked, to him as my master.*" [36] A generation later Peter Bayne published his *Lessons from My Masters: Carlyle, Tennyson, Ruskin;* and the first Browning Societies in the eighties announced the arrival of still another master. Even the novelists, notably George Eliot, had their followers, and many a Victorian sought his personal code of laws from "fictitious histories . . . in place of drawing it direct and pure from the Catechism or the Gospel." [37] Perhaps the most revealing sign of this dependence on literature is to be found in the letters received by every author from unknown disciples. One to Carlyle is representative:

> Honoured Sir,—I am a stranger to you. . . . I was one of those Edinburgh students to whom, as a father to his sons, you addressed words which I have read over at least six times, and mean, while I live, to remember and obey. I have still one plea more. You know that in this country, *when people are perplexed or in doubt, they go to their minister for counsel: you are my minister, my only minister, my honoured and trusted teacher,* and to you I, having for more than a year back ceased to believe as my fathers believed in matters of religion, and being now an inquirer in that field, come for light on the subject of prayer.[38]

When the need for help was so desperate because the pain of doubt was so intense, a man might even cry out for a dictator. It was Charles Kingsley himself, appalled by finding that "verily, in England, doctrines . . . are 'a world gone entirely to chaos,'" who confessed, "I sometimes long for a St. Francis, with a third order of Minors, to lay hold of one's will, soul, and body, and coax, threaten, scourge one along some definite path of doctrine and labor." [39]

4. Reliance on Authority

The deliberate recoil to authority was aided and complemented by a habit of mind, partly inherited, partly acquired, which made re-

36. *Carlyle: Life in London, 1,* chap. 11, p. 296. The italics are mine. In chap. 1, p. 4, Froude speaks of "millions" of readers who looked to him "not for amusement, but for moral guidance."

37. W. R. Greg, "False Morality of Lady Novelists" (1859), *Literary and Social Judgments, 1,* 106.

38. Froude, *Carlyle: First Forty Years, 2,* chap. 1, pp. 19–20. The italics are mine.

39. *Letters and Memories, 1,* 111 (unabridged ed., *1,* 138); cf. *Yeast,* chap. 17, p. 305.

liance on authority a natural tendency. For one thing, the average Victorian was much more likely to defer to the opinions of his "elders and betters" than to question them or think out his own; which is to say that the tradition of respect for the upper classes survived in England much longer than it did in France. The hierarchical structure of society, spared any direct revolutionary attack, remained relatively firm; and the concept of equality never won any general acceptance—least of all from a middle class eager to preserve the social distinctions it was struggling to attain. "The English, of all ranks and classes," wrote Mill in 1858, "are at bottom, in all their feelings, aristocrats. They have the conception of liberty, and set some value on it, but the very idea of equality is strange and offensive to them." [40] Under such conditions it is not surprising, as Taine observed, that the English people were strongly inclined "to adopt the opinions of those above them, and to be governed by them. It is exactly the opposite in France." [41]

But even those who were not so inclined, the staunch liberals and the self-made men determined to reach their own conclusions, often found themselves doing precisely the same thing. For thinking is never easy at best, and still less so at a time when almost every subject was confused by a mass of new facts and novel interpretations. To make matters worse, one was now expected, by himself as well as by others, to have an opinion about everything, to take a position on a score of disputed points in politics, religion, and morals. Not to do so was shameful: it implied indifference to crucial issues or failure to keep abreast of advancing knowledge. Surely, anyone who was a person of importance, or professed to be (viz. any member of the rising middle class), ought to know where he stood on the Oxford Movement or democracy or evolution; what he thought of Carlyle or Mill; whether or not he believed in mesmerism or phrenology. He ought to have a theory of the universe and a view of human nature. "Old Leisure," in the pre-Victorian days of the early century, "was quite a different personage. . . . He was a contemplative, rather stout gentleman . . . of quiet perceptions, undiseased by hypothesis; happy in his inability to know the causes of things,

40. *Letters*, 1, 205.
41. *Notes on England*, pp. 241–2. Bagehot, indeed, specifically says (*The English Constitution*, chap. 1, in *Works*, 4, p. 5) that "the mass of the 'ten-pound' householders did not really form their own opinions," but were "guided in their judgment by the better educated classes"; and goes on to mention their respect for "rank and wealth."

preferring the things themselves." [42] His Victorian child or grandchild, on the other hand, is well represented by the "man of great gifts and requirements" (*sic*) with whom John Tyndall once walked down Regent Street, discussing various theological questions. "I could not accept his views," Tyndall said, "of the origin and destiny of the universe, nor was I prepared to enunciate any definite views of my own. He turned to me at length and said, 'You surely must have a theory of the universe.'" [43] Faced with such expectations, the average man was glad enough to take his ideas from the latest periodical. But *his* ideas, be it noted. A passage on private judgment in one of Newman's sermons shows how neatly one could have his cake and eat it too—save his liberal face and adopt ready-made ideas: "'Private judgment' commonly means passive impression. Most men in this country like opinions to be brought to them, rather than to be at the pains to go out and seek for them." They must have persons "to provide them with their ideas, the clothing of their mind, and that of the best fashion;" for they like to be waited on, "they like to be their own centre." "Hence," he goes on to say, "the extreme influence of periodical publications at this day, quarterly, monthly, or daily; these teach the multitude of men what to think and what to say." [44]

This readiness to depend on literature had another and more creditable source. Many of the middle class, now that they had political standing and social opportunities, were eager to acquire the education, or at least the veneer of culture, which they lacked. For that purpose they found the long essay (in collections or in periodicals) exactly fitted to their need—particularly the *Essays* of Macaulay with their wide range of literary and historical material, and their rapid and simple style:

> Macaulay came upon the world of letters just as the middle classes were expanding into enormous prosperity, were vastly increasing in numbers, and were becoming more alive than they had ever been before to literary interests. His Essays are as good as a library: they make an incomparable manual and vade-

42. George Eliot, *Adam Bede*, 2, chap. 28, p. 339. In editions where the chapters are consecutively numbered, this is chap. 52.

43. *Fragments of Science*, 2, 98–9.

44. "Christ upon the Waters" (1850), *Sermons Preached on Various Occasions* (1898 ed.), pp. 148–9. Cf. Tancred in Disraeli's novel (1847), *Works, 15*, chap. 20, p. 190: "'We live at present under the empire of general ideas, which are extremely powerful. But the public have not invented those ideas. They have adopted them from convenience.'"

mecum for a busy uneducated man, who has curiosity and enlightenment enough to wish to know a little about the great lives
and great thoughts, the shining words and many-coloured complexities of action, that have marked the journey of man through
the ages.[45]

But these *Essays* had originally appeared, for the most part, in the
Edinburgh Review; indeed, most volumes of Victorian essays were
simply collections of articles first printed in the periodicals. Except
for the sermon, the "review-like essay and the essay-like review,"
to use Bagehot's phrase, was the principal form of expository prose.
The need to instruct so many persons, he explained, required a form
long enough to cover a large subject and short enough to make any
laborious analysis conveniently impossible. "The modern man must be
told what to think; shortly, no doubt, but he *must* be told it. The
essay-like criticism of modern times is about the length which he
likes. The *Edinburgh Review*, which began the system, may be said
to be, in this country, the commencement on large topics of suitable
views for sensible persons." [46] The Victorians not only turned to their
prophets for authority in a period of doubt, they depended upon them
in a period of rapidly changing and developing knowledge.

This reliance was further encouraged by another characteristic of
both the age and the people. It was a period of enormous activity
in which practical accomplishment, especially in business, became
the major goal of life. Most men had little time and little inclination
for intellectual pursuits. Furthermore, this anti-intellectualism is almost as much English as it is Victorian. After remarking that there
were some nations so formed for speculation that men originate
doctrines or follow out ideas as readily as they eat or sleep, Newman
went on to say that by contrast the Englishman "bent on action . . .
gets his opinions anyhow, some from the nursery, some at school,
some from the world, and has a zeal for them, because they are his
own. Other men, at least, exercise a judgment upon them, and prove
them by a rule. He does not care to do so, but he takes them
as he finds them, whether they fit together or not, and makes light
of the incongruity, and thinks it a proof of common sense, good sense,
strong shrewd sense, to do so." [47]

45. Morley, "Macaulay," *Critical Miscellanies, 1,* 264-5.
46. "The First Edinburgh Reviewers," *Works, 1,* 7; but see pp. 1-7 for the full
range of Bagehot's argument.
47. "Christ upon the Waters," pp. 149-50. In Taine's *Notes on England,* pp.
312-15, a similar contrast is made specifically between France and England. On

Finally, the dependent habit of mind was powerfully reinforced by the religious education common in Evangelical and Dissenting circles. Ministers and parents felt it a "sacred duty" to impress upon children "the necessity, on pain of reprobation in this world and damnation in the next, of accepting, in the strict and literal sense, every statement contained in the Protestant Bible"; and therefore that "doubt about any of them was a sin, not less reprehensible than a moral delict." [48] In minds subjected to this discipline from early youth, authoritarianism often became a general principle of thought. Huxley knew "many excellent persons" who assumed "that authority is the soundest basis of belief; that merit attaches to a readiness to believe; that the doubting disposition is a bad one, and scepticism a sin; that when good authority has pronounced what is to be believed, and faith has accepted it, reason has no further duty." [49]

5. Tension

Whether to follow the critical mind whatever its destructive effect on religious faith or to follow the will to believe and abandon reason could become for some Victorians, perhaps a majority of the intellectuals, the two horns of a dilemma. They could do neither. No sooner had they concluded, under the influence of science and biblical criticism, that Christianity was a myth or that all supernatural religion was a delusion than they felt the hopes and consolations, so deeply imbedded by the Bible readings and church services of their youth, not only still alive but reviving the more intensely as they were threatened with extinction. The unbeliever had the emotions of the believer. In 1840 James Martineau observed "a simultaneous increase, in the very same class of minds, of theological doubt and of devotional affection," which meant, in effect, that the age was to be what Froude called one of "those trying periods of human history, when devotion and intelligence appear to be opposed." [50] This tension

the anti-intellectualism of business and the worship of common sense, see my next chapter, sec. 1 and start of sec. 2.

48. Huxley, "Prologue" (1892), *Science and Christian Tradition*, p. 22.

49. "On the Advisableness of Improving Natural Knowledge" (1866), *Method and Results*, p. 40.

50. J. E. Carpenter, *James Martineau, Theologian and Teacher* (Boston, 1905), p. 185, from a letter to William Ellery Channing; J. A. Froude, *History of England from the Fall of Wolsey to the Defeat of the Spanish Armada. Reign of Elizabeth* (6 vols. New York, 1871), "Conclusion," *6*, 561. Cf. Lord Acton, "George Eliot's 'Life,'" *The Nineteenth Century*, 17 (1885), 485, where he spoke of her novels "as the emblem of a generation distracted between the intense need of believing and the difficulty of belief."

between the emancipated head and the traditional heart, which can be seen, to greater or less extent, in such different personalities as Tennyson, Kingsley, Arnold, Mill, and Beatrice Webb, is most fully articulated in the poetry of Clough, for Clough refused with scrupulous integrity to suppress, in the interest of either alone, the reality forced upon him by the logic of facts or urged upon him by the deep-seated desires of his religious nature:

> All his religious needs, hopes, aspirations remaining the same, a new view of the universe, with slowly accumulating force, impressed itself irresistibly on his mind, with which not only the intellectual beliefs entwined with these needs and aspirations seemed incompatible, but even these latter fundamentally incongruous. And thus began a conflict between old and new that was to last his life, the various moods of which the series of his religious poems, solemn, passionate, and ironical, accurately expresses.[51]

Behind all these moods lies a rigorous agnosticism. To insist that we have no logical proof of the religious reading of life is true enough, but it is equally true that we have no logical proof of the *scientific* reading of life. Or, in a variant statement, if there are difficulties in the way of faith, there are others in the way of atheism. Clough was one of the earliest examples of that "large class of minds," later described by Pater, which could not believe that the sacred story or a religious philosophy was necessarily erroneous. They thought that those who were quite sure that either or both were false were "unphilosophical through lack of doubt"—failure, that is, to doubt the negative conclusions. "For their part, they make allowance in their scheme of life for a great possibility, and with some of them that bare concession of possibility (the subject of it being what it is) becomes the most important fact in the world. The recognition of it straightway opens wide the door to hope and love."[52] But pos-

51. Sidgwick, "Arthur Hugh Clough," *Miscellaneous Essays and Addresses*, p. 68.

52. Review of *Robert Elsmere* in *Essays from 'The Guardian'* (London, 1910), pp. 67–8, and cf. *Marius the Epicurean*, chap. 19, "The Will as Vision." Clough's most explicit statement is in "Seven Sonnets," No. 7, *Poems*, p. 399. For other examples of this fideistic use of skepticism, see Stanley, *Life of Arnold*, pp. 272–3, letter of February 15, 1832, and a note in chap. 9, p. 491; Tennyson, "The Ancient Sage," lines 57–69; Ruskin, *Works, 36,* 90 (where he employs the related stratagem of Pascal's wager); W. R. Greg, *Enigmas of Life*, pp. v–vii; Fitzjames Stephen, "Women and Scepticism," *Fraser's Magazine, 68* (1863), 681–2; and, apropos of Manicheism, Mill, "Utility of Religion," *Three Essays on Religion*, pp. 116–18.

sibility, not certainty. Again and again through Clough's poems we hear the implicit question: though I have good grounds to deny the absolute authority of logic, does the faith I cling to rest on a valid appeal to the heart, which has its reasons that the reason cannot know? Or does it rest only on the strong desire to believe what I long to believe? Is the religious imagination a faculty of truth or of comforting illusion? He rarely gives one answer without allowing for the possibility of the other. The scales tip—but barely—now to the right, now to the left, as the head intimates its doubts or insists upon them more strongly.

> That there are powers above us I admit;
> It may be true too
> That while we walk the troublous tossing sea,
> That when we see the o'ertopping waves advance,
> And when we feel our feet beneath us sink,
> There are who walk beside us; and the cry
> That rises so spontaneous to the lips,
> The "Help us or we perish," is not nought,
> An evanescent spectrum of disease.
> It may be that in deed and not in fancy,
> A hand that is not ours upstays our steps,
> A voice that is not ours commands the waves,
> Commands the waves, and whispers in our ear,
> O thou of little faith, why didst thou doubt?
> At any rate—
> That there are beings above us, I believe,
> And when we lift up holy hands of prayer,
> I will not say they will not give us aid.[53]

In a complementary poem he finds that it may be true in fancy and not in deed:

> But whether in the uncoloured light of truth
> This inward strong assurance be, indeed,
> More than the self-willed arbitrary creed,
> Manhood's inheritor to the dream of youth;
> Whether to shut out fact because forsooth
> To live were insupportable unfreed,
> Be not or be the service of untruth;
> Whether this vital confidence be more

53. *Poems,* p. 409.

Than his, who upon death's immediate brink
Knowing, perforce determines to ignore;
Or than the bird's, that when the hunter's near,
Burying her eyesight, can forget her fear;
Who about this shall tell us what to think? [54]

One suspects that few·of the intellectuals who turned from logic to feeling in order to save religious belief did so without experiencing the same reservations which these poems suggest, but no one analyzed them more subtly or confessed them more candidly than Arthur Clough.

54. No. 4 of "Seven Sonnets," ibid., p. 398.

Chapter 5

ANTI-INTELLECTUALISM

> Man is sent hither not to question, but to work: "the
> end of man," it was long ago written, "is an Action,
> not a Thought."
>
> *Carlyle* [1]

A PRACTICAL BENT of mind, deep respect for facts, pragmatic skill in
the adaptation of means to ends, a ready appeal to common sense—
and therefore, negatively, an indifference to abstract speculation and
imaginative perception—have always been characteristic of the English
people. What distinguishes the Victorians is that conditions of life
in their period tended to increase this bias, and thus to make anti-
intellectualism a conspicuous attitude of the time. This is not to
forget that many of the Victorians were intellectuals or that the age
of Mill and Darwin made significant contributions to thought. It is
to claim only that middle- and upper-class society was permeated
by a scornful or frightened view of the intellectual life, both speculative and artistic, and the liberal education that fosters it. The
Industrial Revolution alone would have gone far to bring this about;
but when the intellectual climate added its powerful pressure in the
same direction, the result was inevitable.[2]

1. "Characteristics," *Essays*, 3, 25.
2. The more radical sense of the term anti-intellectualism, meaning a doubt or
denial of the capacity to discover ultimate truth or resolve the dilemmas of practical life, does not apply to the mid-Victorians as a whole, though it begins to appear in the last decades of the century: see above, pp. 14–17. In another use of
the term, meaning reliance upon authority or upon inner feeling, conscience, or
intuition rather than upon logical reason, many Victorians may be called anti-
intellectual, but that attitude, which was touched on in the last chapter, is better
defined as anti-rationalism. This chapter is a revised version of my article called
"Victorian Anti-Intellectualism," *Journal of the History of Ideas*, 13 (1952), 291–
313.

1. Business

If "the extremely *practical* character of the English people" made them, as Mill recognized, excel all the nations of Europe "as men of business and *industriels*," their commerical activity, in its turn, deepened this inherited bent.[3] The minds which made the machines, which organized factories and solved the problems of supply and distribution—and did so under high competitive pressure—received an indelible training in practical contrivance. It was, as Carlyle said in 1829, the age of machinery in the inward as well as outward sense of the word; "the age which, with its whole undivided might, forwards, teaches and practises the great art of adapting means to ends."[4] When Mill spoke in 1835 of the celebrity of England resting on her docks, her canals, and her railroads, he added, "In intellect she is distinguished only for a kind of sober good sense . . . and for doing all those things which are best done where man most resembles a machine, with the precision of a machine."[5]

In minds so constituted, and in lives so immersed in business, what counts is tangible results—profits, larger plants or firms, personal advancement, professional and social. The test of value, including that of thought, becomes utility in the narrow sense. The point was made by Coleridge as early as 1817: "We are . . . a busy, enterprising, and commercial nation. The habits attached to this character must, if there exist no adequate counterpoise, inevitably lead us under the specious names of utility, practical knowledge, and so forth, to look at all things through the medium of the market, and to estimate the worth of all pursuits and attainments by their marketable value. In this does the spirit of trade consist."[6]

As a consequence, the mind is focused almost entirely on concrete action, especially in a period of transition demanding particular reforms in social institutions. "The English public," wrote Mill in 1833, "think nobody worth listening to, except in so far as he tells them of something to be *done*, and not only that, but of something which can be done *immediately*. What is more, the only *reasons* they will generally attend to, are those founded on the specific good conse-

3. "Comparison of the Tendencies of French and English Intellect," *The Monthly Repository*, 7, new ser. (1833), 802. The italics are Mill's.

4. "Signs of the Times," *Essays*, 2, 59.

5. "Professor Sedgwick's Discourse on the Studies of the University of Cambridge," *Dissertations*, 1, 96.

6. "A Lay Sermon, Addressed to the Higher and Middle Classes," *Biographia Literaria and Two Lay Sermons*, p. 413.

quences to be expected from the adoption of the specific proposition." [7] A generation later John Morley found what he called the
political spirit, "which is incessantly thinking of present consequences
and the immediately feasible," to be "the strongest element in our
national life; the dominant force, extending its influence over all our
ways of thinking"; with the result that all matters not bearing "more
or less directly and patently upon the material and structural welfare
of the community" were falling out of sight.[8]

The result of these closely related "values"—business, utility, and
practical action—is exactly what Mill pointed out (significantly enough
in the same passage where he spoke of England's celebrity resting
on her docks and railroads), that "philosophy—not any particular
school of philosophy, but philosophy altogether—speculation of any
comprehensive kind, and upon any deep or extensive subject—has
been falling more and more into distastefulness and disrepute among
the educated classes of England." [9] Except in mathematics and science,
there was "not a vestige of a reading and thinking public engaged
in the investigation of truth *as* truth, in the prosecution of thought
for the sake of thought." This no doubt is overstatement, but such a
reading public was probably much smaller, proportionately to those
who read at all, than it had been fifty years earlier. And Mill put his
finger squarely on the direct cause of that decline, which in general
is to be traced to the business mind and its growing influence. There
was no recognition, he said, that from philosophical inquiry into the
nature of man and society, "a single important practical consequence
can follow."

This divorce of theory from practice was conspicuous in politics,
for there the middle classes were not only preoccupied with the
repeal of particular laws that curbed their freedom, but in addition,
with the example of the French Revolution in mind, they could
associate political speculation with abstract theorists meddling in
practical affairs of government—with what disastrous results everyone could see. This had its element of truth, but it was exaggerated,
as Arnold perceived, to a point of out-and-out hostility to all thinkers
whatsoever:

7. "Comparison of the Tendencies of French and English Intellect," p. 802. Cf.
Dissertations, 2, 220.

8. *On Compromise*, pp. 86, 88, 90.

9. "Professor Sedgwick's Discourse," pp. 98–9. The quotations that follow are
on p. 97. Cf. Coleridge, cited in note 6, pp. 403–5, and Carlyle, next note.

The Englishman has been called a political animal, and he values what is political and practical so much that ideas easily become objects of dislike in his eyes, and thinkers "miscreants," because ideas and thinkers have rashly meddled with politics and practice. This would be all very well if the dislike and neglect confined themselves to ideas transported out of their own sphere, and meddling rashly with practice; but they are inevitably extended to ideas as such, and to the whole life of intelligence; practice is everything, a free play of the mind is nothing.[10]

The disparagement of theory in the name of practice extended even into the field where we should least expect it, the physical sciences. As late as 1850, according to Huxley, "practical men" still "believed that the idol whom they worship—rule of thumb—has been the source of the past prosperity, and will suffice for the future welfare of the arts and manufactures. They were of opinion that science is speculative rubbish; that theory and practice have nothing to do with one another; and that the scientific habit of mind is an impediment, rather than an aid, in the conduct of ordinary affairs."[11] The fact is, the Industrial Revolution owed very little to scientific theory. The great inventors—Watt, Stephenson, Arkwright, Hargreaves—had had little mathematics and less science. Their inventions were almost entirely empirical;[12] and the "science" often praised by the practical men is simply the art of mechanical contrivance available to anyone with an ingenious head. When Stephenson was asked how he had invented his machines, especially the locomotive, "he replied that it was due to a power of imagining and conceiving with the utmost precision the different parts, their forms, sizes, and connections, their possible movements . . . *and, by dint of trying, he hit upon the practical combination.*" This method was contrasted by Taine with that of a genuine scientist like Léon Foucault: "*Having one day discovered a proposition of speculative mechanics,* which

10. "The Function of Criticism at the Present Time" (1864), *Essays in Criticism, First Series,* p. 18. Cf. pp. 10–15, where the case of the French Revolution is discussed. In *Sartor Resartus,* Bk. I, chap. 1, p. 7, Carlyle attributed the decline of philosophy to "our mercantile greatness, and invaluable Constitution, impressing a political or other immediately practical tendency on all English culture and endeavour."

11. "Science and Culture" (1880), *Science and Education,* p. 137.

12. This was recognized by the writer of "Plato, Bacon, and Bentham," *Quarterly Review, 61* (1838), 502; and was called to my attention by Professor Marie Boas of Brandeis University.

Huyghens and Lagrange had overlooked, he *worked it out to its final consequences*, and these led him to the idea of his governor."[13] Only after the midcentury did the earlier work of trained scientists like Davy and Faraday become widely known, revealing the practical fruits of scientific theory. And even a generation later Huxley had to attack the notion "that there is a sort of scientific knowledge of direct practical use, which can be studied apart from another sort of scientific knowledge, which is of no practical utility, and which is termed 'pure science.' "[14] It is ironic that the very success of early technology, instead of encouraging scientific research, confirmed the anti-intellectualism that is indigenous to the business mind.

If "deep thinking," even deep scientific thinking, is "quite out of place," as William Sewell dryly remarked, "in a world of railroads and steam-boats, printing-presses, and spinning-jennies,"[15] so of course are the humanities. They fail to pass the same utilitarian test. The important studies become the vocational skills—mining, electricity, surveying, agriculture, bookkeeping, together with the necessary mathematics and a little history. This, indeed, is Bentham's curriculum. It is the new education which the *Edinburgh* and *Westminster Reviews* recommended for the middle class, and the Society for the Diffusion of Useful Knowledge set out to provide.[16] In such a context the humanities are scarcely defensible. In a well-known passage of *The Idea of a University*, Newman imagines the derogatory question of those who take "Utility" as their watchword: "What is the real

13. *Notes on England*, p. 307. The italics are mine. When John Thornton, the Manchester manufacturer, was praising the local inventor of the steam hammer (in Mrs. Gaskell's *North and South*, chap. 10, p. 93), he went on to boast that "we have many among us who, if he were gone, could spring into the breach and carry on the war which compels, and shall compel, all material power to yield to *science*." The italics are mine.

14. "Science and Culture," p. 155.

15. "Carlyle's Works," *Quarterly Review*, 66 (1840), 447. Sewell also noticed the assumption "that prudent practice has no connexion with profound theory." The attribution of this article to Sewell is made by Froude, *Carlyle: Life in London*, 1, chap. 7, 193.

16. Bentham, *Chrestomathia*, in *Works*, 8, 5–191; Sydney Smith, "Edgeworth's Professional Education," *Edinburgh Review*, 15 (1809), 40–53, reprinted in his *Works* (3 vols. London, 1840), 1, 183–99; and the articles on education in the *Westminster Review*, 1 (1824), 43–79, and 4 (1825), 147–76. Cf. the counterattacks, which testify to the same spread of antihumanistic bias, in Peacock's *The Four Ages of Poetry* (1820), ed. H. F. B. Brett-Smith (Boston and New York, 1921), pp. 17–19; and in "Characteristics in the Nineteenth Century," *Fraser's Magazine*, 21 (1840), 160–2.

worth in the market of the article called 'a Liberal Education,' on the supposition that it does not teach us definitely how to advance our manufactures, or to improve our lands, or to better our civil economy; or again, if it does not at once make this man a lawyer, that an engineer, and that a surgeon; or at least if it does not lead to discoveries in chemistry, astronomy, geology, magnetism, and science of every kind?"[17] Tried by that standard, art and philosophy are condemned as useless or patronized as "cultural." A critic in the *Athenaeum* for 1835 charged that "a thorough-paced Utilitarian . . . cannot exactly see the use of Painting and Music; flowers look pretty, but then flowers are of no use."[18] This sounds like a caricature, but a writer in the *Westminster Review* ten years earlier said quite seriously that he would be "glad to be informed, how the universal pursuit of literature and poetry, poetry and literature, is to conduce towards cotton-spinning."[19]

Art is defended, if it is defended, as an ornament or a recreation. Bentham's judgment is standard. After dividing the arts and sciences into those of "amusement and curiosity" and those of "utility," he continues: "By arts and sciences of amusement, I mean those which are ordinarily called the *fine arts*, such as music, poetry, painting, sculpture, architecture, ornamental gardening, &c. &c." Their sole value is the amount of pleasure they yield. "Prejudice apart, the game of push-pin is of equal value with the arts and sciences of music and poetry. If the game of push-pin furnish more pleasure, it is more valuable than either."[20] Moreover, the imagination creates a fancy world very different from the reality grasped by reason and observation. Its "ordinary work consists in exhibiting, for the purpose of amusement, facts, which had indeed no archetypes in nature." Consequently, truth and poetry are always in opposition.[21] As for philosophy, meaning the formal study of metaphysics and episte-

17. Discourse 7, p. 153.
18. No. 418 (October 31, 1835), 817.
19. Vol. 4 (July 1825), 166.
20. *Works*, 2, 253. Cf. Herbert Spencer, *Education*, pp. 72–5. The writer cited in note 12, pp. 504–5, remarks: "It would require a separate article to trace downwards the decline of Art to its present debased condition of a mere slave to pleasure; and it would need another to show how our notion of Education has dwindled from the right formation of the whole man, to the introduction of mere passive notions of outward things—*useful knowledge*, as it is called—into his brain." As the writer implies, the two articles would be intimately connected.
21. *Works*, 6, 256 n.; 2, 253. For Mill's account of Bentham's aesthetics, see his "Bentham," *Dissertations*, 1, 388–90.

mology, that has even less excuse for being. It is a sheer waste of intellectual effort—or worse, a distraction from work. A statement of Ruskin's in *Modern Painters* is the more significant because he was no utilitarian in the specific or general sense of the term: "An affected Thinker, who supposes his thinking of any other importance than as it tends to work, is about the vainest kind of person that can be found in the occupied classes. Nay, I believe that metaphysicians and philosophers are, on the whole, the greatest troubles the world has got to deal with. . . . Busy metaphysicians are always entangling *good* and *active* people, and weaving cobwebs among the finest wheels of the world's business." [22]

If we substitute "university education" for Ruskin's "busy metaphysicians," we have the point of view often adopted by the early industrialists, proud of their class and indifferent to the social ambitions which made Oxford and Cambridge inviting to the next generation. To them a university was a dangerous distraction. It might too easily entangle their good and active sons. The prevalent notion in Manchester of how "to make a lad into a good tradesman" was to catch him young and put him to work. "If he were sent to even the Scotch Universities, he came back unsettled for commercial pursuits: how much more so if he went to Oxford or Cambridge, where he could not be entered till he was eighteen?" [23] In key with that policy, Mrs. Thornton, the mother of a Milton (that is, Manchester) mill owner is distressed when her son begins to read Homer with Mr. Hale. "Classics may do very well," she says, "for men who loiter away their lives in the country or in colleges; but Milton men ought to have their thoughts and powers absorbed in the work of today." [24] The association of learning with idle gentlemen or lazy academics who contribute nothing to the needs of the world can be paralleled in the case of writers. The literary temperament, as defined by Fitzjames Stephen the Benthamite, is "the turn of mind which leads its possessors to sit on a hill retired and make remark upon

22. Vol. 3, chap. 16, in *Works*, 5, 334. The italics, significantly, are Ruskin's.

23. Mrs. Gaskell, *North and South*, chap. 8, pp. 77–8. In his explanation of "the comparative apathy with which the opulent middle-class regards University education," John Morley, "Middle-Class Morality," *Studies in Conduct*, p. 273, noticed the argument that tradesmen consider college training "hinders the promotion of practical business habits," but he thought that "the real argument on which the trader relies in his own mind is that education means loss of time, and loss of time means loss of money, and that this means loss of the one thing that is worth living for."

24. Ibid., chap. 15, p. 132; cf. p. 134.

men and things instead of taking part in the common affairs of life." [25]

To appreciate the handicap of being an intellectual one should glance at Samuel Smiles' popular treatise called *Self-Help* (1859). Throughout the book genius, talent, or native intelligence are minimized and the moral qualities of hard work and persistence exalted. "It is not eminent talent that is required to insure success in any pursuit, so much as purpose—not merely the power to achieve, but the will to labor energetically and perseveringly. Hence energy of will may be defined to be the very central power of character in a man—in a word, it is the man himself." [26] On this premise Smiles adopts an estimate of reading which we shall find again, presently, in Kingsley and Carlyle:

> It is also to be borne in mind that the experience gathered from books, though often valuable, is but of the nature of *learning;* whereas the experience gained from actual life is of the nature of *wisdom;* and a small store of the latter is worth vastly more than any stock of the former. . . .
>
> There were wise, valiant, and true-hearted men bred in England, long before the existence of a reading public. Magna Charta was secured by men who signed the deed with their marks. Though altogether unskilled in the art of deciphering the literary signs by which principles were denominated upon paper, they yet understood and appreciated, and boldly contended for, the things themselves. . . . Many of our most energetic and useful workers have been but sparing readers. Brindley and Stephenson did not learn to read and write until they reached manhood, and yet they did great works and lived manly lives. [27]

To adopt the related attitudes I have been describing is simply to deny, however unconsciously, what Arnold called "the whole life of intelligence." It is to make practice everything, a free play of the mind nothing, and to exalt the man of action at the expense of the thinker and the artist. [28] It is to be a philistine, and philistinism for Arnold was the prime characteristic of bourgeois society. Of the three qualities that went to the making of "a natural, rational life" in the

25. "Mr. Carlyle," *Essays by a Barrister,* p. 243, reprinted from the *Saturday Review* for June 19, 1858.

26. Chap. 8, p. 254; cf. pp. 390–1, 419.

27. Ibid., chap. 11, pp. 359–60.

28. "The Function of Criticism at the Present Time," *Essays in Criticism, First Series,* p. 18.

modern world—the love of industry, trade, and wealth; the love of
the things of the mind; the love of beautiful things—"of these three
factors of modern life, your middle class has no notion of any but
one, the first." [29] In *Culture and Anarchy*, therefore, Arnold set up
the cultivation of the mind, including the aesthetic sensibility, to oppose the anarchical tendencies of thoughtless action, and wrote the
classic protest against Victorian anti-intellectualism.

It was applicable as much to some of the Victorian prophets as
to bourgeois society in general. If Mill and Newman and Bagehot,
Morley and Leslie Stephen were as ready as Arnold to attack the
tyranny of practice and utility, some of their colleagues were so
infected by the glamor, or the requirements, of commercial life that
they became, in varying degrees, apostles of anti-intellectualism. I
refer in particular to Kingsley, Froude, Carlyle, and, of course, Macaulay.

In his lecture "How to Study Natural History" (1846), which contains a eulogy of Bacon and business worthy of Macaulay, Kingsley
thought it quite right not only that practical considerations should
determine the value of any study but that the value should be
measured in pounds, shillings, and pence: "What money will it earn
for a man in after life?—is a question . . . which it is folly to despise.
For if the only answer be: 'None at all,' a man has a right to rejoin:
'Then let me take up some pursuit which will   be of pecuniary
benefit to me some day?'" [30] The beauty of scientific studies is that,
besides drawing the imagination away from an inner world of morbid
fancies and fixing it on external objects, they save you money. Think
how much wealth is lost "for want of a little knowledge of botany,
geology, or chemistry"—mines sought where no mine could be, crops
attempted to be grown where no crops could grow. On the other
hand, hidden treasures are missed, improvements in manufacturing
passed over, all from ignorance of science. "And for the man who
emigrates, and comes in contact with rude nature teeming with
unsuspected wealth, of what incalculable advantage .   " etc. True
enough, England is far behind other nations in "metaphysical and
scholastic science," but what matter? Her practical science has made
her the most powerful and wealthy nation in the world. [31]

29. *Friendship's Garland* (1871), *Culture and Anarchy and Friendship's Garland* (New York, 1901), p. 339.

30. *Scientific Lectures and Essays*, p. 305. The passage on Bacon is quoted
above, p. 44.

31. Ibid., pp. 301, 305, 308.

Some years later Kingsley gave the students of Wellington College a lecture which brings out the full extent of his anti-intellectualism, and relates it to the whole competitive life of the period, though science is still at the back of his mind:

> They say knowledge is power, and so it is. But only the knowledge which you get by observation. Many a man is very learned in books, and has read for years and years, and yet he is useless. He knows *about* all sorts of things, but he can't *do* them. When you set him to do work, he makes a mess of it. He is what is called a pedant: because he has not used his eyes and ears. He has lived in books. He knows nothing of the world about him, or of men and their ways, and therefore he is left behind in the race of life by many a shrewd fellow who is not half as book-learned as he: but who is a shrewd fellow—who keeps his eyes open—who is always picking up new facts, and turning them to some particular use.[32]

After this, Kingsley's protest that he does not mean to undervalue book learning, "no man less," has a hollow ring. Its only possible value is its contribution of new facts capable of being turned to use. The notion that books may so broaden and deepen one's knowledge of life, and so sharpen one's perceptions, that he can live more wisely and judge more intelligently, has dropped out of Kingsley's mind—and to a large extent, out of the Victorian, in fact the modern, mind. In bourgeois society the conception of utility became too narrow to include the great but intangible utility of the humanities.

This is illustrated specifically by Froude. When he succeeded Mill as Chancellor of St. Andrews, his inaugural address was plainly a reply to his predecessor's plea for intellectual and aesthetic culture. He deplored the devotion of so much time and effort in university education "to subjects which have no practical bearing upon life. . . . History, poetry, logic, moral philosophy, classical literature, are excellent as ornament. . . . They may be the amusement of your leisure hereafter; but they will not help you to stand on your feet and walk alone." And since you cannot master all the objects of

32. *Letters and Memories*, 2, 165 (unabridged ed. 2, 161). Cf. Peter Bayne, "Milton," *Contemporary Review*, 22 (1873), 431: "Milton . . . went in due course to Cambridge University, and during those years when the youthful mind is in its stage of richest recipiency, lived among the kind of men who haunt seats of learning. On the whole, the most uninteresting men in existence; whose very knowledge is a learned ignorance; not bees of industry, who have hoarded information by experience, but book-*worms*."

knowledge, and must choose among them, "the only reasonable guide to choice in such matters is utility." [33] What is responsible for such an attitude? Froude gives the answer himself: "In a country like ours, where each child that is born among us finds every acre of land appropriated, a universal 'Not yours' set upon the rich things with which he is surrounded . . . such a child, I say, since he is required to live, has a right to demand such teaching as shall enable him to live with honesty, and take such a place in society as belongs to the faculties which he has brought with him." Such an education will enable him to succeed, if not in overcrowded England, then in the greater English Empire now spreading over the world. "Education always should contemplate this larger sphere," Froude says, echoing Kingsley, "and cultivate the capacities which will command success there." The expansion of business and population, both in turn promoting the expansion of empire, have undermined the life of intelligence.

Even the movement of self-education by means of mechanics' institutes and workingmen's libraries, where the emphasis was largely vocational, is played down by Kingsley in favor of nonintellectual pursuits. Though he defends it against those who argue that it makes young men restless and critical, by attributing those acknowledged faults simply to long hours of stooping over desks and counters in close rooms, his plea for shorter hours and better working conditions is not designed, we discover, to give the men more time and strength for reading. On the contrary, "everything which ministers to the *corpus sanum* will minister also to the *mentem sanam*; and a walk on Durham Downs, a game of cricket, a steamer excursion to Chepstow, shall send them home again happier and wiser men than poring over many wise volumes or hearing many wise lectures." It follows that he backs the early-closing movement "not so much because it enables young men to attend mechanics' institutes, as because it enables them, if they choose, to get a good game of leap-frog"—with a happy effect on their politics as well as their health: "You may smile; but try the experiment, and see how, as the chest expands, the muscles harden . . . and sound sleep refreshes the lad for his next day's work, the temper will become more patient, the spirits more genial; there

33. "Education," *Short Studies,* 2, 464. The quotations that follow are on p. 467. Cf. his remarks in "On Progress," ibid., 2, 373: "The knowledge which a man can use is the only real knowledge, the only knowledge which has life and growth in it, and converts itself into practical power. The rest hangs like dust about the brain, or dries like raindrops off the stones."

will be less tendency to brood angrily over the inequalities of fortune, and to accuse society for evils which as yet she knows not how to cure." [34] This is the company line. More games and less reading will make the employees more energetic—and more docile.

The anti-intellectualism of Carlyle, the master of Froude, and of Kingsley too, in good part, was well established, for other reasons I shall come to, long before he felt the fascination of Manchester. But it was strengthened and given a new basis, as we see in *Past and Present*, by his admiration for industrial achievement. There the burly figure of John Bull, the Man of Practice, inarticulate and ignorant, is pitted against the adroit Man of Theory, clear of utterance, learned, all equipped with logic—"surely he will strike down the game, transfix everywhere the heart of the matter." But lo and behold, "to your astonishment, it turns out oftenest No." It is the stolid, lumbering Bull who comes off victor. Because he has attained to Nature's Fact and followed Nature's regulations, he has built "sea-moles, cotton-trades, railways, fleets and cities." [35] The passage reminds one of Carlyle's earlier attack on the Theoriser in "Characteristics" (1831), but there the contrasting figure was the man of insight and intuition, an intellectual like Goethe. The attack was on rationalism. [36] Here the choice of Bull is a measure of how far industrial progress could induce a Victorian philosopher to discount the value of all thought, logical or intuitive, in favor of common sense, energy, and dogged persistence; and a Victorian critic to prefer action to literature. "Great honour to him whose Epic is a melodious hexameter Iliad. . . . But still greater honour, if his Epic

34. "Great Cities and Their Influence for Good and Evil," *Sanitary and Social Essays*, pp. 210–12. In the upper classes "the immense place which athletic games and out-of-door sports" had taken "in modern English life" was often cited (Lecky, *Map of Life*, chap. 12, pp. 240–2) as one reason why "a genuine love, reverence and enthusiasm for intellectual things" became less common than it had been in the past. Cf. Taine, *Notes on England*, pp. 128, 132–3; Arnold, *Culture and Anarchy*, pp. 61, 160–1. The primary impetus, I think, was the fear of sensuality (discussed below, pp. 359–68) and the hope that sports would distract the mind and fatigue the body: see the anonymous pamphlet *The Science of Life* (Oxford, 1877), pp. 24–5, and Noel Annan, *Leslie Stephen*, pp. 33–4, where he is drawing on Stephen's "Athletic Sports and University Studies," *Fraser's Magazine*, 82 (1870), 691–704. For the emphasis on hunting and field sports among the squirearchy and its anti-intellectual bearing, see below, Chap. 9, sec. 2.

35. Bk. III, chap. 5, pp. 158–60. This passage is an excellent illustration of what is said above (p. 113) about the disparagement of scientific theory.

36. *Essays*, 3, 5–6.

be a mighty Empire . . . a mighty Conquest over Chaos," "written in huge characters on the face of this Planet,—sea-moles, cotton-trades . . . Indian Empires, Americas, New Hollands." "Deeds are greater than Words"—deeds of conquerors and empire-builders, we notice, as well as inventors and businessmen.[37] One analogue of Bull is the dynamic leader who crushes all opposition and imposes his own will on foreigners or subjects. If Dante, Shakespeare, Dr. Johnson, and Goethe were among the *Heroes* of 1841, so were Odin and Napoleon; and after that, Abbot Samson points forward to Dr. Francia, Cromwell, Frederick—or Governor Eyre.[38] So it was that literature, in the broad sense that includes philosophy and history, which Carlyle had once spoken of as the highest of human vocations, as the modern priesthood, lost most of its value: "Life was action, not talk. The speech, the book, the review or newspaper article was so much force expended—force lost to practical usefulness. . . . England had produced her greatest men before she began to have a literature at all. Those Barons who signed their charter by dipping the points of their steel gauntlets in the ink, had more *virtue, manhood,* practical force and wisdom than any of their successors." [39]

The last sentence makes one think of Kingsley or Froude, where the same admiration for strength is allied with the expansion of England to make heroes of Drake and Hawkins—and Rajah Brooke. Amyas Leigh in *Westward Ho!*, who is an "ignorant young savage" without education or intellectual interests, but with "the frame and stature of a Hercules" and a pugnacity that makes him a "most terrible fighter" against his schoolmates and later against the Spaniards, is the "symbol . . . of brave young England longing to wing its way out of its island prison, to discover and to traffic, to colonise and to civilise, until no wind can sweep the earth which does not bear the echoes of an English voice." [40] The complementary patterns are clear: as the Worker able by common sense and perseverance to

37. *Past and Present*, pp. 160–1. Cf. *Latter-Day Pamphlets*, No. 5, p. 186: "Many a highflying speaker and singer whom I have known, has appeared to me much less of a developed man than certain of my mill-owning, agricultural, commercial, mechanical, or otherwise industrial friends, who have held their peace all their days and gone on in the silent state."

38. Tennyson reported in 1848 what he learned from conversation with Carlyle (Hallam Tennyson, *Memoir*, 1, 279): "Goethe once Carlyle's hero, now Cromwell his epitome of human excellence."

39. Froude, *Carlyle: Life in London*, 2, chap. 26, p. 265. Cf. the quotation from Smiles, above, p. 117.

40. *Westward Ho!* chaps. 1 and 2, pp. 8–10, 19. For this anti-intellectual worship of strength, see below, Chap. 9, sec. 4.

build steamboats and railroads is exalted, so also is the Hero able by sheer force of will to found a great commercial nation, at home or abroad.

Finally, there is Macaulay, "the great apostle of the Philistines," whose essay on Bacon is the *locus classicus* of Victorian anti-intellectualism.[41] The glory of Baconian philosophy was its adoption of two watchwords, "Utility and Progress." It aimed at a greater and greater "'relief of man's estate'" by "the multiplying of human enjoyments and the mitigating of human sufferings"; and it has wonderfully succeeded—witness its tremendous achievements in the nineteenth century.[42] Ancient philosophy by contrast "disdained to be useful, and was content to be stationary." It dealt largely in theories of moral perfection designed to form the soul, and it failed to make men virtuous. "Words, and more words, and nothing but words, had been all the fruit of all the toil of all the most renowned sages of sixty generations."[43] As for poetry, meaning the imaginative creation of character and action in either verse or prose, Macaulay had already argued its inevitable decline as society became more enlightened— that is, more aware of the nature of "reality" as it is revealed by observation and analysis in the spirit, and often by the method, of science. For the enlightened mind is certain to detect the fictions of the imagination which once imposed on men in the childhood of the race:

> Poetry produces an illusion on the eye of the mind, as a magic lantern produces an illusion on the eye of the body. And, as the magic lantern acts best in a dark room, poetry effects its purpose

41. The phrase is Arnold's: *Essays in Criticism, First Series*, p. 354. Emerson, in *English Traits* (1856), in *The Works of Ralph Waldo Emerson*, 5, 234–5, uses Macaulay, "who expresses the tone of the English governing classes of the day," as a prime example of anti-intellectualism, and cites the essay on Bacon for evidence. This entire chapter 14 of *English Traits*, called "Literature," might have been entitled "Anti-Intellectualism."

42. *Critical Essays*, 3, 436, for the quotations; pp. 462–3, for the roll call of the achievements. The latter is more prophetic of the future than true at the time: see above, p. 113, on the empirical nature of the great inventions, and the attack, on exactly that line, on Macaulay's high claims for science, *Quarterly Review*, 61 (1838), 501–2.

43. Pages 436–7, 445. Cf. Bentham's remark in the *Deontology* which Arnold quotes in *Culture and Anarchy*, chap. 1, p. 67: "While Xenophon was writing his history and Euclid teaching geometry, Socrates and Plato were talking nonsense under pretence of talking wisdom and morality. This morality of theirs consisted in words; this wisdom of theirs was the denial of matters known to every man's experience."

most completely in a dark age. As the light of knowledge breaks
in upon its exhibitions, as the outlines of certainty become more
and more definite and the shades of probability more and more
distinct, the hues and lineaments of the phantoms which the
poet calls up grow fainter and fainter. We cannot unite the
incompatible advantages of reality and deception, the clear discernment of truth and the exquisite enjoyment of fiction."[44]

2. Democracy, Evangelicalism, and Doubt

As we noticed earlier, democratic theories of popular sovereignty
and the equality of man extended the right of private judgment to
all men.[45] And that meant, in effect, the exalting of natural shrewd-
ness at the expense of the trained intellect. No need for special
knowledge or theoretical analysis: the answers were available to
the common sense of the common man. This notion was encouraged
by the contemporary state of learning. In an age of transition when
established beliefs are questioned and new ones debated, "the divisions among the instructed," as Mill observed, "nullify their authority, and the uninstructed lose their faith in them;" with the result
that "persons who have never studied any branch of knowledge
comprehensively . . . attempt to judge for themselves upon particular
parts of it."[46] That intellectual leveling, so to speak, merged with
democratic dogma to create the state of affairs which Mill described
in *The Spirit of the Age* (1831): "Every dabbler . . . thinks his
opinion as good as another's. . . . It is rather the person who *has*
studied the subject systematically that is regarded as disqualified.
He is a *theorist*: and the word which expresses the highest and noblest
effort of human intelligence is turned into a bye-word of derision.
People pride themselves upon taking a 'plain, matter-of-fact' view of
a subject. . . . Men form their opinions according to natural shrewd-
ness, without any of the advantages of study."[47] In this way political
theory supported the influence of business—how closely can be seen

44. "Milton," *Critical Essays*, 1, 210. The argument that poetry presents an unreal
world of supernatural or/and idealized characters and events goes back to Bacon,
The Advancement of Learning (1605), *The Works of Francis Bacon*, ed. Spedding,
Ellis, and Heath (7 vols. London, 1857–59), 3, 343–4, and to the Royal Society
when it was founded in 1662: see Thomas Sprat, *The History of the Royal Society*
(first ed. 1667; London, 1734), pp. 331, 334, 340.

45. Above, p. 96.

46. *The Spirit of the Age*, p. 17.

47. Ibid., pp. 21–3. See Alexis de Tocqueville, *Democracy in America*, ed.
John C. Spencer (2 vols. New York, 1845), 2, Bk. I, chaps. 1 and 10, for an extensive demonstration of democratic anti-intellectualism.

in a passage of Bagehot's which parallels this one of Mill's, but with a different point of reference. "A man of business hates elaborate trifling: 'If you do not believe *your own* senses,' he will say, 'there is no use in *my* talking to you.' As to the multiplicity of arguments and the complexity of questions, he feels them little: he has a plain, simple—as he would say, 'practical'—way of looking at the matter, and you will never make him comprehend any other." [48]

Another major factor in the intellectual—or we might say the anti-intellectual—environment was Victorian Puritanism. Although the eighteenth-century evangelicals, men like Isaac Milner, Thomas Scott, and John Newton, were concerned with theology, the pietistic core of the Wesleyan movement soon came to the front. In the Clapham Sect emphasis had shifted to works of charity and philanthropy—fighting the slave trade, establishing foreign missions, distributing Bibles. By 1839 Newman could argue, without much exaggeration, that "Evangelical Religion or Puritanism . . . had no intellectual basis; no internal idea, no principle of unity, no theology." [49] And a little later Mark Pattison traced "the professed contempt of all learned inquiry, which was a principle with the Evangelical school" to its protest against the intellectual, if too dry and rational, character of eighteenth-century apologetics: "Evangelism, in its origin, was a reaction against the High-Church 'evidences'; the insurrection of the heart and conscience of man against an arid orthodoxy. It insisted on a 'vital Christianity,' as against the Christianity of books. Its instinct was from the first against intelligence. No text found more favour with it than 'Not many wise, not many learned.'" [50] If we add to this its strongly authoritarian principles—"the assumed infallibility of the

48. "The First Edinburgh Reviewers," *Works*, *1*, 20. Cf. Mill's later passage (review of de Tocqueville, *Dissertations*, *2*, 70), where he attributes the "dogmatism of common sense" as much to the habit of energetic action in a commercial society as to democracy; Huxley and Newman, above, pp. 113 and 105; and Macaulay's praise of common sense in "Lord Bacon," *Critical Essays*, *3*, 463, and in "Mill on Government," *2*, 7, 15. Bagehot's essay brings out the element of anti-intellectualism in the Whig temper, which his own political theory reflects: cf. Crane Brinton, *English Political Thought in the Nineteenth Century* (London, 1949), pp. 182–3; but Bagehot's protest against overactivity in *Physics and Politics* (*Works*, *4*, 563–71) places him with Arnold among the *anti*-anti-intellectuals.

49. *Apologia pro Vita Sua*, Pt. V, p. 200, summarizing a passage in "Prospects of the Anglican Church" (1839), in *Essays Critical and Historical* (2 vols. London, 1911), *1*, 294–8.

50. "Learning in the Church of England" (1863), *Essays*, ed. Henry Nettleship (2 vols. Oxford, 1889), *2*, 268. Cf. Annan, *Leslie Stephen*, pp. 119–22, but notice the qualification on p. 110.

Bible on all questions; the necessity of stifling doubt; the repression of all who stir up theological discussions; the duty of keeping strictly in the old paths . . . and the general depreciation, as an evil to be dreaded, of active and critical inquiry" [51]—we have little difficulty accounting for middle-class philistinism from its religious, no less than its commercial, life.

Indeed, the two are closely connected. Though the exact nature of the relationship between Protestantism and capitalism is complex and not yet entirely clear, it is certain that Puritanism laid great stress both on hard work and on moral discipline (the prerequisites for business efficiency), and neglected, or viewed with suspicion, the worldly distractions of philosophy and art. This was Carlyle's inheritance. It was from his father he first learned "that man was created to work, not to speculate, or feel, or dream." And the maxim was enforced by the teacher's example: "As a man of Speculation . . . he must have gone wild and desperate as Burns: but he was a man of Conduct, and Work keeps all right." [52] This is a relevant illustration of a famous passage in *Culture and Anarchy* where Arnold relates "our preference of doing to thinking" to Puritan ethics: "We may regard this energy driving at practice, this paramount sense of the obligation of duty, self-control, and work, this earnestness in going manfully with the best light we have, as one force. And we may regard the intelligence driving at those ideas which are, after all, the basis of right practice . . . as another force. And these two forces we may regard as in some sense rivals . . . Hebraism and Hellenism, —between these two points of influence moves our world." [53]

In Arnold's period the attraction of Hebraism was more powerful; it was therefore time to Hellenize that the balance might be restored. Mill once spoke of "commercial money-getting business, and religious Puritanism" as the two great influences "which have chiefly shaped the British character since the days of the Stuarts." [54] Plainly they

51. Stopford Brooke, *Life of F. W. Robertson*, p. xii. As the phrasing suggests, this attitude owed a good deal to the fear of speculation, especially in science and biblical criticism, which I go on to discuss just below. Also see above, Chap. 4, end of sec. 4. Brooke's statement was made in the 5th ed., 1868, "Introduction."

52. *Reminiscences*, pp. 5, 9.

53. Chap. 4, pp. 129–30. Like Carlyle, Arnold first met this moral anti-intellectualism in his own home. On Thomas Arnold's preference for "goodness" over "truth," see Frances J. Woodward, *The Doctor's Disciples. A Study of Four Pupils of Arnold of Rugby: Stanley, Gell, Clough, William Arnold* (London and New York, 1954), pp. 5–10.

54. "Inaugural Address at St. Andrew's" (1867), *James & John Stuart Mill on Education*, p. 191.

gave it an anti-intellectual bias. And I mean to include, under that general term, an anti-aesthetic bias as well. Indeed, the context of Mill's remark is the low opinion of art in England as compared with the continent—"business," as he explains, "demanding the whole of the faculties, and whether pursued from duty or the love of gain, regarding as a loss of time whatever does not conduce directly to the end; Puritanism . . . looking upon every feeling of human nature, except fear and reverence for God, as a snare, if not as partaking of sin." [55] Carlyle's father, it may be noted, considered "Poetry, Fiction in general . . . not only idle, but *false* and criminal." [56]

Lastly, there is the frightened reaction which was bound to accompany the outburst of radical thinking. When the foundations of religious and political life were being shaken by new ideas, and Church and State seemed often in peril, the average citizen turned anti-intellectual out of sheer panic. Thought was plainly a dangerous thing—unless it were focused on purely practical concerns. Even the intellectuals grew timorous, as Mill pointed out in the fifties:

> Many . . . are either totally paralysed, or led to confine their exertions to matters of minor detail, by the apprehension that any real freedom of speculation, or any considerable strengthening or enlargement of the thinking faculties of mankind at large, might, by making them unbelievers, be the surest way to render them vicious and miserable. Many, again, having observed in others or experienced in themselves elevated feelings which they imagine incapable of emanating from any other source than religion, have an honest aversion to anything tending, as they think, to dry up the fountain of such feelings. [57]

As a result, they may well "dislike and disparage all philosophy"— exactly the same conclusion that Mill also derived from the worship of canals and railroads.

55. Ibid. Taine, *Notes on England,* p. 258, confirms Mill's contrast of English with European opinion on the value of art: "We all know how in French sketches the artist is raised above the citizen; here, oddly enough, the reverse occurs. Musicians are represented as salaried monkeys, who come to make a noise in a drawing-room. Painters are bearded artisans, unkempt, shabbily-dressed, badly-educated, conceited, hardly one degree raised above photographers. . . . A French moralist would never have occasion to demonstrate that the painter's art is as liberal a profession as that of medicine or law. Probably, in the eyes of the burly John Bull . . . a painter cannot be a gentleman, seeing that he works with his hands."

56. *Reminiscences,* p. 9.

57. "Utility of Religion," *Three Essays on Religion,* pp. 71–2.

There was also the other side of the same coin, the pressure of public opinion. Even if the thinker himself believed that the service of truth was worth any actual, or supposed, ill consequences to society, he was often deterred by the fear of social stigma and its potential threat to his public career, especially if the truth ran counter in any way to Christian orthodoxy. In a society where Mrs. Grundy had become a tyrant, the better part of wisdom for anyone not prepared for martyrdom was to take seriously the advice given ironically by Walter Bagehot: "'Secrete your intellect, use common words, say what you are expected to say,' and you shall be at peace." [58] Was there ever another age where the case against speculation was so strong? At one and the same time, the thinker was threatened both by the fear of what he might do to society and the fear of what society might do to him. Nor was that all. In addition he was threatened by personal distress in a period when thinking led straight to the perplexities and depressions of doubt, a threat which motivated, as we saw, a will to believe strong enough to check or suppress the critical spirit. [59] To save your country, to save your career, to save your peace of mind were the irresistible appeals of anti-intellectualism.

When *Essays and Reviews* challenged the English clergy to re-examine some of their assumptions in the light of biblical criticism, Kingsley's reaction, I suspect, was fairly typical. Not only did he "thrust the book away in disgust" as soon as he found it stirred up old "doubts and puzzles," but when his new curate asked him if he should read it, he told him, "By no means. . . . Do not darken your mind with intellectual puzzles, which may breed disbelief, but can never breed vital religion, or practical usefulness." [60] Twenty years earlier those "doubts and puzzles" had led him to give his future wife a similar piece of advice, one which incidentally reveals how the Romantic cult of childhood and nature could be utilized by a frightened Victorian:

> You may think too much! There is such a thing as mystifying one's self! . . . A child goes straight to its point, and it hardly knows why. . . . Remember that habit, more than reason, will cure one both of mystifying subtlety and morbid fear. . . . The quantity of sounding nonsense in the world is incredible! If you

58. "The Character of Sir Robert Peel" (1856), *Works*, 3, 5. On Mrs. Grundy see below, pp. 397–9.

59. Chap. 4, sec. 2; and also cf. sec. 3.

60. *Letters and Memories*, 2, 138 (unabridged ed., 2, 130–1).

wish to be like a little child, study what a little child could understand—nature; and do what a little child could do—love. Use your senses much, and your mind little. Feed on Nature [for its "moral good" and its reflection of God], and do not *try* to understand it. It will digest itself. It did so when you were a baby. Look round you much. Think little and read less. Never give way to reveries. Have always some employment in your hands. When you are doing nothing at night, pray and praise! [61]

To all this Froude would have given an emphatic "amen." For him the old paths of the eighteenth-century Church, so much criticized by Newman, were the perfection of a healthy religion: "It was orthodox without being theological. Doctrinal problems were little thought of. Religion, as taught in the Church of England, meant moral obedience to the will of God. The speculative part of it was accepted because it was assumed to be true. The creeds were reverentially repeated; but the essential thing was practice." But un- happily this ideal state of affairs was shattered by nineteenth-century inquiry. Religion passed "out of its normal and healthy condition as the authoritative teacher of obedience to the commandments, into active anxiety about the speculative doctrines on which its graces were held to depend." [62] The wording is important. The anxiety, which Froude himself knew so well (it informs his semi-autobiographical *Nemesis of Faith*), threw a nostalgic halo over the age when "doubts about the essentials of the faith were not permitted" and "doctrinal controversies were sleeping" and led Froude into saying that an established creed should not be discussed (only bad men will ques- tion its formularies), and that the test of a religion is not its truth [not now when its truth is so uncertain] but its success—"you look to the work which it is doing." [63] The last clauses, as well as the earlier claim that the essential thing is practice, taken together with Kingsley's appeal to "practical usefulness," show how precisely the fear of speculation in religion and the emphasis of business could come to the same conclusion. Indeed, when we recall the quotations from Kingsley and Froude in the previous section, we see the con- currence demonstrated not merely in the age but in specific in- dividuals.

This is also seen in Carlyle. If his admiration for industrial achieve-

61. Ibid., *1*, 66–70 (unabridged ed., *1*, 87–90).
62. "The Oxford Counter-Reformation," *Short Studies*, 4, 239, 264.
63. Ibid., pp. 237, 238, 242.

ment confirmed his earlier reaction against speculation, what made him abandon, to begin with, the philosophical studies he had pursued ever since he went to Edinburgh in 1809? Partly the influence of Romantic epistemology, the distrust of the "meddling intellect" and the cult of the "heart," the organ of intuitive insight. But it is significant that the essay "Characteristics" (1831), which begins by expounding this Romanticism, ends by dwelling on doubt and its close association with philosophy. Carlyle now considers speculation either directly skeptical in its tendency (the metaphysics of Hume) or at best (German transcendentalism) only an anodyne to doubt, and temporary at that.[64] What he felt he had learned from his own experience between 1809 and 1829 was that metaphysical studies raised more questions than they solved; that "all Speculation is by nature endless, formless, a vortex amid vortices"; and that long years of wandering in mazes of thought made one's whole heart sick.[65] Small wonder he returned, in the "Characteristics," to his father's Puritan teaching, and decided that the only "Profitable Speculation" was, "What is to be done; and How is it to be done," and the right end of life, "not to ask questions, but to do work." [66] With the slightest rewording this becomes, a decade later, the creed of John Bull, the builder of railroads and empires.

Even Carlyle's mean opinion of creative literature, already traced to Puritan and commercial influences, was partly indebted to his struggle with doubt. In the important essay "Biography" (1832), he set up two categories of writing: Reality, meaning the recorded

64. *Essays*, 3, 26.

65. Respectively, "On the Periods of European Culture" (1838), in Edward Dowden, *Transcripts and Studies* (London, 1896), pp. 38–9; *Sartor Resartus*, Bk. II, chap. 9, p. 195; and a letter to Mill, June 13, 1833, *Letters of Thomas Carlyle to John Stuart Mill, John Sterling, and Robert Browning*, p. 57.

66. *Essays*, 3, 27, 28. The analogous tendency to curb speculation in the public interest is illustrated by Edward Hawkins, the provost of Oriel College in the 1830's and 40's. In January 1848 he wrote to Clough—MS letter at Oriel College, printed in G. P. Johari, "Arthur Hugh Clough at Oriel and at University Hall," *PMLA*, 66 (1951), 411—"I am afraid of unrestrained speculation leading to general scepticism—a very unhappy state and one for which God did not design us. In truth you were not born for *speculation*. I am not saying a word against full and fair inquiry. But we are sent into this world not so much to speculate as to serve God and serve Man." Some years earlier in 1839 Clough heard a sermon of Hawkins' which he thought (*Prose Remains*, p. 80) "seemed to say that undergraduates were to mind their Latin and Greek and nothing else"; and Clough went on to remark that "many people here speak of the Union as an institution of very doubtful usefulness."

facts of history or individual lives, and Fiction, whether in prose or verse. The latter is always unsatisfactory, he says, because it produces a tension between imagination and understanding, the imagination urging one to accept as true what the understanding warns him is false: namely, either the supernatural, which he cannot believe at all, or, if that is banished (as it is in modern novels like *Tom Jones* and *Wilhelm Meister*), the made-up story which he can only believe momentarily and must dismiss, the instant he finishes reading, as fictitious because it never really happened.[67] Obviously, Carlyle is failing to recognize the symbolic character of creative literature which can make it at its best a more profound revelation of truth than either biography or history. The strange thing is that he was well aware of the real nature of art. Only a few years before, in 1827, he had said that Shakespeare's plays were not only true, but "truer than reality itself, since the essence of unmixed reality is bodied forth in them under more expressive symbols." [68] And yet by 1833, in a letter to Mill, he could call French memoirs of the Revolution "the highest kind of writing, far higher than any kind of Fiction even of the Shakespeare sort." [69]

Once upon a time, I suggest, Carlyle had believed implicitly in the Christian story, but little by little his understanding had told him that one part of it after another (the virgin birth, the miracles, the vicarious sacrifice) was pure fiction. Oh for a new religion that was entirely true, which one could believe with his whole heart and soul, free of the least conflict between imagination and understanding! In that state of mind, hypersensitive to anything that can possibly be thought false,[70] creative literature will be associated, however unconsciously, with Christian myth, and Carlyle will cry out for a new literature of historical and biographical fact which he can feel is entirely true, which the whole man can believe. This hypothesis is supported by the emphasis on belief in the essay "Biography," written only a year after he published his new religion of natural super-

67. *Essays*, 3, 49–53.

68. "State of German Literature," *Essays*, 1, 51.

69. *Letters* (cited in note 65, above), p. 57. See in general, Hill Shine, *Carlyle's Fusion of Poetry, History, and Religion by 1834*, Chapel Hill, N.C., 1938.

70. Cf. Alton Locke's remark in Kingsley's novel, chap. 38, p. 409, referring to the "mighty gospel of deliverance" in the New Testament: "The thing was too precious, too all-important, to take one tittle of it on trust. I could not bear the consciousness of one hollow spot—the nether fires of doubt glaring through, even at one little crevice."

naturalism in *Sartor Resartus.* "How all-pervading," he says, "om-nipotent, in man's mind [in Carlyle's mind], is the thing we name *Belief.*" That is the fundamental thesis which underlies the critical statements on art:

> Imagination is, after all, but a poor matter when it has to part company with Understanding, and even front it hostilely in flat contradiction. Our mind is divided in twain. . . . Only in so far as Imagination, were it but momentarily, is believed, can there be any use or meaning in it, any enjoyment of it. . . . Whereas *a perennial Belief were enjoyment perennially, and with the whole united soul.*

> True, alas too true, the Poet is still utterly wanting, or all but utterly: nevertheless have we not centuries enough before us to produce him in? Him and much else!—I, for the present, will but predict that chiefly by working more and more on REALITY, and evolving more and more wisely its inexhaustible meanings; and, in brief, *speaking forth in fit utterance whatsoever our whole soul believes, and ceasing to speak forth what thing soever our whole soul does not believe,*—will this high emprise be accomplished, or approximated to.[71]

The poet of the future will write history and biography: a *French Revolution,* a *Cromwell* or *Sterling,* a *Frederick the Great.*

In short, Carlyle's intense need for belief, rising out of his religious problem, made him finally unable to tolerate the literal or technical elements of the fictitious in imaginative literature, and therefore unable any longer to consider that art was truer than reality. Only reality was true. The smallest historical fact in the poorest French memoir became a finer thing than the grandest fictitious event in Shakespeare.[72] While the Victorian identification of poetry with what

71. *Essays,* 3, 50, 53. The italics are mine. Cf. "Diderot," ibid., p. 178, and *Heroes,* Lecture 4, pp. 124–5. This theory of the effect of religious doubt on Carlyle's conception of literature is supported by the letter to Mill quoted above (note 65). Just before saying that French memoirs were superior to Shakespeare, Carlyle urged Mill to escape from his " 'Doubting-Castle' Prison" and find some truth to love. Then, just after it, he wrote that for his part he could now enjoy "no other Poem than the dim, shadowy as yet only *possible* Poem, that hovers for me in every seen Reality" of biography and history, and went on to say that he had wandered long years in endless mazes of speculation till his heart was sick.

72. *Essays,* 3, 54, and "Shooting Niagara: and After?" ibid., 5, 24–5. In both passages, however, Carlyle adopts an argument which undoubtedly supported

was false and the tacit denial that went with it of the symbolic truth of art is mainly to be traced, as in Bentham and Macaulay, to the adoption of scientific criteria,[73] it is also indebted to religious anxiety and the will to believe.

To abandon thought and turn to practical activity was not only a protection against the dangers of speculation, it was the soundest procedure for those already suffering from painful doubts. So it seemed to John Keble when he told Thomas Arnold to put down his objections to certain points in the Thirty-nine Articles "by main force"—that is, to take "a curacy somewhere or other, and cure himself not by physic, *i.e.*, reading and controversy, but by diet and regiment, *i.e.*, holy living." So it also seemed to Arnold when he took Keble's advice and later made a similar recommendation "to a person distressed by sceptical doubts." [74] By moments Kingsley, too, adopted the same expedient. When the insistent questions press upon him—"Is intellectual Science, or the Bible, truth; and All Truth? . . . Are the Fathers and the Tractarians, or the Germans, or the modern Puritans right, and wherein lies the difference between them?"—he recoils from what he calls "that vast, muddy, blind, contradictory book-ocean . . . with its million waves, crying, 'Read! Read! Give up doing, that you may think. Across me is the only path to the isles of the blest, to the temple of wisdom, to the threshold of God's throne!'" "Not so!" he answers. Better far to serve God at home "among the duties and affections of humanity" than to try and reach Him "by weary voyaging on the ocean of intellect." [75] In short, whether to avoid the pain of doubt or to end it, the formula is

---

the influence of doubt in turning his mind from literature to history. When his pantheism led him to consider every object or event a symbolic manifestation of God, purely imaginary objects and events became trivial by comparison.

73. Macaulay's thinking is particularly close to Carlyle's: see above, pp. 123–4 and note 44.

74. Stanley, *Life of Arnold*, chap. 1, pp. 19, 20; and pp. 363–5, from a letter of June 21, 1835.

75. *Letters and Memories* (unabridged ed.), *1*, 111–12. Most of the passage is in the abridged ed., *1*, 87–8. It is significant that even Clough, for all his determination to seek the truth and his horror of evasion, was often swept by the same kind of frustrated and weary anti-intellectualism: see "Amours de Voyage," Canto III, Letter 10, and *Prose Remains*, pp. 384–5. In his case, however, the alternative was sometimes nature (as with Arnold in "The Scholar-Gipsy": below, p. 297) or love (below, pp. 385–9): see "Away, haunt not thou me," *Poems*, p. 24; "July's Farewell," p. 75; "The Bothie of Tober-na-Vuolich," Pt. VIII, lines 112–19, p. 166.

the same: stop thinking and do some simple duty or useful work.

Finally, there is one other argument for the anti-intellectualism of doubt. It runs this way: "Don't speculate, but if you must, don't speculate too much. Beware of pushing arguments to their logical conclusions, or examining first principles too closely. Stop before it's too late." The English, of course, have never been conspicuous for logical rigor, but in the Victorian period there was a conscious effort, personal and public, not merely to discourage the pursuit of truth, but where that was impossible, to check it at a safe distance from subversive conclusions.

So long as speculation threatened to undermine the religious and moral foundations of society, it was wholly natural, however misguided, for society to demand that thought should issue not in a logical but in an orthodox answer. This is the requirement which Mill exposed and attacked in *On Liberty*, though without perhaps sufficient recognition of its underlying cause:

> Who can compute what the world loses in the multitude of promising intellects combined with timid characters, who dare not follow out any bold, vigorous, independent train of thought, lest it should land them in something which would admit of being considered irreligious or immoral? Among them we may occasionally see some man of deep conscientiousness, and subtle and refined understanding, who spends a life in sophisticating with an intellect which he cannot silence, and exhausts the resources of ingenuity in attempting to reconcile the promptings of his conscience and reason with orthodoxy, which yet he does not, perhaps, to the end succeed in doing. No one can be a great thinker who does not recognise, that as a thinker it is his first duty to follow his intellect to whatever conclusions it may lead.[76]

But this was a minority opinion. To most Victorians the first duty was not to upset the apple cart.[77]

But not, I think, entirely from fear of public criticism. If Tennyson can be typical of the mid-Victorian mind in its "incapacity to follow

76. Chap. 2, p. 125.

77. Taine, indeed, claimed (*Notes on England*, p. 314) that even the half-dozen men he met in England who were given to philosophical speculation "paused . . . half way, arriving at no definite conclusion."

any chain of reasoning which seems likely to result in an unpleasant conclusion," [78] was this because the poet was too prudent to risk publicly, or too timid to draw privately, the final deduction? Was it not both? If "the ablest and tenderest minds are afraid to think deeply," as Greg reported, "because they know not where deep thought might land them," are not both fears involved? [79] Was it only deference to public opinion which made "the most sensible and well-informed men" whom Emerson met in England "possess the power of thinking just so far as the bishop in religious matters," and talk with courage and logic on free trade or geology but not on the English Church? [80] Was it not also their own apprehensions, warning them where, and where not, they could pursue the truth in safety without endangering their peace of mind or the stability of their society?

To put the point another way, the public opinion which Mill rapped for curbing free thought was not merely the normal intolerance that characterizes a dominant social group, and especially one like the Victorian middle class, already hostile to speculation for the best of business reasons. It was itself the expression of deep-seated fears. Why had it become, as Ruskin noticed, "a point of politeness not to inquire too deeply into our neighbour's religious opinions; and . . . to waive any close examination into the tenets of faith?" His answer throws a flash of light into the Victorian mind: "The fact is, we distrust each other and ourselves so much, that we dare not press this matter; we know that if . . . we turn to our next neighbour, and put to him some searching or testing question, we shall, in nine cases out of ten, discover him to be only a Christian in his own way, and as far as he thinks proper, and that *he doubts of many things which we ourselves do not believe strongly enough to hear doubted without danger.*" [81] Precisely. It is the danger to their own stability which frightened the Victorians into making searching questions and tenacious inquiry a point of serious indecorum, and one which the individual himself was only too glad to respect. In 1849, in the preface to his novel, Froude reported that English opinion had rejected classical mythology and supernatural stories of medieval saints and witches, but was stop-

78. G. M. Young, *Victorian England*, p. 75. Cf. Geoffrey Tillotson's lecture *English Poetry in the Nineteenth Century* (London, 1945), p. 18.

79. "Kingsley and Carlyle," *Literary and Social Judgments*, 1, 182.

80. *English Traits*, in *Works*, 5, 212–13.

81. *Stones of Venice*, 3, chap. 2, sec. 103, in *Works*, 11, 132. The italics are mine.

ping short—or trying to stop short—of applying the logical analogy to Biblical myth and miracle. "It halts here," he said, "for it is afraid of its conclusions." [82]

A personal experience of Wingfield-Stratford's will give concreteness to these generalizations:

> I had been taught about God by a dear old Victorian clergyman, who explained to me just why God must be. It was extremely simple. The world was so wonderful, that somebody even more wonderful must have made it. Hence God.
>
> I could detect no flaw in this reasoning, but a certain apparent incompleteness. With a faith I never afterwards recovered in the capacity of grown-up people, and particularly reverend grown-ups, to resolve incipient doubt, I proceeded to ask:
>
> "But then, who made God?"
>
> The result was not the explanation I had expected, but an explosion that left me utterly bewildered. I had been brought up in a Christian family. . . . I had been the cause of unutterable grief and disappointment . . . Satan had quite obviously entered into my heart, not without previous encouragement . . .
>
> I had, all unwittingly, blundered into what, to every good Victorian, was the unforgivable sin. It was not, as I half suspected myself, that the unknown God-maker was some one not quite respectable. It was simply that I had pried beneath the surface of a belief, *that I had not known where to stop short of a logical consequence.*

It was not so, as Wingfield-Stratford goes on to point out, in the ages of faith when the medieval schoolmen would leave no question unanswered about the divine nature and attributes. "They had no fear, at the back of their minds, that any danger to faith could lurk in the process of such definition." [83] But his conclusion that Victorian common sense and business instinct dictated the curtailing of thought in the cause of social stability is only half of the truth. The fear at the back of those grown-up minds, which issued in such a horrified outburst, was personal as well as social. Their own peace of mind was at stake.

82. *The Nemesis of Faith*, p. li.
83. *The Victorian Sunset*, pp. 62–3. The italics are mine.

Chapter 6

DOGMATISM

> With all our professions of liberality . . . what tyrants
> we are—what *dogmatists*. Many of us have reached
> the first desirable stage—we have learned to think
> for ourselves. But have we liberated our minds from
> the disposition to exercise inexorable tyranny over the
> thoughts of others?
>
> *E. P. Hood* [1]

OF all Victorian attitudes the hardest for us to take is dogmatism. The imperious pronouncement of debatable doctrines with little or no argument, the bland statement of possibilities as certainties and theories as facts, the assertion of opinion in positive and often arrogant tones—in a word, the voice of the Victorian prophet laying down the law—this sets our teeth on edge. Partly because it insults our intelligence, but much more because it rouses our righteous irritation. For if dogmatism, strictly speaking, is a matter of style, the style betrays —or seems to betray—an insufferable man. When Meredith charged Ruskin with a "monstrous assumption of wisdom" and a "preposterous priestly attitude and inebriate conceit as against adversaries," [2] or when John Morley accused Macaulay of "oracular arrogance, and a rather too thrasonical complacency," they expressed our own moral indignation. [3] And both remarks could have been made with but little qualification of Carlyle or Froude or Thomas Arnold, of Kingsley or Spencer, let alone scores of minor prophets speaking from the pulpits of church and press. It is this dogmatic attitude more than any hypocrisy or bumptious optimism or strait-laced morality which, in default of ade-

1. *The Age and its Architects,* p. 77. The italics are mine.
2. *Letters of George Meredith,* collected and edited by his son (2 vols. New York, 1912), *1,* 200–2.
3. "Macaulay," *Critical Miscellanies, 1,* 257, and cf. 277.

quate understanding of its origins and with no awareness that it was sometimes no more than a mask, has alienated the twentieth century from the Victorians.

It has, of course, always existed in human nature; and the flexible mind, ready to listen to contrary opinions and speak with sweet reasonableness, has hardly been very common. But in the Victorian period the tendency to dogmatize was in an exaggerated phase. For one thing, the eternal ego found itself not only freed from the usual restraints but actually encouraged to consider what it liked or disliked to be absolutely right or wrong. In the second place, there existed certain metaphysical and epistemological theories which rationalized the instinct of the ego and served to warrant the belief that one possessed the Truth, the whole Truth, and nothing but the Truth. Finally, the prophets insisted all the more positively that they were right because their readers, strange as it may seem, liked it that way; and because they themselves, as a matter of fact, were afraid that they were wrong. It was the conjunction at one time of all these factors that made the Victorian age so conspicuously dogmatic.

1. *Opportunity for the Ego*

When Mill spoke of few people having confidence in their own convictions, he added, "few, except the very penetrating, or the very presumptuous." [4] The context was "the age of transition." When old beliefs are being questioned and no new ones have been established, the modest man doubts and the presumptuous man dogmatizes. That state of affairs is nicely revealed by a conversation in *Middlemarch* between old Mrs. Farebrother and Dr. Lydgate:

> "When I was young, Mr. Lydgate, there never was any question about right and wrong. We knew our catechism, and that was enough; we learned our creed and our duty. Every respectable Church person had the same opinions. But now, if you speak out of the Prayer-book itself, you are liable to be contradicted."
>
> "That makes rather a pleasant time of it for those who like to maintain their own point," said Lydgate. [5]

"Pleasant time" is understatement. Say rather, what a magnificent opportunity for the ego to assert itself when nothing is settled and everyone is arguing and no one else seems smart enough to come up with

4. *The Spirit of the Age*, p. 13.
5. Vol. 1, Bk. II, chap. 17, p. 232.

the answers—except me. It is the perfect moment for "every dabbler" to think his own opinion "as good as another's." The fact that he "has never studied politics, for instance, or political economy systematically," does not prevent him (not now when the divisions among the instructed have nullified their authority and robbed them of respect) "from promulgating *with the most unbounded assurance* the crudest opinions." [6] Moreover, he was encouraged to do so by the theory of private judgment.[7] A later reference of Mill's to the dogmatism of "the presumptuous man," rushing "headlong into opinions, always shallow, and as often wrong as right," occurs in a discussion of democratic liberalism. It is one result, he indicates, of persuading ignorant or half-instructed people to assert their liberty of thought, discard all authority, and trust solely to their own judgment, receiving or rejecting ideas according to their own views of the evidence.[8] We should also remember that "half-instructed" people were more common than ever before in a period when self-education had become a popular ideal in the middle classes. Many artisans and clerks were studying in free libraries and mechanics' institutes; many businessmen were picking up a veneer of culture from reading Macaulay or Mill. But a little knowledge is a dogmatical thing. What, asks Kingsley, is "the objection to allowing young men to educate themselves? . . . They become, it is said, discontented, conceited, dogmatical. They take up hasty notions, they condemn fiercely what they have no means of understanding; they are too fond of fine words, of the excitement of spouting themselves, and hearing others spout." [9]

Private judgment and self-education combined, in this age of transition, to produce a dogmatist of genius in Herbert Spencer. Given only elementary schooling and trained from the start to rely completely on his own observation and reasoning, he had little respect, as he says himself, for ancient wisdom, accepted opinions, or scholarly authorities.[10] It was not that he questioned them; for the most part he ignored them—and announced his own judgments the more confidently. He wrote his *Biology* after reading only Carpenter's *Comparative Physiology* (and not the *Origin of Species*); his *Sociology* without knowing Comte or Tylor; his *Ethics* without studying Kant or

6. Mill, *The Spirit of the Age*, p. 21, and cf. p. 17. The italics are mine.
7. See above, pp. 95–6.
8. *The Spirit of the Age*, pp. 30–1.
9. "Great Cities and Their Influence for Good and Evil" (1857), *Sanitary and Social Essays*, p. 210.
10. *Autobiography*, 2, chap. 60, pp. 513–18.

Mill or any moralist except portions of Sidgwick. He was, in short, innocent of book learning, and mainly endowed with the knowledge he picked up at first hand and from which he made his own sweeping generalizations. A few days in Rome were quite sufficient for him to decide that Raphael and Michelangelo had been vastly overrated.[11]

Though they were not self-educated (they were normally university graduates), the popular critics writing for the reviews were themselves "ignorant or half-instructed" in most of the new ideas they were called upon to explain and criticize. Before modern studies had come into the college curriculum, and before the surveys, digests, and histories of every subject which later critics have at their elbow had been written, the Victorian reviewer was in precisely the same condition, at a higher level, as the self-educated artisan.[12] He had so little knowledge of modern art, history, political theory, and philosophy that he could hardly avoid taking up hasty notions or condemning what he did not understand. Leslie Stephen's description of the early Edinburgh reviewers continued to be substantially true during the mid-Victorian period, though in lessening degree as the new knowledge was gradually disseminated and standards of reviewing rose:

> A clever man has turned over the last new book of travels or poetry, or made a sudden incursion into foreign literature or into some passage of history entirely fresh to him, and has given his first impressions with an audacity which almost disarms one by its extraordinary naïveté. . . . Jeffrey wrote about Mrs. Hutchin-

11. Ibid., chap. 42, pp. 219–28. See Josiah Royce, *Herbert Spencer. An Estimate and Review* (New York, 1904), pp. 205–8, and Raymond Mortimer, in *The New Statesman and Nation*, new ser. 24 (1942), 411–12. Cf. Beatrice Webb on Spencer in *My Apprenticeship*, p. 32: "If he had only not dogmatically denied that which he could not perceive or understand, if he had, with sincerity, admitted his own deficiencies of knowledge and perception—perhaps even of reasoning power—if he had had a ray of true humility—what a great and inspiring personality he might have been."

12. Cf. S. Squire Sprigge, writing in 1902, preface to *The Autobiography of Sir Walter Besant*, p. xiv: "It is much easier now than it was in his own young days to get a working knowledge of an author without deep reading. In the 'fifties and 'sixties, if a man wanted to know about—for example—Rabelais or Balzac, he would have to read their works. And he would have to read them all, if he had no well-informed friend to guide him in making a selection. . . . To-day, thanks to Besant, among other men of letters, there are monographs and exact treatises that deal with all accepted classics, so that it is possible for a critic to speak and write as though his reading had been vastly wider than is the case, and at the same time to be fairly correct." And also to be relatively cautious. He knows how much he does not know.

son's "Memoirs" and Pepys's "Diary" as though the books had for the first time revealed to him the existence of Puritans or of courtiers under the Restoration. . . . The young gentlemen who wrote in those days have a jaunty mode of pronouncing upon all conceivable topics without even affecting to have studied the subject.[13]

Even apart from their limited learning, the reviewers picked up an *ex cathedra* tone from the surrounding atmosphere of bumptious optimism and self-congratulation. "Each small scribbler of the great nineteenth century feels his immense superiority over the Addisons and Popes, the Humes and Adam Smiths of that poor benighted period." And this conceit, shared by the reader, made it all the easier for him to adopt the same note of confident assurance. "The young read indiscriminately, digest a small portion of this diluted knowledge, and imbibe *in toto* the easy spirit of decision." [14]

Finally, and most important, the dogmatism not only of professional critics but of all Victorian writers was fostered by the ignorance of the audience. The new reading public, far larger than that of the eighteenth century, had much less knowledge than the analogous audience would have today. In the middle classes there was no tradition of serious reading outside of divinity. What they knew depended largely on their formal education, and that was still very limited. The grammar schools taught little beyond the three R's and the rudiments of Latin grammar. The public schools carried on the work in mathematics and classics, but as late as 1868 they still ignored "modern geography, modern history, modern literature; the English language as a language; the whole circle of the sciences, physical, moral and social." It was possible, Huxley suggested without much exaggeration, to go through any of the great public schools and never hear "that the earth goes round the sun; that England underwent a great revolution in 1688, and France another in 1789; that there once lived certain notable men, called Chaucer, Shakespeare, Milton, Voltaire, Goethe, Schiller." [15]

13. "The First Edinburgh Reviewers" (1878), *Hours in a Library*, 2, 248–9. Herbert Paul in his *Life of Froude* (London, 1905), p. 92, claimed—I suspect quite justly—that most of the critics who in 1856 reviewed the first volumes of Froude's *History of England from the Fall of Wolsey to the Death of Elizabeth* "knew nothing about the subject."

14. Both quotations are from "Our Modern Youth," *Fraser's Magazine, 68* (1863), pp. 121, 122. The whole essay, pp. 115–29, bears on the present topic.

15. "A Liberal Education; and Where to Find It," *Science and Education*, pp. 93–4, for both quotations. Cf. Taine, *Notes on England*, pp. 133–5; Goldwin Smith,

Nor were the limitations of Victorian schools often compensated by home libraries. "Very few middle class people in my childhood," wrote Besant, "had any books to speak of, except a few shelves filled with dreary divinity or old Greek and Latin Classics." [16] Even at Oxford and Cambridge before the reforms of the sixties, the curriculum was largely confined to classics, mathematics, and theology. History as a subject of serious study was not recognized at either university until the last half of the century (the average attendance in 1850 at the modern history course at Oxford was eight). There was even less interest in the few courses that were offered in the natural and social sciences. The study of art was not introduced until 1870 (by Ruskin), and that of modern literatures still later.[17] It is true that the range of studies was wider at the University of London; and that in any event, then as now, formal curricula are not a measure of anyone's knowledge. Most Victorian readers had some contact with the wider and newer areas of learning. But that contact, in the absence of academic stimulus and training, and in the presence of the anti-cultural influences discussed in the last chapter, was rarely more than superficial. "Are they not," asked Bagehot of the English people, "a race with no special education or culture as to the modern world, and too often despising such culture?" [18]

Under these circumstances it would be surprising if the Victorian prophets had not treated their audience with cavalier dogmatism. And there is evidence at hand. Thomas Arnold, accused of "arrogance of tone" in a pamphlet where he brought his knowledge of modern history and of "the laws and literature of foreign nations" to bear on the question of Catholic Emancipation, answered that he did not "consider it to be arrogance to assume that I know more of a particular subject, which I have studied eagerly from a child, than those do who notori-

---

Reminiscences, ed. A. Haultain (New York, 1910), pp. 35–44 on Eton; Lord Clarendon quoted by G. M. Young, *Victorian England*, p. 98; and Walter Besant, *Autobiography*, p. 83, where he says that the lads who came up to Cambridge in the fifties "were wholly ignorant of the world, of society, of literature, of everything."

16. *Autobiography*, p. 37.

17. Smith, *Reminiscences*, p. 99, notices another fact, that "the University, instead of being as it had once been, a place of general learning, science, and education, had become the citadel of ecclesiasticism and the arena of ecclesiastical dispute."

18. *The English Constitution*, chap. 7, in *Works*, 4, pp. 221–2. For further evidence of the low state of general learning, see R. D. Altick, "English Publishing and the Mass Audience in 1852," *Studies in Bibliography*, Papers of the Bibliographical Society of the University of Virginia, 6 (1953–54), 13.

ously do not study it at all." [19] This was a weasel. All that Arnold really says is that it is not arrogance to talk arrogantly to an ignorant audience of what one has studied. He did not answer the accusation— he inadvertently explained why it was true. Ruskin openly confessed, apropos of the charge of "vaingloriousness" brought against his preface to *Pre-Raphaelitism* (1851), "It is quite true, that preface reads haughty enough; but . . . I cannot write with a modesty I do not feel. In speaking of art I shall never be modest any more. I see more and more every day that all over Europe people are utterly ignorant of its first principles, and more *especially* the upper classes; that the perception of it is limited to a few unheard-of artists and amateurs." [20]

The final reference indicates another factor, not the less important for being negative. What an ignorant public encouraged was not checked by the existence of any recognized body of scholars. In an essay on Victorian dogmatism, "The Literary Influence of Academies," Matthew Arnold imputed the freaks and violences of Francis Palgrave's criticism to the fact that he was "speaking before a promiscuous multitude, with the few good judges so scattered through it as to be powerless." Since he was "without any central authority representing high culture and sound judgment," he was "too much left to take his own way." Hence he felt no pressure, in writing his *Handbook* for the exhibition of fine art in 1862, to try his dislikes closely or express them moderately; he could give them free rein. [21] Arnold lays the blame chiefly at the door of English provincialism, cutting off educated men from the latest developments of thought and general standards of judgment in European intellectual circles. [22] Add to this the lack of university faculties equipped to pronounce on subjects like political economy, science, modern literatures, art, and history, and we realize that the dogmatism so easily assumed by a Victorian writer toward his common, and commonly ignorant, readers was not checked by know-

19. Stanley, *Life of Arnold*, p. 224, from a letter of May 29, 1829.

20. *Works, 12*, lii–liii.

21. *Essays in Criticism, First Series*, pp. 82–6.

22. Cf. John Morley, *Recollections, 1*, 69: "The European movement since 1830 was little studied in England by even the leading men, much less by the average." If we mention Coleridge, Carlyle, and DeQuincey, and throw in William Taylor, John Sterling, G. H. Lewes, and Julius Hare, we just about exhaust the English authorities on German literature and philosophy until well along in the century. But see Susanne H. Nobbe, "Some Notes on Anglo-German Studies," *The History of Ideas News Letter, 1*, No. 4 (1955), 2–3, for a considerable list of readers. On French culture I can only think offhand of Mill, Morley, Arnold, and Swinburne before the seventies.

ing that he had to face a body of "good and severe judges." [23] However uninformed the general public may be today on a particular subject, say, the painting of Turner, Tintoretto, Luini, Botticelli, or Carpaccio, no one now can write, as Ruskin did on those five painters, confident that "it was left to me, and to me alone, first to discern, and then to teach" their "excellency and supremacy." [24]

2. The Rationale of Infallibility

"It's no use," said Dr. John Brown, "arguing with Ruskin when he says wild things. I tried once and had to give it up. I had begun saying, 'Now, Ruskin, you surely do not *believe* that?' 'Believe it! Sir, I KNOW it.'" [25] The anecdote reflects the Victorian faith that truth is not only absolute, it is attainable. And once attained, it is, of course, asserted dogmatically. The prophet does not argue or take account of contrary notions or beliefs. He *tells* you in no uncertain terms and with no false modesty of tone, for after all he is not giving an opinion, he is stating, literally, a dogma. "I tell you," begins Ruskin, and then throws in a parenthesis: "—(dogmatically, if you like to call it so, knowing it well)— . . ." [26] "You fancy, doubtless, that I write . . . my 'opinions,'" he remarks on another occasion; "and that one man's opinion is as good as another's. You are much mistaken. When I only opine things, I hold my tongue; and work till I more than opine—until I know them"; and knowing them, can announce, "This is so; you may find it out for yourselves, if you choose; but, however little you may choose it, the thing is still so." "That is what people call my 'arrogance'"—how unjustly! [27] To us arrogance comes from the assumption of absolute wisdom. To Ruskin and other Victorians it comes only from the assumption of absolute wisdom which you do not have. Otherwise the arrogance is not arrogance but justifiable dogmatism. When

23. Arnold's phrase, *Essays in Criticism, First Series*, p. 84. And cf. Besant's account of the Cambridge dons in the fifties, *Autobiography*, p. 81: "These men . . . had for the most part come up from some small country town; they had a very faint tincture of culture; they were quite ignorant of modern literature; they knew absolutely nothing of art. As regards science, their contempt was as colossal as their ignorance. They vegetated at Cambridge; their lectures were elementary and contemptible; they lectured to Freshmen on Euclid, algebra or Greek Testament."

24. "Epilogue" to *Modern Painters, 2*, in *Works, 4*, 355.

25. *Works, 34*, 723.

26. *The Cestus of Aglaia*, in *Works, 19*, chap. 3, p. 89.

27. *Fors Clavigera*, in *Works, 27*, Letter 6, p. 99. Cf. Vol. 28, Letter 43, pp. 107–8.

Matthew Arnold's sister complained that he "was becoming as dogmatic as Ruskin," he told her, "the difference was that Ruskin was
dogmatic and *wrong*." [28] The same attitude is found in his father. Because the points he made in attacking the Oxford Tractarians were
"the most clear and certain truths in existence," Thomas Arnold could
not "speak hesitatingly." "And this may account," he adds, ". . . for
anything which may *seem* harsh or overpositive in my writing against
them." [29]

As these various quotations imply, the Victorian mind in general
was committed to the concept of absolute law. Politics, morals, history,
economics, art, education—all were governed, it was thought, by universal laws or principles true for all times and places; [30] and therefore
to be stated by anyone who knew what they were with serene authority. Broadly speaking, this concept was partly an inheritance from the
long tradition of natural law in both ancient philosophy and medieval
theology; and partly the result of modern (that is, since the seven-
teenth century) scientific thought, reaching out from the physical order
to discover the analogous laws of moral, social, and mental life. [31]

It is the former that explains why Thomas Arnold was ready in all
controversies "to repose with the most undoubting confidence on what
he held to be a general law," and why he always had "real principles
present to his mind . . . which seemed to him so certain, that 'daily
experience could hardly remove his wonder at finding that they did

28. *Letters, 1,* 233. The italics are Arnold's.

29. Stanley, *Life of Arnold,* p. 630, from a letter of December 25, 1841. The
italics are mine.

30. George Brimley in 1855 ("Tennyson's Poems," *Essays,* pp. 85–6) referred
to the age as one "when absolute and universal solutions are sought, not only for
physical phenomena, but also for mental and social,—when not only the movements of the heavenly bodies and the complex relations of the constituent elements
of organic matter, but the course of thought, the growth, decay, and character of
states,—in a word, the whole life of the individual, and the collective life of humanity, are supposed to be traceable to the orderly operation of fixed principles."
A similar statement is in *Life and Letters of Dean* [R.W.] *Church,* ed. Mary C.
Church (London and New York, 1895), p. 146.

31. The paragraphs that follow are intended merely to relate this large and
complex subject to Victorian dogmatism. For natural law, the classic text in England is Book I of Hooker's *Laws of Ecclesiastical Polity* (1594). In the light of
what I go on to say of Thomas Arnold, his admiration for Hooker's theory of law
(but not, of course, for his episcopacy) should be noted: Stanley, *Life of Arnold,*
p. 430 n., note to letter of November 30, 1836. There is a good introduction to the
general subject by A. P. d'Entrèves, *Natural Law* (London, 1951); but the history
of natural law in Victorian thought has still to be written.

not appear so to others.' " [32] Though partly derived from Aristotle, their supreme source was the divinely inspired scriptures. "God's word [was] an ever-living oracle, furnishing to every age those precise rules, principles, and laws of conduct which its actual circumstances may require." [33] Arnold's whole life, it is not too much to say, was an effort "to apply the principles of the Gospel to the legislation and administration of a state" in an age which he saw was becoming more and more secular and utilitarian.[34] And since he knew precisely what those principles were, the application was made, as Mozley remarked, "with a boldness that an evident warrant from the invisible world might produce." [35] If people complained of "violent, harsh, or dogmatical" passages in his sermons, Arnold answered that his "decided tone" was "generally employed in putting forward sentiments of Scripture, not in drawing my own conclusions from it." [36] But it was employed in both; and we must certainly reckon an inspired Bible containing eternal laws of morality now being too often defied or ignored in the selfish and worldly life of the time as a potent cause of Victorian dogmatism.

History too was a revelation of divine law, for "God's dealings with any particular generation of men are but the application of the eternal truths of His Providence to their particular circumstances." [37] It followed that political principles, derived from the study of history, were at one with those derived from Scripture. Natural Law and Divine Law were in harmony. Arnold's liberalism, adopted in opposition at once to both die-hard Toryism and democratic radicalism, was based on "those principles of advance and reform" which he found in every age of the world to be representative "of the cause of wisdom and goodness," and which were confirmed, he thought, by the moral law revealed by Christ.[38] He was prepared to admit, however, that political truths were "not, like moral truths, to be held as *absolutely* certain." [39]

The same tradition of natural law underlies the thinking—and the style—of Carlyle and Ruskin. For they, too, assumed that "a divine

32. Stanley, *Life*, chap. 4, pp. 172, 176.

33. Chap. 4, p. 193, in a letter about Arnold by B. Price.

34. The quotation describes the plan for a book he mentioned to Whately in 1827 (*Life*, chap. 2, p. 46); and cf. the preface to the first volume of his sermons, quoted in the *Life*, pp. 46–7.

35. *Essays Historical and Theological*, 2, 59.

36. *Life*, chap. 2, p. 48.

37. Chap. 4, p. 192, from Price's letter.

38. Chap. 4, p. 174.

39. From the preface to *The History of Rome*, quoted in *Life*, chap. 4, p. 175. The italics are mine.

message, or eternal regulation of the Universe, there verily is, in regard
to every conceivable procedure and affair of man"; and therefore that
"to prosper in this world" a man or a nation must "discern what the
true regulations of the Universe are in regard to him and his pursuit,
and . . . faithfully and steadfastly follow these." [40] The answers might
be hidden to the foolish and wicked, but to the wise and noble-minded
they were clear enough, sufficient for a Carlyle to announce as a
foregone conclusion that "on this side of the Atlantic and on that,
Democracy, we apprehend, is forever impossible! So much, with certainty of loud astonished contradiction from all manner of men at
present, but *with sure appeal to the Law of Nature* and the ever-
abiding Fact, may be suggested and asserted once more. . . . The
Noble in the high place, the Ignoble in the low; that is, in all times
and in all countries, the Almighty Maker's Law." [41]

That is the very note one hears in a remark of Ruskin's about *Fors
Clavigera* that might appropriately stand on the title page of any of
his books, or any of Carlyle's: "It is the assertion of the code of Eternal
Laws which the public mind *must* eventually submit itself to, or die."
Consequently, "the language which seems to you exaggerated . . .
expresses, in its earnestness, facts which you will find to be irrefragably
true, and which no other than such forceful expression could truly
reach." [42]

In other prophets the concept of absolute law derives mainly from
modern science. Starting in the eighteenth century, a host of thinkers
assumed a natural order in human society analogous to that which
Newton had discovered in the physical world. Not only all material
bodies but all social facts were "linked together in the bonds of inevitable laws, which individuals and Governments would obey if they
were once made known to them." [43] The task of the social scientist was

40. *Latter-Day Pamphlets*, No. 1, pp. 16–17. Cf. No. 2, p. 78: "What this Law
of the Universe, or Law made by God, is? Men at one time read it in their Bible.
. . . And if no man could now see it by any Bible, there is written in the heart of
every man an authentic copy of it direct from Heaven itself."

41. Ibid., pp. 21–2. The italics are mine.

42. *Works*, 29, Letter 81, p. 198. Cf. the remark which closes the first essay
of *Unto This Last* (*Works, 17,* 42): "For all this is true, and that not partially nor
theoretically, but everlastingly and practically: all other doctrine than this respecting matters political being false in premises, absurd in deduction, and impossible in practice, consistently with any progressive state of national life."

43. Charles Gide and Charles Rist, *A History of Economic Doctrines*, trans.
R. Richards (Boston and New York, 1948), p. 2, where it is claimed that the
physiocrats were the first to make this assumption.

therefore to discover these laws and proclaim them. Oblivious of the difficulties and complexities which time and later research and a more rigorous scientific method have revealed, they deduced their systems from a few simple truths that seemed axiomatic, and in the literal sense of the term laid down the laws of social life with all the self-assurance of pioneers.[44] Since the young science of political economy, for example, had discovered "the true cause of national prosperity," a disciple (Lecky) could blandly assert that it "demonstrates, beyond the possibility of doubt, that if the property of the rich were confiscated and divided among the poor, the measure would in the end be the most fearful catastrophe that could befall the latter." Or another, like Macaulay, could lament the fact that workingmen do not know "the reasons which irrefragably prove this inequality [of the rich and the poor] to be necessary to the well-being of all classes."[45] In the still younger field of sociology, men like Spencer and H. T. Buckle built up their systems of historical evolution on *the* laws of social and mental development, and treated debatable hypotheses as proven facts. Both, we may remember, proved that war would soon be a thing of the past.[46]

Even in the fields of art and literature we can find the same kind of assumption and presumption. Paralleling his thought in other areas,

44. The psychology was noticed by Kingsley, "The Limits of Exact Science as Applied to History," *The Roman and the Teuton*, in *Works, 10*, 315: "Young sciences, like young men, have their time of wonder, hope, imagination, and of passion too, and haste, and bigotry. Dazzled, and that pardonably, by the beauty of the few laws they may have discovered, they are too apt to erect them into gods, and to explain by them all matters in heaven and earth."

45. Lecky, *History of Rationalism, 2*, 344–5; Macaulay, "The People's Charter," *Complete Writings, 9*, 312. Cf. the editorial in *The Times* for March 1, 1848, referring to the promise of the new French government to secure work for the people by national workshops (quoted in *Letters of Arnold to Clough*, p. 169): "The purport of these fallacious promises and engagements is nothing short of a metamorphosis of the world, and a total change *of all the laws which experience and reflection have demonstrated to be the rules which govern human wealth and human labour, and consequently regulate the conditions of mankind.* To fulfill such promises is not only beyond the power of any Government, but absolutely *contrary to the laws of nature itself.*" The italics are those of the editor of the *Letters*, H. F. Lowry.

46. See above, Chap. 2, p. 42 and note 51. Spencer's dogmatism is exposed by Mill, *Letters, 1*, 310. Justin McCarthy's remark about Buckle (*History of Our Own Times, 2*, 644) is also true of Spencer: "He brought to his task . . . an ardent spirit full of faith in his own theory, and a power of self-will and self-complacency which enabled him to accept as certain and settled every dogma on which he had personally made up his mind."

Ruskin revived the tradition of absolute "rules" which the Romantics
had challenged; and though he rightly took issue with those who
thought there were no standards in art, what he meant by standards was "laws of truth and right . . . just as fixed as those of
harmony in music, or of affinity in chemistry." And since he, Ruskin,
knew what those laws were, it would be ridiculous for him to state
hesitatingly "either preference or principle, respecting pictures." [47]
And worse than ridiculous for the public to challenge or ignore his conclusions. "Until people are ready to receive all I say about art as
'unquestionable,'. . . I don't consider myself to have any reputation
at all worth caring about." [48] One such unquestionable truth, expressed
with the appropriate certainty of tone, was the badness of French
impressionism because it violated one of the prime laws of art—
namely, that objects must be painted with the clarity and detail that
can be seen from the point of observation. [49] In other critics the fixed
principles of art were often, quite literally, scientific principles. In the
aesthetics of Herbert Spencer good art is achieved only when the
artist knows and uses the scientific laws of anatomy, perspective, and
—in order to affect the minds of spectators or readers—psychology. [50]
G. H. Lewes, setting out to give some guidance to young men planning a career in literature, does not call his essays *Advice for Professional Writers* or even *How to Succeed as a Writer*, but *The Principles
of Success in Literature*. For given the native talent, "success is not an
accident." It is certain to reward anyone who knows and follows the
"psychological laws" on which "all Literature is founded," and the
"principles which are true for all peoples and for all times"—which
laws and principles Lewes proceeds confidently to lay down. [51]

As I have implied more than once, the assumption of absolute law
would never have led to dogmatism if men had not been certain they
knew what the law was. That necessary confidence was partly based,

47. Preface to *Modern Painters*, 3, in *Works*, 5, 5.
48. Letter to Furnivall, June 9, 1854, in *Works*, 36, 169.
49. *Modern Painters*, 3, Pt. IV, chap. 16, in *Works*, 5, 318–19; and see index
under modern French painting, ibid., 39, 210. Ruskin did not, of course, consider
Turner an impressionist in the French sense of the term.
50. *Education*, chap. 1, pp. 71–84. With Ruskin's remarks on the impressionists,
cf. Spencer on Chinese painting, pp. 76–7: "In what consists the grotesqueness of
Chinese pictures, unless in their utter disregard of the laws of appearances—in
their absurd linear perspective, and their want of aerial perspective?"
51. Edited F. N. Scott (Boston, 1894), p. 22. The book was first published
serially in 1865 in the *Fortnightly Review*.

as we saw, on the possession of an inspired scripture containing the revelation of God. But it was also founded, especially for those who could not rely on an infallible book, on the possession of an infallible power of insight: either reason or intuition. Both faculties may be used, of course, and were used by the Victorians, with modesty, but the extreme exaltation of both, which was inherited, respectively, from eighteenth-century Rationalism and nineteenth-century Romanticism, provided an epistemological basis for dogmatism. What Beatrice Webb, with special reference to Spencer, called "the defiant pride of intellect" [52] is found in the political economists and the Utilitarians, the positivists and the scientists. But no reliance on reason, however extreme, could issue in such unqualified dogmatism as could that on intuition. The rationalist had, at the least, to arrange some facts to fit his assumptions and employ a logical process of argument. An intuitionist could rely on an immediate vision of truth needing only to be announced with appropriate force. It was natural enough, therefore, that Mill and the philosophers of the school of experience should have protested against what they considered the erection of personal bias into philosophic truth. In the reaction against the eighteenth century, Mill thought the infallibility once accorded to the reasoning elements in human nature was now bestowed upon instinct; [53] with the result that whatever a man felt was true was credited to imagination or intuition, which was considered "to be the voice of Nature and of God, speaking with an authority higher than that of our reason." Consequently, any transcendentalist may "dogmatize at his ease, and instead of proving his propositions, may rail at all who deny them, as bereft of 'the vision and the faculty divine,' or blinded to its plainest revelations by a corrupt heart." [54] That generalization was applied directly to Carlyle by Herbert Spencer: He "never set out from premises and reasoned his way to conclusions, but habitually dealt in intuitions and dogmatic assertions." [55] But that is the rational pot calling the intuitive kettle black.

Carlyle, of course, would have accepted the criticism, and proudly. Nourished on German transcendentalism, he was ready enough to affirm that "the healthy Understanding . . . is not the Logical, argu-

52. *My Apprenticeship*, p. 32.
53. *The Subjection of Women*, chap. 1, p. 430.
54. *Autobiography*, chap. 7, pp. 191, 232–3; "Coleridge," *Dissertations, 1*, 407.
55. *Autobiography, 1*, chap. 22, 441.

mentative, but the Intuitive"; and that its end was "not to prove and find reasons, but to know and believe." [56] Hence the corresponding purpose of his style: not to give reasons but to instill the Truth, once known, by emphatic statement and moral injunction, often the two together. "Know of a truth," he says in a characteristic remark, ". . . that the real Being of whatever was, and whatever is, and whatever will be, is even now and forever. . . . Believe it thou must; understand it thou canst not." [57] The style varies, of course, from one intuitive prophet to another, but all were "declaimers—not reasoners" because "inspiration supersedes all necessity for the slow and cautious processes by which conscientious mortals of the ordinary stamp must painfully work out truth and light." [58] Even Matthew Arnold, for all his attack on "the *eruptive* and the *aggressive* manner in literature," [59] had his own prophetic fist under the urbane glove. He treated the most "difficult problems of individual and social life with an airy dogmatism" and delivered "profound truths and subtle observations with all the dogmatic authority and self-confidence of a prophet." So far as that criticism by Henry Sidgwick, the academic champion of philosophic empiricism, is true (it is somewhat overstated by the professional scholar galled by an amateur who speaks without book or systematic argument), it rests squarely on Arnold's faith in the power of right reason to arrive at the truth, whether about the State or the Bible, education or the Church, criticism or poetry.[60]

The assumption of inspired insight was by no means limited to a few philosophers and intellectuals who had read the German transcen-

56. "Characteristics," *Essays, 3,* 5: cf "State of German Literature," ibid., *1,* 82–3.

57. *Sartor Resartus,* Bk. III, chap. 8, p. 262.

58. W. R. Greg, "Kingsley and Carlyle," *Literary and Social Judgments, 1,* 157.

59. "The Literary Influence of Academies," *Essays in Criticism, First Series,* p. 77.

60. Sidgwick, "The Prophet of Culture," *Miscellaneous Essays and Addresses,* pp. 41, 42. But Arnold's right reason, derived from the tradition of natural law (found in the Stoics, Senancour, and Hooker), should be distinguished from the intuitive inspiration which Carlyle read into Kant's *Vernunft.* The similarity, however, was close enough for another thinker of the empirical school, Fitzjames Stephen, to say—"Mr. Matthew Arnold and His Countrymen," *Saturday Review, 18* (1864), 683–5—that as a transcendentalist, Arnold believes that "the prescriptions of reason are absolute, unchanging, of universal validity." I take the attribution of this article to Stephen from E. K. Brown, *Matthew Arnold: a Study in Conflict* (Chicago, 1948), pp. 207–8. On Arnold's epistemology as well as his belief in a universal order, see Trilling, *Arnold,* pp. 265–6, 272.

dentalists. It is found in most Victorian writers because it was part of the literary tradition. The man of letters was generally considered, and often considered himself, no mere artist or craftsman. He was a *genius* in a period, unlike the eighteenth or the twentieth centuries, when it was thought folly "to say that a man of genius . . . cannot, if he would, understand any object of human science"; when "everybody feels that genius is, in a sort, infallible"; and when young men at Oxford could take *Modern Painters* or *Past and Present* not as good books, not even as authoritative statements of aesthetic and political theory, but as nothing short of "inspired and absolute truth." [61] That environment, in which a writer could hardly escape becoming a fine dogmatist, was created by the transformation, under philosophical or mystical influence, of the natural genius of the eighteenth century— the poet who wrote spontaneously without knowledge of classical literature or the rules of art—into the Romantic Genius of the nineteenth whose imagination was an oracular organ of Truth. This heady doctrine, preached by Wordsworth and Shelley as well as Goethe and Fichte, was adopted from those sources by the Cambridge Apostles. Their leading spirit, F. D. Maurice, formulated it in 1828 in terms which bring out the omniscience of the poet's insight:

> The mind of a poet of the highest order is the most perfect mind that can belong to man. . . . He sympathises with all phenomena by his intuition of all principles; and his mind is a mirror which catches and images the whole scheme and working of the world. . . .
>   He cannot be untrue, for it is his high calling to interpret those universal truths which exist on earth only in the forms of his creation.[62]

One Apostle who listened and believed was Alfred Tennyson, the theory in his case confirmed by his own experience of mystical trance.

61. Sterling in Caroline Fox, *Memories of Old Friends*, ed. H. N. Pym (Philadelphia, 1882), p. 61; Patmore, "Seers, Thinkers, and Talkers," *Religio Poetae*, 1893 (London, 1907), p. 86; J. W. Mackail, *The Life of William Morris*, 1, chap. 2, p. 40.

62. "Byron," *Athenaeum*, 1 (1828), 351. Cf. L. A. Marchand, *The Athenaeum. A Mirror of Victorian Culture* (Chapel Hill, N.C., 1941), pp. 228–50, who called my attention to Maurice's article. On page 237 Marchand speaks of "the dictatorial note of authority in the writers for the quarterlies who saw themselves as the guardians of the gates of literature against the barbaric hordes of triflers who could not 'see true' and who considered literature only a pastime."

In the early "Armageddon," he described the moment when his "soul grew godlike":

> My mind seem'd wing'd with knowledge and the strength
> Of holy musings and immense Ideas,
> Even to Infinitude. . . .
> I was a part of the Unchangeable,
> A scintillation of Eternal Mind,
> Remix'd and burning with its parent fire.
> Yea! in that hour I could have fallen down
> Before my own strong soul and worshipp'd it.[63]

Thus fortified, Tennyson adopted the Apostolic conception of the poet so completely that years later he spoke of feeling like "a priest who can never leave the sanctuary, and whose every word must be consecrated to the service of Him who had touched his lips with the fire of heaven which was to enable him to speak in God's name to his age." [64] If a little less solemnly, Browning too began his career by announcing that he would be "priest and prophet as of old," [65] and though in some ways the influence of Shelley declined, he reaffirmed Shelley's exalted conception of the artist in his introduction to the spurious *Letters* of 1851. The subjective poet aspires to apprehend "all things in their absolute truth. . . . Not what man sees, but what God sees,—the *Ideas* of Plato, seeds of creation lying burningly on the Divine Hand,—it is toward these that he struggles. . . . He is rather a seer, accordingly, than a fashioner, and what he produces will be less a work than an effluence." [66]

It was Carlyle, however, who became the leading advocate of the writer as prophet. In his popular *Heroes and Hero-Worship* the Man of Letters as well as the Poet has his place, and a high one: he is "our most important modern person." He utters forth "the inspired soul of him. . . . I say *inspired;* for what we call 'originality,' 'sincerity,' 'genius,' the heroic quality we have no good name for, signifies that." Whether acknowledged as such or not, "the true literary man," therefore, "is the light of the world; the world's Priest;—guiding it, like a

63. Quoted in Charles Tennyson, *Alfred Tennyson* (New York, 1949), p. 38.

64. Quoted by Harold Nicolson in his *Tennyson* (Boston and New York, 1923), pp. 16–17, from a review of Hallam Tennyson's *Memoir*. Cf. Tennyson's "The Poet."

65. *Pauline,* line 1019.

66. *Complete Works,* p. 1009. Cf. "How It Strikes a Contemporary."

sacred Pillar of Fire, in its dark pilgrimage through the waste of Time." [67] On many a young writer the effect of reading that passage, or others like it in Carlyle's earlier essays, must have been very similar to the effect on many a country clergyman of reading Newman's first *Tract for the Times*,—the sudden discovery that he was no ordinary mortal but a priest possessing supernatural powers of the highest importance to mankind. Though such a discovery may strike a man with awe and profound humility, it may easily have exactly the opposite effect, especially on the writer. For in him more than in the Christian minister it is likely to breed the self-complacency that dogmatizes and the conceit that adds the note of arrogance. When Mill regretted "the things which have been written in late times, as by Carlyle, in exaltation of the literary character . . . that it is the new priesthood, and so on," he pointed to the result: "The consequence of the vulgarisation of these notions has been to make that very feeble and poor minded set of people, taken generally, the writers of this country, so conceited of their function and of themselves, however unworthy of it, and has at the same time made fine people think so much more of them . . . that it has at once inflated their vanity and lowered their ambition." [68]

3. *The Attraction of Dogmatism*

Though dogmatism still flourishes today, it is much less common than it was. The wider knowledge of writers and readers, a greater awareness of the complexity of truth, the historical and relativist point of view, and above all the recognition of how often reason and intuition are only instruments of rationalization—these developments have made it suspect, at least among educated people. But to the Victorians it was not only natural (given the climate of opinion)—it was attractive. They liked it. One might even say they asked for it. The prophets who put on the mantle of infallibility did so as much from public demand as from a personal sense of fitness. The explanation is before us: the pain of doubt and the intense will to believe made the dogmatic assertion of a doctrine a positive virtue. Froude closed his account of how he was saved from atheism by the gospel according to Carlyle with a significant remark: "And the lesson came from one who

67. Lecture 5, pp. 155, 157. For an account of this conception of the writer from another angle, see Raymond Williams, "The Idea of Culture," *Essays in Criticism*, 3 (1953), sec. 3, pp. 252–62.

68. Diary for 1854, *Letters*, 2, 370. Cf. the quotations from Harriet Martineau's "Literary Lionism" (1837) in her *Autobiography*, 1, Period IV, sec. 2, pp. 289–92, and the article on "Professional Enthusiasm," *Saturday Review*, 17 (1864), 157–8.

seemed 'to speak with authority and not as the Scribes,' as if what he said was absolute certainty beyond question or cavil." [69] What *we* find so irritating today was precisely what Froude had to have if he were to be saved. Leslie Stephen was later to notice, apropos of Froude's life of Carlyle, that in spite of the disciple's refined and sensitive temperament, "the dogmatism [of the master] was delightful and comforting, and gave a sense of security. . . . The biography throughout shows that he was even keenly sensible to Carlyle's arrogance, and yet felt it as a valuable support. Carlyle might be rough, but he could sweep away any misgivings with delightful positiveness. . . . *Froude's half-suppressed scepticism made him value the uncompromising dogmatism.*" [70] Much of Macaulay's success may be traced to the same psychology: "The admirer of Macaulay had all the comfort in his studies that a votary of the Roman Catholic Church may have. He had an infallible guide. He had no need to vex himself with doubt, speculation, or even conjecture. This absolute certainty about everything was, beyond question, one great source of Macaulay's popularity." [71] For a smaller audience Ruskin's assurance had the same appeal. In *Fraser's Magazine* for July 1859 it is criticized, but only as the excess of a virtue: "For all his arrogance, dogmatism, and egotism, he is one of the most delightful and instructive of writers; and this because it is partly from a zealous love and a bold and uncompromising assertion of what he believes to be truth, that his arrogance and dogmatism arise." Then follows an extraordinary remark: "For even error, eloquently advocated with the honest conviction that it is truth, is better than truth coldly believed and languidly proclaimed." [72] That is to make the believing state of mind, whatever the belief, true or false, a supreme virtue; [73] and hence to exalt the "bold and uncompromising assertions" that can induce it. Plainly it was not just the inspired prophet who preferred declamation to argument; it was also his troubled and anxious audience.

But to assume a doubting public for whom believing prophets write with a welcome dogmatism is too simple. For the prophets themselves were often plagued with doubt, and their dogmatism was as natural

69. *Carlyle: Life in London, 1,* chap. 11, p. 293.

70. "James Anthony Froude," *Studies of a Biographer, 3,* 249–50. The italics are mine.

71. Justin McCarthy, *A History of Our Own Times, 1,* 530. Cf. Morley, "Macaulay," *Critical Miscellanies, 1,* 277.

72. Vol. *60* (1859), 106.

73. Cf. above, p. 98.

as it was rhetorical. In an age of wavering faith the wish to believe, Mill noticed, leads to a "rather more demonstrative attitude of belief" than people thought necessary "when their personal conviction was more complete." [74] Now they whistle to keep their convictions up. They insist the more loudly because, half-consciously or unconsciously, they know themselves to be uncertain and suspect they are fallible. A remark of Froude's—that even the most ardent ritualist "conceals his misgivings from his own eyes by the passion with which he flings himself into his work"—reveals the psychology in another phase.[75] One might easily substitute "by the passion with which he asserts the undoubted truth" of his faith; and cite in evidence Harriet Martineau's admission that in one of her books she "was unconsciously trying to gain strength of conviction by vigour of assertion." [76] That is what was meant, at the start of this chapter, by saying that a dogmatic style might only *seem* to betray an insufferable man, that it might sometimes be only a mask. It is true enough, as Wingfield-Stratford once said, that "the great Victorians . . . stare back at us, from their frames and pedestals, with an expression of . . . serene—not to say smug—self-assurance," but not, not often, for the reason he gives, because they were "magnificently" free of self-doubt.[77] On the contrary, that expression, in their faces, in their style, was often put on to reassure themselves that what they believed was—of course it was—the absolute truth. Not always. Not in the case of Macaulay or Spencer. But let us glance at five other "great Victorians" famous for their dogmatism.

To turn to Ruskin's letters from his published works, with their explicit claims and implicit assumptions of infallibility, is to hear a succession of cries from a bewildered and sometimes even a humble man. In 1848 he warned his father he was beaten down by the difficulties that stood in the way of his faith. He could not believe in "God's government of the world," and the more he reasoned over the Bible, the more difficulties he found. In a letter of 1859 he wrote to Norton, "Some day, when I've quite made up my mind what to fight for, or whom to fight, I shall do well enough, if I live, but I haven't made up my mind what to fight for." Then followed a series of unanswered questions, ending with "whether it is worth while to ascertain any of

74. "Utility of Religion," *Three Essays on Religion*, p. 71. Cf. W. H. Prescott, *History of the Conquest of Mexico* (3 vols. New York, 1846), 3, 418: "Where there is most doubt, there is often the most dogmatism."

75. "On Progress," *Short Studies*, 2, 366.

76. *Autobiography, 2*, Period V, sec. 2, p. 187.

77. *The Victorian Sunset*, p. 61.

these things; whether one's tongue was ever made to talk with or only to taste with." In the same year he confessed he was "on the whole vacantly puzzled and paralyzed, able only to write a little now and then of old thoughts." In 1861 he was still "an entirely puzzled, help-less, and disgusted old gentleman" and told Mrs. Browning, "I am fighting through all kinds of doubt and wonder; and have no strength —cannot look things in the face—they come instead and grimace at me." [78] His skepticism even intrudes into a formal lecture delivered in 1864. After saying that the age-old moral laws are indisputable truths, he suddenly adds: "For the rest, respecting religions, governments, sciences, arts, you will find that, on the whole, you can know NOTH-ING,—judge nothing; that the best you can do, even though you may be a well-educated person, is to be silent, and strive to be wiser every day. . . . The thoughts even of the wisest are very little more than pertinent questions. To put the difficulty into a clear shape, and exhibit to you the grounds for *in*decision, that is all they can generally do for you!" [79]

It may be so, but it was hardly what Ruskin had been doing for twenty years, or was to do for thirty more. It would be truer to say that in religions, governments, and arts he spent his life exhibiting the grounds of *de*cision, and in no uncertain terms. I do not mean to imply that his claims to infallibility were no more than a desperate psycho-logical expediency, though that may be so. I only argue that the dog-matism had its roots at once in genuine conviction, and in painful doubt, that he possessed the truth.

The same may be said of Ruskin's "master"—and the very archetype of the Victorian dogmatist—Carlyle: throughout his work, passionate insistence on the moral order of the universe and the absolute laws of God; in his letters, evidence of recurrent and distressing uncertainty.[80] The connection between the two was implied by Froude. After refer-ring to his "extraordinary arrogance" and pointing out that if anyone crossed him in argument or dared to contradict him, he could be "rude, disdainful, and imperious," Froude contrasted him with Jeffrey: "Never having had much of a creed himself . . . and having no tend-ency to dogmatism and no impatience of indecision, he thought zeal for creeds and anxiety about positive opinions more and more ludi-

78. *Works, 36,* 90, 313, 327, 357, 363.
79. "Of Kings' Treasuries," *Sesame and Lilies,* in *Works, 18,* 76–7.
80. The evidence for the latter is given above, pp. 73, 84, 130–2; and below, pp. 251–6.

crous." [81] It was because Carlyle *was* so anxious about the positive opinions he held so precariously that he could not brook any one who questioned them. He could only strike him down and reaffirm his own creed with factitious assurance. Through the sixties and seventies his journal is full of sarcastic remarks about scientific atheism: "Man made chemically out of . . . a certain blubber called *protoplasm*. Man descended from the apes, or the shellfish!" [82] Men will have "to return from that, I can tell them," he says in one entry, "or go down altogether into the abyss." But the very next sentence reads: "I find lying deep in me withal some confused but ineradicable flicker of belief that there is a 'particular providence.' Sincerely I do, as it were, believe this, to my own surprise." [83]

In Kingsley the tone of voice is hardly less strident and dictatorial. He had a way of talking, as Hopkins once said (comparing him to another well-known Victorian) "with the air and spirit of a man bouncing up from table with his mouth full of bread and cheese and saying that he meant to stand no blasted nonsense. . . . The effect of this style is a frigid bluster." [84] Was that because all he said had for warrant a divinely inspired Scripture? Attacked on one occasion for the passionate "temper and tone" of his writing, he defended himself by saying: "I believe an old superstition, that things are either right or wrong, and that right means what God commands, and loves, and blesses; and wrong what He forbids and hates, and makes a curse and a road of ruin to those who follow it; and therefore no language is too strong to warn men from the road to ruin." [85] And yet we know that by moments his trust in the Bible seemed "falling to pieces," [86] and that "never . . . at any time did the great and terrible battle of faith and doubt wholly cease within him." [87] And this too, paradoxical as it may seem, provoked the dogmatic tone. There is a revealing passage in a letter of 1855, written in one of his dark moods, when Kingsley was recalling the years from 1844 to 1848. He is now ashamed, he

81. *Carlyle: First Forty Years*, 2, chap. 17, p. 394.

82. Froude, *Carlyle: Life in London*, 2, chap. 31, p. 386; cf. pp. 374, 388, 393–5.

83. Ibid., 2, 395. For another link between doubt and dogmatism in Carlyle, see below, Chap. 9, sec. 6.

84. *The Correspondence of Gerard Manley Hopkins and Richard Watson Dixon*, ed. C. C. Abbott (London, 1935), p. 74.

85. *Letters and Memories*, 1, 231 (unabridged ed., 1, 265–6).

86. From a letter of 1855 quoted by Thorp, *Kingsley*, p. 125.

87. On the word "of one who knew him well," *Letters and Memories*, 2, 206 (not apparently in the unabridged ed.). For further evidence, see above, pp. 74–5, 128–9, and below, p. 257.

says, of "my vanity and haste, my reckless laying down the law and fault finding, my conceited dream that I knew every body's business better than they themselves did." But he looks back to those years, he admits, "with longing, as on a sort of Eden." Shame is countered by envy. It is the weak, bewildered Kingsley longing for the Kingsley whose strength was as the strength of ten because he was infallible. Even now he is not free of the old dogmatism he is criticizing. "I have not lost that vanity," he goes on to say, "often it seems ready to take baser and more childish forms than ever." Now, for example, in this very moment of painful doubt.[88]

The other Victorian whom Hopkins associated with Kingsley was Browning, which is not surprising when we think of Browning's confident affirmation of divine love and immortality, resting on the power of intuition he so often claimed to be the great organ of truth. Nor is it surprising when, on the other hand, we discover the confession he once made in private, that he believed in immortality "if I have any instinct or insight,—if I can retain and rightly reason upon the rare flashes of momentary conviction that come and go in the habitual dusk and doubt of one's life." [89] As R. D. Altick has recently shown, Browning never laid the ghost of Voltairean-Shelleyan antireligion. He abandoned reason because it menaced his precarious faith, and exalted intuition not from any true confidence in its validity but for its power to justify the desires of the heart. He kept reiterating, "as if in an attempt at self-hypnosis: 'I believe . . . I believe . . . I believe . . . of course I believe,'" because he was swept by misgiving; and kept asserting his belief the more dogmatically for the same reason. Altick concludes, "The burly assurance in his voice had no counterpart in his inner being. On the contrary, his famous positiveness in religious matters is a telling clue to his underlying insecurity." And equally the insecurity is a telling clue to the positiveness.[90]

88. This letter, quoted in Thorp, p. 124, is the same one in which he speaks of his trust in the Bible falling to pieces, and also of his political anxieties. Cf. Leslie Stephen, "Charles Kingsley," *Hours in a Library*, 3, 34: "In later years . . . his declarations, if equally dogmatic in form, show less confidence than desire to be confident." His wife (*Letters and Memories*, 2, 206; unabridged ed., 2, 218) somewhat naively imagined it would be "a comfort to other troubled souls to know of the calm assured faith with which at the last, when standing on the very threshold of the next world, he faced death, and was heard repeating again and again, 'It is all right—all under rule.'"

89. *Robert Browning and Julia Wedgwood*, ed. R. Curle (New York, 1937), p. 7, from a letter of June 25, 1864.

90. R. D. Altick, "The Private Life of Robert Browning," *Yale Review, 41* (1952), 257, 259, and passim.

One wonders if something of the sort might be said of Thomas Arnold. Did even he, perhaps, have his fears that the source of certain principles on which he based his writing, the divine will made manifest in an inspired Scripture, might be a delusion? According to Stanley the "intellectual doubts which beset the first opening of his mind to the realities of religious belief" belonged only to the early years at Oxford. After 1820 they "seem to have vanished away and never again to have diverted him." [91] It may be so, and yet his method of resolving them, "to put down the objections by main force"—that is, to abandon the inquiry, give up reading and controversy, and plunge into "the practical duties of a holy life"—looks more like suppression than resolution.[92] Still further, in a telltale footnote Stanley attributes the successful disposal of his doubts to "the joint effect of a healthier frame of mind, when he had entered on practical life, and of the conviction that the view which he eventually adopted was *less encumbered with difficulties than any other.*" [93] Indeed, Arnold himself admitted on one occasion that in the battle of faith, "all that can be done *intellectually* is to point out the *equal* or greater difficulties of atheism or scepticism"; and that a good man "may be perplexed with doubts all his days; nay, his fears lest the Gospel should not be true, may be stronger than his hopes that it will." [94] Could he have had himself in mind? In the last hours before his death he "dwelt with deep solemnity" on the confession of St. Thomas, "as in his life he had dwelt upon it as the great consolation of doubting but faithful hearts." [95] The combination of epithets is striking and exactly descriptive of that state of half-belief which was so characteristic of the age. The *ex cathedra* note of his books and sermons, their "violent, harsh, or dogmatical" tone,[96] is the voice of a man who possessed an absolute set of principles and a doubting heart.[97]

91. *Life,* chap. 2, p. 27.

92. Ibid., chap. 1, pp. 19–20.

93. Chap. 9, p. 491. The italics are mine.

94. *Life,* pp. 272 and 274, from letters of February 15 and March 7, 1832.

95. Ibid., chap. 3, p. 138; and cf. the indication of his own suffering, pp. 364–5, from a letter of June 21, 1835.

96. Chap. 2, p. 48.

97. For the Victorian reaction against dogmatism, see the concluding section of the next chapter (which is also a conclusion to this one), where I discuss the open and flexible mind.

Chapter 7

RIGIDITY

> I am falling foul . . . of John Mill in his modern
> and more humane mood . . . which always makes me
> feel that he is a deserter from the proper principles
> of rigidity and ferocity in which he was brought up.
> *Fitzjames Stephen* [1]

BY AND LARGE, the Victorian mind was rigid. It tended to follow one
line of thought, to look at objects from a single point of view, to shut
out wide interests. It was marked, in Matthew Arnold's analysis, by a
"want of flexibility," an "inaptitude for seeing more than one side of a
thing," an "intense energetic absorption in the particular pursuit" it
was engaged in.[2] I do not mean to imply that one cannot take sides
without being one-sided. A person may have strong convictions which
he defends or advocates strenuously and yet be quite capable of ap-
preciating the appeal of other beliefs or the force of opposing arguments. And this is the case with a number of distinguished thinkers,
notably John Stuart Mill and John Henry Newman. But most Victorians
are well represented by Froude's description of a man who possessed
Newman's Anglo-Catholic convictions without his supple intelligence,
John Keble. Because "his mind moved in the groove of a single order
of ideas, he could not place himself in the position of persons who
disagreed with him, and thus he could never see the strong points of
their arguments." [3]

Another mark of the rigid mind is its adoption of extreme as well as
narrow positions. If there is no effort to examine contrary theories,

1. Quoted in Leslie Stephen, *The Life of James Fitzjames Stephen*, p. 308.
2. *Culture and Anarchy*, chap. 1, p. 49; and see especially the "Preface" and
"The Function of Criticism at the Present Time" in *Essays in Criticism, First
Series*.
3. "The Oxford Counter-Reformation," *Short Studies, 4*, 266–7.

there is little likelihood of compromise or mediation. More than one observer found an "intense tendency to extremes" to be characteristic of the time. In their political, ecclesiastical, and social views, men are "disposed to rush into extravagance. Moderation, self-command, equilibrium, are fearfully wanting." [4] This tendency is even more apparent in matters of judgment, as distinct from those of belief. The Victorian tends to divide ideas and people and actions into tight categories of true-false, good-bad, right-wrong; and not to recognize the mixed character of human experience.

This rigid mind is likely to be dogmatic. Where there is no flexible awareness of various sides to a question, or of possible middle grounds, one side, which may well be extreme, is taken for the whole truth and therefore—given a temperament of sufficient 'blood' and self-confidence —is asserted with corresponding assurance. On the other hand, the dogmatic mind in its turn is certainly rigid. Since Tancred's mother in Disraeli's novel "enjoyed the advantages of knowing exactly what was true in dogma, what just in conduct, and what correct in manners," she was a woman "of fixed opinions, and of firm and compact prejudices." [5] The truth is that we have under view, in both these chapters, a single type of mind which has both characteristics, at least potentially. It is the mind that in various ways was bred by the breakdown of traditional thought and the existence of a mass of new ideas, old ideas, or a mixture of both, on every conceivable subject; with the result that it chose one truth to cling to rigidly and insist upon dogmatically. But there were special factors which tended in particular to nourish one or the other tendency. After the analysis of those bearing directly on its dogmatism, we turn to those that encouraged its narrow one-sidedness, extreme opinion, and categorical judgment.

1. *Sectarian Fervor*

An age in which fundamental conceptions in politics, religion, and morals have to be re-examined is an age of divided opinion. Scores of sects urge their own programs of reconstruction, often through a periodical of their own, and intellectual life becomes as competitive as that of business. The discussion might have been more balanced and rational if the issues at stake had not seemed so crucial that they activated intense emotions of attachment and hostility. When the sta-

4. Hugh Stowell, "The Age We Live In," in *Exeter Hall Lectures*, 6 (1850–51), 50. Cf. William Johnston, *England as It Is, 1*, 221, and the quotation from Mill, below, p. 178.

5. *Tancred*, chap. 2, in *Works, 15*, 19.

bility of society seemed to require the immediate defense or immediate reform of political and religious institutions, there was little chance for disinterested thinking and a dispassionate search for truth. At such a time to hesitate, to balance the pros and cons, to advocate a policy with due recognition of its partial truth or practical difficulties is almost impossible psychologically, and strategically it is fatal. The emotions are too deeply involved; the need to push a particular line of action with rigor, or to oppose another unconditionally, is too imperative.[6] A writer in the *Edinburgh Review* described Thomas Arnold as a man who "could do nothing by halves. . . . Whatever it was on which he was engaged, he threw himself headlong into it, almost bodily, as into a volcano; from whose depths forth he came again— argument and sentiment, emotion and burning words—rolling and thundering." This was due, he adds, not to any arrogance or ill will but to the ardor of his nature [7]—the ardor to save the country from the political revolution inevitable if Tory or Jacobin principles prevailed and the religious disaster if either Anglo-Catholic superstition or Benthamite atheism continued to spread. Because he and John Keble, once close friends, believed "the other in error pernicious to the faith and dangerous to himself," both held and put forward their opinions "with a zeal and tenacity proportionate to their importance." [8] What Stanley wrote of Arnold's sectarian spirit is thus equally true for that of his opponents on the right and on the left: "The vehemence with which he threw himself into a contest against evil, and the confidence with which he assailed it, though it carried him through perplexities to which a more cautious man would have yielded, led him to disregard interests and opinions which a less earnest or a less sanguine reformer would have treated with greater consideration." [9]

Furthermore, when so much was at stake, or seemed to be, one's

6. Cf. Mill, *On Liberty*, chap. 2, p. 148: "Every truth which men of narrow capacity are in earnest about, is sure to be asserted, inculcated, and in many ways even acted on, as if no other truth existed in the world, or at all events none that could limit or qualify the first. I acknowledge that the tendency of all opinions to become sectarian is not cured by the freest discussion, but is often heightened and exacerbated thereby; the truth which ought to have been, but was not, seen, being rejected all the more violently because proclaimed by persons regarded as opponents."

7. Vol. *81* (1845), 206–7, from a review of Stanley's *Life of Arnold*. The author was William Empson: see L. G. Johnson, "On Some Authors of *Edinburgh Review* Articles, 1830–49," *Library*, 5th ser. 7 (1952), 47.

8. Sir J. T. Coleridge, quoted in Stanley, *Life of Arnold*, chap. 1, p. 13.

9. Ibid., chap. 3, p. 89.

estimate of men could be as blind and one-sided as his intellectual commitments. Especially in the case of opponents. Far from being considered, in Mill's fine phrase, "as one's allies; as people climbing the hill on the other side," [10] they became, in varying degrees, enemies of society one could not or would not understand, let alone judge impartially. Thomas Arnold called his essay on the Tractarians "The Oxford Malignants." [11] The Tractarian Keble thought there was something "morally wrong" with those who disagreed with him.[12] We can well believe the friend of Morley's who knew many leaders of Victorian thought and yet could count only five who took pains to master the arguments contrary to their own creeds, or to discern the possible good in the motives and acts of those they believed wrong in opinion.[13]

The one-sidedness bred by sectarian controversy was not limited to the professional thinkers. In a period when traditional beliefs and established authorities (the aristocracy, the Church, the men of learning) were no longer held in unquestioned awe, and all men were being urged to judge for themselves—while at the same time the public was crying out for guidance and almost no one seemed certain of what to believe or what to do—a multitude of amateur prophets stepped forward, some in print but ten times as many in conversation, each with his pet solution. In the midst of clashing interests and opposing theories, as Hood observed in 1851, "every body has his own little *ism*, his own little cockle-boat, by which alone the country can be saved." [14] Tom Brown at Oxford is a case in point. In contrast with his friend Hardy, who would test every theory, "and turn it over, and . . . try to get hold of the whole of it," Tom would rush out "the moment he had seized . . . a new idea . . . and brandish it in the face of all comers, and think himself a traitor to the truth if he wasn't trying to

---

10. Quoted in *The Amberley Papers*, 1, 373.

11. Cf. Stanley, *Life*, chap. 4, p. 171: "With every wish to be impartial, yet his natural temperament [that is, "his keen sense of what he thought evil"] . . . made it difficult for him to place himself completely in another's point of view; and thus he had a tendency to judge individuals, with whom he had no personal acquaintance, from his conception of the party to which they belonged."

12. Froude, "The Oxford Counter-Reformation" p. 268.

13. *Recollections*, 1, 102.

14. *The Age and Its Architects*, p. 80. Cf. Kingsley in 1843, *Letters and Memories*, 1, 87 (unabridged ed., 1, 111): "Hath not every man his own gift? Each hero the appointed witness of some peculiar truth?" In *A French Eton, or Middle-class Education and the State* (first ed. 1864; London and New York, 1892), p. 69, Arnold boasts that *he* has "no pet scheme to press, no crotchet to gratify, no fanatical zeal for giving this or that particular shape to the public establishment of our secondary instruction."

make everybody he met with eat it." [15] His principal "pet idea," and that of all the young liberals in the forties, was nothing less than a "universal democracy," which he thought was the one perfect means of realizing "that age of peace and good-will . . . when the lion should lie down with the kid, and nation should not vex nation any more." This is a fine example of what Morley called the psychology of "ardent spirits . . . in an expectant age":

> Pierced by thought of the ills in the world around them, they are overwhelmed by a noble impatience to remove, to lessen, to abate. Before they have set sail, they insist that they already see some new planet swimming into their ken, they already touch the promised land. An abstract *a priori* notion, formed independently of experience, independently of evidence, is straightway clothed with all the sanctity of absolute principle. Generous aspiration, exalted enthusiasm, is made to do duty for reasoned scrutiny. They seize every fact or circumstance that makes their way, they are blind to every other. Inflexible preconceptions hold the helm. They exaggerate. Their sense of proportion is bad. [16]

Though an "ism" need not be radical and a sect may try to mediate between left and right, the tendency of the age (though mainly in the earlier decades) was toward extreme and unqualified positions. Many Victorians were "downright infidels or downright Christians, thorough Tories or thorough democrats" [17] or, in a larger category that roughly includes both of these, they were Ancients or Moderns. In a period of radical transition, some men bewailed the age "as one of rapid decay; in which the old landmarks are being removed, the old paths lost; in which we are rushing headlong into scepticism and atheism; in which the world and the Church are both in danger; and the last day is at hand." Others, however, gloried in the nineteenth century "as one of rapid progress for good; as the commencement of a new era for humanity; as the inauguration of a Reformation as grand as that of the sixteenth century." [18] Although that was written about 1870 (by Kingsley), it is true of the whole period under discussion. Forty years earlier Mill was aware of exactly the same emotional re-

15. Hughes, chap. 42, p. 486. The quotation that follows is on p. 487.
16. *Notes on Politics and History* (New York, 1914), pp. 21–2. This passage could well apply to system-makers like Bentham, Comte, Buckle, and Spencer. Arnold, *Culture and Anarchy*, chap. 1, pp. 65–7, brings out their narrowness and rigidity, which was as characteristic as their dogmatism, mentioned above, p. 148.
17. Mill, *Letters*, 2, 360.
18. Kingsley, *Westminster Sermons*, No. 8, in *Works*, 28, 85.

actions—he called them "exultation" and "terror"—and noted the resulting hostility toward one another which now inflamed the champions of the past on the one side, and those of the present and future on the other: "The wisdom of ancestors, and the march of intellect, are bandied from mouth to mouth; each phrase originally an expression of respect and homage, each ultimately usurped by the partisans of the opposite catch-word, and in the bitterness of their spirit, turned into the sarcastic jibe of hatred and insult." [19]

That new note of acrimony, so potent in its power to widen the gap between the two camps and fix their respective positions more extremely, has somewhat different sources in each case. It was the dread of violent revolution—that what happened in France from 1789 to 1794 may happen here, *will* happen here if we yield an inch—which created the panicky defense of the status quo (die-hard Toryism) and identified the moderns with revolutionaries.[20] On the other side, the moderns, though not untouched by fear that such a reactionary policy would set off the very revolution it was designed to prevent, were mainly motivated by exasperation with the past and an impatient desire for the clean sweep. "The moment, and the mood of mind, in which men break loose from an error," remarked Mill, "is not, except in natures very happily constituted, the most favourable to those mental processes which are necessary to the investigation of truth. . . . They usually resolve that the new light which has broken in upon them shall be the sole light; and they wilfully and passionately blow out the ancient lamp." [21] Witness, for example, Macaulay's bland dismissal of "the most renowned sages of sixty generations" and his entire commitment to the new light of Baconian philosophy; or Thomas Arnold's first response to liberalism: it shook his family Toryism to pieces and he became for a while "well nigh a Jacobin." [22] By midcentury the moderns had so far captured public opinion as to make allegiance to the traditional a prima facie cause for criticism. "A man is sufficiently

---

19. *The Spirit of the Age*, pp. 1–2. Cf. F. D. Maurice, in the *Athenaeum, 1* (1828), 33: "There are some people who believe our age . . . infinitely the most important the world has ever known. . . . There are others whose interest leads them to laud the wisdom of our ancestors as something altogether superhuman." And cf. Herbert Spencer, *Autobiography, 2*, chap. 60, pp. 516–18.

20. See Bagehot, "The First Edinburgh Reviewers," *Works, 1*, 10–12.

21. *The Spirit of the Age*, p. 15. The text reads "blew," which I take to be a misprint.

22. For Macaulay, see above, p. 123; for Arnold, Stanley, *Life*, p. 541, from a letter of January 24, 1840.

condemned," observed Trollope in 1857, "if it can only be shown that either in politics or religion he does not belong to some new school established within the last score of years. He may then regard himself as rubbish and expect to be carted away. A man is nothing now unless he has within him a full appreciation of the new era. . . . We must laugh at everything that is established." [23] In that frame of mind a new doctrine might well be put forward in its most extreme form out of sheer scorn for the ancients as old fogies—an approach well calculated to increase the inflexibility on the other side by its irritating bravado. In Mill's account of Charles Austen we can see how much the delight of shocking the conservatives contributed to the "youthful fanaticism" of the Benthamites:

> He loved to strike, and even to startle. He knew that decision is the greatest element of effect, and he uttered his opinions with all the decision he could throw into them, never so well pleased as when he astonished any one by their audacity. Very unlike his brother, who made war against the narrower interpretations and applications of the principles they both professed, he, on the contrary, presented the Benthamic doctrines in the most startling form of which they were susceptible, exaggerating everything in them which tended to consequences offensive to any one's preconceived feelings.

And his example was followed by younger proselytes who would "*outrer* whatever was by anybody considered offensive in the doctrines and maxims of Benthamism." [24] This psychology of the avant-garde, so natural to an age of novel ideas and radical theory, is seen, I suspect, in the young Thomas Arnold who "startled" his Tory companions at Oxford "a good deal" by his advanced opinions. [25] And when Tom Brown, a generation later, returned home from Oxford with his head full of notions and beliefs (derived from political economists, High Churchmen, and *Past and Present*) that were certain "to astonish and perplex the mind of that worthy J. P. for the county of Berks, Brown the elder," he must have put them in their most startling form. [26]

23. *Barchester Towers* (New York, 1893), *1*, chap. 13, pp. 144–5. Cf. Clough's protest in "Old things need not be therefore true" (1851), *Poems*, p. 89, though with characteristic flexibility, as the title line indicates, Clough also urged the ancients to "consider it again."

24. *Autobiography*, chap. 3, p. 66.

25. Sir J. T. Coleridge, quoted in Stanley, *Life*, chap. 1, p. 11.

26. Hughes, chap. 35, p. 419.

The one great exception to the inflexibility of the moderns is the mature John Mill. To say that he was an exception that proves the rule is not the easy escape from unwelcome evidence that it often is. For Mill owed his fine capacity to appreciate ancient wisdom and the weak sides of modern thought, and his readiness to examine opposing arguments on every question, to an accident. Had it not been for the nervous breakdown of 1826, he might well have continued in what he called his early state "of intense philosophic intolerance" rising "from the onesidedness of the understanding, seeing nothing myself but the distorted image, thrown back from many most oblique and twisted reflectors, of *one* side only of the truth." [27] But when he blamed his Benthamite education, however unjustly, for his suffering [28] and reacted against Utilitarian principles, he turned with eager sympathy to the opposite school of Coleridge and Carlyle, Goethe and Fichte (which was conservative, religious, concrete and historical, and poetical). There he found much truth along with much error—precisely his new view of Benthamism—and so concluded that in all controversies men seize on only half of the truth.[29] Furthermore, he also reacted against rigidity itself. For he now deliberately tried "to go *all round* every object" which he surveyed, and to place himself "at all points of view, so as to have the best chance of seeing all sides," and thus became for a time "catholic and tolerant in an extreme degree, and thought onesidedness almost the one great evil in human affairs, seeing it was the evil which had been the bane of my own teachers, and was also that of those who were warring against my teachers." [30] The passage reflects a state of uncritical tolerance ("in an extreme degree") which was only temporary; otherwise it expresses perfectly Mill's lasting flexibility of mind. He was, in fact, later charged with being "a deserter from the proper principles of rigidity and ferocity in which he was brought up." [31] But for the accident of his breakdown that desertion might never have occurred.

It is quite true, of course, that many Victorians, blessed with the English talent for compromise and the English distaste for logical extremes, were neither out-and-out ancients nor out-and-out moderns.

27. *Letters*, 1, 87.
28. *Autobiography*, chap. 5, pp. 115–18.
29. "Coleridge," *Dissertations*, 1, 398–403; *Autobiography*, chap. 7, p. 206; *The Spirit of the Age*, p. 15; "Bentham," *Dissertations*, 1, 356–7.
30. *Letters*, 1, 88.
31. Quoted in Leslie Stephen, *The Life of James Fitzjames Stephen*, p. 308.

Thomas Arnold had no sympathy with either the ultra-Tories or the ultra-Liberals and hated the fearful conflict "between the friends and enemies of the old system of things." [32] But he held his own middle ground with inflexible zeal. The rigid mind is narrow and tight, but not necessarily extreme. That was simply a further tendency in a period of radical change.

Extreme one-sidedness was most conspicuous, perhaps, in the great conflict between science and religion. On the one side, the Christian apologists with their backs to the wall, fighting a life and death struggle, had little sympathy with neutrality or compromise; while the scientists for their part, infuriated by what they considered the blind bigotry of their clerical opponents, often talked as if religion were mere superstition and science alone held the key to every truth. [33] The result was that the individual might find himself under the strongest pressure to choose between two extremes. As early as 1843 people like Kingsley were saying: "A question must be tried—Is intellectual Science, or the Bible, truth; and All Truth?" [34] One or the other. When the "march of intellect" was threatening to destroy all religious belief, the defenders of the faith, whether Evangelical or High Church, demanded unequivocal allegiance. Not to be for us was to be against us. Where do *you* stand? That question is implicit in Hugh Stowell's lecture "The Age We Live In" (1850):

> The time is coming when men must hold their opinions with tenacity. . . . The anchorage which will serve for the calm will not serve for the storm.

> Our day is a day of positivity and decision. . . . Every man is being forced to tell us what he is—what he means—whose side he proposes to take. The war-cry has gone forth, "Who is on the Lord's side? Who?" and we shall soon know our foes, and our friends; who are for us, and who are against us; who are for Christ, and who are against Christ. . . . Never was there in our history . . . a crisis when it was more imperative upon all to ponder well

32. Stanley, *Life*, Appendix D, pp. 704–5, from a letter of July 17, 1830.

33. Cf. George Eliot, letter to Charles Bray, July 5, 1859, in Cross, *Life*, 2, 88: "Free-thinkers are scarcely wider than the orthodox in this matter,—they all want to see themselves and their own opinions held up as the true and the lovely."

34. *Letters and Memories, 1,* 88 (unabridged ed., *1,* 112).

the side they intend to elect, and having made their election, to stand to it and by it to the death.[35]

It is not hard to imagine Stowell's opinion of anyone who tried to follow a middle course, the theist, say, or the Broad Churchman with his liberal interpretation of the Bible. "The Word of God," he says, "must be taken altogether, or rejected altogether. . . . The temple of inspiration must stand as a whole, or fall as a whole. Take out one stone, and you endanger and enfeeble the entire structure." [36] Once fear becomes panic, as we ourselves know only too well, the liberal can be crushed between the right and the left. Frederic Harrison gives us a glimpse of what was happening. In 1852 at Oxford he found a group of earnest unbelievers, notably the Positivists, trying to build up some new system of belief on naturalistic lines.

> Then the few men of mind who set themselves to contend with this terrible delusion, take refuge in a narrow bigotry which destroys their service in the fight—they accept as best they may some consistent dogmatism, and for the most part they ignore the earnestness and the great hopes of these unlucky men, and by treating them as shallow sceptics, they drive them into conduct little more excusable. . . .
>
> R——, I fear, has determined to force himself to accept an exclusiveness of creed, a dogmatism which his intellect ought never to have yielded to, in disgust with surrounding errors.

In this intellectual war Broad Churchmen like the young Harrison were deserted. "Those whom we thought for us are against us," gone

35. Hugh Stowell, "The Age We Live In," in *Exeter Hall Lectures, 6* (1850–51), pp. 56–7, 46–7. Compare, on the other side, the agnostic described by Mark Rutherford, *Autobiography*, p. 119, whose "mind so constantly revolved in one circle, and existed so completely by hostility to the prevailing orthodoxy [that is, Christianity], that belief or disbelief in it was the standard by which he judged men." In this atmosphere what we would call a detached and objective examination of religious history is by no means a virtue. A "purely historical tone" seemed to Thomas Arnold (Stanley, *Life*, p. 434, from a letter of February 4, 1837) "painful to a Christian reader" because "neutrality is almost the same as hostility"— almost the same, that is, when faith is fighting a desperate battle. The first question Arnold asks even of a historian of Rome (ibid., pp. 64–5, from a letter of March 3, 1823) is whether he writes "like a Christian or no," and if not, his book will *ipso facto* be a "disgrace" to the historical part of English literature.

36. Stowell, p. 53.

over to one side or the other; indeed he himself could find no one in his college to stand with him on a middle ground.[37]

2. Puritan Judgment

Though Matthew Arnold held sectarianism responsible for much of Victorian rigidity, he thought the chief culprit was Hebraism. In his famous watchwords Hellenism stands for the open mind, free from prejudice or stiffness, bent on following "with flexible activity the whole play of the universal order," reaching through wide learning and intuitive perception toward the highest wisdom. Hebraism, on the contrary, "seizes upon certain plain, capital intimations of the universal order, and rivets itself, one may say, with unequalled grandeur of earnestness and intensity on the study and observance of them." [38] The intimations are those of a fixed moral law, set down in the Word of God and enforced by the powerful voice of conscience.[39] The Puritan possesses the divine truth. He has only to follow it staunchly—and singly. John Knox, in the words of Carlyle, resembled an old Hebrew prophet: "the same inflexibility, intolerance, rigid narrow-looking adherence to God's truth." [40]

It is this tradition among the Evangelicals and Dissenters which largely accounts for the categorical judgment of human beings. Not entirely, because in the heat of sectarian controversy, as we noticed, men were divided into friends or enemies; or historical figures were treated as outright heroes or outright villains.[41] But this bias was implicit in the Puritan temper. The emphasis on moral character allowed little or no consideration for intellectual and aesthetic virtues; and the moral side itself was judged without regard to the mixed nature of human beings, or the relative gravity of moral failings. By the logic of predestination, with its two and only two categories of the elect and the damned, men were either sheep or goats. There were no in-betweens requiring a judicious weighing

37. *Autobiographic Memoirs, 1*, 104–5.

38. *Culture and Anarchy*, chap. 4, pp. 131–2.

39. Ibid., chap. 5, pp. 145–6.

40. *Heroes and Hero-Worship*, Lecture 4, p. 148. The dogmatic side of this reliance on absolute divine law has been brought out in the previous chapter, sec. 2.

41. In Macaulay's *History* the Whigs are angels and the Tories devils; William is white, James II, black. Among the Anglo-Catholics (see Froude, "The Oxford Counter-Reformation," *Short Studies, 4,* 248), Whigs and revolutionists and all their works are Antichrist: Cranmer is a traitor and Milton a name of horror. But Charles I is a holy and blessed martyr.

of the evidence. How constantly Carlyle talks of the just and the unjust, of heroes and quacks, of work and sham work, of the true and the false. All religion is here to remind us, he says, "of the quiet *infinite* difference there is between a Good man and a Bad; to bid us love infinitely the one, abhor and avoid infinitely the other." [42] In an illuminating passage Morley analyzed the rigid character of contemporary judgment:

> Nowhere has Puritanism done us more harm than in . . . leading us to take all breadth, and colour, and diversity, and fine discrimination, out of our judgments of men, reducing them to thin, narrow, and superficial pronouncements upon the letter of their morality, or the precise conformity of their opinions to accepted standards of truth, religious or other. Among other evils which it has inflicted, this inability to conceive of conduct except as either right or wrong, and, correspondingly in the intellectual order, of teaching except as either true or false, is at the bottom of that fatal spirit of *parti-pris* which has led to the rooting of so much injustice, disorder, immobility, and darkness in English intelligence. [43]

Not only is a character much else besides being virtuous or vicious —indeed many great men have not been notable for their morality —but the moral qualities themselves are so various as to preclude any simple attitude of praise or blame. The example Morley offers of the failure to appreciate these considerations is significant, since the choice of Macaulay, the son of a prominent Evangelical, shows how readily Puritanism could support the exaggerations of sectarian judgment: "To a man like Macaulay, for example, criticism was only a tribunal before which men were brought to be decisively tried by one or two inflexible tests, and then sent to join the sheep on the one hand, or the goats on the other. His pages are the record of sentences passed, not the presentation of human characters in all their fulness and colour." [44] In the same vein is Kingsley's answer to his

42. *Past and Present*, Bk. 3, chap. 15, p. 227.
43. "Carlyle," *Critical Miscellanies*, 1, 182.
44. Ibid., p. 184. For the same handling of character in the Victorian novel, see Lord David Cecil, *Early Victorian Novelists* (London, 1934), pp. 101, 127–9, 302. Morley views Carlyle as an exception to this tendency, mainly because of his greater tolerance of sin, in an essay like that on Burns. But if he did not define "good" and "bad" so narrowly, so morally one might say, as the average Evangelical, Carlyle employed the same one-or-the-other pattern of judgment.

daughter when she asked him, "Who was Heine?" "A wicked man, my dear." [45]

Since the smallest moral failings no less than the greatest were considered so much evidence of a dangerous state of the soul, the Puritan judgment did not try to weigh them on the basis of any relative seriousness. They were condemned outright as evil. Kingsley was as famous as Thomas Arnold for his "detestation and abhorrence of sin and wrong-doing, and especially of all little, mean, dirty sins, which most men gloss over"—and some men try to measure judiciously in a flexible scale of values. [46] At Rugby Arnold showed "his loathing and abhorrence of evil" by his "severe rebukes for individual faults" and "the startling earnestness with which he would check in a moment the slightest approach to levity or impertinence." He drew a sharp distinction between "mere amusement and such as encroached on the next day's duties, when, as he pointed out, 'it immediately becomes what St. Paul calls *revelling.*'" "'Nowhere,' he said, in speaking to some boys on bad behaviour during prayers at the boardinghouse, 'nowhere is Satan's work more evidently manifest than in turning holy things to ridicule.'" Even recitations in this world are good or bad, but never passable. Stanley remembered "the pleased look and the cheerful 'Thank you,' which followed upon a successful answer or translation; the fall of his countenance with its deepening severity, the stern elevation of the eyebrows, the sudden 'Sit down' which followed upon the reverse." [47]

3. *The Need for Rigidity*

Arnold's second definition of inflexibility as an intense energetic absorption in one particular pursuit is partly a reflection of Victorian business. Under the high pressure of competitive life—in the professions as well as in trade—there was no time for wide and varied interests. All of a man's energy and attention was required for his work. And this was even made a duty: "Milton men ought to have

45. *Letters and Memories, 1,* 202 (unabridged ed., *1,* 228).

46. Ibid., *2,* 141 (unabridged ed., *2,* 127). For the gravity of small faults, see below, p. 232.

47. The quotations are from Stanley's *Life,* chap. 3, pp. 122, 153. The account of Arnold in Fitzjames Stephen's review of *Tom Brown's School Days,* in *Edinburgh Review, 107* (1858), 183–90, is, in effect, an essay on his rigidity. Among other points, he speaks (p. 183) of his being so anxious for the removal or destruction of anything he thought evil that "he was hardly capable of forming a cool judgment on its extent or intensity."

their thoughts and powers absorbed in the work of to-day," remarks
the mother of John Thornton, the mill owner. Margaret Hale demurs:
"Surely, if the mind is too long directed to one object only, it will
get stiff and rigid, and unable to take in many interests." But Mrs.
Thornton has her answer ready:

> "Having many interests does not suit the life of a Milton manu-
> facturer. It is, or ought to be, enough for him to have one great
> desire, and to bring all the purposes of his life to bear on the
> fulfilment of that."
>
> "And that is—?" asked Mr. Hale.
>
> Her sallow cheek flushed, and her eye lightened, as she an-
> swered—
>
> "To hold and maintain a high, honourable place among the
> merchants of his country—the men of his town." [48]

Mrs. Thornton, of course, was right: that ambition could only be
achieved by concentrated focus and tenacity. The Victorians were
perhaps the most John Bullish generation in English history; which
is to say, with Havelock Ellis, that "they were men of great character;
slow-witted, often dominated by a single aim, with difficulty taking
up new positions, but inflexibly tenacious of the positions once attained"—qualities of inestimable value "in ages of ferocious struggle." [49]

In one of his essays J. B. Mozley described a person who sounds
very much like John Thornton. He was a man who grasped particular
ideas very tightly but did not take in a field of balance and comparison.
What he saw he saw clearly and pointedly, and had no desire to
extend his vision any further.[50] But this Victorian was not a businessman. He was a scholar who had been deeply involved in the religious
problems of the time: Blanco White. After quoting a series of remarks
from White's autobiography—"My doubts seem to increase every
day"; "I feel tired and bewildered"; a reference to prayer that he
may "be defended from the spirit of unbelief" and to a question,
"But what am I to do—am I to shut my eyes and abstain from
further inquiry?"—Mozley continues: "Thus agitated and alternating,
towards the end of 1818 he puts down on paper a formal description
of his faith—what he believed, and what he did not." Then comes

48. Mrs. Gaskell, *North and South*, chap. 15, pp. 132–3.
49. Havelock Ellis, *The Nineteenth Century. An Utopian Retrospect*, p. 151.
50. *Essays Historical and Theological*, 2, 69.

a perceptive comment: "He does it to have a safeguard for himself, a barrier against further assaults, and a *locus standi*." [51] The longing to believe under the painful pressure of doubt leads to a saving belief that is not a conviction but a protection against further distress. Henceforth it will be held by the will (since it is intellectually insecure) and held with a tenacity that can brook no examination of opposing arguments that might reawaken the old anxieties.

It is quite true, as Lecky once said, that human nature has never preferred a flexible search for truth to a rigid attachment to the familiar and traditional, and has always tended to shut out "every consideration that could shake or qualify cherished beliefs." [52] But to Victorian human nature this became something like a necessity. The woman who did not care to know about anybody's views or reasons which would not confirm her in her own could have lived in any age; what is particularly Victorian is her motive: she was determined "in the midst of confusion, to hold tight where she had got footing." [53] That psychology is often found in the letters of Kingsley. As he becomes aware of the disturbing differences between the teaching of St. Paul, St. James, and St. John, he reassures himself by saying that at any rate "some things I see clearly, and hold with *desperate* clutch." [54] But the adjective betrays the panicky fear that even those things are none too clear—not clear enough to be held at arm's length. "I feel," he confesses on another occasion, "a capacity of drifting to sea in me which makes me cling nervously to any little anchor, like subscription [to the Thirty-Nine Articles]. I feel glad of aught that says to me, 'You must teach this and nothing else.'" [55] In one letter he actually makes the link between the psychology of

51. *Ibid.*, pp. 105–6.

52. *Map of Life*, chap. 4, pp. 31–2.

53. Harriet Martineau, *Autobiography*, 2, Period VI, sec. 6, p. 367. Cf. Packe, *Life of Mill*, p. 161, where he speaks of Carlyle "binding himself fast to the rigid masthead of belief" and goes on to say, "His constant preoccupation with the exclusion of opinions not agreeable to his own made him defiant, suspicious and eventually cruel."

54. *Letters and Memories*, 2, 9 (unabridged ed., *1*, 468). The italics are his.

55. Ibid., 2, 205 (unabridged ed., 2, 218). Cf. George Eliot in 1839, when she was still an Evangelical but was experiencing more and more doubt (Cross, *Life*, *1*, 45–6, letter to Miss Lewis, September 4): "A single word is sometimes enough to give an entirely new mould to our thoughts,—at least I find myself so constituted; and therefore to me it is preeminently important to be anchored within the veil, so that outward things may be unable to send me adrift."

doubt and the rigid mind. He has just called the fact that "so few of us deeply believe anything" the curse of our generation, and then continues:

> My friend, we must pray to God to give us faith; faith in some-thing—something that we can live for, and would die for. Then we shall be ready and able to do good in our generation. Our fixed ideas will be to us Archimedes' fulcra in space, from whence, if need be, he could move the world. Get hold of some one truth. Let it blaze in your sky, like a Greenland sun, never setting day or night. Give your soul up to it; see it in everything, and everything in it.[56]

It could be said that sectarianism and Puritanism both tended to fix the mind on some one truth which was seen in everything. But neither of them ever exalted the closed mind into an ideal goal. It took the agony of doubt to do that.

4. The Open and Flexible Mind

At this point we are confronted by a paradox. The Victorian mind was rigid and dogmatic, but it was criticized, we see, by Matthew Arnold and Mill, by Morley and Hughes and J. B. Mozley; and the list could be extended to a score of names.[57] It looks as if the open and flexible mind was also Victorian. Indeed, one might even argue that in one sense it was more Victorian because, unlike the rigid-dogmatic mind with its long history, it was largely indigenous to the nineteenth century. Though by no means new, in fact or theory, it was perhaps more common in the fifties and sixties and more emphatically extolled as a supreme virtue than had ever been the case in the past. Bagehot's essay on Macaulay (1856), Mill's *On Liberty* (1859), Lecky's *Religious Tendencies of the Age* (1860), the *Poems* of Clough (1862), Arnold's *Essays in Criticism* (1865), notably the preface and "The Function of Criticism," followed by his

56. *Letters and Memories, 1,* 113 (unabridged ed., *1,* 141). For a striking con-trast, in this respect, between the Romantics and the Victorians, cf. Keats, letter of September 1819, to George and Georgiana Keats—*The Letters of John Keats,* ed. M. B. Forman (2 vols. London, 1931), *2,* 466: "The only means of strengthen-ing one's intellect is to make up one's mind about nothing—to let the mind be a thoroughfare for all thoughts."

57. They would include F. D. Maurice, Arthur Clough, Walter Bagehot, W. E. H. Lecky, Leslie Stephen, Henry Sidgwick, Mark Pattison, Lord Acton, and Walter Pater.

Culture and Anarchy (1869) and Pater's *Renaissance* (1873)—all struck at one-sided and dogmatic opinions and pled for a more detached and supple intelligence. By 1869 Henry Sidgwick could speak of a remarkable change in intellectual habits during the previous twenty years. He was writing of Clough:

> His point of view and habit of mind are less singular in England in the year 1869 than they were in 1859, and much less than they were in 1849. . . . We are growing . . . more sceptical in the proper sense of the word: we suspend our judgment much more than our predecessors, and much more contentedly: we see that there are many sides to many questions: the opinions that we do hold we hold if not more loosely, at least more at arm's length: we can imagine how they appear to others, and can conceive ourselves not holding them. . . . We are gaining in impartiality and comprehensiveness of sympathy.[58]

In short, it might be said that beneath the dominant tendency of the Victorian mind the opposite ideal was present and gaining momentum until by the sixties it became dominant itself among the intellectuals.[59] The change can be visualized as the swing of a seesaw on the fulcrum of public debate. The very conflict of ideas that issued in dogmatic one-sidedness forced the more intelligent Victorians to recognize that most questions were many-sided. After witnessing the clash of warring sects, men might come to Matthew Arnold's conclusion:

> To try and approach truth on one side after another, not to strive or cry, nor to persist in pressing forward, on any one side, with violence and self-will,—it is only thus, it seems to me, that mortals may hope to gain any vision of the mysterious Goddess, whom we shall never see except in outline, but only thus even in outline. He who will do nothing but fight impetuously towards her on his own, one, favourite, particular line, is inevitably destined to run his head into the folds of the black robe in which she is wrapped.[60]

58. *Miscellaneous Essays and Addresses*, p. 60.

59. Cf. G. M. Young, *Victorian England*, p. 186: "As I see it, the function of the nineteenth century was to disengage the disinterested intelligence, to release it from the entanglements of party and sect—one might almost add, of sex—and to set it operating over the whole range of human life and circumstance."

60. Preface to *Essays in Criticism, First Series*, pp. vii–viii. Cf. John Holloway, *The Victorian Sage* (London, 1953), p. 203, where he remarks that Arnold's work

That passage, with its retention of the Victorian faith in the possibility of truth, defines one type of the open mind and suggests its dialectical method. The theory that truth lies in a mediation between opposing doctrines, both of which are partly true, and that therefore the progress of truth depends on the synthesis of opposites, was perhaps the most influential idea which Coleridge derived from German philosophy (where it was developed especially by Hegel) and passed on directly to both Mill and F. D. Maurice. The latter's *Kingdom of Christ* (1837) is partly an examination of religious opinion in England intended to show that each sect possessed a portion of divine truth in what it asserted, and was wrong in its denial of the truth affirmed by others. All of Maurice's work, in fact, is an attempt to mediate in this way between the right and the left.[61] In 1840 Mill's influential essay on Coleridge attacked "the noisy conflict of half-truths, angrily denying one another," and argued that "in almost every one of the leading controversies, past or present, in social philosophy, both sides were in the right in what they affirmed, though wrong in what they denied; and that if either could have been made to take the other's views in addition to its own, little more would have been needed to make its doctrine correct"[62]—that is to say, if either could have been flexible instead of rigid. Some years later, in 1854, Mill brought his dialectic to bear directly on the intellectual sin of the early Victorians:

> In the last age the writers of reputation and influence were those who took a side, in a very decided manner, on the great questions, religious, moral, metaphysical, and political; who were downright infidels or downright Christians, thorough Tories or thorough democrats, and in that were considered, and were, extreme in their opinions. In the present age the writers of reputation and influence are those who take something from both sides of the great controversies, and make out that neither extreme is right, nor wholly wrong. . . .
>
> This change is explained, and partly justified, by the super-

---

inculcates not a set of beliefs "but simply certain habits and a certain temper of mind," that is, flexible habits and an open temper. His essay, pp. 202–43, explores that thesis.

61. Frederick Maurice, *Life of F. D. Maurice,* 1, 56, 203, 336, 338, and passim; in *The Kingdom of Christ,* see especially the end of the "Introductory Dialogue," and for his debt to Coleridge, the "Dedication."

62. *Dissertations,* 1, 398–9. For the main statements of his dialectic, see above, note 29.

ficiality, and real onesidedness, of the bolder thinkers who preceded. But if I mistake not, the time is now come, or coming,
for a change the reverse way.[63]

This is rather a statement of hope or desire than fact; and after
Darwin, rival battle-lines were again drawn tight. But a change the
reverse way was coming.

Indeed, more of a change than Mill and his fellow Victorians
desired. The only open mind they admired was one with convictions
or at the least in search of convictions. But in the sixties quite another
type of mind began to appear, equally free from rigidity and dogmatism, but free also from any earnest concern for truth. Instead
of a genuine effort at mediation, men began to accept any convenient compromise, however loose and vague. In place of trying to
decide how much validity there was in a given idea, they were
adopting a broad-minded toleration of all ideas regardless of their
intrinsic value. To some extent these related developments were a
product of liberalism. "Many people in our time," wrote John Morley,
the leading disciple of Mill, "have so ill understood the doctrine of
liberty, that in some of the most active circles in society they now
count you a bigot if you hold any proposition to be decidedly and
unmistakably more true than any other." [64] A good liberal is now one
who will look to some 'reasonable' compromise or come to no conclusion at all. But the basic source of this indifference was the historical
relativism that began to emerge about 1870. For once all truths are
considered relative only to a given time and place, they become
simply materials for a history of thought over which the mind plays
with easy flexibility. People are quite willing "to look on collections
of mutually hostile opinions with the same kind of curiosity which they
bestow on a collection of mutually hostile beasts in a menagerie.
They have very faint predilections for one rather than another." [65]
Morley the Victorian was infuriated by this attitude. He called it
"elegant Pyrrhonism" and "light-hearted neutrality"; and he charged
the younger generation with making intellectual sport of the most
serious problems of human existence.

But that was scarcely just. To understand the temper of post-

63. *Letters*, 2, 360–1.
64. "Mr. Mill's Autobiography" (1874), *Critical Miscellanies*, 3, 63.
65. Morley, *On Compromise*, chap. 3, p. 106. This and p. 105 are the references for the remarks that follow. The skeptical effect of the "historic method"
is described in chap. 1, pp. 18–21. As the title suggests, this book is the classic
attack on the new frame of mind.

Victorian skepticism in the seventies, we have to go to someone who knew it from the inside, to a man like W. H. Mallock. In his *New Republic* (1877) he has Mr. Herbert (Ruskin) say to the assembled guests: "What do you do then in this perplexity—this halting between two opinions? Why, you do this. You try to persuade yourselves that neither opinion is of much moment—that the question cannot be decided absolutely—that it should not be decided absolutely—in fact, that it is one of your chief glories that you leave it undecided." [66] There is nothing light-hearted or elegant about that. Weary of the futile struggle to choose between conflicting opinions, the post-Victorians were ready to welcome skepticism because it put an end to the whole business. And having done so, they made a virtue of necessity and boasted, with a convenient appeal to liberalism, of having tolerant and undecided minds. Or they turned cynical out of sheer disillusionment. [67]

But by the nineties, and still more so after Freud showed, or seemed to show, that all convictions were rationalizations of emotional needs, the attitude of elegant skepticism became fashionable; and in the 1920's the open mind—open like a sieve—became a mark of intellectual sophistication. That phase is over. We are now too much in need of beliefs and too envious of anyone who knows what he believes to view Victorian rigidity and dogmatism with much complacent superiority. We are ready to agree with Morley that though "the partisan temperament is no gift in a judge, and it is well for everybody to see that most questions have two sides," it is a pity, to say the least, "never to be sure which side is right, and to remain as 'a cake that is not turned.'" [68] What we want (how to get it is another matter) is precisely the type of mind which Mill conceived of: one that will combine earnestness with tolerance, "the strength of an ordered set of convictions, with that pliability and that receptiveness in face of new truth, which are indispensable to these very convictions being held intelligently and in their best attainable form." [69]

66. Pages 279–80.
67. In 1877 Mark Pattison—"The Age of Reason," *Fortnightly Review*, new ser. 21 (1877), 351—spoke of our "present mood of depression and despondency . . . our cynical indifference, which yawns over its own utterances."
68. *Notes on Politics and History* (New York, 1914), pp. 19–20.
69. This is a summary statement by Morley, "Mr. Mill's Autobiography," p. 62.

Part III

MORAL ATTITUDES

Chapter 8

THE COMMERCIAL SPIRIT

> I do not know any thing more dreadful than a state of
> mind which is, perhaps, the characteristic of this coun-
> try, and which the prosperity of this country so miser-
> ably fosters. I mean that ambitious spirit, to use a great
> word, but I know no other word to express my mean-
> ing—that low ambition which sets every one on the
> look-out to succeed and to rise in life, to amass money,
> to gain power, to depress his rivals, to triumph over
> his hitherto superiors, to affect a consequence and a
> gentility which he had not before.
>
> *Newman, 1836* [1]

THE COMMERCIAL SPIRIT has always existed in human society.
What was peculiar to the nineteenth century was its "overbalance:"
it became the "paramount principle of action in the nation at large." [2]
This emphasis, consequent on the great increase of business activity
which accompanied the Agrarian and Industrial Revolutions, had
emerged before 1830, and by then had become an established fact,
recognized by John Sterling in "The State of Society in England"
(1828) and by Southey in his *Colloquies on Society* (1829). *"Wealth!
wealth! wealth! Praise be to the god of the nineteenth century! The
golden idol! the mighty Mammon!* Such are the accents of the time,
such the cry of the nation. . . . There may be here and there an
individual, who does not spend his heart in labouring for riches; but

1. *Parochial and Plain Sermons*, 8, No. 11, 159.
2. Coleridge, "A Lay Sermon Addressed to the Higher and Middle Classes"
(1817), *Biographia Literaria and Two Lay Sermons*, pp. 424–5. See the whole
sermon passim. The date is one evidence for what I say in the next sentence. Perhaps the best revelation of the commercial spirit in Victorian society is to be found
in three novels of George Eliot's, *The Mill on the Floss* (1860), *Felix Holt* (1866),
and especially *Middlemarch* (1872). Nearly all of the related attitudes described
in this chapter are there embodied in the concreteness of art.

there is nothing approaching to a class of persons actuated by any other desire."[3] As Sterling implies, the worship of Mammon was not confined to business circles. It was almost as common among the landed as the monied aristocracy.[4] It infected all the professions. "Even artists and men of letters, with here and there a brilliant exception, let the bankers' book become more and more the criterion of their being on the right road."[5] Tom Brown discovered that at Oxford itself "the worship of the golden calf was verily and indeed rampant . . . side by side, no doubt, with much that was manly and noble, but tainting more or less the whole life of the place."[6]

1. Respectability

In the middle classes the passion for wealth was closely connected with another, for respectability. Indeed, their economic struggle was focused less on the comforts and luxuries which had hitherto lain beyond their reach than on the respect which money could now command. "From early childhood, the sayings and doings of all around them" indoctrinated the Victorians with "the idea, that wealth and respectability are two sides of the same thing," and prompted "the expenditure of all their energies in money-making."[7] Comparing French with English society, Mill pointed out that in the former "any man who can dress decently may dine with or go to the soirées of anybody, and mix on terms of perfect equality with all whom he meets"; and consequently there was "very little of the artificial demand for mere *money* which the striving and straining for respectability occasions here."[8]

The increasing emphasis on riches produced a new attitude toward poverty. In the past it had been pitied, relieved, or ignored, and only rarely considered an object of scorn or a source of shame. But now Tom Brown at Oxford soon learned "that poverty is a disgrace to a Briton, and that, until you know a man thoroughly, you

3. Sterling, *Essays and Tales*, 2, 25. Cf. Southey, 2, 246.

4. See Stanley, *Life of Arnold*, chap. 6, p. 243; Coleridge, "A Lay Sermon," pp. 416, 430–1; and Carlyle, quoted below, pp. 239–40.

5. J. A. Froude, "On Progress," *Short Studies*, 2, 386–7.

6. Hughes, *Tom Brown at Oxford*, chap. 6, p. 60, reflecting his own impression in the early forties.

7. Spencer, "The Morals of Trade," *Essays: Scientific, Political, and Speculative*, 2, 141; and see the general discussion of the commercial spirit on pp. 139–48. Cf. John Cumming, "The Age We Live In," in *Exeter Hall Lectures*, 3 (1847–48), 364: "To be a 'respectable' man means to be rich."

8. *Letters*, 1, 74. The date is 1833.

must always" assume that "he is the owner of unlimited ready money." His friend Hardy, who was a servitor, not only found himself looked down upon but was so carried along by "the spirit of the place" he became for the first time "ashamed" of being poor.[9]

In itself wealth alone was hardly enough to make a Victorian respectable. He had not only to be rich but to be a gentleman; [10] so that the struggle for money in the middle class was complemented, and to a considerable extent motivated, by the struggle for social advancement.[11] At first, however, in the earlier decades of the century, that was not the case. Disraeli's Millbank, for example, was "a capitalist as anxious to raise a monument of the skill and power of his order as to obtain a return for the great investment"; and he proudly attributed the transformation of forest land into an area of thriving population and large financial returns to Saxon (i.e. middle-class) industry, competing successfully with Norman (i.e. aristocratic) manners.[12] And Mrs. Gaskell's John Thornton wanted only to be the head of a firm that should be known for generations, even in "foreign countries and far-away seas." [13] To be a merchant prince was a far finer thing than to be a gentleman; or, as Wingfield-Stratford put it, men like Bright and Cobden "were too proud to be gentlemen." A respectable British citizen, with top hat and frock coat all complete, was on a level with any lord in the land.[14] But by the 1840's all this was becoming old-fashioned. The younger generation was determined to push—and buy—its way into the upper classes: to exchange trade for a profession and Dissent for the Church of England; to own a gig and, if possible, a country estate, perhaps even a title. Their representative, in contrast to Millbank or Thornton, is Alton Locke's

9. Hughes, *Tom Brown at Oxford*, chap. 5, p. 48, and chap. 8, p. 86. Cf. Sterling, pp. 26, 37; Emerson, *English Traits*, chap. 10, "Wealth," in *Works*, 5, 149–50; and Bulwer Lytton's remark in 1833 (*England and the English*, p. 33): "In other countries poverty is a misfortune,—with us it is a crime."

10. And also, of course, to observe the moral proprieties. The moral component of respectability, which lies outside the commercial spirit, is dealt with later, on pp. 353–8, 419.

11. After attacking "the passion for making money" in the Sermon "God and Mammon," *Westminster Sermons*, in *Works*, 18, 293, Kingsley notes the standard answer (p. 295): "If I wish to rise in life, if I wish my children to rise in life, how can I do it, without making money?"

12. *Coningsby*, in *Works*, 12, chap. 25, pp. 216, 223–4.

13. *North and South*, chap. 50, p. 500. In chap. 20, p. 194, he insists that to be a "true man" is far better than to be a "gentleman."

14. *The Making of a Gentleman* (London, 1938), p. 273.

uncle, who began life as a clerk in a grocery store, then became foreman and married his master's blooming widow, "and rose and rose, year by year, till . . . he was owner of a first-rate grocery establishment in the City, and a pleasant villa near Herne Hill, and had a son . . . at King's College, preparing for Cambridge and the Church—that being now-a-days the approved method of converting a tradesman's son into a gentleman." [15] But the struggle for social advancement, like that for wealth, was not limited to merchants and manufacturers. By 1840 Mill was saying that "that entire unfixedness in the social position of individuals—that treading upon the heels of one another—that habitual dissatisfaction of each with the position he occupies, and eager desire to push himself into the next above it" had become or was becoming a characteristic of the nation. No one seems to care any longer to cultivate "the pleasures or the virtues corresponding to his station in society, but solely to get out of it as quickly as possible." [16]

It was the continued existence of class lines at the same time that the dividing barriers were breaking down, consequent upon the increasing wealth of the bourgeoisie and the declining wealth of the aristocracy, which made this ambition practical, and without which the keen incentive to economic battle would not have existed. The distinguishing feature of the Victorian social structure was its mean between the extremes of equality (in France and the United States)

15. Kingsley, *Alton Locke*, chap. 2, p. 18; cf. the start of chap. 13, p. 147. The older merchant attitude toward the universities, which is found as we might expect in *North and South*, is given above, p. 116. Now, as Hughes says in *Tom Brown at Oxford*, chap. 3, p. 26, in a remark which largely explains the worship of wealth and scorn of poverty at Oxford already noted: "Two out of the three were the sons of rich men who had made their own fortunes, and sent their sons to St. Ambrose's because it was very desirable that the young gentlemen should make good connexions. In fact, the fathers looked upon the University as a good investment, and gloried much in hearing their sons talk familiarly in the vacations of their dear friends Lord Harry This and Sir George That." The analogous career for young girls is described by Thackeray, with reference to Ethel Newcome, in *The Newcomes*, chap. 45, p. 475: "Oh me! what a confession it is, in the very outset of life and blushing brightness of youth's morning, to own that the aim with which a young girl sets out, and the object of her existence, is to marry a rich man; that she was endowed with beauty so that she might buy wealth, and a title with it; that as sure as she has a soul to be saved, her business here on earth is to try and get a rich husband. That is the career for which many a woman is bred and trained."

16. "Democracy in America," *Dissertations*, 2, 65–6, and cf. 14–15.

and of irremovable inequalities (in the East, and still existing, substantially, in most European countries).[17] Either extreme would have
made the struggle to rise unnecessary or futile. But in a system of
removable inequalities, where the aristocracy was prepared to inter-
marry with the new rich and the gentry to accept into county society
(if not at once, in a few years) the commoner who bought an estate,
there existed the indispensable combination of opportunity and incentive. No doubt this had always been true to some extent, but
the system had become noticeably more flexible. It seemed to Frances
Cobbe that "life among all classes in the last generation" (1800–30)
was "much less a struggle than it is with us" because class lines were
then "more marked, and there was very little possibility of rising . . .
into higher grades of society."[18] The contrasting picture of the present
generation was drawn by Ruskin: "The very removal of the massy
bars which once separated one class of society from another, has
rendered it tenfold more shameful in foolish people's, *i.e.*, in most
people's eyes, to remain in the lower grades of it, than ever it was
before. . . . Now that a man may make money, and rise in the
world, and associate himself, unreproached, with people once far
above him . . . it becomes a veritable shame to him to remain in
the state he was born in, and everybody thinks it is his *duty* to try to
be a 'gentleman.' "[19]

We should recognize here the precision and the novelty of the
word "duty." Formerly it had simply meant the obligation to fulfill
one's calling: everyone was "to do his duty in that state of life to
which it had pleased God to call him." But that was alien to both
the principles and the temper of the new era. "To push on, to climb
vigorously on the slippery steps of the social ladder, to raise ourselves
one step or more out of the rank of life in which we were born, is
now converted into a duty."[20] The reference is to the liberal theory

17. Bagehot, "Sterne and Thackeray," *Works*, 2, 190–2.
18. "The Nineteenth Century," *Fraser's Magazine, 69* (1864), 482.
19. "Pre-Raphaelitism" (1851), *Works, 12*, 342. In "Of Kings' Treasuries"
(1864), *Sesame and Lilies*, in *Works, 18*, 54–5, Ruskin points out that the education which parents now want for their children is one which will "lead to
advancement in life." This is another aspect of the antiliberal, vocational attitude
toward education which was discussed in the chapter on anti-intellectualism: see
above, Chap. 5, sec. 1, passim. For another link between that chapter and this
one, see below, note 39.
20. Froude, "England and Her Colonies," *Short Studies, 2*, 206.

that to do the best for yourself was to do the best for society. Social ambition, driving one to the utmost economic effort, was the blessed means of social progress. Beatrice Webb has described the creed of self-advancement as she knew it in her own home:

> It was the bounden duty of every citizen to better his social status; to ignore those beneath him, and to aim steadily at the top rung of the social ladder. Only by this persistent pursuit by each individual of his own and his family's interest would the highest general level of civilisation be attained. . . . No one of the present generation realises with what sincerity and fervour these doctrines were held by the representative men and women of the mid-Victorian middle class.[21]

When duty and respectability combined to make gentility the goal of existence, the phenomenon of snobbery was pervasive. To pretend to be higher in the social scale than one really was, or to cultivate and flatter one's superiors while he despised and insulted his inferiors, without reference in either case to moral or intellectual merits—these were the tendencies which Thackeray in particular explored through all their ramifications, starting with *The Book of Snobs* (1848) and continuing in the novels. One particular form he dissected provides an amusing contrast with the "honest" pride of the early industrialists in their own class. It may be called the snobbish pride of not being snobbish. Mrs. Hobson Newcome "will not bow down to kiss the hand of a haughty aristocracy. She is a merchant's wife and an attorney's daughter. There is no pride about her. Her brother-in-law, poor dear Brian . . . was welcome, after banking-hours, to forsake his own friends for his wife's fine relations, and to dangle after lords and ladies in Mayfair. She had no such absurd vanity—not she." At her own soirées one met something far finer than fashionable people, namely, a motley group of travelers, poets, and painters of dubious genius, collected on the principle she expounds to Colonel Newcome: "If I can be the means—the *humble* means—to bring men of genius together—mind to associate with mind—men of all nations to mingle in *friendly unison*—I shall not have lived *altogether* in vain. . . . I do not say there are not in our own family persons who worship mere wordly rank, and think but of fashion and gaiety; but such, I

---

21. *My Apprenticeship*, p. 13. By the same reasoning it was a woman's duty to make a "good" marriage: see below, pp. 381–2.

trust, will never be the objects in life of me and *my* children. We are but merchants: we seek to be *no more.*" [22]

2. The Bourgeois Dream

In a business society, and one that was strongly under Puritan influence, work was an absolute necessity. Without it there was no hope of achieving the twin goals of life—respectability and salvation. Hence, parents and preachers, writers and lecturers, proclaimed as with a single voice that man was created to work, that everyone had his appointed calling in which he was to labor for God and man, that idleness was a moral and a social sin. Pigeon-shooting aristocrats living in parasitic luxury were special objects of clerical and middle-class scorn. If a man were rich enough not to work, he was to do good works among the poor or serve his country in public office, local or national.[23] And so, after reading hundreds of passages on the necessity and obligation to work, one comes with a start on a remark of Gladstone's: "How are we to secure to labor its due honor? . . . How are we to make ourselves believe . . . that in the sight of God and man labor is honorable and idleness is contemptible?" [24] The desperate tone of almost hopeless insistence betrays the strength of exactly the opposite values. The truth is, however paradoxical it may seem, that the businessman who thought of work as a supreme duty dreamed of retiring from work—into idleness; and those who made the idle aristocrat an object of scorn found him also an object of envy. The son of Alton Locke's old employer, "fired with the great spirit of the nineteenth century . . . resolved to make haste to be rich" so that he could emulate the dozens of men who had begun business long after his old-fashioned, slow-money-making father, and "had now retired to luxurious ease and suburban villas." [25] The hero of Froude's *Nemesis of Faith* lives in a provincial town where there are many "business people, who have either retired from business themselves,

22. *The Newcomes*, chap. 5, p. 45; chap. 8, p. 84.

23. For a full discussion of work, see below, Chap. 10, sec. 4.

24. *The Might of Right. From the Writings of William Ewart Gladstone*, selected by E. E. Brown (Boston, 1880), p. 273. When Lecky noticed a change in public opinion during the reign of Victoria with regard to work (*Map of Life*, chap. 6, p. 64), the best he could claim was that now (in 1899) "young men who are really idle pretend to be busy." On p. 59 he even predicts that in the future "a life of idleness will be regarded with much less tolerance than at present."

25. Kingsley, *Alton Locke*, chap. 10, p. 109.

or have withdrawn their families out of its atmosphere to make idle ladies and gentlemen of them." [26]

These statements explain the paradox. For one thing, the ambitious merchant or manufacturer who exalted work valued idleness as a badge of status: it showed, as the saying went, that one was "a gentleman of independent means." But more important, even as he threw himself ardently into his work, he longed for a life of ease. Not of mere ease—*luxurious* ease. At the heart of the bourgeois dream was the ideal of gracious living, symbolized by the country house. The middle-class businessman longed to escape from drudgery in hideous surroundings into a world of beauty and leisure, a life of dignity and peace, from which sordid anxieties were shut out.[27] This was the vision which the "Goddess of Getting-on" held up before the Bradford captains of industry.

> Your ideal of human life then is, I think, that it should be passed in a *pleasant undulating world*, with iron and coal everywhere underneath it. On each *pleasant bank* of this world is to be a *beautiful mansion*, with two wings; and stables, and coachhouses; *a moderately-sized park;* a *large garden* and hot-houses; and *pleasant carriage* drives through the shrubberies. In this mansion are to live the favoured votaries of the Goddess; the English gentleman, with his *gracious wife*, and his *beautiful family;* he always able to have the boudoir and the jewels for the wife, and the *beautiful ball dresses* for the daughters, and hunters for the sons, and a shooting in the Highlands for himself.[28]

Nothing is said there about social prestige. In the words I have italicized Ruskin defines the kind of life that is dreamed of, utterly removed from the smoke and dirt and grimy battles of the mill. This and no mere do-nothing rest is the content of "idleness."

26. Page 62. Cf. Mr. Bridmain in George Eliot's "The Sad Fortunes of the Reverend Amos Barton" (*Scenes of Clerical Life, 1,* chap. 4, p. 53) who made a moderate fortune in the silk business "that enabled him to retire . . . to study politics, the weather, and the art of conversation at his leisure." Mill, in *The Principles of Political Economy* (Bk. IV, chap. 6, sec. 2, p. 749), speaks of "numbers of individuals" passing over every year "from the class of the occupied rich to that of the unoccupied." Cf. George Orwell, "Dickens," *Critical Essays* (London, 1946), pp. 41–3, on "the strange, empty dream of the eighteenth- and nineteenth-century middle bourgeoisie . . . a dream of *complete idleness.*"

27. Cf. Wingfield-Stratford, *The Making of a Gentleman,* p. 275.

28. "Traffic," *The Crown of Wild Olive,* in *Works, 18,* 453.

3. Success

Much as each was desired, money, respectability, "lovely ease"—
none of them was the chief idol of the commercial spirit or the
major motivation of the economic struggle. The *summum bonum*
for everyone not born into the aristocracy was success. To win the
race of life, to outdistance your competitors, to reach the top and
hold a position in which *you* gave the orders that others executed—
this was the crowning glory. At the end of a hard struggle from
obscurity to the head of a great factory, Mr. Thornton in *North and
South* is proud to say that he has raised himself "to a level from
which he might see and read the great game of worldly success, and
honestly, by such far-sightedness, command more power and influence
than in any other mode of life." That indeed was the "idea" of the
mercantile life from which he had started. " 'Her merchants be like
princes,' " his mother had said, "reading the text aloud, as if it were
a trumpet-call to invite her boy to the struggle." [29] This is not fiction
but fact. Daniel Gooch, engineer and inventor, who rose to be chairman of the Great Western Railway—and Sir Daniel as well—once
quoted to his workmen a sentence his mother had repeated to him
every morning as he went to work, the "beautiful" sentence which
Matthew Arnold treasured "as Mrs. Gooch's Golden Rule, or the
Divine Injunction 'Be ye Perfect' done into British": *"Ever remember,
my dear Dan, that you should look forward to being some day
manager of that concern!"* [30] And with that end in view 20,000 young
men in the year of publication (1859) and 130,000 more in the next
thirty years bought Samuel Smiles' handbook to success called *Self-
Help*.

In this environment failure is the worst fate one can imagine.
"What is it," asks Carlyle, "that the modern English soul does, in
very truth, dread infinitely, and contemplate with entire despair?
What *is* his Hell? . . . With hesitation, with astonishment, I pronounce it to be: The terror of 'Not succeeding.' " [31] "Terror" is scarcely
too strong a word. To be left behind in the race of life was not
only to be defeated, it was to be exposed to the same kind of scorn
and humiliation visited upon poverty (itself a symbol of failure). The
Victorian world "huzzas at prosperity, and turns away from mis-

29. Mrs. Gaskell, *North and South*, chap. 50, p. 500.
30. *Culture and Anarchy*, chap. 2, p. 80.
31. *Past and Present*, Bk. III, chap. 2, p. 146.

fortune as from some contagious disease." [32] Beatrice Webb, a little later, noticed in London society "the making and breaking of personal friendships according to temporary and accidental circumstances in no way connected with personal merit: gracious appreciation and insistent intimacy being succeeded, when failure according to worldly standards occurred, by harsh criticism and cold avoidance." [33] The word "criticism" is revealing. Men who reached the top by their own dogged persistence and concentrated effort could readily attribute the failure of other men to weakness of character. Because "every one who rules himself to decency and sobriety of conduct, and attention to his duties [like me], comes over to our ranks [as I did]," John Thornton is sure that those who fail to do so are "self-indulgent, sensual people" who deserve only "contempt for their poorness of character." That they might not be able to succeed in this special way—might even be successful in another way, by another standard —did not occur to him, or to most Victorians. But Mrs. Gaskell has Margaret say, "The poor men around him—they were poor because they were vicious—out of the pale of his sympathies because they had not his iron nature, and the capabilities that it gives him for being rich." [34]

Social sympathy, indeed, was hardly compatible with the commercial spirit. The cutthroat competition of the time bred a hard and ruthless selfishness that was arraigned by the Victorian moralists. There is Thackeray's acid advice: "If a better place than yours presents itself just beyond your neighbour, elbow him and take it. . . . By pushing steadily, nine hundred and ninety-nine people in a thousand will yield to you. . . . You may be sure of success. If your neighbour's foot obstructs you, stamp on it; and do you suppose he won't take it away?" [35] It is true, no doubt, that some men, perhaps

32. Thackeray, *The Newcomes*, chap. 5, p. 50.

33. *My Apprenticeship*, p. 45. Needless to say, financial failure was the worst disgrace of all: see George Eliot, *The Mill on the Floss*, Bk. II, chap. 7; Bk. III, chaps. 2 and 3.

34. *North and South*, chaps. 10, 11, pp. 96, 98, 101.

35. *The Newcomes*, chap. 8, p. 76. Cf. J. W. Stapleton, *The Great Crime of 1860*, quoted in W. L. Burn, "The Age of Equipoise: England, 1848–1868," *The Nineteenth Century and After*, 146 (1949), p. 213; "In this strife the greatest and the strongest must of necessity be the most unscrupulous. Honour, truth and virtue are sacrificed together. In the battle of life every impediment must first be cast away. Stripped of his clothes the strong and resolute wrestler stands forth naked, slippery, suspicious, on his guard; the living incarnation of concentrated selfishness, modelled by the nineteenth century."

many, felt distaste and even shame for the life they lived, at least in restrospect. Their frame of mind was that of the dying Jacob in Clough's poem:

> Ah me! this eager rivalry of life,
> This cruel conflict for pre-eminence,
> This keen supplanting of the dearest kin,
> Quick seizure and fast unrelaxing hold
> Of vantage-place; the stony-hard resolve,
> The chase, the competition, and the craft
> Which seems to be the poison of our life
> And yet is the condition of our life!
> To have done things on which the eye with shame
> Looks back, the closed hand clutching still the prize!

Not that Jacob and his fellow Victorians were without ethical principles, but the principles were personal rather than social. "I have striven," he goes on to say, "to do my duty to my house and hearth, and to the purpose of my father's race." [36] In this respect, he may be compared with Beatrice Webb's father, railroad magnate and entrepreneur extraordinary, who symbolizes the higher echelons of this society at their best:

> He was an honourable and loyal colleague; he retained throughout his life the close friendship of his partners . . . he never left a colleague in a tight place; he was generous in giving credit to subordinates; he was forgiving to an old enemy who had fallen on evil times. But he thought, felt and acted in terms of personal relationship and not in terms of general principles; he had no clear vision of the public good. "A friend," he would assert, "is a person who would back you up when you were in the wrong, who would give your son a place which he could not have won on his own merits." Any other conduct he scoffed at as moral pedantry. Hence he tended to prefer the welfare of his family and personal friends to the interests of the companies over which he presided, the profits of these companies to the prosperity of his country, the dominance of his own race to the peace of the world. [37]

36. "Jacob," lines 81–90, 95–7, *Poems*, p. 87.

37. *My Apprenticeship*, pp. 5–6. Seventy-five years later the same criticism may be heard of the ethics of capitalist enterprise. Of the United States in particular one critic wrote in 1952—Saul Padover, Dean of the School of Politics, New

But for all the scathing comments of the Victorian critics, the creed of success, like its practitioners, rose to the top; and since 1870—aided, I think, by the steady decline of religious faith—has stood almost unquestioned, even in intellectual circles. An essay called "Success," published in 1860, is not only a full documentation of its amoral values but is also clear evidence of the transition from criticism to enthusiastic acclaim, for its author was a country gentleman, Sir John William Kaye, historian and essayist, and the article appeared in *The Cornhill Magazine*.[38] The opening words mark a change in attitude of immense significance:

> I have a great opinion of successful men; and I am not ashamed to confess it.
>
> It was the fashion, some years ago, to sneer at Success—nay, indeed, sometimes to revile it, as though it were an offence, or at best a pretentious humbug. . . . But a healthier social philosophy is now enthroned amongst us. We have begun to think that men who make their way to the front, becoming rich or famous by the force of their personal characters, must, after all, have something in them. . . . To prostrate oneself before what Success has won, be it power, or riches, or what not, may rightly be called flunkeyism; but to honour what has won success is worthy worship, not to be condemned or restrained. It is veneration for that type of manhood, which most nearly approaches the divine, by reason of its creative energy. It is a good sign of the times that we appreciate it at its true worth.

"But what, it may be asked, is Success? and who is the successful man?" The answer is simple and obvious. If a man "has kept a certain object steadily before him, and has attained it—no matter what the object be—he is a successful man." True, he may not be happier than he was before, and what he has won may give him no satis-

---

School for Social Research, "What's Wrong with American Morals?" *United Nations World* (Feb. 1952), p. 23: "When a nation puts a premium on self, self-advancement and devil-take-the-hindmost, it is bound to discover that the public good is likely to be the major victim. . . . Americans, therefore, may be said to live in a society where social values tend to be pulverized. The individual, under such a system, has two main loyalties: one is to himself and the other to his immediate group."

38. In 2 (1860), 729–41. The quotations that follow are on pp. 729–31, 733–5. For the attribution to Kaye (for which I am indebted to Professor R. D. Altick), see the Bibliography below.

faction. *Vanitas vanitatum!* But that is not the subject of discussion. It is beside the point, for after all "the positive success was there." (And the successful type of manhood, we remember, approaches the divine.) Nor is it relevant to ask if he deserved to win. Addison's Cato is quoted:

> 'Tis not in mortals to command success,
> But I'll do more, Sempronius—I'll deserve it.

But Sir John is more disposed to admire the misquotation:

> 'Tis not in mortals to deserve success,
> But I'll do more, Sempronius—I'll command it.

This does not mean, as he goes on to say later, that one should cut any corners. By all means "keep your hands clean." But "go directly to the point, looking neither to the right nor to the left," and never for a moment forget "the Market-place or the Council-house." Not that we should always be working in one or the other. By taking time off to dine with friends, we may often make a greater stride toward success than by staying at home to post up a ledger.

Then follows a revealing bit of autobiography: "When I was a very young man, I wrote essays in illustration of what I then believed to be the folly of such a course. But as I grow old, every year convinces me more and more that social intercourse, of the right kind, is a material aid to success." That personal change I suggest, is representative of the changing attitude in the age. The naked creed of success is now becoming eminently respectable. In course of time, those who best succeed in being successful will become the men of distinction in modern society.[39]

39. The anti-intellectual implications of this essay are obvious. The quotation from Kingsley, above, Chap. 5, p. 119, specifically exalts the man who succeeds "in the race of life" over the man of learning. And cf. *Yeast* (1851), chap. 6, pp. 90–2, for Kingsley's admiration of Lord Minchampstead, which anticipates the transition I date about 1860: "Naturally keen, ready, business-like, daring, he had carved out his own way through life, and opened his oyster—the world, neither with sword nor pen, but with steam and cotton. . . . From a mill-owner he grew to coal-owner, ship-owner, banker, railway director, money-lender to kings and princes; and last of all, as the summit of his own and his compeer's ambition, to land-owner. He had half-a-dozen estates in as many different counties."

Chapter 9

THE WORSHIP OF FORCE

> . . . new conceptions of man, partly true, partly false,
> but all terminating in the idea of power. Man in the
> civilized world feels a kind of omnipotence.
>
> *E. P. Hood*
>
> I was ever a fighter, so—one fight more.
>
> *Browning* [1]

"THE ENGLISHMAN, armed in his panoply of self-content, and grasping facts with unequalled tenacity, goes on trampling upon acuter sensibilities, but somehow shouldering his way successfully through the troubles of the universe. Strength may be combined with stupidity, but even then it is not to be trifled with." So begins the measured judgment of one eminent Victorian upon another. For Leslie Stephen makes the remark in an essay on Macaulay. He is speaking of Macaulay's sympathy with "some of the most deep-seated tendencies of the national character," and observes that although this led "to a certain brutal insularity," at least we must confess that "he is a thoroughly manly writer."

> He is combative to a fault, but his combativeness is allied to a genuine love of fair-play. When he hates a man, he calls him knave or fool with unflinching frankness, but he never uses a base weapon. . . . His patriotism may be narrow, but it implies faith in the really good qualities, the manliness, the spirit of justice, and the strong moral sense of his countrymen. He is proud of the healthy vigorous stock from which he springs; and the fervour of his enthusiasm, though it may shock a delicate taste, has embodied itself in writings which will long continue

1. Hood, *The Age and Its Architects*, p. 14. He attributes these new conceptions, too narrowly I think, to science. The Browning line is in "Prospice."

to be the typical illustration of qualities of which we are all proud at bottom—indeed, be it said in passing, a good deal too proud.[2]

That is the criticism of the intellectual, but not a modern intellectual; a Victorian intellectual whose roots were in the same soil—indeed, precisely the same soil. Stephen and Macaulay both grew up at Clapham; their fathers were Evangelical businessmen. That explains why, for all his recognition of limitations in Macaulay's standard of values, Stephen is in fundamental agreement with it. He, too, is proud of the English character: of both its physical strength and its moral strength, the very combination that had brought victory to the Ironsides, that now spelled success in the economic struggle for survival.

In this analysis we recognize the familiar lineaments of John Bull. The English, as Carlyle proudly described them in a chapter from *Past and Present* which uses "Mr. Bull" as a national symbol, are Macaulays without a university education or a flair for oratory. They are a strong, silent people, scornful of logic and intellectual pursuits (our dear John is rather stupid, but his stupidity is wiser than the wisdom of philosophers), determined to follow only Nature's fact or Nature's regulations, and wonderfully equipped to fight dragons, be they natural obstacles or human. "Sheer obstinate toughness of muscle; but much more, what we call toughness of heart, which will mean persistence hopeful and even desperate, unsubduable patience, composed candid openness, clearness of mind: all this shall be 'strength' in wrestling your dragon." If actively thwarted, the English strike back with pugnacious power. "Rouse not the Berserkir rage that lies in them! Do you know their Cromwells, Hampdens, their Pyms and Bradshaws? Men very peaceable, but men that can be made very terrible!" Possessed of these great qualities, John Bull has written an unsung epic of "sea-moles, cotton-trades, railways, fleets and cities, Indian Empires, Americas, New Hollands; legible throughout the Solar System;" he has conquered "the largest Empire the Sun ever saw" and earned "mountains of gold ingots."[3] All this, we remember, is Macaulay's boast as well.[4] How fitting that it should

2. "Macaulay," *Hours in a Library*, 2, 374–6.

3. Bk. III, chap. 5, "The English," pp. 159–60, 163, 164. It should be noted that James Brindley, the builder of canals, is chosen as the historical example of a John Bull.

4. See above, pp. 39–40.

have been Carlyle who praised him for having "more force and emphasis in him than any other of my British contemporaries." [5]

Toughness of muscle and toughness of heart. In the Victorian mind the ideal of strength is a combination of force and firmness. On the one hand, there is enormous admiration for the power of machines, and of the men who make them and run them; for the healthy, vigorous body; for the combative and even belligerent temper with its refusal to recognize defeat or mistakes, and its useful assumption that those it dislikes are knaves or weaklings. On the other hand, there is the complementary admiration for "character"—the mastery of the passions, patience and resolution, the controlled energy focused on work.[6] In both cases, Puritanism and the Industrial Revolution are the major points of reference, around which other contributing factors may be grouped.[7]

1. Machines and Men

In Carlyle's account of the English, emphasis falls on the size of their achievement, which is the analogue of John Bull's "bulk and strength": the largest Empire, mountains of gold, huge fleets. This is the Victorian refrain which Arnold satirized in *Culture and Anarchy*.[8] But it was accompanied by another sense of power which is often forgotten: the power of the machine and of the men who dared frame its fearful symmetry. To Carlyle the sound of Manchester awakening on a Monday morning at half-past five, "the rushing-off of its thousand mills, like the boom of an Atlantic tide, ten-thousand times ten-thousand spools and spindles all set humming there" is "sublime as a Niagara." The similes pick up the reference, a moment

5. Froude, *Carlyle: First Forty Years*, 2, chap. 16, p. 373; and cf. chap. 10, p. 231.

6. Cf. Taine, *Notes on England*, pp. 257–8, describing the cartoons in *Punch:* "The most noteworthy personage of all is John Bull, the typical Englishman. . . . He wears top-boots, a low-crowned hat, and carries a cudgel in his hand . . . he is capable of standing his ground against the most vigorous adversary even when it comes to blows. . . . His twinkling or angry eyes, his beetle-brows, the entire expression of his countenance, betray marked animal characteristics and the choleric temperament. His forehead is small, his intellect barren; his ideas are few and petty. . . . By way of compensation, he is gifted with good sense and energy, a fund of good temper, loyalty, perseverance, and determination; that firmness of character, in short, by means of which a man gets on in the world, and renders himself, if not lovable, at least useful."

7. The two kinds of strength are dealt with, respectively, in this chapter and the next.

8. Chap. 1, pp. 50–2.

before, to "the brute Primeval Powers" which the Watts, Arkwrights, and Brindleys have tamed and harnessed to the steam engine. For the present, the path of "this wondrous planet, Earth . . . lies toward *Hercules*, the constellation of *Physical Power*." [9] When Mr. Thornton, the Manchester manufacturer in *North and South*, was explaining the steam-hammer, which recalled to Mr. Hale "some of the wonderful stories of subservient genii in the Arabian Nights," he went on to say: "And this imagination of power, this practical realisation of a gigantic thought, came out of one man's brain in our good town." [10]

But the creative power of the Thorntons, of the men who ran the economic machine, was almost as impressive as that of the inventors. Mr. Hale, coming from the South to Darkshire (that is, Lancashire) was dazzled by "the energy which conquered immense difficulties with ease; the power of the machinery of Milton, the power of the men of Milton, impressed him with a sense of grandeur, which he yielded to without caring to inquire into the details of its exercise." [11] If Carlyle did plenty of inquiring and found some of the details ugly, he was hardly less impressed. He looks at Plugson of Undershot, who is John Bull as mill owner, berates him for his Mammonism, demands he become a noble industrial knight. And yet, "how much is there" in "this Plugson himself."

> Think, how were it, stoodst thou suddenly in his shoes! He has to command a thousand men. . . . For these his thousand men he has to provide raw-material, machinery, arrangement, house-room; and ever at the week's end, wages by due sale. No Civil-List, or Goulburn-Baring Budget has he to fall back upon, for paying of his regiment; he has to pick his supplies from the confused face of the whole Earth and Contemporaneous History, by his dexterity alone.[12]

Plainly Carlyle *has* stood in his shoes, and felt "the mastery, the achieve of the thing." For him the new capitalists were "Sons of the *Jötun*-land; the land of Difficulties Conquered." [13] Better perhaps than

9. "Chartism," *Essays*, 4, 181–2, and "Signs of the Times," 2, 82. In the latter, on p. 74, he remarks: "We are Giants in physical power." The power of man to conquer nature is related above, pp. 40–1, to the optimism of progress.

10. Chap. 10, pp. 92–3.

11. Ibid., chap. 8, pp. 78–9.

12. *Past and Present*, Bk. III, chap. 12, pp. 207–8. Cf. Taine, *Notes on England*, pp. 276–7.

13. *Past and Present*, Bk. IV, chap. 4, p. 276.

any other writer of the age, Carlyle realized "the accumulate manufacturing, commercial, economic *skill*" which made Victorian England
the first great industrial power.[14] Nor were the Plugsons, of course,
unaware of their skill. Mr. Thornton is glad to point out to the
Hales that "We are of a different race from the Greeks, to whom
beauty was everything. . . . Our glory and our beauty arise out of
our inward strength, which makes us victorious over material resistance, and over greater difficulties still." On which Mr. Hale remarks, "You are regular worshippers of Thor." [15]

But more exciting than any scientific or executive strength was
the sense of personal power. Never before had the captains of
industry controlled so many men or so much capital on such a global
scale. "The rapid development of what might be called a new trade,"
remarks Mr. Thornton, "gave those early masters enormous power of
wealth and command. I don't mean merely over the workmen; I mean
over purchasers—over the whole world's market." After giving some
illustrations, he continues:

> I only name such things to show what almost unlimited power
> the manufacturers had about the beginning of this century. The
> men were rendered dizzy by it. . . . There can be no doubt, too,
> of the tyranny they exercised over their work-people. You know
> the proverb, Mr. Hale, "Set a beggar on horseback, and he'll ride
> to the devil"—well, some of these early manufacturers did ride
> to the devil in a magnificent style—crushing human bone and
> flesh under their horses' hoofs without remorse.[16]

But the difference between these early cotton lords and the Victorian
capitalists was not so great as Mr. Thornton supposed. He himself
was enormously proud of having fought his way to a position "from
which he might . . . command more power and influence than in
any other mode of life. Far away, in the East and in the West,
where his person would never be known, his name was to be regarded,
and his wishes to be fulfilled, and his word pass like gold." [17] Nor was

14. "Chartism," *Essays*, 4, 177.
15. Chap. 40, p. 398. Cf. Carlyle's worship of Thor, *Past and Present*, p. 276,
and *Heroes*, Lecture 1, p. 35.
16. Chap. 10, pp. 95–6.
17. Chap. 50, p. 500. Cf. Beatrice Webb, *My Apprenticeship*, pp. 6, 37–8,
43–7, on power as the major goal of commercial life; and also above in my previous chapter, p. 191. I am here focusing on the feeling of power and, just
below, of aggression.

he any the less willing to force his workmen to his own will if he could. "Cromwell would have made a capital mill-owner, Miss Hale. I wish we had him to put down this strike for us." [18] Furthermore, the struggle for power against personal rivals, domestic and foreign competitors, or rebellious hands who joined unions and organized strikes, released the most aggressive impulses; and the more readily because the duties and obligations of the old feudal system were now scrapped, leaving economic life under the new system of laissez-faire at the mercy, in Baldwin Brown's pointed phrase, of "brute force or brain force." [19]

2. The Squirearchy

In upper-class circles, far from Lancashire, there existed a complementary admiration for strength. The idol here was not power but manliness. That was a Victorian requirement for men—just as women had to be womanly.[20] When Mill tried to minimize the difference between the sexes, Leslie Stephen protested that "to a man of ordinary flesh and blood, who had grounded his opinions, not upon books, but upon actual experience of life, such doctrines appear to be not only erroneous, but indicative of a hopeless thinness of character." Mill lacked virility. He needed "some red blood infused into his veins." [21] By contrast, Fielding and Johnson were men, and Macaulay was "a thoroughly manly writer," properly aggressive, rightly proud of "the healthy vigorous stock from which he springs." [22] Adam Bede was "a thorough man," yet if he "had shown less Christian forbearance to young Squire Donnithorne, we should have been more convinced that he was of masculine fibre throughout." [23] Since he knocks the young squire down for his affair with Hetty, the standard of masculinity, as Annan remarks, is certainly high. On the other hand, 'men' like Rousseau, Keats, Shelley—the highly sensitive, delicate, or introspective temperaments—are effeminate. Kingsley's "Thoughts on Shel-

18. Chap. 15, p. 145. The reason why he himself cannot be a Cromwell is given by Mr. Thornton in the passage on the cotton lords. In the next generation, he says (chap. 10, p. 96), more factories and more employers increased the demand for labor, so that "the power of masters and men became more evenly balanced; and now the battle is pretty fairly waged between us."

19. "The Revolution of the Last Quarter of a Century," First Principles, p. 280.

20. On this distinction see Noel Annan, Leslie Stephen, pp. 224–7, to whom I owe the illustrations from Stephen that follow.

21. Life of Fitzjames Stephen, pp. 316–17.

22. "Macaulay," Hours in a Library, 2, 374–6.

23. "George Eliot," Hours in a Library, 3, 221–2.

ley and Byron" are thoughts that "Shelley's nature is utterly womanish," not only in its pity and tenderness but in "the physical distaste for meat and fermented liquors." Only an effeminate age could prefer "the gentle and sensitive vegetarian" to the "sturdy peer proud of his bull neck and his boxing, who kept bears and bull-dogs, drilled Greek ruffians at Missolonghi, and 'had no objection to a pot of beer'; and who might, if he had reformed, have made a gallant English gentleman." [24] "English" should be emphasized. Stephen thought the English undergraduate, playing cricket and rowing, infinitely superior to philosophizing German louts or spindly French intellectuals arguing about politics and art.[25] When Frederick Tennyson and a party of Englishmen—of Tom Browns and Byrons, of Kingsleys and Stephens—fought a cricket match with the crew of the *Bellerophon* on the Parthenopean Hills and "*sacked* the sailors by 90 runs," Edward Fitz-Gerald was delighted. "Is not this pleasant?" he wrote—"the notion of good English blood striving in worn out Italy—I like that such men as Frederick should be abroad: so strong, haughty and passionate. They keep up the English character abroad." [26] Few of the party, one may be sure, were clean-shaven. Down to the late thirties almost everyone shaved, but after that mustaches and beards became the fashion. "There is perhaps some connection," remarks Wingfield-Stratford, "between . . . aggressive manliness and the almost equally aggressive hairiness flaunted by the male sex at this time." [27]

As these quotations suggest, manliness belongs to a tradition which is neither Puritan nor mercantile. It is that of the English squirearchy, both at home and at the public schools and universities, with its cult of games and field sports, and its admiration for physical strength and prowess. The classic text is *Tom Brown's School Days* by Thomas Hughes, in which the Browns are the squires of England, and the hero "the commonest type of English boy of the upper middle class." [28]

24. *Literary and General Lectures and Essays*, pp. 43, 47. Only God may be androgynous. Thomas Hughes, a great champion of manliness, as we shall see in a moment, ended his *Tom Brown's School Days*, p. 441, by noting that only God combined "the love and tenderness and purity" of mothers and sisters with "the strength and courage and wisdom" of fathers and brothers.

25. Annan, *Stephen*, p. 38.

26. *Letters and Literary Remains*, *1*, 71, quoted in Arthur Bryant, *English Saga*, p. 106. The date is March 26, 1841.

27. *The Victorian Sunset*, pp. 77–8. The connection is made by Kingsley in *Yeast*, chap. 3, p. 48.

28. Preface to his *Tom Brown at Oxford*, p. i. In general, see Amy Cruse, *The*

Tom's ambition at Rugby is simply the schoolboy formulation of the family creed: "I want to be A 1 at cricket and football, and all the other games. . . . I want to leave behind me . . . the name of a fellow who never bullied a little boy, or turned his back on a big one." [29] Tom more than held his own in the fist-fighting world of Rugby. He came to it naturally. The first characteristic of the Browns which Hughes mentions is that they "are a fighting family." They may not have wisdom or wit or beauty, but "about their fight there can be no question." For centuries they have been subduing the earth in American forests and Australian uplands, and are now the backbone of an empire on which the sun never sets. They have won renown on every field of battle, from Cressy and Agincourt to Trafalgar and Waterloo. They are as combative at home (in village or family disputes) as they are abroad, and go on "fighting to a green old age." [30] *Tom Brown's School Days* presented almost every Victorian and American boy for two generations with an ideal of life that Hughes summed up in one central statement:

> After all, what would life be without fighting, I should like to know? From the cradle to the grave, fighting, rightly understood, is the business, the real, highest, honestest business of every son of man. . . .
>
> It is no good for Quakers, or any other body of men to uplift their voices against fighting. Human nature is too strong for them, and they don't follow their own precepts. Every soul of them is doing his own piece of fighting, somehow and somewhere. The world might be a better world without fighting, for anything I know, but it wouldn't be our world; and therefore I am dead against crying peace when there is no peace, and isn't meant to

Victorians and Their Reading, chap. 10, "The Browns of England," pp. 204–18; Wingfield-Stratford, *Those Earnest Victorians*, chap. 2, "The Squire and His Relations," pp. 9–20; and the novels of Surtees.

29. Pt. II, chap. 6, pp. 368–9. "Remarkable words," commented Taine when he quoted them (*Notes on England*, p. 127), "and well summarising the ordinary sentiments of an English father and child; science and mental culture occupy the last place; character, heart, courage, strength, and bodily skill are in the first row." As Taine indicates and Hughes makes clear, manliness included certain moral qualities—courage, honesty, and a rough sense of justice, but its chief component was physical strength.

30. Pt. I, chap. 1, pp. 23–7.

be. I am as sorry as any man to see folk fighting the wrong people
and the wrong things, but I'd a deal sooner see them doing that,
than that they should have no fight in them.[31]

If you lose an argument, you do not consider whether perhaps
the victor was right—still less, accept your defeat. You follow the
example of the Browns: "No failures knock them up or make them
hold their hands." [32]

The most famous Brown in the Victorian period was Charles Kingsley, the country squire as muscular clergyman. His family and friends,
he was proud to say, were "hunters and fighters," and he himself, by
God's blessing, "a strong, daring, sporting wild man-of-the-woods." [33]
He lived his life "for Esau and with Esau," hunting, swimming, fishing
—and preaching to the hard-riding squires and hard-fighting soldiers
of Hampshire "a healthful and manly Christianity, one which does not
exalt the feminine virtues to the exclusion of the masculine." It was
this Christianity, which had considerable vogue in Victorian England,
that was dubbed, not too unfairly, Muscular.[34]

31. Pt. II, chap. 5, pp. 334–5. Cf. p. 355: "Fighting with fists is the natural
and English way for English boys to settle their quarrels. What substitute for
it is there, or ever was there, amongst any nation under the sun? What would you
like to see take its place?" There is something of a recantation, however, in the
later *Tom Brown at Oxford*, chap. 11, p. 123. In *Jane Eyre*, chap. 17, p. 175, Miss
Ingram of Ingram Park sums up the philosophy of county society in a single
sentence: "As to the *gentlemen*, let them be solicitous to possess only strength and
valour: let their motto be:—Hunt, shoot, and fight: the rest is not worth a
fillip."

32. Pt. I, chap. 1, pp. 26–7.

33. *Letters and Memories*, 2, 84 (not in unabridged ed.), and *1*, 152 (unabridged
ed., *1*, 180).

34. Ibid., *1*, 63–4 (unabridged ed., *1*, 83–4); *2*, 54 (unabridged ed., *2*, 186);
2, 83–6 (not in unabridged ed.); and (unabridged ed. only) *2*, 212–13, are the
main statements. The quotations in the previous sentence are taken from the second
and the fourth passages. Tom Hughes, as we might suppose, was a muscular
Christian, though critical of its extreme tendencies: see *Tom Brown at Oxford*,
chap. 11, and *The Manliness of Christ*, London, 1879. In his review of *Tom
Brown's School Days—Edinburgh Review*, 107 (1858), 189–93—Fitzjames
Stephen argued that Hughes' portrait of "Dr. Arnold" was Stanley's skeleton
fleshed with Charles Kingsley: Arnold's intellectual qualities, his moral scruples,
his sense of boy wickedness, his indifference toward athletics are entirely omitted;
while on the other hand, he is endowed with Kingsley's faith in muscular Christianity. In America the best representative of the Browns was Theodore Roosevelt. In a review in the *New York Times* (August 16, 1954), p. 15, Orville
Prescott wrote: "Roosevelt rode horseback with his wife, regularly took her
rowing to picnics eight miles away and eight miles back, chopped wood, hiked,

By fighting, the Browns meant not only battling enemies but battling personal discouragement and misfortune. No one of them, especially in those pre-Freudian days,- would have thought of explaining or excusing any failure to fight back or any inability to cope with life as the result of psychic conditioning in childhood. It would have been plain weakness of character. A *man* keeps a stiff upper lip and marches on; only miserable weaklings go under. We may grant what George Brimley said in connection with "Maud," that "to strong men the world is not made bitter by a father's ruin and suicide, by the prevalence of meanness and cruelty, by contemptuous neglect, and general absence of sympathy"; [35] though not without qualifications, since we would recognize that strength of this kind is incompatible with certain qualities we value more highly than the Victorians did, such as sensitivity and humility. What is much harder for us to take is the condemnation of characters who are *not* strong: Brimley calling Shelley, Keats, and Chatterton "morbid, hysterical, spasmodic individuals"; [36] Kingsley finding Shakespeare's sonnets simply "the confession that over and above all his powers he lacked one thing, and knew not what it was, or where to find it—and that was—to be strong"; [37] or Browning dismissing with a fine flourish all those who failed to meet the challenge of life:

> What had I on earth to do
> With the slothful, with the mawkish, the unmanly?
> Like the aimless, helpless, hopeless, did I drivel
> —Being—who?

No, by no means. *He* never turned his back, but marched breast forward, was baffled only to fight better, and greeted the unseen with the cry, "Speed,—fight on, fare ever there as here!" [38] Consonant with such a philosophy is the sympathy with forceful and dynamic personalities that runs through Browning's poetry, and which determined, in part,

swam and played tennis. . . . T.R. preached courage, patriotism, 'aggressiveness in well-doing,' chivalry and the moral necessity for heroic action. 'You can be just as decent as you wish,' he told his children, 'provided you are prepared to fight. If you fight hard enough you are perfectly certain to secure the respect of your playmates for your virtues.' "

35. "Tennyson's Poems," *Essays*, p. 79.

36. Ibid., p. 76; and cf. the quotations from Leslie Stephen in Annan, *Stephen*, pp. 226–7, one of which is: "Sensitive, it may be said, is a polite word for morbid."

37. "The Limits of Exact Science as Applied to History," *The Roman and the Teuton*, in *Works*, 10, 331.

38. "Epilogue" to *Asolando*.

his choice of the two plays he translated from Euripides, in both of which Hercules is the dominating figure.

3. The Major Prophet

Behind Hughes and Kingsley and Browning stands the major Victorian prophet of the "good fight" to whom they are all indebted: Thomas Carlyle. Especially in his later work, after 1832, the same conception of life is repeated again and again. "Man is created to fight; he is perhaps best of all definable as a born soldier; his life 'a battle and a march,' under the right General." "Everywhere we try at least to give the adversary as good as he brings; and, with swift force or slow watchful manoeuvre, extinguish this and the other solecism, leave one solecism less in God's Creation." [39] That attitude has many sources, but the earliest was the same tradition, though in a more violent form, as that so much admired by Kingsley and Hughes. "Annandale had long been a lawless 'Border' Country: the people had ceased from foray-riding, but not from its effects; the 'gallant man' of those districts was still a wild, natural, almost animal man." And Carlyle recounts more than one occasion when arguments were settled or the theft of cattle repaid with physical force. These Scotch Browns were the most fiery, "irascible, indomitable" branch of the family. They had the "toughness and springiness of steel." [40] How strongly they appealed to Carlyle is seen in the essay on Scott:

> Might we not say, Scott, in the new vesture of the nineteenth century, was intrinsically very much the old fighting Borderer of prior centuries; the kind of man Nature did of old make in that birthland of his? In the saddle, with the foray-spear, he would have acquitted himself as he did at the desk with his pen. . . . He too could have fought at Redswire, cracking crowns with the fiercest, if that had been the task; could have harried cattle in Tynedale, repaying injury with compound interest; a right sufficient captain of men. A man without qualms or fantasticalities; a hard-headed, sound-hearted man, of joyous robust temper, looking to the main chance, and fighting direct thitherward; *valde stalwartus homo!* [41]

39. *Past and Present*, Bk. III, chap. 10, p. 190; Bk. II, chap. 12, p. 102. The battle is partly a moral battle in the conscience, as it also is for Hughes: see below, pp. 233–5.
40. *Reminiscences*, pp. 16–18, 26; and on his father, pp. 6–7, 12, 19, 25.
41. *Essays*, 4, 40.

This predisposition attracted Carlyle to other manifestations of strength and gave a coloring to some of his religious and political ideas. In his pantheism we find the conception of Force as the world's soul and animating principle, and therefore the conception of great men as those in whom the divine energy flowed most abundantly.[42] From another facet of Romanticism—specifically from Goethe's *Goëtz von Berlichingen*, Schiller's *Robbers*, Shelley's *Prometheus*, and most of all from the Byronic heroes—he derived his enthusiasm for the superman. At first (in 1829) he condemned contemporary poetry because "beauty is no longer the god it worships, but some brute image of Strength," and cited Byron as the chief example of this "idol-worship," the leading representative in England of the "*Kraftmänner* or Powermen" of the *Sturm und Drang*.[43] But the truth is that Carlyle was deeply imbued with Byronism.[44] For all his injunction in *Sartor* to close one's Byron, he was fascinated by the titanic hero with his superhuman powers of body and will—how much is apparent in his description of Mirabeau: "The fierce wear and tear of such an existence has wasted out the giant oaken strength of Mirabeau. . . . 'A day for this man was more than a week or a month is for others: the mass of things he guided on together was prodigious; from the scheming to the executing not a moment lost.' . . . His death is Titanic, as his life has been!" [45]

In the Mirabeau and the Danton of *The French Revolution* we see the emergence of the Carlylean hero. "As the Stoic's hero was the wise man, the '*sapiens et rex*,' Mr. Carlyle's is the strong man, the 'king, conning, or able man.' His might makes his right. His own power and impetus are his Bible and creed." That interpretation by J. B. Mozley overlooks certain religious and moral components,[46] but Carlyle's pan-

42. *Heroes*, Lecture 1, pp. 8–9, 13; and "The Diamond Necklace," *Essays*, 3, 328.

43. "Signs of the Times," *Essays*, 2, 78, and "Goethe," 1, 218.

44. Even Matthew Arnold hailed Byron ("Byron," *Essays in Criticism, Second Series*, p. 180) as a "puissant and splendid personality," and watched ("Memorial Verses") "with reverential awe . . . the fount of fiery life which served for that Titanic strife." Cf. *On the Study of Celtic Literature*, in *On the Study of Celtic Literature and On Translating Homer* (New York, 1883), sec. 6, pp. 115–20, on Celtic titanism with special reference to Byron.

45. *The French Revolution*, 2, Bk. III, chap. 7, in *Works*, Centenary edition, ed. H. D. Traill (30 vols. New York, 1896–1901), 3, 139–41. The sentence in single quotation marks is quoted from Dumont.

46. "Carlyle's Oliver Cromwell," *Essays, Historical and Theological, 1*, 230. R. H. Hutton, *Contemporary Thought and Thinkers, 1*, 11–13, and James

theism, his Byronism, and his admiration for his fiery ancestors, reinforced by an antidemocratic leaning toward the dictator,[47] made force
the essential characteristic. And that in turn produced a low opinion
of the meek or saintly character, and ultimately of the artistic and
intellectual character, too.

Did this predisposition widen his sympathy with the captains of industry to include their aggressive, as well as their executive, force?
The description of Scott as fighting Borderer—the man without qualms,
hard-headed, looking to the main chance—precisely fits the men who
battled their way to success in the intense commercial warfare of the
period. But any suggestion that Carlyle extended the same admiration
to them seems unlikely. *Past and Present* is a long arraignment of the
mutual hostility of economic life, "cloaked under due laws of war,
named 'fair competition' and so forth." What Carlyle wanted was a
noble chivalry of labor in which the mill owners, united with their
workers in mutual loyalty, should march forth to subdue the forces
of Nature. Captains of Industry, purged of their Mammonism, are
"the true Fighters . . . against Chaos, Necessity, and the Devils and
Jötuns." [48] But who are the Devils and Jötuns? They might be aggressive competitors. Perhaps, after all, Carlyle enjoyed the sheer cut and
thrust of economic war, and admired captains of industry for their
very resemblance to "the old fighting Borderer of prior centuries."
Abbot Samson, the hero of *Past and Present,* is a man "full of cunning
insight" into worldly affairs, "always discerning the road to his object,
be it circuit, be it short-cut, and victoriously travelling forward there-
on," a man whose "noble slow perseverance" is matched by "a strength
of 'subdued rage' calculated to subdue most things." He makes short
work of a threat to the monastery profits:

> We said withal there was a terrible flash of anger in him: witness
> his address to old Herbert the Dean, who in a too thrifty manner
> has erected a windmill for himself on his glebe-lands at Haber-
> don. . . . "I tell thee, it will *not* be without damage to my mills;
> for the Townfolk will go to thy mill, and grind their corn (*bladum*

Martineau, *Essays, Reviews, and Addresses, 1,* 275–7, both substantially agree
with Mozley, though Martineau concludes (p. 277): "He, no doubt, sides on the
whole against the Titans with the gods: but if the Titans make a happy fling,
and send home a mountain or two to the very beard of Zeus, he gets delighted
with the game on any terms and cries, 'Bravo!' "

47. A reference to the later discussion of the hero as dictator is in note 60 of
this chapter.

48. Bk. III, chap. 2, p. 146; Bk. IV, chap. 4, p. 272.

suum) at their own good pleasure; nor can I hinder them, since they are free men. I will allow no new mills on such principle. Away, away; before thou gettest home again, thou shalt see what thy mill has grown to!"—The very reverend the old Dean totters home again, in all haste; tears the mill in pieces by his own *carpentarii*, to save at least the timber; and Abbot Samson's workmen, coming up, find the ground already clear of it.[49]

Any doubt about Carlyle's approval of such tactics is dispelled by his justification of the China War of 1842: "Our friends of China, who guiltily refused to trade . . . had we not to argue with them, in cannon-shot at last, and convince them that they ought to trade!" [50] And the kind of trade which the Chinese were guilty of not carrying on, to the injury of English profits, was—opium. What makes these quotations so significant is the fact that Carlyle was the outspoken critic of the 'immoral' world of ruthless competition. If *his* attitude was ambivalent, we can safely say that few Victorians failed to share, in some degree, his sympathy with the strong arm of capitalism, especially when it involved national power and prestige.

4. *Darwinism, Chauvinism, Racism*

Such sympathy was increased and rationalized when the Darwinians identified the economic struggle for existence with the course of nature. That the stronger should push the weaker to the wall was not only a cosmic fact, it was a beneficent process by which the nation got rid of its liabilities. As early as 1850 Herbert Spencer was happy to point out that the "purifying process" by which animals kill off the sickly, the malformed, and the aged, was equally at work in human society: "The poverty of the incapable, the distresses that come upon the imprudent, the starvation of the idle, and those shvoulderings aside of the weak by the strong, which leave so many 'in shallows and in miseries,' are the decrees of a large, far-seeing benevolence." [51] Small wonder that after *The Origin of Species* came out, Darwin read in a Manchester newspaper, "rather a good squib, showing that I have proved 'might is right,' and therefore that . . . every cheating tradesman is . . . right." [52]

And, also, he added, "that Napoleon is right." For social Darwinism could equally justify war and militarism. It could give philosophical

49. Bk. II, chap. 15, p. 115; chap. 12, p. 100; chap. 15, p. 113.
50. Bk. IV, chap. 3, p. 267.
51. *Social Statics*, p. 323.
52. *Life and Letters*, 2, 56–7, from a letter to Lyell, January 1860.

sanction to the chauvinism that grew up in the second half of the century with the increasing intensity of national rivalries and the scientific development of ever deadlier weapons of destruction. By the middle fifties the proud and combative John Bull was in the mood of boastful belligerence that welcomed the Crimean War, and was later echoed in

> We don't want to fight, but by jingo if we do,
> We've got the men, we've got the guns,
>   we've got the money, too.

But they *would* want to fight if Kingsley and Tennyson had their way. Confessing with obvious satisfaction that he feared he had a little of the wolf-vein in him and in spite of fifteen centuries of civilization, Kingsley wrote off his *Westward Ho!* with maddened speed and called it "a most ruthless, bloodthirsty book . . . (just what the times want, I think)." If he were only younger, he would be there himself, storming the Alma heights. "But I can fight with my pen still (I don't mean in controversy—I am sick of that. If one went on at it, it would make one a very Billingsgate fishwife, screaming and scolding, when one knows one is safe, and then running away when one expects to have one's attack returned).—Not in controversy, but in writing books which will make others fight." [53] The parenthetical remarks remind us that the fighting atmosphere of the Victorian period existed in intellectual, as well as economic and national, life. Only three years earlier, attacked for his criticism of the universities, Kingsley had "returned the blow as hard as I could, my rule being to smash, if possible, all wilful obstacles to anything I have in hand." [54] But that note of brutal violence is largely absent from the controversy of the age, however combative. Thomas Arnold, Macaulay, Ruskin are entirely free of it. They aimed to defeat but not to massacre. It was British chauvinism (supported, as we shall see, by elements latent in Puritanism) which by moments turned men like Kingsley and Froude, Carlyle and Hughes, into storm-troopers and led the British public to buy thirty-one editions of Creasy's *Fifteen Decisive Battles of the World* between

53. *Letters and Memories*, unabridged ed., *1*, 433. The passage in the abridged ed., *1*, 363–4, is incomplete. For Tennyson and the War, see *Maud*, Pt. III. The swashbuckling, pugnacious hero of *Westward Ho!*, Amyas Leigh, is described above in Chap. 5, on p. 122, where I bring out the connection between the worship of force and anti-intellectualism. It is worth noticing that the same prophets (Kingsley, Carlyle, and Froude) are prominent exhibits in both that chapter and this one.
54. *Letters and Memories* (unabridged ed. only), *1*, 267.

1852 and 1882 at least partly for the reason given by Spencer, in order to "revel in accounts of slaughter." [55]

Kingsley's essay "Sir Walter Raleigh and His Time" (1855), a companion piece to *Westward Ho!*, illustrates this temper of mind in significant connection with Protestant and economic nationalism:

> Before this boy's mind, as before all intense English minds of that day, rise, from the first, three fixed ideas, which yet are but one— the Pope, the Spaniard, and America.
>
> The two first are the sworn and internecine enemies (whether they pretend a formal peace or not) of Law and Freedom, Bible and Queen, and all that makes an Englishman's life dear to him. Are they not the incarnations of Antichrist? . . . And America is the new world of boundless wonder and beauty, wealth and fertility, to which these two evil powers arrogate an exclusive and divine right; and God has delivered it into their hands; and they have done evil therein with all their might, till the story of their greed and cruelty rings through all earth and heaven. Is this the will of God? Will he not avenge for these things, as surely as he is the Lord who executeth justice and judgment in the earth? . . .
>
> In whatsoever else he wavered, he never wavered in that creed. He learnt it in his boyhood, while he read Fox's Martyrs beside his mother's knee. He learnt it as a lad, when he saw his neighbours Hawkins and Drake changed by Spanish tyranny and treachery from peaceful merchantmen into fierce scourges of God. [56]

55. *The Man Versus the State* (first ed. 1884; Caldwell, Ohio, 1940), p. 112. In the *Letters and Memories* (2, 78–9; unabridged ed., 2, 47–9), Mrs. Kingsley wrote: "He inherited much of the soldier's spirit, as he inherited soldier blood. . . . He had himself, at one time, thought of the army as a profession, and had spent much time as a boy in drawing plans of fortifications; and even after he took holy orders it was a constant occupation to him, in all his walks and rides, to be planning fortifications . . . No soldier could have read and re-read Hannibal's campaigns, Creasy's Sixteen Decisive Battles, the records of Sir Charles Napier's Indian warfare, or Sir William's magnificent history of the Peninsular War, with keener appreciation. . . . Hence the honor he esteemed it to be invited to preach to the troops at Aldershot, and to lecture to military men there and at Woolwich. His eyes would kindle and fill with tears as he recalled the impression made on him on Whitsunday, 1858, by the sound heard for the first time, and never to be forgotten, of the clank of the officers' swords and spurs, and the regular tramp of the men as they marched into church, stirring him like the sound of a trumpet."

56. *Plays and Puritans*, in *Works, 16*, 88–9. Though I have not read it, I gather (from Kingsley's enthusiastic review, ibid., pp. 211–71, and Leslie Stephen's

Raleigh—this Raleigh—is intended to be an exemplum for Kingsley's own times. New enemies of God—the Old Testament God of battle and vengeance—must again be scourged by his Protestant-English champions lest the wealth and fertility of new Americas be lost.

When this temper was reinforced by the arrogance of white supremacy, it produced some extraordinary fruits. It inspired Carlyle to write his article "The Nigger Question," and led to the defense of Governor Eyre's high-handed and brutal treatment of the natives in Jamaica, in which Carlyle took a leading part.[57] He found Eyre "visibly a brave, gentle, chivalrous, and clear man, whom I would make dictator of Jamaica for the next twenty-five years were I now king of it." [58] In some circles it could even make Rajah Brooke, the conqueror and ruler of Sarawak, a national hero, hailed with sentiments well reflected, I doubt not, in Kingsley's letter to Ludlow:

> I say at once that I think he was utterly right and righteous.
> . . . "Sacrifice of human life?" Prove that it is *human* life. It is
> beast-life. These Dyaks have put on the image of the beast, and
> they must take the consequence. . . . Physical death is no evil. It
> may be a blessing to the survivors. Else, why pestilence, famine,
> Cromwell and Perrot in Ireland, Charlemagne hanging 4000
> Saxons over the Weser Bridge; did not God bless those terrible
> righteous judgments? Do you believe in the Old Testament?
> Surely, then, say, what does that destruction of the Canaanites
> mean? If *it* was right, Rajah Brooke was right. If he be wrong,
> then Moses, Joshua, David, were wrong. . . . You Malays and
> Dyaks of Sarawak, you . . . are the enemies of Christ, the Prince
> of Peace; you are beasts, all the more dangerous, because you have
> a semi-human cunning. I will, like David, "hate you with a perfect

---

essay in *Studies of a Biographer, 3,* 239–48) that the same spirit appears in Froude's *History of England from the Fall of Wolsey to the Death of Elizabeth,* 12 vols. 1856–70.

57. *Essays, 4,* 348–83, first printed in 1849. Mill called it—in "The Negro Question," *Fraser's Magazine, 41* (1850), 25—a eulogy of "the law of force and cunning; the law that whoever is more powerful than another, is 'born lord' of that other, the other being born his 'servant,' who must be 'compelled to work' for him by 'beneficent whip,' if 'other methods avail not.' " Cf. the quotation from Carlyle's *Latter-Day Pamphlets,* below, note 65.

58. Froude, *Carlyle: Life in London, 2,* chap. 31, p. 364. Packe, *Life of Mill,* pp. 464–72, gives a good account of the Jamaica case, and brings Carlyle's "Nigger Question" into connection with it.

hatred, even as though you were *my* enemies." I will blast you out with grape and rockets, "I will beat you as small as the dust before the wind." [59]

Plainly it is not the Malays and the Dyaks who have put on "the image of the beast" but Canon Charles Kingsley. Sadistic brutality of this kind is pathological, and no doubt the desire to "smash 'em good" in Carlyle and Froude as well as Kingsley had personal origins. But nationalism and racism, sanctioned by Old Testament Puritanism and social Darwinism, created an atmosphere in which the normal control of the beast in man could be seriously weakened.[60]

5. Puritanism

Furthermore, Puritanism was itself a direct stimulus to belligerence. Though its conception of life as moral warfare led to a struggle *against* the passions in the Victorian conscience, it also inspired a self-righteous intolerance, based on the belief in divine election, that could *release* the passions and justify the most merciless appeal to force. When Hughes insisted that fighting was "the real, highest, honestest business of every son of man," he explained, in words which show how perfectly the "Puritanism" of Thomas Arnold could be blended at Rugby with the combative instincts of the squirearchy, that "every one who is worth his salt has his enemies, who must be beaten, be they evil thoughts and habits in himself, or spiritual wickedness in high places, or Russians, or Border-ruffians, or Bill, Tom, or Harry, who will not let him live his life in quiet till he has thrashed them." [61] In addition to the inner struggle is the battle against your enemies, political and private as well as national, *who are His enemies, too*, and therefore to be struck down with a good conscience. In the two fat volumes of love letters between Elizabeth Barrett and Robert Browning there is just one quarrel, on the subject of dueling. Elizabeth thinks it utterly un-Christian and stupid. Browning answers, "I must confess that I can conceive of 'combinations of circumstances' in which I see two things only . . . or a Third: a miscreant to be put out the world, my own

---

59. *Letters and Memories, 1,* 374–5 (unabridged ed., *1,* 222–3). Brooke was one of the two people to whom *Westward Ho!* was dedicated, appropriately enough.

60. The admiration of the dictator for authoritarian and antidemocratic reasons, especially by Carlyle, is discussed below, pp. 328–31.

61. *Tom Brown's School Days,* Pt. II, chap. 5, p. 334.

arm and best will to do it; and, perhaps, God to excuse; which is, approve. My Ba, what is Evil, in its unmistakable shape, but a thing to suppress at any price?" [62] The same note is sounded repeatedly by Carlyle. On the one side are the superstitious blockheads and the lazy, sensual masses; on the other, the saints of God, in whom there dwells "a conscious abhorrence and intolerance of Folly, of Baseness, Stupidity, Poltroonery . . . clothed moreover by the beneficent Supreme Powers in what stout appetites, energies, egoisms so-called, are suitable to it;—these latter are your Conquerors, Romans, Normans, Russians, Indo-English." [63] Nor does Carlyle limit such powers to political-military leaders alone. He tells the reader of *Past and Present:* "Where thou findest Ignorance, Stupidity, Brute-mindedness,—yes, there . . . were it with mere dungeons and gibbets and crosses, attack it, I say; smite it wisely, unweariedly, and rest not while thou livest and it lives; but smite, smite, in the name of God! The Highest God, as I understand it, does audibly so command thee." [64] In the same spirit, Kingsley could say that it was no use "telling people what's right . . . If you want to get mankind, if not to heaven, at least out of hell, kick them out." [65] What unspeakable joy and relief, as Greg dryly remarked, for a Christian to discover he was not called upon to control his ag-

---

62. *The Letters of Robert Browning and Elizabeth Barrett Barrett,* 2, 50–1, under date of April 8, 1846.

63. *Past and Present,* Bk. III, chap. 13, p. 213. Cf. Bk. IV, chap. 7, pp. 289–90, where he prophesies that the Mammon worshipers will "be trampled and chained down in whatever terrible ways" by "the elect of the world; the born champions, strong men, and liberatory Samsons . . ."

64. Bk. III, chap. 12, p. 201. In the *Latter-Day Pamphlets,* No. 2, p. 78, his attitude toward revenge is exactly that of Browning.

65. Quoted by Hughes, "Prefatory Memoir," *Alton Locke,* p. xxiii. Cf. his 'Christian' justification of Rajah Brooke (just above) and Carlyle, *Latter-Day Pamphlets,* No. 2, p. 66, where he is discussing negroes: "Brotherhood? No, be the thought far from me. They are Adam's children,—alas yes, I well remember that, and never shall forget it; hence this rage and sorrow. But they have gone over to the dragons; they have quitted the Father's house, and set-up with the Old Serpent: till they return, how can they be brothers? They are enemies, deadly to themselves and to me and to you, till then . . . with tears grown sacred and wrath grown sacred, I will cut them off in the name of God!" In an unpublished essay, written in 1852, Carlyle wrote (Froude, *Carlyle: First Forty Years,* 2, chap. 1, p. 9): "There are a few men who have even at present a certain right, call it rather a certain terrible duty, to be intolerant, and I hope that these will be even more, and that their intolerance will grow ever nobler, diviner, more victorious."

gressive instincts, but only to direct them; "and that once having, or fancying that he has, in view a man or an institution that is God's enemy as well as his, he may hate it with a perfect hatred, and go at it *en sabreur!*" [66]

It was in the name of this jealous God of the Old Testament that Carlyle pronounced the famous dogma that might is right. Might was right because in His universe only what was right was given the strength to succeed. True, injustice might have power enough to conquer temporarily, but in the long run the victory of strength was bound to be the victory of justice.[67] But how long? Carlyle did not say. One might jump the gun, perhaps, and conclude at once that the side of power was the side of God, and the use of force the legitimate weapon against whatever obstructed one's 'just' desires. The doctrine that might is right when the might is just can slide with fatal ease into the belief that might is—right. Or with equal ease, a man's personal desire can be identified with justice.[68]

It is hardly surprising that Cromwell displaced Goethe as Carlyle's major hero. The spirit of the Ironsides flamed again in Victorian veins. Kingsley was proud of the Puritan blood of his forefathers who "fought by Cromwell's side at Naseby and Marston Moor"; FitzGerald, appalled by the candles and stained-glass windows of High Church ritualism, "wanted Oliver and his dragoons to march in and put an end to it all." [69] Tom Brown Hughes, on a visit to Paris, the capital of lubricity, was swept by a frenzy of Puritan destructiveness. "I get mad to smash some of the mirrors on the boulevards and to punch the heads of some of the little coxcombs who sit sipping and smoking all along the Cafe fronts." [70]

66. "Kingsley and Carlyle," *Literary and Social Judgments*, 1, 145–6.

67. For a good exposition see Froude, *Carlyle: Life in London*, 1, chap. 13, pp. 361–2.

68. See Morley, "Carlyle," *Critical Miscellanies*, 1, 166–76, and Leslie Stephen, "Carlyle's Ethics," *Hours in a Library*, 3, 286–92. Basil Willey, *Nineteenth Century Studies*, pp. 130–1, argues that to draw such conclusions is unjust to Carlyle.

69. Kingsley's *Letters and Memories*, 2, 59 (unabridged ed., 2, 24). Cf. 1, 368 (unabridged ed., 1, 440), where he wants the English army of the future to have the fighting power of Cromwell's Ironsides; FitzGerald, *Letters and Literary Remains*, 1, 180, in a letter to Carlyle, September 20, 1847. Mr. Thornton, it will be recalled, longed for a Cromwell to put down the strike in his factory: see above, p. 201.

70. Quoted in E. C. Mack and W. H. G. Armytage, *Thomas Hughes. The Life of the Author of Tom Brown's Schooldays* (London, 1952), p. 176.

6. *Disillusion*

And yet some of the most aggressive Victorians were profoundly insecure. The two most combative writers of the age, as they were called at the time, Carlyle and Kingsley,[71] were deeply troubled with religious doubts, acutely aware of weakness and frustration. Perhaps the paradox is only apparent. At moments when the vision of Nature, blind and indifferent, bringing to life, bringing to death, starts up in mockery of any faith in a loving God and a moral universe, the will to believe dissolves in cynicism. "Life," one says sardonically, "is simply a conflict of wills in which strength alone has any value, in which only the strongest survive; and might is right because there isn't any *moral* right at all." This was one thing Ruskin meant, I think, by saying that while some of the unbelievers he knew were in misery or plodding hesitation, others were driven into "reckless defiance." [72] But the phrase could also describe another type of reaction. At moments when the long struggle to hold or regain a religious faith seems doomed to failure, especially when the old doubts one thought were laid revive again with renewed force, the baffled will breaks out in blind rage, breeding the most violent emotions. In such a mood, not of cynicism but of bitter exasperation, the objective correlative is the destructive force of a conquering hero. Sterling was appalled by the infernal sympathy with which Carlyle described the Reign of Terror in *The French Revolution*. It was, he said, as though he found "the world, and the world's law, and the law of his own nature, so ill a friend to him, that he more sympathizes with almost the worst rebellion against all law, than with almost the best submission to it;" and therefore "thinks . . . a Turgot coldly respectable, while a greedy ruffian Danton, a mass of brutal self-will and reinless appetite, kindles his admiration, and almost his love!" [73] Sterling's initial phrase suggests a three-fold source of exasperation: not only the unrewarded struggle against the world that rejected his *Sartor*, and later listened to, but did not heed, his advice; and the hopeless struggle against the law of his own nature, if we may credit the theory of his impotence (this having obvious relevance to the worship of Danton's strength and his "reinless appetite")—but also the long struggle to recapture his early faith and believe again in the divine law of the world, in which repeated moments of success

71. By Greg, "Kingsley and Carlyle," p. 145.

72. *Modern Painters*, 3, chap. 16, sec. 10, in *Works*, 5, 322. For an example see Clough's *Dipsychus*, scene 5, lines 59–72, 99–102, *Poems*, pp. 249–51.

73. "Carlyle," *Essays and Tales*, 1, 372–3.

were always followed by fresh waves of doubt. All this in a passionate nature like Carlyle's was more than sufficient to make him sympathize with the worst rebellion against all law and take angry delight in other Dantons like Governor Eyre and Dr. Francia. Perhaps it was no accident that in the end he came to believe at heart, I think, in nothing but force. The worship of might took the place of the worship of God.[74]

74. A similar conclusion was reached by a critic in *The Times Literary Supplement* (February 15, 1952), p. 124: "He was religious without a religion; a materialist enraged by his own materialism; a Lear who never came in from the storm. Confined in the dark prison of his egotism, he cried aloud for the light which never came. The God he so often invoked, the eternity he so often proclaimed, eluded him. He filled the silence he was never tired of praising with the clamour of his will. . . . Of the Kingdom of Heaven in Heaven he could catch no glimpse. So what was he left with?—only with Man, and Man's dynamic, power." For a less violent reaction to doubt and despair which also contributed to the worship of force, see below, Chap. 12, sec. 6.

Chapter 10

EARNESTNESS

> Next day [in September 1835] the author of all this hubbub was actually christened. Theobald had proposed to call him George after old Mr. Pontifex, but strange to say, Mr. Pontifex overruled him in favour of the name Ernest. The word "earnest" was just beginning to come into fashion, and he thought the possession of such a name might, like his having been baptised in water from the Jordan, have a permanent effect upon the boy's character, and influence him for good during the more critical periods of his life.
>
> *Butler, The Way of All Flesh* [1]

THE ONE THING, as Macaulay would have put it, which every schoolboy knows about the Victorians is that they were earnest. But what is meant and why they were is less easy to say. A starting point is suggested by the above epigraph from Butler. When a word suddenly comes into fashion to describe a 'good' attitude, it is probably used in protest against some other and well-established attitude which is now discovered to be 'bad'; so that the historical context is more useful than the dictionary for understanding its meaning. If the importance of being earnest was first recognized about 1830—on the threshold of the Victorian era—we can be sure that people had begun to feel a danger or an evil in not being earnest.

The attitude under attack was described by George Eliot in the person of an old gentleman of the pre-Victorian world:

> Old Leisure . . . was a contemplative, rather stout gentleman, of excellent digestion,—of quiet perceptions, undiseased by hypothesis; happy in his inability to know the causes of things, preferring

1. Chap. 18, p. 87.

> the things themselves. . . . He knew nothing of weekday services, and thought none the worse of the Sunday sermon if it allowed him to sleep from the text to the blessing . . . for he had an easy, jolly conscience, broad-backed like himself, and able to carry a great deal of beer or port-wine,—not being made squeamish by doubts and qualms and lofty aspirations. Life was not a task to him, but a sinecure: he fingered the guineas in his pocket, and ate his dinners, and slept the sleep of the irresponsible; for had he not kept up his character by going to church on the Sunday afternoons?

Then follows an illuminating comment:

> Fine old Leisure! Do not be severe upon him, and judge him by our modern standard; he never went to Exeter Hall, or heard a popular preacher, or read "Tracts for the Times" or "Sartor Resartus." [2]

The champions of the modern standard raised their voices at almost the same moment. Exeter Hall, the capitol of Evangelical Puritanism, was opened in 1831 (though the revival had been gaining ground since the French Revolution); the *Tracts for the Times* initiated the Oxford Movement in August of the same year (1833) in which Carlyle's *Sartor Resartus* began to appear in *Fraser's Magazine* for November.

Now, patently, old Leisure was not in earnest. He was not, as one would say, taking life seriously. And that means, we see, that intellectually he has no concern whatever with ideas. He goes to church either to sleep or to repeat the great doctrines of the creed without a moment's attention or an ounce of sincere conviction. He would be equally indifferent, we suspect, to political theories or moral philosophies. He is, indeed, *happy* in his inability to know the causes of things. In the second place, he is living as though his life were entirely self-contained. He is quite oblivious to any larger scheme of human destiny, whether natural or supernatural, and to what duties or responsibilities it might entail. His conscience, therefore, is quite easy; and his daily life is devoted to the enjoyment of sensual pleasures.

If old Leisure was not in earnest, those who judged him so severely "by our modern standard" should be the major prophets of earnestness. And with one omission, that is literally the case. "It is not too much to

2. *Adam Bede*, 2, chap. 28, pp. 339–40. In editions where the chapters are consecutively numbered this is chap. 52.

say," remarks a modern scholar, "that, more than any other single
factor, the Evangelical Movement in the Church of England transformed the whole character of English society and imparted to the
Victorian Age that moral earnestness which was its distinguishing characteristic." [3] This may be true, but when the other factors go unmen-
tioned, we are liable to forget them. To Charles Kingsley, writing in
1851, the "growing moral earnestness" of the age was "in great part
owing . . . to the Anglican movement," and he praised its leaders,
especially Newman, for having "awakened hundreds, perhaps thousands, of cultivated men and women to ask themselves whether God
sent them into the world merely to eat, drink, and be merry." [4] Bagehot
and others traced the "gospel of earnestness" to Carlyle and the Car-
lyleans; [5] while Fitzjames Stephen attributed "the substitution of the
word 'earnest' for its predecessor 'serious'" to Thomas Arnold and his
Rugby students at the universities. [6] (If George Eliot had said that old
Leisure never went to Exeter Hall *or Rugby School,* her list would
have been complete; and the additional date would also have been
right, for Arnold became headmaster in 1828.) Behind all these prophets lay not only the Puritan tradition or its Wesleyan revival, but quite
other forces as well—the sense of crisis, middle-class business, religious doubt.

In these authorities we find the definitions latent in the negatives of
George Eliot. To be in earnest *intellectually* is to have or to seek to
have genuine beliefs about the most fundamental questions in life, and
on no account merely to repeat customary and conventional notions

3. Canon Charles Smyth, "The Evangelical Discipline," in *Ideas and Beliefs
of the Victorians,* p. 98.

4. Preface to the fourth ed., *Yeast,* pp. xv–xvi.

5. "Shakespeare," *Works, 1,* 299; "Macaulay," ibid., *2,* 76. Also see the evidence
of Morley and Martineau, quoted below, p. 256. With Kingsley's statement about
the Tractarians, cf. Froude's about Carlyle (*Carlyle: Life in London, 1,* chap. 11,
p. 291): "To everyone who took life seriously, who wished to make an honourable
use of it, and could not be content with sitting down and making money, his words
were like the morning reveille."

6. Review of "Tom Brown's Schooldays," *Edinburgh Review, 107* (1858), 183.
In the 1862 preface to *Alton Locke,* pp. xc–xci, Kingsley attributed much of the
"increased earnestness and high-mindedness" at the universities "to the late High-
Church movement; much to the influence of Dr. Arnold; much to that of Mr.
Maurice; much to the general increase of civilization throughout the country."
G. M. Young's association of the word (*Victorian England,* p. 14) with an Elizabethan exuberance that includes scented hair, gleaming jewelry, and resplendent
waistcoats seems to me completely mistaken. As I point out below, the ideal of
moral earnestness was partly raised *against* dandyism.

insincerely, or to play with ideas or with words as if the intellectual life were a May-game.

> He was one of those who cannot *but* be in earnest; whom Nature herself has appointed to be sincere. While others walk in formulas and hearsays, contented enough to dwell there, this man could not screen himself in formulas; he was alone with his own soul and the reality of things. . . . From of old, a thousand thoughts, in his pilgrimings and wanderings, had been in this man: What am I? What *is* this unfathomable Thing I live in, which men name Universe? What is Life; what is Death? What am I to believe? What am I to do?[7]

To be in earnest *morally* is to recognize that human existence is not a short interval between birth and death in which one fingers as many guineas as possible and eats all the good dinners he can, but a spiritual pilgrimage from here to eternity in which he is called upon to struggle with all his power against the forces of evil, in his own soul and in society. This is the "real" nature of life.

> Life is real! Life is earnest!
>   And the grave is not its goal;
> Dust thou art, to dust returnest,
>   Was not spoken of the soul.

And that vision entails enormous obligations:

> The predominant characteristic of Dr. Arnold's mind, and that for which above all others we honour him, was his *earnestness*. The idea conveyed by the motto from Schiller, which Carlyle has prefixed to his "Past and Present"—*ernst ist das Leben*—seems to have been, in all its magnificent meaning, perpetually present to his thoughts. Life, in his view of it, was no pilgrimage of pleasure, but a scene of toil, of effort, of appointed work—of grand purposes to be striven for—of vast ends to be achieved—of fearful evils to be uprooted or trampled down—of sacred and mighty principles to be asserted and carried out.[8]

Fundamentally, that conception of life was also held by the Victorian agnostics. Ignore the religious implications, interpret the vast ends as

7. Carlyle, describing Mohammed, *Heroes and Hero-Worship*, Lecture 2, p. 54.
8. W. R. Greg, review of Stanley's *Life*, in *Westminster Review*, 42 (1844), 380. Cf. Carlyle, *Past and Present*, Bk. IV, chap. 7, pp. 290–1. The verse above is a stanza from Longfellow's "Psalm of Life."

those of the human race and the grand purposes the building of the Kingdom of Man, and for Arnold one could substitute Mill or George Eliot, Harriet Martineau or John Morley.

Different as they are, both uses of the term have their common denominator. The prophets of earnestness were attacking a casual, easy-going, superficial, or frivolous attitude, whether in intellectual or in moral life; and demanding that men should think and men should live with a high and serious purpose. What Thomas Arnold longed above all things to give his Rugby students was "moral thoughtfulness,—the inquiring love of truth going along with the devoted love of goodness." [9]

How surprised old Leisure would have been to hear a sermon of Arnold's—if he had stayed awake. And how baffled he would have felt to find himself condemned in his old age for a life no one had questioned before. But the change in value judgment is easy to explain. In the 1830's the most sensitive minds became aware that England was faced by a profound crisis. The intellectual world, the Christian Church, and the social order were all in grave peril, to be averted only by the most earnest search for saving ideas and the most earnest life of moral dedication. And yet people were going about their business —their pleasure rather—as if they had nothing to do but to eat, drink, and be comfortable; which seemed to Newman and the Evangelicals, to Carlyle and Thomas Arnold, not to mention Utilitarians and Broadchurchmen and Cambridge Apostles, just about the best possible way to bring on the destruction that was threatening both Church and State.

1. Intellectual Earnestness

In the background, eighteenth-century rationalism, and in the foreground the passing of Catholic Emancipation, the sharp struggle over the Reform Bill, and the Liberal attack on the Church of England combined, in the early thirties, to shake the security of the English mind. Not only time-honored institutions, but major assumptions in moral and intellectual matters which had been accepted for centuries were suddenly being questioned. Mill proclaimed a state of "intellectual anarchy"; Carlyle talked of an age of doubt in which "Belief, Faith has well-nigh vanished from the world," and the younger generation no longer grows up with any competent theory of the universe, or any definite answers to the questions, "What is man, What

9. Stanley, *Life of Arnold*, chap. 3, p. 116.

are the duties of man?" [10] In the political-economic area problems of
the gravest kind—how to alleviate the increasing misery of the industrial and agricultural workers and to resolve the growing conflict between masters and men—were defying solution. To intelligent minds
this condition was deeply disturbing, both on personal and on social
grounds. They felt it was perilous, for their own stability and that of
society, to sail blindfold and haphazard, without rudder or compass
or chart.[11] A reconstruction of thought was absolutely imperative.
"Clearly enough . . . there *is* want of instruction and light in this mirk
midnight of human affairs; such want as probably for eighteen hundred years there has not been." [12] Clearly enough to the prophets but
not to anyone else. Society was pursuing its worldly goals of ambition
or pleasure in utter indifference to the gravity of the situation. Almost
no one was in earnest, at the very moment when earnestness was the
first and basic requirement for a re-examination of fundamental ideas.
"How have we to regret," moans Carlyle, "not only that men have
'no religion', but that they have next to no reflection; and go about
with heads full of mere extraneous noises, with eyes wide-open but
visionless,—for most part in the somnambulist state!" [13]

In Mill's correspondence at the time, society is divided into the few
"believers" and the many "nonbelievers." In Edinburgh there is only

10. Mill, *The Spirit of the Age*, p. 12; Carlyle, "Characteristics," *Essays*, 3, 29.

11. Cf. Morley, "Carlyle," *Critical Miscellanies, 1*, 137; "One of Mr. Carlyle's
chief and just glories is, that for more than forty years he has clearly seen, and kept
constantly and conspicuously in his own sight and that of his readers, the profoundly important crisis in the midst of which we are living. The moral and social
dissolution in progress about us, and the enormous peril of sailing blindfold and
haphazard, without rudder or compass or chart, have always been fully visible to
him, and it is no fault of his if they have not become equally plain to his contemporaries. The policy of drifting has had no countenance from him."

12. Carlyle, in Froude, *Carlyle: First Forty Years, 2*, chap. 9, p. 202. The date
is 1831.

13. *Past and Present*, Bk. III, chap. 7, p. 174. We begin to see an important
link between this chapter and Chaps. 6 and 7 above. In such critical times an
earnest attachment to a saving idea or a program of reform can easily lead to
dogmatism or/and rigidity, first among the prophets and then presently spreading
through the upper and middle classes as the sense of gravity is recognized. See
in particular Chap. 7, sec. 1, "Sectarian Fervor," especially the opening paragraph (pp. 162–3), where Thomas Arnold is discussed. The writer referred to there
in note 7 goes on to say (ibid.) that Arnold's vehemence of language "was one
of the natural effects of his being so much in earnest." Also see the Mill quotation
in note 6.

"an *odour* of literature and intellect"; in Glasgow, Liverpool, and the like "little else than the *stench* of trade." London is better, bad though it is, because "there are here, in infinitesimal *proportion* indeed, but in absolute *number* more than a very few, actual *believers;* some, whom I . . . could call *true* believers." In another letter Mill speaks of having hoped "that *despair* was the necessary consequence of having no Belief, in a nation at least, though not always in an individual." But apparently that is true only of the nobler spirits. The mass of the well-to-do classes in France, for example, seem entirely able to "make themselves comfortable without either God or Devil either literal or constructive, and are well satisfied to eat their pudding in quiet." Clearly, a "believer" either has some real convictions or is so disturbed by not having any that he is earnestly seeking for light. He is a "sincere, truth-loving person." The "non-believer" (like George Eliot's Leisure, "not being made squeamish by doubts") is either ignoring all basic questions or is not seriously—that is, not sincerely—concerned about the ideas he professes or discusses.[14]

It is the latter, the man of education who is equipped to think and yet refuses to do so, whom Carlyle and Mill find most irritating. They strike at various manifestations of this fatal indifference to truth. There is the repetition of old ideas, especially in religion, which one no longer believes. This is the "beginning of all immorality, or rather it is the impossibility henceforth of any morality whatsoever," since insincerity is corrupting to the whole character. "I do not wonder," says Carlyle, "that the earnest man denounces this, brands it, prosecutes it with inextinguishable aversion." [15] Still more does he denounce the man who views the intellectual life as a kind of sport in which he shows off his skill in debate or in wit, and defends his lack of earnestness as broad-minded toleration: such a man, for example, as Francis Jeffrey, who lived in the old world of Leisure and continued the skeptical tradition of eighteenth-century thought. Jeffrey found Carlyle too "dreadfully in earnest" because "he could not sit down quietly and enjoy himself 'without a theory of the universe in which he could believe'"; naturally enough, since he himself, never having had any strong beliefs, "thought zeal for creeds and anxiety about positive opinions more and more ludicrous. In fact, he regarded discussions which aimed at more than exercising the faculties and exposing intoler-

14. *Letters, 1,* 38, 73–4, 88.
15. *Heroes,* Lecture 4, p. 122.

ance very tiresome and foolish." [16] But to Carlyle this was intellectual dilettantism, and utterly base and reprehensible at a moment when intellectual earnestness was so badly needed. "Dilettantism, hypothesis, speculation, a kind of amateur-search for Truth, toying and coquetting with Truth: this is the sorest sin. The root of all other imaginable sins. It consists in the heart and soul of the man never having been *open* to Truth;—'living in a vain show.' " [17] This was fiddling while England burned. "The time for levity, insincerity, and idle babble and play-acting, in all kinds, is gone by; it is a serious, grave time. Old long-vexed questions, not yet solved in logical words or parliamentary laws, are fast solving themselves in facts, somewhat unblessed to behold!" [18]

To play with words was just as shameful as to play with ideas. The style of wit, paradox, and epigram, so characteristic of eighteenth-century taste and so natural for a dandy, became intolerable. Apropos of an article by Bulwer Lytton in the *Edinburgh Review* (whose editor from 1802 to 1829 was Francis Jeffrey), Mill wrote to the author:

> I first thought it might possibly be Macaulay's. . . . It has much of the same brilliancy, but not his affected and antithetical style, and above all a perception of truth, which he never seems to have,

16. Froude, *Carlyle: Life in London, 1*, chap. 11, p. 295, and *Carlyle: First Forty Years, 2*, chap. 17, p. 394. Cf. Lydgate's remark about Dorothea Brooke (*Middlemarch, 1*, chap. 10, pp. 124–5): "She is a good creature—that fine girl—but a little too earnest. . . . It is troublesome to talk to such women. They are always wanting reasons."

17. *Heroes*, Lecture 2, p. 73. Both forms of intellectual dilettantism described in this paragraph are brought together in a letter of Clough's for August 17, 1845, *Prose Remains*, p. 99: "I believe there is a vicious habit of poking into intellectual questions merely for the fun of it, or the vanity of it, only not quite so common as people make out. At any rate, taking it easy and acquiescing in anything is much more common."

18. *Past and Present*, Bk. III, chap. 13, p. 209. In his "Historic Survey of German Poetry" (1831), *Essays, 2*, 368, he had said that even "honest Scepticism, honest Atheism, is better than the withered lifeless Dilettantism and amateur Eclecticism, which merely toys with all opinions." Newman had the same complaint to make in a sermon on "Christian Zeal" preached in 1834, *Parochial and Plain Sermons, 2*, 383–4: "Positive misbelief is a less odious state of mind than the temper of those who are indifferent to religion, who say that one opinion is as good as the other, and contemn or ridicule those who are in earnest." And he went on to notice the present tendency "to call Zeal by the name of intolerance, and to account intolerance the chief of sins; that is, any earnestness for one opinion above another concerning God's nature, will, and dealings with man."

and a genuine love of the True and the Beautiful. . . . I could not help saying to myself, who would look for these qualities in the *Edinburgh Review?* How the readers of that review must be puzzled and bewildered by a writer who actually takes decided views, who is positively in earnest. . . . Among us [at the *Westminster Review*], you would at least find both writers and readers who are in earnest . . . readers by whom what you write would be taken *au sérieux* and not as a mere play of intellect and fancy.[19]

In Carlyle, more "dreadfully in earnest" than Mill (Mill was simply "in earnest"), this attitude reaches an irritable scorn for men like Lamb and Hazlitt:

How few people speak for Truth's sake, even in its humblest modes! I return from Enfield, where I have seen Lamb, &c. &c. Not one of that class will tell you a straightforward story or even a credible one about any matter under the sun. All must be packed up into epigrammatic contrasts, startling exaggerations, claptraps that will get a plaudit from the galleries! . . . Wearisome, inexpressibly wearisome to me is that sort of clatter; it is not walking (to the end of time you would never advance, for *these persons indeed have no* WHITHER); it is not bounding and frisking in graceful, natural joy; it is dancing—a St. Vitus's dance. Heigh ho! Charles Lamb I sincerely believe to be in some considerable degree insane. . . . His speech wriggles hither and thither with an incessant painful fluctuation, *not an opinion in it, or a fact, or a phrase that you can thank him for.*[20]

19. *Letters, 1,* 102–4. The date is 1836. Cf. Newman, in Wilfrid Ward, *The Life of John Henry, Cardinal Newman* (2 vols. London and New York, 1912), 2, chap. 30, p. 335: "A man should be in earnest, by which I mean he should write not for the sake of writing, but to bring out his thoughts." According to Mill (*Autobiography,* chap. 4, p. 84) it was because the Benthamites wrote with an "air of strong conviction . . . when scarcely any one else seemed to have an equally strong faith in as definite a creed" that they filled "a greater place in the public mind" of the eighteen-twenties and thirties than they later held after "other equally earnest schools of thought" had arisen in England. Cf. F. D. Maurice's comment on the Utilitarians (*Eustace Conway, 1,* 92–3): "The tone of their conversation, after the indifference and want of all public spirit to which one has been used at the university, was quite inspiring."

20. Froude, *Carlyle: First Forty Years, 2,* chap. 9, p. 209. The italics are mine. Cf. *Past and Present,* Bk. III, chap. 3, p. 151, on the fashionable wit. Cf. Clough, "Look you, my simple friend, 'tis one of those," *Poems,* p. 25.

It is because the times are so urgent and so much in need of helpful opinion or fact from persons who have a "whither" (a serious object in mind in what they do or say), that all wit and humor are identified with "levity, insincerity, and idle babble." Plainly the solemn distaste of the Victorians for any joke that touched on things considered grave or sacred is not to be traced simply to the moral proprieties. A friend of Tennyson's recalled a conversation in which "some one made a remark about the fruit being liable to disagree with himself or others, to which another . . . replied with a jocular remark about 'the disturbed districts,' alluding of course to some disorders apprehended or existing in the centres of industry." Tennyson cut in sharply, with a voice and accent like Dr. Arnold's, "I can't joke about so grave a question." [21] Carlyle cannot joke about *any* question. When Lamb made the mistake of telling him there were just two things he regretted in England's history, "First, that Guy Fawkes' plot did not take effect (there would have been so glorious an *explosion*); second, that the Royalists did not hang Milton (then we might have laughed at them)," one shudders to think of the pained expression which appeared on Carlyle's face. His comment is enough: "*Armer Teufel!*" [22]

Finally, the new frame of mind was innately hostile to any literature not seriously—even solemnly—concerned with fundamental questions. Not simply the fashionable novels and light verse which the Minerva Press supplied in abundance, but also the popular work of both Byron and Scott were denounced as "literature of amusement." To Carlyle, Scott was the perfect example of a skeptical dilettante writing simply to entertain "indolent languid men":

> The great Mystery of Existence was not great to him; did not drive him into rocky solitudes to wrestle with it for an answer, to be answered or to perish. . . . One sees not that he believed in anything; nay, he did not even disbelieve; but quietly acquiesced, and made himself at home in a world of conventionalities; the false, the semi-false and the true were alike true in this, that they were there, and had power in their hands more or less. It was well to feel so; and yet not well! We find it written, "Woe to them that

21. Tennyson, *Memoir of Tennyson, 1*, 205. Cf. Ruskin, "The Mystery of Life and Its Arts" (1868), *Sesame and Lilies*, sec. 135, in *Works, 18*, 181: "In time of national distress, of religious trial, of crisis for every interest and hope of humanity —none of us will cease jesting."

22. In Froude (note 20, above), p. 210.

are at ease in Zion"; but surely it is a double woe to them that are at ease in Babel.

Small wonder Carlyle criticizes the Waverley novels for containing nothing "profitable for doctrine, for reproof, for edification, for building up or elevating, in any shape! The sick heart will find no healing here, the darkly-struggling heart no guidance." Clearly, Scott belonged to the easy-going world of old Leisure before the crisis of the thirties. But now "in so extremely serious a Universe as this of ours," in an age "destitute of faith but terrified of scepticism," a speaker must search for "some kind of gospel-tidings." He must be in earnest.[23]

2. Moral Earnestness and the Religious Crisis

Underlying the sectarian differences between Arnold, Newman, and the Evangelicals, there is a fundamental community of aim which springs from their common indebtedness to John Wesley and the religious movement he initiated in the eighteenth century.[24] All of them attack what they call "nominal" Christianity and the slack or feeble conception of moral life that went with it. William Wilberforce called his important book, often considered the Bible of Evangelicalism, *A Practical View of the Prevailing Religious System of Professed Christians, in the Higher and Middle Classes, Contrasted with Real Christianity.* On the prevailing system, a man was considered, and considered himself, a Christian if he professed the main doctrines of the creed and was not guilty of any serious vice. "The title implies no more than a sort of formal, general assent to Christianity in the gross, and a degree of morality in practice, but little, if at all, superior to that for which we look in a good Deist, Mussulman, or Hindoo."[25]

23. "Sir Walter Scott" (1838), *Essays, 4,* 36, 49, 55, 76.

24. See the quotations below from Gladstone in note 26, Clough, pp. 232–3, and Stanley in note 30. There is no satisfactory term to apply to this movement. To call it Evangelical is to introduce a confusion between the movement as a whole and the Evangelical party in the English Church. Puritan is better, but the spirit of piety, reflected in the common designation of "the religion of the heart," marks a clear differentiation from Calvinism, let alone the fact that to call Newman, or even Arnold, a Puritan is rather incongruous. Either the Wesleyan Movement or the Christian Revival would, I think, be better terms (and are sometimes employed in this book), but Evangelical and Puritan have so long been used, and by the Victorians themselves, that I have often adopted them. For a good account of the subject which emphasizes its impact on political and secular life, see Halévy, *England in 1815,* pp. 387–459. There is a useful chapter in Annan's *Leslie Stephen,* pp. 110–29.

25. Chap. 4, sec. 1, p. 109. The first edition came out in 1797.

From Wesley and Whitefield in 1740 to Newman and Arnold in 1830, this was the central evil and not actual disbelief. When Arnold, for example, expressed his fear of an approaching struggle between good and evil "in which there may well happen the greatest trial to the faith of good men that can be imagined," he was not thinking of the spirit of rationalism, and his sermons are not concerned with defending Christian faith. The enemy is the spirit of the world, silently blotting out any true awareness of the Christian destiny of man and the life of moral earnestness it demanded.[26]

That was exemplified, for Wilberforce, in both the upper and middle classes. The aristocracy was not licentious really, or irreligious; it was simply preoccupied with an endless round of amusements—cards, theaters, banquets, hunting. "Christianity," he said, "calls her professors to a state of diligent watchfulness and active services. But the persons of whom we are now speaking, forgetting alike the duties they owe to themselves and to their fellow-creatures, often act as though their condition were meant to be a state of uniform indulgence, and vacant, unprofitable sloth." Complementing this "sober sensuality" was the "sober avarice" and the "sober ambition" of the business and professional world. The successful man was congratulating himself on not being like one who is "a spendthrift or a mere man of pleasure," when all the while he, too, lacked "the true principle of action," and was allowing "personal advancement or the acquisition of wealth" to become objects of supreme desire and predominant pursuit.[27] Even the

26. Stanley, *Life*, chap. 2, p. 42. Cf. Wilberforce's "Introduction," p. iii: "The main object which the writer has in view is, not to convince the sceptic, or to answer the arguments of persons who avowedly oppose the fundamental doctrines of our religion; but to point out the scanty and erroneous system of the bulk of those who belong to the class of orthodox Christians, and to contrast their defective scheme with a representation of what the author apprehends to be real Christianity." Like Arnold, Wilberforce found that "real Christianity" in the Gospels. So did the Tractarians: see R. W. Church, *The Oxford Movement. Twelve Years, 1833–1845* (London and New York, 1891), p. 167. Cf. a passage in Gladstone's essay "The Evangelical Movement," *Gleanings of Past Years, 1843–79* (7 vols. London, 1879), 7, 222–5: "It was common, in my early days," he says (that is, 1810–30), "for morality to be taught without direct derivation from, or reference to, the Person of Christ"; and he goes on to define the religious movement I am describing as "a great revival of what may roughly be called Gospel-preaching in the English Church, extending far beyond the limits of school or party." This is the basic link, he suggests, which connects the Evangelicals with the Tractarians— and both, I would add, with Arnold and his Liberal disciples.

27. *Practical View*, chap. 4, sec. 2, pp. 128–35. Cf. Hannah More, *Practical Piety; or, the Influence of the Religion of the Heart on the Conduct of the Life*

clergy and the intellectuals, in this worldly environment, were living in "practical" or "virtual" atheism—that is, in "a state of insensibility to things as they really are in God's sight." In his sermon contrasting the spirit of the world with "the spirit which is of God," Arnold explained the charge: "Many of us are very seldom in earnest. By this I mean, that the highest part of our minds, and that which judges of the highest things, is generally slumbering or but half awake. We may go through a very busy day, and yet not be, in this true sense, in earnest at all; our best faculties may, as it were, be all the while sleeping or playing." [28] That is to say, our religious awareness and our moral will are both in abeyance, and our conscience is almost as easy as old Leisure's.

This lamentable state had another and related origin. The worldly spirit was silently obliterating whatever it found alien in the Gospels and retaining only what it could assimilate, so that real Christianity was being transformed into something far less demanding—into what Newman called "The Religion of the Day." In his important sermon on that subject, he exposed the moral slackness of its disciples:

> They argue that it is our duty to solace ourselves here (in moderation, of course) with the goods of this life,—that we have only to be thankful while we use them,—that we need not alarm ourselves,—that God is a merciful God,—that amendment is quite sufficient to atone for our offences,—that though we have been irregular in our youth, yet that is a thing gone by,—that we forget it, and therefore God forgets it . . . that we should not be over serious,—that we should have large views on the subject of human nature,—and that we should love all men.

So defined, the teaching of the day, though partially Christian, is really built upon worldly principle. It pretends to be the Gospel, but it has dropped out one whole side of the Gospel. It includes "no true fear of God, no fervent zeal for His honour, no deep hatred of sin." The conscience, which is "a stern, gloomy principle" telling us "of guilt and of prospective punishment" has been superseded by Shaftesbury's moral

---

(1811), chap. 18, "Insensibility to Eternal Things," pp. 247–9, 255–8. This was perhaps the most popular textbook of Evangelical ethics.

28. *Christian Life, Its Course, Its Hindrances, and Its Helps*, No. 17, pp. 180–1; and cf. *Sermons*, *1*, No. 1, pp. 1–12, and Stanley's *Life*, p. 53, letter of November 20, 1819. The charge of insensibility is frequently made by Newman and the Evangelicals: see Newman, *Parochial and Plain Sermons*, *1*, Nos. 5, 8, 26, pp. 57, 111, 338, 349; Wilberforce, chap. 2, sec. 2, p. 45; Hannah More, *Practical Piety*, chap. 18.

sense ("the love of the beautiful") or Bentham's principle of expedience or utility. Accordingly, as its terrors disappear, "then disappear also, in the creed of the day, those fearful images of Divine wrath with which the Scriptures abound." In short, religion has become "pleasant and easy." It has "no seriousness,—and therefore is neither hot nor cold, but (in Scripture language) *lukewarm.*" [29]

Because Newman and the Oxford Movement have been so exclusively identified with Anglo-Catholic doctrine, their central concern with the moral life has been obscured. And because Arnold attacked them both so violently, his fundamental agreement with them has been overlooked. What R. W. Church wrote of the sermons of Newman is equally true (as he himself noted) of Arnold's, and of those of Evangelical preachers like Charles Simeon at Cambridge: "A passionate and sustained earnestness after a high moral rule, seriously realised in conduct, is the dominant character of these sermons. They showed the strong reaction against slackness of fibre in the religious life; . . . the blunted and impaired sense of truth, which reigned with little check in the recognised fashions of professing Christianity; . . . the strange blindness to the real sternness, nay the austerity, of the New Testament." [30]

To be an earnest Christian demanded a tremendous effort to shape the character in the image of Christ. One had to hate the world, the flesh, and the devil, to keep all of God's commandments exactly, and to live "as in the sight of the world to come, as if . . . the ties of this life" were already broken.[31] For such a "frame and temper of mind" the controlling influence is the conscience; for when we set "God in

29. *Parochial Sermons, 1,* No. 24, pp. 312–19; cf. No. 8, pp. 99–100.

30. Church, *The Oxford Movement,* p. 19. Cf. A. P. Stanley, "The Oxford School," *Edinburgh Review, 153* (1881), 310: "What was it again that drew admiring students . . . round Dr. Newman at Oxford? . . . Chiefly the grasp of ethical precepts, the appeals to conscience, the sincere conviction of the value of purity and generosity, in which many of his hearers recognised the reverberations, in a more subtle, though not in a more commanding form, of those stirring discourses which had thrilled them from the pulpit of Rugby." The attribution of this article to Stanley is made by R. E. Prothero and G. G. Bradley, *The Life and Correspondence of Arthur Penrhyn Stanley* (2 vols. New York, 1894), 2, 580. On the ethical impact of the Oxford Movement, note the quotation from Kingsley, above, p. 220, and see in general Amy Cruse, *The Victorians and Their Reading,* chaps. 2 and 3, "The Tractarians" and "The World of Miss Charlotte Yonge."

31. Newman, *Parochial Sermons, 1,* No. 1, pp. 2–3. Cf. Hannah More, *Practical Piety,* chap. 3, p. 54.

Christ before us," as Arnold put it, "tnen the conscience is awake; then we are in earnest." [32] And this "Puritan" or "Nonconformist" conscience, at crucial war with the world, is highly sensitive and "tender"; so much so that Victorians often speak of sin in accents of utter detestation, sometimes even of horror. There was something in Arnold's "very tone and outward aspect, before which anything low, or false, or cruel, instinctively quailed and cowered. . . . That ashy paleness and that awful frown were almost always the expression . . . of deep, ineffable scorn and indignation at the sight of vice and sin." [33] The reference to "anything low, oₗ false, or cruel" reflects the wide interpretation of sin by the tender conscience; in fact, the smallest faults became serious vices when they were seen as the opening wedge through which the worldly spirit might slide into the soul. "In all that relates to God and to himself, the Christian knows of no small faults. He considers all allowed and wilful sins, whatever be their magnitude, as an offence against his Maker. Nothing that offends *him* can be insignificant. Nothing that contributes to fasten on ourselves a wrong habit can be trifling." That is the Evangelical voice of Hannah More,[34] but Arnold and Newman speak from the same conviction. In the "Epilogue" to *Dipsychus*, Arthur Clough, one of Arnold's most devoted disciples at Rugby, argues with his uncle, who clearly belongs to the pre-Victorian world of George Eliot's Leisure. The poem, says Clough, represents "the conflict between the tender conscience and the world," at which his uncle bursts out: "Consciences are often much too tender in your generation—schoolboys' consciences, too! As my old friend the Canon says of the Westminster students, 'They're all so pious.' It's all Arnold's doing; he spoilt the public schools." Clough protests that Westminster had its Cowper (the Evangelical poet) and that his uncle "must not refer it to Arnold, at all at all. Anything that Arnold did in this direction—"

> "Why, my dear boy, how often have I not heard from you, how he used to attack offences, not as offences—the right view—against discipline, but as sin, heinous guilt, I don't know what beside!" . . .

32. *Christian Life*, p. 187. Cf. a remark in Stanley's *Life*, p. 551, from a letter of April 1, 1840: "It is a real pleasure to be brought into communication with any man who is in earnest, and who really looks to God's will as his standard of right and wrong."

33. Stanley, *Life*, chap. 3, p. 158. For the same attitude in Kingsley, see above, p. 173.

34. *Practical Piety*, chap. 11, p. 142.

"If he did err in this way, sir, which I hardly think, I ascribe it to the spirit of the time. The real cause of the evil you complain of, which to a certain extent I admit, was, I take it, the religious movement of the last century, beginning with Wesleyanism, and culminating at last in Puseyism. This over-excitation of the religious sense, resulting in this irrational, almost animal irritability of conscience, was, in many ways, as foreign to Arnold a. it is proper to—"

"Well, well, my dear nephew, if you like to make a theory of it, pray write it out for yourself nicely in full; but your poor old uncle does not like theories, and is moreover sadly sleepy." [35]

Plainly Clough's defense amounts to little more than a denial of Arnold's sole responsibility by claiming that the Puritan revival found parallel expression in the Evangelicals and the Oxford Movement.

When the standard of Christian virtue was placed so high and the range and gravity of sin was so great, the Christian life became in literal fact a life of constant struggle—both to resist temptation and to master the desires of the ego. The Victorian conception of warfare as the main business of man was as deeply rooted in the religious as the political and economic order.[36] "Unless you are struggling, unless you are fighting with yourselves, you are no followers of those who 'through many tribulations entered into the kingdom of God.' A fight is the very token of a Christian. He is a soldier of Christ; high or low, he is this and nothing else." [37] His first objective was to beat down the terrible temptations of worldly and fleshly existence. In that struggle no one was more famous than Arnold of Rugby. Even slight acquaintances were "struck by his absolute wrestling with evil, so that like St. Paul he seemed to be battling with the wicked one." [38]

35. *Poems*, pp. 294–6. On the Rugby conscience, see also Leslie Stephen, "Jowett's Life," *Studies of a Biographer*, 2, 127–8.

36. For the latter see above, Chap. 9, secs. 2–5.

37. Newman, *Discourses Addressed to Mixed Congregations* (1849), No. 6, reprinted in his *Sermons and Discourses* (1839–57), ed. C. F. Harrold, 2, 162.

38. Stanley, *Life*, chap. 2, p. 29. Cf. the quotation from his last sermon, ibid., chap. 10, p. 650: "The real point which concerns us all, is not whether our sin be of one kind or of another, more or less venial, or more or less mischievous in a man's judgment, and to our worldly interests; but whether we struggle against all sin because it is sin; whether we have or have not placed ourselves consciously under the banner of our Lord Jesus Christ, trusting in Him, cleaving to Him, feeding on Him by faith daily, and so resolved, and continually renewing our resolution, to be His faithful soldiers and servants to our lives' end."

Whether successful or not, this is a battle which often appears in Victorian fiction and poetry—dramatized most characteristically perhaps by Thomas Hughes in *Tom Brown at Oxford*.[39]

The complementary form of moral struggle in the conscience was constructive. If the enemy was to be resisted and the soul saved, the armor must be forged beforehand. By an elaborate practice of self-discipline, one had to lay the foundation of good habits and acquire the power of self-control. The day began with a period of self-examination, since only when one knew his "besetting infirmities" and had them constantly in mind could he be ready to deny them.[40] Then followed the actual practice, which was so important one was urged even to make up opportunities of self-sacrifice:

> Rise up then in the morning with the purpose that (please God) the day shall not pass without its self-denial, with a self-denial in innocent pleasures and tastes, if none occurs to mortify sin. Let your very rising from your bed be a self-denial; let your meals be self-denials. Determine to yield to others in things indifferent, to go out of your way in small matters, to inconvenience yourself (so that no direct duty suffers by it), rather than you should not meet with your daily discipline. . . . A man says to himself, "How am I to know I am in earnest?" I would suggest to him, Make some sacrifice, do some distasteful thing, which you are not actually obliged to do (so that it be lawful).

This will not only prove the earnestness of your faith, it will "strengthen your general power of self-mastery" and give you "such an habitual command of yourself, as will be a defence ready prepared when the season of temptation comes."[41] But such a victory over the self required a bitter struggle. "It is a great battle to deny ourselves," wrote Arthur Hallam in 1832, "to abdicate the throne of Self, to surrender

39. See below, p. 354.
40. See Newman, *Parochial Sermons, 1,* Nos. 5 and 18, pp. 67, 232; and Hannah More, "Self-Examination," in *Practical Piety.* There is less asceticism in Arnold.
41. Newman, *Parochial Sermons, 1,* 69–70, from No. 5, "Self-Denial the Test of Religious Earnestness." Cf. More, chap. 6, "Cultivation of a Devotional Spirit." When Ethel May in Charlotte Yonge's *Daisy Chain* (Pt. I, chap. 26, p. 253) says that one should take "the right times for refusing oneself some pleasant thing," Meta Rivers asks, "Would not that be only making up something for oneself?" To which Ethel answers: "No, the Church orders it. . . . I mean one can do little secret things—not read storybooks on those days, or keep some tiresome sort of work for them. It is very trumpery, but it keeps the remembrance, and it is not so much as if one did not heed."

up, not a thought, not an act, not a habit even, but the principle of all thoughts, actions & habits, the principle of self pleasing, which lies fast & deep in the dearest region of our souls. Yet this must be done, or we have not the life of Christ." [42]

It is only within this context that we can understand the severity of parental discipline. So long as the child was too young to practice self-denial, it was plainly the bounden duty of the parent to check the first signs of self-will. Even in circles which had no reverence for John Wesley, his doctrine was approved, "that the wills of the children should be broken," [43]—mainly by constant use of the rod (spare the rod and spoil the child was a Victorian platitude), but also by more refined modes of torture, like those practiced on young Augustus Hare:

> I had a favourite cat called Selma, which I adored, and which followed me about at Lime wherever I went. Aunt Esther saw this, and at once insisted that the cat must be given up to her. I wept over it in agonies of grief: but Aunt Esther insisted. My mother was relentless in saying that I must be taught to give up my own way and pleasure to others; and forced to give it up if I would not do so willingly.

> Hitherto I had never been allowed anything but roast-mutton and rice-pudding for dinner. Now all was changed. The most delicious puddings were talked of—*dilated* on—until I became, not greedy, but exceedingly curious about them. At length *le grand moment* arrived. They were put on the table before me, and then, just as I was going to eat some of them, they were snatched away, and I was told to get up and carry them off to some poor person in the village.

The rationale, written in his mother's journal, was that "the will is the thing that needs being brought into subjection." [44] But we must remember that adults treated themselves in the same way. Sir James Stephen, a leader of the Clapham sect and father of Leslie and Fitzjames, "was inexorably suspicious of pleasure. He drank little; ate the

42. From Letter 13, dated April 28, 1832, in a collection of unpublished letters from Hallam to Emily Tennyson in the Wellesley College Library.

43. E. E. Kellett, *Religion and Life in the Early Victorian Age*, p. 68. Cf. Butler, *The Way of All Flesh*, chap. 5, p. 25; chap. 20, pp. 99–100.

44. Augustus J. C. Hare, *The Years with Mother*, ed. M. Barnes (London, 1952), pp. 27, 43; for other examples, see pp. 26–7, 41–4. This is an abridgment of the first three volumes of Hare's *The Story of My Life* (London, 1896).

lightest of meals; and asking himself once why it was that he continued to take snuff and receiving no satisfactory reply, ceremoniously emptied the box out of the window. 'He once smoked a cigar,' wrote Leslie, 'and found it so delicious that he never smoked again.' " [45] Even on their honeymoon, Sir Guy Morville and his bride Amy, good Anglicans like their creator, Charlotte Yonge, made a "resolution against mere pleasure-hunting"; and when Amy barely escaped a fatal accident on a Swiss mountain they had climbed to enjoy the view, both took it as a solemn warning of God not to break their resolution again. [46]

Only by realizing what a desperate struggle the moral life entailed, both to resist temptation and to train the will, can we do justice to the Victorian taboos, so often and so easily ridiculed: the prohibition of dancing, cards, and the theater; of reading various works of literature, including the comedies of Shakespeare; and of treating anything remotely associated with what was sacred or what was evil with the comic spirit—that is to say, with levity. [47] For when the standard of interior character was so high and the best approximation to it so precariously poised, anything that was not patently innocent or didactic might at the least distract the mind from God and fasten the heart more securely to the world, or at the worst corrupt the soul irredeemably. "Flee from the very shadow of evil," wrote Newman; "you cannot be too careful; better be a little too strict than a little too easy,—it is the safer side." [48] We may say that they played it too safe; or, to use one of the favorite texts of the time, that they made the gate too strait and the way too narrow. But when the spirit of the world was, in fact, laying waste the very life and meaning of the Christian ethic, extreme measures were naturally, if not wisely, taken. There is a remark in one of Newman's sermons

45. Annan, *Leslie Stephen*, p. 14. Cf. the quotation from a tract against smoking, cited by Arnold, "Emerson," *Discourses in America* (London, 1885), pp. 200–1: "Smoking . . . is liked because it gives agreeable sensations. Now it is a positive objection to a thing that it gives agreeable sensations. An earnest man will expressly avoid what gives agreeable sensations."

46. *The Heir of Redclyffe*, chap. 30, p. 380. Aunt Esther Hare, who was the chief instrument of Augustus' discipline, was as hard on herself as she was on him: see *The Years with Mother*, p. 43.

47. See below, pp. 357–8, and also Thomas Arnold's significant attack on comedy in *Christian Life*, No. 17, pp. 183–7. The topic is treated by Maurice J. Quinlan, *Victorian Prelude*, chap. 10, "Censors and Expurgators." This book is a useful study of the moral impact of the Wesleyan movement.

48. *Parochial Sermons*, 1, No. 3, p. 38. Cf. Hannah More, *Practical Piety*, chap. 6, pp. 83–4.

which might well have been addressed to Lytton Strachey and his twentieth-century disciples: "Keep in mind all along that we are Christians and accountable beings, who have fixed principles of right and wrong, *by which all things must be tried*, and have religious habits to be matured within them, *towards which all things are to be made subservient.*" [49]

Finally, the inner life of Christian discipline is the clue to another Victorian phenomenon which now seems so strange, the endless concern with self-improvement. Modern psychology has led us to focus on what we are, not what we should be; and the collapse of the religious tradition with its fixed principles of right and wrong has left us looking rather for a basis than a ceiling for our lives. [50] At the most charitable we find Ruskin's advice to the young dated: "Remember that every day of your early life is ordaining irrevocably, for good or evil, the custom and practice of your soul. . . . Now, therefore, see that no day passes in which you do not make yourself a somewhat better creature: and in order to do that, find out, first, what you are now. Do not think vaguely about it; take pen and paper, and write down as accurate a description of yourself as you can, with the date to it." [51] That might have stood on the title page of *The Daisy Chain*, for Charlotte's Yonge's novel is a study of success and failure in the improvement of character. Even the children themselves are constantly pointing out their faults to one another and exhorting one another to conquer them—*now*, so that later they may have strength to resist the Goliath of evil. Their father, of course, has set the pattern. As Dr. May finishes reading the story of David to Tom and Blanche, he asks:

> "Can you tell me how we may be like the shepherd-boy, David?"
> "There aren't giants now," said Tom.
> "Wrong is a giant," said his little sister.
> "Right, my white May-flower, and what then?"
> "We are to fight," said Tom.
> "Yes, and mind, the giant with all his armour may be some great thing we have to do; but what did David begin with when he was younger?"
> "The lion and the bear."

49. *Parochial Sermons*, 2, 376, from No. 30, "The Danger of Accomplishments." The italics are mine.

50. V. S. Pritchett, *The Living Novel* (London, 1946), p. 80.

51. Preface to *Sesame and Lilies* (1871 ed.), sec. 8, in *Works, 18*, 37–8.

"Aye, and minding his sheep. Perhaps little things, now you are little children, may be like the lion and the bear—so kill them off—get rid of them—cure yourself of whining or dawdling, or whatever it be, and mind your sheep well," said he, smiling sweetly in answer to the children's earnest looks as they caught his meaning, "and if you do, you will not find it near so hard to deal with your great giant struggle when it comes."

The heroine Ethel, with the aid of Margaret's counsel, recognizes her lion and bear to be untidiness and impatience, and begins to wrestle with these "greatest hindrances to her doing anything good and great. Though she was obliged to set to work so many principles and reflections to induce herself to wipe a pen or to sit straight on her chair, that it was like winding up a steam-engine to thread a needle, yet the work *was* being done—she was struggling with her faults, humbled by them, watching them, and overcoming them." [52]

That this concern with self-improvement was not limited to Anglicans or Evangelicals calls attention to a significant fact: the creed of earnestness pushed its way beyond church walls into the community at large. Its ideals penetrated into the homes—and consciences —of half-believers and outright agnostics. This was partly because men retained the ethical fervor of the childhood belief they had discarded.[53] But it was not merely a matter of ingrained habit. In the seventies Mallock noticed that in spite of the growing denial of all religious dogmas, *"and in the places where it has done its work most thoroughly*, a mass of moral earnestness seems to survive untouched." [54] Intellectual radicalism produced a frightened clinging to conservative morals, especially at a time when agnosticism was under attack for its supposed tendency to destroy the moral life. On a famous occasion when George Eliot mentioned the three words which had so long been "inspiring trumpet-calls of men,—the words *God, Immortality, Duty*—" she "pronounced, with terrible earnestness, how inconceivable was the *first*, how unbelievable was the *second*, and yet how peremptory and absolute the *third*." [55] It is partly because

---

52. Pt. I, chap. 10, pp. 87, 91. Cf. Beatrice Webb, *My Apprenticeship*, pp. 67–9.

53. J. A. Symond's father is a good example: Brown, *Life of Symonds*, p. 14. Other illustrations are given by Annan, *Leslie Stephen*, pp. 198, 318.

54. *Is Life Worth Living?* p. 188. The italics are mine.

55. Reported by Frederick Myers, "George Eliot," *Essays: Modern* (London, 1885), pp. 268–9. Cf. David Masson, "The Poems of Arthur Hugh Clough," *Macmillan's Magazine*, 6 (1862), 322: "Many of the most daring sceptics in matters

the first two words have lost their meaning that the third is given such passionate affirmation, in her novels and in contemporary society. Many people alive today can remember the atmosphere of the later Victorian home: "We were a Victorian household, and, in spite of an almost militant agnosticism, attached without the smallest tinge of scepticism or hypocrisy to the ideals of the time: duty, work, abnegation, a stern repression of what was called self-indulgence, a horror and a terror of lapsing from the current code." [56]

3. Moral Earnestness and the Social Crisis

The early Victorians lived under the shadow of revolution. The combination on the one hand of radical-democratic propaganda and acute distress among both agricultural and industrial workers, and on the other of Tory repression or Liberal inaction produced a condition which was steadily threatening between 1815 and 1848, and periodically violent. It became a commonplace to think of the nation as divided against itself between the Rich and the Poor, and to dread the possibility of an English explosion as terrible as that in France.[57] To Carlyle and Thomas Arnold, as to most of their contemporaries, the basic cause of the situation was not economic but moral; and, therefore, though political reform might do something to ease the tension, the fundamental cure lay in a reform of character, the character of the landed and moneyed aristocracy. Any remedy of "the fearful state in which we are living," wrote Arnold, would require "the greatest triumph over selfishness" which man had ever achieved; and Carlyle, finding no real cure in "a Morrison's Pill, Act of Parliament, or remedial measure," called for "a radical universal alteration" of our whole "regimen and way of life." [58]

For at present the landed aristocracy was not only pursuing a selfish life of pleasure, shooting pigeons in the hunting season and going gracefully idle in Mayfair during the London season (the world of the dandies in Regency society and in the novels of Bulwer Lytton and Disraeli, with its gospel of Dilettantism); it was also

---

of theology have been strict and even fanatical in their conformity to the established ethics"; and he goes on to cite Clough as an example: "Even when he doubted in theology most, he was firm and orthodox in his creed as to what is moral, noble and manly."

56. Olivia [Dorothy Strachey Bussy], *Olivia* (London, 1949), p. 13.

57. Cf. above, Chap. 3, sec. 1.

58. Stanley, *Life*, pp. 514–15, from a letter of September 25, 1839; Carlyle, *Past and Present*, Bk. I, chap. 4, pp. 23–4.

charging high rents and maintaining the Corn Laws, at once indifferent to the suffering of the poor and to the lessons of France during 1789–94.[59] In the middle class the gospel of Mammonism, which included a pious belief in laissez-faire, had only one moral command: to pay the worker the exact sum covenanted for. That done, the rich mill owner was free to pursue his career of "making money, fame, or some other figure in the world," and the worker was free to carry on the single-handed struggle to keep himself alive without benefit of government aid—which, as Carlyle dryly remarked, might be freedom "to die by want of food." [60] The world had thus become a fancy bazaar to the aristocracy and a warehouse to the middle class, but to neither was it "a mystic temple and hall of doom," with resulting obligations and duties.[61]

As that implies, the ultimate source of the selfishness corrupting society and spelling revolution seemed to Carlyle exactly the same thing the Puritan leaders called nominal Christianity:

> To speak in the ancient dialect, we "have forgotten God." . . . We have quietly closed our eyes to the eternal Substance of things, and opened them only to the Shows and Shams of things. We quietly believe this Universe to be intrinsically a great unintelligible PERHAPS; extrinsically, clear enough, it is a great, most extensive Cattlefold and Workhouse, with most extensive Kitchen-ranges, Dining-tables,—whereat he is wise who can find a place! All the Truth of this Universe is uncertain; only the profit and loss of it, the pudding and praise of it, are and remain very visible to the practical man. . . .
>
> Man has lost the *soul* out of him. . . . This is verily the plaguespot; centre of the universal Social Gangrene, threatening all modern things with frightful death.[62]

In one word, man has no moral earnestness. He must realize once more the real nature of human existence, poised between two eternities. Then he will rediscover his soul and his conscience; then

59. See *Past and Present*, Bk. III, chap. 8, "Unworking Aristocracy," and Bk. IV, chap. 6, "The Landed." Carlyle's remark (Bk. III, chap. 3, p. 150) on "the impotent, insolent Donothingism in Practice and Saynothingism in Speech" brings together the lack of both moral and intellectual earnestness in the aristocracy.

60. Ibid., Bk. III, chap. 2, "Gospel of Mammonism": see especially pp. 145–7. The last remark is from Bk. III, chap. 13, p. 219.

61. "Characteristics," *Essays*, 3, 31.

62. *Past and Present*, Bk. III, chap. 1, pp. 136–7.

he will recognize that he has "Duties . . . that are alone great, and go up to Heaven and down to Hell," duties to serve God and society in his rank and calling.[63] And so, the end of Dilettantism, the end of Mammonism, and the salvation of the country!

Arnold too, called for the introduction of Christian principles into men's social and civil relations,[64] but Arnold, as we know, was deeply concerned with a religious revival, as were Newman and the Evangelicals, for quite a different reason: because the worldly spirit was threatening not the state of society but the state of Christendom. The appeal for moral earnestness by the Puritan leaders was religious and not social in motivation. Their central aim was to make men good Christians—that is, real instead of nominal Christians—that their immortal souls might be saved. But they were aware that in doing so, they would be making men good citizens—that society might be saved. In this way the social need for moral earnestness gave fresh impetus to the Christian revival and increased its influence.

This, indeed, had been true years earlier at the time of the French Revolution. Up to that date any strong religious fervor had been largely limited to the lower classes, to whom the Wesleyan movement had appealed almost exclusively. But now, when social revolution seemed to be the fruit of atheism and immorality, piety became fashionable. Gladstone remembered hearing "persons of great weight and authority" attribute "a reviving seriousness" in religion among both the clergy and the upper classes of lay society "to a reaction against the horrors and impieties of the first French Revolution in its later stages." [65] In this context Wilberforce was able to add a new and forceful argument for Evangelicalism. Writing in 1797, he could point out that if nominal Christianity were to continue, it must lead to the very catastrophe witnessed "in a neighboring country," where "several of the same causes . . . have at length produced their full effect"; whereas real Christianity would "root out our natural selfishness," which is the "mortal distemper of political communities":

> In whatever class or order of society Christianity prevails, she sets herself to rectify the particular faults, or, if we would speak more distinctly, to counteract the particular mode of selfishness to which that class is liable. Affluence she teaches to be liberal

63. Ibid., Bk. I, chap. 4, p. 26; chap. 6, p. 34; Bk. II, chap. 6, pp. 66–7, from which the quotation is taken; Bk. III, chap. 15, pp. 228–30.

64. The references are given below in note 67.

65. "The Evangelical Movement" (above, note 26), p. 219.

and beneficent; authority to bear its faculties with meekness, and to consider the various cares and obligations belonging to its elevated station as being conditions on which that station is conferred. . . . Those in the humbler walks of life . . . she instructs, in their turn, to be diligent, humble, patient: reminding them that their more lowly path has been allotted to them by the hand of God; that it is their part faithfully to discharge its duties, and contentedly to bear its inconveniences. . . . Such are the blessed effects of Christianity on the temporal well-being of political communities.[66]

This also was Arnold's point of view when, with anxious memories of Arthur Young's travels in France in 1789 and 1790, he recognized that the Christian revival he desired on religious grounds would also "expose the wickedness of that spirit which maintains the game laws, and in agriculture and trade seems to think that there is no such sin as covetousness," and thus would introduce a saving moral earnestness into men's civil relations.[67] Newman was less concerned with the social crisis, but he was well aware that the times were dangerous and that "the especial political evils of the day" had their root "in that principle, which St. Paul calls the root of all evil, the love of money"—for which the countermovement of Christianity was the only corrective.[68] It is thus clear that the critical character of the age and in particular the fear of revolution, first in the 1790's and again from 1819 to 1848, provided an environment which gave the Christian revival some of its motivation and much of its appeal. When this indirect result is taken into account, along with its direct effect (illustrated in Carlyle), the social crisis is seen to have contributed as much, I think, as the religious crisis—perhaps even more—to the formation of moral earnestness.

4. Work

Except for "God," the most popular word in the Victorian vocabulary must have been "work." It was, of course, the means by which some of the central ambitions of a commercial society could be

---

66. *Practical View of Christianity*, chap. 6, pp. 296, 308–10. See in general: Quinlan, *Victorian Prelude*, chap. 3, "Reform or Ruin," and V. Kiernan, "Evangelicalism and the French Revolution," *Past and Present*, 1 (1952), 44–56.

67. Stanley, *Life*, chap. 6, pp. 242–3; cf. pp. 249–50, 251–2, letters of November 1830 and December 24, 1830.

68. *Parochial Sermons*, 2, Nos. 28, 31, pp. 356–7, 392.

realized: money, respectability, and success. But it also became an end in itself, a virtue in its own right. All of Dr. Arnold's children were brought up on the precept, " 'Work.' Not, work at this or that —but, Work." [69] Other children heard a biblical injunction that was endlessly repeated: "Work while it is called Today, for the night cometh when no man can work." By the same token idleness was inexcusable. Ruskin's comment on Millais' painting "Mariana in the Moated Grange" is straight to the point: "If the painter had painted Mariana at work in an unmoated grange, instead of idle in a moated one, it had been more to the purpose—whether of art or life." [70] Even among the landed gentry idleness required an explanation: "Sir Michael had gone to his dressing-room to prepare for dinner after a day of lazy enjoyment; that is perfectly legitimate for an invalid." [71]

This did not mean that one was never to relax. Allowance was made for recreation, in the literal sense that ties it to the pattern of work. Thomas Arnold, on vacation in the Italian lakes, must resist the temptation "to bring one's family and live here . . . abandoning the line of usefulness and activity" which he has in England; he must remember that recreation is intended only "to strengthen us for work to come." [72] Or, in a variation of the same idea, Ruskin thinks playful rest entirely justified "during the reaction after hard labour, and quickened by satisfaction in the accomplished duty or perfected result." [73]

The glorification of work as a supreme virtue, with the accompanying scorn of idleness, was the commonest theme of the prophets of earnestness; for the full meaning of a life of work was identical in outward action (apart from the internal discipline of the character) with a life of moral earnestness. W. R. Greg, writing on what Carlyle had done for his age, concluded:

> He has infused into it something of his own uncompromising earnestness. He has preached up the duty and the dignity of WORK, with an eloquence which has often made the idle shake

69. Thomas Arnold the Younger, *Passages in a Wandering Life* (London, 1900), p. vi.

70. "Notes on Millais," *Works*, 14, 496.

71. M. E. Braddon, *Lady Audley's Secret* (2 vols. Leipzig, 1862), 2, chap. 9, p. 164.

72. Stanley, *Life*, appendix D, sec. 5, pp. 700–1.

73. *Stones of Venice*, 3, chap. 3, sec. 75, in *Works*, 11, 193.

off their idleness, and the frivolous feel ashamed of their frivolity. He has proclaimed, in tones that have stirred many hearts, that in toil, however humble, if honest and hearty, lie our true worth and felicity here below. "Blessed is the man who has found his work," he somewhere says: "let him ask no other blessedness." [74]

These various meanings of the term and their connection with earnestness, first learned by Carlyle in his Puritan home, are brought out more explicitly by Newman in a sermon that starts from the question, "Why were we sent into the world?" Was it merely "to live for ourselves, to live for the lust of the moment . . . without any aim beyond this visible scene? . . . What a contrast is all this to the end of life, as it is set before us in our most holy Faith!" For there we learn that "we are not here, that we may go to bed at night, and get up in the morning, toil for our bread, eat and drink, laugh and joke, sin when we have a mind, and reform when we are tired of sinning, rear a family and die." We are not here, that is, to live like George Eliot's Leisure. On the contrary, "every one who breathes, high and low, educated and ignorant, young and old, man and woman, has a mission, has a work." [75] The word "mission" is important. A Christian was not only to work (as opposed to being idle), but to work in the right spirit—that is, with the sense of having a purpose or mission for which he had special gifts and to which he was dedicated: the service of God in his secular calling. And by doing so, he also served himself because he developed his god-given talent, to the end that he might not be charged at the day of reckoning with the unlit lamp or the ungirt loin. The students at Rugby saw in Arnold a man whose work "was founded on a deep sense of its duty [to God] and its value [to the individual]." From his precept and example they learned "an humble, profound, and most religious consciousness that work is the appointed calling of man on earth, the end for which his various faculties were given, the element in which his nature is ordained to develope itself, and in which his progressive advance towards heaven is to lie." It was that, and not

74. W. R. Greg, "Kingsley and Carlyle," *Literary and Social Judgments*, *1*, 171. The quotation is from *Past and Present*, Bk. III, chap. 11, p. 197.

75. Newman, *Sermons and Discourses*, ed. C. F. Harrold, 2, 153, 155. This sermon, called "God's Will the End of Life," is an excellent statement of the Christian-Victorian theory of work, and is pointedly directed against the worldly, unearnest life of the time. It first appeared in *Discourses Addressed to Mixed Congregations*, 1849.

any mere injunction to work, which the Rugby sons of the gentry found so impressive in the master's teaching. "Every pupil was made to feel that there was *a work for him to do*—that his happiness as well as his duty lay in doing that work well. Hence an indescribable zest was communicated to a young man's feeling about life; a strange joy came over him on discovering that he had the means of being useful." [76] For the upper classes in the thirties, as for old Leisure, this was a novel idea. They had always imagined that "life was not a task . . . but a sinecure." [77]

Such a misapprehension leads directly to the wide gate and the primrose path. For "leisure is the occasion of all evil" and Satan finds work—of a kind—for idle hands to do. Idleness is thus not only a sin because it is an abrogation of God's will, and especially reprehensible in the case of Dives, with his sensual enjoyment of the luxuries of wealth; it is also a dangerous opportunity to take "the first step in the downward path which leads to hell." Work, therefore, has the further value of being a safeguard against temptation—and all the better if it is constant. The man who keeps busy every hour, doing all the duties of his social and family life, "is saved a multitude of sins which have not time to get hold upon him." [78]

Finally, if everyone had his particular work, he also had one in common with all other Christians, a spiritual mission or calling to serve God in His eternal warfare with Satan. To that end he was to set before the world a high example of the Christian spirit: by his conversation, by a scrupulous fulfilment of all his duties, and by helping to carry forward the great battle against social evil and suffering. "Do we not know," asked Arnold in one of his sermons in *Christian Life, "* . . . that there is an infinite voice in the infinite sins and sufferings of millions which proclaims that the contest is raging around us; that every idle moment is treason; that now it

76. Bonamy Price in Stanley, *Life*, chap. 2, pp. 37–8.

77. Cf. James Martineau, "Dr. Arnold," a review of Stanley's *Life, Essays, Reviews, and Addresses* (4 vols. London, 1890), *1*, 63–4: "His general theory of his office may be stated thus:—the peculiar character of the *English gentleman* being assumed as an historical datum, the aim of education should be to penetrate and pervade this with a spirit of Christian self-regulation. He was aware how great was the revolution implied in the accomplishment of this end; that moral heroism must take the place of feudal independence; devout allegiance, of personal self-will; respect for faithful work, of the ambition for careless idleness; manly simplicity and earnestness, of gentlemanly *poco-curanteism* . . ."

78. The quotations are from Newman, *Parochial Sermons, 8*, No. 11, p. 166.

is the time for unceasing efforts; and that not till the victory is gained may Christ's soldiers throw aside their arms, and resign themselves to enjoyment and to rest?" [79] For the upper classes that broad mission centered, in Evangelical minds as well as in Arnold's, on the object for which Wilberforce, among others, had founded the Society for Bettering the Condition and Increasing the Comforts of the Poor. An enormous amount of private charity complemented the long series of Parliamentary measures (prison reform, sanitation, the slave trade, factory acts, mine acts, laws for the prevention of cruelty to children and animals, etc.), and in both fields, a primary motivation was the service of God. [80]

But not the only motivation. Philanthropy and legislation might also serve the cause of social order and lessen the threat of revolution. Indeed, the Puritan doctrine of work would never have been stressed so much, I think, had the prophets not felt that aristocratic idleness had to be exorcized if society were to be saved. The fate of the Idle Aristocracy and therefore of the country fills Carlyle with despair. "A thinking eye discerns ghastly images of ruin, too ghastly for words; a handwriting as of MENE, MENE." And so, "be counselled," he tells them, "ascertain if no work exist for thee on God's Earth; if thou find no commanded-duty there but that of going gracefully idle? Ask, inquire earnestly, with a half-frantic earnestness." They will soon learn that the very possession of the land obliges them "to furnish guidance and governance to England" and to manage their estates, improving the soil and caring for the men who are now "ploughing, ditching, day-drudging; bare of back, empty of stomach, nigh desperate of heart." [81] When Arnold made such a tremendous effort to convince the sons of the gentry that each had "his work and mission in the world" which it was his bounden duty to do, he was thinking almost as much about the needs of England as those of their immortal souls. One of his Rugby sermons leaves no doubt of it. "I know," he says, "and you know also . . . that neglect and selfish carelessness on the one side [that of the Rich], have led to suspicion and bitter hatred on the other [that of the Poor]," so that both classes have come to think of one another as natural enemies. Consequently,

79. *Christian Life*, No. 6, pp. 60–1.

80. For a convenient summary, see Canon Smyth's essay "The Evangelical Discipline," in *Ideas and Beliefs of the Victorians*, pp. 97–104.

81. *Past and Present*, Bk. III, chap. 7, p. 173; chap. 8, pp. 176, 178; Bk. IV, chap. 6, p. 284.

men of wealth and rank [like ourselves] must learn to "instruct, relieve, and improve . . . those who, from poverty and ignorance, have great need that relief and instruction should be given them." Otherwise, "God will soon come and smite the earth with a curse." [82]

The writer, too, in so critical a time had his work to do. On no account was he to live a life of aesthetic pleasure; for the sense of crisis created a literary duty and an artistic conscience. One recalls the attraction Tennyson felt for the Palace of Art and the effort he made, under Apostolic influence, to bring his poetry to bear on the problems of the age. But with uneven success, as the ambiguity of "The Palace of Art" suggests. "Alas for me!" he said to Hallam, "I have more of the Beautiful than the Good!" To which Hallam replied, "Remember to your comfort that God has given you to see the difference. Many a poet has gone on blindly in his artist pride." [83] A generation later Ruskin confessed he felt "tormented between the longing for rest and for lovely life, and the sense of the terrific call of human crime for resistance and of human misery for help"; and he presently found that he could not paint or read or look at minerals, or do anything else he liked, "because of the misery that I know of, and see signs of, where I know it not, which no imagination can interpret too bitterly." Therefore, he would do what he could (in his later political and economic work) "to abate this misery." [84] As with moral earnestness in general, the gospel of work, rooted in Puritanism, was preached with special vigor in a period so desperately in need of social action and intellectual guidance.

In the middle class, where the Puritan tradition was strong, the religious theory of work was a commonplace, but all of its main features were the natural requirements or the natural aims of an industrial society and would have been adopted, in a secular form, regardless of any Christian influence. The arraignment of idleness, the value of work for the development of the individual, and the sense

82. *Sermons*, 2, No. 31, pp. 331–2.

83. *Memoir of Tennyson*, 1, 81. Cf. Carlyle's criticism of Scott, above, p. 227, Kingsley, *Alton Locke*, chap. 1, pp. 2–3, and his criticism of Arnold's *The Strayed Reveller*, in *Fraser's Magazine*, 39 (1849), 578–9 (attributed to him by Thorp, *Kingsley*, p. 192): "What has he taught us? . . . When the world is heaving and moaning in the agonies, either of a death-struggle, or a new birth-hour . . . is he . . . content to sit and fiddle while Rome is burning?" He goes on to complain that Arnold is "taking no active part in God's work."

84. Letter written in 1863, *Works, 36*, 450; *Fors Clavigera, 1*, Letter 1 (1871), in *Works, 27*, 13.

of a mission both to serve society in one's particular calling and to further the larger destinies of the human race, were almost as much the ideals of business as of Protestantism.

In commercial society, needless to say, idleness is a vice. It is the unforgivable—economic—sin. A writer in *Fraser's* for January 1851, celebrating the vast increase of manufacturing, commerce, and wealth, found indications "full of promise for the future, that idleness, whether in the higher or lower classes, will not be much longer tolerated— that it will expose the rich man to contempt, and the poor man to punishment." [85] The contempt for the "unworking" aristocrat which the bourgeois invariably feels is evident in *Past and Present:*

> Is there a man who pretends to live luxuriously housed up; screened from all work . . . he himself to sit serene, amid down-bolsters and appliances, and have all his work and battling done by other men? And such man calls himself a *noble*-man? . . . Here *he* sits; professes, not in sorrow but in pride, that he and his have done no work, time out of mind. It is the law of the land, and is thought to be the law of the Universe, that he, alone of recorded men, shall have no task laid on him, except that of eating his cooked victuals, and not flinging himself out of window.[86]

Plainly, this *noble*-man is nothing but a parasite, living on the work of others; and Carlyle is expressing the outraged sense of injustice— and perhaps the envious scorn—which the workers of the world feel for those whom they support. By middle-class mores all men must work, or at any rate they must have worked in the past (before retirement) for what they possess.

85. Vol. *43*, 14. In like manner the view of recreation noted above (p. 243) is as much a business as a religious view. With the Arnold and Ruskin quotations given there (illustrating the principle laid down by Wilberforce, *Practical View of Christianity*, chap. 7, sec. 1, p. 346), cf. Macaulay's comment on Sunday in his speech on the Ten Hours Bill (Trevelyan, *Life of Lord Macaulay*, 2, 157 n.): "While industry is suspended, while the plow lies in the furrow, while the Exchange is silent, while no smoke ascends from the factory, a process is going on quite as important to the wealth of nations as any process which is performed on more busy days. Man, the machine of machines, the machine compared with which all the contrivances of the Watts and the Arkwrights are worthless, is repairing and winding up, so that he returns to his labors on the Monday with clearer intellect, with livelier spirits, with renewed corporal vigor."

86. Bk. III, chap. 8, p. 179. Cf. Bk. III, chap. 12, p. 202, and Bk. IV, chap. 6, p. 283.

Work is also—in another parallel with religious teaching—the means by which one develops his natural talents and by which his advance toward human perfection can be measured. The struggle to transform natural resources into the finished product, to outdistance one's competitors in the market, or to manage a great concern, demands, and therefore inevitably develops, certain moral and intellectual faculties which come to be thought of as the whole of virtue. "Whatsoever of morality and of intelligence; what of patience, perseverance, faithfulness, of method, insight, ingenuity, energy; in a word, whatsoever of Strength the man had in him will lie written in the Work he does. To work: why, it is to try himself against Nature, and her everlasting unerring Laws; these will tell a true verdict as to the man." And Carlyle goes on at once to speak of cotton spinning, and presently of John Bull and his "railways, fleets and cities." In another passage, where the same industrial qualities are mentioned, Carlyle adds, in words one cannot imagine on the lips of Arnold or Newman, "All these, *all virtues*, in wrestling with the dim brute Powers of Fact, in ordering of thy fellows in such wrestle, *there and elsewhere not at all*, thou wilt continually learn." [87]

One virtue in particular, especially dear to Puritanism, was developed by this discipline—self-denial. When his father died, John Thornton in *North and South* had to leave school and support the family by working in a draper's shop for fifteen shillings a week. "My mother managed so that I put by three out of these fifteen shillings regularly. This made the beginning; this taught me self-denial." Now, when he is a wealthy mill owner, he credits his success to "the habits of life which taught me to despise indulgences not thoroughly earned" and explains the failure of others to climb the ladder as "the natural punishment of dishonestly-enjoyed pleasure, at some former period of their lives. I do not look on self-indulgent, sensual people as worthy of my hatred; I simply look upon them with contempt for their poorness of character." [88] This has precisely the moral flavor of evangelical Christianity, yet it is derived from economic necessity and the will to succeed. Was it an Evangelical who wrote, "To abstain from the enjoyment which is in our power, or to seek distant rather than immediate results, are among the most painful [and necessary] exertions of the human will"? The distant results might have been the enjoyment of heavenly salvation, but in

87. Ibid., Bk. III, chap. 5, pp. 158, 160; chap. 11, p. 198. The italics are mine.
88. Mrs. Gaskell, chap. 10, pp. 97–8.

point of fact they were commercial success and the author was the political economist, Nassau Senior.[89]

Furthermore, surprising as it may seem, the industrial conception of work included the idea of a mission. Manufacturers and workers, it was often said, were engaged in a vast crusade to subdue nature for the benefit of man and thus to strengthen England and further the progress of civilization. No doubt this worthy purpose in its pure form never existed outside the minds of writers like Macaulay, Carlyle, or Kingsley. But many a businessman with one eye on making a fortune sincerely imagined that he was also serving a great cause. Mrs. Gaskell, who had studied Manchester at first hand and knew many of its businessmen, created a mill owner who boasted of the personal power he had attained but also called manufacturers like himself "the great pioneers of civilisation." And it is her experience which is reflected by Margaret Hale's discovery of something large and grand in the interests of the Milton capitalists. "There was much to admire in their forgetfulness of themselves and the present, in their anticipated triumphs over all inanimate matter at some future time, which none of them should live to see." [90]

Moreover the idea of progress, though often limited to material advance, had a wider meaning, as we know, and one which gave all men, not just industrial leaders and workers, a high sense of mission: to take part in the great march and struggle of mankind up from barbarism to civilization. Under the running title of "Life 'a Soldier's Battle'" (Arnold's phrase, we remember, for the *Christian* life), Samuel Smiles, the popular author of *Self-Help*, described the "constant succession of noble workers"—cultivators of the soil, inventors, manufacturers, artisans, poets, philosophers and politicians, all working together to carry society forward to still higher stages.[91] *Past and Present* closes with the inspiring image: "Ploughers, Spinners, Builders; Prophets, Poets, Kings; Brindleys and Goethes, Odins and Arkwrights; all martyrs, and noble men, and gods are of one grand

89. *Political Economy* (first ed. 1836; London, 1872), p. 59.

90. *North and South*, chap. 15, p. 145; chap. 20, pp. 193–4. This suggests that Plugson of Undershot with his noble social purpose—in addition to his ignoble desire to be a millionaire—is not a figment of Carlyle's imagination: see *Past and Present*, Bk. III, chap. 12, p. 208.

91. *Self-Help*, chap. 1, p. 25. This book was a popular summation of industrial ethics for the working class, preaching in simple phrases with illustrative anecdotes the same Puritan-business virtues which Carlyle extolled in Carlylese. There is a useful essay on Smiles by Asa Briggs in *Victorian People*.

Host; immeasurable; marching ever forward since the beginnings of the World. The enormous, all-conquering, flame-crowned Host, noble every soldier in it; sacred, and alone noble." [92] That exalted conception of history gave life a meaning and a significance for the Victorians which we can only envy, and endowed them, for all their anxieties, with a hopeful and buoyant energy that we have never known. "Be inspired," cries Gladstone, brought up under the twin influences of Evangelicalism and business, "with the belief that life is a great and noble calling; not a mean and grovelling thing that we are to shuffle through as we can, but an elevated and lofty destiny." [93]

The Victorian gospel of work, derived from both its religious and economic life and preached the more earnestly because the idea of crisis and the idea of progress both called for dedicated action, found further support from an unexpected quarter. As the difficulties of belief increased, the essence of religion for Christians—and for agnostics the "meaning of life"—came more and more to lie in strenuous labor for the good of society. That was not only a rational alternative to fruitless speculation but also a practical means of exorcizing the mood of ennui and despair which so often accompanied the loss of faith. For these reasons, a religion of work, with or without a supernatural context, came to be, in fact, the actual faith of many Victorians: it could resolve both intellectual perplexity and psychological depression.

Here again Carlyle is the major prophet, for he himself, with the help of Goethe, had discovered the therapy of work in his own struggle with doubt. In *Sartor Resartus*, the desperate mood of Teufelsdröckh is a reflection of his own experience in the "black years" after 1818. But he recognized that the same distress had afflicted Goethe and Byron, and many of the Romantics. *Werther* was the expression of

92. Bk. IV, chap. 8, p. 298. In Mill's essay "Theism," *Three Essays on Religion*, p. 256, the same idea is given a formulation that brings it very close to the religious conception of Christ's soldiers fighting against sin and misery: "A battle is constantly going on, in which the humblest human creature is not incapable of taking some part, between the powers of good and those of evil, and in which every even the smallest help to the right side has its value in promoting the very slow and often almost insensible progress by which good is gradually gaining ground from evil, yet gaining it so visibly at considerable intervals as to promise the very distant but not uncertain final victory of Good." Also, cf. his "Inaugural Address at St. Andrews," *James & John Stuart Mill on Education*, p. 177.

93. Morley, *Life of Gladstone*, 1, 184.

"that nameless Unrest, the blind struggle of a soul in bondage, that high, sad, longing Discontent, which was agitating every bosom" and had driven Goethe "almost to despair." The counterpart in England was "Byron's life-weariness, his moody melancholy, and mad stormful indignation." *Sartor Resartus* was Carlyle's effort to make Byron the last of "the Sentimentalists" who "raged and wailed," by preaching the philosophy he had learned from Goethe's later novel, *Wilhelm Meister:* "For the problem which had been stated in *Werter* [and in "The Everlasting No"], with despair of its solution, is here [and in "The Everlasting Yea"] solved." By opening your Goethe, you can close your Byron.[94]

Starting from a sudden upsurge of protest and defiance—this I will *not* believe, that the universe is a mechanism and man a human automaton—Teufelsdröckh goes on to recover his faith by finding God immanent in nature, or felt in the heart at moments of exaltation when one is filled with love and pity; from which he argues that the voice of conscience is a god-given mandate, saying, *"Work thou in welldoing"*—that is, master the selfish desire for personal happiness and lead a life of dutiful labor. But for all this the chapter ends on quite another note, for the simple reason that Carlyle could not believe in this religious philosophy with any steady conviction. He did not *dis*believe it, often he *did* believe it, but more often he was swept by renewed doubts of any supernatural reality whatever and thrown back again into the Wertherian-Byronic mood. In the very year that *Sartor* was published, he wrote in his journal:

> Wonderful, and alas! most pitiful alternations of belief and unbelief in me.

> For the last year my faith has lain under a most sad eclipse; I have been a considerably worse man than before.

> Oh for faith! Truly the greatest "God announcing miracle" always is faith, and now more than ever. I often look on my mother (nearly the only genuine Believer I know of) with a kind of sacred admiration. Know the worth of Belief. Alas! canst thou acquire none? [95]

94. "Goethe," *Essays, 1,* 217, 218, 224. For the conscious linking of Teufelsdröckh with Werther and Byron, see *Sartor,* Bk. II, chap. 6, title and pp. 156–7. The famous injunction to substitute Goethe for Byron is in chap. 9, p. 192.

95. Froude, *Carlyle: First Forty Years, 2,* chap. 14, pp. 330, 345; chap. 15, p. 354. Although he later spoke in the *Reminiscences,* p. 282, of having conquered

In such circumstance the one way he *could* acquire a faith was pragmatically: by proving its truth in experience.

This principle is announced at the start of the final section. Since "all Speculation is by nature endless, formless, a vortex amid vortices," it is only by an "indubitable certainty of Experience" that conviction can "find any centre to revolve round, and so fashion itself into a system. Most true is it, as a wise man teaches us, that 'Doubt of any sort cannot be removed except by Action.'" [96] But not any action: an unselfish action, something one can call a duty. "Let him who gropes painfully in darkness or uncertain light," he continues, " . . . lay this other precept well to heart, which to me was of invaluable service: 'Do the Duty which lies nearest thee,' which thou knowest to be a Duty! Thy second Duty will already have become clearer." If duty here refers to small and immediate tasks, in the next paragraph it takes on a larger and general meaning applicable to life as a whole: "The Situation that has not its Duty, its Ideal, was never yet occupied by man." The Ideal is not a romantic dream of personal happiness incapable of realization, but a goal, a life purpose, toward which one can strive with all his energy. It is the highest potential attainment which, given the outward conditions and circumstances of life, any individual with a particular talent could hope to reach by concentrated effort and struggle.[97] To discover that Ideal and then to pursue it is not only to do one's duty (the word points the contrast with any egoistic striving for personal happiness), but also to win "Spiritual Enfranchisement" for the vital energies of life, so long dammed up and paralyzed by doubt and indecision. Hence the final exhortation which climaxes the chapter:

> I too could now say to myself: Be no longer a Chaos, but a World, or even Worldkin. Produce! Produce! Were it but the pitifullest infinitesimal fraction of a Product, produce it, in God's name! 'Tis the utmost thou hast in thee: out with it, then. Up,

---

"all my scepticisms, agonising doubtings" in the year 1825 (i.e. before he started *Sartor*), he went on at once to say: "I had, in effect, gained an immense victory; and, *for a number of years*, had, in spite of nerves and chagrins, a constant inward happiness . . . which *essentially* remains with me still, *though far oftener eclipsed, and lying deeper down, than then.*" The italics are mine. Even in the chapter "The Everlasting Yea," when he refers to the struggle for belief "in an Atheistic Century" (p. 184), he admits that to me "was given, if not Victory, yet the consciousness of Battle, and the resolve to persevere therein."

96. *Sartor*, Bk. II, chap. 9, pp. 195–6. The wise man is Goethe. The quotations that follow are on pp. 196–7.

97. See Bk. II, chap. 4, p. 119.

up! Whatsoever thy hand findeth to do, do it with thy whole
might. Work while it is called Today; for the Night cometh,
wherein no man can work.

Out of its context, who would not suppose that this was the Sunday
sermon of an Evangelical preacher? or, still more likely, the daily
chant of the Captains of Industry to their hands? Puritanism, business, and doubt met together to write the gospel of work. In this
passage the moral—and psychological—value, it should be noticed,
lies not in what one actually produces but in struggling with all one's
might to achieve the utmost one has in him to produce. This is perfectly calculated to answer the sense of futility—the what-can-I-
accomplish-anyway feeling—which is integral to the mood of despondency. And when the creative challenge is added, the sick soul is ready
to respond to the "Up, up!"

Although this ethic could stand alone, as we shall see, Carlyle
links it to his religious faith by the pragmatism which argues that
the gospel of work will prove its credentials and show by practice
that the mandate of conscience, *"Work thou in Welldoing,"* is God-
given. The argument, I think, was mainly psychological. By im-
mersing himself in action, conceived as the pursuit of any immediate
duty or of the larger work he was best fitted to do, he could quiet
his inner anxiety (the reiterated imperatives of the final paragraph
—Produce! Produce!—have a note that is almost frantic) and gain
a sense of health and well-being. Then, in that happier state of mind
he could feel that really all was well; and surely there was a God;
and obviously this ethical creed which gave him peace was His will.
That last conclusion was all the easier to draw since the ethic of
work which he found in Goethe was so similar to the ethic he had
learned in his Puritan home.

Against this background we can readily understand why idleness
for Carlyle was something worse than a sin. It was "perpetual despair." [98] For it opened the door not to evil temptations, as it did for
Newman and the Evangelicals, but to "self-listenings, self-questionings,
impotently painful dubitations, all this fatal nosology of spiritual
maladies, so rife in our day." [99] No wonder he praised the religion
of the monks for being free from "a diseased self-introspection, an

98. *Past and Present*, Bk. III, chap. 11, p. 196.

99. *Life of Sterling* (1851), Pt. I, chap. 1, p. 6. For examples of Carlyle struggling against this disease, see Froude, *Carlyle: First Forty Years*, 2, chap. 4, pp.
81–2, and *Letters, 1826–1836*, pp. 313–14.

agonising inquiry." [100] Their duties were clear; above all, their supreme duty to work. Indeed, "properly speaking, all true Work is Religion: and whatsoever Religion is not Work may go and dwell among the Brahmins, Antinomians, Spinning Dervishes, or where it will; with me it shall have no harbour." This exaggerated statement of the ancient maxim *Laborare est Orare*, which had been emphasized by the Puritan moralists of the Reformation, occurs in the chapters "Labour" and "Reward" in *Past and Present*,[101] where the final message of "The Everlasting Yea" is expanded and cast into a simpler form. After the opening paragraph speaks of idleness as "perpetual despair," and the next announces that "the latest Gospel in this world is, Know thy work and do it," the central passages follows:

> It has been written, "an endless significance lies in Work"; a man perfects himself by working. Foul jungles are cleared away, fair seedfields rise instead, and stately cities; and withal the man himself first ceases to be a jungle and foul unwholesome desert thereby. Consider how, even in the meanest sorts of Labour, the whole soul of a man is composed into a kind of real harmony, the instant he sets himself to work! Doubt, Desire, Sorrow, Remorse, Indignation, Despair itself, all these like hell-dogs lie beleaguering the soul of the poor dayworker, as of every man: but he bends himself with free valour against his task, and all these are stilled, all these shrink murmuring far off into their caves. The man is now a man. The blessed glow of Labour in him, is it not as purifying fire, wherein all poison is burnt up, and of sour smoke itself there is made bright blessed flame! [102]

Industrial activity, reclaiming land and building cities, is also "withal" the means of curing doubt and despair; and the two great results of work are linked in the repeated image of the cleared jungle.[103] More

100. *Past and Present*, Bk. II, chap. 4, p. 60.
101. Specifically in Bk. III, chap. 12, p. 200.
102. Bk. III, chap. 11, p. 196. Cf. Bk. I, chap. 6, pp. 37–8.
103. Cf. the paragraph just below this (pp. 197–8), where Goethe's "Doubt, of whatever kind, can be ended by Action alone" is again quoted, and the action is plainly industrial. This is also true, I think, of the conclusion to "The Everlasting Yea" (quoted just above), since Carlyle must have had business in the back of his mind at least when he chose the term "Produce" instead of "Work" or "Labor" or "Toil." A little earlier (Bk. II, chap. 4, p. 118) he had spoken with satisfaction of a new era of "Industrialism and the Government of the Wisest." The passage

than that, its two moral functions are united in the phrase about
man perfecting himself by work: he develops his natural talents
and composes the psyche. Needless to say, Carlyle places this life
of earnest endeavor in a religious context. But he does not say, work
because it is the will of God. He says, work and you will end your
misery and forward the progress of civilization—and remember, too,
that "all true Work is sacred" and labor is a "god-given Force," and
the worker's wages "do yet lie in Heaven or else Nowhere." [104] That,
I think, places the sanctions of work for the mature Carlyle in their
true order of importance.

This ethic, whose supernatural setting could be adopted or ignored
or held in willing suspension of disbelief, was precisely what the
Victorian intellectuals most needed. It offered the welcome possibility
of by-passing the difficulties of belief by finding the essence of religion or the purpose of life in the pursuit of a creative task, suited
to one's own nature and socially valuable. And it promised a blessed
release from the mood of subjective ennui. Carlyle was not, of course,
its only source, but it is significant that Harriet Martineau thought
he "infused into the mind of the English nation a sincerity, earnestness, healthfulness and courage which can be appreciated only by
those who are old enough to tell what was our morbid state when
Byron was the representative of our temper"; and that Morley
considered his central achievement to have been the "neutralisation
of Byron," the deliverance of England from "the mood of Byronism,"
by setting up the counter ideal of "labour in a high spirit, duty done,
and right service performed in fortitudinous temper." [105]

When religious perplexity was so common, Christian apologetics
often relied on the kind of pragmatism adopted by Carlyle. In the
midst of wandering doubts about this or that particular doctrine,

---

has, in fact, been used (by Lewis and Maude, *The English Middle Classes*, p. 52,
and Wingfield-Stratford, *Those Earnest Victorians*, p. 107) to describe the industrial life of the time, which is to wrest it out of its context but not to misread its
secondary implication. For Tennyson's recommendation of industrial work to cure
despair, see below, pp. 259–60.

104. Bk. III, chap. 11, p. 197; chap. 12, pp. 201, 203.

105. Martineau, *Autobiography*, *1*, Period IV, sec. 2, p. 387; Morley, "Carlyle,"
Critical Miscellanies, *1*, 156, 162. The close connection between this religion of
work and the anti-intellectualism of doubt described above in Chap. 5, sec. 2,
will be apparent. Carlyle and Kingsley (who will be cited in a moment) are central figures in both discussions. But the focus there was on the revulsion against
speculation; here it is on the point of recoil, to the outer tasks of an earnest life.

or even of the reality of religion altogether, the safest course was not to look for their resolution, but "meekly to do God's will." [106] The conclusion to "The Everlasting Yea" is rephrased by Kingsley in more Christian terms: "God has given you a great talent, whereby you may get an honest livelihood. Take *that* as God's call to you, and follow it out. . . . And how to fear God I know not better than by working on at the speciality which He has given us, trusting to Him to make it of use to His creatures. . . . Therefore fret not nor be of doubtful mind. But just do the duty which lies nearest." [107] And Kingsley kept giving himself the same advice. After describing the battle between faith and materialism which "has gone on in me since childhood," filling him with fear that he should "end by a desperate lunge into one extreme or the other," he suddenly throws up his hands and cries out with relief:

> But after all, what is speculation to practice? What does God require of us, but to do justly, to love mercy, and to walk humbly with Him? The longer I live this seems to me more important, and all other questions less so. If we can but live the simple right life—
>
> Do the work that's nearest,
>   Though it's dull at whiles;
> Helping, when we meet them,
>   Lame dogs over stiles.[108]

Laymen like Clough and Ruskin, religiously oriented but acutely aware of the dead end of theological speculation, find the only basis

106. See Newman, "Obedience the Remedy for Religious Perplexity," *Parochial Sermons, 1*, No. 18, pp. 228–43. Cf. Arnold, in Stanley's *Life*, pp. 271–3, letter of February 15, 1832, and pp. 363–5, letter of June 21, 1835.

107. *Letters and Memories, 2*, 107 (unabridged ed., *2*, 91). Cf. *1*, 111 (unabridged ed., *1*, 138): In the midst of falling creeds and warring doctrines, still, at any rate, he says, he can hear God's voice through the roar, "He that doeth my will shall know of the doctrine whether it be of God." Cf. Masson, "The Poems of Arthur Hugh Clough," *Macmillan's Magazine, 6* (1862), p. 321: " 'Do the law and thou shalt know the doctrine,' is the profound aphorism of Scripture itself— an aphorism the attenuated form of which, in modern religious casuistry, is that, if the doubter will only persevere in the routine of plain and minute duties lying before him, and will abstain as far as he can, during this regimen, from the questionings that have been perplexing him, he will find light unawares breaking in upon him."

108. *Letters and Memories, 2*, 57 (unabridged ed., *2*, 19). Cf. *1*, 87–9, and *2*, 7–9 (unabridged ed., *1*, 112–13 and 467–8).

of religious belief in the simple life of earnest endeavor. It is not the thinkers but the workers, in Ruskin's famous lecture, who have solved "The Mystery of Life and Its Arts." They alone know that religion is founded "on rational, effective, humble, and helpful action." But unfortunately there are girls, he says (and he would have said men and women had he been speaking to an adult audience), who waste their time in

> grievous and vain meditation over the meaning of the great Book, of which no syllable was ever yet to be understood but through a deed; all the . . . glory of their pure consciences warped into fruitless agony concerning questions which the laws of common serviceable life would have either solved for them in an instant, or kept out of their way. Give such a girl any true work that will make her active in the dawn, and weary at night, with the consciousness that her fellow-creatures have indeed been the better for her day, and the powerless sorrow of her enthusiasm will transform itself into a majesty of radiant and beneficent peace.[109]

From here it is only a step to holding the religious reference, as I put it earlier, in willing suspension of disbelief or abandoning it altogether. There may be a God—and maybe not. And if there is, is there a life after death? in a heaven? or a hell? Let us forget the insoluble questions and plunge into some useful career. By the fifties "the higher class of thinkers . . . for the most part have given up the peculiarly Christian doctrines, and indeed nearly all thought of a future life . . . and set themselves actively to improve this world and do as much good in it as they can." [110] This philosophy in more Carlylean terms is reflected in Leslie Stephen's remark about his brother: "Work, I might almost say, was his religion. 'Be strong and of a good courage' was the ultimate moral which he drew from doubts and difficulties. . . . Set to work upon the job that lies next to your hand, and so long as you are working well and vigorously, you will not be troubled with the vapours." [111] At the end of the century Lecky could say that more and more men had come to "base

109. *Sesame and Lilies*, sec. 140, in *Works, 18*, 185, 186. See also the whole lecture. For Clough, see "Qui Laborat, Orat," *Poems*, pp. 12–13, and "Notes on the Religious Tradition," *Prose Remains*, p. 418.

110. Ruskin, *Works, 36*, 137; and cf. the description of Mr. George, p. 139.

111. *Life of Fitzjames Stephen*, pp. 453–4.

their moral life on some strong unselfish interest for the benefit of their kind. In active, useful and unselfish work they find the best refuge from the perplexities of belief and the best field for the cultivation of their moral nature, and work done for the benefit of others seldom fails to react powerfully on their own happiness." [112]

Between a rational reorientation of the doubting mind from speculation to conduct and the emotional recoil from the mood of despair to the therapy of action, no sharp line can be drawn. But where the note of personal pain is heard, especially with reference to introspection, the psychological motive of escape is clearly present. We can hear it, for example, in Tennyson's assertion that "the persevering performance of daily duty [was] the best medicine for paralysing doubts, and the safest shelter under the storms either of practical or of speculative life"; [113] or in the frantic tone with which Norman May, in *The Daisy Chain*, longs to cast behind him the criticisms and doubts which had overwhelmed him at Oxford:

> "I must be away from it all, and go to the simplest, hardest work, beginning from the rudiments, and forgetting subtle arguments."
> "Forgetting your*self*," said Ethel.
> "Right. I want to have no leisure to think about myself," said Norman. "I am never so happy as at such times."

Idleness, we remember, is "perpetual despair." And to make the cure doubly promising, Norman has found a life-purpose to work for in the conversion of South Sea islanders. [114] But if the saving task lay in the field of industrial development, it could seem the more valuable to most Victorians (as it did to Carlyle) and therefore the more effective as therapy. In "Locksley Hall" the protagonist's mood of self-pity, disgust, and bitter isolation, so reminiscent of Teufels-

112. *Map of Life*, chap. 11, p. 228. In chap. 5, pp. 58–9, he emphasizes the influence in this direction of Goethe.

113. W. E. Gladstone, " 'Locksley Hall' and the Jubilee," *Nineteenth Century*, 21 (1887), 4.

114. Pt. II, chap. 16, p. 461. Cf. George Eliot, "Janet's Repentance," *Scenes of Clerical Life*, 2, chap. 24, p. 146: "No wonder the sick-room and the lazaretto have so often been a refuge from the tossings of intellectual doubt,—a place of repose for the worn and wounded spirit. Here is a duty about which all creeds and all philosophies are at one; here, at least, the conscience will not be dogged by doubt, the benign impulse will not be checked by adverse theory; here you may begin to act without settling one preliminary question."

dröckh,[115] has its explicit source in the loss of Amy and not of faith, but he, too, must "wither in despair" unless he "mix with action. After the momentary longing to escape to "some retreat deep in yonder shining Orient," he turns back to nineteenth-century Europe and feels the quickening urge to belong to its dynamic civilization:

> Not in vain the distance beacons. Forward,
>   forward let us range,
> Let the great world spin for ever down the
>   ringing grooves of change.
> Thro' the shadow of the globe we sweep
>   into the younger day:
> Better fifty years of Europe than a cycle
>   of Cathay.
> Mother-Age (for mine I knew not) help me as
>   when life begun:
> Rift the hills, and roll the waters, flash
>   the lightnings, weigh the Sun.

The poem is neither a celebration of progress, as we usually read it today, nor the expression of a "Werterian and unhealthy" sensibility, as it was often read at the time.[116] Its theme is the resolution of a mood of depression (which existed quite aside from any experience of frustrated love) by an inspiring call to join imaginatively, if not literally, in an active life devoted to the cause of human progress. "The spirit of the poem," wrote Kingsley—and he had reason to perceive it—"is simply anti-Werterian. It is man rising out of sickness into health—not conquered by Werterism, but conquering his selfish sorrow, and the moral and intellectual paralysis which it produces, by faith and hope—faith in the progress of science and civilisation, hope in the final triumph of good." [117]

But action of some kind, no matter what, is essential if one is not to "wither in despair." The passion for work was sometimes nothing but the desire to numb the sensibility and suppress anxiety by plunging into some form of activity without reference to any moral values,

115. W. D. Templeman, "Tennyson's *Locksley Hall* and Carlyle," *Booker Memorial Studies,* ed. Hill Shine (Chapel Hill, N.C., 1950), pp. 34–59, argues that *Sartor* is the source of the poem, but that seems to me unlikely.

116. According to Kingsley, "Tennyson," *Literary and General Essays,* p. 114.

117. Ibid. On p. 115 he adds, "There are, in fact, only two deliverances from Werterism possible in the nineteenth century; one is into Popery, and the other is— 'Forward, forward, let us range,' " etc.

however rationalized it might be as the "right path" or a duty or a contribution to social progress—even as the will of God. The enormous production of the Victorian writers, far greater than anything we are now accustomed to, volume after volume, scores of reviews and articles, thousands of letters, is simply astonishing. And in many cases —both the Arnolds, for example, as well as Kingsley, Mill, and Huxley —extensive literary production was achieved in addition to a regular job. The explanation lies partly in their optimism—their confidence in the power of the mind to resolve every problem and of the individual to influence the course of events regardless of political or economic forces; and in their deep conviction that a critical age of transition and an uneducated democracy required immediate guidance in many areas. But there was also their frantic need to bury their doubts and anxieties under the distraction of objective and constant activity.

Would Carlyle's later life have been filled with so much writing done under such nervous strain if he had found the spiritual peace he talked about? He must often have written from the same motive once acknowledged by Symonds (who was perhaps the Victorian who suffered most from "moods of speculative negation . . . abysses of depression"): "This letter has been the work of a long wet day. Tired as I am, I feel the better for writing myself out. . . . We must make the machine of the brain go. It does not do to let it stop. Whatever happens, energise." [118] Kingsley once described a rather different day, crowded with earnest work in the service of God: "See how much a day can do! I have since nine this morning, cut wood for an hour; spent an hour and more in prayer and humiliation, and thereby established a chastened but happy tone, which lasts till now; written six or seven pages of a difficult part of my essay; taught in the school; thought over many things while walking; gone round two-thirds of the parish visiting and doctoring; and written all this. Such days are lives—and happy ones." But suddenly in the next sentence he added: "One has no time to be miserable"—and the work is

118. Brown, *Life of Symonds*, pp. 238–9. Cf. p. 244 on the anodyne of fatigue, and pp. 295–6 on work as the salvation of the soul, i.e. of the psyche. A recent comment on another Victorian famous for the amount of his writing, Anthony Trollope—in a review of A. O. J. Cockshut, *Anthony Trollope. A Critical Study* (London, 1955), in *The Times Literary Supplement* (Sept. 23, 1955), p. 550— calls attention to "his underlying pessimism, his lack of solid belief in anything except the power of work by which he kept both his pessimism and his doubts at bay."

instantly seen to be compulsive. "Do not be afraid of my overworking myself," he wrote to his wife. "If I stop, I go down. I must work." [119] But even work was not enough, for after it was done, he would often rush into violent physical recreation, running to hounds on foot, leaping hedges and ditches for five hours at a stretch, as though he dared not rest for a single moment. One of his former pupils at Eversley remembered that "except during sleep . . . repose seemed impossible to him for body or mind" and observed that his "impetuous, restless, nervous" energy made constant movement "almost a necessity." [120] In Froude's essay "On Progress," there is a revealing explanation of the contrast between the quiet life of an eighteenth-century parson and the feverish activity of a modern clergyman. Where the former assumed the truths he preached, the latter has to wrestle with uncertainties, and therefore "conceals his misgivings from his own eyes by the passion with which he flings himself into his work." Today the clergy are "building and restoring churches, writing books and tracts; persuading themselves and others with spasmodic agony that the thing they love is not dead, but sleeping." [121] For the Victorians intense activity was both a rational method of attacking the anxieties of the time, and an irrational method of escaping them. Or rather, trying to escape. The record of exhaustion and collapse, sometimes requiring long periods of convalescence for recuperation, is extensive. But the breakdowns, which were regularly attributed to overwork, were "rather due," as Lecky dryly observed, "to anxiety." [122]

119. *Letters and Memories*, 1, 63, 70 (unabridged ed., 1, 83, 90).
120. Ibid., 1, 262–5 (unabridged ed., 1, 300–3).
121. *Short Studies*, 2, 366–7.
122. *Map of Life*, chap. 16, p. 332.

Chapter 11

ENTHUSIASM

> To labour in elevating the genius of action, as exhibited in the more practical world of politics and laws—to refine the coarse, and to ennoble the low; this, sir, it seems to me, is the true moral which the infirmities of this present time the most demand, and which the English writer . . . ought to place unceasingly before him. . . . His great aim for England shall be . . . to inculcate a venerating enthusiasm for the true and ethereal springs of Greatness and of Virtue.
>
> *Bulwer Lytton, 1833* [1]

IT IS HARDLY SURPRISING that Thomas Arnold should have thought "our common temper . . . but too generally cold, and selfish, and worldly." What is unexpected is the cure he once suggested. Instead of appealing for self-denial and the performance of duty, he recommended the reading of poetry because it could arouse "all the highest and purest feelings of our nature." It could have the same effect as some occurrence that puts us above ourselves, and awakens "our devotion, our admiration, or our love," or of some distress that calls for pity, or an emergency that demands "the sacrifice of our own comfort, or interest, or credit, for the sake of others." Any such experience, he said, acts upon us like poetry: "It exalts and ennobles us, and puts us into a higher state of mind than that which we are commonly living in." [2] That higher state of mind, in which the selfish

1. *England and the English*, p. 195.
2. Preface to *Poetry of Common Life* (1831), reprinted in *The Miscellaneous Works of Thomas Arnold* (London, 1845), pp. 252–3. Cf. Coleridge, "The Statesman's Manual," *Biographia Literaria and Two Lay Sermons*, p. 318: "For what is enthusiasm but the oblivion and swallowing-up of self in an object dearer than self, or in an idea more vivid?" And he goes on to describe "the genuine enthusiasm of morals, religion and patriotism" as an "enlargement and elevation of the soul above its mere self."

desires of the ego, far from having to be conquered by the moral will, are swept aside by the selfless impulse of the "noble" emotions, is a state of enthusiasm. And though in itself ephemeral, it has lasting effects. By "winding up to a high pitch those feelings of an elevated kind which are already in the character," the "exciting enthusiasm" of music gives them "a glow and a fervour, which, though transitory at its utmost height, is precious for sustaining them at other times." [3]

In significant contrast with that of moral earnestness, the ethic of enthusiasm assumes that human nature is good; that the organ of virtue is the sensibility rather than the conscience; and that the moral life depends, not on the arduous struggle to master the passions and compel the will to a life of duty, but on the vitality of the noble emotions, inspiring the delighted service of a high ideal. But however different in basic assumptions, this ethic should not be thought of as an alternative, still less as a rival, to that of earnestness. Both were held by most Victorians, with the stress falling more often and more strongly on earnestness. Tennyson, Carlyle, Kingsley, Macaulay, both the Arnolds found a place for enthusiasm in their ethical creed, sometimes a large one. [4] That was the majority group. On the other hand, the minority group, the men who substituted "noble" for "earnest" as the term of highest praise for a man or a life—Mill, Morley, Dickens, Browning, George Eliot—were far from condemning the contrasting mode of earnestness; and they shared to some extent (George Eliot to a large one), its concern for moral discipline and the performance of duty. For although the two attitudes may exist separately, indeed may even be incompatible if pushed to extremes, and although they have their roots in different traditions, the one Puritan and mercantile, the other romantic and aristocratic, they could perfectly well be combined. When Mill said that it was "quite possible to cultivate the conscience and the sentiments too," and make men ashamed not only of actual wrong but of the absence of "high feelings" and "noble aims," he was stating a basic assumption of nearly all mid-Victorians, though his emphasis was falling on enthusiasm. [5]

3. Mill, *Autobiography*, chap. 5, p. 122. Also see the quotation from Mill in note 8, below.

4. In his *Matthew Arnold*, pp. 340–4, Lionel Trilling sets the negative morality of self-control against the positive morality of generous impulse, but he does not sufficiently allow for their combination, and seems to associate Arnold too exclusively with the former. Arnold's enthusiasm is brought out later in the present chapter.

5. "Inaugural Address at St. Andrews," *James & John Stuart Mill on Education,*

The combination seems natural enough when we realize that most "enthusiastic" Victorians grew up in Evangelical or Dissenting homes, and when we discover that some of the same motivating factors which called for earnestness called also for enthusiasm.

The cult of enthusiasm appears in a number of related forms. The central one is a theory of moral education. The function of all teachers, including those who write for adults, is to present the imagination with objects calculated to call forth the noble emotions. In Ruskin's summary of the aims of education (which underscores the interwoven character of Victorian morality), the first and basic one is to make boys and girls "practically serviceable to other creatures" by not allowing them to run too long "in the paddock before they are broken" and training them early to do "such work as they are able for." The second is to give them "the faculties of admiration, hope and love" (the principal noble emotions) through "the study of beautiful Nature; the sight and history of noble persons; and the setting forth of noble objects of action." [6]

When a Victorian was inspired in these ways to become a "noble" person, he might have in mind either of two ideals of character. Where the quickening objects are nature in its pastoral forms, or music that is sensuous and melodic, or images of the misery or goodness of man, the emotions kindled are those of love in the sense of pity for human beings suffering under misfortune, admiration for what is good and gracious in human nature, and, hence, hope for the human situation. In this mood of warm sympathy the moral ideal is benevolence.[7] But where the inciting objects are mountain scenery, stirring and triumphant music, heroic men and heroic action, the mood produced is one of excited aspiration. In the presence of what is sublime one is swept by an exhilarating sense of reaching up, of

---

p. 192. The two attitudes may, indeed, be fused if one feels an ardent enthusiasm for a life of moral earnestness: see below, p. 273, and note 29.

6. *Fors Clavigera*, Letter 67, in *Works, 28*, 655–6.

7. See Ruskin, "The Moral of Landscape," *Modern Painters, 3* (1856), Pt. IV, chap. 17, secs. 18, 26, 30, in *Works, 5*, 367, 371–2, 376, where the inciting object is nature. This passage is of special value because Ruskin is contrasting the ethic of enthusiasm with that of the earnestness he learned in his Evangelical home. In his early "Essay on Literature," *Works, 1*, 365–6, he ascribes the moral influence of Scott's novels to their power of so bringing our "good feelings" into play that "we become, for the time, spirits altogether benevolent, altogether just, hating vice, loving virtue . . . lamenting the misfortune, rejoicing in the welfare of others." By the standard of moral earnestness, however, Scott's novels will be thought devoid of moral influence: see Carlyle's remarks above, pp. 227–8.

breaking through human limitations, of possessing within himself tremendous potentialities. He feels the dynamic desire for what the Romantics called the ideal and the infinite, and Shelley popularized as "the desire of the moth for the star." He longs to be a *great* man —as distinct from a benevolent man. In this mood of high enthusiasm, the moral ideal, which now inspires *passionate* admiration, love, and hope, is either that of nobility or else the development of all one's powers to their highest potentiality.[8]

Finally, enthusiasm sets up a standard of judgment which may be called moral optimism. The right attitude is one which recognizes and praises whatsoever things are lovely, admirable, and hopeful in human life and human beings. The wrong attitude, which but too plainly shows the presence of the ignoble emotions of anger, scorn, or hopelessness, is critical, satiric, pessimistic—even realistic. One must adopt an optimistic view of man and the universe.

8. Though these moods, especially the second, are transient, their impact may have lasting effect, as Mill points out in *The Subjection of Women*, chap. 3, p. 500: "The capability of that lofty enthusiasm which takes the human being out of his every-day character, reacts upon the daily character itself. His aspirations and powers when he is in this exceptional state, become the type with which he compares, and by which he estimates, his sentiments and proceedings at other times: and his habitual purposes assume a character moulded by and assimilated to the moments of lofty excitement, although those, from the physical nature of a human being, can only be transient."

It may be admitted that the term enthusiasm means "rapturous intensity of feeling in favour of a person, principle, cause, etc." (*O.E.D.*) and is therefore only applicable, strictly speaking, to the second and higher level. That, indeed, is its normal use in Victorian criticism; and it is specifically set apart, sometimes, from the milder mood of kindness and pity: see Charlotte Yonge, preface to *A Book of Golden Deeds*, p. 5, and W. R. Greg, "False Morality of Lady Novelists," *Literary and Social Judgments*, 1, 106, where he speaks of our owing to novels "the perception of the beautiful, the enthusiasm for the grand." But since what is normally called enthusiasm is simply a higher degree of the same psychological experience that perceives the beautiful and feels benevolence (the emotional transcendence of self and its worldly temper), I see no reason why the term should not be applied to both levels. On one occasion, at least, it was used for the lower level: In George Eliot's *Daniel Deronda*, 3, chap. 63, p. 277, Gwendolen's dependence on Deronda "tended to rouse in him the enthusiasm of self-martyring pity." At any rate, the use of the term in the broad sense I propose has the great advantage of giving us one word that may be placed against earnestness to define the other moral attitude that was conspicuous in the period. And for that there *is* contemporary authority: see the quotations from Mill and W. R. Greg below, p. 299, where enthusiasm and earnestness are used as complementary terms.

1. *Idealism and the Education of the Feelings*

The Victorians inherited the cult of noble emotions from the Romantics: from the Rousseauistic faith in the goodness of human nature and the spontaneous flowering of the moral sentiments, so long as they were uncorrupted by the "evil" influences of civilization and unrestrained by authoritarian discipline. (Rousseau and Wesley can be thought of as the immediate fountainheads of the two great streams of Victorian morality.) It was the earlier Wordsworth, under the influence of Rousseau—the later Wordsworth became more and more earnest—who carried this morality alive into the Victorian heart, referring its inspiration to the direct or vicarious experience (the latter through art and poetry) of the beauty or grandeur of nature and man, and defining its central doctrine:

> We live by Admiration, Hope, and Love;
> And, even as these are well and wisely fixed,
> In dignity of being we ascend.[9]

This teaching remained vital, to give the broadest reason first, because many Victorians felt the need, as John Morley explained, for some effective agency to nourish "the diviner mind" and keep alive the love of the Ideal in a society becoming more and more "scientific in method, rationalistic in spirit, and utilitarian in purpose." That need could be satisfied, he went on to say, by literature. By itself literature could not make a good man, but to the moral foundation of "restraint and discipline," it could add the very education of the feelings which our modern civilization was ignoring or repudiating: "the cultivation of the sympathies and imagination, the quickening of the moral sensibilities, and the enlargement of the moral vision."[10]

In Victorian culture, as Morley defined it, the principal ingredient was Benthamism, and Bentham had specifically denied the validity of the feelings and the effectiveness of sympathy (the only disinterested motive he recognized) as sanctions of morality. The only

9. *The Excursion*, Bk. IV, lines 763–5, frequently quoted by Ruskin: see *Fors Clavigera*, Letter 5, in *Works*, 27, 90, where other references are cited in the note.

10. "On the Study of Literature," *Studies in Literature*, pp. 201–2; and cf. the important passage in his essay on Browning's *Ring and the Book*, ibid., pp. 268–9. The dates are 1887 and 1869, but the point of view is mid-Victorian, as the following paragraphs will show.

valid sanction was self-interest, properly trained and enlightened. His disciple James Mill "regarded as an aberration of the moral standard of modern [Romantic] times . . . the great stress laid upon feeling. Feelings, as such, he considered to be no proper subjects of praise or blame. Right and wrong, good and bad, he regarded as qualities solely of conduct—of acts and omissions." [11] In this faith his son John Stuart was brought up. He and his Benthamite friends did not expect the regeneration of mankind from any direct action on the moral sentiments, "but from the effect of educated intellect, enlightening the selfish feelings." [12] It was the nervous breakdown of 1826 which revolutionized Mill's ethics; for if he failed to understand its main cause,[13] the cause he assumed (that his education had been too exclusively intellectual) forced him to conclude that the moral sentiments needed to be cultivated as well as the reason. Only when they were nourished and enriched from the earliest years could they be created in sufficient strength to survive the corrosive influence of the analytical mind. Henceforth "the cultivation of the feelings" became one of the cardinal points in his ethical and philosophical creed, and he began, under the further influence of Wordsworth, to recognize "the importance of poetry and art as instruments of human culture." [14]

This personal experience is reflected in the famous essay on Bentham (1838). There Mill charged the master with overlooking not only "the moral part of man's nature, in the strict sense of the term"— that is, the conscience (this is the central point of the attack on Bentham by the earnest Victorians)—but also the sense of honor, the love of beauty, and especially "the love of *loving*, the need of a sympathising support, or of objects of admiration and reverence." [15] These omissions, together with the doctrine of self-interest, exposed Benthamism to the scorn of "the more enthusiastic and generous minds." [16] Sterling's Arthur Coningsby thought it a most degrading

11. John Mill, *Autobiography*, chap. 2, p. 41; cf. chap. 4, p. 93.

12. Ibid., chap. 4, p. 94.

13. See above, Chap. 3, note 73.

14. *Autobiography*, chap. 5, p. 122. The analysis of his education is on pp. 115–18.

15. *Dissertations*, 1, 360.

16. Mill, "Remarks on Bentham's Philosophy," which is appendix B to Bulwer Lytton's *England and the English*, p. 372. For Mill's authorship, see his *Autobiography*, chap. 6, p. 168. These "Remarks," pp. 365–75, are, in effect, the first draft of the later essay. Appendix C, pp. 376–80, on James Mill, written, I assume,

moral theory because it made no allowance for "the nobler sympathies and convictions of mankind." [17] Eustace Conway in Maurice's early novel goes through a Benthamite period in which he is ready to sacrifice the "gentle sympathies and kindly affections" and might have become "an intellectual all-in-all" but for the fact that "impulses of deeper mood would come to him in solitude, and sometimes . . . disturbed him with the joy of elevated thoughts." [18]

This reaction against Benthamism was complemented by the reaction against the industrial environment. A society that placed supreme value upon "her docks, her canals, her railroads" was distinguished, Mill pointed out, "for a kind of sober good sense, free from extravagance, but also devoid of lofty aspirations." [19] Indeed, the utilitarian spirit of business was innately hostile to idealism for the best of all business reasons: it was impractical. To Macaulay the ancient philosophy was immeasurably inferior to the Baconian philosophy because it "dealt largely in theories of moral perfection, which were so sublime that they never could be more than theories." While Plato aimed to exalt man into a god, Bacon thought only of supplying our vulgar wants. "The former aim was noble; but the latter was attainable. . . . An acre in Middlesex is better than a principality in Utopia." [20] Furthermore, the counteremphasis on idealism was needed to check the commercial, as well as the utilitarian, spirit of middle-class society. A world in which money and respectability were the related goals of social life, and national greatness was symbolized by the Exhibition of 1851, seemed to some Victorians a travesty of what

---

by Bulwer Lytton himself, concludes: "He rather discontents us with vice than kindles our enthusiasm for virtue. He possesses but little of
'The vision and the faculty divine;'—
nor is it through his writings, admirable as they are, that we are taught
'To feel that we are greater than we know.'"
Both lines are quotations from Wordsworth.

17. *Arthur Coningsby* (3 vols. London, 1833), *3*, 378.

18. *Eustace Conway: or, the Brother and Sister* (1834), *1*, 142, 228. The quoted allusions to "The Poet's Epitaph" and the "Lines" on Tintern Abbey again show Wordsworth being called on to oppose Benthamism: cf. note 16 above.

19. "Professor Sedgwick's Discourse on the Studies of the University of Cambridge," *Dissertations, 1*, 96–7.

20. "Lord Bacon," *Critical Essays, 3*, 436–7, 458–60. Cf. Morley, "Byron," *Critical Miscellanies, 1*, 205: "That intense practicalness which seems to have done so many great things for us, and yet at the same moment mysteriously to have robbed us of all, forbids us even to cast a glance at what is no more than an aspiration."

personal and national success ought to mean. More than once Mill
noticed the contrast between French and English society: in the
former, elevated sentiments were the current coin of human intercourse but accompanied by an easy-going conscience; in the latter,
a strict conscience but an absence of "high feelings" and the assumption that conduct is "always directed towards low and petty
objects." [21] In the last section of his address at St. Andrews, where he
turned to "the education of the feelings, and the cultivation of the
beautiful," [22] Mill described the type of character produced by the
two influences which had chiefly shaped the British temperament since
the days of the Stuarts, commercial money-getting business and
Puritanism:

> One of the commonest types of character among us is that of
> a man all whose ambition is self-regarding; who has no higher
> purpose in life than to enrich or raise in the world himself and
> his family; who never dreams of making the good of his fellow-
> creatures or of his country an habitual object, further than giving
> away, annually or from time to time, certain sums in charity; but
> who has a conscience sincerely alive to whatever is generally
> considered wrong, and would scruple to use any very illegitimate
> means for attaining his self-interested objects.

The conclusion is that earnestness and enthusiasm should be combined:

> It is quite possible to cultivate the conscience and the sentiments
> too. Nothing hinders us from so training a man that he will not,
> even for a disinterested purpose, violate the moral law, and also
> feeding and encouraging those high feelings, on which we mainly
> rely for lifting men above low and sordid objects, and giving
> them a higher conception of what constitutes success in life.
> . . . It is worth training them to feel, not only actual wrong or
> actual meanness, but the absence of noble aims and endeavours,
> as not merely blameable but also degrading.

To that end the great instruments of education are poetry, and all
literature so far as it is "poetical and artistic." [23]

21. *Autobiography*, chap. 2, pp. 49–50.
22. "Inaugural Address," p. 189. The quotations that follow are on pp. 191–3.
23. Cf. Ruskin's definition of poetry, *Modern Painters*, 3 (1856), Pt. IV, chap.
1, sec. 13, in *Works*, 5, 28, which begins: "I come . . . to the conclusion, that
poetry is 'the suggestion, by the imagination, of noble grounds for noble emotions.' " This enthusiastic theory of poetry may be contrasted with the earnest

Since a moment before Mill had been tracing the low opinion of art to the business character of the age, this corrective seems a little quixotic. The cry for idealism, especially where poetry was advocated as its inciting means, was designed, I think, less to convert the middle classes to nobler aims than to protect the rest of society—gentlemen and intellectuals—from being infected by the utilitarian and commercial spirit. It is significant that no sooner has Mill said that self-regarding men should be trained to feel "the absence of noble aims" than he adds, with a telltale shift from "them" to "we," "and if unfortunately those by whom we are surrounded do not share our aspirations, perhaps disapprove the conduct to which we are prompted by them," we may "sustain ourselves by the ideal sympathy of the great characters in history, or even in fiction."[24] It was with that object in mind that Tennyson wrote the *Idylls of the King*. "My father felt strongly," his son remarked, referring to the poem, "that only under the inspiration of ideals . . . can a man combat the cynical indifference, the intellectual selfishness, the sloth of will, the utilitarian materialism of a transition age." That is to say, only so can a man of finer feelings—a man like Tennyson—ward off the insidious influence of the environment.[25]

As a matter of fact, we know that for society as a whole Mill never relied on art alone to quicken the altruistic emotions or create an ideal goal. For such ends he and his fellow rationalists depended on a Religion of Humanity in which man took the place of God as the object of devoted love and service: "The idealization of our earthly life, the

---

theory that poetry should provide moral lessons: see Morley, second reference in note 10. On p. 196 Mill makes the further point that the very theory of art, for all who understand it, has an uplifting influence. For by its "conception of an ideal Beauty, to be eternally aimed at, though surpassing what can be actually attained . . . it trains us never to be completely satisfied with imperfection in what we ourselves do and are: to idealize, as much as possible, every work we do, and most of all, our own characters and lives."

24. Page 193. Cf. George Eliot, speaking of Lydgate in *Middlemarch*, 2, chap. 45, p. 256: "A man conscious of enthusiasm for worthy aims is sustained under petty hostilities by the memory of great workers who had to fight their way not without wounds, and who hover in his mind as patron saints, invisibly helping."

25. *Memoir of Tennyson*, 2, 129. Cf. Kingsley, "Heroism," *Sanitary and Social Essays*, pp. 249–50. To Elizabeth Barrett—*Letters*, ed. F. G. Kenyon (2 vols. New York and London, 1897), *1*, 48—the great value of a poem like Talfourd's *Ion* whose "moral tone is very noble" was not its effect on society so much as its welcome reassurance to a cultured reader. It sent, she said, "a grand and touching harmony into the midst of the full discord of this utilitarian age."

cultivation of a high conception of what *it* may be made, is . . .
capable of supplying a poetry, and, in the best sense of the word, a
religion, equally fitted to exalt the feelings, and (with the same aid
from education) still better calculated to ennoble the conduct, than
any belief respecting the unseen powers." [26] That is certainly open to
serious question—if one has a choice. But if not, if supernatural beliefs
are becoming more and more tenuous and yet their loss is felt to be a
dangerous threat to the moral nature, one may well agree with Mill
that the image of perfected humanity may so stimulate the noble emotions of admiration, love, and hope as to be a possible substitute for
Christianity. The English followers of Comte, whether whole-hearted
disciples like Congreve and Harrison or less orthodox adherents like
Mill, Morley, and George Eliot, adopted a secular ethic of enthusiasm
to save the moral foundations of society in an age of doubt; but they
also recognized its direct and salutary effect on an age of commercialism.

Apart from a specific Religion of Humanity, the cultivation of the
feelings by an ideal image was promoted indirectly by the decline of
ecclesiastic and parental discipline. Through the century the starting
point of moral education continued to change. The old ascetic training
in which the "supreme object was to discipline and strengthen the
will, to accustom men habitually to repudiate the pleasurable and
accept the painful, to mortify the most natural tastes and affections,
to narrow and weaken the empire of the desires," was gradually dis-
appearing, as life grew more comfortable and luxurious, and as the
religious beliefs on which self-discipline rested steadily gave way.[27]
For the same reasons parental discipline also declined, to be given its
death-blow presently by the arrival of Freud. More and more the education of the desires took the place of educating the will. The object
became, as Lecky said, "to make the path of virtue the natural, the
easy, the pleasing one" by presenting the imagination with ideal pictures of action and character that would quicken the noble emotions.

26. "Utility of Religion," *Three Essays on Religion*, p. 105.

27. Lecky, *The Map of Life*, chap. 12, pp. 245–51, under the running title, "Two
Forms of Education." The quotation below is on p. 246. In his *History of European
Morals* (first ed. 1869; 2 vols. New York, 1903), *1*, 187–9, Lecky contrasts "two
great divisions of character" (which correspond "very nearly to the Stoical and
Epicurean temperaments"—and very nearly to the earnest and enthusiastic temperaments), and then goes on to associate them respectively with "two distinct
theories of education," one aiming to strengthen the will, the other, "which was
never more prevalent than in the present day" [1869], to guide the desires. For a
useful example of how the latter might be done, see Ruskin, "Education," *Time
and Tide*, Letter 16, in *Works*, 17, 398–9.

Normally, ideal action and character, as we shall see in a moment, were either "benevolent" or "noble," but it was possible, perhaps not uncommon, to react with enthusiasm to an image of moral earnestness. In a Victorian like George Eliot, brought up in Evangelicalism and yet filled with Romantic ardor, the creed of strict conduct, the renunciation of self, and a dedicated pursuit of social duty could become a sublime object of passionate devotion. Under the influence of Thomas à Kempis that organic fusion of the two poles of Victorian morality takes place in Maggie Tulliver, a portrait of the author as a young girl. It enables her to surmount the enervating effect of her environment and resolve the depression it had induced.[28] In Matthew Arnold this therapy is applied to the despairs of religious skepticism:

> Long fed on boundless hopes, O race of man,
> How angrily thou spurn'st all simpler fare!
> "Christ," some one says, "was human as we are;
> No judge eyes us from Heaven, our sin to scan;
>
> "We live no more, when we have done our span."—
> "Well, then, for Christ," thou answerest, "who can care?
> From sin, which Heaven records not, why forbear?
> Live we like brutes our life without a plan!"
>
> So answerest thou; but why not rather say:
> "Hath man no second life?—*Pitch this one high!*
> Sits there no judge in Heaven, our sin to see?—
>
> "*More strictly, then, the inward judge obey!*
> *Was Christ a man like us? Ah! let us try*
> *If we then, too, can be such men as he!*"

Arnold called this "The Better Part." But his original title was "Anti-Desperation."[29]

2. Sympathy and Benevolence

In the reaction against Hobbes, eighteenth-century thought had stressed the moral value of sympathy and the virtue of benevolence. The ethical theories of Shaftesbury, Hume, Adam Smith, and even

28. *The Mill on the Floss*, 2, Bk. IV, chaps. 1, 3.

29. *Poetical Works*, p. 170. In Carlyle, too, there is a strain of aspiration directed toward the ideal of earnestness: for example, *Sartor Resartus*, Bk. II, chap. 9, pp. 196–7; *Past and Present*, Bk. I, chap. 6, pp. 37–8; Bk. III, chaps. 11 and 12, pp. 199–200, 205–6.

Bentham, had assumed in human nature a disinterested feeling of sympathy with the joys and sorrows of others; [30] but the last three had viewed it more as a negative principle that helped to curb selfishness than a positive faculty to be cultivated. Most English thinkers, John Mill complained, seem to have regarded the sympathies "as necessary evils, required for keeping men's actions benevolent and compassionate." [31] In literature, "the man of feeling" had made his appearance in Steele, Mackenzie, even Pope; and the current of charity and good will in the work of Goldsmith, Richardson, and Sterne had been deepened by the influence of Rousseau until it became an important element in the Romantic temper. But the cult of benevolence took a new direction in the nineteenth century when the misery of the industrial workers became sufficiently apparent to demand redress—and all the more so because it constituted a threat to social order. If one solution proposed (by Carlyle and Dr. Arnold, as we have seen) was a more earnest sense of social duty, another lay in quickening the moral sensibility to an acute sympathy for suffering humanity. This approach was immediately inspired by the harsh and inhuman spirit which had seemed to characterize the Tory and Benthamite efforts to meet the situation. The world of the Six Acts, of frequent executions, of workhouse Bastilles, provoked, as Bagehot first suggested, a violent reaction: "The unfeeling obtuseness of the early part of this century was to be corrected by an extreme—perhaps an excessive—sensibility to human suffering in the years which have followed. There was most adequate reason for the sentiment in its origin, and it had a great task to perform in ameliorating harsh customs and repealing dreadful penalties." [32] In this reaction, the tradition of benevolence reached its peak and added its powerful influence to that of moral earnestness in promoting Victorian charity and social legislation.

Bagehot's remarks occur, appropriately enough, in his essay on Dickens, for Dickens was recognized as a major prophet of sympathetic feeling and benevolent action. As early as 1838 the *Edinburgh Review* was praising him for "his comprehensive spirit of humanity" and the "tendency of his writings . . . to make us practically benevolent—to excite our sympathy in behalf of the aggrieved and suffering in all classes; and especially in those who are most removed from ob-

30. For a useful summary see W. J. Bate, *From Classic to Romantic* (Cambridge, Mass., 1946), pp. 131–41.

31. *Autobiography*. chap. 5, p. 128.

32. "Charles Dickens," *Works*, 2, 269–70. I am indebted for the reference to Humphry House, *The Dickens World*, p. 47.

servation." [33] This ethical message is related, in a significant way, to the negative character of Dickens' social criticism. He attacked various abuses—prisons, boarding schools, the Court of Chancery—but he had no positive theory of reform. For him, as for Stephen Blackpool, "It's aw a muddle." The only remedy he could think of was to melt the cold indifference of the fashionable world and the hard, two-fisted insensitivity of the Gradgrinds by the warm breath of pity and kindness; and by that inspiration stimulate an active life of private charity. It is Mr. Jarndyce rescuing the family of Coavinses from destitution who is the symbol of reform by benevolence, and Scrooge's conversion multiplied thousands of times is the panacea Dickens offers. In short, if the intellect is baffled, one turns to the heart. Benevolence thrives in a period of social distress and political uncertainty.[34]

Dickens often speaks of it in Christian terms, but Christian benevolence, based on a will dedicated to the service of God, is quite another thing. In Christian thought acts of charity are not the spontaneous expression of a good heart, but performances of religious duty. Dickens' heroes, however, "are all good-*natured*, and seem to act as they do because they cannot act otherwise. Not one of them has a moral policy, or a considered opinion about why he does good." [35] That Dickens could identify this Romantic benevolence with Christian benevolence marks the decline of the older and sterner faith on which the latter had been based. In commenting on the novels as the expression of lower-middle class attitudes, Fitzjames Stephen pointed out that the class which "had once found a voice for its religious sentiments in Puritanism, with stern conceptions of duty and of a divine order of the universe," was now turning to a "kind of vapid philanthropic sentiment which calls itself undenominational; a creed of maudlin benevolence from which all the deeper and sterner elements of religious belief have been carefully purged away." [36]

That criticism, indeed, is representative of the general opposition to the cult of benevolence which appeared in the 1840's. Earnest Vic-

33. Vol. 68, 77–8.

34. William O. Aydelotte, "The England of Marx and Mill as Reflected in Fiction," *Journal of Economic History, 8,* Supplement (1948), 42–58, brings out another factor in his discussion of Dickens, Kingsley, Mrs. Gaskell, and Disraeli, namely that a political conservatism which was fearful of both collectivism and democracy naturally limited its action to pleas for philanthropy and mutual understanding.

35. House, p. 39.

36. Leslie Stephen, *Life of Fitzjames Stephen,* p. 157, paraphrasing an article by his brother.

torians like Clough were alarmed lest a kind heart and occasional acts of charity might become the sole requirement of the moral life, to the serious neglect of self-discipline and strenuous work. "It is a good deal forgotten that we came into this world to do, not kindness to others, but our own duty, to live soberly, righteously, and godly, not benevolently, philanthropically, and tenderheartedly. To earn his own bread honestly—in the strictest sense of the word *honestly*—to do plain straightforward work or business well and thoroughly . . . is really quite a sufficient task for the ordinary mortal." [37] In Carlyle a strident attack is directed against the displacement of stern moral judgment by a "beautiful" pity. For to him the humane treatment of sinners and criminals was nothing but "a blind loquacious pruriency of indiscriminate Philanthropism substituting itself, with much self-laudation, for the silent divinely awful sense of Right and Wrong;—testifying too clearly that here is no longer a divine sense of Right and Wrong." [38]

The tendency of benevolence to obliterate that distinction was largely a late Victorian development. At the time another tendency was more apparent, its ready decline into sentimentality and the enjoyment of the tender emotions for their own sake. The sentimental in art is betrayed by an emotional expression in excess of what the object of love or pity would normally arouse; or by the exaggeration of the benevolent character through bestowing upon it an incredibly warm heart that irradiates the soul with extraordinary kindness and pity. Both forms of sentimentality merge in the tears—tears of joy and tears of "sweet sorrow"—which flow through the Victorian novel whenever a loving heart catches a glimpse of either goodness or suffering. After Mr. Jarndyce has been generous enough to excuse Harold Skimpole for misconduct because he is a child, Esther's comment shows the unabashed release of the sentimentality latent in benevolence: "It was so delicious to see the clouds about his bright face clearing, and to see him so heartily pleased, and to know, as it was impossible not to know, that the source of his pleasure was the goodness which was tortured by condemning, or mistrusting, or secretly accusing any one, that I saw the tears in Ada's eyes, while she echoed his laugh, and felt them in my own." [39] As to Dickens' deathbeds, Stephen thought them an indulgence in "the luxury of grief"; since once the full Christian meaning of death is lost sight of (its relation to sin and divine

37. *Prose Remains*, p. 171, undated but placed between entries for 1849 and 1850. Also, cf. p. 411.

38. *Latter-Day Pamphlets*, No. 2, called "Model Prisons," p. 51.

39. *Bleak House*, 1, chap. 6, 82.

judgment and hell), it may become a mere occasion for sentimental vaporings.[40] But at least Dickens' pathos had a social purpose. The heart that is purified by pity for the dead may be readier to feel pity for the living.[41] It also had a religious purpose. The death scenes which fill the Victorian novels are clearly connected with the religious crisis. They are intended to help the reader sustain his faith by dissolving religious doubt in a solution of warm sentiment. When the heart is so strongly moved, the skeptical intellect is silenced; and when feelings of profound love and pity are centered on a beautiful soul who is gone forever, the least religious affirmation, the slightest reference to heaven or angels, or to reunion with those who have gone before (and no decent deathbed in any novel was without them) was sufficient to invoke a powerful sense of reassurance.[42]

The deterioration of benevolence into sentimentality, consequent upon the decline of Christian vitality, was also affected by middle-class business. "In business begad," says Barnes Newcome, "there are no friends and no enemies at all. I leave all my sentiment on the other side of Temple Bar" [43]—with the result that the sentiment broke out on "the other side" all the more emotionally. The taut nerves rebounded, the hard temper melted into tears. But the compensation was also motivated by guilt. A business society dedicated to the political principle of laissez-faire and the economic principle that there must be no interference with the iron laws of supply and demand needed to feel that in spite of appearances its heart was tender. If it was doing little to relieve the suffering of the poor, at any rate it was feeling very sympathetic. To the needling of the conscience it received from many of the Victorian prophets, from Froude, for example, in The Nemesis of

40. Fitzjames Stephen (reference in note 36), p. 158; and cf. House, p. 132.

41. Kathleen Tillotson in an interesting discussion of Dickens' pathos, Novels of the Eighteen-Forties, pp. 47–53, also points out that Nell, Smike, Jo, even Paul, are all in different ways social victims.

42. See, for a good example, the famous death of "dear, gentle, patient, noble Nell" in The Old Curiosity Shop, chap. 71, pp. 555–6. The ultimate expression of this desire to make the deathbed serve the cause of antiskepticism is the "miracle" which sometimes occurs just before the last moment: the dying character hears the actual sound of heavenly music or catches his first sight of the loved ones who are waiting for him. See Little Nell, ibid., start of chap. 72, p. 557; Milly in George Eliot's "The Sad Fortunes of the Rev. Amos Barton," Scenes of Clerical Life, 1, chap. 8, p. 99; Margaret in Charlotte Yonge's The Daisy Chain, Pt. II, chap. 25, p. 575; Muriel in Mrs. Craik's John Halifax, Gentleman, chap. 28, p. 393.

43. Thackeray, The Newcomes, chap. 64, p. 669.

Faith—"How can a man grow rich, except on the spoils of others' labour? His boasted prudence and economy, what is it but the most skilfully availing himself of their necessities, most resolutely closing up his heart against their cries to him for help?" [44]—to such an attack there was a ready answer. The heart was *not* closed up; why, it even bursts into tears at the sight of suffering and death. But they were not tears of genuine pity. They were tears of purgation. And thus "purified," one could return next day to business as usual. "It has been often noticed," said Lecky, "that the exaggerated sentimentality which sheds passionate tears over the fictitious sorrows of a novel or a play is no certain sign of a benevolent and unselfish nature, and is quite compatible with much indifference to real sorrows and much indisposition to make efforts for their alleviation." [45] Quite compatible, I suggest, because the tears make it *unnecessary* to make any efforts for alleviation. [46]

Benevolence need not, however, degenerate into sentimentality. It does not do so, or very slightly, in the work of George Eliot, the other major Victorian besides Dickens who made its promotion a central aim of fiction. The reason is that for Eliot the essential thing, the foundation of genuine benevolence, is not feeling as such but understanding. It originates in a clear and compassionate perception of human suffering, which then quickens the natural emotions of pity and love; with the result that the emotions are commensurate with what such an object would normally arouse and warrant, and not, as in sentimentalism, too intense for an object which is but dimly perceived. The contrast may be made in another way that brings out the ethical difference. The sentimental indulgence of pity and love is really self-centered —one enjoys feeling a burst of kindness for those less fortunate than himself—whereas George Eliot's benevolence presupposes a forgetfulness of self in the recognition of our common humanity. The distinction meant a reemphasis on sympathy as the power of entering into the feelings of another, especially in sorrow or trouble; and consequently experiencing not only pity and love but also patience, tolerance, and forbearance. Sympathetic feeling is fellow-feeling. Her approach is summarized in a passage from *Adam Bede* which has the added value, for our purposes, of taking the "earnest" reformer to task for his lack of benevolence:

44. Page 51.
45. Lecky, *The Map of Life*, chap. 12, p. 260.
46. For other types of sentimentality, see the Index, below.

These fellow-mortals, every one, must be accepted as they are, —you can neither straighten their noses, nor brighten their wit, nor rectify their dispositions; and it is these people—amongst whom your life is passed—that it is needful you should tolerate, pity, and love; it is these more or less ugly, stupid, inconsistent people, whose movements of goodness you should be able to admire, for whom you should cherish all possible hopes, all possible patience . . . who can be cheered and helped onward by your fellow-feeling, your forbearance, your outspoken, brave justice.[47]

The context is a discussion of fiction which develops her characteristic defense of realism. "My artistic bent," she said elsewhere, "is directed not at all to the presentation of eminently irreproachable characters, but to the presentation of mixed human beings in such a way as to call forth tolerant judgment, pity, and sympathy."[48]

Her purpose was partly social amelioration. Though the artist should not propose concrete remedies for particular evils, he should give reform its animating spirit by rousing "the nobler emotions, which make mankind desire the social right."[49] But George Eliot had a wider object in mind which she shared with many of her contemporaries in the fifties and sixties, to heal the divisive effect of the sectarian spirit, especially in the area of religion. In the clash of warring doctrines, "speculative truth begins to appear but a shadow of individual minds. Agreement between intellects seems unattainable, and we turn to the *truth of feeling* as the only universal bond of union"—the truth, that is, of those sympathetic feelings which draw men together.[50] The date is 1843. When Baldwin Brown gave his lectures in 1870 entitled "The Revolution of the Last Quarter of a Century," he thought that "during the last generation, ecclesiastical and theological ideas have steadily declined as a basis of fellowship and co-operation, while spiritual ideas have taken their place. Men are increasingly drawn together by that which belongs to the sphere of the sympathies . . . while they attach less and less importance to merely intellectual agreement."[51] To further that movement was the central aim of George Eliot's work.

47. Vol. *1*, chap. 17, p. 245.
48. Cross, *George Eliot's Life*, *1*, 326, from a letter to Blackwood, February 18, 1857.
49. Ibid., *3*, 268, from a letter to Mrs. Taylor, July 18, 1878.
50. Ibid., *1*, 92, from a letter to Sara Hennell, October 19, 1843.
51. *First Principles*, p. 336.

If art does not enlarge men's sympathies, it does nothing morally. I have had heart-cutting experience that *opinions* are a poor cement between human souls; and the only effect I ardently long to produce by my writings is, that those who read them should be better able to *imagine* and to *feel* the pains and the joys of those who differ from themselves in everything but the broad fact of being struggling, erring, human creatures.[52]

To imagine and feel our common humanity is to call forth the binding emotions of pity and love.

Under the influence of Victorian benevolence, however motivated, the moral judgment of a strict conscience, taking the ten commandments for its standard, lost its central authority. It was attacked because it ignored other moral qualities over and above technical virtue, noble emotions which might even thrive in characters by no means free from sin; and because it encouraged a holier-than-thou self-righteousness that was fatal to the development of compassion. Nowhere has Puritanism done us more harm, wrote John Morley in 1870, than in reducing our judgments of men "to thin, narrow, and superficial pronouncements upon the letter of their morality . . . as if we had no faculties of sympathy, no sense for the beauty of character, no feeling for broad force and full-pulsing vitality." Still worse, it has "hardened the hearts and parched the sympathies of men by blasts from theological deserts." Fortunately, "a wholesome rebellion is afoot" that will bring back "wide sympathy and many-coloured appreciativeness" into our judgment of human beings.[53]

But as Morley recognized, "this broad and poetic criticism" had special dangers. It might be carried too far, to a point at which sympathy would become the only reaction and moral judgment be abandoned entirely. This is what happened in the post-Victorian development of aestheticism. Pater was happy to observe that unlike Dante (and, we may add, unlike George Eliot) Botticelli gave a detached and "attractive" picture of men and women in their mixed and uncertain condition. His morality was "*all* sympathy." [54] Correlative with that prin-

---

52. Cross, *Life*, 2, 88, from a letter to Charles Bray, July 5, 1859.

53. "Carlyle," *Critical Miscellanies*, 1, 182–5.

54. "Sandro Botticelli," *The Renaissance*, p. 58. A. C. Benson, *Walter Pater* (London, 1906), p. 48, remarked that his principles "tend to the refinement and enlargement of the moral nature . . . by substituting sympathy for conscience." This, of course, is exactly what Carlyle had claimed was happening about 1850: see above, p. 276. The italics in the Pater quotation are mine.

ciple, Pater announced another: that the end of life was not action, however motivated, whether by the conscience or the sensibility, but simply contemplation, "*being* as distinct from *doing*—a certain disposition of the mind." The artist, therefore, was "not to teach lessons, or enforce rules, or even to stimulate us to noble ends; but to withdraw the thoughts for a little while from the mere machinery of life, to fix them, with appropriate emotions . . . 'on the great and universal passions of men.'" [55] That is the pure aesthetic attitude. Some years earlier Matthew Arnold had felt its fascination, and had rejected it because he was a mid-Victorian. The poet who interprets the natural world, he had said, as distinct from one who interprets the moral world, "goes into religion and out of religion, into society and out of society, not from the motives which impel men in general, but to feel what it is all like; he is thus hardly a moral agent. . . . Assuredly it is not in this temperament that the active virtues have their rise. On the contrary, this temperament, considered in itself alone, indisposes for the discharge of them." [56] But what to Arnold was a serious criticism became a virtue to Pater and the aesthetes who were revolting against mid-Victorianism. In the early Yeats sympathetic contemplation took the place of both action and judgment. The philosophy of Dante was that "of soldiers, of men of the world, of priests busy with government, of all who, because of the absorption in active life, have been persuaded to judge and to punish"; while that of Blake is the philosophy of "artists and poets, who are taught by the nature of their craft to sympathise with all living things, and . . . to come at last to forget good and evil in an absorbing vision of the happy and the unhappy." [57]

3. *Nobility*

In Mary Mitford's letters she describes two men, both of whom are called noble: Richard Porson was "a noble nature unhappily wasted— . . . a kind, careless, generous, open-hearted creature." But Daniel Webster, who stopped his own career to put his brother through school and college, was a great man. "This total self-sacrifice and self-oblivion

---

55. "Wordsworth" (1874), *Appreciations*, pp. 61–2. In later life Pater became more conservative. The close of his essay on "Style" (1888), ibid., p. 36, marks a reaction back to the didacticism of enthusiastic theory. Still later, he even criticized Wilde—review of *Dorian Gray*, in *Sketches and Reviews* (New York, 1919), p. 128—because his heroes were limited by lacking a "sense of sin."

56. "Maurice de Guerin," *Essays in Criticism, First Series*, pp. 124, 126.

57. "William Blake," *Essays* (New York, 1924), pp. 158–9.

does seem to me the very finest thing I ever heard in my life. Is it not *noble in the highest degree?*" [58] A similar distinction is found in Mill. His early zeal for the good of mankind did not have its root, he said, "in genuine benevolence, or sympathy with mankind. . . . Nor was it connected with any high enthusiasm for *ideal nobleness.*" [59] At the top level of intensity the mood of aspiration issues in a more exalted conception of character. Nobility takes the place of benevolence. [60]

Its central characteristic, clearly enough, is self-sacrifice, but in a sense quite different from the usual meaning of Christian self-sacrifice. The latter is better termed self-renunciation. It is a discipline and a way of life, an act of the will. Noble self-sacrifice is best described by Mary Mitford's synonym of self-oblivion. Under the impact of enthusiasm all selfish concern is transcended by ardent devotion to a person or a cause. This, too, of course, may be Christian; indeed, the term enthusiasm was intimately connected with religious mysticism or fanaticism. The distinction I am making is between the conscious and demanding earnestness of self-renunciation and the spontaneous enthusiasm of self-oblivion. Charlotte Yonge spoke of "golden deeds" which showed "such entire absorption in others that self is not so much renounced as forgotten." [61] But the service of "an object dearer than self" requires courage and effort; and with courage goes fortitude under misfortune, defeat, or personal attack. Other noble qualities are those of pride in its favorable meaning: the sense of dignity, self-respect, and personal honor. These various attributes are sometimes drawn loosely together under the all-inclusive virtue of magnanimity, the Aristotelian greatness of soul which raises one above everything that is petty, mean, or commonplace. [62]

Those who exalted this ideal were uncomfortably aware that a new class was rising to political power whose standards of conduct were distinctly and definitely not noble. The criticism came from two quarters: from the aristocracy or its middle-class friends who wanted to maintain what was literally, in its origin, the code of the nobleman;

58. *The Life of Mary Russell Mitford*, ed. A. G. L'Estrange, 3, 155; 101–2. The italics are mine.

59. *Autobiography*, chap. 4, p. 92. The italics are mine.

60. Although the adjective "noble," in the broad sense of "fine" or "admirable," may be used, as we see, for a benevolent man or action, it was more often applied to a person or a deed that had the quality of nobility I go on to describe.

61. Charlotte Yonge, *A Book of Golden Deeds*, p. 1.

62. It is thus clear that what is noble is also "grand," "great," or "heroic"; and nobility is often called "moral grandeur," "moral greatness," and sometimes "heroism."

and from the middle-class intellectuals who wanted to inject into a Puritan, commercial society a higher sense of social service, or to inspire noble opposition to its demand for conformity.

The attitude of the first group is reflected by its emphasis on gentility; for some of the talk about the necessity of being a gentleman was not mere social snobbery. If the merchant or manufacturer was barred from the world of fashion, it was not only because he lacked the social manners of a gentleman; it was also because he lacked, or was supposed to lack, the moral sentiments of a gentleman. Taine noticed the assumption. The English believe, he said, that "the monied man and the man of business is inclined to selfishness; he has not the disinterestedness, the large and generous views which suit a chief of the country; he does not know how to sink self, and think of the public." To the English, he went on to say, rephrasing the idea in positive form, "a real gentleman is a real noble, a man worthy of commanding, upright, disinterested, capable of exposing himself and even of sacrificing himself for those whom he leads." [63] All who held that belief could only view the coming of democracy with alarm. Up till then the aristocracy, besides governing the country, had placed before the nation —in theory at least and to some extent in fact—their high conception of character. "That noble way of thinking and behaving" which is a gift of nature to some individuals, wrote Arnold in his essay "Democracy," had been generated in aristocracies "by the possession of power, by the importance and responsibility of high station, by habitual dealing with great things, by being placed above the necessity of constantly struggling for little things." The governing class had therefore set "an invaluable example of qualities without which no really high welfare can exist." But now society was coming more and more under the control of the monied man and the man of business. In the age of democracy, "who or what," Arnold asked, "will give a high tone to the nation? . . . That is the grave question." [64]

One answer he goes on to give is rather surprising: the establishment by the state of national schools modeled on Eton, Harrow, and Rugby but intended for the middle class. Novel though it seemed, the idea was derived from his father, and specifically from a sermon, "Christian Education," in which the famous headmaster, thinking always of the education of Christian *gentlemen,* had dilated on the

63. *Notes on England,* pp. 172, 175.
64. *Mixed Essays,* pp. 4–5, 20. Cf. *Friendship's Garland* (1871), *Culture & Anarchy and Friendship's Garland* (New York, 1901), Letter 9, pp. 286–8.

advantages of *great* places of education: "There is, or ought to be, something very ennobling in being connected with any establishment at once ancient and magnificent; where all about us, and all the associations belonging to the objects around us, should be great, splendid, and elevating." And he went on to liken the influence of a celebrated school to that of a great estate where even the walls and the trees, let alone the portrait gallery, remind a boy that he is "born of an old and illustrious race." [65] In a word, Rugby keeps the aristocratic ideal alive. And if the father was as eager as the son to curtail the political power of the aristocracy, he wanted no less to preserve the legitimate influence of its "great and good qualities" in the democratic society that was emerging.[66] To that end Matthew would have the state establish new Rugbys in which the middle classes could acquire "the sense of belonging to great and honourable seats of learning. . . . This sense would be an educational influence for them of the highest value. It would really augment their self-respect and moral force." [67] And in Arnold's mind, for all his stress on intellectual culture, that is the primary purpose of middle-class education: "To the middle class, the grand aim of education should be to give largeness of soul and personal dignity." [68]

At that point Arnold joins hands with an ally he never acknowledged (because he identified him too closely with the Benthamites): John Mill. But Mill, who never went to a public school and had grown up under his father's anti-aristocratic influence, derived the ideal of nobility from Greek and Roman sources (as both the Arnolds did, too, in part), and used it to criticize the religious and commercial life of the middle class. "Christian morality (so-called)," he wrote in *On Liberty*, ". . . is negative rather than positive; passive rather than active." Its aim is "Innocence rather than Nobleness; Abstinence from Evil, rather than energetic Pursuit of Good." In its precepts "thou shall not" is much stronger than "thou shalt." By its primary motivation, the hope of heaven and the fear of hell, it nourishes an "essentially selfish character." What little recognition of public duty obtains in modern morality is therefore derived from classical thought; and "in the morality of private life, whatever exists of magnanimity, highmindedness,

---

65. *Sermons*, 3, 186–7. The passage is quoted in Stanley, *Life of Arnold*, chap. 3, p. 96; and cf. p. 137.

66. Stanley, *Life*, p. 256, from a letter of March 20, 1831.

67. *Mixed Essays*, p. 26.

68. *A French Eton, or Middle-Class Education and the State* (London and New York, 1892), pp. 62–3.

personal dignity, even the sense of honour, is derived from the purely human, not the religious part of our education." [69] This is hardly the whole truth about Christian ethics (as Mill admits in the qualification of "so-called") or even the truth about the ethics of the Christian revival in the nineteenth century, where the obligations of social duty were certainly emphasized. But there is no doubt that in Evangelical and Dissenting circles the revival often degenerated into a negative and self-centered form which invited reaction, and opened the way, especially in nonreligious minds, to exalting the noble champion of Humanity or civilization over the timid soul who found "abstinence safer and easier than action." [70]

The middle classes needed more nobility for another reason. They were too much given to the calculated pursuit of the main chance, and had therefore created a period "essentially unheroic . . . more prolific of prudence than of elevated feeling—an age in which generous enthusiasm is dead." [71] Such a temper of mind was entirely consonant with Bentham's conception of society as a collection of individuals owing nothing to one another beyond the strict keeping of contractual obligations, and where the general good was best promoted by the free competition of all men seeking their own interests—seeking them prudently, of course, since honesty is the best policy. On such a philosophy, "how," asked Carlyle, "can a man act heroically?" "Whatsoever is noble, divine, inspired, drops thereby out of life." [72] And Lecky agreed that the principle of utility could not rise to "the conception of the purely disinterested," which is "the principle of . . . heroism." The age, therefore, "exhibits a marked decline in the spirit of self-sacrifice"; its character has become "mercenary, venal, and unheroic." This he thought was the great shadow resting on the otherwise brilliant picture of our progress in rationalism and industry.[73] The effort to remove or

69. Chap. 2, pp. 145–6.

70. See W. R. Greg, "Good People," *Literary and Social Judgments*, especially 2, 205–8; and Beatrice Webb, *My Apprenticeship*, p. 83, where she decided that while "Christianity certainly made one more egotistical, more desirous to secure one's own salvation," the new Religion of Humanity "removes the thoughts from that wee bit of the world called self to the great whole." The egotistical tendency of the Evangelicals is often noted by George Eliot, most unsparingly in the portrait of Bulstrode in *Middlemarch*.

71. William Johnston, *England as It Is* (1851), quoted by W. R. Greg in his review, *Edinburgh Review*, 93 (1851), 335. Cf. Kingsley, "Heroism," *Sanitary and Social Essays*, p. 249.

72. *Heroes and Hero-Worship*, Lecture 5, p. 173.

73. *History of Rationalism*, 2, 353–4.

reduce that shadow which called for educating the noble emotions called also for the ideal of nobility.[74]

Finally, this ideal was provoked by the intolerance of the Puritan-business class, since those who differed from them in opinion needed an heroic character to resist their intimidations. The panicky fear that free and disinterested speculation, by leading to unorthodox conclusions, would shake the foundations of morality and endanger the social order, 'justified' every effort—as it often does today in the area of political thought—to silence the individual. To oppose that pressure and speak the truth, however heretical, required the courage to endure obloquy and perhaps to sacrifice one's social position. When Lyell, after hesitating, announced his support of the *Origin of Species*, Darwin wrote, "Considering his age, his former views and *position in society*, I think his conduct has been heroic." [75] Some of Mill's most living pages are devoted to the right purpose of education: not as at present in the Church, the Universities, and in almost every dissenting community, that the student should become a disciple to carry away "a particular set of opinions," but that he "should go forth determined and qualified to seek truth ardently, vigorously, and disinterestedly . . . and that, by a free communion with the thoughts and deeds of the great minds which preceded him, he be inspired . . . with the courage to dare all which truth and conscience require." For the latter purpose in particular, Mill urges the value of ancient literature:

> It brings before us the thoughts and actions of many great minds, minds of many various orders of greatness, and these related and exhibited in a manner tenfold more impressive, tenfold more calculated to call forth high aspirations, than in any modern literature. . . . It is incalculable what we owe to this, the sole ennobling feature in the slavish, mechanical thing which the moderns call education. Nor is it to be forgotten among the benefits of familiarity with the monuments of antiquity, and especially those of Greece, that we are taught by it to appreciate and to admire intrinsic greatness, amidst opinions, habits, and institutions most remote from ours; and are thus trained . . . to a habit of free, open sympathy with powers of mind and nobleness of character, howsoever exemplified.[76]

74. See below, Chap. 12, sec. 3, where this point is developed in more detail.
75. *Life and Letters*, 2, 119, from a letter to Asa Gray, July 22, 1860. The italics are mine.
76. "Civilization" (1836), in *Dissertations*, *1*, 196–7, 202–3. Cf. pp. 194–5, where he quotes an important passage from *Eustace Conway*, *2*, 79–81, in which

Both the Arnolds would have applauded this estimate of classical studies, for they found in Homer and Sophocles and Thucydides the same saving ideal of nobility which they also associated with the aristocracy. In the great public schools those two traditions merged, to be supplemented in the Victorian period by that of Christian earnestness.

4. Self-Development

Though the focus is fundamentally different, the ideal of self-development is found side by side with that of self-sacrifice, and its major champions are also Arnold and Mill. Those Victorians, however, who made the fully developed individual an object of aspiration had two distinct things in mind. One was Goethe's doctrine of *Bildung*, which he had derived from the Hellenic revival of the later eighteenth century, and particularly from Winckelmann's *History of Ancient Art* (1764). In *Wilhelm Meister* he had set up the Greek ideal of a complete and harmonious development of one's nature, in which body and soul, reason and emotion and imagination, should find their integral places in a fully realized personality. At the same time a similar idea of self-development emerged from the Romantic reaction against rationalism and authority. Let each man be "alive with his whole being." "Let each become all that he was created capable of being; expand, if possible, to his full growth . . . and show himself at length in his own shape and stature, be these what they may." [77] This is something fundamentally different, because here the ultimate purpose is to produce an individual, a unique man, rather than a perfectly developed specimen of human nature. But because both ideals advocated the cultivation of all one's faculties, either could appeal to a Victorian conscious of forces in the age that were producing "incomplete and mutilated men."

Chief among these forces was Puritan earnestness. To the intellectuals, the human being formed on that pattern was not only a travesty of what human beings ought to be and might be; he was also odious.

F. D. Maurice calls on the universities to "aim at something noble; make your system such that a great man may be formed by it." His purpose, however, is more to counteract the commercial-utilitarian spirit I spoke of in the previous paragraph than the pressure of conformity. On the noble influence of classical literature, also see Mill's footnote in "Democracy in America," *Dissertations*, 2, 69 n.

77. Carlyle, first essay on Richter (1827), *Essays, 1,* 19. But for Carlyle this was a passing phase; his moral earnestness soon condemned any such amoral ideal.

"A highly developed moral nature joined to an undeveloped intellectual nature, an undeveloped artistic nature, and a very limited religious nature, is of necessity repulsive. It represents a bit of human nature— a good bit, of course, but a bit only—in disproportionate, unnatural, and revolting prominence."[78]·That indictment by Bagehot in 1864 could have been an epigraph (it may even have been the original idea) for *Culture and Anarchy*, published five years later. In his preface Arnold announced that all he had to say about Hebraism and Hellenism had "for its main result to show how our Puritans, ancient and modern . . . have developed one side of their humanity at the expense of all others, and have become incomplete and mutilated men in consequence." Where the goal of Hebraism was a character in which the moral "obligation of duty, self-control, and work" was developed to its highest point, that of Hellenism (and of Culture) was a character in which no one power was developed at the expense of the rest but "*all* the powers which make the beauty and worth of human nature" reached "harmonious expansion." Arnold's point of reference is left in no doubt: "The immense spiritual significance of the Greeks is due to their having been inspired with this central and happy idea of the essential character of human perfection"—an idea Arnold derived from Goethe as well as from the classics themselves.[79]

Its adoption was facilitated by the whole movement of naturalism, dating from the Renaissance, and gaining momentum rapidly in the nineteenth century. When an other-worldly orientation declines, the natural life of man reasserts its ancient-pagan importance, and ascetic discipline is discarded for the free development of all the faculties. With his keen awareness of the secular and naturalistic drift of the age, Newman analyzed the attitude of "the world" in his sermon "Nature and Grace":

> Its highest idea of man lies in the order of nature; its pattern man is the natural man. . . . It sees that nature has a number of tendencies, inclinations, and passions; and because these are natural, it thinks that each of them may be indulged for its own sake. . . . The devotional feeling and the intellect, and the flesh, have each its claim upon us, and each must have play, if the Creator is to be duly honoured. It does not understand, it will not admit, that impulses and propensities, which are found in

78. Bagehot, "Wordsworth, Tennyson, and Browning," *Works, 1,* 236.
79. Preface, p. 11; chap. 1, pp. 48, 54; chap. 4, p. 129.

our nature, as God created it, may nevertheless, if indulged, become sins, on the ground that He has subjected them to higher principles.[80]

In short, because the world is not Christian, it cannot believe in asceticism. It believes in freedom of development. This is explicit in Edward Dowden's essay "The Scientific Movement and Literature." On the assumption that "scientific habits of thought must dispose men to seek for a natural rather than a miraculous or traditional foundation for morality," Dowden argues that "the scientific [that is, naturalistic] doctrine of self-development" must "for ever replace the false ethics of self-mortification." "Among our human instincts, passions, affections,—the aesthetic sensibilities, the intellect, the conscience, the religious emotions, an order and hierarchy are indeed indispensable; but not one citizen in our little state of man shall be disfranchised or dishonoured." [81]

With that philosophy Mill was in complete agreement. In his writings, indeed, the corrective of self-development was given its widest application. Early in life, reacting against the one-sided character of his Benthamite education, which had made him almost a "reasoning machine," he decided that intellectual culture "had consequences which required to be corrected, by joining other kinds of cultivation with it. The maintenance of a due balance among the faculties, now seemed to me of primary importance." [82] This conviction was deepened by his social observation. The pressure on the individual, unusually strong in this period, to adopt prescribed—and circumscribed—patterns of life provoked his fine plea for individuality in the essay On Liberty: "Human nature is not a machine to be built after a model, and set to do exactly the work prescribed for it, but a tree, which requires to grow and develop itself on all sides, according to the tendency of the inward forces which make it a living thing." [83] From that assumption too, Mill was critical of the type of character produced by a Puritan-commercial society. The man who combines a strict conscience with the ambition to raise himself a step or two on the social ladder is far removed from what a man "ought to be," since he lacks the moral-aesthetic development of the sentiments so needful not only

80. *Discourses Addressed to Mixed Congregations* (1849), in *Sermons and Discourses*, ed. Harrold, 2, 167–8.

81. *Studies in Literature*, pp. 116–18.

82. *Autobiography*, chaps. 4 and 5, pp. 92, 121–2.

83. Page 157. See the whole of chap. 3, "Of Individuality."

to the nobility, but "to the completeness, of the human being." [84] A sharper criticism of Puritanism (again in *On Liberty*) was made in terms similar to Arnold's juxtaposition of Hebraism and Hellenism. To the "pinched and hidebound type of human character" which results from the ascetic discipline of the will, Mill opposes "a different type of human excellence from the Calvinistic": a conception of humanity as having its nature bestowed on it that "all human faculties . . . might be cultivated and unfolded, not rooted out and consumed." "There is a Greek ideal of self-development, which the Platonic and Christian ideal of self-government blends with, but does not supersede"—blends with because it includes the conscience among the faculties to be cultivated. Men should grow up, he says a moment later, "to the mental, moral, and aesthetic stature of which their nature is capable." The link with Arnold includes even Mill's recognition of Goethe as a modern champion of self-development. [85]

Nevertheless, Mill's interpretation of this ideal is neither Greek nor Goethean—nor Arnoldian: it is Romantic. The discussion occurs in the chapter called "Of Individuality"; and the sentence that precedes and defines the contrast between Greek self-development and Christian self-government is one which Arnold would instantly have repudiated: " 'Pagan self-assertion' is one of the elements of human worth, as well as 'Christian self-denial.' " What Mill wanted was freedom for the individual to go his own way and live his own life; freedom, in short, to cultivate and call forth all that was unique in himself, within the limits imposed by the rights and interests of others. Development meant the development of his special capacities for intellectual, moral, and aesthetic life, not their harmonious flowering in a balanced personality. The latter was specifically attacked in the same year in which he wrote the first draft of *On Liberty*:

> To me it seems that nothing can be so alien and (to coin a word) antipathetic to the modern mind as Goethe's ideal of life. He wished life itself, and the nature of every cultivated individual in it, to be rounded off and made symmetrical like a Greek temple or a Greek drama. . . . As well might he attempt to cut down

84. "Inaugural Address," pp. 189, 192. On p. 189 he divides education into three divisions: intellectual, moral, and aesthetic.

85. Chap. 3, pp. 160–1, 168. The reference to Goethe is in the account of *On Liberty* in *Autobiography*, chap. 7, p. 217. Cf. Beatrice Webb, *My Apprenticeship*, p. 84, where she sets Goethe's plan "to develop the whole of your nature" against "an earnest attempt to silence and put down what is vile in you."

Shakespeare or a Gothic cathedral to the Greek model, as to give a rounded completeness to any considerable modern life. Not symmetry, but bold, free expansion in all directions is demanded by the needs of modern life and the instincts of the modern mind.[86]

One may compare Arnold: "Greece did not err in having the idea of beauty, harmony, and complete human perfection, so present and paramount."[87] The epithet "harmonious" for development echoes through his pages as constantly as "individual" does through Mill's.

The difference goes back ultimately to a different evaluation of modern life. In the same chapter, "Of Individuality," Mill contrasted the progressive principle with the despotism of custom. In the East and especially in China the force of custom has kept society almost stationary over many centuries. In Europe a remarkable diversity of character and culture, favoring many kinds of individual development, has kept the western family of nations an improving one. For Mill and those who shared his faith in progress, self-development meant self-expansion.[88] But other Victorians who had less zeal for progress and more distaste for contemporary life, and who knew the pains of depression and ennui—men like Arnold, J. A. Symonds, and Walter Pater—turned their gaze often backward with nostalgia to the ancient world. For them the Greek conception of rounded development, demanding as it does a certain detachment and a studied concern to shape one's life like a work of art, was a natural ideal.[89]

5. Aspiration without an Object

If we look closely at Victorian aspiration, we discover that the ideal object, whether a great cause or an exalted conception of human nature, is often vague and sometimes nonexistent. When that is the case, aspiration has changed its character and its dynamics. For where there is no definite goal, it becomes an end in itself: an exciting experience instead of an inspiring one, its motivation no longer being the desire to live on a higher plane, but simply to live passionately. Far from transcending the self, one is delighted to feel his own poten-

86. From the 1854 diary, *Letters*, 2, 368. Cf. F. A. Hayek, *John Stuart Mill and Harriet Taylor*, pp. 225–6.

87. *Culture and Anarchy*, chap. 1, p. 55.

88. *On Liberty*, chap. 3, pp. 171–4. Cf. Lecky, *History of Rationalism*, 2, 348–51, and Dowden, *Studies in Literature*, pp. 116, 118.

89. Symonds, *Studies of the Greek Poets, First Series* (London, 1873), pp. 414–17; Pater, "Winckelmann," *The Renaissance*, especially the concluding paragraphs where he discusses Goethe and Hellenic culture.

tial power and greatness. The eye is focused not on an ideal but on oneself in glorious pursuit of an ideal—some ideal or other. Under these conditions, aspiration is often combined with vivid sensuous experience of all kinds, since it is merely one way of satisfying the general appetite for life which asserts its sway when energy has no recognized goal.

The best comment on these tendencies, which appear in some of Tennyson and much of Browning, is in *Middlemarch*. In that novel Dorothea Brooke is a person who, like Saint Theresa, "soared after some illimitable satisfaction, some object which would never justify weariness, which would reconcile self-despair with the rapturous consciousness of life beyond self." But she could not transform *some* object into *an* object. "I should like," she says, "to make life beautiful,—I mean everybody's life." This is a feeling and not an idea with a content, for a moment later she says, "I cannot help believing in glorious things in a blind sort of way." "Dorothea's heart," remarks George Eliot, was always "giving out ardour." Precisely. The aspiration is directly expressed as emotion, since the head has found no object it can set up as a goal.[90] Ladislaw's temperament is less volatile, but he, too, dreamed of some "indeterminate loftiest thing" which alone would be "worthy of continuous effort." [91] All this is the very form and pressure of the time. The Oxford graduates of the fifties, Frederic Harrison remembered, fancied they had a call—"though from what or Whom, to what or whither," they had "no distinct idea." In a letter written on his twenty-first birthday, apropos of his inability to choose a line of action, he describes his psychological condition as one "when strong feelings are at work, and yet are clouded and confused. When the mind broods over some idea, and yet the suggestions that are called forth are vague and indistinct and contrary and unsifted." [92] Without a focus the emotions can hardly be clear or coherent. In the "Prelude" to *Middlemarch* Dorothea is compared to St. Theresa. They are both passionate, ideal natures demanding epic lives. But where St. Theresa found her epos in the reform of a religious order, many modern Theresas have found "no epic life . . . of far-resonant action; perhaps only a life of mistakes, the offspring of a certain spiritual grandeur ill-matched with the meanness of opportunity. . . . *For these later-born Theresas were helped by no coherent social faith and order*

90. Vol. *1*, Prelude and chaps. 1 and 22, pp. 1, 304–6.
91. Vol. *2*, chap. 46, p. 263.
92. *Autobiographic Memoirs*, *1*, 110.

*which could perform the function of knowledge for the ardently will-
ing soul."* [93] The fact is that an age which knew the Romantic taste,
and the Victorian desire, for ideal aspirations was also an age of transition in which the old ideals were vanishing and new ones were many
and half-formed. Aspiration could not easily find its objective correlative, whether a great cause to serve or a high character to strive for. It
tended to jump from one aim to another, or to look to a vague humanitarianism, an 1 therefore to become, when the end proved elusive, an
end in itself. Dorothea was "enamoured of intensity and greatness." [94]
If she yearned to renounce her self in a noble cause, it was really the
vision of playing a great role, and not a vivid sense of the objective,
that captured her imagination. George Eliot had pointed this out in the
case of Maggie Tulliver: "From what you know of her, you will not
be surprised that she threw some exaggeration and wilfulness, some
pride and impetuosity, even into her self-renunciation: her own life
was still a drama for her, in which she demanded of herself that her
part should be played with intensity." [95]

With appropriate modifications to fit the case, most of this might be
said of Browning's aspiring heroes. Many of them are preoccupied—
Browning is preoccupied—with the glamorous vision of superior beings
striving for great ends.

> That low man seeks a little thing to do,
> Sees it and does it:
> This high man, with a great thing to pursue,
> Dies ere he knows it.

Just what the great thing is hardly seems to matter (it takes innumerable forms), and *why* it is great, if it is, remains uncertain. The truth
is that what is "great" is the aspiring itself, and the fine sense of superiority to low men without ideals.

> What I aspired to be,
> And was not, comforts me:
> A brute I might have been, but would not sink i' the scale. [96]

93. The italics are mine. Frances Cobbe, "The Nineteenth Century," *Fraser's
Magazine*, 69 (1864), 494, describes the representative young Victorian as a man
who "has the very finest aspirations in all directions, but has no particular creed
as yet, political, religious, moral, or aesthetic."

94. Vol. *1*, chap. 1, p. 5.

95. *The Mill on the Floss*, 2, Bk. IV, chap. 3, p. 33.

96. The verses quoted are from "A Grammarian's Funeral," lines 113–16,
and "Rabbi Ben Ezra," lines 40–2.

This philosophy of the imperfect, of "success in failure," takes on a color of rationalization. Far from depressing the ego, failure can be made a proof of its greatness, a reassuring sign that one had, in fact, aimed above any low goal that might have been achieved. "Failure after long perseverance," says Dorothea, "is much grander than never to have a striving good enough to be called a failure." [97]

Santayana's essay on Browning is the classic statement of the case. Browning had "no idea of an intelligible good which the phases of life might approach and with reference to which they might constitute a progress." Aspiration with all its fine sense of intensity and greatness thus became an end in itself; and Browning's popularity rested on his power to invoke the rhythm and compulsion of general striving.[98] As Robert Buchanan put it, unconsciously illustrating the truth of this criticism, Browning succeeds "in stirring the soul of the spectator with . . . concentrated emotion and spiritual exaltation." [99] Plainly, this excitement of aspiration is simply a phase of the excitement of passionate feeling; and Santayana's main point is that Browning offers, in lieu of any ideal, the vivid expression of intense and fragmentary experience.[100] In "Rabbi Ben Ezra" it is not only the striving but the mere sensation of being intensely alive and active that is celebrated. "Welcome . . . each sting that bids nor sit nor stand but go!"

How readily the two went together can be seen in some poems of Tennyson's. In the allegory of "The Voyage," written to the text "Life is the search after the ideal" (as he phrased it), the sailors dedicate their lives to the pursuit of "one fair Vision." But what vision?

> For one fair Vision ever fled
>   Down the waste waters day and night,
>   And still we follow'd where she led,

97. Vol. *1*, chap. 22, p. 308.

98. "The Poetry of Barbarism," *Interpretations of Poetry and Religion* (New York, 1900), pp. 191, 204. Like George Eliot, Santayana (pp. 215–16) attributes this aspiration without an object to the lack of any coherent philosophy outside of science.

99. Quoted by Frederick J. Furnivall, *A Bibliography of Robert Browning, from 1833 to 1881*, Browning Society Papers, No. 2 (London, 1881), p. 100.

100. Had he known it, he would have quoted Matthew Arnold's letter (*Letters of Arnold to Clough*, p. 97): "As Browning is a man with a moderate gift passionately desiring movement and fulness, and obtaining but a confused multitudinousness, so Keats with a very high gift, is yet also consumed by this desire. . . . They will not be patient neither understand that they must begin with an Idea of the world in order not to be prevailed over by the world's multitudinousness."

> In hope to gain upon her flight.
> Her face was evermore unseen,
>   And fixt upon the far sea-line;
> But each man murmur'd, "O my Queen,
>   I follow till I make thee mine."
>
> And now we lost her, now she gleam'd
>   Like Fancy made of golden air,
> Now nearer to the prow she seem'd
>   Like Virtue firm, like Knowledge fair,
> Now high on waves that idly burst
>   Like Heavenly Hope she crown'd the sea,
> And now, the bloodless point reversed,
>   She bore the blade of Liberty.

And the poem ends:

> Again to colder climes we came,
>   For still we follow'd where she led;
> Now mate is blind and captain lame,
>   And half the crew are sick or dead,
> But, blind or lame or sick or sound,
>   We follow that which flies before;
> We know the merry world is round,
>   And we may sail for evermore.

Sailing evermore in pursuit of a face "evermore unseen" takes place, we notice, in a "merry" world—surely a very curious adjective. But just above, Tennyson has said, "We loved the glories of the world"— that is, the whole exciting experience of the voyage, struggling against the elements, scudding past strange lands of "nutmeg rocks and isles of clove," or "hills and scarlet-mingled woods," plunging into endless and exciting adventures.

In the "Ulysses" the hero and his men set forth in old age on a last voyage, determined to achieve "some work of noble note." But *what* work is never defined. It is "evermore unseen." And as one focuses closely on what follows, he notices that Ulysses' real object seems to be new and stirring experiences:

> Come, my friends,
> 'Tis not too late to seek a newer world.
> Push off, and sitting well in order smite

> The sounding furrows; for my purpose holds
> To sail beyond the sunset, and the baths
> Of all the western stars, until I die.
> It may be that the gulfs will wash us down;
> It may be we shall touch the Happy Isles,
> And see the great Achilles, whom we knew.
> Tho' much is taken, much abides; and tho'
> We are not now that strength which in old days
> Moved earth and heaven, that which we are, we are,—
> One equal temper of heroic hearts,
> Made weak by time and fate, but strong in will
> To strive, to seek, to find, and not to yield.

In this context, with the noble work forgotten (and all the more so because it was undefined), the last lines express simply the thrill of aspiration; and therefore readily merge with the general excitement of sailing always beyond the sunset, ever into newer worlds. This, indeed, is the same amoral purpose which Ulysses confesses quite frankly earlier in the poem:

> I cannot rest from travel; I will drink
> Life to the lees. All times I have enjoy'd
> Greatly, have suffer'd greatly, both with those
> That loved me, and alone. . . .
> For always roaming with a hungry heart
> Much have I seen and known. . . .
> How dull it is to pause, to make an end,
> To rust unburnish'd, not to shine in use!
> As tho' to breathe were life. Life piled on life
> Were all too little, and of one to me
> Little remains; but every hour is saved
> From that eternal silence, something more,
> A bringer of new things; and vile it were
> For some three suns to store and hoard myself,
> And this gray spirit yearning in desire
> To follow knowledge like a sinking star,
> Beyond the utmost bound of human thought.

Not to sit nor stand but go, on endless adventures brave and new, tasting the glories of the world, with a heart ever hungry for new knowledge—this is the real incitement that drives this Faustian Ulysses forth on another voyage.[101]

Arnold's "Scholar-Gipsy" provides a good analogy. What Arnold wants to do—what the poem purports to do—is to offer a generation sick with fatigue and languid doubt an image of one who has what we alas have not, "*one* aim, *one* business, *one* desire." But the scholar-gipsy, in point of fact, has no aim. He is busy drifting through the lovely Oxford countryside enjoying its beauty. Try as he may, Arnold simply cannot imagine a particular goal that can cure the Victorian malaise. All he can do is to turn to sensuous experience, and like his gipsy "plunge deeper into the bowering wood"—exactly as Ulysses (as Tennyson) plunges into the more exciting experience of the voyage.[102] The combination is precisely what we might expect—what we find in fact in Browning—from an age which felt the deep need for ideals and then turned, when they could not be objectified (I do not say, of course, that this was always the case) to the grandeur of aspiration itself and/or the sheer excitement of vivid experience.

6. Moral Optimism

To be an enthusiast in any of the ways we have been examining is to adopt a standard of judgment which may be called moral optimism. The 'good' man, whether as person or artist, is one who recognizes the beauty and greatness of human nature and therefore is filled with the 'good' emotions of admiration, love, and hope. The 'bad' man or 'bad' artist sees only what is dark and ugly and thus expresses the 'bad' emotions of captious criticism, mockery, or scorn instead of admiration; anger or hatred instead of love; gloomy despondency and pessimism instead of hope. In short, men come to be judged by their attitude toward life. It must be optimistic. Consider the extraordinary reception of Kingsley as Professor of Modern History at Cambridge:

101. Although Tennyson said (Hallam Tennyson, *Memoir*, 1, 196) that the poem "was written soon after Arthur Hallam's death, and gave my feeling about the need of going forward, and braving the struggle of life," it seems to me rather to express Tennyson's need to escape into experience: to forget his grief and his religious perplexities in the distraction of tasting life to the lees.

102. Arnold also, no doubt, found "spiritual refreshment" in nature: cf. above, pp. 80–1. This factor is overlooked in the remarks on the poem by F. R. Leavis, with which I otherwise agree: "Mr. Eliot and Milton," *Sewanee Review*, 57 (1949), 27. I do not think the text supports the philosophical interpretations of E. K. Brown, Lionel Trilling, and Wilson Knight.

Kingsley preached without seeming to do so. History was his text. The men and women of History were the words that built up his sermon. *He loved men and women, you felt that. He never sneered at their faults.* He had a deep, sad pity for them; he would even laugh a little, goodhumoredly, at the comical side of some of them, for he was full of humor: but anything like a sneer one never heard. Hence, partly, his great power. *Again, he had such a warm, passionate admiration for fine deeds.* His eye used to glisten, his voice in its remarkable sea-like modulations to swell like an organ as he recounted something great, till his audience listened—quiet, spell-bound, fixed, till the climax came, and then rushed into a cheer before they were well aware of it.[103]

That is hardly the response he would have met with today when enthusiasm is so entirely out of fashion—indeed, suspect. But in 1860, when the emotions of love and admiration were noble and those of sneering reprehensible, Kingsley could bring down the galleries.[104]

Optimism originated, as a specific moral quality, in the Romantic reaction against the critical and skeptical temper of the eighteenth century, represented in its extreme form by Goethe's Mephistopheles. To Carlyle, Mephistopheles was the spirit of Voltaire: "His wit and sarcasm are unlimited; the cool heartfelt contempt with which he despises all things, human and divine, might make the fortune of half a dozen 'fellows about town'. . . . With lynx vision, he descries at a glance the ridiculous, the unsuitable, the bad; but for the solemn, the noble, the worthy, he is blind as his ancient Mother. . . . He can believe in nothing, but in his own self-conceit, and in the indestructible baseness, folly and hypocrisy of men." [105] As that implies, the Romantic reaction meant the reaffirmation of those solemn and noble and worthy elements in human nature, of the goodness and the greatness of man, which were denied by the critical intellect but affirmed by the responsive heart and the sympathetic imagination.

Mephistopheles not only had a destructive wit, he had the "shrewd, all-informed intellect" of an attorney; it could contradict but it could not affirm. The need for positive and constructive beliefs accompanied

103. *Letters and Memories*, 2, 133 (apparently not in the unabridged ed.). The italics are mine.

104. Another professor (C. B. Tinker of Yale) was wildly applauded in 1923 at the close of his course in nineteenth-century poetry for telling the graduating students to go out and greet the unseen with a leer.

105. "Goethe's Helena," *Essays*, 1, 157.

the need for positive and constructive attitudes, and intellectual earnestness united with enthusiasm to form a common front against negativism—and specifically, in many cases, against dilettantism, since the man of the world (Mephistopheles "has the manners of a gentleman" and "knows the world") [106] is at once indifferent to truth and cynical about human nature. In a letter to Bulwer Lytton, Mill imagines how the readers of the *Edinburgh Review* for 1836 must have been puzzled and bewildered by an article of his because, expecting only a clever and sophisticated play of the intellect, they found "a writer who actually takes decided views, who is positively in earnest, and is capable of downright admiration and even enthusiasm!" [107] Some years later, in W. R. Greg's portrait of Benjamin Constant we see the Victorian anti-Christ, a living Mephistopheles: "He was a second Voltaire . . . profoundly cynical and profoundly sceptical, he loved nothing and believed in nothing . . . no deep affection—no absorbing passion—no earnest or solemn thought—seems ever to have entered his heart." But the influence of Mme. de Staël nearly converted him into a good Victorian: "She made him at once almost earnest and enthusiastic. For the first time we find in his letters a tone of seriousness and a capacity for admiration." [108]

To admire—which is to say, *not* to criticize, still less to ridicule— was the first requirement which enthusiasm brought into English taste. By the eighteen-twenties it was adopted by Mary Mitford (in later life the friend of Ruskin and Mrs. Browning) and brought to bear on her contemporaries. Sir Thomas Talfourd, the author of *Ion*, was a man who "takes people at their best, and sets forth their beauties instead of their defects. I never met—not even in Walter Scott—with such lenient sympathy, such indulgence to human frailty, or such cordial delight in the beautiful and the good. . . . He has a talent for admiration and enjoyment." On the other hand, Maria Edgeworth had "too great a proneness to find bad motives for good actions, too great a contempt for that virtuous enthusiasm, which is the loveliest rose in the chaplet of youth." [109] Like Carlyle, she attacked the Byronic state

106. Ibid. Cf. George Eliot, *Daniel Deronda*, 2, chap. 40, p. 300: "that antipole of all enthusiasm called 'a man of the world.'"

107. *Letters, 1,* 102–3.

108. "Madame de Staël," *Literary and Social Judgments, 1,* 56–9.

109. *The Life of Mary Russell Mitford, 2,* 116; *1,* 257. Cf. George Eliot, letter to J. Sibree, February 1848, in Cross, *Life, 1,* 134–5: "You and Carlyle . . . are the only two people who feel just as I would have them,—who can glory in what is actually great and beautiful without putting forth any cold reservations and

of mind rather than Byron's immorality, but with a significant difference. Although in one remark she condemned his life-weariness and
lack of courage, her main objection fell on his being "too melancholy
—too morbid—too sneering"; on his heartless and gloomy sentiments,
his "derisive mockery—the tossing about of all good feeling, so gibing
and so Voltaire-ish." [110] To Carlyle Byronism needed the corrective of
an ethic which would break the mood of despair and transform the
selfish and self-defeating search for happiness into an active life of
duty. To Miss Mitford, Byronism was a cynical and pessimistic attitude
which needed the corrective of a warmer spirit and a juster, because
sunnier, view of life. Her own greatest blessing she thought was her
"constitutional buoyancy of spirits, the aptness to hope, the will to be
happy." And that blessing was increased, she said, by her own mis-
fortunes because they showed her "how much goodness and kindness
exist in the world." [111]

The hostility to derisive mockery, and to wit and ridicule in general,
was strongly impressed on the Victorian mind. From the earnest point
of view wit was a plain sign of levity, reprehensible in the face of a
social crisis, and outright immoral if it dealt with things evil.[112] The
enthusiastic demand for warm and generous sentiments made it the
sure mark of a cold or perverted heart. The right attitude was expressed by Ruskin in a passage which suggests, however, that the
wrong attitude still existed: "The chief bar to the action of imagination, and stop to all greatness in this present age of ours, is its mean
and shallow love of jest; so that if there be in any good and lofty work
a flaw, failing, or undipped vulnerable part, where sarcasm may stick
or stay, it is caught at, and pointed at, and buzzed about, and fixed
upon, and stung into, as a recent wound is by flies. . . . Men dare
not open their hearts to us, if we are to broil them on a thorn-fire." [113]

The same charge is placed in a larger context by George Eliot's essay
"Debasing the Moral Currency." The moral currency is "all the grander
deeds and aims of men . . . every sacred, heroic, and pathetic theme
which serves to make up the treasure of human admiration, hope, and

---

incredulities to save their credit for wisdom. I am all the more delighted with
your enthusiasm because I didn't expect it."

110. Vol. *1*, 193, 267–8; *2*, 85, 178.

111. Vol. *2*, 51–2.

112. See above, pp. 225–7, 236–7.

113. *Modern Painters*, 2 (1846), Pt. III, sec. 2, chap. 3, par. 10, in *Works*, 4,
258.

love"; the debasement is the work of the "burlesquing spirit," the "habits of contempt and exultant gibing" at "all historic beauty, majesty, and pathos" which lower "the value of every inspiring fact and tradition." What makes these habits of ridicule all the more reprehensible is that "our civilization, considered as a splendid material fabric, is helplessly in peril without the spiritual police of sentiments or ideal feelings." [114] Historically, the importance of this essay is that it corrects the impression we get from Victorian literature; for the literature, written to guide or to inspire, is almost entirely free (Thackeray is a partial exception) from the "derisive mockery—the tossing about of all good feeling" which was common enough in the literary tradition of 1820 which Mary Mitford was attacking. It shows, together with Ruskin's comment, that the spirit of Voltaire and Byron persisted in Victorian life and conversation when earnestness and enthusiasm had checked its appearance in print. Certainly there were forces in the age—notably the critical spirit, the influence of Benthamism, the competitive life of business, the dogmatic temper—which may well have combined, as one writer claimed in 1863, to wither "the faculty of admiration, the source of some of our truest enjoyments and most elevated emotions." Instead of feeling "overwhelmed by the presence of the sublime," the younger generation "judge, compare, and criticise." [115]

Though less culpable than the critical or sarcastic frame of mind, one that was rebellious, pessimistic, or even realistic was perhaps more irritating to the Victorian moralists, since it deepened instead of relieving the mood of anxiety and depression. In Arnold's criticism, for example, where the central demand is that works of art shall "inspirit and rejoice," Wordsworth's superiority to Leopardi is traced to his "sound and profound sense 'Of joy in widest commonalty spread'; whereas Leopardi remains with his thoughts ever fixed upon the *essenza insanabile*, upon the *acerbo, indegno mistero delle cose*." One view of life is "healthful and true," the other is not. [116] In like manner, Charlotte Brontë's *Villette* is a disagreeable book "because the writer's

114. In *Impressions of Theophrastus Such* (1879), in *Works, 11*, 103–4, 106–8.
115. "Our Modern Youth," *Fraser's Magazine, 68* (1863), 116–18.
116. The main statement is in the preface to the 1853 edition of his poetry: see *Poetical Works*, p. xviii. The Wordsworth-Leopardi contrast is in "Byron," *Essays in Criticism, Second Series*, pp. 190–2. The Italian may be translated as "the unhealthy essence, upon the bitter, unworthy mystery of things." Arnold's similar view of Schopenhauer is in the preface to *Last Essays on Church and Religion*, pp. 174–5.

mind contains nothing but hunger, rebellion, and rage." [117] Even the movement of realism as it was growing up in France and Russia is distasteful to Arnold because it emphasizes the weakness of man at the expense of his ideal potentialities. It is here that his taste—and mid-Victorian taste in general—is farthest removed from that of the twentieth century, though there are some signs at present of a reaction. But when Arnold finds *Anna Karenina* a "piece of life" and not "a work of art," and agrees with Sainte-Beuve that Flaubert is inferior to George Sand because in him "the ideal has ceased, the lyric vein is dried up" (*Madame Bovary* is "a work of *petrified feeling*" whose atmosphere is one "of bitterness, irony, impotence; not a personage in the book to rejoice or console us"); or when he quotes with approval Joubert's dictum that "fiction has no business to exist unless it is more beautiful than reality," and laments the publication of Dowden's biography of Shelley because, by revealing the seamy side of his life, it has tarnished our former image of the "delightful" Shelley, the "ideal" Shelley, the "beautiful and lovable Shelley"—when Arnold adopts these judgments we have to remember how strongly the burden of depression could reinforce the demand for moral optimism. [118]

His point of view was by no means unique. However far from meeting Arnold's standard herself, Charlotte Brontë criticized Balzac because he was "forever holding up in strong light our defects, and . . . rarely draws forth our better qualities," and found that George Sand, for all her lack of Balzac's subtle analysis of motive, had a better nature: "Her brain is larger, her heart warmer than his." [119] Mary Gladstone thought *Anna Karenina* "a wretchedly melancholy tragic novel with marvellously delicate human insight but surely, I earnestly trust, with too low a view of our nature." [120] At a moment when contemporary life was exhibiting the selfish, acquisitive side of human nature, any dark view of man could only reduce one's faith in goodness and nobility to the level of a shaky trust. The need was for reassurance. Dowden found that the failure of Lydgate in *Middle-*

117. *Letters, 1,* 34; cf. *Letters of Arnold to Clough,* p. 132.

118. "Count Leo Tolstoi," *Essays in Criticism, Second Series,* pp. 253, 260, 276; "Joubert," ibid., *First Series,* p. 340; "Shelley," ibid., *Second Series,* pp. 213, 245.

119. Mrs. Gaskell, *Life of Charlotte Brontë,* chap. 22, p. 318.

120. *Diaries and Letters,* ed. Lucy Masterman (London, 1930), p. 371. Cf. Amy Cruse, *The Victorians and Their Reading,* pp. 414–16, where she cites this judgment in a discussion of the demand for a happy ending. The remark was made in 1885, but like Arnold's comments on this novel and on *Madame Bovary,* which were made in 1887, it reflects a mid-Victorian point of view.

march "impoverishes the spirit as the failure of light at morning does."
Fortunately that novel was followed by the corrective and counterpoise of *Daniel Deronda*, which closes by showing us "how two
natures can be ennobled and enlarged." [121]

Pushed to an extreme, the standard of moral optimism could find
fault with the introduction into art of anything that was ugly and
painful, and lead to what Ruskin called "Purism," an idealization of
life which creates an unreal world of sentimental beauty. The mass
of Victorian art, painting and poetry especially, is infected by this tendency. Purism and French naturalism are at opposite poles. A middle
position was adopted by the more intelligent critics. Art should not
omit what is ugly or evil, but it should emphasize what is good and
great. It should be ideal in the sense that it should embody a vision
either of potential beauty, of what man and nature strive to be, or
of that actual beauty which both have occasionally achieved. Ruskin
gives the general standard: "Great art dwells on all that is beautiful;
but false art omits or changes all that is ugly. Great art accepts
Nature as she is, but directs the eyes and thoughts to what is most
perfect in her; false art saves itself the trouble of direction by re-
moving or altering whatever it thinks objectionable." [122] In Morley
this principle is extended from the artist to the man, and the beautiful
is identified with the noble:

121. "George Eliot," *Studies in Literature*, pp. 283–4. With Arnold's comparison
of Wordsworth with Leopardi, cf. the comparison of Clough's "Bothie" with his
"Amours de Voyage"—"Poems by A. H. Clough," *North British Review*, 37 (1862),
340–1, attributed to W. Y. Sellar by H. F. Lowry, *Letters of Arnold to Clough*,
p. 96: "Into the one poem the author seems to have thrown all the sanguine buoyancy; into the other, all the weary, hopeless feelings of his life"; and the writer
goes on to say that the power displayed in the latter is often "the power of insight
into the under-side of human nature—into the doubts, weakness, and self-deception
which underlie that aspect of things on which it is most pleasant, and perhaps
most profitable, to dwell. There is often a jar produced on the feeling of the
reader by some bitter or weary expression of despondency or self-distrust, after
some transient outburst of the old enthusiasm."

122. *Modern Painters*, 3 (1856), Pt. IV, chap. 3, sec. 13, in *Works*, 5, 57. On
Purism, see chap. 6. The main discussion of the three classes of artists is in *Stones
of Venice*, 2, chap. 6, secs. 51–63, in *Works*, 10, 221–31. Ruskin's middle position
is adopted by G. H. Lewes, "Realism in Art," *Westminster Review*, 70 (1858),
493–5; by George Eliot (see *Adam Bede*, 1, chaps. 17, 19, pp. 248–9, 294–5),
under Ruskin's influence as well as Lewes': see Cross, *Life*, 2, 5, letter to Sara
Hennell, January 17, 1858, and her review of *Modern Painters*, 3, in *Westminster
Review*, 65 (1856), 625–33; by Leslie Stephen, "The Duties of Authors," *Social
Rights and Duties* (2 vols. London and New York, 1896), 2, 167–76; and by J. A.
Symonds, "Realism and Idealism," *Essays*, pp. 108–27.

There is no need to plant oneself in a fool's paradise, with no eye for the weakness of men, the futility of their hopes, the irony of their fate, the dominion of the satyr and the tiger in their hearts. . . . All this we may see and show that we see, and yet so throw it behind the weightier facts of nobleness and sacrifice, of the boundless gifts which fraternal union has given, and has the power of giving, as to kindle in every breast, not callous to exalted impressions, the glow of sympathetic endeavour, and of serene exultation in the bond that makes "precious the soul of man to man." [123]

123. "Carlyle," *Critical Miscellanies, 1,* 189.

Chapter 12

HERO WORSHIP

> The Victorians . . . carried admiration to the highest
> pitch. They marshalled it, they defined it, they turned it
> from a virtue into a religion, and called it Hero Wor-
> ship.
>
> *Edmund Gosse* [1]

THOUGH it has always existed and is still alive today—too much so
under Western eyes—hero worship is a nineteenth-century phenomenon. At no other time would it have been called "the basis of all
possible good, religious or social, for mankind." [2] In no other age were
men so often told to take "the great ones of the earth" as models for
imitation, or provided with so many books with titles like *Heroes and
Hero-Worship, Lectures on Great Men, A Book of Golden Deeds,
The Red Book of Heroes.* Heroic myth was as popular as heroic
biography. Tales of medieval knights and legendary heroes, Greek and
Roman, Celtic and Norse, were widely read—in new editions of
Malory and Froissart, in the poetry of Tennyson, Arnold, and the
Pre-Raphaelites. In actual life to meet a great man, or look on anything he possessed, was an overwhelming experience. "One man is so
little," a lecturer told his audience, "that you see him a thousand times
without caring to ask his name; another man is so great, that if you
have once exchanged a word with him while living, or possess 'a hair
of him' when dead, it is something of which you are proud." [3] Even
Macaulay, who lamented the propensity to "Boswellism," could imagine
"the breathless silence" in which we should listen to Milton's slightest

1. "The Agony of the Victorian Age," *Edinburgh Review, 228* (1918), 295.

2. Carlyle, *Heroes and Hero-Worship,* Lecture 4, p. 123; and see an even larger
claim in the essay on Scott, *Essays, 4,* 24.

3. William Arthur, "Heroes," in *Exeter Hall Lectures, 6* (London, 1851),
p. 289.

word, "the passionate veneration with which we should kneel to kiss his hand and weep upon it." [4]

One reason for the enormous vogue of hero worship is before us: the cult of enthusiasm. For hero worship, in the words of its major prophet, is "*infinite* admiration," and the worshiper an enthusiast who "can love his hero or sage without measure, and idealise, and so, in a sense, idolise him." [5] That marks a striking reversal of the rationalistic attitude in the previous century. When Hume and Gibbon submitted the heroic to the cold glance of reason, they tended to see it as a mask to hide selfish ambition or else a patent form of madness and delusion (that is, of enthusiasm in the derogatory sense). [6] But when enthusiasm became a virtue second only to earnestness, the Romantic-Victorian eye brought with it the power to see man as a hero and the heart to respond with the appropriate worship.

But this was hardly more than the essential foundation. Other constructive factors had their roots, like enthusiasm, in the Romantic outlook. There was the important distinction in kind and not merely in degree between great men and ordinary men. Amid the dull millions "are scattered here and there superior natures." They are the geniuses of Romantic theory, more demigods than men, possessed of supreme wisdom and extraordinary powers of action. [7] In the same period, the revolt of Romantic individualism against authority created sublime figures like Manfred and Prometheus—or Milton's Satan as conceived by Blake and Shelley—endowed with superhuman powers of heroic courage and endurance. These related conceptions could readily, if not logically, be merged with the Protestant idea of the elect, and Carlyle is witness to the curious but fruitful alliance of Romanticism and Puritanism behind the Victorian tendency to think of men in two categories, heroes and ordinary mortals.

4. "Milton," *Critical Essays, 1,* 265.

5. Carlyle, "Goethe's Works," *Essays, 2,* 391. Cf. Ruskin, *The Art of England,* Lecture 2, in *Works, 33,* 292: "The three romantic passions are those by which you are told, in Wordsworth's aphoristic line, that the life of the soul is fed:—'We live by Admiration, Hope, and Love.' Admiration, meaning primarily all the forms of Hero Worship . . ."

6. Hume in particular is attacked for his denigration of heroism: by Coleridge, "The Statesman's Manual," *Biographia Literaria and Two Lay Sermons,* p. 318; by Carlyle, *Heroes,* Lecture 6, pp. 227–8 (cf. Lecture 2, pp. 43–4, where Gibbon is in his mind), and *Past and Present,* Bk. IV, chap. 1, p. 239; by Kingsley, "Sir Walter Raleigh and His Time," *Plays and Puritans,* in *Works, 16,* 92–3, 134 (and cf. "Froude's History of England," ibid., pp. 212–13, on Gibbon and Voltaire).

7. The quoted phrase is Carlyle's, "Boswell's Life of Johnson," *Essays, 3,* 89. Cf. in general, above, pp. 152–4, where the Romantic genius is discussed.

The literary background of Shelley's *Prometheus* is the Hellenic revival of the later eighteenth century, which modified neoclassical taste by introducing a new strain of the wild and primitive. The mythology of Versailles was transformed into the mythology of Homer; the gods of Greece ceased to be rococo toys and became, along with their later counterparts, the gods of Norse and German legend, Titanic symbols of power and beauty. Natural geniuses like Shakespeare and Homer were no longer criticized for "irregularities" and rude simplicity; and Homer, it was suggested—now greatly to his credit—was a strolling bard writing a kind of epic folk-poetry.[8] That brought the Hellenic revival into direct relation with the revival of the ballad, announced by Bishop Percy's *Reliques of Ancient English Poetry* (1765), and together they evoked the taste for heroic legend. Their meeting-point in Scott became a commonplace of Victorian criticism. Scott was born with "a spirit in itself naturally of the heroic or epic order"; it was then awakened to consciousness by an excited reading of Percy's *Reliques;* and the result, in *Marmion, The Lady of the Lake,* and the other romances, was poetry which approached the popular epic and "revived the Homeric inspiration."[9] A generation later Macaulay's *Lays of Ancient Rome* (1842), in which Horatius defends the bridge, were written under the converging influences of the *Iliad,* the old ballads, and Sir Walter Scott, not to mention Macaulay's own enthusiasm for the grandeur that was Rome.[10]

All of these literary sources, including Macaulay's *Lays,* were discussed in Matthew Arnold's lectures *On Translating Homer* (1861–62), for their subject was heroic poetry, or, to use his own critical term, the grand style. "The grand style,—but what *is* the grand style?" Arnold was loath to define it very exactly. It arises, he said, "when a noble nature, poetically gifted, treats with simplicity or with severity a serious subject." That at least indicates the large meaning of the term. Style in this sense is the embodiment of a vision of life not only

8. See the summary in Douglas Bush, *Mythology and the Romantic Tradition in English Poetry* (Cambridge, Mass., 1937), pp. 44–50.

9. J. C. Shairp, "The Homeric Spirit in Walter Scott," *Aspects of Poetry,* pp. 384, 389, 391, and passim.

10. See the end of Macaulay's preface. Thomas Arnold's youthful enthusiasm for Homeric heroes and ballad poetry leading to the writing of a long poem on Simon de Montfort in imitation of Scott's *Marmion* (Stanley, *Life,* p. 3) shows the same merging influences a generation earlier, and suggests the paternal background of Matthew's lectures, referred to in the next paragraph. In *Past and Present,* Bk. II, chap. 17, pp. 131–2, Carlyle brings together the *Iliad* and *Robin Hood's Garland* as two collections of "Heroic Ballads."

in diction and rhythm, but also in character, action, and apothegm. When the style is grand, form and content are noble and exalted. And to write it with sincerity the poet himself must have a noble nature. The masters who fulfill these requirements are Homer, Pindar, Sophocles, Virgil, Dante, Milton—and also Phidias and Michelangelo, who were included because Arnold adopted the term from art criticism, specifically from Joshua Reynolds' *Discourses on Art* (1769–90).[11] In the grand style, which Reynolds also called the epic style, "some eminent instance of heroic action, or heroic suffering," was the right subject, to be found most readily in "the great events of Greek and Roman fable and history"; and "the effect of the capital works of Michael Angelo" was said to correspond perfectly "to what Bouchardon said he felt from reading Homer; his whole frame appeared to himself to be enlarged, and all nature which surrounded him, diminished to atoms." [12] In the famous chapter of *Modern Painters*, "Touching the 'Grand Style,'" Ruskin adopted his conception of great art from Reynolds: It is the work of "men in a state of enthusiasm" —that is, of "men who feel *strongly* and *nobly*," and "it is like the writing of Homer," especially in its delineation "of the human character and form in their utmost, or heroic, strength and beauty." [13] In short, the criticism of Arnold and Ruskin embodied the heroic tradition as it came down to the Victorians from both the art schools of Europe and the literary revival of Homer and the ballad.

This is the intellectual background. To most Victorians, ignorant of aesthetic theories and literary movements, the image of the hero came directly from Scott's re-creation of the feudal past; from Byron's *Childe Harold*, where the "aspirations of the mind after greatness and true glory" were kindled by a portrait gallery of great men, ancient and modern; [14] and most of all, from the Napoleonic wars. Frederic Harrison, brought up from the country at the age of seven to see Queen Victoria's coronation, gives us a glimpse into the post-war

11. *On Translating Homer*, in *On the Study of Celtic Literature and On Translating Homer* (New York, 1883), pp. 264–5, for the definition; pp. 167, 205, for the list of masters. The influence of Reynolds is pointed out by Lionel Trilling, *Matthew Arnold*, pp. 173–4, to whom I am indebted here.

12. *Fifteen Discourses Delivered in the Royal Academy* (Everyman Library, London and New York, 1906), pp. 41, 47, 66–7.

13. *Modern Painters*, 3 (1856), Pt. IV, chap. 1, secs. 17, 18, in *Works*, 5, 32–3. For Ruskin's early reading of Scott as well as Homer, see below, pp. 326–7.

14. Hazlitt, "Byron," *The Spirit of the Age* (1825), in *Miscellaneous Works* (5 vols. New York, 1859), 5, 101–3, shows the heroic reading of the poem.

sensibility: "I can recall now my awe and wonder when we came up to, and actually engaged in conversation with, a gigantic life-guardsman. What a glorious and mighty being he seemed to me! . . . Marshal Soult, Wellington's opponent in the Peninsula, was the special envoy of France at the Coronation; Prince Esterhazy, in his diamond suit, was the Ambassador of Austria; and the procession contained crowds of men who had fought in the long wars or taken part in the great historic events of the first thirty years of the nineteenth century." [15]

Though only one was present on that occasion, there were three great men of that era whose fame alone would have made the whole society hero conscious. "Oh, what a man!" wrote Mary Mitford of Napoleon. "I would have given a limb . . . to have been concealed somewhere just to have heard him conversing and dictating." [16] But in English eyes Nelson and Wellington were *the* heroes of the age. Nelson's achievement, Carlyle had written in one of his first biographies, "raised the admiration of his countrymen to enthusiasm" and made his name synonymous with "that of a HERO." [17] Wellington by his very presence in England from 1815 to 1852, and his explicit illustration of the principle emphasized by Carlyle that the great man was a genius capable of being either a soldier or a statesman, was the greatest single argument for Victorian hero worship. He became, said Harrison, "a sort of ultimate arbiter; and discussions usually were closed by—'the Duke agrees to it!', 'the Duke will see to it!', 'the Duke says it must be done!'" [18] Tennyson's *Ode* springs from the same soil:

> Mourn for the man of long-enduring blood,
> The statesman-warrior, moderate, resolute,
> Whole in himself, a common good.
> Mourn for the man of amplest influence. . . .
> Great in council and great in war,
> Foremost captain of his time. . . .
> O good gray head which all men knew,

15. *Autobiographic Memoirs*, 1, 25.

16. *Life*, ed. L'Estrange, 3, 189. For Carlyle he and Goethe are the two great men of the century: "Goethe's Works," *Essays*, 2, 398–9; and though criticized for personal ambition, Napoleon takes his place in the *Heroes*, Lecture 6.

17. "Nelson" (1822), *Montaigne and Other Essays, Chiefly Biographical* (London, 1897), pp. 75, 91.

18. *Autobiographic Memoirs*, 1, 26.

O voice from which their omens all men drew. . . .
The long self-sacrifice of life is o'er.
The great World-victor's victor will be seen no more.[19]

When the Victorian period began, all the prerequisites for hero worship were present: the enthusiastic temper, the conception of the superior being, the revival of Homeric mythology and medieval ballad, the identification of great art with the grand style, the popularity of Scott and Byron, and the living presence of Napoleonic soldiers and sailors. But traditions die without nourishment, and this one throve. For it answered, or it promised to answer, some of the deepest needs and problems of the age. In the fifty years after 1830 the worship of the hero was a major factor in English culture.[20]

1. Messiah

In a period of radical transition when men feel lost in a maze of ideas, they look to a savior. The problems to be solved are so vast and difficult that he must be more than an ordinary mortal; and the need for guidance is so imperative that he will not simply be applauded and respected, he will be looked up to with profound gratitude and reverence. "Are these times for great legislators and great conquerors?" asks Coningsby in Disraeli's novel; and Sidonia answers, "When were they wanted more? . . . From the throne to the hovel all call for a guide." A few years later, in 1851, Henry Atkinson was writing to Harriet Martineau, "The world is ripe if there were but the towering genius that would speak to it. . . . O! that some great teacher would arise, and make himself heard from the mountain top!" And Kingsley in the same year described England as "a chaos of noble materials . . . all confused, it is true,—polarized, jarring, and chaotic . . . but only waiting for the one inspiring Spirit to organize, and unite, and consecrate this chaos into the noblest polity the world

19. "Ode on the Death of the Duke of Wellington," stanza 4. In stanza 6, there is a eulogy of Nelson.

20. As the paragraphs above dealing with Homer, Scott, and Arnold would suggest, I include the taste for heroic literature in all its forms (epic, myth, romances, novels, and biography) under the general subject of hero worship. Though a person may enjoy Malory and reject any enthusiastic admiration for great men, real or fictional, I doubt if that was often the case among the Victorians, however natural it may be for modern readers. At that time, the enjoyment of heroic stories and the worship of heroes tended to merge, each encouraging the other; and both grew out of the same social and intellectual milieu.

ever saw realized!" [21] This need for a Messiah is the central motivation of Carlyle's *Heroes:*

> I liken common languid Times, with their unbelief, distress, perplexity, with their languid doubting characters and embarrassed circumstances, impotently crumbling-down into ever worse distress towards final ruin;—all this I liken to dry dead fuel, waiting for the lightning out of Heaven that shall kindle it. The great man . . . is the lightning. His word is the wise healing word which all can believe in. . . . In all epochs of the world's history, we shall find the Great Man to have been the indispensable saviour of his epoch.[22]

For this epoch the savior, he thought, had already appeared. His name was Goethe. For when Carlyle had opened his *Wilhelm Meister,* he had found the saving message which became the first injunction of the Carlylean philosophy: know your work and do it, and so conquer the misery of introspection and doubt. No wonder he spoke of Goethe "like an enthusiast." "But for him," as he told Crabb Robinson, "he should not now be alive. He owes everything to him!" [23] Plainly he owed him also the second injunction of the Carlylean philosophy, equally effective for the same therapy: find your hero and follow him. It is the tremendous gratitude one feels for the man who has rescued his soul from the Victorian purgatory which exalts the savior into a hero and makes the rescued a hero-worshiping disciple. "He alone can love, with a right gratitude and genuine loyalty of soul, the Hero-Teacher who has delivered him out of darkness into light." [24] And if the saving message made a supernatural belief, whether orthodox or liberal, credible to an anxious Victorian, the gratitude could easily become infinite admiration. "At a time when a religion

21. *Coningsby,* chap. 19, in *Works, 12,* 158; Harriet Martineau's *Autobiography, 2,* Period VI, sec. 6, p. 369; *Yeast,* chap. 17, p. 294.

22. Lecture 1, p. 13.

23. *Diary, Reminiscences, and Correspondence of Henry Crabb Robinson,* ed. T. Sadler (3 vols. London, 1869), *3,* 2.

24. *Heroes,* Lecture 4, p. 126. No doubt there was plenty of vanity and mean curiosity in the "Literary Lionism" which had become conspicuous enough by 1839 to warrant a long article in the *Westminster Review* (*32,* 261–81) but it was partly traced by the writer, Harriet Martineau (on p. 263), to the "strong, personal gratitude" felt for an author who "had opened up a spring of fresh ideas, furnished a solution of some doubt." The main passages are reprinted in her *Autobiography, 1,* Period IV, sec. 2, 271–97. On literary lionism and hero worship, see also Carlyle's essay on Scott, *Essays, 4,* 22–4.

which can no longer be believed clashes with a scepticism full of
danger to conduct," wrote Mrs. Humphry Ward, "every such witness
as Grey [T. H. Green] to the power of a new and coming truth
holds a special place in the hearts of men who can neither accept
fairy tales, nor reconcile themselves to a world without faith." [25]

The need for a messiah underlies the inspiration to *be* a hero, as
well as the impulse to find one. Carlyle's fifth lecture is a call to
men of letters to realize their genius and become leaders of society
in religion and politics.[26] Disraeli's *Coningsby* might have had for
subtitle, "Or, The Making of a Hero." It is the story of how a young
man of high birth, fully awake to the confusion around him but ignorant of how to meet it, is converted to the philosophy of the heroic.
His reply to Sidonia's insistence on the need for great prophets, legislators, conquerors—that an individual can do little against public
opinion and that in any case he himself is too young—is answered by
a roll-call of young men who changed the world, ending with the
rhetorical flourish, "The History of Heroes is the History of Youth."

> "Ah!" said Coningsby, "I should like to be a great man."
>
> The stranger threw at him a scrutinising glance. . . . He said
> in a voice of almost solemn melody,
>
> "Nurture your mind with great thoughts. To believe in the
> heroic makes heroes."
>
> "You seem to me a hero," said Coningsby, in a tone of real
> feeling.

Sidonia's words fall on fertile ground. Coningsby already had a well-
developed sentiment of veneration, but he had found no guide to
admire among his elders. "He had found age only perplexed and
desponding." Perhaps the leadership *must* devolve upon youth. Later
in the book the conscious adoption of his heroic destiny occurs as
he is walking through the streets of London, trying to throw off a
worried concern for his personal fame and fortune. Suddenly he says
to himself: "The power of man, his greatness and his glory, depend
on essential qualities. Brains every day become more precious than

25. *Robert Elsmere*, chap. 44, p. 600. The remark is late (1888), but Froude's
attitude toward Carlyle in the 1840's was precisely the same: see above, pp. 101–2.

26. Cf. Thackeray, "Madame Sand and the New Apocalypse," *The Paris Sketch
Book* (1840), in *Works*, 5, 189, where he speaks of every scribbler being "convinced of the necessity of a new 'Messianism,'" and ready to recite his own Apocalypse to anyone who will listen. The movement, as with all literary movements,
was more conscious and more extreme in France than in England.

blood. You must give men new ideas, you must teach them new words, you must modify their manners, you must change their laws, you must root out prejudices, subvert convictions, if you wish to be great." [27]

But before he and his Young England friends can become great, they are forced to denounce "the frigid theories of a generalising age that have destroyed the individuality of man." [28] The reference is partly to the democratic theory which reduced political leaders to instruments of the will of the people; but mainly to the scientific conception of history as a vast and interrelated play of cultural forces under the impersonal control of historical laws. On that conception, the individual leader, far from being a genius different in kind from the ordinary person, was simply the man who was in a position to hasten the development which in any case would have occurred eventually. Instead of being the dynamic creator of an age, he was himself the product of contemporary conditions. This was already a "sign of the times" when Carlyle published his essay in 1829.

> Speak to any small man of a high, majestic Reformation, of a high majestic Luther; and forthwith he sets about "accounting" for it; how the "circumstances of the time" called for such a character, and found him, we suppose, standing girt and road-ready, to do its errand; how the "circumstances of the time" created, fashioned, floated him quietly along into the result; how, in short, this small man, had he been there, could have performed the like himself! For it is the "force of circumstances" that does everything; the force of one man can do nothing. [29]

It was explicitly to attack that philosophy of history, according to Froude, that Carlyle wrote the *Heroes;* [30] and if that is too simple, attack it he had to before he could inaugurate his hero worship. A generation later the new professor of history at Cambridge, Charles Kingsley, opened his course with a lecture on one of the most controversial topics of the time, "The Limits of Exact Science as Applied to History." After rapping the "laissez-faire School of Political Economy" and the French Socialist School for their confident assumption that man was the creature of circumstances, he claimed

27. Chap. 19, in *Works, 12,* 158–68; chap. 73, in *13,* 197–8. Also see chap. 35, in *12,* 317–19.
28. Chap. 76, in *13,* 225–6.
29. *Essays, 2,* 75.
30. *Carlyle: Life in London, 1,* chap. 7, pp. 175–6.

that mankind alone of all species had the faculty of producing, from time to time, "individuals immeasurably superior to the average in some point or other, whom we call men of genius," and that the course of history was determined by these "extraordinary few." A Mohammed, a Luther, a Bacon, a Napoleon had changed the thoughts and habits of millions. And what *had* been could be again.[31] The Victorian who looked for a messiah or dreamed of becoming one had to repudiate any theory that denied the supreme influence of the hero in history.

2. Revelation

None of Carlyle's pronouncements on hero worship was more important than a statement in *Sartor Resartus:* "Great men are the inspired (speaking and acting) Texts of that divine BOOK OF REVELATION, whereof a Chapter is completed from epoch to epoch, and by some named HISTORY."[32] One could say that that passage was itself the inspired text on which Carlyle preached his sermons, ten years later, *On Heroes and Hero-Worship.* For there the opening paragraph defined universal history as the history of the great men "sent into the world" to be "the modellers, patterns, and in a wide sense creators, of whatsoever the general mass of men contrived to do or to attain." The hero, that is to say, and in the literal sense, is a messiah: "A messenger he, sent from the Infinite Unknown with tidings to us. . . . Really his utterances, are they not a kind of 'revelation'? . . . God has made many revelations: but this man too, has not God made him, the latest and newest of all? The 'inspiration of the Almighty giveth *him* understanding': we must listen before all to him." Listen—and worship. If by act and word the hero is a revelation of God, hero worship is a religion; or more exactly, the basis of all religion. "Heartfelt prostrate admiration, submission, burning, boundless, for a noblest godlike Form of Man,—is not that the germ of Christianity itself?"[33]

Behind this quasimystical point of view, so difficult for us to understand, lay various ideas which are now largely dead: the prophetic tradition of the Old Testament, the religious reading of history, first formulated by Augustine and widely held by the Puritans, and the powerful strain of pantheism in transcendental thought. But the reason

---

31. *The Roman and the Teuton,* in *Works, 10,* 326–9.
32. Bk. II, chap. 8, p. 177.
33. Lecture 1, pp. 1, 11; Lecture 2, pp. 45–6.

why these influences were active was the intense will to believe, in an age demanding tangible evidence of religious truth. When traditional faith declines and the Bible is reduced to a human document full of superstition and the Church is no longer a divine temple, God is sought in nature and in history. His spirit is felt rolling through all things or his beauty is found reflected in natural beauty; his will is seen active in human affairs, working out in time his divine purposes or fulfilling his moral law in the rise and fall of nations. "The Eternal Bible and God's-Book" in which every man "can and must, *with his own eyes,* see the God's-Finger writing" is "Universal History." [34] Many who would not have gone so far as that were glad enough to turn to history for welcome signs of God's providence and justice. And if to history, then also to the great men who were his divine instruments. When Kingsley urged his future wife to the study of God, he mentioned three ways of doing so: from nature, where you will find "the countenance of God" in "every line of beauty, every association, every moral reflection;" from "His dealings in History"; and "from His image as developed in Christ the Ideal, and in all good men—great good men." [35]

Kingsley might just as well have written, "His dealings in myth" and "His image in legendary heroes"; for heroic mythology satisfied the same need as heroic biography for a natural revelation. Indeed, the very presence of God or the gods, of heroes descended from gods or fighting for a divine cause, and of noble deeds readily identified with one or another aspect of Christian ethics, made a religious reading of heroic legend entirely natural. Moreover, the new theories of evolution in which the Divine Idea was thought of as clothed in different forms from age to age suggested that mythology was a phase in the development of the religious imagination, and therefore a permanent source of spiritual truths. "You must not fancy," wrote Kingsley in the preface to *The Heroes, or Greek Fairy Tales*

34. *Past and Present*, Bk. IV, chap. 1, p. 240. The italics are mine.
35. *Letters and Memories*, *1*, 67–8 (unabridged ed., *1*, 88). Cf. the important passage in Carlyle's *Heroes*, Lecture 5, pp. 162–3, where, after speaking of the writers of poems and books as "the real working effective Church of a modern country," he goes on to cite the poet of nature and the biographer of heroes as authors who bring us manifestations "of the great Maker of the Universe." For other examples of great men viewed as "a kind of revelation of God," see F. D. Maurice, preface to Kingsley's *The Saint's Tragedy* (London, 1848), p. viii; E. P. Hood, *The Uses of Biography*, pp. 194–5; Frederic Myers, *Lectures on Great Men*, pp. 47–51.

(1856), " . . . that because these old Greeks were heathens, therefore God did not care for them, and taught them nothing. The Bible tells us that it was not so, but that God's mercy is over all his works, and that He understands the hearts of all people, and fashions all their works." [36] In the later lecture entitled "Heroism" he described Theseus ridding the land of robbers and Perseus slaying the Gorgon as figures of "divine moral beauty"; and argued that far from contradicting the Christian ideal, they harmonized with its expression in chivalry.[37] It followed, therefore, that the Greek myths, the sagas of our old forefathers the Northmen (the Eddas, the *Voluspà*, and *Beowulf*), the Roman *fabulae*, and chivalric romances were all, in various degrees, religious books. They could make children "love noble deeds, and trust in God to help them through." [38] At a time when the Bible and the Church were no longer able to satisfy the religious instinct of many Victorians, heroic legend, like nature and great men, could be welcomed as another manifestation of the divine spirit working in the world.

3. *Moral Inspiration*

To the Victorians a hero might be a messiah or he might be a revelation of God, but he was certain to be a man of the highest moral stature, and therefore of enormous importance to a period in which the alarming increase of both the commercial spirit and religious doubt made moral inspiration a primary need. In a few words written in 1838, Mill put his finger squarely on the major function of heroic literature, in the past and—so be it—in the present. Once upon a time, he said, the "old romances, whether of chivalry or of faëry" had "filled the youthful imagination with pictures of heroic men, and of what are at least as much wanted, heroic women," and so helped to make the noblest minds noble and common minds responsive to nobility. "And *this* is education." But now the old books have been banished in favor of "catalogues of physical facts and theological dogmas," and the popular novels of the day "teach nothing but (what is already too soon learnt from actual life) lessons of worldliness, with at most

36. *The Heroes*, pp. xiii–xiv.
37. *Sanitary and Social Essays*, pp. 231–32.
38. *The Heroes*, p. xix. See also his essay on "The Poetry of Sacred and Legendary Art," *Literary and General Essays*, pp. 187–98. A good guide to the Victorian reading of myth is Ruskin's *The Queen of the Air: Being a Study of the Greek Myths of Cloud and Storm* (1869); see in particular the opening statements, secs. 1–9, in *Works, 19*, 295–303.

the huckstering virtues which conduce to getting on in the world."
Hence the significance of the *Letters from Palmyra*, which Mill is
reviewing; for "greatly is any book to be valued, which in this age,
and in a form suited to it, does its part towards keeping alive the
chivalrous spirit, which was the best part of the old romances; towards
giving to the aspirations of the young and susceptible a noble direction, and keeping present to the mind an exalted standard of worth,
by placing before it heroes and heroines worthy of the name." [39]

This conviction was completely shared by Tennyson. Not only did
he consider that boys educated in science and modern languages
"ought to be made to study the old stories of heroism," but he
claimed to have designed the *Idylls* with its pictures of heroism as an
antidote to the selfishness and materialism of the age:

> All ages are ages of transition, but this is an awful moment of
> transition. It seems to me as if there were much less of the old
> reverence and chivalrous feeling in the world than there used
> to be. I am old and I may be wrong, for this generation has
> assuredly some spirit of chivalry. We see it in acts of heroism
> by land and sea, in fights against the slave trade, in our Arctic
> voyages, in philanthropy, etc. The truth is that the wave advances
> and recedes. I tried in my "Idylls" to teach men these things, and
> the need of the Ideal. [40]

With a similar intention, Charlotte Yonge hoped that her *Book of
Golden Deeds* would fasten the minds of young people on actions
whose object was not "promotion, wealth, or success" but the service
of others in "the spirit of heroism and self-devotion." [41]

When Froude adopted this notion of hero worship as a check to
the commercial spirit, he introduced a novel idea, that of modern
heroes suitable for modern inspiration. This idea was prompted by
the problem which anyone had to face who aspired to more than
a mere negative abstaining from wrong. He was told, Froude says,
to be noble; but "what was nobleness? and where are the examples?"
Where can he find a "modern ideal which shall be to him what the
heroes were to the young Greek or Roman, or the martyrs to the

---

39. "A Prophecy," *Dissertations*, *1*, 284–5, which is a selection from his review—
Westminster Review, 28 (1838), 436–70—of *Letters of Lucius Manlius Piso, from
Palmyra, to His Friend, Marcus Curtius, at Rome*, 2 vols. New York, 1837.
40. Hallam Tennyson, *Memoir of Tennyson*, 2, 129, 337, 349.
41. Page 1.

Middle-Age Christian?" Those old models, framed for an aristocratic order, had no relevance for burghers or artisans. Now in the age of business and democracy, "the old hero-worship has vanished with the need of it; but no other has risen in its stead, and without it we [of the middle class] wander in the dark." Or worse, we follow the all too explicit ideal which is preached by the "keen-eyed children of this world": that "the business of man in it is to get on, to thrive, to prosper, to have riches in possession." The great need of the age, therefore, is a whole series of biographies of lawyers, merchants, landlords, workmen, each of whom is the type of his profession at its best. Then we could say to a boy, "Read that; there is a man—such a man as you ought to be; read it, meditate on it; see what he was, and how he made himself what he was, and try and be yourself like him." In short, a new pantheon, men of the people transformed into pure heroes, should take the place of the old and old-fashioned one with its kings and knights and Christian martyrs.[42]

The use of hero worship to correct the ills of a commercial society was not limited to general moral inspiration. Surprising as it seeems today, it was brought forward as the solution for two major economic problems. In the same essay, "Representative Men," Froude goes on to mention the mounting warfare between the masters and their workmen. Like most Victorians, he did not think it could be dealt with by legislation. What was needed was a strong realization on both sides of those moral obligations and duties which it was the function of the Church and not the State to look to. But the Church was silent, afraid to give offense. What, then, could resolve the conflict of capital and labor into an harmonious partnership? "Far off we seem to see a time when the lives, the actions of the really great —great good masters, great good landlords, great good working men —will be laid out once more before their several orders, laid out in the name of God, as once the saints' lives were; and the same sounds shall be heard in factory and in counting-house as once sounded through abbey, chapel, and cathedral aisle—'Look at these men; bless God for them, and follow them.'"[43]

The full implications of this approach to the economic problem

42. "Representative Men" (1850), *Short Studies*, 1, 579, 581, 583–4, 587, 590–1, 600. For a cognate idea, that Hakluyt's *Voyages* might be a modern prose epic with the same inspiring effect on the common people which the old epics had on "the royally or nobly born," see his "England's Forgotten Worthies," ibid., pp. 446–8.

43. Ibid., pp. 595–6.

were developed by Carlyle and Ruskin. Their appeal to the captains of industry to be heroes and to their men to be hero worshipers now seems ludicrously innocent, but they seriously hoped that in this way the two antagonistic classes could form a common "chivalry of labor," marching together, armed with the new weapons of technology, against the recalcitrant forces of nature in a new crusade for civilization. Carlyle in particular took feudalism as his point of reference and contrasted the old "noble devout-hearted Chevalier" with the new "ignoble godless Bucanier and Chactaw Indian." The Bucanier enlists his thousand men, leads them to "victory over Cotton," hangs up the scalps in his own wigwam, the hundred thousands at his banker's, and disbands his regiment. William the Norman conquered England and said to his men: "Noble fighters, this is the land we have gained; be I Lord in it . . . and be ye Loyal Men around me in it; and we will stand by one another, as soldiers round a captain, for again we shall have need of one another!" And so the moral: that the Captains of Industry, in imitation of "the Cliffords, Fitzadelms and Chivalry Fighters," should become noble knights, placing the welfare of their men and the good of society above any selfish desire for wealth and success. Then the workers would become noble workers, serving their captains with patience and loyalty. And so peace on earth in every factory, office, and shop.[44] The fantastic nature of this plan was recognized by Mill in his comment on *Past and Present*, and Carlyle himself came to realize its futility.[45] But in an age of decaying feudalism and ardent hero worship it could seem a practical solution to a major problem.

The condition of the industrial workers inspired a complementary appeal to the upper classes. Whether Protestant or humanitarian in spirit, the movement to ameliorate the condition of the masses found the ideals of chivalry directly to the purpose. In his speech on sanitary reform, Kingsley called on every one of his hearers to be "a knight-errant or lady-errant" even now in the nineteenth century, for the alleviation of misery among the poor is a noble work, a chivalrous work—"just as chivalrous as if you lived in any old fairy land, such

44. *Past and Present*, Bk. III, chap. 10, pp. 191–3; Bk. IV, chap. 7, p. 289. For Ruskin's similar appeal, see *Unto This Last* (1860), first essay, in *Works*, 17, 25–42; and "Traffic," *The Crown of Wild Olive* (1866), in *Works*, 18, 448–50.

45. *Principles of Political Economy*, Bk. IV, chap. 7, pp. 752–7. Packe, *Life of Mill*, p. 307, claims that Harriet Taylor more or less dictated the comment. For Carlyle's later disillusionment, see *Last Words of Thomas Carlyle on Trades-Unions, Promoterism and the Signs of the Times* (Edinburgh, 1882), pp. 15, 44–5.

as Spenser talked of in his 'Faerie Queene.'"[46] Or Malory, he might have said, in his *Morte d'Arthur*. Sir Edward Strachey ended the introduction to his popular edition of Malory by pointing its contemporary relevance: "We must remember that our nineteenth century world is yet far from cleared of the monstrous powers of evil, which still oppress and devour the weak." Let us all unite, therefore, "in the true spirit of chivalry" to serve "the poor, the weak, and the oppressed."[47] When fear and guilt were making people acutely conscious of lower-class suffering, the role of the philanthropist took on an importance, even a necessity, which called for the rhetoric of heroism. It was a foregone conclusion that the knights of Tennyson's Round Table should "ride abroad redressing human wrongs."

Arnold's Preface to the 1853 *Poems*—his most important critical statement—is a plea for modern poetry in the grand style. The young poet should take the "great works of Homer, Aeschylus, and Virgil" as his models, and write of "some noble action of a heroic time." The intention was primarily didactic. Arnold believed that the grand style was "tonic and fortifying": it could form the character; it could "compose and elevate the mind."[48] Hence the remarks in the Preface about the "moral impression left by a great action treated as a whole," and the power of "some noble and significant action . . . to affect what is permanent in the human soul."[49] In pleading for such a poetry, Arnold was thinking not of businessmen needing nobler motives but of men like himself, the "we" of "The Scholar-Gipsy," burdened by sick fatigue and languid doubt, needing something to quicken their energies and give a new impetus to the moral life—something like his own poem in the grand style, "Sohrab and Rustum," published in this very volume. Just after the Preface was completed, he wrote to Clough:

> I am glad you like the Gipsy Scholar—but what does it *do* for you? Homer *animates*—Shakespeare *animates*—in its poor way I

46. *Letters and Memories*, 2, 110–11 (apparently not in the unabridged ed.).

47. *Morte Darthur. Sir Thomas Malory's Book of King Arthur and His Noble Knights of the Round Table: The Text of Caxton* (1868; London, 1889), p. xxxvii. For an extended use of knightly imagery, including modern St. Georges rescuing distressed persons attacked by the dragon Poverty, see Thackeray, "De Juventute," *Roundabout Papers*, in *Works*, 12, 229–30.

48. *On Translating Homer*, in *On the Study of Celtic Literature and On Translating Homer* (New York, 1883), pp. 157, 197; *Letters of Arnold to Clough*, p. 100.

49. *Poems*, pp. xxviii–xxix.

think Sohrab and Rustum *animates*—the Gipsy Scholar at best awakens a pleasing melancholy. But this is not what we want.

> The complaining millions of men
> Darken in labour and pain—

what they want is something to *animate* and *ennoble* them—not merely to add zest to their melancholy or grace to their dreams. I believe a feeling of this kind is the basis of my nature—and of my poetics

—that is, the poetics of his Preface, where poetry in the grand style is called for to take the place of the subjective poetry of doubt and melancholy.[50] Earlier in the same year he had sent Clough a more explicit statement:

> Miss Brontë has written a hideous undelightful convulsed constricted novel. . . . She is so entirely—what Margaret Fuller was partially—a fire without aliment—one of the most distressing barren sights one can witness. Religion or devotion or whatever it is to be called may be impossible for such people now: but they have at any rate not found a substitute for it and it was better for the world when they comforted themselves with it. . . . It gives you an insight into the *heaven born* character of Waverley and Indiana and such like when you read the undeniably powerful but most un-heaven-born productions of the present people—Thackeray—the woman Stowe etc. . . . I read Homer and toujours Homer.[51]

It is quite right, I think, to see a connection between, on the one hand, finding a substitute for religion, and on the other, the heaven-born character of Scott's *Waverley* and George Sand's *Indiana*—as well as the *Iliad* and *Odyssey*. A little earlier Arnold had said that modern poetry could subsist only "by becoming a complete magister vitae as

50. *Letters of Arnold to Clough,* p. 146; *Poetical Works,* pp. xvii, xxiv. This is not the whole truth about Arnold's nature or his poetics. His nature included a strong leaven of moral earnestness, and he could think of poetry as a powerful application of moral ideas to life. But the ideal of aristocratic nobility was also, as we know, part of his nature (see above, pp. 283-4) and that ideal was the natural analogue of the grand style in art. Tinker and Lowry, *The Poetry of Arnold* (full reference below, note 93), p. 273, misinterpret the letter, I think, to mean that an aptitude for pleasing melancholy is the basis of his nature and his poetics.

51. *Letters of Arnold to Clough,* pp. 132-3.

the poetry of the ancients did: by including, as theirs did, religion
with poetry, instead of existing as poetry only, and leaving religious
wants to be supplied by the Christian religion"; and that such a poetry
must be written in the "plain direct and severe" manner of the grand
style.[52]

The pattern of thought illustrated here in one eminent Victorian was
not uncommon; for when God was dead, the gods and heroes of history
or of myth could take his place and save the moral sum of things.
What Mary Sibree said of herself—that under George Eliot's influence
her interest shifted from Christianity "towards manifestations of nobility," like that of the Marquis von Posa in *Don Carlos*, who roused
in her "an enthusiasm for heroism and virtue"—was true, I think, of
many Victorians, especially late Victorians.[53] For young John Mill,
brought up an agnostic, the character of Socrates stood in his mind
"as a model of ideal excellence"; and later on the lives of heroic
persons who had been benefactors of mankind—he mentions in particular Condorcet's biography of Turgot—were "memorials of past
nobleness and greatness," from which he drew "strength and ani-
mation." [54] More than once he spoke of sustaining one's aspirations
for a noble life by "the ideal sympathy of the great characters in
history, or even in fiction": "The idea that Socrates, or Howard or
Washington, or Antoninus, or Christ, would have sympathized with
us, or that we are attempting to do our part in the spirit in which
they did theirs, has operated on the very best minds, as a strong
incentive to act up to their highest feelings and convictions." [55] Mill
was thus prepared, for all his dislike of the authoritarianism in
Comte's Religion of Humanity, to sympathize wholeheartedly with
the calendar of great men that Comte designed as a substitute for the

52. Ibid., p. 124. It is worth noticing that when Arnold repeats this plea in
the Preface to the *Poems* of 1853, the reason given (*Poetical Works*, p. xxii) is
that otherwise, if any elaborate imagery is used, "the grandiose effect of the whole"
will be impaired.

53. Cross, *George Eliot's Life*, 1, 375, appendix.

54. *Autobiography*, chap. 2, p. 39; chap. 4, pp. 95–6, where poetry, enthusiasm,
and hero worship are brought together; chap. 5, p. 114. Not all his early heroes,
however, were philosophers. He was started off (Packe, *Life of Mill*, pp. 21–2)
on "true accounts of resourceful, energetic men who overcame their difficulties"—
Drake, Philip of Macedon, Frederick the Great—and on histories containing
"heroic achievements" like the defense of the Knights of Malta against the Turks.

55. "Utility of Religion," *Three Essays on Religion*, p. 109. Cf. the "Inaugural
Address at St. Andrews," *James & John Stuart Mill on Education*, p. 193; and
Comte and Positivism, p. 136.

Catholic calendar of saints. His list of heroes and benefactors of mankind, serving as objects of veneration to supplement the worship of man, each with his "day," included the most illustrious names in science and literature, in religion, philosophy, and politics.[56] In 1892 the English Comtists, under the leadership of Frederic Harrison, published *The New Calendar of Great Men*, containing biographical sketches of all 558 names in Comte's list. It became their manual of devotion. In the meanwhile its inspiration had been partly supplied by memorial addresses which commemorated "Great Heroes from Alfred to Washington," given on the centenaries of their deaths; and by organized expeditions to the birthplaces, homes, or tombs of great men in England and France. But the expeditions had another name which underscores the link between the decline of religious, and the rise of hero, worship. They were called "pilgrimages."

> One of the most popular forms of commemoration which we instituted was that of a pilgrimage to the home, or tomb, and associations of great men, and visits to scenes of historic interest. The most elaborate of these were visits to Stratford-on-Avon and its neighbourhood, to Oxford, Cambridge, and Huntingdon, to Paris, Winchester, and Canterbury. . . . In every case, the design was . . . to give a serious tone and that religious consecration which befits a genuine pilgrimage by filling our minds with reverence for the immortal spirit whose footsteps we were seeking to trace.[57]

Though Ruskin was no Comtist, and clung rather desperately to theism, we know that he gave "the sight and history of noble persons" a central place in an education designed to develop the faculties of "admiration, love, and hope." For this purpose he planned a textbook on "the history of five cities: Athens, Rome, Venice, Florence, and London." There, he says, young people "shall learn . . . what has been beautifully and bravely done; and they shall know the lives of the heroes and heroines in truth and naturalness; and shall be taught to remember the greatest of them on the days of their birth and death; so that the year shall have its full calendar of reverent Memory."[58] The Comtist calendar of great men was simply one ex-

---

56. *Comte and Positivism*, pp. 115–17.

57. Frederic Harrison, *Autobiographic Memoirs*, 2, 288. Cf. "Modern Pilgrimages," in his *Realities and Ideals, Social, Political, Literary and Artistic* (New York, 1908), pp. 175–9.

58. *Fors Clavigera*, Letters 8 and 9, in *Works*, 27, 143, 156–7. For the general statement on education, see above, p. 265.

pression of a general movement of thought in which hero worship and its moral inspiration inherited the functions once fulfilled by a living Church.

4. Patriotism

No Victorian would have called patriotism, as Dr. Johnson did, the last refuge of a scoundrel. He would probably have cried, "Woe to those who fancy it fine to turn cosmopolite," and have found patriotism "a righteous and a God-given feeling." [59] The change in attitude, which came with the increasing nationalism of the nineteenth century, brought with it the glorification of English heroes. At first they were those of the Napoleonic wars. Napier wrote the *History of the War in the Peninsula* (1828–40) to enshrine the exploits of the British army, "great in themselves, great in their consequences, abounding with signal examples of heroic courage and devoted zeal." [60] In the fifties the national heroes came out of the Crimea; and presently—for this Protestant, commercial, and naval country—became the great Elizabethans. Kingsley conceived his *Westward Ho!* not only as a fighting sermon to quicken the nationalism of 1854 but as a prose epic of England's seadogs. He wrote it, he said, in memory of the Drakes and Hawkinses, the Raleighs and Gilberts, and a host more of "forgotten worthies" to whom England "owes her commerce, her colonies, her very existence," and of "their voyages and their battles . . . their heroic lives and no less heroic deaths." It was a theme "fit rather to have been sung than said, and to have proclaimed to all true English hearts . . . the same great message which the songs of Troy, and the Persian wars, and the trophies of Marathon and Salamis, spoke to the hearts of all true Greeks of old." [61]

But as long as patriotism aroused heroic attitudes of devotion and self-sacrifice (now almost destroyed under the glaring light of modern psychology), it could also be utilized for moral purposes. Though repudiating the extremes of provinciality and chauvinism, Mill and Lecky and George Eliot emphasized its power to arouse a fine enthusiasm. "Not only the nobleness of a nation depends on the presence of this national consciousness, but also the nobleness of each individual citizen. Our dignity and rectitude are proportioned

59. Kingsley, *Letters and Memories, 1,* 173 (unabridged ed., *1,* 200).

60. Preface to *History of the War in the Peninsula and in the South of France. From the Year 1807 to the Year 1814.* (4 vols. Philadelphia, 1842), p. x.

61. *Westward Ho!* chap. 1, pp. 2–3. Cf. Froude, "England's Forgotten Worthies" (note 42, above).

to our sense of relationship with something great, admirable, pregnant with high possibilities, worthy of sacrifice, a continual inspiration to self-repression and discipline by the presentation of aims larger and more attractive to our generous part than the securing of personal ease or prosperity." [62] The biographies of great Englishmen, therefore, could provide the same kind of counteroffensive which heroic legend was called on to perform. By studying the "sterlingly great characters, such as England had, in times gone by," wrote Baldwin Brown in *The Uses of Biography*, we might have less "to do than unfortunately we have with the . . . miserable huckstering spirit of the day" and yearn "less for outward show and delusive appearances." And in addition, all of us would be helping "to make England truly great, more respected abroad, and happier and more united at home." [63] As the last remark suggests, the nationalistic and the moralistic functions of patriotic hero worship tended to merge, and in the concreteness of experience a great soldier or statesman was an inspiration to a noble life—for the glory of England. When Kingsley drove home the moral of "The Argonauts," that no hero ever did a noble deed for gold, he pointed to the Spartans who fought and died at Thermopylae, the great Elizabethan sailors, and the young men who went to the Crimea "leaving wealth, and comfort, and a pleasant home, and all that money can give . . . that they might fight for their country and their Queen." [64]

5. Politics

In conservative-aristocratic circles, where the dread of bourgeois democracy was strongest, heroic literature acquired the value of a political symbol. Medieval romance in particular could be read as the image of a feudal society in striking contrast to the new order that was pushing it aside, and of an ideal which still might be revived. To the Young Englanders, led by Lord John Manners and George Smythe, the novels of Scott (which translated the politics of Burke into character and action) were almost as highly valued as those of Disraeli; and their bible was the major treatise written on chivalry during the century, Kenelm Digby's *The Broadstone of Honour; or, Rules*

62. George Eliot, "The Modern Hep! Hep! Hep!" *The Impressions of Theophrastus Such*, in *Works*, *11*, 190; and see the previous paragraph. For Mill, "Coleridge," *Dissertations*, *1*, 419–21; for Lecky, *History of European Morals*, (first ed. 1869; 2 vols. New York, 1903), *1*, 173, 177–8, 200–1.

63. *On the Uses of Biography*, pp. 6–7.

64. *The Heroes*, pp. 71–3.

for the Gentlemen of England.[65] When Charlotte Yonge's *Heir of Red-clyffe* appeared in 1853, they took Sir Guy Morville as "the embodiment of their vision of a latter-day knight"; [66] naturally enough, since the author, sharing their sympathy with the aristocratic-chivalric tradition, had consciously created Sir Guy as the inheritor of medieval ideals. Malory's *Morte d'Arthur* and Fouqué's *Sintram* were his favorite books, Sir Galahad his favorite hero, and King Charles the martyr whom he would have "served . . . half like a knight's devotion to his lady-love, half like devotion to a saint." He rules his Redclyffe tenants with a care that justifies their "strong feudal feeling" of loyalty, and sacrifices his life for his cousin Philip like a true knight.[67] This medievalism was further encouraged by the High Church Movement that naturally appealed to the same minds. (The alliance of Tory politics with Anglican Christianity appears in Miss Yonge and the Young Englanders as well as in Keble and Newman; with Roman Catholicism in Digby.) At Oxford William Morris and Burne-Jones were led on from their reading of *Tracts for the Times* and the *Acta Sanctorum* to a "rapid and prodigious assimilation of mediaeval chronicles and romances," including Fouqué's *Sintram,* Malory, and Froissart. This prepared the way for their enthusiastic reception of *The Heir of Redclyffe,* which they adopted "as a pattern for actual life," and directly inspired, under the immediate proximity to Littlemore, where Newman had founded an Anglican monastery, their dream of a brotherhood with Sir Galahad as patron saint and a "Crusade and Holy Warfare against the age" as its end and aim.[68] If they passed presently from religious and social to artistic goals, the medieval focus in their art on knights and saints had its roots in the Anglican-aristocratic tradition.

The link between Tory politics and heroic literature can also be found in conservative circles of the middle class. Ruskin, to take the most famous example, began his *Praeterita* with a defiant profession of faith: "I am, and my father was before me, a violent Tory of the old school;—Walter Scott's school, that is to say, and Homer's. I name these two out of the numberless great Tory writers, because they were my own two masters. I had Walter Scott's novels, and the *Iliad* (Pope's translation), for constant reading when I was a child . . ." They taught him, as he goes on to say, "a most sincere

---

65. See Amy Cruse, *The Victorians and Their Reading,* pp. 138–42.
66. Ibid., p. 52.
67. Chaps. 5, 22, 30, pp. 60, 274, 388.
68. J. W. Mackail, *The Life of William Morris,* chap. 2, *I,* 39, 41, 43, 65.

love of kings, and dislike of everybody who attempted to disobey them," and that kings and king-loving persons did more work than anybody else and in proportion to their doings got less. But as he toured England with his father and visited the castles he had read of, he began to realize that the old ideals were forgotten.

> Having formed my notion of kinghood chiefly from the Fitz-James of the *Lady of the Lake*, and of noblesse from the Douglas there, and the Douglas in *Marmion*, a painful wonder soon arose in my child-mind, why the castles should now be always empty. Tantallon was there; but no Archibald of Angus:—Stirling, but no Knight of Snowdoun. The galleries and gardens of England were beautiful to see—but his Lordship and her Ladyship were always in town, said the housekeepers and gardeners. Deep yearning took hold of me for a kind of "Restoration," which I began slowly to feel that Charles the Second had not altogether effected, though I always wore a gilded oak-apple very piously in my button-hole on the 29th of May.[69]

Ruskin's lecture "The Future of England," given at Woolwich in 1869, is one illustration of his effort to give that yearning practical effect. He was speaking, as he said, on the eve of "a great political crisis" in which "a struggle is approaching between the newly-risen power of democracy and the apparently departing power of feudalism; and another struggle, no less imminent, and far more dangerous, between wealth and pauperism." After noticing the alarming decline of reverence for one's superiors among the masses, which he blames on the failure of the aristocracy to provide the wise government they had once given the nation, he goes on to raise the standard of a "second Restoration." Let the Lords "be lords indeed, and give us laws—dukes indeed, and give us guiding—princes indeed, and give us beginning of truer dynasty." And then he addresses his audience directly: "I, one of the lower people of your country, ask of you in their name,—you whom I will not any more call soldiers, but by the truer name of Knights;—Equites of England—how many yet of you are there . . . who still retain the ancient and eternal purpose of knighthood, to subdue the wicked, and aid the weak? To them, be they few or many, we English people call for help to the wretchedness, and for rule over the baseness, of multitudes desolate and deceived."[70] Tory paternalism found its natural expression in the heroic image.

---

69. Vol. *1*, chap. 1, secs. 1, 3, 7, in *Works, 35,* 13–15, 17.
70. *The Crown of Wild Olive,* in *Works, 18,* 494, 499. This passage is clearly

Though in this period of the second Reform Bill, Carlyle could talk in the same way about the wisdom of restoring the aristocracy to power,[71] his first and characteristic reaction against democracy led to a very different alternative: to the hero as absolute ruler, and the hero worship of men like Cromwell, Frederick the Great, and William the Conqueror. This looks like fascism—and sometimes it was; but Carlyle's conception of the hero king was not what we would mean by a dictator, and his criticism of democracy in its Victorian form had sufficient validity to make the counterimage more appealing than it would be now.

In theory, at any rate, Carlyle's political hero was not merely a man of force and courage, he was "the truest-hearted, justest, the Noblest Man." Gifted with superior intelligence and virtue, he could see the "wisest, fittest" thing to be done; and therefore the thing which it well behooved the rest of us, "with right loyal thankfulness," to do. If he was not so gifted, if his real concern was with personal power and glory, he was not a hero at all, but a sham hero.[72] As Carlyle saw it, the French Revolution was an entirely justifiable revolt against unheroic leadership. But it issued unfortunately, however naturally, in a rejection of all leadership and a desperate attempt by the people to govern themselves. In violent reaction against an authority which had been unjustly used, men cried out for no authority at all, that is, for liberty and equality. But the liberty meant a laissez-faire policy which allowed the worker to be exploited by the capitalist. The equality assumed that a great nation could be well governed by a Parliament chosen by the populace, when in fact Parliamentary action, he thought with some truth, was bound to be "a compromise between conflicting opinions, and therefore uncertain, inadequate, alternately rash or feeble, certain to end in disaster at all critical times when a clear eye and a firm hand was needed at the helm." Moreover, the kind of Parliament which the people would elect would not be composed of the wisest and fittest to govern, but of M.P.'s like themselves with little education and no political experience. It is quite true that Carlyle overlooked the fact that power can corrupt even good men, that he had no proposal by which benevolent leaders were to be found and installed, and that he com-

related to the moral humanitarianism mentioned above, pp. 319–20, but its political theme brings it into this section.

71. "Inaugural Address at Edinburgh" (1866), *Essays*, 4, 462–5; and "Shooting Niagara," ibid., 5, 18–23.

72. The quoted phrases are from *Heroes*, Lecture 6, p. 197.

pletely ignored the educative values of self-government on which
Mill laid such wise emphasis. But he pointed a finger at the weak
sides of democracy.[73]

How readily his political theory could build on the existing tradition
of hero worship is clear from a passage in *Tom Brown at Oxford*.
In the first flush of social idealism, Tom had become an ardent supporter of universal democracy, which was to bring about "that age
of peace and good-will which men had dreamt of in all times." Hardy
takes him aside, asks what he means by democracy. Well, he means
at the least that "every man should have a share in the government
of his country."

> Hardy, seeming to acquiesce . . . decoyed his innocent guest
> away from the thought of democracy for a few minutes, by
> holding up to him the flag of hero-worship, in which worship
> Tom was, of course, a sedulous believer. . . .
>
> "You long for the rule of the ablest man, everywhere, at all
> times? To find your ablest man, and then give him power, and
> obey him—that you hold to be about the highest act of wisdom
> which a nation can be capable of?"
>
> "Yes; and you know you believe that too, Hardy, just as firmly
> as I do."
>
> "I hope so. But then, how about our universal democracy, and
> every man having a share in the government of his country? . . .
> Will that find our wisest governor for us—letting all the foolishest
> men in the nation have a say as to who he is to be?" [74]

In the same years, the early forties, just after Carlyle gave his
lectures, the hero-governor alternative to democracy had a further
and more compelling appeal. Since the time of the French Revolution
democracy had been associated with mob violence and the con-
fiscation of property; and now in the Chartist Movement with its
democratic platform the same disastrous results seemed apparent, in
fact or in prospect. In that context Carlyle's remarks in the "Hero
as King" must have carried special impact: "Disorder is dissolution,
death. No chaos but it seeks a *centre* to revolve round. While man
is man, some Cromwell or Napoleon is the necessary finish of a
Sansculottism. . . . In rebellious ages, when Kingship itself seems

73. These ideas, constantly reiterated throughout Carlyle's later works, are
summarized by Froude, *Carlyle: Life in London, 1*, chap. 13, pp. 359–64, from
which the quotation is taken.
74. Chap. 42, pp. 487–8.

dead and abolished, Cromwell, Napoleon step-forth again as Kings. The history of these men is what we have now to look at, as our last phasis of Heroism."[75] Nor is it only the hero who is a bulwark against "the confused wreck of things crumbling and even crashing and tumbling all round us in these revolutionary ages."[76] So is hero worship, since it exorcises the antisocial forces of personal or class ambition, bred by the doctrines of liberty and equality, and in their place calls forth the uniting emotions of loyalty and reverence for one great man who is our common leader.[77]

At times, however, this theory takes on a rather different coloring. The hero has a tendency to become the embodiment of sheer force and the exponent not of justice but of his own self-will, and the people no longer to be men of sufficient "heroic mind" to recognize and reverence true greatness, but stupid blockheads who are in great need of the horsewhip.[78] In the chapter of *Past and Present* on democracy which proposes the redefinition of liberty as freedom from stupidity, cowardice, and folly through obeying, or being forced to obey, "a wiser man," the said wiser man turns out to be the man on the white horse who installs a military despotism. "Sweep away thy constitutional, sentimental and other cobwebberies; look eye to eye, if thou still have any eye, in the face of this burly William Bastard: thou wilt see a fellow of most flashing discernment, of most strong lion-heart;—in whom, as it were, within a frame of oak and iron, the gods have planted the soul of 'a man of genius'!"[79] Three years later Carlyle met Mazzini, the great European champion of democracy. What he said was reported by Margaret Fuller: "All Carlyle's talk that evening . . . was a defence of mere force, success the test of right. If people would not behave well, put collars round their necks. Find a hero, and let them be his slaves. It was very Titanic and Anticelestial."[80] Carlyle's antidemocratic passion united, we see, with his admiration for force to turn his hero worship, by moments at least, into the worship of the führer.

And he was far from unique. Though few Victorians in liberal England openly advocated such a political philosophy, there is good evidence of its existence. In the fifties Samuel Smiles protested against

75. Page 204.
76. Page 15.
77. *Sartor Resartus*, Bk. III, chap. 7, p. 251; "Chartism," *Essays*, 4, 159–60.
78. The most notorious illustration is the essay called "Dr. Francia," *Essays*, 4, 261–321. Cf. above, Chap. 9, secs. 3–6.
79. Bk. III, chap. 13, pp. 212–14.
80. Froude, *Carlyle: Life in London, 1*, chap. 15, p. 402.

an old fallacy that was turning up again, the doctrine that "we are to wait for Caesars, and when they are found, 'happy the people who recognize and follow them'"—which is a quotation from a new life of Caesar by the outstanding dictator of the age, Napoleon III.[81] In the year 1859 Mill was condemning "the sort of 'hero-worship' which applauds the strong man of genius for forcibly seizing on the government of the world and making it do his bidding in spite of itself."[82] A little later, when Huxley noticed that men took sides on the Jamaica Question according to "their deepest political convictions," he described the opposing parties in these revealing terms:

> The hero-worshippers who believe that the world is to be governed by its great men, who are to lead the little ones, justly if they can; but if not, unjustly drive or kick them the right way, will sympathise with Mr. Eyre.
> The other sect (to which I belong) who look upon hero-worship as no better than any other idolatry, and upon the attitude of mind of the hero-worshipper as essentially immoral; who think it is better for a man to go wrong in freedom than to go right in chains; who look upon the observance of inflexible justice as between man and man as of far greater importance than even the preservation of social order, will believe that Mr. Eyre has committed one of the greatest crimes of which a person in authority can be guilty.[83]

The very expression "hero worship" has now become a purely political term, the badge, I suspect, of a sizable part of the middle class, the John Bull-ish part, proud of its power and frightened by the threat of democratic and socialistic thought.[84]

6. Compensation

Irrespective of any desire for a messiah or divine revelation or moral sanctions, regardless of patriotism or politics, the Victorians wanted to think about heroes. They wanted to read heroic literature

81. *Self-Help*, chap. 1, pp. 23–4.
82. *On Liberty*, chap. 3, p. 166.
83. Leonard Huxley, *Life and Letters of Thomas Henry Huxley*, 1, chap. 20, pp. 303–4. The date is 1866.
84. In 1881 Lord Acton—*Letters of Lord Acton to Mary, Daughter of the Right Hon. W. E. Gladstone*, ed. Herbert Paul (London, 1904), p. 70—remarked, apropos of Carlyle and Froude as historians, "The doctrine of heroes, the doctrine that will is above law, comes next in atrocity to the doctrine that the flag covers the goods."

—and the artists wanted to write it—because it satisfied a purely emotional need as imperious as any desire they had for didactic inspiration. It served them precisely as Scott served the people of Cowfold in Mark Rutherford's novel. By introducing them into a "society of noble friends," he not only added to the ordinary motives which prompted Cowfold action a thousand higher motives, he also transported them into another world and another age far away from Cowfold cares.[85] The same dual purpose is seen in Arnold's theory of the grand style. Its supreme function, to "inspirit and rejoice the reader," meant more than its power to animate and ennoble. "For the Muses," he went on at once to say, quoting Hesiod, "were born that they might be 'a forgetfulness of evils, and a truce from cares.'" Later, in the central statement, the modern poet was told to turn away from an age so wanting in moral grandeur, so full of spiritual discomfort, and "to delight himself with the contemplation of some noble action of a heroic time, and to enable others, through his representation of it, to delight in it also." Plainly the delight is that of being forgetful as much as feeling inspirited.[86] The extraordinary popularity of Greek myths and medieval legends, of Kingsley's *Heroes* and Tennyson's *Idylls* and Morris' *Jason*, and all the volumes of Golden Deeds and Ages of Fable lay in their fortuitous power to give the anxious Victorians, weighed down by the commercial meanness and the intellectual difficulties of the time, the two things they most desired: inspiration and escape.

The escape had the special attraction of a flight *from* thwarted impulses *to* an ideal fulfillment. Surprising as it seems (because we associate the Victorians with forceful energy) the upper levels of social and intellectual life suffered from a marked feeling of impotence and timidity. What Tancred said of his contemporaries—that is, Disraeli's—was a common complaint: "No one has confidence in himself; on the contrary, every one has a mean idea of his own strength and has no reliance on his own judgment. Men obey a general impulse, they bow before an external necessity, whether for resistance or action. Individuality is dead; there is a want of inward and personal energy in man; and that is what people feel and mean when they go about complaining there is no faith." [87] That state of

85. *The Revolution in Tanner's Lane* (first ed. 1887; 10th ed. London, n.d.), p. 277.

86. Preface to *Poems* (1853), in *Poetical Works*, pp. xviii, xxix–xxx.

87. Chap. 20, in *Works*, 15, 190. The date is 1847. In addition to the extensive evidence that follows, there is Bagehot's observation in "Mr. Clough's Poems"

mind is attributable partly to the ennui and frustration which accompanied the collapse of traditional belief, and partly to certain philosophical theories and social conditions (referred to here as "external necessity"). Whatever its origin, the mood of weakness found the anti-self in the image of the hero, strong in both decisive force and mastery of circumstance.

Its appeal to the Arnolds of the "Scholar-Gipsy," with their endless hesitations and vague resolves that bear no fruit because not clearly willed, could be assumed even without the added evidence from other poems:

> I too have long'd for trenchant force,
> And will like a dividing spear;
> Have praised the keen, unscrupulous course,
> Which knows no doubt, which feels no fear.
>
> Those sterner spirits let me prize,
> Who, though the tendence of the whole
> They less than us might recognize,
> Kept, more than us, their strength of soul.
>
> Yes, be the second Cato prais'd!
> Not that he took the course to die—
> But that, when 'gainst himself he rais'd
> His arm, he rais'd it dauntlessly.
>
> And, Byron! let us dare admire,
> If not thy fierce and turbid song,
> Yet that, in anguish, doubt, desire,
> Thy fiery courage still was strong. . . .
>
> Our bane, disguise it as we may,
> Is weakness, is a faltering course.[88]

The heroes invoked by Arnold in "Rugby Chapel" are "beacons of hope" not only for what they may do (to inspire our "fainting, dispirited race") but for what they are—or rather, are not:

(1862), *Works*, *1*, 175: "In the present state of the world . . . there is a superfluity of persons who have all the knowledge, all the culture, all the requisite taste, —all the tools, in short, of achievement, but who are deficient in the latent impulse and secret vigor which alone can turn such instruments to account."

88. "A Farewell," lines 33–6, and "Courage," lines 9–20, 25–6.

> Languor is not in your heart,
> Weakness is not in your word,
> Weariness not on your brow.[89]

A letter of Kingsley's in which he describes one of the periodic depressions that left him fatigued in body and mind and crying out for "life, life!" ends with the remark, "I wish I could see your father once! I like to look in the faces of strong good men, and to hear the tones of their voice. I don't mind what they say. It is the men themselves I love to contemplate." [90] Their strength is manifested especially in vigorous action. To the intellectual, submerged and baffled by the sterile analysis of modern problems and doubts, feeling by moments so lacking in blood, so emasculated, the heroic life was a vitalizing image. Carlyle was thinking of himself as well as his contemporaries when he traced the popularity of Scott to the fact that, living in an age "fallen into spiritual langour, destitute of belief, yet terrified at Scepticism; reduced to live a stinted half-life . . . the reader was carried back to rough strong times, wherein those maladies of ours had not yet arisen. Brawny fighters, all cased in buff and iron, their hearts too sheathed in oak and triple brass . . . went forth in the most determined manner, nothing doubting. The reader sighed, *yet not without a reflex solacement:* 'O, that I too had lived in those times, had never known these logic-cobwebs, this doubt, this sickliness; and been and felt myself alive among men alive!' " [91]

The analogue in critical theory is objective art. The general influence of Romanticism, reinforced by the introspective and analytical pressures of the time, made a subjective account of the mind so popular it was called " 'the highest thing that one can attempt in the way of poetry' "; [92] so natural that the two major poems of the

89. Lines 193–5. The implied contrast with "our" gives the repeated "your" a secondary stress. In Clough's "Review of Some Poems by Alexander Smith and Matthew Arnold," *Prose Remains*, pp. 372, 374, he sees the two poets as representative, respectively, of "unquestioning, unhesitating confidence" and "ascetic and timid self-culture"; speaks of there being something "of an over-educated weakness of purpose in Western Europe"; and expresses his "preference for the picture of simple, strong, and certain [in Smith's poetry], rather than of subtle, shifting, and dubious feelings [in Arnold's]." Since he and Arnold were two of a kind, this shows Clough's longing for the anti-self.

90. *Letters and Memories*, 2, 115 (unabridged ed., 2, 94).

91. "Sir Walter Scott," *Essays*, 4, 56. The italics are mine. Cf. 4, 50.

92. David Masson, as quoted by Arnold in the 1853 Preface, *Poetical Works*, p. xxiv. The source is Masson's "Theories of Poetry and a New Poet," *North British Review, 19* (1853), 338, partly reprinted in his *Essays* (Cambridge, 1856).

age, *In Memoriam* (1850) and "Empedocles on Etna" (1852), are subjective accounts of the Victorian soul, in which the poet

> Tells us his misery's birth and growth and signs,
>   And how the dying spark of hope was fed,
>   And how the breast was soothed, and how the head,
> And all his hourly varied anodynes.

No wonder Arnold, who was describing *In Memoriam*, I take it, in those lines,[93] and who rejected his own "Empedocles" because it was a story of inner suffering unrelieved by action, insisted that the grand style and not "an allegory of the state of one's own mind" was the right form of poetry, and cited the contrast between early Greek art and the later fragments of Empedocles: "The calm, the cheerfulness, the disinterested objectivity have disappeared: the dialogue of the mind with itself has commenced; modern problems have presented themselves; we hear already the doubts, we witness the discouragement, of Hamlet and of Faust." [94] His successor at Oxford as professor of poetry, J. C. Shairp, recommended "the bracing atmosphere of Homer, and Shakespeare, and Scott" as the most effective antidote against the whole subjective tendency of modern poetry and fiction, "so weakening, so morbidly self-conscious, so unhealthily introspective"; and another Victorian critic praised the poets of the Middle Ages because they were little addicted to "dissection of the passions, reflections upon the operations of their own minds, morbid self-anatomy," and thus wrote a dramatic art far superior to the "analytic" art of modern Europe.[95] It was that point of view, I suggest, which led Arnold to turn from "Empedocles" to *Sohrab and Rustum* and *Balder Dead*, and Tennyson from *In Memoriam* and *Maud* to the *Idylls;* and which directed the Pre-Raphaelite poets to Greek and medieval legend. For the same reason the public welcomed the new

93. "The Scholar-Gipsy," lines 187–90. The case for Tennyson has been well argued by C. B. Tinker and H. F. Lowry, *The Poetry of Matthew Arnold: a Commentary* (London and New York, 1940), pp. 209–11.

94. Preface to 1853 edition of *Poems,* in *Poetical Works,* xvii–xix, xxiv.

95. Shairp, "The Homeric Spirit in Walter Scott," *Aspects of Poetry,* pp. 405–6; "Gothic Art—John Ruskin," *London Quarterly Review,* 7 (1856–57), 490. Cf. Yeats' account—*The Autobiography of William Butler Yeats* (New York, 1938), p. 131—of standing before the statues of Mausolus and Artemisia in the British Museum, seeing them as "images of an unpremeditated joyous energy, that neither I nor any other man, racked by doubt and inquiry, can achieve," and longing to create once more a simple, objective art like that "in some old Scots ballads, or . . . Arthurian Romance."

narrative poetry. On the face of it, no one would expect a man like John Morley, so deeply concerned with social problems and political causes, to find anything to praise in the Pre-Raphaelites. But he hailed "such a poet as Mr. Morris" at a time "when lovers of poetry are overwearied with excess of purely subjective verse . . . We nowhere see in his work the enfeebling influences of the little doubtings, and little believings, and little wonderings, whose thin wail sounds in a conventional manner through so much of our current writing, whether in prose or verse, weakening life and distorting art. Mr. Morris's central quality is a vigorous and healthy objectivity." [96]

The complement of feeling indecisive and morbidly introspective is the sense of being small and inconsequential, caught in the iron grip of huge social or physical forces, with one's potential greatness thwarted and dammed up. In that state of mind the image of the hero in all his free, creative power is enormously attractive. One's faith in man is revived, if not as an intellectual conviction, at least as an emotional attitude. And one feels personally released from the bonds of "Fate and Circumstance"; even capable of heroic action.

> Yet now, when boldest wills give place,
> When Fate and Circumstance are strong,
> And in their rush the human race
> Are swept, like huddling sheep, along;
>
> Those sterner spirits let me prize,
> Who, though the tendence of the whole
> They less than us might recognize,
> Kept, more than us, their strength of soul.[97]

"Circumstance" refers, I take it, to the social determinism which the Victorians inherited from eighteenth-century rationalism (mind and character are built up by the influence of the environment) and

96. *Fortnightly Review*, new ser. 3 (1868), 713–14. Cf. Kingsley, "Poems of Matthew Arnold," *Fraser's Magazine*, 49 (1854), 140 (attributed to him by Thorp, *Kingsley*, p. 195): "All that the singer can do, unless he chooses to degrade his powers, by setting to rhyme the spiritual dyspepsia of an unhealthy and nerveless time, is to betake himself to the greater dead; to reproduce, as well as he can, their thoughts, their forms; perhaps to awaken men to admire—to make them imitate is now hopeless—the noble deeds of their forefathers." This, he says, is a common point of view with which he largely agrees.

97. Arnold, "Courage," lines 5–12.

which was reinforced by the scientific conception of history. Its psychological impact was described by Carlyle: "Yes, Reader, all this that thou hast so often heard about 'force of circumstances,' 'the creature of the time,' 'balancing of motives,' and who knows what melancholy stuff to the like purport, *wherein thou, as in a nightmare Dream, sittest paralysed, and hast no force left,*—was in very truth . . . little other than a hag-ridden vision of death-sleep." The remark occurs in the essay on Boswell's *Johnson,* where Carlyle is claiming that the life of every great man preaches "these gladdest tidings" that he "is not the thrall of Circumstances, of Necessity, but the victorious subduer thereof"—preaches them *"to the eye and heart and whole man."* Not by argument addressed to the intellect, but through the immediate vision of a triumphant hero can the reader feel the inner joy of renewed energy and freedom.[98]

Another theory which raised a paralyzing nightmare was the conception of man as a human automaton, whose actions and thoughts were controlled by the total physical environment. No one can read Victorian literature without recognizing the painful, indeed agonizing, sense of being caught in a vast mechanism of scientific law. "The advancing tide of matter threatens to drown their souls; the tightening grip of law impedes their freedom." [99] In such a state of apprehension the hero embodies everything one longs to hold on to: the self-reliance, the moral character freely choosing the nobler course of action, the dynamic power of the human will. It is significant that when Arnold's niece, Mrs. Humphry Ward, spoke of Amiel (who was born in 1828) as representative of a generation "more widely conscious than its predecessors of the limitations of the human mind, and of the iron pressure of man's physical environment," she at once added, "But at the same time—paradox as it may seem—more conscious of man's greatness, more deeply thrilled by the spectacle of the nobility and beauty interwoven with the universe." [100] The paradox was only ap-

98. *Essays, 3,* 90–1. The italics are mine. Cf. James Martineau, "Personal Influences on Present Theology," *Essays, Reviews, and Addresses, 1,* 278: "In a world of mere 'general laws,' it would ever remain a melancholy thing to see living heroes and saints struck down at the altar of 'historical tendency' by some shadowy dagger of necessity. Love, enthusiasm, devotion, need some concrete and living object; if not to command their allegiance, at least to turn it from sorrow into joy."

99. Cf. above, pp. 70–1, where the quotation (from Huxley) is given at greater length.

100. Introduction to her translation of *Amiel's Journal* (first ed. 1885; New York, n.d.), p. liii.

parent. In Pater the two points of view were consciously related. One function of art, he suggested, was the alleviation of the scientific nightmare by the picture of noble human beings nobly facing the cosmic tragedy: "The chief factor in the thoughts of the modern mind concerning itself is the intricacy, the universality of natural law, even in the moral order. . . . Can art represent men and women in these bewildering toils *so as to give the spirit at least an equivalent for the sense of freedom?* . . . Natural laws we shall never modify, embarrass us as they may; but there is still something in the nobler or less noble attitude with which we watch their fatal combinations." [101] There is still compensation, that is to say, in heroic literature.

Quite apart, however, from all speculative theories of the nature of man and society, the social life of England, as the intellectuals observed it, was pushing the individual, especially the great individual, to the wall. The common complaint is that the age was becoming "the paradise of little men, and the purgatory of great ones"; that "a great career is hardly possible any longer" because "the world tends to become more comfortable for the mass, and more uncomfortable for those of any natural gift or distinction"; that "the general tendency of things throughout the world is to render mediocrity the ascendant power among mankind." [102] All this seemed the inevitable result of the new democracy, political and social, which greatly increased the competition for positions of authority and prestige, and gave the average man, speaking through the voice of public opinion—mass public opinion—tremendous influence over thought and conduct. "In ancient history," wrote Mill, "in the Middle Ages, and in a diminishing degree through the long transition from feudality to the present time, the individual was a power in himself; and if he had either great talents or a high social position, he was a considerable power. At present individuals are lost in the crowd." [103] In a passage on the force of public opinion, which Mill quoted at length, the French historian Guizot drew a significant contrast between the old feudalism and the new democracy:

> We have lived for half a century under the empire of general ideas, more and more accredited and powerful. . . . There has

101. "Winckelmann" (1867), *The Renaissance*, pp. 244–5. The italics are mine.
102. Newman, "Who's to Blame?" *Discussion and Arguments on Various Subjects* (London, 1882), p. 343; Arnold, *Letters to Clough*, p. 122; Mill, *On Liberty*, chap. 3, p. 165.
103. *On Liberty*, p. 165.

resulted a certain weakness, a certain effeminacy, in our minds and characters. Individual convictions and will are wanting in energy and confidence in themselves. Men assent to a prevailing opinion, obey a general impulse, yield to an external necessity. Whether for resistance or for action, each has but a mean idea of his own strength, a feeble reliance on his own judgment. Individuality, the inward and personal energy of man, is weak and timid. Amidst the progress of public liberty, many seem to have lost the proud and invigorating sentiment of their own personal liberty.

In the Middle Ages, however, though morality was far inferior, "individuality was strong, will was energetic." [104] That the philosophers exaggerated the democratic threat to personal freedom and initiative may well be true. But it is irrelevant. All that was needed to turn men's minds nostalgically to "some noble action of an heroic time" (especially a feudal time) was the depressing conviction that the individual was withering and the world was more and more.[105]

What made the situation worse—and the reaction the more compelling—was that "great qualities," let alone great individuals, were being lost in the advancing tide of mercantile and social ambition.

> The brave, impetuous heart yields everywhere
> To the subtle, contriving head;
> Great qualities are trodden down,
> And littleness united
> Is become invincible.[106]

But once upon a time, before the Deluge, there were heroes. Through thee, wrote Arnold of his father,

> through thee I believe
> In the noble and great who are gone;
> Pure souls honour'd and blest
> By former ages, who else—
> Such, so soulless, so poor,
> Is the race of men whom I see—

104. Quoted by Mill, "Guizot's Essays and Lectures on History," *Dissertations*, 2, 267.

105. The reference is to Tennyson's "Locksley Hall," line 142. Cf. Kingsley, cited in note 96 above: "It is not an aristocratic age, an age of heroes; but a democratic one, in which men think and act in masses."

106. Arnold, "Empedocles on Etna," Act II, lines 90–4.

> Seem'd but a dream of the heart,
> Seem'd but a cry of desire.
> Yes! I believe that there lived
> Others like thee in the past,
> Not like the men of the crowd
> Who all round me to-day
> Bluster or cringe, and make life
> Hideous, and arid, and vile;
> But souls temper'd with fire,
> Fervent, heroic, and good,
> Helpers and friends of mankind.[107]

Clearly, they are still a dream of the heart and a cry of desire.

The truce from cares which the Victorians found in contemplating the hero is a truce from the cares of living in a world where one feels an acute sense of weakness, whether engendered by indecision and enervating analysis (of abstract ideas or personal distress) or by the cramping pressure of "fate and circumstance." The reaction is psychological and nostalgic. But hero worship was equally indebted—and in the same minds, as we have seen, notably in the case of Arnold—to a reaction against the same general environment which was didactic and positive; which sought to meet the moral needs of a period of doubt and bourgeois democracy by exalting the hero, whether in history or in legend. It was because the heroic image could serve so ambiguously as message and as compensation that it won so conspicuous a place in the Victorian imagination.

107. "Rugby Chapel," lines 145–61.

Chapter 13

LOVE

> Love for the maiden, crown'd with marriage, no re-
> grets for aught that has been,
> Household happiness, gracious children, debtless com-
> petence, golden mean.
>
> *Tennyson* [1]

The Angel in the House—there in the title of Coventry Patmore's famous poem is the essential character of Victorian love (though not its only form in the period): the passion that was very much tempered by reverence and confined to the home—that is, to potential or actual marriage—and the object that was scarcely mortal. Otherwise love was not love but lust. This conception looks like a curious blending of Protestant earnestness and Romantic enthusiasm, with a strong assist from chivalric literature (as ready a source for woman worship as for hero worship). But seeds explain nothing apart from the receptive soil. The circumstances of Victorian society made bliss connubial; and, indeed, even apart from love, decreed the exaltation of family life and feminine character.

1. *Home, Sweet Home*

At the center of Victorian life was the family. Its ritual is well known: the gathering of the whole household for family prayers, the attendance together at church on Sunday morning, the reading aloud in the evenings, the annual family vacation. On the living-room table lay family magazines and the family photograph album. Since women have always been concerned with the home, this special development in the Victorian period must be attributed to a reorientation of the masculine attitude. In the eighteenth century the coffee house had

1. "Vastness," stanza 12.

341

often been the center of man's social life. There he smoked, dined, wrote letters, discussed politics and literature, and got drunk. A manual for gentlemen, written in 1778, urged them to beware "of thinking domestic pleasures, cares, and duties, beneath their notice." [2] The radical change which occurred in the next century was recorded and partly explained by Mill in 1869:

> The association of men with women in daily life is much closer and more complete than it ever was before. Men's life is more domestic. Formerly, their pleasures and chosen occupations were among men, and in men's company: their wives had but a fragment of their lives. At the present time, the progress of civilization, and the turn of opinion against the rough amusements and convivial excesses which formerly occupied most men in their hours of relaxation—together with (it must be said) the improved tone of modern feeling as to the reciprocity of duty which binds the husband towards the wife—have thrown the man very much more upon home and its inmates, for his personal and social pleasures: while the kind and degree of improvement which has been made in women's education, has made them in some degree capable of being his companions in ideas and mental tastes. [3]

Better education was hardly a factor before the fifties, but the reaction against convivial excesses and the greater sense of duty may be traced to the Evangelical revival. Moreover, life became more domestic than it had been earlier because of the mere existence of large families. The improvement in medical knowledge and standards of sanitation, reducing infant mortality, and the general ignorance of contraceptives (because information lay under the severest social and legal restraints) increased the size and complicated the problems of the home. Men were required to give far more time and attention to the business of the family; and in the middle class that necessity was reinforced by ambition. Now that work had become the means not simply of maintaining a family but of raising it on the social ladder, fathers were preoccupied with getting their sons into the "best" colleges at Oxford and Cambridge or setting them up in a good profession, and marrying their daughters to gentlemen of birth. [4]

2. See H. V. Routh, *Money, Morals and Manners as Revealed in Modern Literature*, chap. 10, "The Idea of Home," p. 143, where the quotation may be found.

3. *The Subjection of Women*, chap. 4, p. 540.

4. Cf. Mr. Vincy's remark in *Middlemarch, I*, chap. 13, p. 173: "It's a good British feeling to try and raise your family a little: in my opinion, it's a father's

But none of this goes to the root of the matter, for the greater *amount* of family life and thought would not in itself have created "that peculiar sense of solemnity" with which, in the eyes of a typical Victorian like Thomas Arnold, "the very *idea* of family life was invested." [5] That idea was the conception of the home as a source of virtues and emotions which were nowhere else to be found, least of all in business and society.[6] And that in turn made it a place radically different from the surrounding world. It was much more than a house where one stopped at night for temporary rest and recreation—or procreation—in the midst of a busy career. It was a place apart, a walled garden, in which certain virtues too easily crushed by modern life could be preserved, and certain desires of the heart too much thwarted be fulfilled. Here is Ruskin's definition in *Sesame and Lilies:*

> This is the true nature of home—it is the place of Peace; the shelter, not only from all injury, but from all terror, doubt, and division. In so far as it is not this, it is not home; so far as the anxieties of the outer life penetrate into it, and the inconsistently-minded, unknown, unloved, or hostile society of the outer world is allowed by either husband or wife to cross the threshold, it ceases to be home; it is then only a part of that outer world which you have roofed over, and lighted fire in. But so far as it is a sacred place, a vestal temple, a temple of the hearth watched over by Household Gods . . . so far as it is this, and roof and fire are types only of a nobler shade and light,—shade as of the rock in a weary land, and light as of the Pharos in the stormy sea;—so far it vindicates the name, and fulfils the praise, of Home.[7]

The final metaphors of shade and light underscore the dual character of the Victorian home and reflect its psychological and ethical appeals. It was both a shelter *from* the anxieties of modern life, a place of peace where the longings of the soul might be realized (if not in fact, in imagination), and a shelter *for* those moral and spiritual values which the commercial spirit and the critical spirit were threatening to destroy, and therefore also a sacred place, a temple.

duty to give his sons a fine chance." Cf. Mrs. Craik, *John Halifax, Gentleman,* chap. 29, p. 412. See, in general, above, Chap. 8, sec. 1.

5. Stanley, *Life of Arnold,* chap. 4, p. 205. The italics are mine.

6. Cf. Routh, *Money, Morals and Manners,* p. 142.

7. "Of Queens' Gardens," sec. 68, in *Works, 18,* 122. This lecture of Ruskin's is the most important single document I know for the characteristic idealization of love, woman, and the home in Victorian thought.

The peace it promised was partly, to vary Ruskin's metaphor, that of a rock in the midst of a rushing stream. As most traditional beliefs and institutions on which stability depends were being questioned or transformed, the Victorian clung the harder to the oldest of all traditions and stressed its ordered hierarchy and daily ritual. Here at any rate was something firm to stand on. But this, I think, was largely unconscious. The conscious association of family life with security took another form. The home became the place where one *had* been at peace and childhood a blessed time when truth was certain and doubt with its divisive effects unknown. In the "strange ways of feeling and thought" that in later life enveloped Pater's child in the house and left him isolated and alone, he felt "the wistful yearning towards home." [8] So did the skeptic in Froude's essay on homesickness, who looked back to what was literally a paradise:

> God has given us each our own Paradise, our own old childhood, over which the old glories linger—to which our own hearts cling, as all we have ever known of Heaven upon earth. And there, as all earth's weary wayfarers turn back their toil-jaded eyes, so do the poor speculators, one of whom is this writer, whose thoughts have gone astray, who has been sent out like the raven from the window of the ark, and flown to and fro over the ocean of speculation, finding no place for his soul to rest, no pause for his aching wings, turn back in thought, at least, to that old time of peace—that village church—that child-faith—which, once lost, is never gained again—strange mystery—is never gained again—with sad and weary longing!

Plainly nostalgia of this kind helped to idealize the Victorian home. [9]

A more important factor, working to the same end, was the impact of modern business. In the recoil from the City, the home was irradiated by the light of a pastoral imagination. It could seem a country of peace and innocence where life was kind and duty natural.

8. *Miscellaneous Studies. A Series of Essays* (New York, 1900), p. 154.

9. *The Nemesis of Faith*, p. 116; and cf. a similar passage quoted above, p. 86. The "essay" is on pp. 108–17. The nostalgia was felt not only by the "speculators" but also, as Froude implies, by "earth's weary wayfarers." The rapid increase of emigration to the colonies brought the homesickness of the exile into many a letter. In the same essay, Froude wrote (p. 110): "Far round the earth as their life callings may have scattered men, here is their treasure, for here their heart has been"; and here they often return as if to tie up the "broken links" so that the family may go together to "the long home where they shall never part again."

For something that abode endued
   With temple-like repose, an air
Of life's kind purposes pursued
   With order'd freedom sweet and fair.
A tent pitch'd in a world not right
   It seem'd, whose inmates, every one,
On tranquil faces bore the light
   Of duties beautifully done.[10]

In a sermon of Baldwin Brown's, women are told to remember the need of "world-weary men" and therefore to "pray, think, strive to make a home something like a bright, serene, restful, joyful nook of heaven in an unheavenly world." [11]

In the home so conceived, man could recover the humanity he seemed to be losing. Under the intense pressure of competitive life, he felt more and more like a money-making machine, or a cog in the vast mechanism of modern business. He was haunted, as Routh has said, by a specter staring back at him in the mirror, a hard-faced, dwarfish caricature of himself, unpleasantly like the economic man.[12] His emotions of pity and love seemed to be drying up; he was losing the sense of relatedness as superiors, inferiors, and equals were becoming actual or potential enemies. But in the home he might escape from this inhuman world, at least for part of every day (which was all he wanted). He might feel his heart beating again in the atmosphere of domestic affection and the binding companionship of a family. It is significant that when Carlyle described the world of big business, he called it "a world alien, not your world . . . not a home at all, of hearts and faces who are yours, whose you are" and said that to live in it was to be "without father, without child, without brother." [13] But the hour strikes and all that is lost may be found again: "When we come home, we lay aside our mask and drop our tools, and are no longer lawyers, sailors, soldiers, statesmen, clergymen, but only men. We fall again into our most human relations, which, after all, are the whole of what belongs to us as we are ourselves, and alone have the key-note of our hearts. There our skill, if skill we have, is exercised with real gladness on

10. Patmore, "The Angel in the House," Bk. I, end of Canto I, *Poems*, p. 69. Cf. Bk. II, Canto III, opening poem, p. 154.

11. *Young Men and Maidens. A Pastoral for the Times* (London, 1871), pp. 38–9.

12. *Money, Morals and Manners*, pp. 141, 147–8.

13. *Past and Present*, Bk. IV, chap. 4, p. 274. Cf. above, Chap. 3, start of sec. 6, on economic isolation.

home subjects. . . . We cease the struggle in the race of the world, and give our hearts leave and leisure to love." [14]

Or at a lower social and economic level, one escapes from a cold, domineering Scrooge to the freedom and warmth of the family hearth. Mark Rutherford was simply a more intellectual Mr. Wemmick when he cultivated a deliberate dissociation of his personality so that his "true self" should not be stained by contact with the self that was subjected to the petty spite and brutal tyranny of an office. Then on the stroke of seven he could become himself again: "I was on equal terms with my friends; I was Ellen's husband; I was, in short, a man." And he goes on to speak of happy evenings reading aloud with his wife.[15] Small wonder the Victorian home was sentimentalized. In the reaction from a heartless world, the domestic emotions were released too strongly and indulged too eagerly. Indeed, it may be only by the unabashed display of feeling that one can prove unmistakably to all the world, himself included, that he has a heart. Barnes Newcome knew his audience when he lectured at the Athenaeum on Mrs. Hemans and the poetry of the affections:

> A public man, a commercial man as we well know, yet his heart is in his home, and his joy in his affections: the presence of this immense assembly here this evening; of the industrious capitalists; of the intelligent middle class; of the pride and mainstay of England, the operatives of Newcome; these surrounded by their wives and their children (a graceful bow to the bonnets to the right of the platform), show that they, too, have hearts to feel, and homes to cherish; that they, too, feel the love of women, the innocence of children, the love of song! [16]

The Victorian home was not only a peaceful, it was a sacred, place. When the Christian tradition as it was formally embodied in ecclesiastical rites and theological dogmas was losing its hold on contemporary society, and the influence of the pastorate was declining, the living church more and more became the "temple of the hearth." [17] This was

14. Froude, *The Nemesis of Faith*, pp. 112–13.

15. *Mark Rutherford's Deliverance*, chap. 8, pp. 106–7. Mr. Wemmick is Mr. Jagger's clerk in Dickens' *Great Expectations*.

16. Thackeray, *The Newcomes*, chap. 66, pp. 687–8.

17. Cf. G. K. Chesterton, *Autobiography* (New York, 1936), p. 20, speaking of the Victorians: "Theirs was the first generation that ever asked its children to worship the hearth without the altar." He went on to say that "this was equally true, whether they went to church at eleven o'clock . . . or were reverently agnostic or latitudinarian."

not entirely a metaphor. By the use of Christian Platonism, the home was sanctified. As it was a sacred place for Ruskin because its roof and fire were types of a nobler shade and light, so for Baldwin Brown it was made by God, like the first man, "after a divine original." [18] To Kingsley all domestic relations were "given us to teach us their divine antitypes [God the Father, Christ the husband of the one corporate person the Church, and all men children of the same Heavenly Father]: and therefore . . . it is only in proportion as we appreciate and understand the types that we can understand the antitypes." He was even ready to imply that a bachelor was at some disadvantage: "Fully to understand the meaning of 'a Father in Heaven' we must be fathers ourselves; to know how Christ loved the Church, we must have wives to love, and love them." And to be religious, especially for a woman, we must do good in those simple everyday relations and duties of the family "which are most divine because they are most human." [19] In this way the moral authority and inspiration of the church was being transferred to the home without any apparent break with the Christian tradition.

For the agnostics, also, the home became a temple—a secular temple. For them the family was the basic source of those altruistic emotions they relied upon to take the place of the Christian ethic. It was there, they thought, that all who had thrown off the trammels of superstition might learn the "sentiment (1) of *attachment*, comradeship, fellowship, (2) of *reverence* for those who can teach us, guide, and elevate us, (3) of *love* which urges us to protect, help, and cherish those to whom we owe our lives and better natures." [20] No doubt one might, in fact, learn quite different things, as Mill pointed out, but in its best forms he too recognized the family as "a school of sympathy, tenderness, and loving forgetfulness of self." [21] As such, it was the foundation for the Religion of Humanity. These generous sentiments, once learned in the home, might be extended later to the human race and the future of civilization.[22]

18. *The Home Life: in the Light of Its Divine Idea*, p. 8.

19. Kingsley, *Letters and Memories*, *1*, 166, 222, 361–2 (unabridged ed., *1*, 190, 255, 431).

20. Frederic Harrison, lecture on "Family Life," *On Society* (London, 1918), p. 33. The lecture was given in 1893, but the point of view goes back at least to the sixties: see the next notes.

21. *The Subjection of Women*, chap. 2, p. 469.

22. This paragraph, it will be noticed, is closely related to a passage in Chap. 11, "Enthusiasm," pp. 271–2, above. Harrison, Mill, and George Eliot, like most of the agnostics who advocate a Religion of Humanity in some form or other, were

But whether a sacred temple or a secular temple, the home as a storehouse of moral and spiritual values was as much an answer to increasing commercialism as to declining religion. Indeed, it might be said that mainly on the shoulders of its priestess, the wife and mother, fell the burden of stemming the amoral and irreligious drift of modern industrial society.

2. Woman

Of the three conceptions of woman current in the Victorian period, the best known is that of the submissive wife whose whole excuse for being was to love, honor, obey—and amuse—her lord and master, and to manage his household and bring up his children. In that role her character and her life were completely distinct from his:

> Man for the field and woman for the hearth;
> Man for the sword, and for the needle she;
> Man with the head, and woman with the heart;
> Man to command, and woman to obey;
> All else confusion.

Against that conservative view, spoken by the Prince's father in Tennyson's poem,[23] the Princess Ida represents the most advanced thought. She is the "new woman," in revolt against her legal and social bondage (and against the boredom of life in homes where servants and nurses now do all the household chores), and demanding equal rights with men: the same education, the same suffrage, the same opportunity for professional and political careers. Ida's passionate oration closes with a prophecy which Tennyson hardly imagined would come true:

> Everywhere
> Two heads in council, two beside the hearth,
> Two in the tangled business of the world,
> Two in the liberal offices of life,
> Two plummets dropt for one to sound the abyss

---

partly indebted for their ideas on the family (and therefore also on woman) to Auguste Comte's *Système de politique positive, ou traité de sociologie, instituant la religion de l'humanité* (4 vols. Paris, 1851–54). For a convenient summary by Comte himself see *A General View of Positivism*, translated by J. H. Bridges (London, 1865), chap. 4, "The Influence of Positivism upon Women."

23. *The Princess* (1847), Pt. V, lines 437–41. See John Killham, *Tennyson and "The Princess": Reflections of an Age* (London, 1958) for an illuminating account of the whole question.

> Of science and the secrets of the mind;
> Musician, painter, sculptor, critic, more.[24]

Between these two poles there was a middle position entirely characteristic of the time in its mediation between conservative and radical
thinking. By all means let us remove the legal disabilities and give
"more breadth of culture"; but higher education is unwise, the vote
is dubious, and professional careers are dangerous. For after all woman
is *not* man; she has her own nature and function in life, not inferior
to his but entirely different; and the only test to apply to the "woman
question" is simply, "Does this study or this activity help or injure her
womanhood?" That is Tennyson's stand, expounded by the Prince and
Ida at the close of the poem. Together they

> Will clear away the parasitic forms
> That seem to keep her up but drag her down—
> Will leave her space to burgeon out of all
> Within her—let her make herself her own
> To give or keep, to live and learn and be
> All that not harms distinctive womanhood.
> For woman is not undevelopt man,
> But diverse.

Let be with the proud watchword of "equal,"

> seeing either sex alone
> Is half itself, and in true marriage lies
> Nor equal, nor unequal. Each fulfils
> Defect in each.[25]

What is meant by "distinctive womanhood" and what defect in man
the woman should fulfill are only implied by Tennyson. The answers
are spelled out in Ruskin's important lecture "Of Queens' Gardens" in
1865. There he begins by rejecting the notion both that woman is "the
shadow and attendant image of her lord, owing him a thoughtless and
servile obedience," and that she has a feminine mission and feminine
rights that entitle her to a career in the world like man's. Her true
function is to guide and uplift her more worldly and intellectual mate:
"His intellect is for speculation and invention; his energy for adven-

24. Ibid., Pt. II, lines 155–61. Amy Cruse, *The Victorians and Their Reading,*
chap. 16, gives a good sketch of "The New Woman," with many illustrations from
contemporary literature.
25. *The Princess,* Pt. VII, lines 253–60, 283–6.

ture, for war, and for conquest, wherever war is just, wherever conquest necessary. But the woman's power is for rule, not for battle,—and her intellect is not for invention or creation, but for sweet ordering, arrangement, and decision." Although this lofty theory had been gaining ground through the 1850's, Ruskin is aware that he is challenging the ordinary assumptions of male superiority and command. He marshals his evidence. In Shakespeare and Scott, in Dante and Homer, women are "infallibly faithful and wise counsellors"; and by their virtue and wisdom men are redeemed from weakness or vice. Then, with their role defined, he proceeds at once to his description of the home, since it is women so conceived who make it a temple and a school of virtue. The more reason, therefore, to keep it a walled garden. While the man in his rough work must encounter all peril and trial, and often be subdued or misled, and always hardened, "he guards the woman from all this; within his house, as ruled by her, unless she herself has sought it, need enter no danger, no temptation, no cause of error or offence." [26]

This woman worship, as it came to be called in the sixties, was as much indebted to the need for fresh sources of moral inspiration as it was to Romanticism in general. In a sketch by Lancelot Smith, the hero of Kingsley's *Yeast* (made, it should be noted, when his only bible was Bacon), Woman was portrayed walking across a desert, the half-risen sun at her back and a cross in her right hand, "emblem of self-sacrifice." In the foreground were scattered groups of men. As they caught sight of this "new and divine ideal of her sex,"

> the scholar dropt his book, the miser his gold, the savage his weapons; even in the visage of the half-slumbering sot some nobler recollection seemed wistfully to struggle into life. . . . The sage . . . watched with a thoughtful smile that preacher more mighty than himself. A youth, decked out in the most fantastic fopperies of the middle age, stood with clasped hands and brimming eyes, as remorse and pleasure struggled in his face; and as

26. "Of Queens' Gardens," sec. 68 in *Works, 18,* 111–22. With the last remark cf. George Eliot in "Amos Barton," *Scenes of Clerical Life, 1,* chap. 7, p. 85: "A loving woman's world lies within the four walls of her own home; and it is only through her husband that she is in any electric communication with the world beyond." In *Silas Marner* the bad habits of Godfrey and Dunstan Cass are attributed mainly to their growing up in a home without a mother (chap. 3, pp. 30–1), and Godfrey longs to marry Nancy Lammeter because she "would make home lovely" and help him conquer his weakness of will (chap. 3, pp. 39–41)—which is exactly what she does effect after the marriage (chap. 17, pp. 207–8).

he looked, the fierce sensual features seemed to melt, and his flesh came again to him like the flesh of a little child.

The drawing is entitled "Triumph of Woman." [27] Other writers emphasized a more specific mission in more mundane terms: to counteract the debasing influence on religion as well as morals of a masculine life preoccupied with worldly goods and worldly ambitions. Mrs. Sara Ellis, whose *Daughters of England, Wives of England,* and *Women of England* were standard manuals, brought that argument to bear directly on the "Behaviour to Husbands." Since the life of men, especially businessmen, is tending, she said, to lower and degrade the mind, to make its aims purely material, and to encourage a selfish concern for one's own interests, a wife should be supremely solicitous for the advancement of her husband's intellectual, moral, and spiritual nature. She should be "a companion who will raise the tone of his mind from . . . low anxieties, and vulgar cares" and will "lead his thoughts to expatiate or repose on those subjects which convey a feeling of identity with a higher state of existence beyond this present life." [28] Indeed, the moral elevation of man became so closely identified with this feminine duty that a moralist like Baldwin Brown in his sermons called *The Home Life* was ready to blame women for the deterioration of men under the hardening influence of business. They have themselves succumbed to mean desires for money and family position; or they have been seduced by the ridiculous phantom of woman's rights when their true power, the birthright they would sell for a mess of pottage, is the "power to love, to serve, to save." But many, thank God, are still faithful to their trust: "I know women whose hearts are an unfailing fountain of courage and inspiration to the hard-pressed man, who but

27. Chap. 10, pp. 148–50. Kingsley was one of the leading exponents (along with Ruskin, Tennyson, Patmore, and—more moderately—George Eliot) of this view of woman. See his statement in 1870 (*Letters and Memories,* 2, 283: unabridged ed., 2, 330): He will continue, he says, "to set forth in every book I write (as I have done for twenty-five years) woman as the teacher, the natural and therefore divine guide, purifier, inspirer of the man."

This woman worship was not, of course, universal. It is less likely to be found among "earnest" Victorians than "enthusiastic" Victorians. It is conspicuously absent from Macaulay, Carlyle, Trollope, and both the Arnolds, and from Mill as a general principle (Mrs. Taylor is a very special case!). In "Emancipation—Black and White," (1865), *Science and Education,* pp. 68–9, Huxley protested against "the new woman-worship which so many sentimentalists and some philosophers are desirous of setting up."

28. *The Wives of England. Their Relative Duties, Domestic Influence, and Social Obligations* (London, 1843), pp. 99–100.

for them must be worsted in life's battle . . . and who send forth
husband or brother each morning with new strength for his conflict,
armed, as the lady armed her knight of old, with a shield which he
may not stain in any unseemly conflicts, and a sword which he dares
only use against the enemies of truth, righteousness and God." Like
the hero, the angel in the house serves, or should serve, to preserve
and quicken the moral idealism so badly needed in an age of selfish
greed and fierce competition.[29]

This accounts (as Brown's remark would suggest) for the wide
hostility to her emancipation. Feminist claims to intellectual equality
with man and to the same education and professional opportunity
were attacked by liberals—let alone conservatives; partly, no doubt,
to forestall competition, but much more to prevent what they honestly
believed would mean the irreparable loss of a vital moral influence.
Lancelot Smith is the more eager to assert his mental superiority over
Argemone, the heroine of *Yeast* (who imagined there was no intellectual difference between the sexes), and at the same time to look up
to her "as infallible and inspired" on all "questions of morality, of taste,
of feeling," because he longs to teach her "where her true kingdom
lay,—that the heart, and not the brain, enshrines the priceless pearl
of womanhood." [30] Even a perfectly commonplace writer like Edwin
Hood calls a chapter of *The Age and Its Architects* "Woman the Reformer" and begins by announcing: "The hope of society is in woman!
The hope of the age is in woman! On her depends mainly the righting
of wrongs, the correcting of sins, and the success of all missions," and
goes on, therefore, to condemn the utterly mistaken tendency now
growing up to encourage women to enter professional and political
careers.[31] All this is touched with melodramatic and sentimental exaggeration, but many intelligent women—George Eliot, Mrs. Humphry
Ward, Mrs. Lynn Linton, Beatrice Potter Webb, for example—viewed
with uneasiness or apprehension any emancipation of their sex which
would weaken its moral influence by distracting attention to the outside world or by coarsening the feminine nature itself.[32]

29. Brown, pp. 23–5. For the hero, see above, pp. 316–18. Other reasons for
exalting the role and character of woman are dealt with below, in sec. 4 on "Love."

30. Chap. 10, pp. 143–5.

31. Pages 393, 400. The particular sins woman is to correct (pp. 393–4)—
revolution, prostitution, and atheism—are major anxieties of the period. For prostitution, see below in this Chapter, sec. 3.

32. The main document is "An Appeal against Female Suffrage," *The Nineteenth Century*, 25 (1889), 781–8, signed by about 100 women, including Mrs.

However conceived, the Victorian woman was not Venus, nor was meant to be. If it was only the feminists who rejected love—and often dressed accordingly—their more conservative sisters were not exactly objects of desire. Their sexual attraction was kept under wraps, many and voluminous. To employ it, except obliquely, was to run the risk of being considered "fast." Victorian ideas about sex were—very Victorian.

3. Sex

In the Victorian home swarming with children sex was a secret. It was the skeleton in the parental chamber. No one mentioned it. Any untoward questions were answered with a white lie (it was the great age of the stork) or a shocked rebuke. From none of his elders— parent, teacher, or minister—did the Victorian child hear "so much as one word in explanation of the true nature and functions of the re- productive organs." [33] This conspiracy of silence was partly a mistaken effort to protect the child, especially the boy, from temptation (initially from masturbation, which was condemned on grounds of health as well as morals), but at bottom it sprang from a personal feeling of revulsion. For the sexual act was associated by many wives only with a duty and by most husbands with a necessary if pleasurable yielding to one's baser nature: by few, therefore, with an innocent and joyful experience. The silence which first aroused in the child a vague sense of shame was in fact a reflection of parental shame,[34] and one suspects that some women, at any rate, would have been happy if the stork had been a reality.

At school the knowledge acquired by the boy (most girls, it would seem, knew nothing before their marriage night) came to him in whis- pers and in a form which confirmed his first impression that sex was something nasty. When he reached puberty, the elders finally spoke,

---

T. H. Huxley, Mrs. Leslie Stephen, Mrs. Matthew Arnold, Mrs. Walter Bagehot, and Mrs. Arnold Toynbee, as well as all of those cited in the text except George Eliot. For her, see Cross' *Life*, 3, 346, in his summary of her character and ideas. There is an account of this "Appeal" by Beatrice Webb, *My Apprenticeship*, pp. 302–4.

33. *The Science of Life*, p. 9. Some letters to the author by Ruskin were re- printed in *Arrows of the Chace*, in *Works*, 34, 526–31. In what follows I have drawn, in part, on this illuminating pamphlet.

34. George Eliot (*Middlemarch*, 1, chap. 15, 195) speaks of Lydgate being brought up with "a general sense of secrecy and obscenity in connection with his internal structure."

vaguely but pointedly, about "uncleanness" of body and mind. Parental letters echoed what he heard in sermons. Although learning is important, wrote Patmore to his son, other things are more so: to be honest "and to be *pure*, (you know what I mean). . . . When the other boys say and do dirty things (as many boys at all great schools will) remember those words of Jesus Christ, 'The pure in heart shall see God'—that is to say they will go to heaven." [35] And he might well have mentioned—many parents did—the source of Galahad's famous strength. As this implies, premarital continence for men (it was, of course, *de rigueur* for women) was an ideal which was widely held; and though more honored in the breach, no doubt, than in the observance, it was at any rate honored to an extent unknown in the past. Tom Brown at Oxford, attracted by the charms of a barmaid, reacts in a way which his eighteenth-century predecessors would have thought ridiculous. He tries to fight down the temptation. In Hughes' comment, the symbolism of the storm, the metaphors of evil spirits and still small voice, wild beast and true man, are the typical notes of the Victorian struggle for chastity:

> We have most of us walked the like marches at one time or another of our lives. . . . Times they were of blinding and driving storm, and howling winds, out of which voices as of evil spirits spoke close in our ears—tauntingly, temptingly whispering to the mischievous wild beast which lurks in the bottom of all our hearts. . . .
>
> And all the while . . . was there not the still small voice—never to be altogether silenced by the roarings of the tempest of passion, by the evil voices, by our own violent attempts to stifle it —the still small voice appealing to the man, the true man, within us, which is made in the image of God—calling on him to assert his dominion over the wild beast—to obey, and conquer, and live? [36]

To keep body and mind untainted, the boy was taught to view women as objects of the greatest respect and even awe. He was to think of them as sisters, whether they lived in palaces or "in the cold sepulchre of shame." [37] He was to consider nice women (like his sister and his

35. Derek Patmore, *The Life and Times of Coventry Patmore* (London, 1949), p. 110.

36. Chap. 15, p. 183.

37. E. P. Hood, *The Age and Its Architects*, p. 396. Cf. Ruskin, *Fors Clavigera*, Letter 81, in *Works, 28,* 81.

mother, like his future bride) as creatures more like angels than human beings—an image wonderfully calculated not only to dissociate
love from sex, but to turn love into worship, and worship of purity. An
English lady like Mrs. Pendennis, with her "tranquil beauty . . . and
that simplicity and dignity which a perfect purity and innocence are
sure to bestow," was the "most complete of all Heaven's subjects in
this world" and therefore the most wholesome influence one could
possibly have. For in such "angelical natures there is something awful,
as well as beautiful, to contemplate"; at their feet "the wildest and
fiercest of us must fall down and humble ourselves, in admiration of
that adorable purity which never seems to do or to think wrong." [38]
This patterned reaction could be so instilled into a sensitive boy like
Frederick Robertson that he could feel even marriage to be a kind of
desecration: "The beings that floated before me, robed in vestures
more delicate than mine, were beings of another order. The thought
of one of them becoming mine was not rapture but pain . . . At seven
years old, woman was a sacred dream, of which I would not talk.
Marriage was a degradation. I remember being quite angry on hearing
it said of a lovely Swede—the loveliest being I ever saw—that she was
likely to get married in England." Robertson was far from laughing at
such romantic feelings. He knew from his own experience that they
could "keep a man all his youth through, before a higher faith has
been called into being, from every species of vicious and low indulgence." [39] But of all women in the world, the most pure—and the most
useful as a sanction for adolescent chastity—was Mother. Every young
Victorian heard his father's voice sounding in his conscience, "Remember your dear, good mother, and never do anything, think anything,
imagine anything she would be ashamed of." In that way filial love,
already increased in the Victorian family by the repression of sexual
emotions, was exaggerated in the cause of moral censorship and control. What still exists in the debased form of "mommism" is found in the
Prince's description of his mother in *The Princess:*

> No angel, but a dearer being, all dipt
> In angel instincts, breathing Paradise,
> Interpreter between the gods and men,
> Who look'd all native to her place, and yet
> On tiptoe seem'd to touch upon a sphere

38. Thackeray's novel, chap. 2, in *Works,* 2, 13.
39. Brooke, *Life of F. W. Robertson,* p. 53.

> Too gross to tread, and all male minds perforce
> Sway'd to her from their orbits as they moved,
> And girdled her with music. Happy he
> With such a mother! faith in womankind
> Beats with his blood, and trust in all things high
> Comes easy to him, and tho' he trip and fall
> He shall not blind his soul with clay.[40]

It goes without saying that after marriage, quite as much as before, the Victorian ethic made fidelity the supreme virtue and sexual irregularity the blackest of sins. For a man to be called a moral person came to mean, almost entirely, that he was "not impure in conduct." Adultery, especially in the case of a wife, and no matter what the extenuating circumstances, was spoken of with horror. A "feeble and erring woman" became, in fact, a social outcast.[41]

This ethic of purity—which remained in full force until Freud and the disrupting effect of war on moral standards and the widening knowledge of contraceptives combined about 1920 to undermine its prestige, though not to end its influence—was accompanied by a phenomenon which is notorious: Victorian prudery. The term has come to be used loosely and broadly to cover all efforts to conceal the facts of life: the demand for expurgated editions of English classics, the drawing up of indexes of books or authors not to be read, especially by girls, the powerful condemnation (and hence in effect prohibition) of any candid treatment of sex in literature, the insistence that conversation be impeccably proper, even to the point of banning any words which could conceivably carry a sexual suggestion, and the chilling disapproval of the slightest approach to levity—all this is called prudery, and treated today with ridicule. But much of it, however silly and unwise, was quite free from what alone deserves the charge, namely, an affectation of purity which is basically insincere.[42] Most of it was simply an excessive censorship intended to protect and support the code of chastity, or to prevent the embarrassment of looking at

40. Pt. VII, lines 301–12. Cf., for another example, Kingsley's passage in "Heroism," *Sanitary and Social Essays*, pp. 247–8, where he finds the diseased world wholesome to him "because, whatever else it is or is not full of, it is at least full of mothers."

41. The phrases quoted are from W. R. Greg, who expresses the criticism of a small and liberal minority: "False Morality of Lady Novelists," *Literary and Social Judgments*, 1, 136–7.

42. I therefore deal with prudery in Chap. 14, "Hypocrisy": see pp. 408–9 and 419.

what was felt to be shameful. Consider, for example, the censorship of literature by a person like Charlotte Brontë, certainly no prude—indeed, the object of some strong criticism for the freedom with which she spoke of sex. She has recommended a list of poets to a correspondent who wanted advice, and then continues: "Now don't be startled at the names of Shakespeare and Byron. Both these were great men, and their works are like themselves. You will know how to choose the good, and to avoid the evil; the finest passages are always the purest, the bad are invariably revolting; you will never wish to read them over twice. Omit the comedies of Shakespeare and the 'Don Juan,' perhaps the 'Cain,' of Byron, though the latter is a magnificent poem." [43] The fear of Shakespeare is also found in the young George Eliot, who thought "we have need of as nice a power of distillation as the bee, to suck nothing but honey from his pages." [44] The best solution, perhaps, was expurgation; and most Victorians read the plays in Thomas Bowdler's *Family Shakespeare*.[45]

The ban on levity has the same origin. Levity is what Queen Victoria found "not amusing." It is light treatment of serious things, especially sexual evil. Thomas Arnold was as famous as his queen for the "startling earnestness with which he would check in a moment the slightest approach to levity"—which is likely to arouse some levity of our own unless we recall his acute and painful sense of the immorality (dirty jokes, masturbation, even sodomy) that existed in the public schools.[46] Charlotte Brontë, with Branwell in her mind, found Thackeray's lecture on Fielding very painful.

> Had Thackeray owned a son, grown, or growing up, and a son, brilliant but reckless—would he have spoken in that light way of courses that lead to disgrace and the grave? . . . I believe, if only

43. Mrs. Gaskell, *Life of Charlotte Brontë*, chap. 7, p. 85. The date is 1834.

44. Cross, *George Eliot's Life*, 1, 38, in a letter to Miss Lewis, March 16, 1839.

45. There is an interesting essay on censorship and the Victorian novel by Kathleen Tillotson, *Novels of the Eighteen-Forties*, pp. 54–73. Mrs. Tillotson argues that the high points of squeamishness were the twenties and the sixties, which agrees with my findings. (For the sixties, see below, pp. 367–8.) But the general attitude runs right through the age, as her sources (pp. 60–2) and mine (just cited and others that follow) both show. Also see Christie, *The Transition from Aristocracy, 1832–1867*, pp. 77–87.

46. Stanley, *Life of Arnold*, chap. 3, p. 122. For his sense of evil in the school, see chap. 3, pp. 99, 153, 155; chap. 5, pp. 235 and 238, letters dated June 28 and August 24, 1830; and for the general state of affairs in the public schools as late as the 1870's, see the pamphlet *The Science of Life*, pp. 9–11.

once the prospect of a promising life blasted on the outset by wild ways had passed close under his eyes, he never *could* have spoken with such levity of what led to its piteous destruction. . . . The true lover of his race ought to devote his vigour to guard and protect; he should sweep away every lure with a kind of rage at its treachery.[47]

It follows that the alliance of levity and seriousness which appeals so strongly to the modern sensibility could only be distressing to the Victorians, or, at best, an inexplicable combination of disparates. Nothing seemed to Ruskin "more mysterious in the history of the human mind than the manner in which gross and ludicrous images are mingled with the most solemn subjects in the work of the Middle Ages"; and although some examples may be excused, others "are clearly the result of vice and sensuality." Specifically, how shall we account for a man like Chaucer, in the very midst of thoughts of beauty, "pure and wild like that of an April morning," inserting "jesting passages which stoop to play with evil?" or for that tendency to degenerate in later centuries into "forms of humour which render some of quite the greatest, wisest, and most moral of English writers now almost useless for our youth?" [48]

The whole campaign, whether prudish or honestly protective, was wrong-headed enough, no doubt, since sexual passion is not to be controlled by concealment and censorship. But the effort was natural enough at a time when so white a purity was demanded that only extreme measures seemed capable of preserving it from taint or corruption. Thackeray might satirize prudery, but he was ready enough to praise *Punch* because it contained nothing unfit for little boys at school to read, or for women to enjoy without blushing: "We like that our matrons and girls should be pure." [49] No doubt, wrote Leslie Stephen, "prudery is a bad thing," but it is not so bad as the prurience of Sterne, the laxness of Fielding, the unwholesome atmosphere of Balzac.[50]

47. Mrs. Gaskell, *Life of Charlotte Brontë*, chap. 26, pp. 381–2.

48. *Stones of Venice*, 3, chap. 3, sec. 70, in *Works, 11*, 189; *Lectures on Art*, No. I, sec. 14 (and cf. 15 on Shakespeare), in *Works, 20*, 29–30. Ruskin's remarks suggest, I think, what Matthew Arnold meant, or partly meant, when he criticized Chaucer, in "The Study of Poetry," for lacking "high seriousness."

49. *The Book of Snobs*, chap. 13, in *Works, 6*, 347; "Two or Three Theatres at Paris," *Punch, 16* (1849), 75, reprinted in *Works, 6*, 151.

50. Annan, *Stephen*, p. 228.

There is, of course, no mystery about the primary source of the ethic of purity and the social taboos that accompanied it. The Evangelical revival in a middle class now strong enough to impose its mores on society, and all the more determined to do so because of its disgusted reaction against the license of the Regency, is the crucial factor.[51] And when the family was treasured so highly, a code that would protect its integrity from centrifugal temptation would be doubly welcomed. But neither explanation accounts for the unmistakable note of horror and fear that runs through so many of the texts I have quoted. One gets the impression that the frame of mind which was shaped by Puritan and family influence must have been acerbated by something new and dangerous in the environment. There must have been immediate signs that the sexual impulse was threatening to overflow the traditional dykes; signs so ominous that men felt it could be checked only by the most severe and repressive code. As we look more closely at Victorian life, we can see good cause, theoretical and actual, for a frightened reaction, and one which not only intensified the demand for chastity, the severe punishment for extramarital relations, and the program of censorship, but also promoted a new attitude toward love.

The first source of worry was the popularity of what was pointedly called "the literature of prostitution." All through the period the violence with which Balzac, Sue, and George Sand—and toward its end Gautier, Baudelaire, and Zola—were condemned reveals something much more than an outraged Puritan conscience.[52] It betrays the fear of their influence. The potential perils of such literature were felt and analyzed as early as 1819 in Hannah More's *Moral Sketches:* "Such fascinating qualities are lavished on the seducer, and such attractive graces on the seduced, that the images indulged with delight by the

51 See above, Chap. 10, sec. 2, especially pp. 236–7; and the reference there to Quinlan's book in note 47. Thackeray's lecture "George the Fourth" (1861) is an excellent index to the Victorian view of the Regency, combining a solemn attack on the king, the court, and the dandies with reiterated praise of purity, love, and domesticity. "What is it to be a gentleman?" he asks in the final paragraph (*Works*, 7, 710). "Is it to have lofty aims, to lead a pure life, to keep your honour virgin; to have the esteem of your fellow-citizens, and the love of your fireside; to bear good fortune meekly; to suffer evil with constancy; and through evil or good to maintain truth always?" Whoever has these qualities "we will salute as gentleman."

52. There is a convenient survey by C. R. Decker, *The Victorian Conscience* (New York, 1952), but as the title implies, Decker traces the hostility entirely to the Evangelical movement. George Brimley, *Essays*, p. 233, speaks of French novels as "the properly styled 'literature of prostitution.' "

fancy, carry on the reader imperceptibly to a point which is not so far from their indulgence in the act as some imagine." Moreover, the violation of the seventh commandment is often "reduced to a venial fault, for which the irresistibleness of the temptation is shamelessly, but too successfully pleaded." Nor is that the extent of the evil. She could, she says, give actual instances where the reading of French fiction has led to the breach of solemn vows, and she thinks it highly probable, therefore, that it has contributed to the alarming increase of divorce. This, no doubt, is to reason too closely, but most Victorians would have thought such results all too possible and been ready enough to agree with Hannah More's demand for the forcible exclusion of such literature from family reading.[53] But in spite of—or perhaps because of—reiterated attacks of this kind, in sermons and tracts and periodical reviews, French novels in the thirties were on sale in the most respectable London bookstores and finding their way into the circulating libraries—"nay, into *ladies' book clubs*"; and in the fifties a familiar acquaintance with even the worst class of French fiction was commonly displayed in the best society.[54] Matthew Arnold, for all his admiration of France and of George Sand, came to speak of the insidious attraction of the French ideal of *l'homme sensuel moyen* and the French worship of the goddess of Lubricity:

> That goddess has always been a sufficient power amongst man-kind, and her worship was generally supposed to need restraining rather than encouraging. But here is now a whole popular litera-ture, nay, and art too, in France at her service! stimulations and suggestions by her and to her meet one in it at every turn. . . . M. Renan himself seems half inclined to apologise for not having paid her more attention. . . . "Nature," he cries, "cares nothing about chastity." What a slap in the face to the sticklers for "What-soever things are pure"!

The sticklers are the saving remnant dedicated to combating the un-soundness of the majority. They must stand fast, and maintain that "the worship of the great goddess Lubricity . . . is against nature,

53. "Unprofitable Reading," *The Works of Hannah More* (11 vols. London, 1853), *11*, 111–14. Cf. G. H. Lewes, *The Life and Works of Goethe* (first ed. 1855; London and New York, 1908), p. 523: "If we in this nineteenth century often carry our exclusion of subjects to the point of prudery, that error is a virtue compared with the demoralising license exhibited in French literature."

54. "French Novels," *Quarterly Review, 56* (1836), 66; and Brimley, *Essays*, p. 233.

LOVE   361

human nature, and that it is ruin." [55] Clearly, if Arnold's belief in the
virtue of chastity was derived from his father and the Christian revival, the passionate emphasis he gave it sprang from his fear of
French contamination.

A second source of anxiety was the philosophy, and to some extent
the open practice, especially in America, of what was called free love.
The theory was first formulated by the Utopian socialists, from Godwin, Mary Wollstonecraft, and Shelley to Fourier, Owen, and the
Saint-Simonians, as a protest against the institution of marriage as it
then existed. Shelley began his note on free love in *Queen Mab*
(1813): "Not even the intercourse of the sexes is exempt from the
despotism of positive institution." As in the old political order, here
too there was no freedom or equality, and therefore no happiness. For
"love withers under constraint: its very essence is liberty: it is compatible neither with obedience, jealousy, nor fear: it is there most
pure, perfect, and unlimited, where its votaries live in confidence,
equality, and unreserve." But equality was a far cry from the social
and legal arrangements then existing between husband and wife; and
liberty to escape from an unhappy marriage was almost impossible.
Shelley shouts his defiance of the established order: "A husband and
wife ought to continue so long united as they love each other: any law
which should bind them to cohabitation for cne moment after the
decay of their affection would be a most intolerable tyranny, and the
most unworthy of toleration. . . . Love is free: to promise for ever to
love the same woman is not less absurd than to promise to believe
the same creed." [56]

It follows that if marriage is to be retained, divorce for incompati-
bility must be accepted, legally and socially; or if marriage is abolished, some new "system of license," to use Fourier's alarming phrase,
should be established whereby mutual love, publicly acknowledged,
should constitute the sole requirement for living together—a system
actually put into practice in some of the Fourierist communities in the
United States. Among the later Saint-Simonians, led by Enfantin, the
principle of "the rehabilitation of the flesh" (from its disparagement in
Christian thought) was, indeed, pushed to a point where it justified

55. "Numbers," *Discourses in America* (London, 1885), pp. 40–1, 56–7. This
attitude toward France had appeared in 1873 in *Literature and Dogma:* see note
63, below.

56. *Complete Poetical Works,* ed. Thomas Hutchinson (New York, 1933), pp.
796–7. As usual Shelley is here indebted to Godwin: see H. N. Brailsford, *Shelley,
Godwin, and Their Circle* (New York and London, 1913), pp. 138–40.

"men and women giving themselves to several without ceasing to be united as a couple."[57] No English socialist went so far, but Shelley talked of the fanatical idea of chastity excluding young men from the society of modest and accomplished women, and thus promoting prostitution; and Robert Owen, besides advocating freedom of divorce at the will of either party, defined chastity as sexual intercourse with affection.[58]

Though not socialists, the "friends of the species" who gathered in the thirties around W. J. Fox, the Unitarian minister—among them Harriet Taylor and John Mill—were ardent critics of marriage; and the institution was subjected to hostile analysis in a series of essays, by Fox and William Adams, in the Unitarian periodical, *The Monthly Repository*.[59] Moreover, when Fox and Eliza Flower practiced what they advocated, Mrs. Fox's complaint to her husband's congregation precipitated an open battle over the claims of free love and fidelity. Carlyle, faithfully reflecting public opinion, spoke with disgust of "a flight of really wretched-looking 'friends of the species' [he mentions Mill, Mrs. Taylor, and Fox], who (in writing and deed) struggle not in favour of Duty being *done*, but against Duty of any sort almost being *required*. A singular creed this; but I can assure you a very observable one here in these days."[60] It was also observable, a little later, in the households of John Chapman, George Henry Lewes, and Thornton Hunt; and George Eliot became the outstanding exponent, in the public mind, of the doctrine of free love.[61] Then, in the very year of her union with Lewes, 1854, appeared a work by Dr. G. R. Drysdale called *The Elements of Social Science: Physical, Sexual, and Natural*

57. Henri, Comte de Saint-Simon, *Selected Writings*, ed. and trans. F. M. H. Markham (Oxford, 1952), p. xxxviii.

58. Shelley, *Works*, p. 798; Owen's definition of chastity is quoted by Mill: F. A. Hayek, *John Stuart Mill and Harriet Taylor*, pp. 74, 291 n. 3.

59. See Packe's chapter entitled "Friends of the Species" in his *Life of Mill*, pp. 115–54; Francis E. Mineka, *The Dissidence of Dissent: the Monthly Repository, 1806–1838* (Chapel Hill, 1944), pp. 369–71; and Mill's essay in Hayek, chap. 3, "On Marriage and Divorce."

60. *Letters, 1826–1836*, pp. 464–5. Names there omitted are supplied by Hayek, p. 82. In the *Latter-Day Pamphlets* (1850), pp. 24–5, Carlyle publicly inveighed against the spread of French theories of enfranchisement which, among other things, would abolish the old sacrament of marriage in favor of a "new Sacrament, that of *Divorce*, which we . . . spout-of on our platforms."

61. Joan Bennett, *George Eliot* (Cambridge, 1948), pp. 45–6, 65. For the liberal view of love in Feuerbach's *The Essence of Christianity*, which George Eliot translated in 1854, see Gordon S. Haight, *George Eliot & John Chapman* (New Haven, 1940), pp. 80–1.

Religion, in which the author argued that "if a man and a woman conceive a passion for each other, they should be morally entitled to indulge it, without binding themselves together for life," and supplied a fairly detailed account of the best methods for doing so without contracting children. This was not an obscure medical treatise; it went through twelve editions in the next twenty years.[62] By the middle seventies Matthew Arnold, after noticing the growing violation of the seventh commandment, went on to say: "Not practice alone is against the old strictness of rule, but theory; we have argumentative systems of free love and of re-habilitation of the flesh. Even philosophers like Mr. Mill, having to tell us that for special reasons they had in fact observed the Seventh Commandment, think it right to add that this they did, 'although we did not consider the ordinances of society binding, on a subject so entirely personal.'" To Arnold this freedom was but the mask of bondage. Anyone who believes the theory of free love is like the man who believes the harlot when she says, "stolen waters are sweet, and bread eaten in secret is pleasant. . . . He knows not that the dead are there, and that her guests are in the depths of hell." [63]

Meanwhile the theory was widely publicized in the novels of George Sand (who had come under Saint-Simonian influence) and was thus brought forcibly into the general consciousness. People who had never heard of Fourier or Enfantin, of Fox or Drysdale, were well aware of what Carlyle called "a *new* astonishing Phallus-Worship, with universal Balzac-Sand melodies and litanies . . . with its finer sensibilities of the heart, and 'great satisfying loves,' . . . and universal Sacrament of Divorce." [64] In 1840, with an unctuous irony that now sets our teeth

62. For the quotation, 1872 ed., p. 368. Drysdale was a socialist and a Neo-Malthusian who saw what he preached as an important means toward a happier and healthier society. His protest on pp. 1–8 against exalting the intellect over the body illustrates the socialist "rehabilitation of the flesh." On the subject of birth control (pp. 346–53), he is in the line that runs from Francis Place and Mill in the twenties to Bradlaugh and the Neo-Malthusian League in the seventies: see J. A. Banks, *Prosperity and Parenthood,* chaps. 2, 10.

63. *God and the Bible* (first ed., 1875; New York, 1895), chap. 3, p. 133. I have supplemented Arnold's quotation from *Proverbs* 9:18 by adding 9:17, which he obviously had in mind. The quotation from Mill is from his *Autobiography,* chap. 7, p. 194. Cf. a similar passage in *Literature and Dogma,* chap. 11, pp. 322–5, where Arnold again cites the insidious influence of France (cf. note 55 above).

64. *Latter-Day Pamphlets,* No. 2, pp. 81–2; and cf. p. 80. Carlyle has merged (perhaps deliberately because he saw no real distinction between them) the serious attack on marriage and the sympathy with extramarital lovers in George Sand

on edge, Thackeray described "Madame Sand's . . . eloquent attack
on marriage, in the charming novel of 'Indiana'."

> What a tender suffering creature is Indiana; how little her husband
> appreciates that gentleness which he is crushing by his tyranny and
> brutal scorn; how natural it is that, in the absence of his sympathy,
> she, poor clinging confiding creature, should seek elsewhere for
> shelter; how cautious should we be, to call criminal—to visit with
> too heavy a censure—an act which is one of the natural impulses
> of a tender heart, that seeks but for a worthy object of love.

In *Valentine* young men and maidens are accorded "the same tender
licence"; in *Lélia* we have "a regular topsyturvyfication of morality, a
thieves' and prostitutes' apotheosis." [65] And this was the foreign
writer everyone had heard of and almost everyone was reading. No
wonder her name was "for many years 'a word of fear' in British households." [66]

Finally, the major reason why sex was so frightening to the Vic-

---

(see the next note) with the neutral presentation of free, in the sense of illicit, love
in Balzac. This essay is primarily aimed at the cult of benevolence (see above,
Chap. 11, sec. 2); but the love of Man and the love of woman—a woman—both
belonged to the radical-liberal tradition, and are found together in Shelley, the
Saint-Simonians, and the "Friends of the Species," as well as George Sand. Carlyle's full text reads: "with its finer sensibilities of the heart, and 'great satisfying
loves,' with its sacred kiss of peace for scoundrel and hero alike, with its all-
embracing Brotherhood, and universal Sacrament of Divorce."

65. "Madame Sand and the New Apocalypse," *The Paris Sketch Book*, in *Works*,
5, 189–91. Her actual position is well summed up in a passage from *Jacques*
(Paris, 1857), Pt. I, Letter 6, p. 36, which was called to my attention by Gordon
Haight of Yale. Jacques writes to Sylvia: "Je n'ai pas changé d'avis, je ne me suis
pas réconcilié avec la société, et le mariage est toujours, selon moi, une de plus
barbares institutions qu'elle ait ébauchées. Je ne doute pas qu'il ne soit aboli, si
l'espèce humaine fait quelque progrès vers la justice et la raison; un lien plus
humain et non moins sacré remplacera celui-là, et saura assurer l'existence des
enfants qui naîtront d'un homme et d'une femme, sans enchaîner à jamais la liberté
de l'un et de l'autre."

66. F. W. H. Myers, *Essays: Modern* (London, 1885), pp. 71–2. There is some
account of the frightened reception of George Sand in Decker, *The Victorian Conscience* (above, note 52). A general study of her reputation and influence among
the Victorians has still to be written. I have the impression that she was the most
widely read of all foreign authors except perhaps Goethe. The whole subject of
free love in Victorian life and thought would make a valuable monograph. The
only connected treatments I have found are: "The Free Love System," *The Living
Age*, 2d ser. *10* (1855), 815–21, and the article by Robert Briffault in the *Encyclo-
pedia of Social Sciences*, where there is a short bibliography.

torians was the glaring fact that gave practical edge to the theoretical dangers of French novels and social theories—that sexual license in England not only existed on a large scale but seemed to be increasing. In 1867 Francis Newman wrote in *Fraser's Magazine:* "That libertinism of the most demoralizing character flourishes in London, in Paris, and in New York, cannot be a secret; nor that it is confined to no grade of society. But alas, the chief cities do but impress the imagination more, by the scale of the evil." The reference is partly to prostitution, which will be considered in a moment, but it is also to adultery and seduction. Newman goes on to remark that what makes the evil more intractable is that the offenders often appeal to "a theory upheld by earnest persons of both sexes, hitherto wholly guiltless of transgression against the received moralities," a theory that has arisen on both sides of the Atlantic "concerning 'free love,' which, however variously applied, in every case would supersede marriage." Those who invoke it do so sometimes because they honestly consider sexual union a private affair with which the state has no right to interfere, but more often as an excuse for the free indulgence of passion. The "Parisian licentiousness" of our upper ten thousand (the world of *Vanity Fair*) shows that "their 'free love' from the very first deliberately intends to abandon the loved object, as an inconvenience and an obstacle to ambition." [67] The attitude was not limited to the upper ten thousand. A recurrent theme in the Victorian novel is the seduction of lower-class girls by the Henry Bellinghams and Arthur Donnithornes, the J. Steerforths and Barnes Newcomes.[68] In 1857 Dr. William Acton said that no one acquainted with rural life would deny that seduction was "a sport and a habit with vast numbers of men, married . . . and single, placed above the ranks of labour." [69] Among Oxford undergraduates the prevailing mores were somewhat higher:

> Adultery and Seduction, they avowed, were utter scoundrelism. It was needless to say a word more about them. *At least* (said one) if a gentleman *did* seduce a poor girl, at any rate he ought not to abandon her, but to make her an allowance, to look after her now and then; to maintain her child, if he had one by her; in short, he must honourably take the consequences of his own act. Nevertheless, on the whole, they did not approve of seduction. A

67. "Marriage Laws," reprinted in his *Miscellanies*, 3, 222–3, 235–6.

68. Other novels that deal with this subject are cited by Amy Cruse, *The Victorians and Their Reading*, p. 356.

69. *Prostitution, Considered in Its Moral, Social, and Sanitary Aspects*, p. 175.

man could not exactly put the woman back where she had been. It was really a shame to spoil a girl's after-chances. But as to Fornication, that was quite another thing. A man found a woman already spoiled; he did not do her any harm, poor creature! [70]

What these texts imply is more than confirmed by statistics. In a single year (1851) 42,000 illegitimate children were born in England and Wales; and on that basis it was estimated that "one in twelve of the unmarried females in the country above the age of puberty have strayed from the path of virtue." [71]

The context of these remarks by Acton and Newman is prostitution, since the fallen woman, made an outcast by the Victorian code of purity, had little else to turn to for support. But seduction was only one of many factors leading through the middle nineteenth century to the alarming increase of what came to be called "The Great Social Evil." The growth of industrial cities providing a cover of secrecy, the starvation wages of women at the lowest economic level, the maintenance of large armed forces, and the social ambition which required the postponement of marriage until a young man could afford to live like a gentleman were important causes. By 1850 there were at least 50,000 prostitutes known to the police in England and Scotland, 8,000 in London alone.[72] In the sixties Taine reported that in the Haymarket and the Strand "every hundred steps one jostles twenty harlots" and called prostitution "the real plague-spot of English society." [73] Beginning about 1840 and rapidly increasing after 1850, a long series of books and articles brought the problem into the open [74] and drove home the points explicitly made by two writers on the subject: that "the prevalence of this vice tends, in a variety of ways, to the deterioration of national character,—and to the consequent exposure of the nations among whom it abounds to weakness, decline, and fall"—and

70. F. W. Newman, "Remedies for the Great Social Evil" (1869), Miscellanies, 3, 275. Cf. Mr. Tryan's life at college, in George Eliot, "Janet's Repentance," Scenes of Clerical Life, 2, chap. 18, pp. 109–11. Acton, pp. 168–9, refers to "the ruinous effects of a college career on fathers and sons."

71. Acton, p. 18.

72. "Prostitution," Westminster Review, 53 (1850), 475.

73. Notes on England, p. 36; and cf. pp. 44–6.

74. From only a brief search for bibliography, I found 16 books and 26 articles on prostitution published in England and Scotland between 1840 and 1870, and there must have been many more. In comparison the publication during the previous thirty years (1810–40) was very slight.

that unless it were dealt with promptly from many angles of attack, "the patient will be extinct before the disease is eradicated." [75]

One approach to the problem is found in an article entitled "Prostitution" in the *Westminster Review* for 1850. Although not sanguine about the results, the author thought something might be accomplished if licentious literature were excluded from the curriculum and boys brought up with "the same watchful attention to purity" that was given to girls.[76] In Newman's tract "Remedies for the Great Social Evil" a series of pointed questions addressed to young men is intended to give practical support to the thesis that if they were chaste, the pernicious trade of the harlot would not exist: could they bear to have their mothers and sisters know what they were doing? did they want to become hypocrites and liars? was it "just in a man to expect in a wife an antenuptial chastity, if he do not come chaste to her"? should he not feel self-degraded by what "he would regard as self-degradation in her"? Furthermore, since "the School Classics perniciously inflame passion in boys and young men," as do "many approved English poems, plays, sculptures, and paintings," all such temptations should be as rigidly barred from them as they are from girls. Newman turns with something like suppressed rage on anyone who dares call him a prude. "With eight thousand harlots in London alone, what utter nonsense is such talk! It is clear that many of us are early and profoundly corrupted: no one can tell how small a spark may cause explosion." That remark should be kept in mind by anyone tempted to

75. Ralph Wardlaw, *Lectures on Female Prostitution* (Glasgow, 1842), quoted in William Logan, *The Great Social Evil* (London, 1871), p. 114; and Acton, pp. viii–ix. Cf. John S. Smith, who begins his *Social Aspects* (1850), pp. 1–33, by reminding an age given to self-congratulation that the greatest nations of the past have ultimately fallen, and that the only possible way for England to avoid that fate is to avoid its causes as revealed in history, and ends his chapter on immorality, pp. 75–6: "The whole array of history, speaking through Greece, Rome, France, Charles II courts, and George Barnwell ballads, is there to proclaim that, of all the plagues that human sin creates to scourge itself, there is none so paralyzing to the individual body and mind, so disastrous to the national safety, and poisonous to the High and the True in man, as immorality." For other evidence of a frightened awareness of sexual immorality in England, see Macaulay, "Leigh Hunt" (1841), *Critical Essays*, 4, 361; Bagehot, *Physics and Politics* (1872), No. 5, in *Works*, 4, 571; Mallock, *The New Republic* (1877), pp. 41–2; and Morley, quoted on the next page.

76. *Westminster Review*, 53 (1850), 479. The author of this important article (pp. 448–506) was W. R. Greg: see the Bibliography below, under his name.

ridicule Victorian "prudery" wholesale, or to trace it simply to middle-class Evangelical morality.[77]

In 1866 John Morley wrote a review of Swinburne's *Poems and Ballads* which has come to be a classic example of the Nonconformist conscience at its worst. "No language is too strong," he said (and showed it in nearly every sentence), "to condemn the mixed vileness and childishness of depicting the spurious passion of a putrescent imagination, the unnamed lusts of sated wantons." For here was a poet "tuning his lyre in a stye," grovelling "among the nameless, shameless abominations which inspire him with frensied delight," and much more to the same purpose. But in the midst of this tirade, Morley paused to say that if Swinburne were simply "a rebel against the fat-headed Philistines and poor-blooded Puritans who insist that all poetry should be such as may be wisely placed in the hands of girls of eighteen, and is fit for the use of Sunday schools, he would have all wise and enlarged readers on his side. . . . It is a good thing to vindicate passion, and the strong and large and rightful pleasures of sense, against the narrow and inhuman tyranny of shrivelled anchorites." But no, what Swinburne has done is to "set up the pleasures of sense in the seat of the reason they have dethroned"; or, more pointedly still, he has crammed his book "with pieces which many a professional vendor of filthy prints might blush to sell."[78] The man who wrote that review was no prude and no Puritan. He was simply a very typical Victorian terrified, as he said elsewhere, by "the most awful influx the world ever saw of furious provocatives to unbridled sensuality and riotous animalism."[79]

To re-read the *Idylls of the King* against this background of fear, bred by French literature, theories of free love, and the acute awareness of "unbridled sensuality," is to realize at once the full implications of Tennyson's description of the poem as an "old imperfect tale, new-old, and shadowing Sense at war with Soul."[80] For the poem is the study of how a society founded on the highest moral ideals, above all,

77. Newman, "Remedies for the Great Social Evil," pp. 276–7. Other writers make the same case for censorship for the same general reason: see Acton, *Prostitution*, p. 168, and the author of *The Science of Life*, pp. 17–18. We have here the reason for the increase of "prudery" in the sixties which Mrs. Tillotson (see above, note 45) notices without explanation.

78. *Saturday Review, 22* (August 4, 1866), 145–7.

79. Quoted by F. W. Hirst, *Early Life & Letters of John Morley* (2 vols. London, 1927), *1,* 10.

80. "To the Queen," published as an epilogue in the 1872–73 edition of Tennyson's works, lines 36–7.

that of purity, is gradually undermined and corrupted by adultery and fornication. In the central speech which concluded the first edition of 1859, King Arthur reminds the guilty Guinevere of the vow his knights had taken:

> To reverence the King, as if he were
> Their conscience, and their conscience as their King,
> To break the heathen and uphold the Christ,
> To ride abroad redressing human wrongs . . .
> To lead sweet lives in purest chastity,
> To love one maiden only, cleave to her,
> And worship her by years of noble deeds,
> Until they won her. . . .

"And all this throve," he says, "before I wedded thee." But

> Then came thy shameful sin with Lancelot;
> Then came the sin of Tristram and Isolt;
> Then others, following these my mightiest knights,
> And drawing foul ensample from fair names,
> Sinn'd also, till the loathsome opposite
> Of all my heart had destined did obtain,
> And all thro' thee! [81]

Furthermore, from these sins of the flesh sprang other sins—murder, deceit, disloyalty, atheism—until the Table Round was ultimately broken by civil war and the victory of the barbarians in the last great battle in the west. The final word is spoken by Arthur:

> For I, being simple, thought to work His will,
> And have but stricken with the sword in vain,
> And all whereon I lean'd in wife and friend
> Is traitor to my peace, and all my realm
> Reels back into the beast, and is no more. [82]

Again and again that conclusion is anticipated. In "Merlin and Vivian" the magician who gained his wisdom because

> he kept his mind on one sole aim,
> Nor ever touch'd fierce wine, nor tasted flesh,
> Nor own'd a sensual wish,

---

81. "Guinevere," lines 465–8, 471–4, 484–90.
82. "The Passing of Arthur," lines 22–6.

is seduced and betrayed by the harlot of the court. And though he
denies Vivian's calumnies against the knights—no one is stainless
except Arthur, and "is he man at all?"—the best Merlin can say is that
all were "brave, and many generous, and some chaste." [83] In "Pelleas
and Ettarre" the young knight who has sent his friend Gawain to press
his suit finds him in the willing arms of Ettarre; and presently, when
he remarks to Sir Percivale that Ettarre is as false as Guinevere is true,
is dumbfounded by the astonished expression on Sir Percivale's face:

> And he shrank and wail'd,
> "Is the Queen false?" and Percivale was mute.
> "Have any of our Round Table held their vows?"
> And Percivale made answer not a word.
> "Is the King true?" "The King!" said Percivale.
> "Why, then, let men couple at once with wolves." [84]

In "The Last Tournament," pointedly called "The Tournament of the
Dead Innocence," the hero Tristram, who has wedded easily and all
as easily left his bride to take another Isolt for mistress, sings the new
philosophy of love:

> New life, new love, to suit the newer day;
> New loves are sweet as those that went before.
> Free love—free field—we love but while we may.

How ridiculous, he cries, for Arthur to have tried to bind "free manhood" with inviolable vows. "The wide world laughs at it. . . . We are
not angels here nor shall be. . . . My soul, we love but while we
may." One can hardly escape reading the message of the Red Knight
to the King as Tennyson's own speech of bitter disillusion to an age
whose ideal of purity seems to be nothing but a hypocritical mask to
hide its sensuality:

> Tell thou the King and all his liars that I
> Have founded my Round Table in the North,
> And whatsoever his own knights have sworn
> My knights have sworn the counter to it—and say
> My tower is full of harlots, like his court,
> But mine are worthier, seeing they profess
> To be none other than themselves—and say

83. Lines 624–6, 779, 815; and see the whole passage, lines 689–836.
84. Lines 521–6.

> My knights are all adulterers like his own,
> But mine are truer, seeing they profess
> To be none other; and say his hour is come,
> The heathen are upon him, his long lance
> Broken, and his Excalibur a straw.[85]

If this picture of the decline and fall of a civilization was largely the expression of Tennyson's somber observation of contemporary life,[86] it was also—inevitably, coming from the mouth of the poet laureate—a horrible warning. The didactic intention of stemming the tide, or trying to, is manifest in the introduction of two moral lessons, two cures, one might say, for the disease. The first is the reaffirmation, in the strongest possible terms, of the code of purity, embodied in the lives of a few knights and ladies—notably Arthur and Galahad, Enid and Elaine—and expounded with all its anathemas by the King himself in the speech to Guinevere. There, after quoting the knightly vow,

> To lead sweet lives in purest chastity,
> To love one maiden only, cleave to her,

he pronounces judgment upon the Queen in tones far more Victorian than Celtic:

85. Lines 279–81, 690–98, 77–88. With Tristram's distortion for sensual reasons of the doctrine of free love, compare F. W. Newman's statement, four years earlier, on p. 365 above. Between the early *Idylls* and those of the late sixties stands the "Lucretius," written in 1865. Its central theme is the erotic effect of the love potion given Lucretius by his wife. But to imagine that Tennyson was trying "to imitate the libertinism and daring of Swinburne's *Poems and Ballads*" is preposterous. On the contrary, he talks the language of Morley's review: see lines 52–5, 156–63. Lucretius (lines 164 ff.) says of his erotic dreams that like crowds in an hour of civic tumult, they bear the keepers down and throng "far into that council-hall where sit the best and stateliest of the land." It is the council-hall of Camelot—and Westminster. And so, since (lines 219–22, 231–2),

> . . . now it seems some unseen monster lays
> His vast and filthy hands upon my will,
> Wrenching it backward into his, and spoils
> My bliss in being. . . .
> Why should I, beastlike as I find myself,
> Not manlike end myself?

The same monster laid his hands on Arthur's court and thwarted Arthur's will.

86. Cf. S. C. Burchell, "Tennyson's 'Allegory in the Distance,'" *PMLA*, 68 (1953), 418–24. Burchell rightly brings forward other sources of Tennyson's despair, especially the pride, greed, and selfishness of a commercial society. All I claim is that sexual immorality is the central evil in Tennyson's mind.

> I hold that man the worst of public foes
> Who either for his own or children's sake,
> To save his blood from scandal, lets the wife
> Whom he knows false abide and rule the house:
> For being thro' his cowardice allow'd
> Her station, taken everywhere for pure,
> She like a new disease, unknown to men,
> Creeps, no precaution used, among the crowd,
> Makes wicked lightnings of her eyes, and saps
> The fealty of our friends, and stirs the pulse
> With devil's leaps, and poisons half the young.

As he departs, Arthur (who remarks in passing that he "was ever virgin save for thee") cannot so much as take her hand, since his own flesh, "here looking down on thine polluted, cries, 'I loathe thee.'" And Guinevere herself, bowed in bitter repentance, completely concurs in his judgment, even to the admission that

> The shadow of another cleaves to me,
> And makes me one pollution.[87]

It is only by keeping vividly in mind the merging influence of the Puritan revival, the exaltation of the family, and the acute fear of sex, that an age like ours, which sets no great value on chastity and views marriage as a problem in adjustment and forbearance between equals, can tolerate this passage, or avoid finding Arthur more of an insufferable prig than an ideal man.

The second cure for the disease of the age also appears in this central speech of the poem. Arthur knows no greater power, he says, of keeping down "the base in man" than "the maiden passion for a maid." [88] From the fear of sex we pass directly to the exaltation of love.

4. Love

At the house party in Mallock's *New Republic*, one subject of discussion is love. "I know a little of the love poetry of this and of other times," remarks Mr. Allen, "and the poetry of this has always seemed to me far—far the highest. It has seemed to me to give the passion so much more meaning, and such a much greater influence over all life." He is thinking especially, he says, of two contemporary poets:

87. "Guinevere," lines 509–19, 550–4, 613–14.
88. Lines 474–7.

Shakespeare may of course have exhibited the working of love more powerfully than they; yet I am sure he could never have conceived its meaning and its nature so deeply. No heroine of his could have understood Mrs. Browning's *Sonnets from the Portuguese;* nor any hero of his her husband's love lyrics. What seems to me the thing so peculiarly modern, is this notion of love as something which, once truly attained, would, as Browning says,

> make Time break,
> Letting us pent-up creatures through
> Into Eternity, our due.[89]

This is to make love not only the supreme experience of life but its end and object—the very means by which the soul is saved. The fullest statement is in "Cristina," written well before Browning met Elizabeth Barrett:

> Doubt you if, in some such moment,
>   As she fixed me, she felt clearly,
> Ages past the soul existed,
>   Here an age 't is resting merely,
> And hence fleets again for ages,
>   While the true end, sole and single,
> It stops here for is, this love-way,
>   With some other soul to mingle?
>
> Else it loses what it lived for,
>   And eternally must lose it;
> Better ends may be in prospect,
>   Deeper blisses (if you choose it),
> But this life's end and this love-bliss
>   Have been lost here.

The "moment" is the critical moment when the lover meets his soulmate, the one person in the wide world who was made for him or her, made to be loved forever, here and hereafter. After finding one's affinity, to draw back, like Cristina, out of timidity or apathy or any consideration of "the world's honours," is failure in life. Success is to seize the predestined moment and to love on, even if love is unrequited (as here), even if the beloved is dead—always to be faithful until, in

89. Pages 240–1. This is Mallock's own opinion: cf. *Is Life Worth Living?* p. 103.

heaven, the perfect union is achieved or renewed. This extraordinary conception, though often expressed more moderately, is found in many other Victorian poets, notably Tennyson, Patmore, and Rossetti. And in hundreds of novels—for in fiction, too, what seemed modern at the time was the same preoccupation. In the work of Scott, as Ruskin and Bagehot observed, love and marriage had been viewed as simply constituents of human happiness. Now, in the modern novel, they had often become its sole object, the most important business of life.[90]

Literature, of course, and especially the literature of love, is not a transcript of reality. But it is significant that Taine cited Major Dobbin, the lover of Amelia in *Vanity Fair*, who waited fifteen years without hope because for him there was but one woman in the world, as representative of what he had observed in England—but not in France. "Many do not marry in consequence of a thwarted inclination, and continue to live with their eldest brother. . . . One who was mentioned to me, very distinguished, was supplanted by a titled rival; during two years apprehensions were felt for his reason. He went to China and to Australia; at present he occupies a high post, he has been made a baronet, he presides over important business, but he is unmarried." [91] It is fair to say, I think, that the woman who insisted, for all Carlyle's growling, that men and women were born "for the chief purpose of falling in love, or being fallen in love with" was a rather typical Victorian.[92]

90. Ruskin, "Fiction, Fair and Foul," sec. I, par. 21, in *Works, 34,* 284–5; Bagehot, "The Waverley Novels," *Works,* 2, 199–201. Even Trollope, for all his common sense, seems to approve of Johnny Eames' resolve in *The Small House at Allington* (first ed. 1864; 3 vols. New York, 1893), *1,* chap. 4, p. 49, that once having loved Lily Dale, "it behoved him, as a true man, to love her on to the end" even though she should refuse to marry him; and he seems to agree with Lady Julia (3, chap. 15, p. 230) when she says to him after Lily's refusal, "To have loved truly, even though you shall have loved in vain, will be a consolation when you are as old as I am." Cf. Tennyson, *Maud,* part 1, sec. xi; *In Memoriam,* No. 27, though he is there thinking of his love for Arthur Hallam.

91. *Notes on England,* pp. 96–7. Cf. Yeats' attitude toward Maude Gonne, *The Autobiography of William Butler Yeats* (New York, 1938), pp. 341, 368. Taine might equally have cited Squire Dale and Lord De Guest in *The Small House at Allington* (see previous note), 2, chap. 13, pp. 197–8: "The story of their lives had been so far the same; each had loved, and each had been disappointed, and then each had remained single through life."

92. Froude, *Carlyle: Life in London, 1,* chap. 8, p. 216. Cf. Ruskin, "Fiction, Fair and Foul," p. 284 n. The only essay I know on Victorian love (and this is limited by the special approach of the book) is by Joseph Wood Krutch in *The Modern Temper* (New York, 1929), chap. 4, "Love—or the Life and Death of a Value."

The whole attitude is exactly what we call Romantic, and it was, in fact, a direct inheritance from Romanticism: partly from its naturalism, which found the instincts good and appealed to the feelings or the heart as the supreme guide to conduct and wisdom; partly from its idealism, whether Platonic or chivalric. The study of Victorian love is the study of how this tradition, embodied mainly in the works of Rousseau, Shelley, and George Sand, was domesticated under the powerful influence of Evangelical and family sentiment, and then emphasized, as a protection against, or a solution for, some major concerns of the time: sensuality, the marriage market, the painful mood of baffled thought, and the decline of religious faith.

In the literature of love written in the forties and fifties there occurs a persistent note of reconstruction. It takes the form of antithesis. Love is not something carnal and evil to be ashamed of but something pure and beautiful; it is not a temptation to be struggled against but a great ethical force which can protect men from lust and even strengthen and purify the moral will; it is not an experience limited to courtship but continues throughout life, animating husband and wife no less than the lover and his lass. The motivation is obvious. If men are to be saved from the sensuality that threatens society, love must be distinguished from sex and given its rightful place and influence within the code of purity. When Sir Guy Morville in *The Heir of Redclyffe* (1853) discovers that Amy is the being he had dreamt of, the one woman he would love forever, Charlotte Yonge stops to point out: "Sternly as he was wont to treat his impulses, he did not look on his affection as an earthborn fancy, liable to draw him from higher things, and, therefore, to be combatted; he deemed her rather a guide and guard whose love might arm him, soothe him, and encourage him." [93]

The leaders of this new orientation were Kingsley and Patmore; its principal manifestoes *Yeast* (1851) and *The Angel in the House* (1855, 1856). In *Yeast* the story of Lancelot Smith is a thinly disguised account of Kingsley's own experience; and the heroine, Argemone, is a portrait of Fanny Grenfell, whom he married in 1844. Before he met her, his education in sex was Lancelot's. He had read Byron by stealth and been forced by his private tutor to read Ovid, Tibullus, and Martial.

All conversation on the subject of love had been prudishly avoided, as usual, by his parents and teacher. The parts of the Bible which spoke of it had been always kept out of his sight. Love had been

93. Chap. 13, p. 179.

to him, practically, ground tabooed and "carnal." What was to be expected? Just what happened—if woman's beauty had nothing holy in it, why should his fondness for it? Just what happens every day—that he had to sow his wild oats for himself, and eat the fruit therof, and the dirt thereof also.[94]

From this period of debauchery with its acute sense of guilt, Kingsley was rescued by falling in love; and upon his marriage he discovered that sexual experience could be exactly the opposite of all he had been told and all he had known: it could be an innocent and joyous thing. And the love of a good woman could strengthen and apparently purify the whole nature. How outrageous to call it carnal! Love was a natural desire, given by God, and the body the intended means by which, under the control of the soul, that desire was to be realized. From then on Kingsley was determined to preach "that higher and spiritual view of marriage" which was so different, as he says in 1848, from "that vulgar and carnal conception of it which is common"; and to show that the most passionate love could be the purest, if only its object were legitimate and worthy.[95] This is the major theme of his literary work. As in *Yeast*, the leading characters of all his novels are saved, or lost, depending on their understanding of love and marriage and their consequent attitude toward women. Everywhere the moral is that while passion alone may drag one down to hell, passion lifted to a higher level by reverence and devotion is the gate to heaven.[96] In this way Kingsley brought love within the code of purity and made it even a sanction for premarital chastity. To sow one's wild oats was not merely a sin against God, it was a sin against the pure woman one would some day meet and marry, bringing with it tortured memories, like those which afflicted Lancelot:

> The contact of her stainless innocence, the growing certainty that the destiny of that innocence was irrevocably bound up with his own, made him shrink from her whenever he remembered his own guilty career. . . . To think . . . that she would bring to him what he could never, never bring to her!—The thought was unbearable. . . . How gladly, at those moments, he would have welcomed centuries of a material hell, to escape from the more

94. *Yeast*, chap. 1, p. 4. For the autobiographical reading, see Thorp, *Kingsley*, p. 15; and for my next statement, *Letters and Memories, 1*, 30 (unabridged ed., *1*, 45–6, 53).

95. *Letters and Memories, 1*, 71, 160–7 (only the second passage is in the unabridged ed., *1*, 186–91). Cf. *Yeast*, chap. 7, pp. 108–13.

96. Cf. Leslie Stephen, "Charles Kingsley," *Hours in a Library, 3*, 36–8.

awful spiritual hell within him,—to buy back that pearl of innocence which he had cast recklessly to be trampled under the feet
of his own swinish passions! [97]

Kingsley's presentation of love was just a little too outspoken to be
quite wholesome. Patmore expressed the same ideas with more delicacy
in the enormously popular *Angel in the House*. He began with a claim
to originality:

> The richest realm of all the earth
>   Is counted still a heathen land:
> Lo, I, like Joshua, now go forth
>   To give it into Israel's hand. . . .
> From love's abysmal ether rare
>   If I to men have here made known
> New truths, they, like new stars, were there
>   Before, though not yet written down.[98]

One truth in particular: that love was an uplifting experience—the
love that idealizes and worships not only the maiden but the wife as
well. The fact is, he says later, "lovers are the fountains of morality,"
though that is still "a star too deep-enskied for all to see." And again,
although "strong passions mean weak will,"

>   he
> Who truly knows the strength and bliss
>   Which are in love, will own with me
>   No passion but a virtue 'tis.
> Few hear my word; it soars above
>   The subtlest senses of the swarm
> Of wretched things which know not love,
>   Their Psyche still a wingless worm.

Few, that is, now recognize this truth. Few would give his answer to
the question that follows:

> You love? That's high as you shall go;
>   For 'tis as true as Gospel text,

---

97. *Yeast*, chap. 10, pp. 146–7. See above, p. 350, where I quote from this
chapter to illustrate the "woman-worship" which I was there relating (in sec. 2)
to the general need for nonreligious sources of ethical strength, and the particular
need to counteract the influence of commercial life. As we now see, it was also
inspired by the theory of love as a bulwark against sensuality.

98. Bk. I, Canto I, *Poems*, p. 65.

Not noble then is never so,
    Either in this world or the next.[99]

Only by realizing how closely love was associated with passion, and
passion with weakness of will and sensuality, can we imagine the surprise and delight of Victorian readers at such a happy synthesis of love
and virtue. Moreover, so conceived, love is a powerful protection
against what should only be called lust or shame. The sanction for
premarital chastity offered by Kingsley reappears:

Prospective Faith

They safely walk in darkest ways
    Whose youth is lighted from above,
Where, through the senses' silvery haze,
    Dawns the veil'd moon of nuptial love.
Who is the happy husband? He
    Who, scanning his unwedded life,
Thanks Heaven, with a conscience free,
    'Twas faithful to his future wife.[100]

In the same cause Patmore utilizes the Romantic idea of elective
affinities. His hero says he

never went to Ball, or Fête,
    Or Show, but in pursuit express
        Of my predestinated mate;
And thus to me, who had in sight
    The happy chance upon the cards,
Each beauty blossom'd in the light
    Of tender personal regards.

It is hardly surprising that when "by heavenly chance express" he
meets "the destined maid," her name is Honoria. Even if "fate Love's
dear ambition mar," the rejected lover has the consolation of knowing
that "Love, won or lost, is countless gain," since in both cases it "leaves
the heart more generous, dignified, and pure." [101] But in this poem a
happy courtship is crowned by a marriage in which love continues to
uplift and protect.

99. Canto XI, p. 125; Canto III, pp. 78–9.
100. Canto V, p. 91.
101. Canto II, p. 75; Canto III, p. 77; Canto V, pp. 90–1.

In short, one might say that Patmore was fighting fire with fire, the
fire of hell with that of the hearth. He would shame "the music of the
Sirens" with the "sweeter song" of Orpheus,

> Till ev'n the witless Gadarene,
>   Preferring Christ to swine, shall know
> That life is sweetest when it's clean.

He would exalt the ideal passion of his hero over the mere idealism
of Plato and the mere passion of Anacreon.[102] He would write a love
poetry, as George Brimley pointed out in his review of *The Angel in
the House,* that would "rival and outweigh any real attraction which
the properly styled 'literature of prostitution' may have for any but
mauvais sujets," for it would snatch the wand from Comus and reverse
all his mightiest charms.[103]

A year before this review George Brimley had written an essay on
Tennyson in which he praised the love poems that had appeared in
the volumes of 1832 and 1842: "The Miller's Daughter," "The Gar-
dener's Daughter," "The Lord of Burleigh," and the rest. Those idylls
are now viewed as sickly examples of domestic sentiment, and I have
no doubt that Tennyson intended simply to celebrate the beauties of
connubial affection. But Brimley, writing in 1855, saw them as a contribution to the reconstruction of love he was to notice, a year later,
in Patmore. "Mr. Tennyson's glory," he said, "is to have portrayed passion with a feminine purity; to have spiritualised the voluptuousness
of the senses and the imagination by a manly reverence for woman's
worth." Wherever his works have depicted love in its various influences
upon character, the passion shown in operation has been a "purifying,
strengthening, sustaining power," one which "allies itself with conscience and reason, and braces instead of debilitating the will." [104] If
that was hardly more than latent in the domestic idylls, it was clearly
affirmed in the Arthurian *Idylls* of 1859. After mentioning the vow

102. Bk. II, Canto I, pp. 142–3.

103. *Essays,* pp. 233–4. Some years later, after his own arguments for premarital chastity, quoted above, p. 367, Francis Newman added another remedy
for the "Great Social Evil" (*Miscellanies,* 3, 277): young men should be told that
"a true love marriage purifies the debased imagination; that is the first gain. It
teaches, practically, how empty is carnal, how solid is spiritual delight. . . . If
young men knew what is the constant joy of a simple loving wife, they would not
be such fools as to defer or sacrifice it for frivolous luxury, much less for hired
embraces." They ought to read, he might have said, *The Angel in the House.*

104. *Essays,* pp. 61, 73–4.

imposed on his knights to live sweet lives in purest chastity and love one maiden only, Arthur continues:

> I knew
> Of no more subtle master under heaven
> Than is the maiden passion for a maid,
> Not only to keep down the base in man,
> But teach high thought, and amiable words
> And courtliness, and the desire of fame,
> And love of truth, and all that makes a man.

Then at once this 'high' love is placed against Guinevere's "shameful sin with Lancelot" and its fatal influence through the court until

> the loathsome opposite
> Of all my heart had destined did obtain—

the opposite, that is, of what would have been true if Guinevere had loved him with the chivalric devotion he had felt for her.[105] Or which Enid felt for Geraint and Elaine for Lancelot. A few years later Ruskin was to call love "in its purity . . . the source of the highest and purest mortal happiness" and to describe it as "the *purifying* passion of the soul" (for indeed "there is no true conqueror of Lust but Love"). And he, too, was to find in the old chivalrous devotion of the knight to his lady a type of the surest safeguard against "all wayward and wicked passion." [106] Earlier than either, a writer in the *Westminster Review* for 1850, arguing for premarital chastity, asked what would be the result on the general tone of society were young men to gratify the sexual desire as soon as it arose:

> Where should we find that reverence for the female sex, that tenderness towards their feelings, that deep devotion of the heart to them, which is the beautiful and purifying part of love? Is it not certain that all of delicate and chivalric which still pervades our sentiments towards women, may be traced to *repressed*, and therefore hallowed and elevated passion? . . . And what, in these

105. "Guinevere," lines 474–90.

106. *Time and Tide* (1867), Letter 10, in *Works, 17*, 362, where he quotes *The Angel in the House;* "Of Queens' Gardens" (1865), *Works, 18*, 119–20, and see his note on p. 138, where he wishes that a true order of chivalry might be instituted "for our English youth of certain ranks." The remark I have placed in a parenthesis is from one of the letters to the author of *The Science of Life,* in *Works, 34*, 527.

days, can preserve chastity, save some relic of chivalrous devotion? Are we not all aware that a young man can have no safeguard against sensuality and low intrigue, like an early, virtuous, and passionate attachment? [107]

The ingenious argument of this pre-Freudian passage is circular: repress sexual desire and you will preserve all the reverence, tenderness, and chivalric devotion to women which makes love beautiful and purifying; and then, the ideal preserved, you can form a virtuous and passionate (that is, romantic but unconsummated) attachment which will save you from sensuality. The subject of the article was the cause and cure of prostitution.

Paradoxical as it may seem, the Victorian emphasis on romantic and wedded love was as much a protest against marriage as it was a means of protecting it from extramarital temptations. In this respect it was a revolt of the heart against a system which denied its impulses, and which, in the absence of love, was a source of personal distress and social evil. In 1854 G. R. Drysdale described the contemporary situation: "A great proportion of the marriages we see around us, did not take place from love at all, but from some interested motive, such as wealth, social position, or other advantages; and in fact it is *rare* to see a marriage in which true love has been the predominating feeling on both sides." It was therefore "chiefly in works of fiction" that "the romance and impetuosity of love" were to be met with; for there "people indulge in a day-dream of what should be the feelings between the sexes." [108] But in the best fiction—notably in Thackeray, George Eliot, Trollope, and Charlotte Brontë—it was not a daydream people found but a passionate insistence that those feelings should be a reality, and a bitter arraignment of the system that ignored them.

In a society so permeated by the commercial spirit, love could be blatantly thrust aside if it interfered with more important values. "It would not signify about her being in love," says Mrs. Davilow in *Daniel Deronda*, speaking of her daughter, "if she would only accept the right person." Her brother-in-law, Mr. Gascoigne, a respected minister in the Church of England, takes even higher ground. When Gwendolen is hesitating to marry Grandcourt, for whom she has no affection whatever, he feels called upon to speak bluntly: "You hold

---

107. *Westminster Review*, 53 (1850), 480 (article attributed to W. R. Greg: see Bibliography).

108. *The Elements of Social Science*, p. 357.

your fortune in your own hands,—a fortune such as rarely happens to a girl in your circumstances,—a fortune in fact which almost takes the question out of the range of mere personal feeling, and makes your acceptance of it a duty. If Providence offers you power and position,—especially when unclogged by any conditions that are repugnant to you,—your course is one of responsibility, into which caprice must not enter." In pointed contrast with that philosophy, Catherine Arrowpoint in the same novel asserts the claim of love and marries the unacceptable musician, Herr Klesmer.[109] Other girls were less successful (Beatrix Potter was told she could not marry a publisher because he was in trade),[110] or were forced into unions they abhorred. Marriage would not be a happy institution, wrote Mill, until there was not only equality of rights on both sides but also "that full freedom of choice which as yet is very incomplete anywhere, and in most countries does not exist at all on the woman's side."[111]

Even the marriage of friendship, based on community of taste and interest and often justified for women because their great function— and their only career—was that of wife and mother, was arraigned in Charlotte Brontë. It was Hamlet without the Prince. Jane Eyre, for all her admiration of St. John Rivers and her desire to work with him in a foreign mission, refuses his proposal because they "did not love each other as man and wife should." "Can I," she asks herself, "receive from him the bridal ring, endure all the forms of love . . . and know that the spirit was quite absent? . . . No: such a martyrdom would be monstrous."[112]

The unhappiness of loveless marriages, whether made by personal choice or parental command, is documented through the literature of the time. The Lydgates, the Grandcourts, the Dombeys, the Kennedys, and the Barnes Newcomes are the readiest examples that come to mind. In every case, the intention is to preach the moral which Ethel Newcome learned from the experience of Barnes and Clara: that

109. Vol. 1, chap. 9, p. 123; chap. 13, p. 190; chap. 22, pp. 334–40. Cf. Clough's direct attack on allowing duty instead of love to dictate the choice of a husband or wife: "Thought may well be ever ranging," Poems, p. 26.

110. Margaret Lane, The Tale of Beatrix Potter (London and New York, 1946), p. 68.

111. Letters, 2, 241.

112. Chap. 34, p. 408. Though less sharply, the same note sounds in Trollope: see Bell Dale's rejection of her cousin Bernard in The Small House at Allington (1864) and Mary Lowther's of Harry Gilmore near the beginning of The Vicar of Bullhampton (1870). In the latter case especially the girl's friends find her scruples ridiculous.

since marriages of convenience issued in personal misery and made one or both partners cruel and selfish and cold, it was both foolish and wrong to marry without love. Or to put it in positive form, it was wise as well as romantic to make love the sanction of marriage, and therefore the supreme object to search for, the jewel more precious than gold.[113]

To find it and be frustrated by the system is a recurrent and tragic —perhaps one should say melodramatic—theme in Tennyson's poetry. In "Edwin Morris" the rendezvous of a penniless young painter with the daughter of a manufacturer is suddenly interrupted:

> While we stood like fools
> Embracing, all at once a score of pugs
> And poodles yell'd within, and out they came,
> Trustees and aunts and uncles. "What, with him!
> Go," shrill'd the cotton-spinning chorus; "him!" . . .
> Again with hands of wild rejection, "Go!—
> Girl, get you in!" She went—and in one month
> They wedded her to sixty thousand pounds,
> To lands in Kent and messuages in York,
> And slight Sir Robert with his watery smile
> And educated whisker.[114]

In *Maud* a similar interruption, made with the same purpose, results in murder. In "Locksley Hall," where the lovers are torn apart because Amy is the "puppet to a father's threat, and servile to a shrewish tongue," the man's "despair" is matched by the woman's suffering, married to a hunting squire who drinks too much. The indictment is summed up:

> Cursed be the social wants that sin
>   against the strength of youth!
> Cursed be the social lies that warp us
>   from the living truth!

113. Thackeray, *The Newcomes,* chap. 59, p. 626. For an extended arraignment of the Victorian marriage-market, see the whole of this chapter and chaps. 28 and 58. The central theme of Trollope's Parliamentary novels would seem to be love vs. ambition (measured in terms of money, social position, and power): see especially the study of Lady Laura Kennedy's unhappy marriage in *Phineas Finn* (1869) and *Phineas Redux* (1874), and the discussions in *The Eustace Diamonds* (1873), near the end of chap. 13. For the considerable amount of domestic poisoning going on in Victorian homes, see E. E. Kellett, *As I Remember,* pp. 232–5.
114. Lines 118–29.

> Cursed be the sickly forms that err from
>   honest Nature's rule!
> Cursed be the gold that gilds the
>   straiten'd forehead of the fool! [115]

Another and more damaging charge is brought against

> the woman-markets of the west,
> Where our Caucasians let themselves be sold,

in Tennyson's later study of frustrated love, "Aylmer's Field," written in the sixties when he was preoccupied with the problem of sensuality. After the protagonist Leolin is turned away by Edith's father because he is poor, he denounces "this filthy marriage-hindering Mammon" on the grounds that it "made the harlot of the cities":

> Nature crost
> Was mother of the foul adulteries
> That saturate soul with body. . . .
> He had known a man, a quintessence of man,
> The life of all—who madly loved—and he,
> Thwarted by one of these old father-fools,
> Had rioted his life out, and made an end. [116]

In other ways as well the marriage system was a factor in the increase of prostitution,—and therefore in the countermovement to exalt the importance of love. Not only did marriage without love increase "the great social evil"—so did the long engagements of the time. When a gentleman was expected to provide his wife with a carriage and to associate with men of wealth, the average age at which he could afford to marry was almost thirty. [117] The result, pointed out in *The Times* for

115. Lines 42, 59–62.

116. Lines 348–9, 373–7, 388–91. Hallam Tennyson, *A Memoir of Tennyson*, 2, 9, wrote of this poem: "My father always felt a prophet's righteous wrath against this form of selfishness [pride of wealth]; and no one can read his terrible denunciations of such pride trampling on a holy human love, without being aware that the poet's heart burnt within him while at work on this tale of wrong."

117. J. A. Banks, *Prosperity and Parenthood*, p. 48. For the social and financial requirements, see chaps. 3–4 of this valuable study. "According to the doctrines that are going now-a-days," says Captain Marrable in Trollope's *The Vicar of Bullhampton* (first ed. 1870; 2 vols. New York, 1906), *1*, chap. 21, p. 207, "it will be held soon that a gentleman can't marry unless he has got £3000 a year. It is the most heartless, damnable teaching that ever came up."

May 7, 1857, was that thousands were "living in sin . . . almost with-out a thought of the misery they are causing, and the curse they are laying up for themselves." They know they are sinning, they know— or should know—that they are increasing the demand for, and conse-quently the supply of, prostitutes, but "they dare not offend their family, alienate their friends, and lose their social position by making what the world calls an imprudent marriage. The very feeling which Heaven has given as a chief purifier of man's nature is darkening their conscience and hardening their heart, because the law of society contra-dicts the law of God." By all means, therefore, let us encourage earlier marriages, however poor they may be—marriages of love.[118] What makes this statement of special significance is the range of its context. Love is here exalted as a corrective for two of the major evils of the time: prostitution and a marriage system dominated by the commercial spirit.

By the sixties the system was beginning to break down. When the nineteenth-century current of freedom and individualism, innately hostile to social controls, was aided by the literary movement just examined, and strengthened by the support of the emancipated woman, the decline of marriages for convenience became a sign of the times. "We are beginning to see," wrote Frances Cobbe in 1864, "that the canon that 'marriage must hallow love' has a converse quite equally sacred, and that 'love also must hallow marriage.'"[119]

Love is not associated normally with the intellectual life. The prophets might recommend it, as they did, to cure the evils of sensual-ity and the marriage market, but that they themselves should have made it an idol is not what we should have expected. Yet under the circumstances it was natural enough. In an age of transition in which crucial problems, both practical and theoretical, exercised the thinking mind at the expense of the sensibility and in which baffled thought so often issued in a feeling of impotence and a mood of despair, the thinker could find in love a resolution of psychological tensions, and a religion, naturalistic or Platonic, to take the place of Christianity. This is the source, primarily, to which we owe the major love poetry of the age, and Browning's in particular.

The formation of Browning's ideas on the subject can be studied in the early philosophical poems. Paracelsus had subdued his life to one purpose, the aspiration to KNOW,

118. Quoted by Acton, *Prostitution*, pp. 170–1.
119. "The Nineteenth Century," *Fraser's Magazine*, 69 (1864), 493.

> consenting fully
> All passionate impulses its soil was formed
> To rear, should wither.

But knowledge attained had brought no happiness, and he remembers
with pain that

> there was a time
> When yet this wolfish hunger after knowledge
> Set not remorselessly love's claims aside.
> This heart was human once.

In that frame of mind he is ready enough to welcome Aprile, who
has aspired only to LOVE, and to draw the conclusion that both aspirations are necessary for the full development of man:

> *Par.* Die not, Aprile! We must never part.
> Are we not halves of one dissevered world,
> Whom this strange chance unites once more?
> Part? never!
> Till thou the lover, know; and I, the knower,
> Love—until both are saved.[120]

The same prayer, essentially, in more prosaic form was made by
Kingsley in 1848: "Would to God that . . . woman's heart would
help to deliver man from bondage to his own tyrannous and all-too-
exclusive brain—from our idolatry of mere dead laws and printed
books—from our daily sin of looking at men, not as our struggling
and suffering brothers, but as mere symbols of certain formulae, in-
carnations of sets of opinions." [121]

A deliverance of precisely this kind had occurred in the early
thirties when John Mill met Harriet Taylor. The extravagance of
Mill's passion and his idealization of "that woman" (Carlyle's epithet)
is clearly related to an education which had made him, on his own
confession, almost a reasoning machine. The emotional nature starved
for so long burst forth the more intensely.[122]

120. *Paracelsus*, Act II, lines 113–15, 123–6, 633–7. In this poem love is not so
much a human passion as a Shelleyan-Christian love of man: see the essay on
Paracelsus by William O. Raymond, *The Infinite Moment and Other Essays in
Robert Browning* (Toronto, 1950), chap. 9.

121. "On English Literature" (1848), *Literary and General Essays*, pp. 258–9.

122. *Autobiography*, chap. 4, p. 92, for the reasoning machine; chap. 5, p. 149,
and chap. 6, pp. 156–60, for the extravagant passion. Clough's "July's Farewell,"

For the intellectual burdened with a sense of weakness, stemming partly from lack of 'blood' and partly from the frustration of long analysis and reading and debate, the image of woman could take on the character of a Phidian statue. She could become an incarnation of the simplicity and force of elemental nature, possessed of the very strength man lacks—and to which he eagerly turns: "Tito . . . felt himself strangely in subjection to Romola with that simplicity of hers: he felt for the first time, without defining it to himself, that loving awe in the presence of noble womanhood, which is perhaps something like the worship paid of old to a great nature-goddess, who was not all-knowing but whose life and power were something deeper and more primordial than knowledge." [123] Though the analogy would be rough, one is tempted to substitute Browning and Pauline. The first published poem of Browning's begins:

> Pauline, mine own, bend o'er me—thy soft breast
> Shall pant to mine—bend o'er me—thy sweet eyes,
> And loosened hair and breathing lips, and arms
> Drawing me to thee—these build up a screen
> To shut me in with thee, and from all fear;
> So that I might unlock the sleepless brood
> Of fancies from my soul, their lurking-place,
> Nor doubt that each would pass, ne'er to return
> To one so watched, so loved and so secured.

The brood of fancies he proceeds to unlock are those which followed from his reading of Voltaire and Shelley, destructive attacks on the Evangelical faith inherited from his mother and wild dreams of liberty which later collapsed, both leaving him in an "aimless, hopeless state" —a state he would have escaped if, "doubting nothing," he

> had been led by thee,
> Through youth, and saved, as one at length awaked
> Who has slept through a peril. Ah vain, vain!

But it is not vain, perhaps, to hope that even now her love may save him, if only he will cease to "look within" or trust his "vain self, vague intuition—draining soul's wine alone in the still night."

Poems, p. 75, is an excellent illustration of a weary intellectual rushing from Oxford into the arms of love and nature. With special reference to the Kingsley quotation, cf. "The Bothie of Tober-na-Vuolich," Pt. VIII, lines 111–19, p. 166.

123. George Eliot, *Romola, 1*, Bk. I, chap. 9, p. 134.

> No more of this! We will go hand in hand,
> I with thee, even as a child—love's slave,
> Looking no farther than his liege commands.[124]

The poem was addressed to Eliza Flower, but it defines precisely the attitude of worship and dependence which he later adopted toward Elizabeth Barrett. "I should like to breathe and move and live," he wrote to her, "by your allowance and pleasure." And again, "Give me your counsel at all times, beloved: I am wholly open to your desires, and teaching, and direction. Try what you can make of me." When he speaks, in an unconscious echo from *Pauline*, of her hand being in his, he at once corrects himself: "rather mine in yours." Then, "all will be well." [125] Some years later, in one of his finest love poems, he expressed the same kind of desire:

> I would I could adopt your will,
>   See with your eyes, and set my heart
> Beating by yours, and drink my fill
>   At your soul's springs,—your part my part
> In life, for good and ill.[126]

It would be foolish to push the argument too hard, either in Browning's own life or in the period. There are many psychological factors which lead to a masculine dependence on a strong feminine will, real or imagined, and turn a woman—and a wife—into a guardian angel. I only suggest that one of them was the weakness consequent upon a baffled search for truth.[127]

At its extreme, the intellectual struggle could result, as we know, in a sick state of skeptical negation. Without a theory of life or action to sustain the will to live, lost in a wasteland of loneliness and despair, the sensitive mind could turn to love as the only value left to hold onto. Here at least was an anchor for the soul and a refuge from cosmic and social isolation. "Scepticism is my spirit," cries out Symonds. "In my sorest needs I have had no actual faith, and have said to destruction, 'Thou art my sister.' To the skirts of human love

---

124. *Pauline*, lines 1–9, 36–8, 50, 937–40, 947–9.

125. *The Letters of Robert Browning and Elizabeth Barrett*, 2, 98, 232, 545; and cf. 2, 117, 201, 268, 425. This point has been stressed by Betty Miller, *Robert Browning: a Portrait* (London, 1952), pp. 115–17.

126. "Two in the Campagna," stanza 9.

127. Arnold's attitude toward Marguerite is another example: see Lionel Trilling, *Arnold*, pp. 125–9, and the note to p. 128 on nineteenth-century novelists.

I have clung, and I cling blindly. But all else is chaos." In a letter of 1867 to his wife, in which he describes the "*ennui* or soul-sickness" he is suffering from, he writes: "You and I together must be strong in the world: be it what it is to be for us—or if we are weak, we are still together." [128] The same note is heard at the end of "Dover Beach," after the melancholy, long, withdrawing roar of the Sea of Faith:

> Ah, love, let us be true
> To one another! for the world, which seems
> To lie before us like a land of dreams,
> So various, so beautiful, so new,
> Hath really neither joy, nor love, nor light,
> Nor certitude, nor peace, nor help for pain;
> And we are here as on a darkling plain
> Swept with confused alarms of struggle and flight,
> Where ignorant armies clash by night.

In an earlier poem of Arnold's a more romantic love is invoked as a refuge from the loneliness which he felt so acutely:

> Two bleeding hearts,
> Wounded by men, by fortune tried,
> Outwearied with their lonely parts,
> Vow to beat henceforth side by side.
>
> The world to them was stern and drear;
> Their lot was but to weep and moan.
> Ah, let them keep their faith sincere,
> For neither could subsist alone! [129]

Finally, the cult of love and the idealization of woman is related, in another way, to the problem of doubt—doubt of traditional Christianity, and the resulting will to believe. When the religious emotions of worship were denied a divine object, they could readily turn to a human one, to a hero or a heroine; and romantic love, called on to fill the vacuum, could take on a new fervor and importance. Leslie Stephen adored Julia Duckworth because what he sought in marriage, as Noel Annan has said, was "a living image before whom he could

---

128. Brown, *Life of J. A. Symonds*, pp. 185, 238.
129. "Euphrosyne," lines 5–12. On Arnold's loneliness, see above, end of Chap. 3. I have inserted the semicolon after "drear," as it stood in the original text. There is no punctuation in *Poetical Works*, p. 203.

pour out the flood of devotion that could find no outlet in religion. He idealised her and longed to sacrifice himself for her." In one of his letters begging her to marry him, he wrote: "You must let me tell you that I do and always shall feel for you something which I can only call reverence as well as love. *Think* me silly if you please. . . . You see, I have not got any saints and you must not be angry if I put you in the place where my saints ought to be." [130]

That is the highly conscious analysis of an acknowledged agnostic. But I wonder if the same psychology was not working on a less conscious level in the far larger body of Christians who were troubled by religious doubts. It would be an obvious mistake, though not a stupid one, to imagine that Stephen's letter had been addressed by Browning to Elizabeth Barrett; for Browning's religious worries and anxieties, which had led him to turn away from speculation to the love of a strong personality, could also lead him to turn from doubt to a religion of love. But of a different kind from Stephen's. What for Stephen was a *substitute* for religious experience, for Browning *was* a religious experience, and therefore a powerful confirmation of divine reality. In his poetry the love of woman is not only strikingly analogous to the love of God—the attitude of worship, the acceptance of rejection (in her will is our peace), the lasting devotion—it is also explicitly identified with religion by making it the symbolic representation of divine love and merging the two in a typically Romantic distortion of Platonism. The woman in "Dîs Aliter Visum" reproaches her lover who had refused to seize the critical moment:

> Was there naught better than to enjoy?
>   No feat which, done, would make time break,
> And let us pent-up creatures through
>   Into eternity, our due?
> No forcing earth teach heaven's employ?

130. Annan, *Stephen*, p. 75. Cf. R. H. Hutton, "The Magnanimity of Unbelief," *Contemporary Thought and Thinkers*, 1, 301: "The failure to recognise the divine love and righteousness, will lead those who miss them to exaggerate the worth and value of human love and righteousness"; and Ruskin, "Fiction, Fair and Foul" (above, note 90), p. 286, protesting against the exaltation of love in the modern novel: "An era like ours, which has with diligence and ostentation swept its heart clear of all the passions once known as loyalty, patriotism, and piety, necessarily magnifies the apparent force of the one remaining sentiment which sighs through the barren chambers, or clings inextricably round the chasms of ruin."

> No wise beginning, here and now,
>> What cannot grow complete (earth's feat)
> And heaven must finish, there and then? . . .
>
> No grasping at love, gaining a share
>> O' the sole spark from God's life at strife
> With death, so, sure of range above
>> The limits here? For us and love,
> Failure; but, when God fails, despair.[131]

Equally, when love succeeds, it is a foretaste (and therefore a guarantee) of heavenly life; and as such can sweep away all anxieties in a rush of emotion at once erotic and spiritual. As Mr. Rose remarks in Mallock's *New Republic*, the goddess of love in its distinctly modern form is no longer the Aphrodite of the Greeks or the Mary of the Christians. "*She is a mysterious hybrid being, in whose veins is the blood of both of them.*" [132] She is, that is to say, an angel in the house.

No doubt this deification of love was partly an apologia for sex in a period when sex was evil; when, so to speak, it could not be taken straight or could not be contemplated naked; or, more important, when it was so closely connected with emotions of guilt and shame—for the most part, religious guilt and shame. Under such conditions, to be able to rationalize love as a sacrament is to free oneself from every repressive fear; and to transform what was evil, praise God, into something holy and divine. When Patmore was torn between the pagan philosophy of his father and the stern Puritanism of his mother—and between the sensuous and religious sides of his

131. Lines 116–23, 126–30. For his most explicit statement of this "Platonism," see "Summum Bonum."

132. Page 243. To put it more accurately, she is not a hybrid but the natural descendant of the family of Platonists, Pantheists, and amorous Christian mystics. Besides Browning, this sanctification of love is conspicuous in D. G. Rossetti (mainly in "The House of Life"; and see Graham Hough, *The Last Romantics*, pp. 74–82); in Patmore (besides the poetry, see "The Precursor" and "Ancient and Modern Ideas of Purity," in *Religio Poetae*); and in Kingsley (see *Letters and Memories*, *1*, 71, 160–7, 222–9, *2*, 116–19; unabridged ed., *1*, 186–91, 255–60, for the middle references—I cannot find the first and fourth in this ed.). Cf. the analogous deification of the hero, above, Chap. 12, sec. 2, and in this chapter the Platonizing of the Victorian home, p. 347. If marriage, as Kingsley puts it (first reference), is a spiritual and paradisaic state "like the kingdom of heaven," it might logically follow that romantic and physical love would continue in heaven. That idea is found in Kingsley, Browning, and Rossetti.

own nature—he resolved the conflict by adopting the amorous mysticism of the *Song of Songs*. Anyone who knows the story of Kingsley's early life can imagine the relief he felt when he decided that sexual desires were not human and evil, but human and spiritual, and that by giving himself up to love in childlike simplicity and self-abandonment, man was "readmitted into the very garden of the Lord." [133]

But for anyone aware of Kingsley's lifelong struggle with doubt, the word "readmitted" strikes with a further implication. For the sanctification of love and woman could rescue a worried Victorian from sliding into disbelief by reassuring him of a divine world, manifested here in the flesh, so to speak. The heroine of Patmore's poem is a woman around whose "footsteps blow the authentic airs of Paradise":

> Her disposition is devout,
>   Her countenance angelical;
> The best things that the best believe
>   Are in her face so kindly writ
> The faithless, seeing her, conceive
>   Not only heaven, but hope of it.

And therefore,

> Doubts of eternity ne'er cross
> The Lover's mind, divinely clear.[134]

Some years earlier, as the Victorian period began, a Romantic genius named Teufelsdröckh, who had been taught that "all women were holy, were heavenly," found himself imprisoned in a material universe from which God and human freedom were both excluded, leaving him in a state of agony and despair. In this crisis he met a beautiful maiden named Blumine and fell madly in love. "Did not her presence bring with it airs from Heaven? As from Aeolian Harps in the breath of dawn . . . unearthly music was around him, and lapped him into untried balmy Rest. Pale Doubt fled away to the distance; Life bloomed-up with happiness and hope. The past, then, was all a haggard dream; he had been in the Garden of Eden, then, and could not discern it! But lo now, the black walls of his prison melt away;

133. *Letters and Memories,* 1, 164 (unabridged ed., 1, 189). Cf. *Yeast,* chap. 7, p. 112.

134. *The Angel in the House,* Bk. I, Canto III, in *Poems,* p. 77; Canto IV, p. 83; Canto VII, p. 100.

the captive is alive, is free." [135] Blumine departed and Jane Welsh was no substitute. Carlyle did not find his salvation in love. But many Victorians, consciously or otherwise, were able to quiet their anxious doubts by finding an angel in the house.

To reflect for a moment on the preceding discussion is to realize with special force how much and how curiously the dynamics of an age affect the human mind. That Victorian ideas about religion or politics or education should have been closely related to the environment is only what we should expect. But offhand, we might not have supposed that such personal and elemental feelings as those about love and women would have been so strongly influenced by the hard competitive world of business or by the pressure of intellection and doubt. The Industrial Revolution creates the large, impersonal city and makes considerable wealth a requirement as well as a sanction for marriage. These factors contribute to an alarming increase of prostitution; a fact which, in turn, contributes to a strong protective movement in morals (a code of purity, censorship, and prudery) and an effort to idealize love and woman, including the mother, in the cause of purer conduct. And that is only one pattern, and an oversimplified one. It is equally true that the Industrial Revolution created a psychological and amoral atmosphere for which an idealized home with its high priestess offered a compensating sense of humanity and moral direction. And still, to all that must be added the parallel impulse to exalt the feminine nature and find a "divinity" in love which sprang from the needs of the baffled intellect. Our most personal attitudes are deeply affected by elements in the environment which seem to have no connection with them at all.

135. *Sartor Resartus*, Bk. II, chap. 5, pp. 133, 143.

Chapter 14

HYPOCRISY

> The want of independence of mind, the shutting their
> eyes and professing to believe what they do not, the
> running blindly together in herds, for fear of some
> obscure danger and horror if they go alone, is so
> eminently a vice of the English, I think, of the last
> hundred years . . . that I cannot but praise a person
> whose one effort seems to have been to deal per-
> fectly honestly and sincerely with herself.
>
> > *Matthew Arnold in 1855,*
> > *referring to Harriet Martineau*

> Perhaps there never was a more moral man than
> Mr. Pecksniff; especially in his conversation and cor-
> respondence. . . . His genius lay in ensnaring parents
> and guardians, and pocketing premiums.
>
> > *Dickens, Martin Chuzzlewit*

> If they smell a rat about the precincts of a cherished
> institution, they will always stop their noses to it if
> they can.
>
> > *Butler, on the Erewhonians* [1]

OF ALL THE CRITICISMS brought against them by the Lytton
Stracheys of the twentieth century, the Victorians would have pleaded
guilty to only one. They would have defended or excused their optimism, their dogmatism, their appeal to force, their strait-laced
morality, but they would have confessed to an unfortunate strain of
hypocrisy. To understand the charge, it must be broken down into
three specific counts. One, they concealed or suppressed their true
convictions and their natural tastes. They said the 'right' thing or
did the 'right' thing: they sacrificed sincerity to propriety. Second,

1. Arnold, *Letters, 1,* 51; Dickens, *Martin Chuzzlewit, 1,* chap. 2, pp. 14–15;
Butler, *Erewhon,* chap. 18, p. 182.

and worse, they pretended to be better than they were. They passed themselves off as being incredibly pious and moral; they talked noble sentiments and lived—quite otherwise. Finally, they refused to look at life candidly. They shut their eyes to whatever was ugly or unpleasant and pretended it didn't exist. Conformity, moral pretension, and evasion—those are the hallmarks of Victorian hypocrisy.

Now the leading Victorians, as I said, would have agreed to this bill of particulars, but they would have challenged the wholesale implications of duplicity and cowardice. For they recognized, as modern critics have not, that the circumstances were often extenuating and the motivation by no means always culpable. For one thing, hypocrisy might not be conscious and calculated (for the sake of personal gain). It might very well be unconscious or half-conscious: a conforming to the conventions out of sheer habit, or an understandable piece of self-deception. Furthermore, even when the deception was deliberate, it might be practiced for disinterested reasons, because one honestly believed that candor would do more harm than good; or from pardonable self-protection, because otherwise one might not be able to hold his job or support his family. And as for evasion, one might refuse to look at certain facts from sheer terror quite as much as from selfish prudence. In short, if we are to charge the Victorians with hypocrisy, the term must not carry its usual connotations of guilt. It should be used as they themselves used it for the most part, as a synonym for insincerity. It should be written 'hypocrisy.'

1. *Conformity*

In any society which is ambitious and at the same time unsure of itself because it is new, conventions assume enormous force. For his part, the individual himself is only too eager to find something to rely on, and to avoid any ideas or behavior which by distinguishing him from his class—or the class just above—might make him look like an outsider or an upstart. In Mill's analysis of "our times,"

> the individual or the family do not ask themselves—what do I prefer? or, what would suit my character and disposition? . . . They ask themselves, what is suitable to my position? what is usually done by persons of my station and pecuniary circumstances? or (worse still) what is usually done by persons of a station and circumstances superior to mine? . . . Even in what

people do for pleasure, conformity is the first thing thought of
. . . peculiarity of taste, eccentricity of conduct, are shunned
equally with crimes.[2]

"I do not mean," he explains, "that they choose what is customary in
preference to what suits their own inclination. It does not occur to
them to have any inclination except for what is customary." That is
an overstatement; the choice was often conscious. But much of the
time, no doubt, social conformity was a kind of sincere insincerity.
People adopted the conventions because from long training and habit
they themselves were conventional. "By dint of not following their own
nature," Mill continues, "they have no nature to follow . . . and are
generally without either opinions or feelings of home growth, or
properly their own." "They" could be the Dodsons of George Eliot's
Mill on the Floss, whose religion "consisted in revering whatever was
customary and respectable. . . . A Dodson would not be taxed with
the omission of anything that was becoming, or that belonged to that
eternal fitness of things which was plainly indicated in the practice of
the most substantial parishioners, and in the family traditions." There
was nothing deliberately insincere about this. A Dodson was an
honest Dodson, but in many respects he could not "be himself." [3]

One of the leading proprieties, I need hardly say, was religious
conformity. No one could be respectable who did not go to church,
and for ultrarespectability to the Church of England. But here, too,

2. *On Liberty*, chap. 3, p. 159. Cf. G. M. Young, *Victorian England*, pp. 23–4:
"Not only were the middle classes drawing apart from the poor, each stratum, in
a steady competition, was drawing away from the stratum next below, accentuating
its newly acquired refinements, and enforcing them with censorious vigilance.
The capriciousness, the over-emphasis, of Victorian propriety betrays its source."

3. Vol. 2, Bk. IV, chap. 1, pp. 5–6. Cf. Charlotte Brontë, speaking of Blanche
Ingram, the county beauty (*Jane Eyre*, chap. 18, pp. 181–2): "She was not genuine . . . nothing bloomed spontaneously on that soil; no unforced natural fruit
delighted by its freshness . . . she never offered, nor had, an opinion of her own."
By intended contrast, her rival Jane Eyre (chap. 14, p. 130) is not only frank and
sincere, but consciously takes "nature" for her guide in defiance of several well-
established conventions, much to the dismay of some good Victorian readers.
Clough's lines beginning (*Poems*, p. 27),

> Duty—that's to say complying
> With whate'er's expected here,

strike more sharply at this stunting of "sturdy limbs that Nature gave" by adding
the suggestion that to make conformity a duty is a tacit repudiation of the real
nature of duty.

habit and training played an important part. The conservatism of the English temper, its instinctive attachment to custom and tradition, its love of old associations, reinforced in this period by frightened reaction against radical innovation, kept many a person repeating the time-honored formulas he had learned in childhood without any clear awareness that in point of fact he no longer believed them. It is worth remembering that more than one Victorian was startled to discover that he was an agnostic. His belief had silently withered away while he had been professing it sincerely enough but not genuinely. "The change which takes place," wrote Leslie Stephen with his own experience in mind, "is not, in fact, an abandonment of beliefs seriously held and firmly implanted in the mind, but a gradual recognition of the truth that you never really held them." [4]

The proper thing to do is not only what the individual *wants* to do in order to belong to good society, or what he *does* do out of ingrained habit; it is also what he *must* do if he is to avoid social stigma. Mill's analysis began: "In our times, from the highest class of society down to the lowest, every one lives as under the eye of a hostile and dreaded censorship." [5] The censorship is bourgeois public opinion demanding that the proprieties be observed—or else! Bagehot described its despotism:

> You may talk of the tyranny of Nero and Tiberius; but the real tyranny is the tyranny of your next-door neighbor. . . . Public opinion is a permeating influence, and it exacts obedience to itself; it requires us to think other men's thoughts, to speak other men's words, to follow other men's habits. Of course, if we do not, no formal ban issues; no corporeal pain, no coarse penalty of a barbarous society is inflicted on the offender: but we are called "eccentric"; there is a gentle murmur of "most unfortunate ideas," "singular young man," "well-intentioned, I dare say; but unsafe, sir, quite unsafe." [6]

What is peculiar to the period is not that Mrs. Grundy was abroad —she always has been, as Bagehot's generalization implies—but that after being laughed at by society in 1798 she became so highly respected, so all-powerful a Victorian deity. [7] Those who have arrived

4. "An Apology for Plainspeaking," *Essays on Freethinking and Plainspeaking,* p. 375. Cf. *Henry Sidgwick: a Memoir,* pp. 74–5.

5. *On Liberty,* p. 159.

6. "The Character of Sir Robert Peel," *Works,* 3, 4–5.

7. Mrs. Grundy first appeared in Thomas Morton's play called *Speed the Plough*

have the best of reasons to guard the hard-won circle of respectability from vulgar intruders and to condemn any breach of the conventions which they themselves have cultivated so assiduously. Moreover, a middle class strongly under Wesleyan influence naturally laid
special emphasis on moral respectability and actively tried to enforce
the ethical standards of the Puritan revival.[8] But I think the primary
source of Mrs. Grundy's power was the fear reflected in the final
murmur which Bagehot hears: "But unsafe, sir, quite unsafe." Then,
as recently in the United States, intolerance and Star Chamber pro-
cedures were the result of panic in narrow and illiberal minds. The
Victorian middle class, as we have seen more than once in this book,
was ridden by fear: fear of radical politics (manhood suffrage as well
as socialism) because it threatened the bourgeois state of 1832; fear
of atheism because it might dissolve the moral sanctions on which
society rested; fear of sensuality because it menaced the family. So
motivated, it employed the full force of social stigma and ostracism
against any real or supposed deviation from political, moral, or religious orthodoxy. Huxley remembered how his Evangelical elders
referred in tones of horror to the skeptics and infidels who trusted in
carnal reason and doubted that the world was made in six days;
and how he was taught to believe that to question any statement in the
Bible was "a sin not less reprehensible than a moral delict." Among
his contemporaries nine hundred out of every thousand, he thought,
were brought up in this way, to add their voices in turn to the shower
of verbal missiles hurled at anyone suspected of any religious doubt.[9]

(1798). For her Victorian power, cf. William Johnston, *England as It Is* (1851), *1*,
223, quoting Arthur Helps: "This age is, indeed, he says, free from fear of the
faggot or the torture; but, he adds, 'fear of the social circle, fear of the newspaper,
fear of being odd, fear of what may be thought of people who never did think,
still greater fear of what somebody may say—are not these things a clinging dress
of torture?' And, again, he complains that we live 'in continual fear and danger
of the meanest aspects of public opinion.'"

8. In 1859 Mill noticed (*On Liberty*, chap. 3, p. 170) that a strong movement
of moral reform had set in, that there was "a philanthropic spirit abroad, for the
exercise of which there is no more inviting field than the moral and prudential
improvement of our fellow-creatures. These tendencies of the times cause the
public to be more disposed than at most former periods to prescribe general rules
of conduct, and endeavour to make every one conform to the approved standard."
Cf. chap. 1, pp. 100–1.

9. "Prologue" to *Controverted Questions*, reprinted in *Science and Christian
Tradition*, pp. 21–2.

Nor was that all the punishment one had to fear. He might well be dismissed from his job or excluded from a career suitable to his education and abilities.[10] When Froude published *The Nemesis of Faith* in 1849, he was not only abused by the newspapers "in the tone of the Dominican inquisition" because he denied the plenary inspiration of the Bible, but was forced to withdraw from a post as schoolmaster for which he had been selected by the Council of University College.[11]

A better breeding ground for hypocrisy could hardly be imagined. The *smart* man was happy to conform and play the game. The *average* man bowed with stolid acquiescence, like the London merchant Taine knew who was willing enough when he was in Paris on business to amuse himself on Sunday as freely as anyone else but would not do so at home for fear of what the neighbors would say.[12] The *conscientious* man was faced by the cruel alternative of either suffering the extreme penalties of confessing his real opinions or else of living a life of concealment and deception. Even were he willing to encounter the sacrifices and risks of nonconformity for himself, he would hesitate to impose them on his family. "Whoever has a wife and children has given hostages to Mrs. Grundy. The approbation of that potentate may be a matter of indifference to him, but it is of great importance to his wife." So it was that even the most courageous and unselfish of Victorians could find themselves involved in a measure of insincerity they hated.[13]

10. Mill, *Autobiography*, chap. 2, p. 37, where he thinks such cases are becoming fewer. But that was written in 1853 or 1854 (see Packe, *Life of Mill*, p. 369). The loss of means of subsistence for unpopular opinions is stated as a contemporary fact in *On Liberty* (1859), chap. 2, pp. 122–3, and *The Subjection of Women* (1869), chap. 4, p. 534.

11. Hayek, *John Stuart Mill and Harriet Taylor*, pp. 142, 301 n. 61.

12. *Notes on England*, pp. 238–9. And even at Paris on one occasion, when he was accompanied by his wife and daughters, he gave up all "gaiety,. good fellowship" on Sunday and became "stiff, starched, a perfect pattern of propriety."

13. Mill, *The Subjection of Women*, chap. 4, p. 535. The fear of public opinion and its destructive power was one cause, as we have seen (Chap. 5, sec. 2), for Victorian anti-intellectualism: i.e., the stopping short of logical conclusions or the outright refraining from speculation on first principles. A passage in *On Liberty*, chap. 2, p. 124, adds another: "Those who avoid this alternative [of fitting their own conclusions to propositions which they have internally renounced], do so by narrowing their thoughts and interest to things which can be spoken of without venturing within the region of principles, that is, to small practical matters." To escape insincerity one turns anti-intellectual.

Cocial ambitions and social pressures were so characteristic of the time we forget that to some extent, especially in the area of religion, the Victorians adopted an equivocal position irrespective of what was proper or prudent. By silence or outward profession they conformed to orthodox opinion for what they honestly considered good reasons, —which were sometimes rationalizations, no doubt, but not always, or entirely. Many men distinguished for their wisdom and virtue who were complete skeptics at heart nevertheless refrained, according to Mill, from any avowal of their religious disbelief, "less from personal considerations, than from a conscientious . . . apprehension, lest by speaking out what would tend to weaken existing beliefs, and by consequence (as they suppose) existing restraints, they should do harm instead of good." [14] Mill himself had once adopted this kind of accommodation and argued that infidels should "abstain from either directly attacking, or indirectly undermining Christianity," because otherwise they would be "shaking the only firm convictions and feelings of duty" which people had without providing any substitute.[15] Another Victorian, Henry Sidgwick, no less famous than Mill for intellectual integrity, concealed his disbelief in immortality because he thought "the general loss of such a hope, from the minds of average human beings as now constituted," might result in the dissolution of society.[16] In addition to the moral argument for reticence, there was also the honest reluctance to rob people of a faith they still enjoyed. "Reverent and kindly minds" shrank "from giving an unnecessary shock to the faith which comforts many sorely tried souls"; and all the more so at a time when doubt and disbelief were so painful. Can any duty to truth possibly require us to inflict keen distress on other human beings, and especially on "those to whom we are bound by the tenderest and most consecrated ties?" [17]

The fact is that the Victorian agnostics, and even the theists, were on the spot. They were caught in an impossible dilemma. They could neither speak out nor be silent with a good conscience. To be honest involved the guilty sense of perhaps undermining the moral foundations of society or depriving people of their spiritual comforts; to be reticent was to feel like a hypocrite. "It is a most painful position

14. *Autobiography*, chap. 2, p. 38. Cf. the passage from his "Utility of Religion," quoted earlier, p. 127.

15. *Letters, 1*, 5. The date is 1831.

16. *Henry Sidgwick: a Memoir*, p. 357.

17. Leslie Stephen, "An Apology for Plainspeaking," p. 369; John Morley, *On Compromise*, chap. 4, p. 122.

to a conscientious and cultivated mind," wrote Mill, "to be drawn in contrary directions by the two noblest of all objects of pursuit, truth, and the general good." [18]

The apparent conformity of reticence was complemented by the actual conformity of profession. More and more as the years passed the Victorian churches were filled by men who did not believe the prayers they said or the creeds they repeated. Many of them, no doubt, were actuated by worldly motives, but some at least found justification in the same "good" reasons that were used in defense of reticence, though the pinch of insincerity was naturally sharper when overt profession was made. They could feel (as some unbelievers do today in the 1950's) that a church was so vital for social and family stability that their attendance and support was something like a duty—though to many an unpleasant duty, involving, as it did, a consciousness of duplicity.[19] The Victorian dilemma is seen in Trollope's Mr. Quickenham, Q.C. When he stayed away from church he felt "a sting of conscience in that he was neglecting a duty"; and when he did go, he felt "the presence of some unsatisfactory feelings of imposture." [20]

It is true, however, that insincere profession was sometimes less defensible and more justly to be called hypocritical. With nice irony Carlyle once explained how the followers of Voltaire discovered he had gone too far in his attack on religion. It was not really a superfluity and a nuisance. On the contrary, "being a great sanction to civil morality," it was of real use "for keeping society in order, at least the lower classes, who have not the feeling of Honour in due force." As the fear of revolution increased in the thirties and forties, the "advanced Liberal" recommended his fellow men "to believe in God, that so Chartism might abate, and the Manchester Operatives be got to spin peaceably!" [21] Is hell a fiction? Of course, but it is such a useful fiction for the proletariat—useful to us, that is—we must pretend to believe it and maintain its truth.[22] And so with all the other

18. "Utility of Religion," *Three Essays on Religion*, p. 71. Cf. Morley, ibid., pp. 122–3, and a poem of Hardy's called "The Problem."

19. See Morley, chap. 4, pp. 139–40, though his judgment is harsher than mine; and cf. Hardy's later outline for an article to be called "The Hard Case of Would-Be-Religious. By Sinceritas," in Florence E. Hardy, *The Later Years of Thomas Hardy, 1892–1928* (New York, 1930), pp. 121–2.

20. *The Vicar of Bullhampton* (first ed. 1870; 2 vols. New York, 1906), 2, chap. 5, p. 47.

21. Carlyle, "Goethe," *Essays, 1*, 215–16; *Past and Present*, Bk. III, chap. 15, p. 228.

22. Morley, *On Compromise*, chap. 2, pp. 30–2. Cf. E. E. Kellett, *As I Remem-*

articles of the supernatural system. More common, perhaps, than this deliberate hypocrisy was the unconscious hypocrisy of men who supported Christianity and fought atheism from the same selfish motives, but disguised them from themselves. Belfort Bax remembered how the conventional arguments against free thought were topped off by an additional point: that if it prevailed, there would be no security for property and its interests. "Now it was this sort of remark," he says, "thrown in . . . as a make-weight, that first opened my eyes to the subconscious insincerity or unconscious hypocrisy of much of middle-class public opinion on these subjects." [23] But side by side with such hypocritical expediency, conscious or unconscious, was the disinterested profession of men who honestly felt they would do more harm than good to the *whole* of society by refusing to support a church. [24]

The problem of religious conformity was most acute and most painful, naturally enough, among the clergy. The minister of God who found his faith giving way could neither remain silent nor stay at home on Sunday. He had to practice some degree of hypocrisy in the pulpit, in the very presence of God, so to speak, or else resign his living when resignation might well mean ruin for himself and his family. It is the hard case of Mr. Hale in *North and South* and of Robert Elsmere in Mrs. Ward's novel; of the Erewhonian priests; and of the man described by Kellett—forty years old, with a wife and two children, who had entered the ministry with happy confidence at twenty-three and now found himself battered by misgivings:

---

ber, p. 103: Except for a few bold spirits like Mill and Harriet Martineau, "unbelievers held that, as religion was necessary to keep the lower classes in order, the pretence must be maintained that all the better people were devout Christians. . . . One of the most justly censurable features of the early Victorian age was this reticence, which is one of the few characteristics of the time really deserving to be called hypocrisy. For the sake of political expediency . . . scores of leading men disguised their real opinions and pretended to an orthodoxy to which they could lay no real claim."

23. E. Belfort Bax, *Reminiscences*, pp. 17–18.

24. The new historical point of view made this kind of compromise all the easier to follow. If all religions were so many attempts to embody a higher moral law which could save man from the slavery of unregulated passion, we need not hesitate to attend a church even if we do not believe its formularies. What is literally false is at any rate symbolically true. This was George Eliot's defense of conformity (Cross's *Life*, 3, 179, from a letter to Cross, October 20, 1873), though qualified by the provision that it must not be accompanied "by a consciousness of hypocrisy." One must really be able, I take it, to read the dogma as a symbol.

The struggle was almost visible in his face, and was indeed painful. Like Arthur Hallam, "he fought his doubts," but unlike him, gathered no strength. More and more "perplexed in faith," he found it quite impossible to "beat his music out." But he had no private income, and the prospect of a refuge outside his church was remote. To resign was to exchange security for uncertainty, and a small but sufficient living for the real danger of starvation. What added to his trouble was the impossibility of making the few friends to whom he confided his difficulties understand them. The hard-headed men thought him a fool to imperil his position for mere fantastic scruples; and to the truly religious the doubts were sins, to be crushed down.

This man took the plunge and resigned from the church.[25] He must have been one in a thousand. Of the other nine hundred and ninety-nine, a few, no doubt, were cowards and time-servers, but the vast majority stayed uncomfortably where they were and did their unhappy best to ignore the dogmas they disbelieved, or to give them a private interpretation in line with modern thought. The latter expedient—recommended by both Arnold and Mill[26]—could, however, be a boomerang. As Mark Rutherford found out from personal experience, "the preacher who . . . uses a vocabulary which has a certain definite meaning, and has had this meaning for centuries . . . cannot stay to put his own interpretation upon it whenever it is upon his lips, and so his hearers . . . imagine him to be much more orthodox than he really is." His very effort to avoid hypocrisy landed him in a hypocritical position.[27] Kellett records a striking case of this irony. A minister preached the sermons of F. W. Robertson or Horace Bushnell word for word because he found it impossible any longer "to write out and learn, as *his own* thoughts," Christian doctrines he did not believe.[28]

Conformity for "good" reasons or for self-protection is a conscious process. But a good deal of religious 'hypocrisy' was unconscious or half-conscious. "What we have to complain of," wrote Carlyle in the *Latter-Day Pamphlets*, "is that . . . every man lies,—with blasphe-

25. Kellett, *As I Remember*, p. 351. The main passages in *Robert Elsmere* are in chap. 27, pp. 394, 401–2, and chap. 30, pp. 432–3. In Butler's *Erewhon*, the priests appear in chap. 15, pp. 155–8, but see the whole chapter for an essay on religious hypocrisy. Also, cf. "A Clergyman's Doubts," in his *Notebooks*, pp. 304–8.

26. *Last Essays on Church and Religion*, No. 1, pp. 209–13; "Inaugural Address at St. Andrews," *James & John Stuart Mill on Education*, p. 188.

27. *Autobiography*, chap. 4, p. 41.

28. Kellett, pp. 349–50.

mous audacity, and does not know that he is lying. . . . The light of our inner eyesight is gone out. . . . 'Cant and even sincere Cant': O Heaven, when a man doing his sincerest is still but canting! For this is the sad condition of the insincere man." [29] What is meant is not the sincere insincerity mentioned earlier that sprang from conservatism and ingrained habit. Sincere canting is self-deception. This is brought out plainly in Carlyle's account of Sterling's ordination, published a year later, where the loss of "inner eyesight" is again noticed: "No man of Sterling's veracity, had he clearly consulted his own heart, or had his own heart been capable of clearly responding, and not been dazzled and bewildered by transient fantasies and theosophic moonshine, could have undertaken this function." [30] But it was not easy for a thoughtful Victorian to consult his own heart clearly. His vision was blurred or blinded by a powerful current of emotion: the fear of finding there an ominous and horrible doubt, or, to put it in positive form, of finding a ghastly suspicion that atheism and materialism were true, and human life, therefore, a meaningless existence in a meaningless universe. In that state of mind self-deception was all but impossible to avoid, and the refuge of 'believing' what one needed so desperately to believe almost inescapable. In the preface to *Yeast* Kingsley told the whole story in two perceptive sentences:

> The mass . . . are fancying that they are still adhering to the old creeds, the old church, to the honoured patriarchs of English Protestantism. . . . To me they seem . . . to be losing most fearfully and rapidly the living spirit of Christianity, and to be, for that very reason, clinging all the more convulsively—and who can blame them?—to the outward letter of it, whether High Church or Evangelical; unconscious, all the while, that they are sinking out of real living belief, into . . . dead self-deceiving belief-in-believing.[31]

2. Moral Pretension

Although everyone at times pretends to be better than he is, even to himself, the Victorians were more given to this type of deception than we are. They lived in a period of much higher standards of

29. No. 8, pp. 309–10. On p. 312 he speaks of human speech being "false to a degree never witnessed in this world till lately . . . false with consciousness of being sincere!"

30. *Life of Sterling*, Pt. II, chap. 2, p. 105.

31. Page xxii.

conduct—too high for human nature. As men were required to support Christianity by church attendance and active charity, and to accept the moral ideals of earnestness, enthusiasm, and sexual purity, the gap between profession and practice, or between profession and the genuine character, widened to an unusual extent. But here again we encounter various kinds and degrees of insincerity. When Sir Walter Scott contrasted the eighteenth century with his own time (1827), he remarked that men were "now under the necessity of being actuated, or at least appearing to be so, by nobler motives than their predecessors proposed to themselves." [32] The second alternative involves conscious duplicity, but the first only self-deception or sincere insincerity.

The discrepancy between Sunday and Monday was the most conspicuous example of "that utter divorce," as Froude put it, "between practice and profession which has made the entire life of modern England a frightful lie." [33] The same man who on Sunday was a pious and devout Christian, pillar of the Church, supporter of foreign missions, distributor of Bibles, on Monday was the tough businessman and hard bargainer whose creed was "Each for himself . . . The devil take the hindmost, o!" [34] In words echoed by all the prophets, Kingsley charged the Victorians with the hypocrisy of worshiping one god and following another: "It is most sad, but most certain, that we are like those Pharisees of old in this . . . that we too have made up our mind that we can serve God and Mammon at once; that the very classes among us who are most utterly given up to money-making, are the very classes which, in all denominations, make the loudest religious profession; that our churches and chapels are crowded on Sundays by people whose souls are set, the whole week through, upon gain and nothing but gain." [35] Clearly the revival of Evangelical Christianity existing side by side in the middle classes with the new commercial spirit and a political economy of self-interest and unlimited competition widened the eternal disparity between ideals and reality.

No doubt the situation bred its quota of outright hypocrites, like those in Clough's acid poem who repeat the ten commandments with cynical qualifications:

32. *Miscellaneous Prose Works* (6 vols. Edinburgh, 1827), 3, 517.
33. *The Nemesis of Faith*, p. lii.
34. Clough, "In the Great Metropolis," *Poems*, p. 91.
35. Sermon 26, "God and Mammon," *Westminster Sermons*, in *Works*, 28, 293–4.

> Thou shalt not steal; an empty feat,
> When it's so lucrative to cheat;

and so with the other nine.[36] But the representative servant of God
and Mammon, as Kingsley suggests, was a Pharisee. He imagined,
sincerely enough, that although he was sometimes a sinner (like everyone else), he was a true servant of God. He was not being virtuous
and pious because to be so was to win social prestige, or supporting
the Church because its precepts of honesty, work, and charity would
fend off revolution and make for good efficiency—and good profits.
No, these utilitarian advantages—so he persuaded himself—were simply by-products of the Christian life he adopted from the highest
motives. A striking illustration of this psychology occurs (the source
could hardly be more significant) in this very sermon of Kingsley's.
After contrasting the two goals of seeking the good things of this
world and seeking first the kingdom of God, and calling his congregation to "the noble life, the pure life . . . the heroic life, the
Godlike life," he paused to ask, "How will this help you to rise in
life?" But he did not answer, "Not at all. It will help you to rise to a
far higher and heavenly life, here and hereafter." No. His answer was
much more reassuring:

> The very good things of this world—wealth, honour, power, and
> the rest, for the sake of which worldly men quarrel, and envy,
> and slander, and bully, and cringe, and commit all basenesses and
> crimes—all these shall come to you of their own accord by the
> providence of your Father in heaven and by His everlasting
> Laws, if you will but learn and do God's will, and lead the
> Christlike and the Godlike life. . . . You shall find that godliness
> hath the promise of this life, as well as of the life which is to
> come.[37]

You have your cake and you eat it too. I do not mean that Kingsley
is advocating the Christian life simply for worldly reasons he has
disguised from himself: he believed in its intrinsic and spiritual value.
But, still, to recommend it in these terms and in this sermon—to say,
in effect, don't serve Mammon, serve God because He can give you
all that Mammon promises and heaven too—is, I submit, a subtle
form of the very disease he is attacking.

Sometimes the servant of these twin gods was aware of a divided

36. "The Latest Decalogue," *Poems*, pp. 60–1.
37. Pages 297–8.

allegiance. His conscience troubled him—not enough, it is true, to force him to change his way of life, but enough to make his Sunday professions at least a sincere expression of what he wanted to be, of what he honestly thought he *ought* to be. His role of pious Christian was motivated by guilt: it was a restitution—sufficient unto the soul of him—for his commercial sins. This was the man, George Gissing thought, whom foreign critics had in mind when they called the English hypocritical. But the right term was "pharisaic":

> The blatant upstart who builds a church . . . may have lied and cheated for every sovereign he possesses; he may have polluted his life with uncleanness; he may have perpetrated many kinds of cruelty and baseness—but all these things has he done against his conscience, and, as soon as the opportunity comes, he will make atonement for them in the way suggested by such faith as he has, the way approved by public opinion. His religion, strictly defined, is *an ineradicable belief in his own religiousness.*

Precisely. Religion, in the full sense, is incompatible with any hypocrisy, but "religiousness" is not. Gissing continues: "When, at public dinners and elsewhere, he tuned his voice to the note of edification, this man did not utter the lie of the hypocrite; he *meant every word he said.*" [38] But he was deceiving himself as well as others. Sometimes this psychology took a more subtle and more pardonable form. Beatrice Webb's father, the railway magnate, spent his days living by "the ethics of capitalist enterprise," but he went to church regularly, took the sacrament, and prayed night and morning, repeating "the prayer taught him at his mother's lap—'Gentle Jesus, meek and mild, look upon a little child,' etc." In that way, to that extent, he repudiated the moral environment in which he lived, and struggled against "the sins of the world and the flesh" in which he was immersed. [39] The pious businessman who professed Christian virtues he ignored in practice might be a fine hypocrite, but he was more likely to be a Pharisee, concealing his worldly motives from himself or proving that at heart he was really a good Christian by a gesture of atonement or repudiation.

The commercial spirit was not responsible, however, for the most

38. *The Private Papers of Henry Ryecroft* (first ed. 1903; London, 1914), "Winter," sec. 20, pp. 274–5. The remarks on page 277 show that Gissing is discussing the situation prior to 1873.

39. *My Apprenticeship*, pp. 5–7.

odious forms of moral pretension: the unctuous mouthing of pious
sentiments and a sanctimonious prudery. Both must be traced mainly
to Puritanism. For when the saintly character became the ideal of
religious life, those who could give a reasonable facsimile thereof
possessed a ready means of gaining enormous respect or of masking
a worldly or vicious career. The old charge, first heard in the seven-
teenth century, was renewed in the nineteenth, when "cant" and
"hypocrisy" were hurled at Methodists and Evangelicals, not without
some justice,[40] and "canting hypocrites" were conspicuous in the
contemporary novel. There was the immortal Mr. Pecksniff, that
"most exemplary man, fuller of virtuous precept than a copy-book,"
whose dress and manner and very tone of voice, "all tended to the
same purpose, and cried aloud, 'Behold the moral Pecksniff!'"—and
whose "genius lay in ensnaring parents and guardians, and pocketing
premiums." [41] And there was Mr. Brocklehurst who had "a Master to
serve whose kingdom is not of this world," and whose mission as
head of the charity school of Lowood was to mortify the lusts of the
flesh, but not his own or his family's—his pupils'; and which in
their case he defines as the craving for anything that might cost
him a single extra penny, like sufficient food or decent dress.[42] Unlike
these "coarse hypocrites" who consciously affect godliness in order
to impose on society, George Eliot's Bulstrode persuades himself
that the evil he has done has been a service to God.[43]

The pretension to excessive piety and virtue often took a particular
form peculiar to the period. When a new middle class, determined
to be proper, was too unsure of itself to risk anything that might
be thought vulgar, and when Evangelicalism and the fear of sensuality
encouraged a rigid censorship, the affectation of prudery was certain
to occur.[44] The prude raises his hands in holy horror at such a nasty
remark—a gesture well calculated to impress all present with the
extraordinary propriety and moral delicacy of a person so readily

40. See George Eliot, "Janet's Repentance," *Scenes of Clerical Life*, chaps. 1–4.
41. See *Martin Chuzzlewit*, chap. 2. The quotations are on *1*, 14–15.
42. *Jane Eyre*, chap. 7, p. 59.
43. George Eliot makes this contrast herself in *Middlemarch*, *3*, chap. 61, 122.
A full analysis of Evangelical insincerity is given in her essay, "Evangelical Teaching: Dr. Cumming," *Westminster Review*, *64* (1855), 436–62.
44. The first cause is well brought out by Lionel Stevenson on pp. 259–62 of his
illuminating article, "Prude's Progress," *Virginia Quarterly Review*, *13* (1937),
257–70, but I do not think he lays sufficient stress on Evangelicalism. The censorship, which is usually included under "prudery," is discussed above, pp. 356–7.

shocked. Hence the association of prudery with cant among intelligent critics, though not in the public at large.[45] But it may also warrant the charge of outright hypocrisy, for the prude may be obsessed with what he is pretending to shut out of his mind. To feel shocked can be a mode of surreptitious enjoyment. Certainly to separate male and female authors in a library or drape the legs of a piano is to betray an abnormal preoccupation with sex; or, as a modern psychiatrist has put it, to pervert—that is, to sexualize—the normal inhibitions of modesty.[46] This "prurient prudery" (Charles Reade's phrase)[47] is the exact reflection of an age given at once to both excessive admiration of purity and excessive concern, out of anxiety or desire, with the indulgence of passion.

But the Puritan revival issued in less reprehensible forms of insincerity. Besides encouraging some people to put on a mask of impeccable virtue, it forced many more to try to appear, or to try to be, more Christlike than they were. In Evangelical and Dissenting circles the child was exposed to a discipline that put a premium on piety, for piety was the indispensable mark of conversion. When Jane Eyre makes the honest but shocking confession to Mr. Brocklehurst that she does not like the Psalms, she is put in her place at once with the example of an angelic child:

> "I have a little boy, younger than you, who knows six Psalms by heart: and when you ask him which he would rather have, a ginger-bread nut to eat, or a verse of a Psalm to learn, he says: 'Oh! the verse of a Psalm! angels sing Psalms;' says he, 'I wish to be a little angel here below;' he then gets two nuts in recompense for his infant piety."
>
> "Psalms are not interesting," I remarked.
>
> "That proves you have a wicked heart; and you must pray to God to change it: to give you a new and clean one: to take away your heart of stone and give you a heart of flesh."

45. Besides the evidence in Stevenson, pp. 257–8, see E. P. Hood, *The Age and Its Architects*, p. 408. In "English Morality," *Monthly Repository*, new ser. 7 (1833), 784, the same charge is leveled at the nation: "England is a prude among nations. As long as she preserves external propriety, she plumes herself on the possession of superior virtue" and shakes her head at flirting France, etc. etc.

46. Edward Glover, "Victorian Ideas of Sex," in *Ideas and Beliefs of the Victorians*, pp. 363–4.

47. Quoted by Kellett, *As I Remember*, p. 344.

She must pray, that is, for conversion.[48] And converted the child
would be if anxious parents and insistent ministers, with inquisition
and terrifying accounts of what happened to those who did not
experience God, had anything to do with it.[49] The result was to be
expected: one *was* converted, willy-nilly. Either he "answered the
pious man according to his piety, and thus practised a defensive
deception," like Mr. Brocklehurst's child, or he persuaded himself, or
tried to, that he had been saved, like Mark Rutherford at the age of
fourteen:

> I was told it was time I became converted. . . . I knew that I
> had to be "a child of God," and after a time professed myself
> to be one, but I cannot call to mind that I was anything else
> than I always had been, save that I was perhaps a little more
> hypocritical; not in the sense that I professed to others what
> I knew I did not believe, but in the sense that I professed it
> to myself. I was obliged to declare myself convinced of sin;
> convinced of the efficacy of the atonement; convinced that I
> was forgiven; convinced that the Holy Ghost was shed abroad in
> my heart; and convinced of a great many other things which
> were the merest phrases.[50]

And he was obliged, of course, to act accordingly. This might be
called being taught to deceive yourself. Since it paid off so hand-
somely in prestige, it was not a habit one would easily forget.

But apart from conversion as such, and in all religious quarters,
children were brought up to hear such constant emphasis on duty
and self-sacrifice, on benevolence and sympathy, and such constant
disapproval of any criticism whatever of those they should love and
respect, especially parents, brothers, and sisters, that they were under
the necessity not only of being actuated by noble motives but of *not*
being actuated by any which were selfish, mean, or destructive. As ε
result, they became adept, as Phyllis Bottome remembered, at rationaliz-
ing pleasure: "Duty, to children of my education, was set dangerously
high and off the track of natural life, so that it became a smoke screen
for our wishes. God was an ace we had up our sleeves and played
at convenient moments. I thought, or I believed that I thought be-

48. Chap. 4, p. 27.
49. See E. E. Kellett, *Religion and Life in the Early Victorian Age,* pp. 74–6,
from whom the quotation that follows just below is taken.
50. *Autobiography,* chap. 1, pp. 9–10. W. H. White was fourteen in 1846.

cause I *wished*, that it was my duty to stay at Swanscombe, helping my father and mother." [51] Self-deception was complemented by sincere insincerity. Through long training one might come in time to express fine sentiments spontaneously, free from any sense whatever that he was concealing the contradictory feelings he must in some degree have had; for those feelings were now deeply repressed. In *The Daisy Chain*, Richard and Margaret May have occasion to discuss their much more successful juniors. Norman has had a brilliant career at Oxford, where Richard was unable to finish. Ethel has displaced Margaret as the father's favorite daughter, a position of special significance because Dr. May is a widower. But not a word of criticism is uttered, not a hint appears of the least trace of envy in their hearts. Instead, first they praise Ethel and then they praise Norman. And the author, Charlotte Yonge, is at pains to emphasize their complete sincerity: "The elder brother and sister, who might have had some jealousy of the superiority of their juniors, spent a good happy hour in dwelling on the shining qualities they loved so heartily." [52] Plainly, Miss Yonge has been so trained to suppress the normal feelings of jealousy that she can believe they do not exist in good characters. Or, if we imagine the incident as occurring in actual life, we could say that although Richard and Margaret were not being genuine, they were not consciously pretending to be saints, nor even practicing any self-deception; and that the artificial character had become the only one they had.

Charlotte Yonge was simply a good Christian. In ardent and earnest Christians, under the powerful influence of the Puritan revival, the necessity for superhuman virtue was much greater, with a proportionate increase of insincerity. When every action, every word, every thought, no matter how small or apparently trivial, must conform to the will of God, when the least failing was a sin, condemned by the tender conscience, a vital Christian had to strive for a purity of life, both outer and inner, that could not possibly be attained, even approximately, without a constant and drastic suppression of "impurities." Outwardly, he could never relax from his appointed calling of witness to divine truth by the example of his character and action. He had to show by everything he said and everything he did that he, at any rate, had brought his "whole life into obedience to Him

51. *Search for a Soul* (New York, 1948), p. 301. Miss Bottome was not born until 1882, but the same point is made by Clough in 1849, "Amours de Voyage," Canto II, lines 272–5, *Poems*, p. 195.

52. Pt. II, chap. 7, p. 366.

whose world we live in, and who has purchased us with His blood."
It is true, continues Thomas Hughes, describing the ideal as he heard
it preached by Thomas Arnold, that a boy indoctrinated in such a
creed might seem at first to be a bit of a prig and a Pharisee, but after
a year or two the " 'thoughtful life' has become habitual to him, and
fits him as easily as his skin." [53] As easily, perhaps, but by no means
so naturally. Take the master himself. He gave the impression of a man
who knew what others only believed, who realized the operation of
something more than human in his abhorrence of evil and his love of
good. "The earnestness of his religious convictions and feelings *were
ever bursting forth,* so as to make it strongly felt that his life, both
outward and inward, was rooted in God." [54] No one who has read
Stanley's biography sympathetically, free from the malicious bias of
Lytton Strachey, could believe that Arnold was posing. His passionate
devotion to the cause of God is unquestionable. And yet the impression he gave was not the whole truth. We know on his own confession
what we might well suspect, that there were days when "all the feelings or principles of belief or of religion altogether" were in utter
abeyance; and when, pleased with external and worldly comforts,
without having a particle of Christian principle in his mind, he was
"living a life of virtual Atheism." [55] On such days did he keep to his
bed? or did he stride to his pulpit and into his classroom with gesture
and countenance and speech that showed his life was rooted in God?
Even on "good" days, it was impossible, surely, for Arnold's religious
convictions and feelings to be forever bursting forth naturally. A
strain of self-deception, even sometimes just a trace of *conscious* deception in a good cause, were inevitable.

This is equally true of the inner life. Here an Evangelical Christian
had to face the tremendous question of motives, since it was but too
easy, so subtle are the temptations of the world, to do the right
thing for the wrong reason: to be good because it was prudent, to do
a hard duty for the praise and respect it would evoke, to criticize an
erring brother because you disliked him, and so on. Let a man catch
a single glimpse of such selfish motives and he could not doubt that
God was aware of them too; and that his soul was corrupt and its

53. Preface to the 6th ed., *Tom Brown's School Days,* pp. 16–17. The general
background is in Chap. 10 above, sec. 2.

54. Stanley, *Life of Arnold,* chap. 2, pp. 28–9, 38. The italics are mine.

55. Ibid., p. 53, from a letter of November 20, 1819; and cf. the later remark,
quoted above, p. 160, where one strongly suspects he was drawing on personal
knowledge.

punishment certain and terrifying. But—what one doesn't know
With the best of intentions to perform the duty of self-examination,
one might not look too closely. With half-conscious or even unconscious self-deception, he might effectively hide the selfish motive
from himself and therefore also—in psychological fact—from God.
In 1847 Arthur Helps quoted a passage from Hazlitt's essay "On
Cant and Hypocrisy." By "making us accountable for every word,
thought, or action, under no less a responsibility than our everlasting
future welfare or misery," Hazlitt had written, Calvinism had "added
incalculably to the difficulties of self-knowledge . . . and made it
almost impossible to distinguish the boundaries between the true and
false, in judging of human conduct and motives. A religious man
is afraid of looking into the state of his soul, lest at the same time
he should reveal it to Heaven; and tries to persuade himself that by
shutting his eyes to his true character and feelings, they will remain
a profound secret both here and hereafter. This is a strong engine
and irresistible inducement to self-deception." [56]

3. Evasion

Strictly speaking (as the last quotation reminds us), all forms of
self-deception involve evasion. The intense desire to cling to Christianity or to be a model Christian, with the correlative fears of finding
doubt in the mind or evil in the heart, and the general pressure to
adopt noble attitudes, made clear-eyed self-examination rare and
difficult. Whatever threatened needs so great or social requirements so
strong was shut out from consciousness. But this is not what we mean
by charging the Victorians with evasion. We mean a process of deliberately ignoring whatever was unpleasant, and pretending it did
not exist; which led in turn to the further insincerity of pretending
that the happy view of things was the whole truth. In a word, they
conveniently looked the other way. The charge was made most
sharply by Ruskin in 1856. Any effort to attain a real knowledge of
ourselves or the existing state of things was being thwarted, he said, by
"a fear of disagreeable facts and conscious shrinking from clearness
of light which . . . increase gradually into a species of instinctive
terror at all truth, and love of glosses, veils, and decorative lies of
every sort." [57] For the Victorians, the disagreeable facts were primarily

56. *Sketches and Essays; and Winterslow* (London, 1872), p. 30, quoted in
Helps, *Friends in Counsel, First Series*, 1, chap. 3, 51.
57. *Modern Painters*, 3 (1856), Pt. IV, chap. 4, sec. 3, in *Works*, 5, 71.

those of sex, and the terrifying truth the state of religion. But there were other facts, which may first be noticed, like the suffering of the poor and the ugliness of human nature, which called for veils and decorative lies, not so much from fear—though that enters in—as from a shallow and insistent optimism.

In the years after 1850 a realist like Hardy, who believed that "if way to the Better there be, it exacts a full look at the Worst," found himself a peculiar and isolated figure:

> When the clouds' swoln bosoms echo back the
>   shouts of the many and strong
> That things are all as they best may be, save
>   a few to be right ere long,
> And my eyes have not the vision in them to
>   discern what to these is so clear,
> The blot seems straightway in me alone; one
>   better he were not here. . . .
>
> Their dawns bring lusty joys, it seems; their
>   evenings all that is sweet;
> Our times are blessed times, they cry; Life
>   shapes it as is most meet,
> And nothing is much the matter.

This is the "robustious, swaggering optimism" which Hardy once spoke of as "cowardly and insincere." [58] The "many and strong" would not look at the other side of the picture, and labeled anyone who did —who questioned the blessings of English liberty, or the virtues of English civilization, or doubted if change was entirely progress or progress entirely upward—a pessimist. For, after all, nothing *was* much the matter for *them*. The Victorians were well off, as Kingsley dryly observed, unless they happened to be "Dorsetshire labourers— or Spitalfields weavers—or colliery children—or marching soldiers— or, I am afraid, one half of English souls this day." [59] But that was the

58. The poem is "In Tenebris, II"; the remark is in William Archer, "Real Conversations: II—with Mr. Thomas Hardy," *Pall Mall Magazine, 23* (1901), 535. Cf. Hardy's observation (work cited in note 19, above), p. 183: "The motto or practice of the optimists is: Blind the eyes to the real malady, and use empirical panaceas to suppress the symptoms." Although the poem and the remarks were made much later in his life, they accurately reflect the atmosphere of the fifties and sixties when he was growing up.

59. *Yeast*, chap. 2, p. 29.

other half whom one could ignore. When large-scale production and laissez-faire economics had brought the captains of industry undreamed of wealth and power, and had made England top nation, it was hardly to be expected that the cost in human suffering should not have been overlooked. Macaulay's reply to Southey's indictment of the system is a tissue of evasions: he never comes to grips with the central charge that the poor are being exploited by the rich.[60] He was not by any means a callous person, indifferent to suffering or injustice; and later on he voted for the Ten Hours Bill. But he could not risk an honest examination of facts and arguments that might cast a shadow of criticism upon so splendid an industrial achievement, let alone suggest countermeasures (like those which Southey wanted the Government to take) that might impede its further progress. What the Macaulays used sophistry to deny the Podsnaps refused even to recognize. Mr. Podsnap, who "had thriven exceedingly in the Marine Insurance way," had a happy method of getting rid of all disagreeables with a convenient, "I don't want to know about it; I don't choose to discuss it; I don't admit it!" As he stands on the hearth rug after a good dinner, he is approached by "a stray personage of a meek demeanour" (too unimportant to have a name). This personage makes "a highly unpolite remark; no less than a reference to the circumstance that some half-dozen people had lately died in the streets, of starvation."

> "I don't believe it," said Mr. Podsnap, putting it behind him.
> The meek man was afraid we must take it as proved, because there were the Inquests and the Registrar's returns.
> "Then it was their own fault," said Mr. Podsnap. . . .
> The man of meek demeanour intimated that truly it would seem from the facts, as if starvation had been forced upon the culprits in question—as if, in their wretched manner, they had made their weak protests against it—as if they would have taken the liberty of staving it off if they could—as if they would rather not have been starved upon the whole, if perfectly agreeable to all parties.
> "There is not," said Mr. Podsnap, flushing angrily,—"there is not a country in the world, sir, where so noble a provision is made for the poor as in this country."

60. "Southey's Colloquies on Society," *Critical Essays*, 2, 132–87. For one telling example, see his misrepresentation of Southey's passage on Mammon's temples, p. 149.

The meek man was quite willing to concede that, but perhaps it rendered the matter even worse, as showing that there must be something appallingly wrong somewhere.

"Where?" said Mr. Podsnap.

The meek man hinted, Wouldn't it be well to try, very seriously, to find out where?

"Ah!" said Mr. Podsnap. "Easy to say somewhere; not so easy to say where! But I see what you are driving at. I knew it from the first. Centralisation. No. Never with my consent. Not English." . . .

"And you know, at least I hope you know," said Mr. Podsnap, with severity, "that Providence has declared that you shall have the poor always with you? . . . Besides . . . the subject is a very disagreeable one. I will go so far as to say it is an odious one. It is not one to be introduced among our wives and young persons, and I—" He finished with that flourish of his arm which added more expressively than any words, And I remove it from the face of the earth.[61]

Another type of evasion was indebted to another kind of optimism, the confident or sentimental view of man that came down to the Victorians from the Romantics; that is, from the new enthusiasm with which they looked at human nature, and which in turn, as we have seen, was out of sympathy with any views that were critical and dark. The evasive effect of what I have called moral optimism is brought out by a passage in J. C. Shairp's essay "The Moral Motive Power":

Shrewd observers of human nature are often keen to discern the weaknesses and foibles of men, and even to exaggerate them, but slow to perceive those finer traits of heart which lie deeper. The apprehension of character with which the student should begin, and which his moral studies ought to deepen, is something very different from this. It is an eye open to see, a heart sensitive to feel, the higher excellencies of human nature, as they have existed, and still exist in the best of the race.[62]

61. *Our Mutual Friend, 1,* Bk. I, chap. 11, pp. 134, 146–8. It will be recalled that Mr. Podsnap is equally blind to any defects in the English nation and the British constitution: see above, in Chap. 2, sec. 3, where the discussion of optimism and national pride is another facet of the present topic. The essence of Podsnappery is the evasion of anything disagreeable.

62. *Studies in Poetry and Philosophy,* pp. 321–2.

This does not mean, he insists, that the darker side of human nature should be ignored. But to make the "main end of moral teaching," as he does, the contemplation of what is noble and ideal is tacitly to limit the range of vision. And to make the principal end of art the quickening of the noble emotions by an ideal image is to run the danger of purism.[63] " 'But, Mr. Mellot,' " says Honoria to the painter in *Yeast*, " 'why have you been so unfaithful to your original? why have you, like all artists, been trying to soften and refine on your model?'—— 'Because, my dear lady, we are bound to see everything in its ideal—not as it is, but as it ought to be, and will be, when the vices of this pitiful civilized world are exploded.' " [64]

Mellot's model was Tregarva, the gamekeeper. Enthusiasm transformed men into heroes, and the need for moral inspiration justified the omission of the clay feet. In developing a heart sensitive to the higher excellencies of human nature, there is one influence, continues Shairp, more potent than moral teaching:

> To have seen and known lives which have embodied these fair qualities, to have felt the touch of their human goodness, to have companioned with those
>
> > "Whose soul the holy forms
> > Of young imagination hath kept pure;"
>
> to have fed on high thoughts, and been familiar with the examples of the heroes, the sages, the saints of all time, so as to believe that such lives were once on earth, and are not impossible even now,—these are, beyond all teaching, the "virtue-making" powers.

And if the lives of ancient heroes, why not also of modern heroes? The notorious evasions of Victorian biography owed something to Mrs. Grundy, forcing the biographer to omit anything which might seem unbecoming; but their main source lay in a theory of biography conditioned by the anxieties of the time. When the impact of religion was declining and that of commercialism increasing, the aim of the biographer was not to deepen the reader's insight into human nature but to give him, in the revealing words of one critic, "the assurance of the certainty of something better than we are." [65] As Tennyson

63. See above, last paragraph of Chap. 11.
64. Chap. 3, p. 59.
65. Hood, *The Uses of Biography*, p. 195.

created his Arthur an ideal man in order to combat the selfishness and
materialism of the age,[66] so his son, largely with the same purpose,
created Tennyson himself, in the official biography, as King Arthur
in modern dress. If a writer so far forgot his function as to expose
a man's weakness, an outburst of indignation showed how strongly
the public wanted to keep its heroes inspiring as well as proper. Lock-
hart was censured not only for indiscretion but for making Scott
"unheroic"; Dowden for tarnishing the ideal image of Shelley so that
"never again will it have the same pureness and beauty which it
had formerly." [67]

Complementing the effect of enthusiasm, and partly under its influence, the development of religious liberalism encouraged the same
optimistic view of human nature. It turned attention to the brighter
side of the Gospel and emphasized its tidings of comfort and its
precepts of love; so much so that "all darker, deeper views of man's
condition and prospects" were comparatively forgotten.[68] That remark
of Newman's is well borne out by Kingsley, who is the perfect type of
the Broad Church liberal. To him the essential idea of Protestantism
was not the corruption of man by original sin, but "the dignity
and divinity of man as God made him." It followed that the purpose
of the incarnation was not his redemption by supernatural means, but
the making known to him his divine position and divine privileges
that he might realize the eternal union with God which self-will alone
can break asunder. "Evil, as such, has no existence; but men can and
do resist God's will . . . and so punish themselves by getting into
disharmony with their own constitution and that of the universe."
But only temporarily. For God in his infinite mercy (his wrath is
rarely mentioned by Kingsley) is "baffling all the lawlessness and self-
will of the spirits whom He has made," so that ultimately all men
are inheritors of the kingdom of heaven. Like Maurice, therefore,
Kingsley was a universalist; and like Maurice, too, he repudiated the
doctrine of hell.[69] Needless to say, in sermon after sermon one looks
almost in vain for any recognition of human weakness or spiritual

66. Hallam Tennyson, *Memoir of Tennyson*, 2, 128–9.

67. Carlyle, "Sir Walter Scott," *Essays, 4,* 29, though Carlyle himself is out of
sympathy with the criticism; Matthew Arnold, "Shelley," *Essays in Criticism,
Second Series,* p. 213.

68. Newman, "The Religion of the Day," *Parochial and Plain Sermons, 1,* 311.

69. *Yeast,* chap. 3, p. 48; *Letters and Memories, 2,* 64–5 (unabridged ed., *2,*
28). See the fuller description of Kingsley's theology in sec. 6 of my article called
"The Issue between Kingsley and Newman," *Theology Today, 4* (1947), 80–101,
where Kingsley is seen as the embodiment of the religious liberalism Newman was
attacking.

poverty, of the emptiness and wretchedness of life. And the omission is deliberate and conscious. As early as 1842 he had written to his future wife:

> There are two ways of looking at every occurrence—a bright and a dark side. Two modes of action— Which is most worthy of a rational being, a Christian and a friend? It is absurd, as a rational being, to torture one's self unnecessarily. It is inconsistent in a Christian to see God's wrath, rather than His mercy in everything. . . . Never begin to look darkly at a subject, without checking yourself and saying, "Is there not a bright side to this? Has not God promised the bright side to me? Is not my happiness in my own power? Do I not know that I am ruining my mind and endangering the happiness of those I love—by looking at the wrong side?" [70]

One particular element in human nature that was notoriously ignored was, of course, the sexual passion, for there shame, fear, and the proprieties united to draw a veil of silence or a gloss of euphemism over the facts of life. So far as the motive was not virtue but the appearance of virtue, and what was condemned was not sin but open sin, the evasion was patently hypocritical. This was nicely hit by Thackeray in *Vanity Fair:*

> We must pass over a part of Mrs. Rebecca Crawley's biography with that lightness and delicacy which the world demands—the moral world, that has, perhaps, no particular objection to vice, but an insuperable repugnance to hearing vice called by its proper name. . . . A polite public will no more bear to read an authentic description of vice than a truly-refined English or American female will permit the word "breeches" to be pronounced in her chaste hearing. . . . I defy any one to say that our Becky, who has certainly some vices, has not been presented to the public in a perfectly genteel and inoffensive manner. [71]

As that suggests, the prudery of evasion was more indebted to middle-class gentility than to the Puritan revival. "A truly refined mind," says Mrs. General in *Little Dorrit,* "will seem to be ignorant of the existence of anything that is not perfectly proper, placid, and pleasant." [72]

70. *Letters and Memories,* 1, 65 (unabridged ed., *1, 86*)
71. Chap. 64, p. 624.
72. Vol. 2, chap. 41, p. 50. Cf. 2, chap. 38, p. 22: "Even her propriety could not dispute that there was impropriety in the world; but Mrs. General's way of getting

But it was quite possible to condemn that attitude and at the same time condemn any open description of vice. A critic who had no patience with "the immoral prudery that will not face the facts of human nature itself, and falsifies them to the young" was equally ready to complain about the present fashion of dwelling upon unclean topics and ugly things in the naturalistic novel—"as if lack of reticence and want of decorum were the hall-mark of power and life, and not the brand of vulgarity and poverty of mind." The date of that remark is 1896, but the judgment is Victorian.[73] Nor was reserve simply a matter of decorum. A man might look at the facts of life clearly enough and honestly decide that in the face of ominous threats to the moral stability of society (from French literature, theories of free love, and prostitution), such facts ought to be concealed. When W. R. Greg, for example, admitted that the liaisons which filled French novels were far from being unknown among ourselves, he added, that in England "at least they have no *recognised* existence: wisely or unwisely, they are usually ignored both in general society and in literature designed for general reading. . . . If the writer of fiction uses them at all, he is obliged to use them with the utmost reticence and moderation." Presently, with reference to George Sand's *Elle et Lui*, he goes on to say that "nothing can be more disgraceful than the things revealed—except the revelation of them."[74] Partly, no doubt, because it was improper, but largely, I think, because it was dangerous: it encouraged sensuality.

---

rid of it was to put it out of sight, and make believe that there was no such thing. This was another of her ways of forming a mind—to cram all articles of difficulty into cupboards, lock them up, and say they had no existence. It was the easiest way, and, beyond all comparison, the properest. Mrs. General was not to be told of anything shocking. Accidents, miseries, and offences were never to be mentioned before her. Passion was to go to sleep in the presence of Mrs. General, and blood was to change to milk and water." Plainly, Mrs. General is sister to Mr. Podsnap; and, indeed, along with other ugly things Mr. Podsnap would not hear mentioned (above, note 61, p. 140) was anything "calculated to call a blush into the cheek of a young person." In a new middle class the hard facts of both economic and sexual life were equally taboo.

73. M. G. Tuttiet (Maxwell Gray), quoted in *Nineteenth-Century Opinion*, ed. Michael Goodwin (London, 1951), p. 170. Cf. Wingfield-Stratford, *Those Earnest Victorians*, p. 160: "The Victorians might have pleaded that their reticence about sex was no more misplaced than the desire of the Greek dramatist to get his killing done 'off.' The modern flaunting of passion and sex-appeal would have struck them as not only wicked, but vulgar."

74. "French Fiction: the Lowest Deep," *Literary and Social Judgments, 1,* 188, 225. The italics are his.

There is also the other side of the same coin. When the beauty of romantic and connubial love is exalted, mainly to counteract the attraction of lust, its passion may be minimized or excluded, leaving only its sentiment—or sentimentality—to stand for the whole truth. There is a direct connection between Patmore's statement,

> Strong passions mean weak will, and he
> Who truly knows the strength and bliss
> Which are in love, will own with me
> No passion but a virtue 'tis,

and the recurrent sentimentalism of his poem.[75] Or, where the passions appear, they must be properly clothed if the ideal character of love is to be preserved. To strip off "the concealing and adorning drapery of fancy and grace" meant for Greg the reduction of love to its "mere beggarly material elements"; [76] and George Brimley was certain that there were "feelings upon which the light and air cannot dwell without tainting them." [77] Even as late as 1914, in an essay called "Victorian Hypocrisy" the new man of the twentieth century who "thinks reserve is used for things we are ashamed to speak of" and asks aggressively, "What is there to be ashamed of in sex?" is met with the answer: "Nothing to be ashamed of (except its perversion), but much which is too sacred, personal, delicate, potent, and marvellous to be mentioned at random." [78]

Finally, the exaltation of love tended to exclude violent or ugly emotions which may be aroused by sexual attraction or repulsion: hate, jealousy, cruelty, as well as lust. They are incompatible with ideal sentiment. Because Leslie Stephen equated love with monogamous bliss, when it appeared in the guise of a destroyer he averted his eyes.[79] With reference to Tennyson in particular, Morley spoke of the limitation of Victorian poetry to "the ethics of the rectory parlour set to sweet music, the respectable aspirations of the sentimental curate married to exquisite verse, the everlasting glorification of domestic sentiment in blameless princes and others . . . as if domestic sentiment included and summed up the whole throng of passions, emotions, strife, and desire" and went on to praise *The Ring and the Book* (1869) in very un-Victorian tones (outside of aesthetic circles): "In

75. "The Angel in the House," Bk. I, Canto III, *Poems*, p. 78.
76. "French Fiction," p. 227.
77. Review of "The Angel in the House," *Essays*, p. 229.
78. Annie W. Allen, *Atlantic Monthly, 114* (1914), 187.
79. Annan, *Stephen*, p. 240.

the tragedy of Pompilia we are taken far from the serene and homely region in which some of our teachers would fain have it that the whole moral universe can be snugly pent up. We see the black passions of man at their blackest; hate . . . cruelty . . . greediness, lust, craft." [80]

Though we are less aware of it because we are less concerned in this area with the truth, it is probable that Victorian evasion was more common in religion than anywhere else. The conviction that faith was essential if society were not to collapse, and the intense will to believe in order to escape the personal distress of doubt or to preserve the personal comforts of a creed—these currents of emotion, which led as we have seen to insincere profession, led also to blinking any serious examination of whatever might weaken or undermine religious belief. The close connection between both types of insincerity is brought out in a passage of Froude's *Carlyle*. Half mankind, he says, had been betrayed into materialism. The other half, shivering at so blank a prospect, were "pretending to believe, or believing that they believed, becoming hypocrites, conscious or unconscious . . . not daring to look the facts in the face, so that the very sense of truth was withered in them." [81] The "facts" were of two kinds: those of traditional Christianity and those of science and biblical criticism. Men were saying to themselves, better accept the established creed and avoid any awkward questions about its meaning or validity; and certainly avoid looking at the other side of the picture. Shut your eyes to how much error there is in Christianity and to how much truth there is in atheism—those are the two related imperatives of religious evasion.

The first is well illustrated by the average Cambridge don of the fifties as Leslie Stephen remembered him. "He was rational enough to see that the old orthodox position was untenable. He did not believe in Hell, or in 'verbal inspiration' or the 'real presence'." But he considered himself to be a genuine believer. He assumed "that somehow or other the old dogmas could be explained away or 'rationalised' or 'spiritualised'" and that "in some sense or other" he could accept them. But he "did not ask too closely in what sense. . . . He shut his eyes to the great difficulties or took the answer for granted." [82] Not to have done so—to have undertaken a serious examination of the foundations of belief—that would have been too great a risk to his moral and

80. "On 'The Ring and the Book,'" *Studies in Literature*, pp. 256–7.
81. *Carlyle: Life in London*, 2, chap. 26, p. 261.
82. F. W. Maitland, *The Life and Letters of Leslie Stephen* (London, 1906), pp. 150–2.

psychological stability. He needed the support and comfort of a creed, and he needed to keep the mind free from explicit and painful doubts. For the latter purpose evasion could be carried still further. More than one Victorian openly advised his contemporaries not to attack their doubts but to suppress them by the simple expedient of ignoring them. When Thomas Arnold was asked for advice by a person who found the existence of evil a distressing argument against believing in God, he told her that all speculations of this kind which can only lead to perplexity "are to be repressed by the will." And if that were impossible, the doubts they raised "should be kept, I think, to ourselves, and not talked of even to our nearest friends, when we once understand their true nature. Talking about them gives them a sort of reality which otherwise they would not have; just like talking about our dreams. We should act and speak, and try to feel as if they had no existence, and then in most cases they do cease to exist after a time." A man of Arnold's integrity could only have advocated so gross an evasion because, as he says in the next sentence, such doubts "are the most grievous affliction with which human nature is visited." [83] When that was so—and when Freud had not yet explained the perils of repression—such an expedient was understandable enough.

The complementary refusal to face subversive facts or theories springs from the fear that they cannot be met, or the appalling suspicion that they are true. The reaction of Gladstone to the progress of science and the questions it raised about the nature of man and the universe must have been a common one. Because instinct told him "that the advance of natural explanation, whether legitimately or not, would be in some degree at the expense of the supernatural," he stood aside "from any full or serious examination of the details of the scientific movement . . . safe and steadfast within the citadel of Tradition." [84] In like manner, clerical defenders of the faith were given to ducking a serious criticism of the books they attacked. Henry Atkinson complained, I doubt not justly enough, that the reviewers of his *Letters on the Laws of Man's Nature and Development* were merely abusing the book with unsupported charges of "shallow" and "superficial," when, in point of fact, they were afraid that there was substance in the midst of it and danger to the existing state of things. "They dare not

83. Stanley, *Life of Arnold*, pp. 363, 365, from a letter of June 21, 1835. Cf. Keble's advice to Arnold himself when certain doubts made him hesitate to take orders (chap. 1, p. 20): he should "put down the objections by main force, whenever they arise in his mind."

84. Morley, *Life of Gladstone*, 1, 209.

honestly face the facts, and meet the argument which they declare to be too superficial to deceive any one. They dare not honestly and fairly do it." [85] In a variation of the same psychology, one might insist that if materialism were true, it should be concealed or ignored. "Sincerely, for my own part," wrote Charlotte Brontë, with reference to the same book, "do I wish to find and know the Truth; but if this be Truth, well may she guard herself with mysteries, and cover herself with a veil." [86] Still more astonishing is the proposal made by Beatrice Webb: "Even if the instinctive faith in a mysterious goodness is a fiction of the mind, would it not on the whole be happier to live by the light of this delusion, *and blind oneself wilfully to the awful vision of unmeaning misery?*" [87] Though she herself thought it would be difficult to direct a life on that basis, many Victorians must have attempted to do so. Ruskin was right: the terror of truth led to the love of glosses, veils, and decorative lies of some desperate kinds.

4. Anti-Hypocrisy

Of all Victorian attitudes none was so often attacked by the Victorians themselves as hypocrisy. Indeed, much of the evidence for calling the age hypocritical comes, as we have seen, from the hostile criticism of Carlyle, Mill, Morley, Froude, and others. Nor is this the only case where an attitude is thrown into relief by the protest or satire it provoked at the time. A glance back over the preceding chapters would show that nearly every fault and failing of the Victorian mind was exposed by the Victorians themselves. The general reason is clear. The very fact that they saw the period as one of radical transition made the major thinkers acutely conscious of their age and highly sensitive to the loss of old values or the adoption of new ones that seemed to spell a deterioration of the moral or intellectual life. The worship of material progress, the anti-intellectualism, the dogmatism, the commercial spirit, the exaltation of force, the marriage market, and the insincerities of conformity, moral pretension, and evasion—all of these Victorian weaknesses were recognized and attacked more clearly and vigorously than anyone today exposes the shortcomings of our own time. Why modern criticism by contrast is so limited, in amount

85. Quoted in Harriet Martineau, *Autobiography*, 2, Period VI, sec. 6, p. 368. Cf. Stopford Brooke, *Life of F. W. Robertson*, p. xii, accusing the Evangelicals "of shutting the eyes to difficulties, and of answering opponents without the requisite knowledge": a charge made in the "Introduction," 5th ed. (1868).

86. Mrs. Gaskell, *Life of Charlotte Brontë*, chap. 23, p. 329.

87. *My Apprenticeship*, p. 90, from her diary for 1883. The italics are mine.

and quality, is a complex question. The acceptance out of habit or indifference of "evils" that have been inherited from the nineteenth century, the lack of confidence in human reason, and the suspicion that the individual critic can accomplish little in the face of mass propaganda or vast economic forces no one can control would be among the relevant factors. But whatever the reasons, we are now in a position to recognize the most admirable quality of the Victorian mind at its best: its readiness to submit society to close critical analysis and to judge it in the light of Western culture. No doubt this led by moments to an irrational and reactionary desire to sweep back the tide and return to the good old days. But on the whole the Victorian thinkers assumed the responsibility of providing their age with the kind of criticism that should be and must be the work of the intellectuals—teachers, artists, writers, scholars—if any standards higher than expediency and comfort are to prevail.

Nowhere was this truer than in their vigorous demand for sincerity, since they had special reasons for finding the vice of hypocrisy particularly irritating. The contemporary tendency to profess the old beliefs insincerely, out of habit or fear, especially in religion, and to evade the new difficulties or counterarguments, or at least to practice reserve about saying what in any way was radical, aroused the righteous wrath of progressive minds, and all the more so because they themselves often suffered from the social stigma visited on all freethinkers.

In their angry reaction we can distinguish two lines of attack, represented respectively by Mill and Carlyle. For a time the two men joined forces on the basis of a common "love of truth" and "a common contempt for the insincere professions with which men were veiling from themselves and from one another their emptiness of spiritual belief." [88] But "love of truth" contains an ambiguity; its meaning depends on which word is emphasized. For Mill and the rational, liberal school the *truth* is paramount. All forms of insincere profession and evasion which put social utility or personal advantage above the supreme obligation to think freely and speak freely, or which sacrifice reason to emotion, are anathema. They are thwarting the progress of man. And so the intellectual liberals set up the cry, "Seek the truth whatever it is and speak it courageously. Say what you honestly think." On the other hand, moderns like Carlyle who were less devoted to the march of mind, or who found themselves in some doubt about what they did

88. Froude, *Carlyle: First Forty Years*, 2, chap. 12, p. 273; and cf. Charles Buller's letter, chap. 10, pp. 235–6.

think, laid their emphasis on the *love* of truth. What they wanted was a society composed of sincere, truth-loving persons even though what they held were wrong. Or, to put it another way, the truth they valued was truth of character more than knowledge. A man should avoid all forms of false profession or evasion simply because he ought to be true to himself. He should say what he honestly thinks because as a man, and not merely as a thinker, he ought to be sincere. In short, for these critics the curse of hypocrisy lay in its dangerous effect on the moral rather than the intellectual life of the time.

The major text of the first school is the second chapter of *On Liberty*, with its incisive attack on the tyranny of public opinion. The ringing sentences are still very much alive: "Our merely social intolerance kills no one, roots out no opinions, but induces men to disguise them, or to abstain from any active effort for their diffusion." By "the ban placed on all inquiry which does not end in the orthodox conclusions" the progress of truth is retarded: error is preserved, free from attack; the mental development of potential thinkers is cramped and the reason cowed. "We may occasionally see some man of deep conscientiousness, and subtle and refined understanding, who spends a life in sophisticating with an intellect which he cannot silence, and exhausts the resources of ingenuity in attempting to reconcile the promptings of his conscience and reason with orthodoxy, which yet he does not, perhaps, to the end succeed in doing." [89]

On Liberty was hardly published before a fresh wave of panic and intolerance, following upon the publication of *The Origin of Species* and *Essays and Reviews*, carried conformity and evasion to a high point and provoked a broadside attack on Victorian hypocrisy from the scientists and their sympathizers. Its initiation might be dated in 1862 when a club was founded in London to bring together "scientific and philosophic men . . . who care to know and speak the truth." No one was to be admitted who was "not 'thorough' in the sense of being free from the suspicion of temporising and professing opinions on official grounds." Huxley was president and Kingsley vice-president.[90] After a few meetings, the "Philosophical Club" went to pieces, but the concerted opinion it reflected got expressed through the following

89. Chap. 2, pp. 123–5.
90. The club is described by George Eliot in Cross' *Life*, 2, 269–70, 275, letters to Sara Hennell, November 26, 1862, and March 9, 1863. Huxley refers to it (Leonard Huxley, *Life of T. H. Huxley*, 1, 214) as a "Society for the propagation of common honesty in all parts of the world." The plan originated in Cambridge.

years in a series of essays arguing the case for veracity at whatever cost and heaping scorn on all who placed prudence or comfort ahead of truth. The principal writers were Leslie Stephen, W. K. Clifford, Samuel Butler, John Morley (whose *On Compromise* in 1874 is the classic protest against all forms of reserve and evasion) and above all, in the light of his influence, T. H. Huxley. Always a man who liked a fight, and in the present case infuriated by the obloquy heaped on the defenders of evolution and the cowardice of time-serving scientists who would not brave the ignorant clamor, Huxley struck out with all his rhetorical power against "liars and hypocrites." It is significant that when he came to America in 1876, the ovation he received was less for the scientist than for the champion "of freedom and sincerity in thought and word against shams and self-deceptions of every kind. It was not so much the preacher of new doctrines who was welcomed, as the apostle of veracity." [91]

Like many apostles he was not entirely fair to the old school; nor were Stephen and Clifford. After saying that the devil was a liar from the beginning, Huxley continues: "If we set out in life with pretending to know that which we do not know; with professing to accept for proof evidence which we are well aware is inadequate; with wilfully shutting our eyes and our ears to facts which militate against this or that comfortable hypothesis; we are assuredly doing our best to deserve the same character." [92] But this is to make a gratuitous assumption: that the "believer" has agreed to play the game by the same rules which the scientist has adopted and is therefore cheating. But many sincere believers, J. H. Newman let us say, were wholly unwilling to make scientific proof the basis of religious belief. The proof they relied on—mystical experience or various forms of intuition (such as Newman's illative sense)—could be defended on good philosophical grounds. And their refusal to follow logic to an agnostic conclusion was by no means a willful disregard of what threatened a comfortable hypothesis. It was the rejection of exactly that type of evidence which they considered entirely inadequate. The fact is that the positivists were so certain that all subjective evidence of spiritual reality was a delusion and honest belief could only be given to what was capable of scientific demonstration that they could hardly avoid accusing anyone who adopted a belief "without logically satisfactory evidence" of

91. Huxley, *Life, 1,* 494.
92. "Prologue" to *Controverted Questions,* reprinted in *Science and Christian Tradition,* p. 54.

being "immoral," and anyone who maintained a supernatural faith of living in a "cloudcastle of sweet illusions and darling lies." [93] This is the swing of the pendulum with a vengeance. Not the disbelievers or the half-believers who pretended to believe, but the genuine believers themselves are now accused of shuffling and evasion. But though overstated in this way, the shoe undoubtedly fitted a good many feet, as we have seen, and not a few Victorians adopted Huxley's rules and then refused to keep them. The persistent exposure of such hypocrisy by the agnostics, and their complementary challenge to be courageous and honest, finished off what Mill had begun.

The other school which attacked insincerity and demanded intellectual integrity did so quite apart from, or over and above, the relation of either to the cause of truth. Here the cause was moral character, and the school the apostles of earnestness. For not to be in earnest, it will be recalled, was to adopt conventional notions one did not seriously examine or genuinely believe. It was to be a dilettante playing with ideas, without any real convictions about man's relation to society or the universe. [94]

More than anyone else, Carlyle was infuriated by that kind of worldly insincerity—so much so that he was prepared to admire even a man who spoke error so long as he honestly believed it. His tribute in *Heroes and Hero-Worship* to the Benthamism he hated is a significant illustration of his attitude. He praised it for its "laying-down of cant" and its fearless committal to what it found true. "It seems to me, all deniers of Godhood, and all lip-believers of it, are bound to be Benthamites, if they have courage and honesty." Indeed, for this reason and this only, that it openly affirmed what all the world, "in a cowardly half-and-half manner," was tending to believe, Carlyle was willing to bestow his greatest compliment on a philosophy he thought was false and call it heroic, "though a Heroism with its *eyes* put out!" [95] The qualification does not invalidate the important identification of the heroic and the sincere which runs all through the *Heroes*: "Sincerity, a deep, great, genuine sincerity, is the first characteristic of all men

93. Huxley, "Agnosticism and Christianity," in *Science and Christian Tradition*, p. 310; W. K. Clifford, "The Ethics of Belief," *Lectures and Essays*, 2, 186. Also cf. Clifford, "Right and Wrong," pp. 175–6; Stephen, "An Apology for Plainspeaking," *Essays on Freethinking and Plainspeaking*, pp. 372, 388, 402–3.

94. Above, Chap. 10, sec. 1.

95. *Heroes and Hero-Worship*, Lecture 5, pp. 172–3.

in any way heroic." Contrariwise, the insincere man, though he profess the highest truths, "*is* himself a falsehood." [96] The standard of value is most clearly laid down in a comment on Emerson's *Essays* in 1841:

> I love Emerson's book, not for its detached opinions, not even for the scheme of the general world he has framed for himself . . . but simply because it is his own book; because there is a tone of veracity, an unmistakable air of its being *his* (wheresoever he may have found, discovered, borrowed, or begged it), and a real utterance of a human soul, not a mere echo of such. . . . Really, in any country, all sunk crown deep in cant, twaddle, and hollow traditionality, is not the first man that will begin to speak the truth—any truth—a new and newest era? [97]

The *tone* of veracity is more important than the veracity; any belief is valuable so it be genuine. Sterling was dead right when he said that Carlyle dwelled more on the spirit with which a man held a creed than on the creed itself, on "the degree of seriousness and devotion in the believer's mind—rather than the quality and amount of truth which his belief embodies." [98]

That would not have been the case, I suggest, if Carlyle had had any strong convictions of his own. When a man detests hypocrisy but does not know exactly what he believes himself, he lays supreme importance on the honest search for truth or the honest confession of uncertainty. What Froude said of Carlyle could be applied not only to himself but to Clough and Tennyson, and even to Mill (in the years just after his early beliefs collapsed), that he thought it his highest duty "to see facts as they actually were, and, if that was impossible, at least to desire to see them, to be sincere with his own soul." [99] Conversely, a man should honestly face whatever doubts he had and try to resolve them. Even when questioning God's existence, Carlyle's Teufelsdröckh was "the Servant of Goodness, the Servant of God," because, as he says, "I never-

96. Ibid., Lecture 2, pp. 45, 73.
97. Froude, *Carlyle: Life in London*, 1, chap. 8, p. 220.
98. "Carlyle," *Essays and Tales*, 1, 281.
99. *Carlyle: Life in London*, 2, chap. 17, pp. 16–17. In the years when he himself was unsure of his beliefs, Mill adopted Carlyle's point of view: see his praise of "sincere, earnest, and truth-loving" persons (*Letters*, 1, 88, 92) and especially his assertion (pp. 32–3) that one sincere mind speaking what it believes to be true is "perhaps more profitable to the hearer or reader, than much sounder doctrine delivered without intensity of conviction." All quotations are from letters written to Carlyle.

theless still loved Truth, and would bate no jot of my allegiance to her." [100] So too with Tennyson's Hallam:

> He fought his doubts and gather'd strength,
>   He would not make his judgment blind,
>   He faced the spectres of the mind
> And laid them; thus he came at length
>
> To find a stronger faith his own,[101]

—and also to prove that there lived more faith, potentially, in honest doubt than in the professions of many a Christian who purchased his belief by evasion. But Tennyson is not really defending instrumental skepticism. He is defending the character of honest doubters who are being condemned as wicked sinners or bad citizens by insincere Christians. He means to suggest that Hallam would have been an admirable man even had he failed to lay the specters of the mind—a man, let us say, like Tennyson himself.

If those who were uncertain of the truth emphasized the virtue of sincerity, those who came after, the post-Victorian and modern skeptics who have doubted even the possibility of reaching the truth, have made it the supreme virtue. From Carlyle and Tennyson it is only a step to the attitude defined by Dobrée in 1934:

> In our present confusion our only hope is *to be scrupulously honest with ourselves,* so honest as to doubt our own minds and the conclusions they arrive at. Most of us have ceased to believe, except provisionally, in truths, and we feel that *what is important is not so much truth as the way our minds move towards truths.*[102]

The circle comes round, though the ends do not meet. First, men believe sincerely in the established truths. Then, as those truths are undermined by new knowledge or new political forces, the conservatives pretend to believe the old creeds and evade the difficulties: doubt and "hypocrisy" are born together. Next comes the reaction. The champions of new truth demand intellectual candor—that a man deal honestly with others. But those who remain in doubt, and still more those who come to doubt the mind itself, demand personal sincerity— that a man deal honestly with himself.

100. *Sartor Resartus*, Bk. II, chap. 7, p. 161.
101. *In Memoriam*, No. 96.
102. *Modern Prose Style* (Oxford, 1934), p. 220. The italics are mine.

BIBLIOGRAPHY

THIS bibliography makes no attempt to list all the books and articles used in this study but only those quoted three or more times, or those of sufficient importance to warrant inclusion in even a short bibliography on the Victorian frame of mind. When two years are given, the first year (in parenthesis) is that of the first edition; the second, that of the edition cited.

ACTON, SIR J. E. E. D., first Lord Acton, "George Eliot's Life," *Nineteenth Century*, 17 (1885), 464–85.

ACTON, WILLIAM, *Prostitution, Considered in Its Moral, Social & Sanitary Aspects, in London and Other Large Cities*, London, 1857.

"The Age We Live In," *Fraser's Magazine*, 24 (1841), 1–15.

The Amberley Papers. The Letters and Diaries of Lord and Lady Amberley, ed. Bertrand and Patricia Russell, 2 vols. London, 1937.

ANNAN, NOEL GILROY, *Leslie Stephen. His Thought and Character in Relation to His Time*, London, 1951.

ARNOLD, MATTHEW, *Culture and Anarchy*, ed. J. Dover Wilson, Cambridge, 1932.

—— *Essays in Criticism, First Series* (1865), London, 1875.

—— *Essays in Criticism, Second Series* (1888), London and New York, 1891.

—— *Last Essays on Church & Religion* (1877), bound with *St. Paul & Protestantism*, New York, 1894.

—— *Letters, 1848–1888*, ed. G. W. E. Russell, 2 vols. London and New York, 1901.

—— *The Letters of Matthew Arnold to Arthur Hugh Clough*, ed. H. F. Lowry, London and New York, 1932.

—— *Literature & Dogma. An Essay towards a Better Apprehension of the Bible* (1873), New York, 1883.

—— *Mixed Essays, Irish Essays, and Others*, New York, 1896. *Mixed Essays* was first published in 1879, *Irish Essays* in 1882.

—— *Poetical Works*, ed. C. B. Tinker and H. F. Lowry, London and New York, 1950.

ARNOLD, THOMAS, *Sermons* (1829–34), 3 vols. London, 1844–45.

ARNOLD, THOMAS, *Christian Life, Its Course, Its Hindrances, and Its Helps* (1841), London, 1849.

—— *Life and Correspondence.* See Stanley, A. P.

ARTHUR, WILLIAM, "Heroes," *Exeter Hall Lectures, 6* (1850–51), 289–338. See also under *Lectures.*

BAGEHOT, WALTER, *Works,* ed. Forrest Morgan, 5 vols. Hartford, Conn., 1891.

BANKS, J. A., *Prosperity and Parenthood. A Study of Family Planning among the Victorian Middle Classes,* London, 1954.

BAX, E. BELFORT, *Reminiscences and Reflections of a Mid and Late Victorian,* New York, 1920.

BESANT, WALTER, *Autobiography,* ed. S. Squire Sprigge, London, 1902.

BRIGGS, ASA, *Victorian People. Some Reassessments of People, Institutions, Ideas and Events, 1851–1867,* London, 1954.

BRIMLEY, GEORGE, *Essays,* ed. W. G. Clark (1858), London, 1882.

BRONTË, CHARLOTTE, *Jane Eyre* (1847), Everyman's Library, London and New York, 1908.

BROOKE, STOPFORD, *Life and Letters of Frederick W. Robertson* (1865) bound with *Lectures and Addresses,* New York, n.d.

BROWN, HORATIO F., *John Addington Symonds. A Biography,* London, 1903.

BROWN, JAMES BALDWIN, *The Home Life: in the Light of Its Divine Idea* (1866), New York, 1867.

—— *On the Uses of Biography,* London, 1871.

—— "The Revolution of the Last Quarter of a Century," in *First Principles of Ecclesiastical Truth. Essays on the Church and Society,* London, 1871. Four lectures entitled "The Intellectual Revolution," "The Social Revolution," "The Ecclesiastical Revolution," and "The Theological Revolution," delivered in the winter of 1869–70.

—— *Young Men and Maidens. A Pastoral for the Times,* London, 1871.

BROWNING, ROBERT, *The Complete Poetic and Dramatic Works* (Cambridge Edition), Boston and New York, 1895.

—— *The Letters of Robert Browning and Elizabeth Barrett Barrett, 1845–1846,* 2 vols. New York and London, 1899.

BRYANT, ARTHUR, *English Saga (1840–1940),* London, 1940.

BUCKLE, HENRY THOMAS, *History of Civilization in England* (1857–61), 3 vols. London, 1882.

BUCKLEY, JEROME H., *The Victorian Temper. A Study in Literary Culture,* Cambridge, Mass., 1951.

BURY, J. B., *The Idea of Progress. An Inquiry into Its Origin and Growth*, London, 1920.

BUTLER, SAMUEL, *Erewhon, or over the Range* (1872), Everyman's Library, New York, 1927.

—— *Note-Books,* ed. Henry Festing Jones (1912), New York, 1917.

—— *The Way of All Flesh* (1903), Everyman's Library, New York, 1927. Written between 1872 and 1884.

CARLYLE, THOMAS, "Characteristics" (1831), in *Essays* (next entry), 3, 1–43.

—— *Critical and Miscellaneous Essays* (1838), 5 vols. in the Centenary Edition of Carlyle's *Works,* ed. H. D. Traill, 30 vols. New York, 1896–1901. Referred to as *Essays* in the notes.

—— *Latter-Day Pamphlets* (1850), in the Centenary Edition, London, 1907.

—— *Letters, 1826–1836,* ed. C. E. Norton, London and New York, 1889.

—— *Letters to John Stuart Mill, John Sterling, and Robert Browning,* ed. A. Carlyle, London, 1923.

—— *The Life of John Sterling* (1851), in the Centenary Edition, New York, 1900.

—— *On Heroes, Hero-Worship, and the Heroic in History* (1841), in the Centenary Edition, London, 1897.

—— *Past and Present* (1843), in the Centenary Edition, London, 1897.

—— *Reminiscences* (1881), Everyman's Library, London and New York, 1932.

—— *Sartor Resartus. The Life and Opinions of Herr Teufelsdröckh* (1834), ed. C. F. Harrold, New York, 1937. Written between 1830 and 1831, and first published in *Fraser's Magazine* from November 1833 to August 1834.

—— "Signs of the Times" (1829), in *Essays,* 2, 56–82.

"Characteristics in the Nineteenth Century," *Fraser's Magazine,* 21 (1840), 147–64.

CHRISTIE, O. F., *The Transition from Aristocracy, 1832–1867,* New York and London, 1928.

CLIFFORD, W. K., *Lectures and Essays,* ed. Leslie Stephen and Frederick Pollock, 2 vols. London, 1879.

CLOUGH, ARTHUR HUGH, *Poems,* ed. H. F. Lowry, A. L. P. Norrington, and F. L. Mulhauser, Oxford, 1951.

—— *Prose Remains, with a Selection from His Letters and a Memoir,* ed. by his wife (1869), London and New York, 1888.

COBBE, FRANCES POWER, "The Nineteenth Century," *Fraser's Magazine*, 69 (1864), 481–94. Reprinted under the title "Decemnovenarianism" in the author's *Studies New and Old of Ethical and Social Subjects*, London, 1865.

COLERIDGE, SAMUEL TAYLOR, *Two Lay Sermons* (1816, 1817), bound with his *Biographia Literaria*, London, 1898.

MRS. CRAIK (*née* Dinah Maria Mulock), *John Halifax, Gentleman* (1856), Collin's Pocket Classics, London and Glasgow, n.d.

CROSS, J. W., *George Eliot's Life as Related in Her Letters and Journals* (1885), 3 vols. New York. Vols. *22–24* of her *Works:* see under Eliot, George.

CRUSE, AMY, *The Victorians and Their Reading*, Boston and New York, 1935.

CUMMING, JOHN, "The Age We Live In," in *Exeter Hall Lectures*, 3 (1847–48), 337–68. See below under *Lectures*.

DARWIN, CHARLES, *The Origin of Species by Means of Natural Selection, and The Descent of Man*, New York, Modern Library, n.d.

DARWIN, FRANCIS, *The Life and Letters of Charles Darwin*, 2 vols. New York, 1887.

DICEY, A. V., *Lectures on the Relation between Law & Public Opinion in England during the Nineteenth Century*, London and New York, 1905.

DICKENS, CHARLES, *Writings, with Critical and Bibliographical Introductions by Edwin Percy Whipple and Others*, 32 vols. Boston and New York, 1894. All quotations from the novels are from this edition.

DISRAELI, BENJAMIN, *Coningsby, or the New Generation* (1844). Vols. *12, 13* of his *Works*, ed. Edmund Goose and Robert Arnot, 20 vols. London and New York, 1904.

—— *Sybil, or the Two Nations* (1845), in *Works*, Vols. *14, 15*.

—— *Tancred, or the New Crusade* (1847), in *Works*, Vols. *15, 16*.

DOWDEN, EDWARD, *Studies in Literature, 1789–1877* (1878), London, 1899.

DRYSDALE, GEORGE R., *The Elements of Social Science; or, Physical, Sexual, and Natural Religion. An Exposition of the True Cause and Only Cure of Poverty, Prostitution, and Celibacy. By a Doctor of Medicine* (1854), London, 1872. Published anonymously. Attributed to Drysdale in the *Library of Congress Catalogue of Printed Cards*, 1944.

Early Victorian England, 1830–1865, ed. G. M. Young, 2 vols. London 1934.

ELIOT, GEORGE, *Works*, Illustrated Cabinet Edition, 24 vols. New York, n.d. All quotations from the novels are from this edition.

—— *Impressions of Theophrastus Such* (1879), in *Works*, Vol. 11.

—— *Life.* See under Cross, J. W.

ELLIOTT-BINNS, L. E., *Religion in the Victorian Era*, London, 1936.

ELLIS, HAVELOCK, *The Nineteenth Century. An Utopian Retrospect*, Boston and London, 1901.

EMERSON, RALPH WALDO, *English Traits* (1856), Vol. 5 of *Works*, 14 vols. Boston and New York, 1883.

Exeter Hall Lectures. See under *Lectures.*

"The First Half of the Nineteenth Century," *Fraser's Magazine*, 43 (1851), 1–15.

FITZGERALD, EDWARD, *Letters and Literary Remains*, ed. William A. Wright, 3 vols. London and New York, 1889.

FROUDE, JAMES ANTHONY, *The Nemesis of Faith* (1849), with an introduction by William G. Hutchison, London and New York, 1904.

—— *Short Studies on Great Subjects*, 4 vols. London, 1888.

—— *Thomas Carlyle. A History of the First Forty Years of His Life, 1795–1835*, 2 vols. London, 1882.

—— *Thomas Carlyle. A History of His Life in London, 1834–1881*, 2 vols. London, 1884.

GASKELL, ELIZABETH, *The Life of Charlotte Brontë* (1857), Everyman's Library, London and New York, 1908.

—— *North and South* (1855), Vol. 4 of *Works*, 8 vols. London, 1906.

GLADSTONE, WILLIAM EWART, *Gleanings of Past Years, 1843–1878*, 7 vols. London, 1879.

GOSSE, SIR EDMUND, *Father and Son. A Study of Two Temperaments*, London, 1907.

GREG, WILLIAM RATHBONE, "British and Foreign Characteristics" (1863), in his *Literary and Social Judgments* (1868), 4th ed. 2 vols. (London, 1877), *1*, 62–101.

—— "The Life and Correspondence of Thomas Arnold, D.D.," *Westminster Review*, 42 (1844), 363–81, reprinted in his *Essays on Political and Social Science* (2 vols. London, 1853), *1*, 47–80.

—— "England as It Is," *Edinburgh Review*, 93 (1851), 305–39, reprinted in his *Essays on Political and Social Science, 1*, 297–343. Review of a book by William Johnston: see below under Johnston.

—— *Enigmas of Life* (1872), London, 1889.

—— "French Fiction: the Lowest Deep" (1860), in his *Literary and Social Judgments, 1*, 184–230.

GREG, WILLIAM RATHBONE, "Kingsley and Carlyle" (1860), in his *Literary and Social Judgments*, *1*, 143–83.

—— "Life at High Pressure" (1875), in his *Literary and Social Judgments*, *2*, 262–88.

—— "Prostitution," *Westminster Review*, *53* (1850), 448–506, reprinted as *The Great Sin of Great Cities*, London, 1853. The reprint, which was published anonymously, is attributed to Greg in the British Museum Catalogue.

HALÉVY, ELIE, *A History of the English People in the Nineteenth Century*, trans. E. I. Watkin and D. A. Barker, 6 vols. 1924–51. See especially Vol. *1*, *England in 1815*; Vols. *3* and *4* (Pt. I), covering the years from 1830 to 1852.

HARRISON, FREDERIC, *Autobiographic Memoirs*, 2 vols. London, 1911.

—— "A Few Words about the Nineteenth Century" (1882), reprinted in *The Choice of Books and Other Literary Pieces* (London and New York, 1896), pp. 417–47.

HAYEK, F. A., *John Stuart Mill and Harriet Taylor. Their Correspondence and Subsequent Marriage*, London, 1951.

HELPS, SIR ARTHUR, *Friends in Council. First Series* (1847), 2 vols. London, 1857.

—— *Friends in Council. A New Series* (1859), 2d ed. 2 vols. London, 1859.

HIRST, F. W., *Early Life and Letters of John Morley*, 2 vols. London, 1927.

HOLLAND, SIR HENRY, "The Progress and Spirit of Physical Science," *Edinburgh Review*, *108* (1858), 71–104, reprinted in his *Essays on Scientific and Other Subjects Contributed to the Edinburgh and Quarterly Reviews*, London, 1862.

HOOD, EDWIN P., *The Age and Its Architects. Ten Chapters on the English People, in Relation to the Times* (1850), London, 1852.

—— *The Uses of Biography, Romantic, Philosophic, and Didactic*, London, 1852.

HOUGH, GRAHAM, *The Last Romantics*, London, 1949.

HOUSE, HUMPHRY, *The Dickens World*, London and New York, 1942.

HUGHES, THOMAS, "Prefatory Memoir," in the 1876 ed. of Charles Kingsley, *Alton Locke:* see below.

—— *Tom Brown at Oxford* (1861), Nelson Classics, London and New York, n.d.

—— *Tom Brown's School Days* (1856), Philadelphia, n.d. Hughes wrote an important preface to the 6th ed., 1868.

HUTTON, RICHARD HOLT, *Aspects of Religious and Scientific Thought. Selected from the "Spectator,"* ed. Elizabeth M. Roscoe, London and New York, 1899.

—— *Criticisms on Contemporary Thought and Thinkers. Selected from the "Spectator,"* 2 vols. London and New York, 1900.

HUXLEY, LEONARD, *Life and Letters of Thomas Henry Huxley,* 2 vols. New York, 1901.

HUXLEY, THOMAS HENRY, *Evolution and Ethics and Other Essays* (1894), New York, 1898.

—— "The Progress of Science, 1837–1887" (1887), in *Method and Results. Essays* (New York, 1898), pp. 42–129.

—— *Science and Christian Tradition. Essays* (1893), New York, 1898.

—— *Science and Education. Essays* (1893), New York, 1898.

Ideas and Beliefs of the Victorians. An Historic Revaluation of the Victorian Age, London, 1949. A series of talks given by British scholars on the B.B.C. Third Program in 1948.

JOHNSTON, WILLIAM, *England as It Is, Political, Social, and Industrial, in the Middle of the Nineteenth Century,* 2 vols. London, 1851.

KAYE, SIR JOHN WILLIAM, "Success," *Cornhill Magazine,* 2 (1860), 729–41, reprinted in his *The Essays of an Optimist* (London, 1870), pp. 77–111.

KELLETT, E. E., *As I Remember,* London, 1936.

—— *Ex Libris. Confessions of a Constant Reader,* London, 1940.

—— *Religion and Life in the Early Victorian Age,* London, 1938.

KINGSLEY, CHARLES, *Alton Locke, Tailor and Poet* (1850), in Vol. 3 of his *Works,* 28 vols. London, 1880–85. The important prefaces to the 1856 and 1862 editions are reprinted here, pp. lxxxix–cxvii.

—— *The Heroes; or, Greek Fairy Tales for My Children* (1856), in *Works,* Vol. 7.

—— *His Letters and Memories of His Life,* ed. Fanny Kingsley, 2 vols. London, 1877. Though referred to in my notes as the unabridged edition, there is a good deal of material to be found in the abridged edition (the next item) which is not, apparently, in this edition. The different arrangement of the material and the lack of good indexes make it difficult to determine whether or not a passage in one edition is in the other. There is great need for a bibliographical article on the differences between the two editions.

—— *His Letters, and Memories of His Life,* ed. by his wife (1879), 2 vols. New York, 1900. Known as the abridged edition.

KINGSLEY, CHARLES, *Literary and General Lectures and Essays* (1880), in *Works*, Vol. 20.

—— *Sanitary and Social Lectures and Essays* (1880), in *Works*, Vol. 18.

—— *Scientific Lectures and Essays* (1885), in *Works*, Vol. 19.

—— *Westward Ho!* (1855), in *Works*, Vol. 6.

—— *Yeast. A Problem* (1851), in *Works*, Vol. 2.

LECKY, W. E. H., *History of the Rise and Influence of the Spirit of Rationalism in Europe* (1865), 2 vols. New York, 1903.

—— *The Map of Life. Conduct and Character* (1899), London and New York, 1921.

—— *The Religious Tendencies of the Age*, London, 1860. Published anonymously. For proof of Lecky's authorship, see *A Memoir of William Edward Hartpole Lecky. By His Wife* (London and New York, 1909), pp. 19–21.

Lectures before the Young Men's Christian Association in Exeter Hall, 20 vols. London, 1845–65.

LEROY, GAYLORD C., *Perplexed Prophets. Six Nineteenth-Century British Authors*, Philadelphia, 1953.

LEWIS, ROY, AND ANGUS MAUDE, *The English Middle Classes*, London, 1949.

LOGAN, WILLIAM, *The Great Social Evil. Its Causes, Extent, Results, and Remedies*, London, 1871.

LYTTON, EDWARD BULWER, *England and the English* (1833), London and New York, 1874. Charles Kingsley wrote a short preface to the 1874 edition.

MACAULAY, THOMAS BABINGTON, *The Complete Writings*, ed. Lady Trevelyan, 20 vols. in 10, New York, *ca.* 1898.

—— *Critical, Historical, and Miscellaneous Essays*, 6 vols. in 3, Boston, 1878.

—— Letter on democracy, *Review of Reviews and World's Work*, 90 (July 1934), 38–9.

MACKAIL, J. W., *The Life of William Morris* (1899), World's Classics, 2 vols. in 1, London and New York, 1950.

MALLOCK, W. H., *Is Life Worth Living?* New York, 1879.

—— *The New Republic, or Culture, Faith, and Philosophy in an English Country House* (1877), with an introduction by Sir John Squire, Rosemary Library, London, n.d.

MARTINEAU, HARRIET, *Autobiography, with Memorials by Maria Weston Chapman* (2 vols., comprising all that Harriet Martineau wrote, were first published in 1857), 3 vols. London, 1877.

MARTINEAU, JAMES, *Essays, Reviews, and Addresses*, 4 vols. London, 1890–91.

MAURICE, FREDERICK DENISON, *Eustace Conway, or The Brother and Sister*, 3 vols. London, 1834.

—— *The Kingdom of Christ, or Hints on the Principles, Ordinances, & Constitution of the Catholic Church* (1837), Everyman's Library, 2 vols. London and New York, n.d.

MAURICE, SIR J. FREDERICK, *The Life of Frederick Denison Maurice, Chiefly Told in His Own Letters*, 2 vols. London, 1884.

MCCARTHY, JUSTIN, *A History of Our Own Times from the Accession of Queen Victoria to the General Election of 1880* (1879–80), 2 vols. New York, n.d.

Meliora. A Quarterly Review of Social Science in Its Ethical, Economical, Political, and Ameliorative Aspects, 12 vols. London, 1859–69. Vols. 7 and 8 are both dated 1865.

MILL, JOHN STUART, *Auguste Comte and Positivism* (1865), London, 1882.

—— *Autobiography* (1873), with an appendix of unpublished speeches and a preface by Harold Laski, World's Classics, London, 1924.

—— "Comparison of the Tendencies of French and English Intellect," *Monthly Repository*, new ser. 7 (1833), 800–804.

—— *Dissertations and Discussions, Political, Philosophical, and Historical*, 4 vols. London, 1875.

—— "Inaugural Address at St. Andrews" (1867), in *James & John Stuart Mill on Education*, ed. F. A. Cavenagh, Cambridge, 1931.

—— *Letters*, ed. H. S. R. Elliot, 2 vols. London and New York, 1910.

—— *On Liberty* (1859). See below under *Utilitarianism*.

—— *Principles of Political Economy with Some of Their Applications to Social Philosophy* (1848), ed. Sir W. J. Ashley, London and New York, 1909. See especially the chapters "Of Property," "General Characteristics of a Progressive State of Wealth," "Of the Stationary State," "On the Probable Futurity of the Labouring Classes," and the last four on the function and power of government.

—— *The Spirit of the Age*, ed. F. A. von Hayek, Chicago, 1942. Articles reprinted from the *Examiner*, January–May 1831.

—— *The Subjection of Women* (1869), reprinted in *On Liberty, Representative Government, The Subjection of Women*, World's Classics, London, 1912.

MILL, JOHN STUART, *Three Essays on Religion* (1874), 2d ed. London, 1874. "Nature" and "The Utility of Religion" were written between 1850 and 1858; "Theism," between 1868 and 1870.

—— *Utilitarianism, Liberty, and Representative Government*, with an introduction by A. D. Lindsay, Everyman's Library, new ed. New York and London, 1950.

MITFORD, MARY RUSSELL, *Life . . . Related in a Selection from Her Letters*, ed. A. G. L'Estrange, 3 vols. London, 1870.

MORE, HANNAH, *Practical Piety; or, the Influence of the Religion of the Heart on the Conduct of the Life* (1811), Boston, 1811.

MORLEY, JOHN, VISCOUNT MORLEY, *Critical Miscellanies*, 4 vols. London, 1886 (for Vols. *1–3*), and New York, 1908 (for Vol. *4*).

—— *The Life of William Ewart Gladstone*, 3 vols. New York and London, 1903. See especially Bk. II, chap. 6, "Characteristics."

—— *Modern Characteristics. A Series of Short Essays from the "Saturday Review,"* London, 1865. Published anonymously. See Hirst, *Early Life of Morley* (listed above), *1*, 47–9.

—— *On Compromise* (1874), London, 1923.

—— *Recollections*, 2 vols. London, 1917. See especially Bk. I, "The Republic of Letters," in which chap. 2, "Spirit of the Time," is of special interest.

—— *Studies in Conduct. Short Essays from the "Saturday Review,"* London, 1867. Published anonymously. See F. W. Knickerbocker, *Free Minds: John Morley and His Friends* (Cambridge, Mass., 1943), p. 76.

—— *Studies in Literature*, London, 1890.

MOZLEY, J. B., *Essays, Historical and Theological* (1878), 2 vols. London, 1892.

MYERS, FREDERIC, *Lectures on Great Men* (1856), London, 1877.

NEWMAN, FRANCIS W., *Miscellanies: Chiefly Addresses, Academical and Historical*, 5 vols. London, 1889.

NEWMAN, JOHN HENRY, *Apologia pro Vita Sua*, ed. Wilfrid Ward (1864), London and New York, 1913.

—— *Sermons and Discourses*, ed. C. F. Harrold, 2 vols. London and New York, 1949.

—— *The Idea of a University Defined and Illustrated* (1852), London and New York, 1901.

—— *Parochial and Plain Sermons* (1868), 8 vols. London, 1872–79. Sermons preached between 1825 and 1843.

PACKE, MICHAEL ST. JOHN, *The Life of John Stuart Mill*, London, 1954.

PATER, WALTER, *Appreciations. With an Essay on Style* (1889), London and New York, 1900.

——— *The Renaissance. Studies in Art and Poetry* (1873), New York, 1899.

PATMORE, COVENTRY, *The Angel in the House* (1854, 1856), in *Poems,* ed. Frederick Page, London and New York, 1949.

PATTISON, MARK, *Memoirs,* London, 1885.

QUINLAN, MAURICE J., *Victorian Prelude. A History of English Manners, 1700–1830,* New York, 1941.

RANDALL, JOHN HERMAN, JR., *The Making of the Modern Mind,* 2d ed. Boston, 1940.

READE, WILLIAM WINWOOD, *The Martyrdom of Man* (1872), 10th ed. New York, n.d.

ROUTH, H. V., *Money, Morals and Manners as Revealed in Modern Literature,* London, 1935.

——— *Towards the Twentieth Century. Essays in the Spiritual History of the Nineteenth,* New York and Cambridge, 1937.

RUSKIN, JOHN, *Works,* ed. E. T. Cook and A. D. O. Wedderburn, 39 vols. London, 1902–12.

RUTHERFORD, MARK (William Hale White), *The Autobiography of Mark Rutherford, Dissenting Minister* (1881), 15th ed. London, n.d.

——— *Mark Rutherford's Deliverance. Being the Second Part of His Autobiography* (1885), 13th imp. London, n.d.

The Science of Life. A Pamphlet Addressed to All Members of the Universities of Oxford and Cambridge, London and Oxford, 1877.

SHAIRP, J. C., *Aspects of Poetry. Being Lectures Delivered at Oxford,* Oxford, 1881.

——— *Studies in Poetry and Philosophy* (1868), Edinburgh, 1886.

SIDGWICK, ARTHUR AND ELEANOR, eds., *Henry Sidgwick. A Memoir,* London, 1906.

SIDGWICK, HENRY, *Miscellaneous Essays and Addresses,* London and New York, 1904.

SMILES, SAMUEL, *Self-Help; with Illustrations of Character, Conduct, and Perseverance* (1859), Chicago, 1881.

SMITH, GOLDWIN, *Reminiscences,* ed. A. Haultain, New York, 1910.

SMITH, JOHN S., *Social Aspects,* London, 1850.

SOMERVELL, D. C., *English Thought in the Nineteenth Century,* London, 1929.

SOUTHEY, ROBERT, *Sir Thomas More: or, Colloquies on the Progress and Prospects of Society,* 2 vols. London, 1829.

SPENCER, HERBERT, *An Autobiography*, 2 vols. New York, 1904.

―――― *Education: Intellectual, Moral, and Physical* (1861), New York, 1890.

―――― *Essays: Scientific, Political, and Speculative* (1858–63), 2 vols. London and Edinburgh, 1868.

―――― *Social Statics; or, the Conditions Essential to Human Happiness*, London, 1851.

STANLEY, ARTHUR PENRHYN, *The Life and Correspondence of Thomas Arnold, D.D., Head-Master of Rugby* (1844), London, 1904.

STEPHEN, SIR JAMES FITZJAMES, *Essays. By a Barrister*, London, 1862.

―――― "Tom Brown's Schooldays," *Edinburgh Review*, 107 (1858), 172–93. The attribution is made by Leslie Stephen, *Life* (just below), p. 484.

STEPHEN, LESLIE, *Essays on Freethinking and Plainspeaking* (1873), New York and London, 1905.

―――― *Hours in a Library* (1874–79), 3 vols. New York and London, 1899.

―――― *The Life of Sir James Fitzjames Stephen*, London, 1895.

―――― "Some Early Impressions," *Atlantic Monthly*, 92 (1903), 305–17, 527–38.

―――― *Studies of a Biographer*, 4 vols. London, 1898–1902.

STERLING, JOHN, *Arthur Coningsby. A Novel*, 3 vols. London, 1833.

―――― *Essays and Tales*, ed. J. C. Hare, 2 vols. London, 1848.

―――― "Carlyle's Works," *Westminster Review*, 33 (1839), 1–68, reprinted in his *Essays and Tales*, 1, 252–381.

―――― "Poems by Alfred Tennyson," *Quarterly Review*, 70 (1842), 385–416, reprinted in his *Essays and Tales*, 1, 422–62.

STEVENSON, LIONEL, "Prude's Progress," *Virginia Quarterly Review*, 13 (1937), 257–70.

STOWELL, HUGH, "The Age We Live In: Its Tendencies and Its Exigencies," *Exeter Hall Lectures*, 6 (1850–51), 41–74.

SYMONDS, JOHN ADDINGTON, *Essays, Speculative and Suggestive* (1890), London, 1907.

―――― Life. See above under Brown, Horatio F.

TAINE, HIPPOLYTE, *Notes on England*, trans. W. F. Rae, London, 1872. Written between 1861 and 1871 and published serially in *Le Temps*, 1871. A fuller translation by Edward Hyams appeared in 1957.

TENNYSON, ALFRED LORD, *The Poetic and Dramatic Works*, ed. W. J. Rolfe, Boston and New York, 1898.

TENNYSON, HALLAM, *Alfred Lord Tennyson. A Memoir* (1897), 2 vols. in one, New York, 1905.

THACKERAY, WILLIAM MAKEPEACE, *The Newcomes. Memoirs of a Most Respectable Family* (1855), Vol. 8 of his *Works, with Biographical Introductions by His Daughter, Anne Ritchie*, 13 vols. New York and London, 1898.

—— *Vanity Fair. A Novel Without a Hero* (1848), in *Works*, Vol. 1.

THORP, MARGARET FARRAND, *Charles Kingsley, 1819–1875*, Princeton, 1937.

TILLOTSON, KATHLEEN, *Novels of the Eighteen-Forties*, Oxford, 1954.

TODD, MARGARET G., *Windyhaugh. A Novel* (1898), Edinburgh and London, 1899. Published under the pseudonym of Graham Travers. The time of the story (see p. 31) is the eighteen-sixties.

TREVELYAN, G. M., *English Social History. A Survey of Six Centuries, Chaucer to Queen Victoria*, London and New York, 1942. Chaps. 17 and 18 are on the Victorian period. There is an illustrated edition (4 vols. 1949) in which Vol. 4 covers the nineteenth century.

TREVELYAN, G. O., *The Life and Letters of Lord Macaulay*, 2 vols. New York, 1876.

TRILLING, LIONEL, *Matthew Arnold*, New York and London, 1949.

TROLLOPE, ANTHONY, *The Chronicles of Barsetshire*, 13 vols. New York, 1893.

—— *The Parliamentary Novels*, 17 vols. New York, 1893.

TUPPER, MARTIN, *Proverbial Philosophy: a Book of Thoughts and Arguments, Originally Treated* (1838), New York, 1846.

TYNDALL, JOHN, *Fragments of Science for Unscientific People* (1871), 2 vols. New York, 1899.

VAUGHAN, ROBERT, *The Age of Great Cities: or, Modern Civilization Viewed in Its Relation to Intelligence, Morals, and Religion*, London, 1843.

WADE, JOHN, *England's Greatness. Its Rise and Progress in Government, Laws, Religion, and Social Life; Argiculture, Commerce, and Manufactures; Science, Literature, and the Arts. From the Earliest Period to the Peace of Paris*, London, 1856.

—— *History of the Middle and Working Classes; with a Popular Exposition of the Economical and Political Principles which have Influenced the Past and Present Condition of the Industrious Orders*, London, 1833.

WARD, MRS. HUMPHRY, *Robert Elsmere* (1888), Chicago and New York, n.d.

WARD, WILFRID, "The Time-Spirit of the Nineteenth Century," *Edinburgh Review*, 194 (1901), 92–131, reprinted in his *Problems and Persons* (London and New York, 1903), pp. 1–65.

WEBB, BEATRICE, *My Apprenticeship* (1926), London and New York, 1950.

WHITEHEAD, ALFRED NORTH, *Science and the Modern World* (1925), New York, 1939. The chapters bearing most directly on this study are "The Romantic Reaction," "The Nineteenth Century," "Religion and Science," and "Requisites for Social Progress."

WILBERFORCE, WILLIAM, *A Practical View of the Prevailing Religious System of Professed Christians, in the Higher and Middle Classes, Contrasted with Real Christianity* (1797), American Tract Society, New York, n.d.

WILLEY, BASIL, *Nineteenth Century Studies*, London, 1949.

WINGFIELD-STRATFORD, ESMÉ, *Those Earnest Victorians*, New York, 1930.

—— *The Victorian Sunset*, New York, 1932.

WOOD, H. G., *Belief and Unbelief since 1850*, Cambridge, 1955.

YONGE, CHARLOTTE, *A Book of Golden Deeds of All Times and All Lands* (1864), Everyman's Library, London, 1910.

—— *The Daisy Chain, or Aspirations. A Family Chronicle* (1856), London, 1915.

—— *The Heir of Redclyffe* (1853), Everyman's Library, London and New York, 1909.

YOUNG, G. M., *Daylight and Champaign. Essays*, London, 1937.

—— *Victorian England. Portrait of an Age*, London and New York, 1937. A revision and expansion of the last essay in *Early Victorian England*: see above.

Addenda

ALTICK, RICHARD D., *The English Common Reader. A Social History of the Mass Reading Public, 1800–1900*, Chicago, 1957.

FOX, CAROLINE, *Memories of Old Friends*, ed. H. N. Pym, and including fourteen letters by J. S. Mill, Philadelphia, 1882.

RIESMAN, DAVID, *The Lonely Crowd. A Study of the Changing American Character*, New Haven, 1950.

WILLEY, BASIL, *More Nineteenth Century Studies. A Group of Honest Doubters*, London, 1956.

WILLIAMS, RAYMOND, *Culture and Society, 1780–1950*, London, 1958.

Index

Lightning Source UK Ltd.
Milton Keynes UK
14 October 2010

161264UK00001B/1/P

9 780300 001228